RELIGION FOR A NEW GENERATION

RELIGION FOR A NEW GENERATION

Jacob Needleman
San Francisco State College

A. K. Bierman
San Francisco State College

James A. Gould
University of South Florida

The Macmillan Company, New York

The Macmillan Company
866 Third Avenue, New York, New York 10022
Collier-Macmillan Canada, Ltd., Toronto, Ontario

Library of Congress catalog card number: 72-77149

Printing: 1 2 3 4 5 6 7 8   Year: 3 4 5 6 7 8 9

For Rafe and Eve, the new generation.

J. N.

To my parents, Elsie Cecilia Kalmer Bierman and Arthur Gustav Bierman, in whose lives religion found Eden's own soil.

A. K. B.

For Stephanie—the beautiful, free, and joyous spirit.

J. A. G.

Preface

There is need for a new kind of anthology of religious thought.

The study of religion in our schools used to be a fairly comfortable discipline, clearly delimited and, in a certain sense, relatively innocuous. Enrollment was mainly by students preparing either for the ministry or for specialized academic careers. For these students, many excellent texts existed that presented Western religion in the light of modern scholarship and current intellectual categories.

Now, that has all changed. In a bewildering burst of energy, the younger generation has begun to turn in all directions for a religious understanding of themselves and the universe—from the religions of Asia and mysticism to occultism, drugs, and magic. A veritable flood of books has appeared in response to this new hunger for religious and metaphysical ideas: translations of sacred texts from all traditions, hundreds of new comparative studies, and a very great number of highly personal and speculative tracts purporting to deal with the deepest spiritual questions that man can ask.

At the same time, Western religious institutions are shaking at the foundations, and Western religions are searching for a way into the social realities of the day: war, the problem of racial injustice, poverty, the destruction of the environment, the breakdown of traditional family life, and the questioning of all forms of authority. Without pausing to fit themselves into familiar theological molds, often without even becoming acquainted with them, men have begun to speak out about religion in books and in actions that have captured the attention of the world.

Almost every student now wishes for a better understanding of religion in all its myriad aspects, both to satisfy his mind and to aid his search for himself. The need is obvious, therefore, for a new kind of text in our colleges and universities. It must respond to the personal search among our young people yet at the same time enable the instructor to provide the intellectual discipline that his students need if their interest in the religious is to be based on more than emotion.

To accomplish this, an anthology must represent the best of a wide spectrum of religious writings. Few instructors can reasonably be expected to have gone through all the material now available concerning, for example, astrology or Tibetan Buddhism or the traditions of esotericism. One or two bad experiences with this sort of material, which in the past has often been so presented as to justify every brand of religious charlatanry imaginable, has soured numerous instructors seriously interested in understanding the present burgeoning of religion among the new generation. It is understandable, therefore, that no anthologies have yet appeared that attempt to present what is intellectually invaluable in this whole area.

The aim of this text is to present teachable material that illuminates both major directions of the new religious mind: the movement toward the experience of inwardness and the movement outward into the vortex of external problems now threatening the existence of civilized man. Many of the selections in this book will be new and unfamiliar to the instructor, more so than for many of his students. It must be so. Otherwise, we, as editors, would have utterly compromised our purpose.

In the process of making our selections, we considered writings from all epochs and all traditions, our main requirement being that the selections express ideas that open fresh channels of thought about the new sense of religion. Needless to say, the amount of material before us was staggering: worlds within worlds. We had to resign ourselves to committing many sins of omission in the hope of minimizing our sins of commission.

The result, we hope, is a text that will serve the many and various young people now demanding introductory courses in tune with the new feeling for religion. But this book is also intended for use in other academic disciplines, for what aspect of human knowledge and endeavor can be fully studied apart from the question of man's search for a more fundamental reality?

Therefore, considering the vastness of the subject as against the limitedness of our own minds, we will gratefully welcome all comments and suggestions, not only from within the field of religion but also from psychologists, philosophers, anthropologists, historians—anyone, specialist or student, who wishes to see this most extraordinary phenomenon of our time more adequately represented in future editions of this book.

Our thanks to Judy Barkan, Bill Garrett, and Camille Ginette for their generous help in the task of preparing the manuscript, and to Louise Kanter for bibliographical help.

J. N.
A. K. B.
J. A. G.

Contents

Chapter Summary: (1) Analysis of reasons for interest in Eastern religions, with summary of doctrinal attractions. (2) First-hand example of young Americans engaged in Eastern religious practice. (3) Appraisal of drug phenomenon, which spans all religious interests among the young. (4) The Jesus movement—a critical appraisal, centering on the movement as a counter-drug tendency. (5) First-hand example of Jesus movement. (6) General critique of commune movement, its ideals and failures.

IS THERE A SUBSTITUTE FOR RELIGION?

Chapter Summary: This chapter explores modern attempts to deny the *sui generis* nature of religion. (1), (2), (3), and (4) Representative attempts to explain religion by reduction to other aspects of human life. (5), (6), and (7) Three contemporary efforts to find a substitute for religion.

THREE   Religion and the Current Crisis

WAR AND THE NATIONS

THE CRISIS OF RACE

THE CRISIS OF ECOLOGY

THE CRISIS OF SEXUALITY: WOMAN AND GOD

FOUR   The Religious Diagnosis of Man

Chapter Summary: This chapter presents the religious view of human failure and possibility. (1) The Asian point of view, (2) the Catholic, and (3) a powerful Protestant statement that has influenced a whole generation. (4) Nietzsche's attack on "tender-minded" religion, especially in its Christian forms. The chapter is for discussion of the "tough-minded" aspect of religion.

FIVE Spiritual Discipline: Methods of Religious Search

Chapter Summary: This chapter concerns the means employed by religion for psychological change. (1) and (2) Contemporary discussions of the method of meditation as seen from a Buddhist and Christian perspective. (3) Contemporary example of the relationship to a spiritual master. (4) Issues involved in seeing religious struggle in psychological terms and also relation of the modern interest in spiritual techniques to classic Western concepts such as virtue and repentance. (5) Religion of Judaism in the perspective of what might be called a "spiritual strategy" and attack on the cult of experience as against dutiful action. (6) Indication that the tradition of Western philosophy may once have been connected more closely to spiritual practice than it now is.

SIX Toward a Sacred Universe: Religion and the Cosmic

Chapter Summary: The issue of this chapter is whether the nature of the universe is a question that has religious import. (1) The classic statement from the perspective of scientism—the universe is meaningless; meaning resides only in man. (2) Revelation of the presuppositions of this view, the tendency of modern science to see death everywhere. (3) Careful exposition of the metaphysical limitations of science from a positivist point of view that leaves room for faith and a religious metaphysic. (4) An influential speculation attempting to bring together religious eschatology and modern science. (5) A coherent picture of an ancient and vastly influential Indian system, showing how the view of the cosmos is related to spiritual meditation. (6) Analysis of the history of the divorce between science and religious metaphysics and call for a return of the latter.

SEVEN   The Sacred Word

Chapter Summary: What is necessary in order to bring the Bible back to life for modern man? Is it possible? (1) A classic statement of the dangers of literal reading interpretation and the need to find "higher" meaning. (2) From an existentialist point of view, why this must be so, and what psychological response is necessary in order to understand scripture. (3) The classic modern statement of reinterpretation. (4) The problem in the light of contemporary linguistic analysis. (5) A brief attempt to understand a personal and political crisis in terms of scripture. (6) The idea of "levels of meaning" applied to a work of literature with which everyone is familiar but that possibly few have seen as religious.

EIGHT   The Struggle with Death

Chapter Summary: (1) A powerful personal statement of the horror of death. (2) The justification of death and the inability of man to accept it. (3) A summary of all the philosophical and religious issues surrounding the meaning of death, advancing the thesis that it is death that gives life meaning. (4) An analysis of how the medieval Christians connected the problem of death with man's wrong relationship to the body. (5) The classic modern analysis of the anxiety before death and the existential posture that it is necessary for man to assume.

Introduction

For many people, it was once part of growing up to reject religion, with all its apparent dogmatism, its comforting world-views, and its rituals. In those days and for those people, it seemed a part of courage to embrace the scientific concept of the universe and of man : that was almost the definition of realism and clear-mindedness. The vast cosmos was a blind cave, in one tiny corner of which a metaphysical freak called man lived, suffered, and died while projecting into the darkness his fantasies of a universal intelligence. It was the mission of science to show man the truth about the cave and its ironclad laws of mindless energy and indifferent matter.

Those days were only yesterday, and those people were ourselves. Today, however, with the world almost in ruins and the meaninglessness of everyday life pressing in, it no longer seems courageous or even reasonable to affirm that modern man has grasped the essential scheme of reality. And as it is impossible to return to the narrow and often sentimental sense that we used to have of religion, there has arisen a hunger for a wider and deeper sense of the religious. The search is for a view of the universe and of man in which great meaning is not purchased at the price of alienation from either nature or the intellect and in which the perception of human life as a spiritual task does not mean denying either the vital energies of the body or the claims of a true morality.

The religions of the East—Hinduism, Buddhism, and certain aspects of Islam—have lately served us well in this search for a wider understanding of the nature of religion, as many of the selections in this book will show. Against these formulations—ancient, but new to us—most of the objections that used to be raised against religion no longer carry weight. And we are thereby compelled to look again at our own religious traditions, seeking to understand the force they may once have had.

With our eyes opened by the Eastern religions, the entire Western tradition emerges as though out of a dark night of our own making. As we break loose a little from the mental associations that dull us to the teachings of Moses and Jesus, the history of Western man appears as a struggle to live according to ideas as sacred and objective as anything brought forth out of India, China, or Tibet. And we find ourselves freer to discover in St. Paul, or in Shakespeare, or in the builders of the Gothic cathedrals real impetus for

1

pondering the sense and aim of our own life on earth. That is surely one of the functions of religious tradition: to provide a man with ideas and impressions that can jar him for a moment out of the circle of everyday thinking and compel him to search for himself.

The present text shows us this side of religion. But it also shows the arena in which this search for oneself must now take place: under the threat of atomic war, amid the monstrous misapplications of scientific technology and the conflicts of race, sex, and generation. At the end of the previous century, Nietzsche called out loudly for a "revaluation of all values." In this book, the student will find a wide basis for pondering whether this revaluation, which is necessary to the survival of man, is now taking place. Will it come from a new sense of the horror of war or from a new perception of the inherent violence in unregenerate human nature? From a sudden questioning of the meaning of sexuality or from a new understanding of the difficulty of love? From an extraordinary experience or from a fresh entry into ordinary experience? From outrage or from insight? From action or from contemplation? From innovation or from the rediscovery of tradition?

These are all religious questions, and not only matter for psychologists, sociologists, historians, or scientists. They are religious questions because in the emergency of our time they are now part of the basic question of the meaning of one's life, a question that one asks not only in class but alone in one's room. It is the purpose of this anthology to respect the new energy in such questions both by presenting a wide range of contemporary responses to them and by trying to show how they bring new vitality to our own perennial religious ideals.

J. N.

The New Generation's "Spiritual Revolution"

INTRODUCTION

The "spiritual revolution," as it has been called, began as a distinct phenomenon in San Francisco in the early 1960s. Zen Buddhism had already become respectable throughout the Western world, due in large measure to the writings of D. T. Suzuki. On a popular level, the writers of the Beat generation had fastened on certain dramatic aspects of Zen and other Eastern religions and used them in their outcry against the value system of contemporary America. Against this very mixed intellectual background, there arose among the young a fascination with and then a dependence on psychedelic drugs, along with a profound reaction against the Vietnam war, technology, and almost every other aspect of modern society, from food to sexual mores to social injustice and organized religion.

Suddenly, God was no longer "dead." Now free to ask simple, fundamental questions of life, the younger generation groped for metaphysical answers within systems of thought as disconnected as possible from the religion of their parents. But however awkward, naive, or impatient this groping, it was nevertheless answered by the arrival in America, particularly in California, of numerous other Eastern teachings and spiritual leaders. In addition to providing what the younger generation felt it wanted from religion, these teachings also tapped into the widespread interest in the occult that has always existed among us in this country. The result was that Eastern religious ideas now began to enter into the stream of American thought with unprecedented speed.

In what way, precisely, had our Western religious forms become ripe for this challenge from Asia? In the first selection in this chapter, **Jacob Needleman** attempts to analyze this issue. Often, one approaches Eastern religion by asking what it has to offer that we do not have. In this selection, however, the question is slightly different: do these new teachings offer something that we once had but have now lost sight of? This is an important qualification that to an extent counters the compulsion people sometimes feel to choose between Eastern and Western religious ideas. Is there a way to understand Buddhism, Hinduism, or Sufism (the mystical aspect of Islam) such that the sense of our own religious traditions is deepened?

The real religious path requires more than concepts, however extraordinary they may be. One of the most interesting experiments in establishing a practical Eastern religion on American soil is now taking place at Zen Center in California. Zen Center was the first community of Western men and women (almost all of them young) directed by a Japanese Zen Master. Here, in the second selection in this chapter, the **students of San Francisco Zen Center** write about their work of building and running an American Zen monastery and how this tested their understanding of the principles of Buddhism. In a quite matter-of-fact way, this selection reveals some of the problems young Americans face who seriously wish to live according to non-Western religious ideas.

We then move to the question of drugs, which has colored almost every aspect of the new generation's religious renaissance. **Kenneth Keniston** (third selection in the chapter) attempts to place the move toward drugs in the context of the psychological and social difficulties that all young men and women face today. To the extent to which he succeeds in this, his essay brings us to the haunting question of whether the whole "spiritual revolution" is not a manifestation of the weaknesses in our social order. Can a true religious rebirth arise in a society where even normal human needs are withheld from the young? Can the disillusioned young really be serious about the great struggle for self-transformation—or is their search the sort that Keniston describes as a craving for experience?

According to **James Nolan**, the author of our fourth selection, the answer is clear. The young, at least those who have come to be known as Jesus freaks, are simply starved for a task in a social order that considers the absence of work the greatest human blessing. His article compels us to ask what religious passion really is. Is it like any other passion, save that it has "God" for its object? Or is religious feeling a totally transformed human emotion? If the latter, then—according to Nolan—the devout young are very far from a real return to religious depth. If the former, then it is only because our society has impoverished our emotional life that the religious revolution has been born—we are a subnormal people craving for feeling rather than meaning or God or inner transformation. **Lowell Streiker's** first-hand account of one Jesus organization, the fifth selection in this chapter, confirms Nolan's opinion. Then, what *is* a Christian? Are the students at Zen Center closer to Christianity than the Jesus freaks? We shall find some rich thought on this question later in the text.

Finally, **Paul Kagan**, in the conclusion of his study of California's utopian experiments, asks a question about the "spiritual revolution," the answer to which may well determine whether or not it represents a new hope. Is there a way of life that fulfills both the rational and the mystical needs of man and that brings together both the outer and the inner man? Traditions have existed, he writes in the sixth selection in this chapter, that have contained the means by which men could learn about their needs, motivations, purpose, and place in the universe and that have understood the necessity that people come together in a community in search of individual wholeness. The need, he says, is for real ideas that do not lead merely to reaction against present ills, thus heightening the schism of society, or to a return to the outer forms of past societies, but rather to an awareness of all the warring parts of human nature. He suggests that it is this awareness alone that can heal man and lead him to right action.

J. N.

Suggested Readings

Bellah, Robert N. *Beyond Belief: Essays on Religion in a Post-Traditional World*. New York: Harper & Row, 1970.

Cox, Harvey. *Feast of Fools.* Cambridge, Mass.: Harvard University Press, 1969.

Das, Baba Ram. *Be Here Now.* New York: Crown Publishers, 1971.

Ellwood, Robert S. *The Return of the Magus.* New York: Prentice-Hall, 1972.

King, W. L. "Eastern Religions: New Interest and Influence." *Annals of the American Academy*, 387 (January 1970), 66–76.

Needleman, Jacob. *The New Religions.* New York: Pocket Books, 1972.

Roszhak, Theodore. *The Making of a Counter Culture.* New York: Anchor Books, 1970.

———. *Sources.* New York: Harper & Row, 1971.

Woods, Richard. *The Occult Revolution.* New York: Herder & Herder, 1971.

Young America Turns Eastward

Jacob Needleman

Jacob Needleman (1934–   ) teaches philosophy and comparative religion at San Francisco State College. His recent book *The New Religions* is a report and analysis of the "spiritual revolution" among the new generation. He is also author of *Being-in-the-World,* a critical study of existential psychoanalysis, and general editor of the Penguin Metaphysical Library.

A WIDER SENSE OF PSYCHOLOGY

During my years of teaching philosophy I witnessed at close hand the birth of the hippie movement, the flower children, the drug scene and everything that went with it. I was quite convinced that the drugs led nowhere and I still am convinced of that; but what I underestimated was the sincerity of these young people with regard to the religions of the East. I think this book will rather clearly show the nature of that sincerity. I see now that conventional psychological analysis of this interest is really of secondary importance, especially as the religious systems we shall be dealing with contain their own psychodynamic categories, which in many cases strike much deeper, in my opinion, than those formulated by twentieth-century Europeans like Freud, Jung, or Heidegger.

I am sure it would make many of us less uncomfortable if we could subject this interest in the new religions to a comprehensive psychological study. It can be done; I myself was doing it for several years. But even apart from the fact that . . . our modern idea of psychology is seriously challenged by these new teachings, we should miss the whole point if such analysis were a main concern of ours. These teachings resonate with something in people which is utterly untouched by everything else in our society, something which "makes no sense" from one point of view, but which makes the most essential and urgent sense in the world from another point of view.

The reader who wishes to fit these new teachings into familiar psychological, sociological or literary categories is, I am afraid, in for some bad moments. I recall one winter afternoon several years ago in New York discussing Jewish mystical communities with the great scholar Abraham Heschel at a time when he was working on the translation of a particular Hasidic text. He pounded his finger on a stack of manuscript in front of him and quoted something he had just translated: "God is not nice, He is not an uncle. God is an earthquake." Many of those we shall be quoting, the young as well as the older, the hippies as well as the established members of the community, including some highly articulate and urbane people, have been struck by just such an earthquake. We shall often find, if we have the patience and the sensitivity, that they are speaking from a very particular "place" in themselves. We may even find—as

I found to my own surprise—that they are speaking *to* a similar "place" in ourselves.

Not long ago I discussed some of my findings with a very large group of interested psychiatrists and clinicians at the Langley-Porter Neuropsychiatric Institute in San Francisco. I am sure there were many reasons why they came to hear about the new religions. Certainly one of these reasons was that so many of their younger patients are deeply involved in the literature of this "spiritual explosion." But in their questions and in the discussions I had with them afterward, they made it clear to me that their motives were not only professional. They themselves were searching for ways to come in touch with something deeper in themselves, something of which, they felt, modern psychology was largely ignorant. Like many of us, they saw very little for themselves in the Judaism and Christianity of our society; indeed, from their professional perspective they judged much of contemporary religion as psychologically harmful. Was there something in the religions of the East, they asked, which could really call forth those human depths and heights which neither psychology nor Western religion seemed able to reach? If so, how, they wanted to know, could they come in touch with it? The directness and clarity of their questions brought me up short once again. Not only had I underestimated the sincerity of the younger followers of the new teachings, I had seriously underestimated the hunger in these people—trained, intelligent professionals who had staked their careers on the European psychological view of man—for a new sort of psychology and a new way of searching for the purpose and sense of their existence. . . .

. . . .

Inasmuch as the condition of a society, its hopes and aspirations, are reflected in the condition of its religion, it is America and the West as a whole which stand to benefit from this "invasion from the East," and not just our religious forms. When our younger people rebel against our institutions, they are rebelling against our hopes both for ourselves and for them. If we wish to understand their hopes and the nature of the world they seek to live in, we must understand something about these new religions.

. . . .

THE AGONIES OF RELIGIOUS "RELEVANCE"

What, then, have they found, these followers of the new religious teachings? It is possible that a serious look at them and at the people involved in them will change our whole idea of religion.

Who will deny that some such change is necessary? When God was recently pronounced dead it was not because people were no longer asking fundamental questions about life and death, human identity, suffering, and meaninglessness. On the contrary. Never before have men been more desperate about these questions.

True, our established religions are alive to this desperation. They are in agony because of it. We see them twisting and turning, seeking to change form without altering their essence. They wish to become *relevant* to the times, for the times are torturing us all.

But how are they, how is religion, to do this? We are tortured—agreed. The scientific world-view, recently so full of hope, has left men stranded in a flood of forces and events they do not understand, far less control. Psychiatry has lost its messianic aura, and therapists themselves are among the most tormented by the times. In the social sciences, there exists a brilliant gloom of unconnected theories and shattered predictions. Biology and medicine promise revolutionary discoveries and procedures, but meanwhile we suffer and die as before; and our doctors are as frightened as we.

And we cling violently to forms of life which, perhaps, were not even meaningful to us in quieter times.

So, when religion, in the name of relevance, seeks to adjust itself to the times, the question is bound to arise: is the leader being led? As church and synagogue turn to psychiatry, the scientific world-view, or social action, are they not turning toward what has failed and is failing? And has not the very failure of these non-religious enterprises shifted the common mind back to a renewed interest in the religious?

Men turn to religion and find, to their ultimate dismay, that religion turns to them, to their sciences, their ideas of action and accomplishment, and their language. This is what is known as secularization: the effort by religion to be "relevant," to "solve" human problems, to make men "*happy*."

How, one asks, could this aim be wrong? Should religion strive to be irrelevant, out of touch? Should it try to make men *un*happy? And in any case, by rigidly maintaining the purity of its traditional forms does it not simply become spinsterish and, finally, extinct? Who needs the dull sentiment of antique languages and meaningless rituals? Who needs a system of moral behavior which no one can or will follow?

Certainly, such questions require that we keep an open mind toward anything new which could refresh our understanding of the religious process. We want to know: what do these Eastern teachings say about man's existential situation, his place in the universe, his relationship to God? What do they promise? What do they demand? What sorts of people do they attract and what have these people experienced? Who are the leaders, what manner of people are they? We shall try not only to understand their doctrines, but to get a feel of their activity.

THE SENSE OF ASIAN TEACHINGS

Most of these teachings are sourced in Asia. Therefore, if we wish to know what they have brought to America, we have to begin by understanding something about Eastern religion.

Almost all the religions of Asia have one thing in common: "self-centeredness." Their goal is always release from suffering, *my* suffering as well as the suffering of humanity. Their cosmology and metaphysics, their imperatives to act morally or to serve God, are almost always instrumental toward this goal. What is true or good is what helps me out of my suffering; what is false or evil is what locks me in it. The well-known Buddhist simile expresses this exactly: the human situation is that of a man who has been struck in the chest by a poisoned arrow. He does not waste time trying to discover who shot it or why;

he is not interested in learning what the arrow is made of. He wishes only to get it out of his chest so that he will not die.

What is this suffering? And how is this goal any different from the contemporary Western effort to make men happy, which we have just characterized as "secularization"? The answer to this question involves an idea that is markedly alien to our modern minds: *the satisfaction of desire is not happiness.*

Because human desires are so multiform and contradictory, the satisfaction of one is always at the expense of another. And even if it were possible to satisfy all our desires, it would still be a contradictory and chaotic satisfaction corresponding to the contradictory and chaotic condition of the desires themselves. Contradictory satisfaction is what we call inner conflict, and the modern man experiences inner conflict as suffering.

In religious literature the desires—physical as well as emotional and mental, the wishes, hopes, fears, and so forth—are often symbolized by animals. It is as though within man there were a thousand animals each seeking its own food and comfort. Some of these animals are, moreover, the very food that the others seek. *What is called "pleasure" or satisfaction is the feeding of one or another of these animals.*

Thus, in this view, man's suffering is based on the mistake of identifying his whole self with these animals as they appear in him and make their wants known by howling for their food. No sooner is one fed than another appears, hungrier than ever, and sometimes hungry for the very food that has just been given his predecessor—and is therefore no longer available. By identifying himself with these animals, man forfeits the possibility of inner unity and wholeness, a possibility which represents another level of existence for him.

In these traditions, this level is variously spoken of as "higher" or "deeper" or "inner." It is that level from which consciousness can control and care for the animals in a way that corresponds to their true needs as part of a whole. In its function as master, this level of consciousness is spoken of as a special force; as guardian it is called knowledge; as action in the world it is known as love or service. It is *able, conscious,* and *beneficent:* i.e., "divine."

According to Eastern psychology, there is something in man which he squanders by understanding himself to be no more than these animals, a sort of energy or life which he ignorantly gives to them, and which they really do not need or use. To turn that energy to its proper use, to direct it toward the work of integration and awareness is one of the primal functions of religious discipline. But it is much, much harder to do than one thinks, for there is always an animal in man, a kind of monkey, perhaps, which imitates the real work and which wants to *feel* whole rather than *be* whole.

In this perspective, religion becomes "secularized" when its main concern is more to feed than to control the animals—that is, when its concern is primarily with the external conditions of human life. In this sense what we ordinarily call happiness is the exact opposite of what the Eastern traditions understand by release from suffering.

In Eastern thought these animals, these desires, are much more various than we might suspect. Physical desires—for ordinary food and drink, warmth, sexual gratification, etc.—comprise only a small fraction of the total. Some others are: the desire for praise and recognition, the wish to be superior, the fear of pain, the desire for security, the wish to control others, the desire to be desired, the desire to express oneself, the fear of the unknown, etc., etc. The list is very long, and relatively few religions become secularized in the sense of seeking to gratify only the basic physical desires. The difficulty is that certain non-physical desires are identified and officially sanctioned as corresponding to the inner or divine in man, whereas in reality they are merely "animals" on a level with all the others.

When this happens all the other animals go hungry, and when they are hungry enough they go crazy.

Religions have, for example, existed for the sole purpose of allaying man's fear of the unknown. This often takes the form of scholastic or highly rationalistic and doctrinaire systems of belief and explanation. Some anthropologists and religionists have even theorized that this is the fundamental purpose of religion at all times. Of course, from the perspective we are now presenting, this view is superficial.

Closely related to this, religions have existed for the purpose of making man feel secure and "cared for." At present this is a very popular form of religion and a very popular view of the function of all religion. Modern psychology gives this view of religion its blessing because, in our age, it has "officially sanctioned" the desire for recognition and "love" as the real inner spring of the human psyche. This has been done by labeling this desire a "need."

... The central thrust of Eastern religion is toward the *transformation of desire*, not satisfaction of desires. At its purest, it is a radical and constant movement inward, into the "self." Thus, the contemporary idea of "relevance" —which by and large has to do with the satisfaction of certain desires, or the allaying of certain fears—is antagonistic to the sense of Eastern religion. And thus the revolution in religion that is brewing among these new teachings in America is one that may run directly counter to the direction of contemporary religious reform.

No one can say that this "inward turn" is not also central to the Judaeo-Christian tradition, but it is also certainly true that this dimension of Western religion has been overlaid or neglected. Therefore, in looking at these new teachings we will want to know what light they can throw on our own traditions. Perhaps the East has to come West in this way for the West to rediscover the sense of its own religion.

WHY NOW? WHY HERE?

It is, in any case, this "inward turn" which has drawn so many Americans to these new religious teachings. What has happened to our culture and to our religions to make this inward turn so necessary? If we can begin to answer this question, we shall see something of the significance of this whole movement.

Here we immediately face an interesting difficulty. It is easy enough to argue that technology, affluence, the routinization of religion, and the like have stifled a deep longing in man, a "dark" side of his nature which is now welling forth to claim its own. From there, it is but one step to our "approving" of these new teachings because they satisfy an "irrational" need in the psyche of all men. We might even go so far as to argue that we must transform our view of reality by liberating our inherent attunement with the magical and by abandoning what has been called the "myth of objective consciousness." This has been done, and brilliantly, by Theodore Roszak in his book, *The Making of a Counter Culture*.

But to take this approach is, in the last analysis, to confess that we really do not wish to be serious about religion. It means that we have relied upon modern psychology or sociology to tell us what our possibilities are and which of them are not being realized in our society. Or, it means relying on our own feelings of frustration to tell us what reality should be like, or upon our responses to literature and art, themselves produced by men like us.

THE INCLUSION OF THE MIND

The terribly embarrassing thing about the great religions of the world is that *they* pass judgment on *us*, and that the moment we begin to pass judgment upon them without having submitted to their instruction, there is a real question whether we can understand them at all. Even to put the matter like this is already to have come upon one of the most striking ways in which the new teachings may change our contemporary concept of religion. To put it succinctly: they bring the idea that our mind, and the power of thought itself, is wretchedly inept without exposure to a spiritual discipline.

The exclusion of the mind from the religious process is one of the central characteristics of our religious forms. It was not always so, but by and large it is so now. We may be willing to grant religion the power to move us and stir us to the "depths" of our emotions, but we reserve the autonomy of our reasoning for ourselves. If we wish to train our minds, we know where to go, and it is not to religion.

Our popular religious forms long ago acquiesced to this. They spoke of human depravity, sin, faithlessness, immorality—but not so much of stupidity, illusion and bad thinking. It is true that Christianity and Judaism are essentially religions of the will, but the intellect was always understood as in the service of the will. Today, however, they, the will and the intellect, are tacitly recognized as separate.

Not so for the Eastern religions. Returning for a moment to our metaphor of the animals as symbols of human desires, the Eastern religions tell us that each animal has its own practical intelligence which operates only to procure its "food," namely, the satisfaction of desire. Thus, when we are at the mercy of these animals our intelligence is also at their mercy. And as they are interested in pleasure and not in truth, so our minds inevitably follow the line of pleasure and attraction. Logic is a whore serving anyone who can pay the price.

The "inward turn" of the Eastern religions may thus be understood in part as the effort to include the mind in the process of psychological regeneration. "Who are *they* to train *my* mind!" one might say. Quite a legitimate question, but the problem is how are we to find out *who* "they" are? What in ourselves or in others do *we* trust to ascertain the truth: do we know? are we sure? That is the question which immediately comes back at us from the Eastern religions, and which used to come back at man from the Judaeo-Christian tradition.

To put the point another way, the established religions of the day tend to emphasize choice and action. But under the Eastern diagnosis of the human condition, choice without intellectual freedom is only impulse, the impulse of the animal. We might agree with that, but not with the added stipulation that we lack intellectual freedom outside of a spiritual discipline. In short, the Eastern religions tell us, as did Plato, that we are chained by our subjectivity. It is therefore quite wrong to see even our most ecstatic bursts of subjective feeling as a step toward spiritual regeneration in the Eastern sense.

Here I must hasten to say that when I speak of "our" religions, I am speaking of church and synagogue, not of what takes place in Western monasteries or convents. At the same time, it is also indicative of our idea of religion that monasticism is by and large considered on the fringe, as secondary to church religion. Of course, this is a complete reversal of the historical relationship between church and monastery, where the latter was the source of life of the former. Today, most of us tend to think of monks and nuns as a bit odd, rather than as holy people.

THE RETURN OF THE PRACTICAL

Which brings us to the second main point about our contemporary religious forms, namely, the absence in them of practical technique, method and discipline. Various rituals, prayers, services and the like no longer function as part of the mechanics of the religious process, but mainly as an emotional "lift," something to help us return to our ordinary life feeling better, psychologically more secure. In this way they help to preserve the quality of the life we lead, rather than transform it.

This general forgetting of the instrumental nature of religious forms is in a way really quite bizarre. It is as though millions of people suffering from a painful disease were to gather together to hear someone read a textbook of medical treatment in which the means necessary to cure their disease were carefully spelled out. It is as though they were all to take great comfort in that book and in what they heard, going through their lives knowing that their disease could be cured, quoting passages to their friends, preaching the wonders of this great book, and returning to their congregation from time to time to hear more of the inspiring diagnosis and treatment read to them. Meanwhile, of course, the disease worsens and they eventually die of it, smiling in grateful hope as on their deathbed someone reads to them yet another passage from the text. Perhaps for some a troubling thought crosses their minds as their eyes close for the last time: "Haven't I forgotten something? Something important? Haven't I forgotten actually to undergo treatment?"

It is impossible to say when this forgetting of the fundamentally instrumental nature of religious forms began in the West. But obviously the general clergy— priests, ministers, and rabbis—forgot it quite as much as their congregations. No wonder the young became disillusioned with religion. They heard exhortations, commandments, prescriptions by the basketful, but nobody was telling them *how to be able* to follow them. I do not say they formulated it this way to themselves, but they—and not only they—saw the absurd discrepancy between the ideal preached in their churches and the actual behavior of men, behavior which seemed reinforced rather than seriously challenged by religion.

The Eastern teachings which are attracting so much interest in this country have by and large preserved this instrumental aspect of religion. That is why they come to us with such things as meditation techniques, physical and psychological exercises, and why they tend to emphasize the necessity of a *guru,* or master. It takes no great research to discover that practical psychological methods were always a central part of Christianity and Judaism, and that they still exist in monastic settings or, for example, among certain communities such as the Jewish Hasidim. The point is only that this aspect of religion has been forgotten by almost all other Westerners.

It is only because it was forgotten that Judaism and Christianity were so shaken by psychoanalysis and various other movements in modern psychology. Compared, for example, to the early Christian diagnosis of the inner human condition, Freud's "exposé" of the nature of human motivation is a very weak tea indeed. For one thing—and this is the very least of it—he retained his trust in the power of reason, his own, and observation, also his own, to arrive at the truth about human psychology. But for the early Christians, and for several of the most interesting new teachings, the power of thinking and observing clearly is a quality only of a higher state of consciousness, and not something that man is able to rely on without work in a spiritual discipline.

The main point here, however, is that because the instrumental nature of religious forms was forgotten, the science of psychology suddenly appeared as something *new.* Such an absurdity could only arise on the basis of a total misunderstanding or ignorance of the history of Judaeo-Christian thought and practice. One need only glance again at the writings of Augustine, Eckhardt, the Eastern Orthodox Fathers, or the great rabbis to confirm this point.

THE MODERN UNDERESTIMATION OF MAN

Modern psychology did indeed bring one thing that was new, namely, an underestimation of human possibility. Which brings us to our third point about the nature of contemporary religion.

There is really a tremendous irony at this point. Because religion forgot the instrumental function of its forms, these forms changed to accommodate the ordinary desires of men—as we pointed out in discussing the idea of "secularization." As a result of this forgetting and this change of form, religion was no longer able to effect the essential improvement of human life. Observing this, various "original thinkers" immediately concluded that religion was a fraud and began to produce, by the dozens, their own methods for improving human life. For they quite accurately saw that what men were getting out of religion (religion which was no longer instrumental) could be gotten faster without all the rituals, "mumbo jumbo," metaphysics, and so forth, all of which originally formed part of the instrumentality of the Judaic and Christian *Way,* but whose essential function nobody seemed really to understand. To return for a moment to a medical metaphor, it was as though patients and doctors began to insist that medicine taste good and make one *feel* rather than *be* well, and as though certain clever benefactors of mankind discovered that this could be done more effectively by removing from the medicines precisely those ingredients which had genuine therapeutic properties.

What modern psychology offered as an improvement of human life was precisely that quality of life which drove men originally to the instrumentalities of religion, the only addition being the conviction that this was the highest quality of life one could realistically expect. Religion was dismissed as an illusion —and indeed the religion which psychologists dismissed was perhaps illusory because it had forgotten its practical function and had lost its instrumental forms. Thus psychology became much more efficient than religion which, pursuing the same goals as this new science, found itself hampered by "outworn" beliefs and rituals. Modern psychology began to lead religion. The destruction of religious forms proceeded at an accelerated pace, and the underestimation of human possibility became fixed in our society.

It is only partially true that this estimation of man was based on a premature acceptance of human limitation, itself based on a mistaken extrapolation from the failure of non-instrumental religion. To be sure, there were some thinkers, not in the majority, who claimed that all man could ever hope for was the illusion of freedom, the partial gratification of instinctual desires and a more or less tolerable, though meaningless, existence between oblivions. The freedom, immortality, higher consciousness and inner unity spoken of by religions was to them a romantic dream. At least they tried to some degree to avoid replacing this so-called romantic dream with a naïve belief in their own innate, fully developed powers.

Not so the majority of psychologists. They coupled their underestimation of man's possibilities with an emphatic overestimation of man's and their own actual psychological condition. Simply to mention one example, Freud's whole theory of dreams, parapraxes and neurotic symptomology is based on the assumption that there is a basic unity of purpose underlying all human behavior, and that everything man does is an expression, though unconscious, of this instinctual unity. Since it is precisely this unity which many of the Eastern religions call into question, from their perspective it is Freud's assumption which is the romantic dream. He once said, "Man has always known he possessed spirit; I had to show him he was also an animal." Unfortunately, he settled for only *one* animal, whereas the fundamental religious diagnosis of man is that he is an entire menagerie.

Blithely accepting the "tough-minded" scientific view that there are no purposes in the external world, psychoanalysis substituted the rather sentimental belief that there is nothing but purpose and intention in the psychic world. At least the positivists made a clean sweep of all purpose, inner and outer, and after them one could much more clearly see the dust bowl of modern thought for what it was.

Coupled with this assumption that everything in one's psychic life had "meaning" was the psychologists' belief that they were able to ascertain this meaning, to control their own feelings toward the patient, and to communicate the truth to the patient in a way that could be effective—all this being the general sort of thing which a spiritual master does, but toward an aim entirely different than "mental health" and only after he himself has submitted his life (including his mind) to the instrumental rigors of a spiritual path.

One obvious aspect of the modern, Western concept of religion was its picture of a "holy" man. He was nicer, kinder, gentler, more moral, perhaps, than other men—but more intelligent? more perceptive? Emotionally stronger? psychologically more balanced? more creative? more unified? Were not these "*secular*" properties of men? Again, it is the Eastern religions with their practical methods involving work with the body, the attention, the intellect and memory, the training of the emotions, which have begun to supplant this simplistic picture of holiness. Till now, it has been entirely possible for many of us to be surprised if not slightly offended by the idea that Jesus Christ had a mind as well as a heart, and to be genuinely astonished that almost all of the enduring art in the world has been produced by men with obvious religious ties.

Summing up, there are three ways in which Western, and particularly American, religions are vulnerable to correction by the religions of the East: exclusion of the mind, the absence of religious techniques and methods, and the underestimation of human possibility. One could cite still more ways in which our religious forms have moved away from their original direction, but these, perhaps, are enough to have exposed as well some of the conditions of our American culture which make it ripe for the invasion from the East.

The Making of an American Zen Monastery

The Students of San Francisco Zen Center

WINTER AND SPRING

Turning this wild land and old resort buildings into an actual functioning practice center with a Zen Master, other teachers, and the right conditions for Zen practice, was a job that surpassed in time and effort any boundaries we imagined.

. . . Much of the moment by moment responsibility for finding a way to live together, to complete the necessary work, and to develop a Zen practice rested with the students themselves, some of whom had very little Zen experience. But with the help of Suzuki Roshi and the older students, and perhaps because of the balance and communal feelings inherent when people meditate together, things developed well.

In late May and June Suzuki Roshi was able to be at Zenshinji more of the time. One of the most helpful experiences for the students was to work with him or just to watch him working. This was the first time most of the students had had the opportunity to be around him for more than a period or two of meditation a day in San Francisco. The need for such an opportunity was the main reason we began Zen Mountain Center.

From *The Wind Bell* (Fall, 1967), pp. 2–16. Reprinted with permission of *The Wind Bell*, organ of Zen Center of San Francisco.

Roshi has had considerable experience in Japan with stone masonry and the caprices of mountain streams because he has lived at two or more remote temples. But it was not just his skill in moving huge stones to direct the course of a stream, or in shaping stones to rebuild the large supporting wall under the bridge that affected the students so directly. It was the energy and attention with which he did his work. He seemed able to work without rest all day long, even when moving bigger stones than anyone else, and by mid-day to completely tire out the strapping students who were working with him. Everyone wondered what his secret was. One student who was helping him finally observed that Roshi was always at rest, unless he was directly pushing on a stone, and that even when he fell he was relaxed and found his balance naturally. Suzuki Roshi is very modest, even embarrassed about this and says that he is too attached to hard work; but to the students he is what they hoped a Zen Master would be like.

. . .

All the work in these two months was directed toward the opening of the summer practice period in July and August. Three jobs took priority over all others. Though urgently needed, the building of a new kitchen and other jobs had to wait. The first was putting in a new floor for a zendo on the ground floor of the dormitory building. This became a bigger job than was expected because the sixty-year-old building had slid toward the stream and everything was out of level. This first zendo seated thirty-six students and was not adequate for the overflow work crews who came down from Zen Center for the weekends. So the deck on the east side of the building which overlooked the intersection of the two streams was turned into an outside extension of the zendo that seated another thirty-five students. This was also used while the new floor was being laid. During the practice period this first zendo and deck were further rebuilt and modified and were used as the guest dining room during the fall guest season. This winter it will serve as the common room for the students.

The second job was turning the upstairs level of the same building into a dormitory for male students. This also we thought would be a small job, but the replastering and painting took several weeks. The third job was converting the former office, bar and lounge into the main zendo which would seat seventy people. This was completed the night before the opening ceremony. All of the construction on the zendo was being done while Suzuki Roshi was completing work on the caved-in bridge wall. Tassajara remained open to guests during the rebuilding and remodeling. The kitchen had to prepare three meals a day for the forty guests in addition to the vegetarian meals for the students.

At the same time in San Francisco we were trying to cope with the quantity of applications for the practice period that were coming in. More than two hundred applications were received—many more than we had expected—and daily, people came into the office at Zen Center or walked or drove into Tassajara over the trails and the precipitous road, asking if they could stay for the practice period. We required of the prospective students some experience in zazen, straight-forwardness, an ability to convince us of a serious interest in Zen, the balance to respond quickly and honestly to disconcerting questions, the willingness to sit first at Zen Center or with some other Zen group, and finally the determination necessary to sit through the three (now five) days of tangaryo (all days sitting, with breaks only for meals, to face oneself and one's reasons for wanting to practice Zen life). Out of all the applicants about 85 were chosen. Only 70 of these students were willing to enter the first tangaryo; about 55 stayed through it; by August there were 68 students and 4 priests.

SUZUKI ROSHI WRITES ON THE PRACTICE PERIOD

Through the practice period Buddha's way will be known in America. The practice period originated with Buddha's sangha (community of disciples) during the rainy season in India when the monks could not go wandering from village to village begging and teaching. In Japan only certain Zen temples are given the privilege of being able to hold practice periods. Now this indispensable practice has begun in America and it must not be discontinued. Each year we must have at least one practice period; it is indispensable for the students at Zenshinji and for the existence of Zenshinji itself. Strict observation of the practice period with qualified teachers and qualified students is one of the foundations of Zen Buddhism and is the most important reason we started Tassajara.

There are not many teachers in this world, and there are many students. Of course teachers and students are not different, but we must begin with a teacher. The teacher works and practices under the same conditions as the students. But there is some difference. The student perceiving this difference is shown the way to the Buddha in himself and the Buddha in his teacher. This is the most fundamental way to help others. So direct contact with the teacher, listening to his lectures, working with him, receiving personal instruction, is very important. By this we can go beyond any physical, mental or emotional ideas we have about practice. It is possible to practice by yourself, but when we practice in a group we can help each other; and by practicing with people under the same conditions we can eliminate self-centered practice. When there are not many teachers, group practice is the only way possible to have direct contact with a teacher.

The purpose of group practice is not the observation of rules and rituals. Although the rules do allow you to focus on your practice, and to live according to the essentials needed to practice together, the purpose is to obtain freedom beyond rules and ceremony, to have naturalness, a natural order of body and mind.

To live in this world means to exist under some condition moment after moment. We should have the flexibility of mind to adjust our being to these conditions so that when we do change our attitudes or circumstances, there will still be a fundamental imperturbability to our minds and bodies. This imperturbability gives us absolute freedom and we should practice our way until we obtain this. Group practice is the short cut to the imperturbable mind which is beyond concepts of personal or impersonal, formal or informal.

At first group practice seems restricting, but later you will find the freedom in it. At the same time, of course, it is easier to observe some rules rather than to practice your individual way or to practice in various ways. A person may be said to be a good Zen student if he knows his own way in its true sense; but it is very difficult to know what your own way is. For finding what your own way is, group practice is best. For example, a woman will go to a store thinking that she knows exactly what she wants. But when she gets there and sees all those things, she may no longer know exactly what she wants. So she may buy many things, and end up wasting money. So we limit our life to find our true way. It may be how to know your way in the grocery store! Of course the best way is to use something when you have it; and if you buy things, at least you can use them until you know why you don't want them. Then you will have some sense of choosing things as your own.

So through group practice you find out how to know your own way. For example, Buddhist ceremonies are too complicated to do perfectly and so in our observance of them we can see our own way and not just the way of the ceremony. And in learning to accommodate ourselves to the practice of others and to our teachers, we will find out how to communicate with others and with all worlds and their various Buddhas. This is not just verbal communication. It is more direct than that. It is person to person and beyond any specific way. This is known as the Bodhisattva's way.

THE FIRST PRACTICE PERIOD

In the evening before the practice period opened, the first ordination ceremony at Zenshinji took place when Dick Baker had his head shaved, was given the name Zentatsu Myoyu, and was appointed Shuso or head student for the first practice period. The next day at one o'clock, Bishop Sumi Roshi, Suzuki Roshi, Katagiri Sensei, Kato Sensei, and Maezumi Sensei opened the practice period and installed the Buddha in the zendo. This ceremony gave the students a sense of respect for the tradition which brought Buddhism and the teachers to them, and also an awareness that what is Japanese in Zen cannot be made American all at once. If the tree that has been transplanted at Tassajara is stripped of its branches and bark it will die, but if it is nourished and allowed to take root the new soil of America will subtly bring the tree into accord with its new life.

But the students also learned that they could not leave all the changes and adaptations up to Suzuki Roshi's successors. These adaptations can only have life if they are guided by Suzuki Roshi's sense of and insistence on keeping the essentials of Buddhism intact.

This sense of how Buddhism should exist in America was in sharp focus during the practice period when we were faced over and over again with details like: Do we wear robes or not, and what kind of robes? Shall this ceremony be simplified? How? Shall it be in English? Should we chant in English or Japanese? Japanese has more resonance but English we can understand. Should there be three, five, or seven days of tangaryo? How much zazen, study time, work time should there be? Should the organization and spirit of the practice be along the lines of original Buddhism, or present-day Buddhism in Japan, or what combination of these? How strict should the practice be made? Should we follow the Soto way completely, or should we apply the approaches of various schools according to the needs of the students? To what extent should the experience of zazen, koans, mantras, and the other techniques of Buddhism be used? These questions, many of which may seem superficial, actually helped to deepen our real experimental unknown practice (the student himself doesn't know what will unfold next in his practice), suggested guidelines that pervaded our whole practice, and perhaps prepared some of the ground for Buddhism in America.

TANGARYO

The practice period began with every student doing tangaryo. Previously we had debated whether tangaryo should be three days or the seven which is traditional in Japan. Since many students had insufficient experience in just sitting, three days was decided upon for entering the monastery during the practice period, and five days thereafter.

The students were not told what to expect from tangaryo. Suzuki Roshi liked it that the American students could come less prepared for tangaryo than their Japanese counterparts, because they could come without preconceptions. All Roshi said was, "Be prepared to sit." And that we did, for three days straight from four in the morning until ten at night with no breaks except for eating.

If you go through tangaryo the value of this experience is apparent. It tested us to our utmost in a way most of us had never experienced before. And yet we knew the test was an encounter with ourselves in a way and in a situation which could only help us. Many experiences come out of a practice like this. After tangaryo there was a kind of alert joyful feeling at Tassajara that lasted throughout the practice period.

But if you have not been through tangaryo it is difficult to understand it. The advice to just "be prepared to sit" means that the student should be inwardly prepared to have an experience that, like most life experiences, there are no guidelines for, and that you must structure and solve for yourself. The student must decide for himself how long he is going to sit in one position, how long he will change his position, with what dignity and composure can he live during the time of tangaryo, and how he should react to his own confidence and discouragements. It is a kind of time/space experiment which the student freely enters into by himself, in which his own functionings become the unavoidable subject of his attention. It is here that he decides whether this practice which throws his self and being into such relief is what he can and wants to do.

THE SCHEDULE

The daily schedule is the first problem the new American student faces. The usual attitude towards schedules is that they are trifling and irritating. But it is important that the schedule in a Zen monastery become second nature so that the student does not have to think about the details of time, but only concentrate on what has to be done and how to do it. So Zen practice is limited to essentials so that things are done for themselves, in terms of the relationships within the situation, and not in terms of what your limited self, or small ego, thinks should be done.

For example, the wake-up bell is rung only 15 minutes before you should be in the zendo. This gives just enough time to dress and wash and get to the zendo during the second round of the han (wooden sounding board), and little time to consider how you feel about getting up. So what is hardest on the beginning student is dealing with the lack of personal time he has to think about things. You learn to have everything you need moment after moment without thinking about yourself, and so gain the awareness that at each moment you are perfect.

The daily schedule for students was: rise at 4 a.m. 50 minutes of zazen beginning at 4 : 20, breakfast, a three-hour work period, mid-day zazen, lunch, rest period, study period, a two-hour work period, bath time, supper, lecture, and one or two more periods of zazen before bed at 9 : 45.

We experimented with the sechedule several times during the month of July trying to find out how tight the schedule should be and what combinations of zazen, work, study and rest time were most satisfactory. A Japanese monastery schedule cannot be adopted without modifications since a schedule for American students must be related somehow to the life they had before coming to the monastery. It must make some sense to them and must be related to their own limitations and Zen experience, particularly during this first incubation period; otherwise they cannot follow the schedule at all. By the beginning of August we had a good working schedule that still followed the basic patterns of Chinese and Japanese monasteries enough that a professor who had been a long-time student of Zen both in this country and in Japan, and who was a student at Zen Mountain Center during this period, said, "Tassajara has everything Japan has and more."

TIME SOUNDS

In a Zen monastery the day begins just before sunrise with the sound of a hand bell and then a wooden board being struck by a mallet. Bedtime comes sometime after dark with the slower ringing of the same bell. The times and activities of the day are sounded throughout the monastery by a combination of either the han, a piece of ash planking 4 inches thick with a concave surface in the middle which is struck with a wooden mallet; the bronze bell, which is made from a wooden mold carved especially for the bell and then discarded; or the drum, which is more than 3 feet in diameter and was made from a single tree trunk. These were paid for by a contribution from the Soto Zen Headquarters in Japan and were engraved or carved with Zen Mountain Center in Japanese and dated "In the time of Shunryu." Their design originated over 1000 years ago in China and has remained the same since, except for the drum support which was heightened for Americans.

The basic sound pattern lasts fifteen minutes and is composed of three rounds on either the han or bell, with each round having a different number of beats in it. But often the sound was a combination of several instruments. Lunch is announced by three such rounds on the han and the food is brought after three rolls on the drum (Buddha's thunder). The time is sounded in the early morning and late evening by hitting the drum once for each hour and the bell once, twice, or three times, depending on which third of the hour it is.

Several students were given the responsibility for hitting the instruments. The daily schedule was such that each sound or series of sounds had to begin and end on time so that the students could place themselves accordingly. At first the students found it difficult to be so in tune with time. The moment a sound began they had to immediately begin to change what they were doing so that they could be punctual for the next period and everyone could begin at the same time.

. . .

FOOD AND MEALS

In the spring and summer we experimented with the basic diet at Tassajara. We had two styles of food, Japanese and American, and ideas, both Buddhist and our own. The first was that you should eat only what you need, and as simple as possible protecting your health; and second, that you should eat what is offered, without discrimination, but that a simple, non-meat diet is preferred. Working with these things, several combinations were tried out, and the final diet was chosen for its spiritual and nutritious qualities, not its nationalistic ones. The food was vegetarian, but because of the great amount of outside work that was done, and because of the need to balance the transition from the previous diet of the students to the new monastery diet, such protein staples as eggs and cheese were added to the diet. The soup usually had miso, a paste made from fermented soy beans, in it, because of the high protein content of soy beans. On the other hand, brown rice was used instead of white because of the great nutrient value of the rice hull, despite the apathy with which Japanese usually greet brown rice at first.

Our desire to be simple and to hold to Buddhist traditions where possible, determined what foods should be eaten at specific times. On alternate days breakfast consisted of either gruel, pickles and fruit, or hot cereal, a hard boiled egg and fruit. Lunch was soup, salad and bread, and fruit for dessert; dinner was brown rice, salad and another vegetable. Seconds were served on the grains, the soup at lunch, and the salad at dinner.

How the food was prepared was determined by tradition and by the experience of Ed Brown and Bill Kwong, the cooks. The gruel was made from rice cooked with leftover vegetables and soup, and has become the favorite meal of the students. The bread was both leavened and unleavened; the salad was made of various kinds of greens and had one of many kinds of dressing on it, ranging from garlic to honey and vinegar. Some of the guests who ate with us in the zendo were disappointed that we ate so well.

Ed was so involved in making the kitchen work and finding it necessary to make rules that he wrote:

> A dull knife will not cut,
> Nor a cracked bowl hold water.
> Putting your mind and body in order,
> How useful everything becomes.
>
> Looking for the knife
> Which is not there—
> How hard to find.
>
> Washing rice, kneading bread,
> Chopping carrots, peeling oranges,
> Slicing pickles, saving crumbs,
> No time for living, no time to die.

These were the rules for his helpers. "That's what the kitchen does to you, you know," says Ed.

The meals were eaten in silence using an oryoki, or set of bowls and utensils. The oryoki is comprised of three bowls that can be set into one another, chopsticks, a spoon, a setsu (utensil for scraping and washing bowls), a sheath that holds the utensils, a napkin, a dishtowel, and a large cloth in which to wrap all the bowls, utensils and cloths together. Each act in eating with an oryoki is prescribed: how to untie the wrapping cloth with certain fingers, folding the corners so that a square is formed under the bowls, how the bowls and utensils are taken out and placed, how to hold the bowls while eating, how each bowl is washed with water that is poured into the largest bowl by a server and how the water is poured from bowl to bowl until each utensil and bowl is washed and dried except for the last which is emptied into a bucket the server returns with, and finally how the various pieces are reassembled into the oryoki and the ends of the wrapping cloth are retied in a half-bow.

But the use of the oryoki is more than Zen etiquette. When each act is accounted for you become aware of each moment and of the difference between one moment and the next. It is perhaps the simplest possible way to eat (no dishes to wash) and each motion is reduced to the absolute essentials. It requires concentration and attention—an alert clear mind—to eat this way. You no longer have to be bothered with what you *should* do moment after moment and are able to act perfectly in each moment without thought, to be able to just eat when you eat.

Eating with an oryoki becomes an important opportunity in our practice. At first the students' reactions were that they were being programmed, even though eating with an oryoki was a Buddhist tradition that originated with Buddha carrying his bowl in his sleeve. But many students left Tassajara with the feeling that perhaps the most important thing they'd learned there was how to eat in a satisfying and simple manner.

SESSHIN

The practice period ended with an intensive seven-day sesshin; 40 to 50 minute periods of sitting meditation (zazen) alternated with 10 to 15 minutes of walking meditation (kinhin) from 4 a.m. to 10 p.m. Interposed between the 18 hours of zazen and kinhin were three meals, a tea service, an hour work period, a half-hour for bathing, and two lectures. There was no talking except for the minimum necessary during work period, and, of course, the student could speak to the Roshi during dokusan (sanzen, or personal instruction) or the discussion that followed the lectures.

The students looked forward to sesshin with anticipation and dread. Sesshin demands a great deal: the schedule is long and hard enough that each student is required to fully explore and make use of his sources of energy. But sesshin is not so hard once you are actually participating in it. You have to be attentive to only one thing, and there is much satisfaction in concentrating on your practice intensively with others.

Zazen should permeate one's life so that everything becomes practice. This is the point of sesshin. And sesshin also gives one the opportunity to focus, with a minimum of distraction, on the essence of one's life or life problems, or on a koan or mantram, and, more particularly, to let the happenings of one's mind and body come and go without interference, until one knows his mind and body before it takes on any activity or knows any form, until one knows emptiness itself. We say, "to know your original face."

Suzuki Roshi meditated with the students and lectured twice a day. The lectures were on the Prajna Paramita Sutra (which we chant several times daily), the Genjo Koan by Dogen Zenji, and the meaning of zazen and practice. They were often followed by questions and discussion. . . .

When Suzuki Roshi was not in the zendo he was giving dokusan (personal instruction). Anything may happen in dokusan, from questions to complete silence, and what does happen is between the Roshi and the students and is not talked about with others.

Sesshin ended with a formal question and answer ceremony in which the students presented questions to Suzuki Roshi about Zen and their practice before all the other students. Students stood together on one side of the zendo and each in turn walked to the front, bowed to Roshi and presented his question in a strong voice. Each received an answer from the Roshi, thanked him and returned to make way for the next questioner.

Some of the questions and their answers were:

"For the big mind the bridge flows. If everything has such independence, how can we find our responsibility?" "Your responsibility is on your own, under your own feet."

"If there is no beginning, no end, and no existence, what is the use of a question?" "To call back something which is unknown; to address Buddha."

"Docho Roshi, do you have some question?" "Yes, I have a question. Why are you so serious?"

"Using the mantram you gave me I broke through one dam of spiritual tension. Should I continue to use this mantram to break through further dams?" "As long as you are directed single-heartedly to your attainment you can use that mantram. You cannot use it for other purposes."

"In Zen we often hear of doing what one must do rather than what one wants to do. Is it possible to know what one must do before one has the desire to do it?" "Your teacher will put you in those circumstances. Follow our way. At first you think you are following the way, but soon you will drive the way."

"Why is it necessary to have some unusual experience in order to practice Buddhism?" "To open up your mind wider and wider."

SHUSO CEREMONY

Suzuki Roshi described the Shuso Ceremony in this way: "Each practice period we appoint a Shuso to be head of training and leader of the disciples. For the student the experience of being Shuso, head of the monks, and being tested by the other students in the Discussion Ceremony marks the second stage in priesthood. For this first practice period at Tassajara, Zentatsu Myoyu (Richard Baker) was appointed Shuso. He was the first priest appointed Shuso in America."

The Discussion Ceremony is very old. It originated in China and still exists in Japan. However, in Japan it is often more of a formality than anything else— the Shuso is often a young student without the experience necessary to answer questions about Zen that presuppose some maturity. The young Shuso is given the answers to questions which have been given out to the students.

In America the ceremony has returned closer to its original content and feeling. Zentatsu, Richard Baker, is well into his practice and somewhat older than his Japanese counterpart. No questions were given out. Chino Sensei told the students to choose questions which demonstrated their own understanding of Zen and which probed the understanding of the Shuso. The question could be discussed until they felt the matter was resolved. Sensei described the ceremony as Zen "combat." Something was obviously expected from the Shuso and the zendo was charged with skeptical excitement—how can a student answer questions usually asked a Roshi—about to be resolved one way or another.

The priests sat together on the altar-platform in scarlet robes and ceremonial kesas. A strange bamboo root stick, called a Vajra (Diamond-Lightning) Staff, which had been made by Chino Sensei, rested on a low table in front of Suzuki Roshi. After chanting and offering incense, Dick walked slowly to face Docho (Abbot Suzuki) Roshi, bowed and received the Vajra Staff from his teacher. He returned to his seat on Docho Roshi's right, pounded twice on the tatami with his staff and announced, "I am ready for your questions."

The first student began a long stare at the Shuso, leaped to his feet, stamped and shouted *KWATZ!* Then he turned slowly and formally and walked toward the door. There was a tense pause and the Shuso asked, "Do you have anything else to say?" The student turned, stamped, and walked back, bowed to the Shuso, and sat down.

Student after student brought forth his question to the Shuso. "What do you make of my transparency?" "What transparency," answered the Shuso, "You seem to be there to me. I can't see the wall through you." Or from another student, "Why did Suzuki Roshi come to San Francisco?" The Shuso answered, "Buddhism neither comes nor goes. Suzuki Roshi can study Zen as well here as in Japan. The question is, what is this 'you' that you think comes and goes?" Sometimes there was a debate: a student said, "I don't accept your 'if' in that answer." "You are right," said the Shuso, "No 'if.'" And the student, "Me asking, you answering—is that a comparison?" The Shuso answered, "No 'me,' no 'you'—just questioning is all that exists here." The atmosphere lost none of its solemnity and power, but changed slowly to admiration for the Shuso and to gratitude for the pulsing life that has carried the ancient Zen traditions to Tassajara.

When all the students had presented their questions, Chino Sensei said, "In a vale of these deep mountains a disciple of Buddha comes to teach. Let us hear congratulations." Congratulations came spontaneously from the students throughout the zendo. Bishop Sumi Roshi gave a short moving talk. Docho Roshi concluded the ceremony with his congratulations, saying how he felt the ceremony was a beautiful expression of his faith in the Shuso and in Tassajara.

Drug Use and Student Values
Kenneth Keniston

Kenneth Keniston (1930–   ) teaches at Yale University and is especially interested in the problems of American youth. His works include *The Study of Lives, The Uncommitted: Alienated Youth in American Society,* and *Young Radicals: Notes on Committed Youth.*

Student drug-users are generally treated by the mass media as an alien wart upon the student body of America. The use of drugs to alter psychic states, associated in the public mind with the abuse of narcotics, conjures up images of moral lepers and Mafia members. These images, in turn, help prevent any real understanding of the actual meanings and functions of drug use among a small minority of today's students.

In the comments to follow, I will argue that student drug use is closely related to the dominant pressures on American students, and is but a *variant* of values that are shared by many and perhaps most American undergraduates today. To be sure, only a small minority turn toward drugs; but the members of this minority group are but first-cousins to the more "normal" college student. In particular, the student drug-user shares with his non-drug-using classmates an active search for meaning through intense personal experience.

In order to understand the values shared by many American college students, we must begin by considering some of the pressures that affect today's students. With regard to drug use, two pressures are particularly important: the pressure toward cognitive professionalism, and the pressure toward psychological numbing.

COGNITIVE PROFESSIONALISM

The past two decades have seen a revolution in our expectations about college students. Rising standards of academic performance in primary and secondary schools, the "baby boom" of the war, the slowness with which major American universities have expanded their size—all have resulted in increasing selectivity by the admissions offices of the most prestigious American colleges and universities. Furthermore, once a student is admitted to college, higher admission standards have meant that more could be demanded of him; students who a generation ago would have done "A" work now find themselves doing only "C" work with the same effort. The sheer volume of required reading and writing has increased enormously; in addition, the quality of work expected has grown

From a paper presented by Kenneth Keniston at the National Association of Student Personnel Administrators Drug Education Conference, Washington, D.C., November 7–8, 1966. The NASPA Drug Education Project is supported by Contract No. FDA 67–3, with the Food and Drug Administration, Department of Health, Education and Welfare. Reprinted by permission.

by leaps and bounds. Finally, for a growing number of young Americans, college is but a stepping stone to professional and graduate school after college; and, as a result, consistent academic performance in college increasingly becomes a prerequisite for admission to a desirable business school, medical school, law school or graduate school.

Not only have academic pressures mounted in the past generation, but these pressures have become more and more cognitive. What matters, increasingly, to admissions committees and college graders is the kind of highly intellectual, abstracting, reasoning ability that enables a student to do well on college boards, graduate records and other admissions tests, and—once he is in college or graduate school—to turn out consistently high grades that will enable him to overcome the next academic hurdle. And while such intellectual and cognitive talents are highly rewarded, colleges increasingly frown upon emotional, affective, non-intellectual and passionate forms of expression. What is rewarded is the ability to delay, postpone and defer gratification in the interests of higher education tomorrow.

In contrast to these cognitive demands, there are extremely few countervailing pressures to become more feeling, morally responsible, courageous, artistically perceptive, emotionally balanced or interpersonally subtle human beings. On the contrary, the most visible pressures on today's students are, in many ways, anti-emotional, impersonal, quantitative and numerical. The tangible rewards of our college world—scholarships, admission to graduate school, fellowships and acclaim—go for that rather narrow kind of cognitive functioning involved in writing good final examinations, being good at multiple choice tests and getting good grades. Furthermore, the tangible rewards of the post-collegiate professional world also demand a similar kind of cognitive functioning, at least in the early years. Thus, it is the outstanding college and graduate student who goes on to coveted appointments in desirable hospitals, law firms, business, faculties and scientific laboratories.

This pressure for cognitive professionalism is closely related to the increasing "seriousness" of American college students. Many observers have commented on the gradual decline of student enthusiasm for such traditional American student pastimes as fraternities, football games, popularity contests and panty raids. At least at the more selective colleges, the reason for this decline is obvious: the pre-professional student has neither time nor motivation for the traditional pranks of his parents' generation. To survive and prosper in today's technological world, he must work with unremitting diligence to "be really good in his field."

Increasingly, then, one of the major pressures on American students is a pressure to perform well academically, to postpone and delay emotional satisfactions until they are older, to refine and sharpen continually their cognitive abilities. As a result, students today probably work harder than students in any other previous generation; a bad course or a bad year means to many of them that will not get into graduate school. Taking a year off increasingly means running the danger of getting drafted and being sent to Vietnam.

In describing these pressures, I have used the word "performance" advisedly. A "performance" suggests an activity that is alien, that is done on a stage in order to impress others, that is, a role played for an audience's applause. And to many students, of course, this quality of mild "alienness" pervades much of their intellectual and academic activities.

Thus, while the systematic quest for cognitive competence occupies much of the time and effort of the pre-professional student at today's selective colleges, this pursuit does little to inform the student about life's wider purposes. One of the peculiar characteristics of professional competence is that even when competence is attained, all of the other really important questions remain unanswered: what life is all about, what really matters, what to stand for, how much to stand for, what is meaningful, relevant and important, what is meaningless, valueless and false. Thus, for many students, the pursuit of professional competence must be supplemented by another, more private and less academic quest for the meaning of life. Academic efforts seem, to a large number of students, divorced from the really important "existential" and "ultimate" questions. In this way, the student's private search for meaning, significance and relevance is experienced as unconnected with or opposed to his public exertions for grades, academic success and professional competence. How students search for significance and relevance, of course, varies enormously from individual to individual; but, as I will later suggest, drug use seems—to a small group of students—a pathway to the pursuit of meaning.

STIMULUS FLOODING AND PSYCHOLOGICAL NUMBING

Every society contains pressures and demands which its members simply take for granted. Thus, the pressure for extremely high levels of cognitive efficiency seems to most of us a necessary and an even desirable aspect of modern society. Our response to the second social pressure I want to discuss is even more unreflective and automatic. This second pressure has to do with the sheer quantity, variety and intensity of external stimulation, imagery and excitation to which most Americans are subjected. For lack of a better label, I will term our condition one of increasing "stimulus flooding."

Most individuals in most societies have at some point in their lives had the experience of being so overcome by external stimulation and internal feelings that they gradually find themselves growing numb and unfeeling. Medical students, for example, commonly report that after their first and often intense reactions to the cadaver in the dissecting room, they simply "stop feeling anything" with regard to the object of their dissection. Or we have all had the experience of listening to so much good music, seeing so many fine paintings, being so overwhelmed by excellent cooking that we find ourselves simply unable to respond further to new stimuli. Similarly, at moments of extreme psychic pain and anguish, most individuals "go numb," no longer perceiving the full implications of a catastrophic situation or no longer experiencing the full range of their own feelings. This lowered responsiveness, which I will call "psychological numbing," seems causally related to the variety, persistence and intensity of psychological flooding. In a calm and tranquil field of vision, we notice the slightest motion. In a moving field, only the grossest of movements are apparent to us.

One of the conditions of life in any modern technological society is continual sensory, intellectual and emotional stimulation which produces or requires a high tendency toward psychological numbing. Some of you, I am sure, have had the experience of returning to urban American life from a calm and tranquil pastoral setting. Initially, we respond by being virtually overwhelmed with the clamor of people, sights, sounds, images and colors that demand our attention and our response. The beauty and the ugliness of the landscape continually strike us; each of the millions of faces in our great cities has written on it the tragi-comic record of a unique life history; each sound evokes a resonant chord within us. Such periods, however, tend to be transient and fleeting; often they give way to a sense of numbness, of non-responsiveness, and of profound inattention to the very stimuli which earlier evoked so much in us. We settle in; we do not notice any more.

This psychological numbing operates, I submit, at a great variety of levels for modern man. Our experience from childhood onward with the constantly flickering images and sounds of television, films, radio, newspapers, paperbacks, neon signs, advertisements and sound trucks numbs us to many of the sights and sounds of our civilization. The exposure of the most intelligent men to a vast variety of iedologies, value systems, philosophies, political creeds, superstitions, religions and faiths numbs us, I think, to the unique claims to validity and the special spiritual and intellectual values of each one: we move among values and ideologies as in a two-dimensional landscape. Similarly, the availability to us in novels, films, television, theatre and opera of moments of high passion, tragedy, joy, exaltation and sadness often ends by numbing us to our own feelings and the feelings of others.

In all these respects, modern men confront the difficult problem of keeping "stimulation" from without to a manageable level, while at the same time protecting themselves against being overwhelmed by their own inner responses to the stimuli from the outer world. Defenses or barriers against both internal and external stimulation are, of course, essential in order for us to preserve our intactness and integrity as personalities. From earliest childhood, children develop thresholds of responsiveness and barriers against stimulation in order to protect themselves against being overwhelmed by inner or outer excitement. Similarly, in adulthood, comparable barriers, thresholds and defenses are necessary, especially when we find ourselves in situations of intense stimulation.

I do not mean to suggest that the quantity of stimulation in modern society is alone responsible for psychological numbing. Certainly the quality, kind and variety of stimuli determine how we respond to them; in addition, our own excitability, responsivity, sensitivity and openness are crucial factors in determining what defenses we need against stimulus flooding. But I am arguing that the quantity, intensity and variety of inputs to which the average American is subjected in an average day probably have no precedent in any other historical society; everywhere we turn we are surrounded by signs, sounds and people actively clamoring for our response. Thus, to survive with calm and intactness in the modern world, we all require an armor, a protective shell, a screen, a capacity to "close off," ignore or deny our attention to the many stimuli of our physical and social world. Such numbing is necessary and useful for most of us, most of the time. The problem arises, however, because the shells we erect to protect ourselves from the clamors of the inner and outer world often prove harder and less permeable than we had originally wanted.

Thus, in at least a minority of Americans, the normal capacity to defend oneself against undue stimulation and inner excitation is exaggerated and automatized, so that it not only protects but walls off the individual from inner and outer experience. In such individuals, there develops an acute sense of being trapped in their own shells, unable to break through their defenses to make "contact" with experience or with other people, a sense of being excessively armored, separated from their own activities as by an invisible screen, estranged from their own feelings and from potentially emotion-arousing experiences in the world. Presumably most of us have had some inkling of this feeling of inner deadness and outer flatness, especially in times of great fatigue, let-down, or depression. The world seems cold and two-dimensional; food and life have lost their savor; our activities are merely "going through the motions," our experiences lack vividness, three-dimensionality and intensity. Above all, we feel trapped or shut in our own subjectivity.

Such feelings are, I believe, relatively common among college students, and particularly so at moments of intense stress, loss, depression, discouragement and gloom. It is at such times that the gap between the public pursuit of professional competence and the private search for meaning seems widest; it is also at these times that the chasm between the individual and his own experience seems most unbridgable.

Each of the two pressures I have discussed—cognitive professionalism and stimulus flooding—evokes characteristic responses among today's American college students. The pressure for cognitive professional competence leads to a search for meaning in other areas of life; the feeling and fear of psychological numbing lead to a pursuit, even a cult, of experience for its own sake. And the use and abuse of psychoactive drugs by students is closely related to these two themes in student values.

THE SEARCH FOR MEANING

Among today's self-conscious college students, the statement "I'm having an identity crisis" has become a kind of verbal badge of honor, a notch in the gun, a scalp at the belt. But although the term "identity crisis" can be easily parodied and misused, it points to fundamental issues of adolescence in all societies that are particularly heightened in our own society. Since academic pursuits, on the whole, tell the student so little about life's ultimate purposes, students are turned back upon their own resources to answer questions like "What does life mean? What kind of a person am I? Where am I going? Where do I come from? What really matters?"

Obviously, our society does not attempt to provide young Americans ready-made and neatly packaged answers to these questions. Rather, we expect that students will, in general, arrive at individual solutions to the riddles of life, and, indeed, we sometimes deliberately design our educational systems so as to provoke and challenge students to profound replies. Yet at the same time, we insist that students occupy themselves with getting good grades and getting ahead in the academic world, pursuits that often seem to have relatively little to do with "ultimate" questions. Thus, students often feel obligated to turn away from their academic pursuits toward a private quest for identity or search for meaning.

To understand this search for meaning, we must recall that many of the traditional avenues to meaning and significance have dried up. Traditional religious faith is not, for most sophisticated undergraduates, a means of ascertaining the meaning of life: traditional religions often seem to students to be worn out, insincere, or superficial. Similarly the great classic political ideologies, whether they be political liberalism, conservatism, Marxism or Fascism, arouse relatively little interest among most undergraduates. Nor does the "American Way of Life," as epitomized by 100% Americanism and free enterprise, stir most students to enthusiasm, much less provide them with answers about life's ultimate purposes.

At the same time, many traditional campus activities have lost their centrality as guidelines for or rehearsal of life's ultimate purposes. There was a day when the quest for popularity seemed to a great many undergraduates a reflection of a broader philosophy of life in which the most important goal was to make friends, to be popular and to influence people. Today, the pursuit of popularity and social success is declining in importance, and even those who pursue friendship and social skills most avidly are likely to recognize their limitations as ultimate values. Upward mobility, another ancient American goal, has also lost much of its savor. More and more students arrive in college already "ahead in the world," from well-situated middle-class families, and not particularly worried about status and upward mobility. Nor does the old American dream of giving one's children "a better chance" make great sense of life to a generation that has been born and bred amid affluence, and that rarely imagines a society in which starvation, unemployment or depression will be major possibilities.

One by one, then, many of the traditional sources of meaning have disappeared, at the very same time that academic life itself, because of its intense pressure and professional specialization, seems to many students increasingly irrelevant to their major existential concerns. Where, then, do students turn?

THE CULT OF EXPERIENCE

The cult of experience has often been discussed as a defining characteristic of American youth cultures. Central to this cult is a focus on the present—on today, on the here-and-now. Thus, rather than to defer gratification and enjoyment for a distant future, immediate pleasure and satisfaction are emphasized. Rather than reverence for the traditions of the past, experience in the present is stressed. Psychologically, then, such human qualities as control, planning, waiting, saving and postponing on the one hand, and revering, recalling, remembering and respecting on the other, are equally de-emphasized. In contrast, activity, adventure, responsiveness, genuineness, spontaneity and sentience are the new experiential values. Since neither the future nor the past can be assumed to hold life's meaning, the meaning of life must be sought within present experience, within the self, within its activity and responsiveness in the here-and-now.

The cult of experience has many variants and forms, most of them visible in one aspect or another on most American campuses. One such variant is what is often termed "student existentialism." At the more intellectually sophisticated campuses, this outlook manifests itself in an intense interest in Existential writers like Sartre and Camus. But at a variety of other colleges, it is evident by student discussions of the importance of simple human commitments as contrasted with absolute values, and by a pervasively high estimation of such human qualities as authenticity, genuineness, sincerity and directness, which are contrasted with phoniness, inauthenticity, artificiality and hypocrisy. This student existentialism is humanistic rather than religious, and its most immediate goals are love, intimacy, directness, immediacy, empathy and sympathy for one's fellow man. Thus, what matters is interpersonal honesty, "really being yourself," and genuineness, and what is most unacceptable is fraudulence, "role playing," "playing games."

The same focus on simple human experiences in the present is seen in a variety of other student values. Consider, for example, the great growth in interest in the arts—music, poetry, sculpture, drama, the film as art. Or recall the importance to many students of nature—that is, of wilderness, of the rapidly disappearing natural beauty of this country. Sex, too, is related to the same theme; for sex is above all that human experience that seems to require directness and immediacy, and that cannot be forced. Similarly, the focus by many students on family life—their willingness to sacrifice other goals for the creation and maintenance of a good family and a "productive" relationship with their future wives—these too are variations on the same experiential theme.

DISAFFILIATION AND DRUGS

The two student values I have discussed—the search for meaning and the cult of experience—are intimately related to the pressures I have outlined earlier. The search for meaning is made more urgent by the amount of time and energy the average student must spend in pre-professional academic pursuits that often appear to him irrelevant to his basic concerns. And the cult of experience is intensified by the fear or feeling in many undergraduates that, instead of becoming more open to themselves and to experience, they are becoming increasingly numbed and closed off from all that is exciting and beautiful. Both of these values are, as well, related to the use and abuse of drugs by students. For such is the cultism and propaganda that surrounds drugs, especially the hallucinogens, that many students have come to feel the states induced by these drugs will automatically produce a revelation of life's meaning, or at least an experience which itself will be highly significant and illuminating. Similarly, to the undergraduate who feels himself unduly walled-off from experience, drugs like the hallucinogens and the amphetamines (which intensify and alter ordinary states of consciousness) may seem a chemical sledgehammer for breaking out of his shell.

Obviously, despite the congruence of drug use with important student values in American colleges, the vast majority of American students do not seek meaning and experience primarily via psychoactive compounds. There are other values in most students that conflict sharply with drug use—for example, a kind of "do-it-yourselfism" that strongly rejects "artificial" and "chemical" means of altering psychic states; a sense of social responsibility that enjoins the student against doing socially disapproved things like abusing drugs; and—perhaps most important—a legitimate fear of the possible bad affects of drug use. Social and geographic factors also contribute to the low incidence of drug use. On many campuses, drugs are simply not available; on other campuses, the prevalent value system (e.g., religious fundamentalism) is completely at odds with the use of psychoactive compounds. Thus, despite the presence of some values which are consistent with drug use, most students have other values that argue against drug use. It is only a minority who are persuaded to choose drugs as a primary means of searching for meaning.

I doubt that it is possible to present an exact portrait of *the* type of student who is likely to use and abuse drugs. My own experience with student drug-users convinces me that there are many different motives for drug use and abuse, and there are many different factors—psychological, sociological, cultural and situational—that determine whether one student will use drugs while another will not. But despite the diversity of student types who *may* become involved in drug use, there is, I believe, one type that is particularly prone to drug abuse. Students of this type have, I think, particularly few values that militate against drug use and particularly strong motivations that incline them toward drugs, especially the hallucinogens. I will call such students "disaffiliates."

Elsewhere I have attempted a more comprehensive description of disaffiliates or "alienated" students. Here I will merely summarize some of the factors that predispose these students toward drug abuse. The defining characteristic of the disaffiliate is his generalized rejection of prevalent American values, which he rejects largely on esthetic, cultural and "humanistic" grounds. Such students are rarely political activists, and they are rarely concerned with the issues of economic, social and political justice that agitate many of their classmates. For these students, the problem is not political or social, but esthetic: American society is ugly, trashy, cheap and commercial; it is dehumanizing; its middle-class values are seen as arbitrary, materialistic, narrow and hypocritical. Thus, those conventional values which deem experimentation with drugs—or experimentation of all kinds—illicit are strongly rejected by disaffiliates; for them, what matters is somehow to seek a way out of the "air-conditioned nightmare" of American society.

A second characteristic of disaffiliates is a more or less intense feeling of estrangement from their own experience. Such students are highly aware of the masks, facades and defenses people erect to protect themselves; and not only do they criticize these "defenses" in others, but even more strongly in themselves. Any "defense" that might prevent awareness of inner life must be rooted out and destroyed: self-deception, lack of self-awareness and any "phoniness" with regard to oneself are cardinal sins. But despite their efforts to make contact with their "real" selves and to have "genuine" experiences, disaffiliates often feel separated from both self and others. They experience themselves as separated from others by a grey opaque filter, by invisible screens and curtains, by protective shells and crusts that prevent them from the fullness of experience. They recriminate themselves for their lack of feeling expressiveness, spontaneity and genuineness. One such student described human relations as being like people trying to contact and touch each other through airtight space suits; another talked of a wax that was poured over all of his experience preventing him from genuine contact with it. These feelings of estrangement are often accompanied by considerable depression and a strong sense of personal isolation. Indeed, depression, following the loss of an important relationship, is commonly found in the immediate background of the student who begins to abuse drugs. For the student with intensified feelings of estrangement from himself and others, drugs that promise to heighten experience seem a tempting way out of his shell.

A third relevant characteristic of disaffiliates is a fantasy of fusion and merger, which contrasts sharply with their current feelings of estrangement. In the background, many of these students have a concept of an almost mystical fusion with nature, with their own inner lives, or above all with other people—a kind of communication that requires no words, a kind of oneness with nature or the world that has characterized intense religious experience for centuries, a special kind of automatic oneness with another. For an undergraduate with an especial longing for oneness with others, the hallucinogens are especially tempting. For one characteristic of the drug experience is a weakening or breaking down of the boundaries of the self such that many individuals in fact report feelings of oneness, merger and fusion with others.

On several grounds, then, the disaffiliate is strongly attracted by drugs. Arguments based on traditional American values against drug use carry little weight for him; on the contrary, he values most in himself his own rebellion against such "middle-class" standards. His frequent feelings of estrangement from experience lead him to seek means of breaking through the walls, shells, filters and barriers that separate him from the world. And his fantasy of fusion disposes him to seek out chemical instruments that will increase his "oneness" with others. For such students, who are young, searching, uncommitted and anti-conventional, drug use is primarily a way of searching for meaning via the chemical intensification of personal experience.

DRUG USE AND STUDENT VALUES

In portraying one type of student who is predisposed toward the abuse of psychoactive compounds, and in relating drug use to more general student values, I do not mean to portray all American students as potential drug users, nor to decry the student values which may be interpreted to support drug use. On the contrary, I am convinced that the search for meaning through experience is an important and valid search, although I personally doubt that present experience is itself enough to provide "the meaning of life." Similarly, even those students who actively abuse drugs are seeking, I think, legitimate ends through unwise means. It will not do, therefore, to repudiate students who misuse drugs as moral lepers and "addicts" without trying to understand their motives for drug use, and the values and goals they pursue. These motives are rarely simply antisocial or "thrill-seeking." On the contrary, they almost always involve a legitimate (if misguided) search for ultimate meaning and contact with the world. In dealing with individual drug users, then, we must attempt to provide the student with alternate routes to attain his valid goals. And since drug use is notoriously hazardous and uncertain, it should not prove impossible to suggest better avenues toward meaning and experience than drugs. Even Dick Alpert commented . . . that he considers the use of LSD a "crutch;" we must help our students to understand that this is so.

In addition, we need to appreciate that students who use and abuse drugs are reacting not only to the individual circumstances of their past and present lives, but to dilemmas that confront their entire generation. It would of course be wrong to identify drug use *solely* with cultural and historical pressures. But it would be equally wrong to emphasize the individual psychodynamics of student drug-users in such a way as to avoid confronting the possibility that the rising rate of student drug use is a commentary upon our educational system and upon our entire society. Although student drug-users are a small minority, they point to the inability of our colleges and our society to enlist the commitments of a talented minority. If we could understand why, it might point not only to how we could "cure" drug-users, but, even more important, how we might "cure" colleges and society.

As for counseling student drug-users—potential and actual—I think it import-ant to acknowledge that the question of drug use is, in the last analysis, not a medical issue, but an existential, philosophical and ethical issue. Student drug-users are, as a group, extremely knowledgeable about the possible bad effects of drug use; they can usually teach their counselors, deans and advisors a good deal about the potential bad side effects of drugs. They will argue—with considerable validity—that society does not prohibit the use of other psychoactive compounds (e.g., alcohol, tobacco) which in some ways are far more dangerous than many of the hallucinogens or amphetamines. In the last analysis, then, whether one chooses or not to use drugs, in full consciousness of their possible bad effects and the legal implications of drug use, becomes an existential rather than a medical decision. It is a matter of how one chooses to live one's life, how one hopes to seek experience, where and how one searches for meaning. To be sure, I doubt that we can hope to persuade students that drugs are ethically, humanly or existentially undesirable if they are not already persuaded. But I think we can at least help the student to confront the fact that in using drugs he is making a statement about how he wants to live his life. And we can, perhaps, in our own lives and by our own examples, suggest that moral courage, a critical awareness of the defects of our society, a capacity for intense experience and the ability to relate genuinely to other people are not the exclusive possessions of drug-users.

In the long run, then, those of use who are critical of student drug abuse must demonstrate to our students that there are better and more lasting ways to experience the fullness, the depth, the variety and the richness of life than that of ingesting psychoactive chemicals. It would be a pity, for example, to allow the advocates of LSD to take exclusive possession of the term "consciousness-expansion." Consciousness-expansion seems to me not the sole prerogative of psychoactive compounds, but of education in its fullest sense. The giants of our intellectual tradition were men who combined critical consciousness of their own societies with a capacity for experience and relatedness. And they were consciousness-expanders par excellence in their attempts to lead their fellows out of ignorance to a clearer perception of truth, beauty and reality.

Thus, insofar as we can truly and honestly help our students to become educated in the fullest sense, we will be able to provide alternative routes to the pursuit of meaning, the quest for experience and the expansion of consciousness. Obviously, much of what passes for higher education in America fails to accom-plish any of these high objectives. As long as it continues to fail, I suspect that drugs will continue to be a problem on our campuses and in our society.

The Jesus Freaks

James Nolan

James Nolan (1947–   ) is a poet from New Orleans now living in California.

Swept along in the squall of *Peace on Right Now You-Name-It Against The War* placards at the Spring Offensive in San Francisco waved a flimsy blue poster with drippy red lettering that read *Jesus: A Bridge Over Troubled Waters.* The bearer wasn't a collared cleric or a Youth Fellowshipper chalking up merit points for heaven, but a scroungy, ponchoed, bell-bottomed veteran of the streets. Anyone at all familiar with what is happening in California simply nodded a recognition—ah, a Jesus-freak—accepted his tract and plowed on to the polo field. A few stopped and stared, obviously shaken to their Sunday School roots by the very idea of freak evangelism, a fairly new breed in the hip-liberation menagerie. But there he was, marching right-on along with the red armbands, the lavender headbands, the brown berets, the black berets, the inverted flags, the hardstepping women, the saffron robes and the green earth insignias. And this barefoot boy with his flimsy blue bridge-over-troubled-waters certainly did not seem to have come at the wrong time or to the wrong place with whatever message he had to give America in the Seventies.

The message of Jesus-freaks, in case you haven't been able to skim their tracts or sit still through their spiel, is simply down-home, Jesus-is-the-way, evangelical fundamentalism delivered with flower-child innocence and visionary fervor. The movement is incredibly broad-based. There are over 200 Jesus communes in California alone, a Jesus headquarters coffeehouse or headshop in every major city in the country, and missionary troops in motion everywhere, converting, founding, funding and then moving on. The large wall map at the Christian World Liberation Front in Berkeley is studded with pinheads marking the places where the movement has taken root, giving you the same they're-really-out-there feeling of a Howard Johnson's placemat map. Despite the bare feet and patches, it really is big time stuff, concentrated mostly along the West Coast in Vancouver, Seattle, the Bay Area and Los Angeles, with another con-tingent distributed throughout the South. Most Jesus communes publish amateurish underground newspapers and bear names like the folksy Children of God Soul Clinic, the obscure Koinonia Community, and the clever House of the Risen Son.

American blow-your-mind, zappo-revolutionary kids are literally flocking into these fundamentalist conversion parlors and coming out with handfuls of psychedelic-looking tracts, a "Biblical" set of morals and big Billy James Hargis friend-do-you-know-the-Lord grins. The Jesus houses offer a place to crash indefinitely, free food and free medical care, a toothbrush and comb, enough to do and more than enough to believe in; and there's usually a Mother or Daddy figure who, despite the preaching and soul-saving, really seems to care, and won't make you cut your hair. All in all, it's an unbeatable combination if you're 18 years old, a runaway from some cowtown Paducah or plastic Executive Oaks, used to dropping acid by the six-pack, alone and penniless in the ghetto-zoo, . . . testing around for some ultimate reality trip, with nothing to do and no place in particular to do it.

The Jesus trip is particularly attractive to children brought up in staunchly religious homes (there are many former Catholics and Baptists) or to kids reared on suburban textbook agnosticism, the ones who are lost even before they've found anything to be lost from. Most of the converted are between 14 and 20, and they possess an amazingly glowing energy and commitment, all shining as though they've just washed their hair. Maybe the Jesus movement is only a later version of Love-Generation-Haight-Ashbury optimism, the flowers-and-trans-cendence stage of growing up American, that will eventually turn the same worn path to skepticism and militancy when they reach 23.

But it can't be this alone. There is a great difference between an imported novelty fetish like, say, Hare Krishna—which is essentially hip faddism in search of faith, a turn-on that soon burns itself out into a religion of Indian-print bedspreads and incense, and deeply ingrained, evangelical Christianity—upon which, they tell us, this Nation of Ours was founded and the West was Won. They are partially right, of course. And, even if Jesus was not in cahoots with Christopher Columbus and Kit Carson, Bible Belt Christianity is not simply another American fad—it runs too deep in too many people. Like that trout-fishing cabin in Utah, it is at least what part of America is all about. Whether the new masses of Jesus-freaks are only visiting or whether they plan to stay, they are pitching their tents very close to one of the main arteries of the American heart.

Jesus-freaks have introduced only a few real variations to Bible-pounding, tent-revival, fundamentalist Christianity, among them street language (Jesus is no longer Lord and Savior but Leader and Liberator) and the communal life-style. But over-arching all else is a passionate belief that the world will end with-in their lifetime while Jesus returns to rapture them off to a very literal heaven with streets of gold and angels twanging on electric-amp harps, the thought of which clouds their eyes and leaves them murmuring "fa-a-ar out."

Fundamentalists are a tricky lot. Between the ages of 6 and 12 I probably gave my life to Christ about two or three hundred times in the fundamentalist church in New Orleans that I was combed and bow-tied off to every Sunday morning. *Are you washed in the blood of the lamb? Do you recognize yourself as a miserable sinner wretched in God's sight? Are you ready to get down on your knees and accept Jesus into your heart as your own personal savior? All those ready to make a decision for Christ, just step on up to the front of the church and praise* deedum deedum deedee. Sunday morning was bringing in the sheaves (and usually the same old ones), followed by the Sunday evening Saved for Christ Scoreboard, followed by Bible study with Dixie cups of punch and cookies, everyone feverishly fanning himself in the sultry New Orleans night with picture fans of Jesus-in-the-Garden-of-Gethsemane supplied by a local mortuary. It was a hell of a way to grow up, I suppose, but I eventually felt secure enough in my solid-rock salvation to sneak off to the drugstore from Bible study to read *Playboy,* though not without the puffy red face of the preacher following me in my mind, exhorting me to give my life to Christ again.

The fundamentalist works on an appeal to guilt, which suburban drop-outs are particularly full of, on a thundering fear of hell and a candy-sweet promise of heaven, on a complete negation of any other possible means to happiness, and on a repetition of phrases so unrelenting as to make a Madison Avenue advertiser stutter. You either give in or walk out. His pitch is an express train with only one stop: your salvation. All questions are answered by vague and enigmatic Bible quotations followed by chapter and verse number so that you cannot *possibly* doubt their truth, and key simplicities are underlined in verbal red. If you protest even the slightest, you are told that Satan has planted his seed in your brain, a notion with disturbing implications to be sure, and, if you protest too much, you are told that you are possessed of a demon from which only the blood of Jesus Christ can deliver you. Then it starts all over again, back to original sin and the goddamned Garden of Eden. In the end, if you become a passive enough listener, you are rewarded with a paperback Bible, the converter tape-loop is shut-off, pleasantries are exchanged about automobiles or summer vacations, and you can leave, promising to read the Bible and "look over" the tract.

I o.d.'d on peanut butter when I was 10 and fundamentalism when I was 12 and haven't been able to stand the taste of either since. Every time I hear the familiar strains of one of those mournful old hymns, I gag on years of undigested punch and cookies. I can make no pretense about my feelings about fundamentalist theology, fundamentalist evangelism and the whole fundamentalist fandango of faith-healing, Bible-beating and tent-shouting: it's hogwash. It is a political opiate and a psychological crutch. Fundamentalism is truly the wading pool of religious faith, reserved for the fearful, the guilt-ridden and the childish, for those unprepared to dive, to make their faith leap into a political reality or mystical depth.

In America, fundamentalism has always been associated with the forces of political reaction, with the blathering God-on-our-side cross and flag confusers, and, even worse, with the phony racketeers of religious ecstacy, the Elmer Gantrys of *Miracle* magazine or the Oral Roberts variety who feed on the hopelessness of uneducated minorities who cough up ten dollars a month or more so that some sleazy preacher with a slick-backed pompadour and sequin jacket will pray over miniature healing aprons to cure them of their vitamin deficiencies and other ghetto diseases, all of which is nothing less than a kind of lower-class voodoo. Most peculiar about Jesus-freaks is the combined tradition of middle-class hypocrisy and lower-class viciousness out of which they bloom, with their flowers and smiles and God-bless-you's. The sources and purveyors of this tradition were the first to prey upon this open-armed innocence, with the greasy *Miracle* magazine and the staid *Christianity Today* being among the first to report the Jesus Movement.

Fundamentalist theologian Carl F. H. Henry writes in *Christianity Today* that Jesus-freaks have "succeeded in redirecting the revolutionary enthusiasm of not a few converts into recreative channels and toward durable Christian goals." Few young Jesus-freaks understand the perspective in which their leaders and elders see them: they just want to stand in white robes on mountain tops and wait for the light show of the Second Coming. They do not see themselves as long-haired chalk-ups on the large conversion scoreboard, as part of a power-game whose rules, goals and techniques have not changed one bit in the last hundred years or more. After all, they are told, we are not of this world.

Reverend Blessit of "His Place" on Sunset Strip in Los Angeles is a particularly flashy example of this Campus Crusade for Christ mentality, boutiqued over with paste-board psychedelic finish and restocked on the shelves as the Real Thing for the Youth Market, the Uncola of religious persuasion, bearing about as close a resemblance to anything revolutionary as those cleverly advertised, insipid little cheese-nothings, Screaming Yellow Zonkers, had to the nutrition revolution.

This plasticine selling-of-the-revolution is operating on all levels now, and is particularly aimed at media-impressionable teeny- and micro-boppers. And it should be no surprise that the evangelism industry—which has used everything from Motown to motel-drawers in the past to push its product—should shift into the third-gear of its get-with-it campaign and begin strutting its stuff with a hippie-drug-cult border around it. Reverend Blessit, duded up in bell-bottoms and his "hippie vest," does the rock-festival circuit, bringing in the sheaves by sowing psychedeic brochures, sandwiches with tracts tucked inside, and frothing around on stage with such big-name Decisions for Christ as the manager of the Chambers Brothers. The marriage of Pop myths and evangelism is almost as perfect a union as the one between Hollywood and establishment politics, both based on the manipulation of empty media myths to extort either souls or votes from the star-struck masses.

Even Pat Boone, who was last seen posing for the covers of Pony Tail autograph albums, has white-bucked it back on the scene, and now peppers his ever-wholesome sermonettes with hip argot as he conducts mass baptisms in his Beverly Hills swimming pool, walking with floppy flipper feet and chlorinated eyes down the paths of righteousness.

Sitting around the nicely table-clothed, properly-set dinner table at Harvest House "commune" in San Francisco brought an incredible psychological flashback to my punch-and-cookie years in Youth Fellowship. The feeling was amazingly the same, a sort of strained institutional good humor. Pass the biscuits and praise the Lord. Talking with the soft-spoken, Alabamabred Oliver Heath, an ordained minister of the Southern Baptist Church and graduate of the Golden Gate Theological Seminary in Marin County, a fundamentalist school which is the seedbed of the Jesus movement in northern California, while his Louisiana-bred wife, Mary Louise padded about in fluffy pink bedroom slippers and curlers serving up cornbread and potluck, it really felt like a corner of Kansas pocketed by cosmic mistakes in the teeming heavy freak scene of Haight-Ashbury.

A shaggy young hippie-type in a corner was for some reason knotted into a red tie and starched white collar with an ill-fitting grey sport-coat, and kept giving me that strangled home-for-the-holidays look which I remember only too well. He looked as though he were trying to win the keys to the family car for the night by painfully self-conscious good behavior. Oliver kept interrupting our discussion of original sin and repentance to deliver stern reprimands to various scruffies: "Eric, you know you're not allowed to smoke in here, put that cigarette out!" and "Dennis, don't you have a comb!" Eric, the communal scapegoat, at 17 is so disoriented by his 100 or more acid trips that he would bring back groceries to the wrong apartment door, and therefore, the others explained, could not be trusted, so everyone prayed constantly for his soul to be purged of its demons. And Dennis was having Satan's seed planted in his brain by such Little Rascals' naughties as not coming home right after school but sneaking off to some suspicious Haight hash house, where he brushed shoulders with the devil's crowd, all fanged and horned and high on the Killer Weed.

At Harvest House there was much talk of the Enemy, who was on guard at all times, waiting for any opportunity to slither into their midst like some green gaseous malevolence sent from below. A young girl named Rose Marie, who seemed to become upset often, pleaded to the others that she needed to be left alone when she was disturbed, but the others insisted that such was the easiest time for Satan to stick a lie into her head. *The devil gonna git your soul, honey.* Huddling like a small child in a large, overstuffed armchair, Rose Marie seemed close to freaking out.

Like a camp shower room, all the towels in the bathroom were pegged and labeled, *Mary, Johnny, Sue* and so forth; and for some reason that simpy Sunday School picture of Jesus-in-the-Garden-of-Gethsemane was iconed over the toothbrush rack, probably to remind early morning brushers of their oft-bannered slogan: *after Jesus, everything else is toothpaste.* The orderly atmosphere, I was informed, was enforced in order to keep the "children" together —but not too together, for according to the strict precepts of Biblical morality (no screwing without a license), the boys and girls are carefully chaperoned and sleep in segregated quarters because "too much friction between the sexes tends to distract from the Lord's work."

The Lord's work at Harvest House consists of putting out a Jesus newspaper called the *Oracle* (which is an almost campy, religious, calendar-art revival of the old Haight-Ashbury *Oracle*), running a free store, printing tracts, helping to manage three adjoining communes in the city, and evangelizing in the streets. After Bible study at a local church that evening, the commune regathered for a sort of community encounter with each other. One wide-eyed young man confessed that, when he thought of all the things he had done wrong that very day, it was like going up and hitting God right in the mouth, WHAMMM. A very pregnant girl offered that, since she had become a Christian, she couldn't associate with her friends—they are "so steeped in sin," as she had been. Oliver told the group: "If you think I'm a phony, if you think I'm dishonest, if you think I'm not like Jesus, tell me now." Everyone beamed. A 17-year-old volunteered that he now felt closer to his parents (since he accepted Jesus) than ever before, and that his father had taught him not to lie and, even after all the acid and all the meth, that still made sense.

Spontaneous eruptions of conscience continued for about an hour, moving around the room like some T-group rendition of the White Tornado. My heart sank. Here it all was—the entire American mythology of growing up, freaking out, and running away; the well-powdered, Bible-preaching forces of Aunt Em, Aunt Sally, Miss Crabtree, confronting the primitive scraggly-haired, dirty faces of the perverse, freedom-loving Dorothy, Huck Finn and Our Gang; and Aunt Sally was winning. Dorothy had finally made it back to hug her Aunt Em and gasp about the bad dreams she had just tripped through. The high school dropouts in the room were all going back to school, the rest were getting jobs and re-establishing contact with their parents or going home. Intuitively I realized what the Jesus trip really meant to a lot of these kids; it is a way of getting back to Kansas from the tortured and confusing psychedelic world of surreal low-life munchkins, witches and wizards, back to the comfort and reassurance of your own backyard. Back from the drop-a-tab, crash pad spirituality of cross-country hitching, of protesting and confronting, of open-ended grooving that somehow always ended with the needle, getting busted, having your head swagger-sticked open, or getting pregnant. I didn't, I couldn't have any more questions of these people.

I still think Aunt Sally with her comb and her toothbrush and her Bible is a stifling bitch, but I know those dead-ends that the river can lead to, and that sometimes you have to try to get back to where you once belonged. This, Oliver explained to me, is the function of Harvest House and others like it: it is a hospital, a half-way house back to stability and wholeness through, he added, Jesus Christ. There is a time to argue theology, and I think his is wrong. There is a time to argue politics, and I think, whether he knows it or not, his are reactionary. There is a time to argue the revolution, and the Jesus movement is definitely *not* where it's happening. But there is also a time to shut up and let people heal. And this, if Harvest House can accomplish it, may be worth all the rest.

The Jesus movement's recognition of, and struggle with, the literal presence of the Satanic forces of darkness is a phenomenon precedented in America only by Cotton Mather's persecution of his neighbors as witches in Salem over two hundred and fifty years ago. Mather's account of the witch epidemic, *Wonders of the Invisible World,* a book which has puzzled and fascinated history and theology students for centuries, would make complete sense to these people. That's how freaked-out certain elements in the movement *really* are. Ecstatic religious practices, such as speaking in tongues (*glossolalia*), rolling on the floor, and raising arms heavenward and shouting, are common in the movement—although many prefer to sit with their legs crossed and study the Bible.

The Pentecostals, who speak in tongues and writhe about, have been making quite an impact lately not only in Protestant circles but also in Catholicism, but most Jesus people feel as estranged from the established Pentecostal churches as they do from their icier Methodist brethren. Margaret Ravick, the remarkable Big Mama of the Koinonia Community in Santa Cruz, says that when she listened to her first tape of Pentecostals she accidentally played the thing backwards, and for at least two weeks that is what she thought it sounded like to speak in tongues. Speaking in tongues is simply the gibberish, or angelic secret language, that descends on certain individuals in ecstatic fits of spiritual communication. Although they feel that psychedelics are the instruments of Satan, it certainly seems that their widespread use has been the very thing which has turned most Jesus people on to the realities of the spiritual realm. For the ecstatics, acid is almost a conversion prerequisite. The kids have the visions and blow out; and the evangelists put them together again by explaining what their visions mean—structuring, out of a nightmarish morass of tripping, a Biblical value system of significances, interpretations and codes, functioning as a poor man's Jung to the overloaded and chaotically explored psyches of acid-heads.

Identifying itself with the armies of God, Koinonia Community is currently waging war with the Satanist churches in Santa Cruz, which they say are everywhere. Recently it exorcised, in the name of Jesus Christ, a particular accident-ridden location on the main highway after discovering that a coven of witches and warlocks lives only a few yards away. Koinonia claims that the Satanist churches are becoming tightly organized, cutting their hair and mustering their energies for the final knock-down, drag-out battle with God. A crew-cut, collared priest was recently turned away from their doors because Michael, who possesses the gift of discerning evil spirits because he was once occupied by one, detected him to be a spy of Satan. The community later linked the priest to a large Satanist church in the area.

According to this particular band of Jesus people (who assert that they were there before the plastic Jesus-freak movement started and will be there when it is over), the occult is the devil's map of the spiritual world, and the Bible of course is God's map. They believe that the real battle being waged in California is not between reactionary Reaganism and the people, or between pollution and ecology, but between the forces of God and those of Satan; and this is one of the first battles of the Apocalypse, or the final separation of light from darkness. The state not being big enough for both of them, perhaps they'll swagger out the swinging saloon door all holstered up for a showdown, shoot-it-out, mini-Armageddon, with black cloaks flying and brandished crosses gleaming in some wildly surrealistic alcove on the dramatically appropriate California coastline.

Examined closely, the Jesus movement really separates into three distinct directions: the ecstatics, who live in relative seclusion; the do-good evangelists, who run the Jesus crashpads; and the quasi-politicos, who bait left-wing causes and occasionally disrupt radical rallies and congregations, while insisting they are apolitical. "Everyone says we're something we're not," protests Jeanette, a worker at the Christian World Liberation Front in Berkeley. "The right-wing says we're a bunch of long-haired communists and the left-wing says we're reactionaries."

Because the Jesus movement does claim apoliticism, it has attracted numerous disillusioned campus radicals and street revolutionaries who now argue that nothing can be accomplished on *that level*. "I don't believe in the peace movement," said a young Jesus-freak handing me a tract at the spring offensive, "but I believe in Jesus who can bring peace." Jeanette, who was, strangely enough, turned on to drugs by fellow workers at the Campus Crusade for Christ in southern California and did not repent until her third dope bust, feels that Jesus is a non-political answer. But the CWLF newspaper, *Right On,* and the reams of tracts which CWLF prints and distributes are nothing but half-baked and awkward attempts at political relevancy, written from a perspective which dissolves every issue into the world cynicism and downright doomsday-preaching of the fundamentalist salvation formula.

In an age of choose-your-apocalypse—ecological, political, thermonuclear, social, famine, over-population, natural disaster (experts say it's *all* about to happen) this doomsday-preaching has an infantile appeal. It is the chief drawing card of the hippie-evangelist as he whips out his Book of Revelation and rattles through a cookbook account of how it all will come to pass. "I'll be so disappointed if the world doesn't end soon," one Jesus person told with a look of gleeful death-obsession on his face. The end is so near, one tract advises, that there is no point even in getting married—stay celibate until Armageddon and save it all up for the Second Coming.

The Jesus movement must not be confused with the left-wing underground church, which preaches the full exercise of the Christian social conscience against the war and against oppression of any kind, which affirms the celebration of life on earth, not the other-wordly negation of it. The Free Church in Berkeley and

Glide Memorial in San Francisco, two Bay Area underground churches, have been at constant odds with the Jesus people. One Sunday last autumn the Jesus-freaks stormed Glide with posters announcing: "This Congregation Uses Jesus but Does not Honor Him as Lord" and pushed tracts titled, "Glide into Hell." The week before, a band of Jesus people made up of members of the CWLF, the Jesus Mobilization Committee of Marin, and other Bay Area communes started such a row at the West Coast SDS conference that they were bodily removed from the gathering. Whenever the members of the God Squad *do* express a political sentiment, in some evangelical attempt at relevancy, it is consistently reactionary. The CWLF's attitude toward Women's Liberation is, according to *Right On,* that "the real power of a woman is in loving a man. Let Jesus free you from yourself and free you to love a man. When you love a man, you will known what it is to be a woman. And you will see how only God can liberate women." As far as Gay Liberation is concerned, they simply feel that it is an "awful thing to do." And they do not allow homosexual couples to spend the night on their premises.

Despite the see-through veil of apoliticism and despite hard-sell pseudo-militancy, the Jesus movement is rife for a takeover by right-wing sugar-daddies. Already they control a small part of it. The Jesus newspaper, *For Real,* published in Buena Park, California, by the Living Issues Foundation, is "a dedicated effort to counteract the evil influences on campuses today by radical and anti-God elements. . . . *For Real* takes aim at that large fringe element who are being influenced by what the agitators are saying." Sandwiched between the turn-on-with-Jesus spreads, the Jesus-rock advertisements, and the pseudo-relevant articles on Leary and Women's Lib, *For Real* contains pro-militaristic, anti-welfare, capitalist harangues.

As to the financial source of all these free newspapers, free pass-outs, free food and lodging, the Jesus people respond with big lilies-of-the-field smiles: the Lord Provideth. And the Lord worketh in some pretty mysterious ways, they'll say, reeling out stories of $10 bills wrapped in toilet paper sent in the mail every month, commune members' back paychecks arriving miraculously on rent day as the landlord menacingly twirls his moustache, $50 for car payments sent from churches back home in Alabama. Despite their patches-and-leftovers life style, Jesus people usually have an impressive business set-up. One example is Harvest House which, together with Zion's Inn, a Jesus commune in nearby Marin County, has formed the Solid Rock Construction Company, which does housepainting. Most of the communes have prospered because of a Calvinist dedication to hard work and self-improvement, making carpenters, printers and soup-makers of the aimless kids who stumble in. The kids seem to enjoy the work, bustling about with sacks of flour and bundles of paper with a door-to-door-for-McCarthy cheerfulness. After all, with no dope or sex or Zap Comix or TV, what else is there to do?

Suddenly, Jesus is everywhere. Jesus buttons, Jesus sweatshirts, Honk-if-you-love-Jesus bumper-stickers, Jesus day-glo posters, Jesus on the cover of the *Whole Earth Supplement,* Jesus comics, the Jesus look, *Jesus Christ, Superstar,* Jesus rock.

Jesus is even more popular than John Lennon. Put your hand in the hand of the man from Galilee, how I changed from Krishna to Christ, how I lost 300 lbs. and saved my marriage with Jesus. Somehow fundamentalist evangelism has caught up with mass media and is plastering stickers, converting rock stars and plugging in amps all over the place.

As people lose their grip on the revolution, they seem to be grasping for absolutes. In the heavily moralistic South, the Jesus line seems appropriate—else no one would listen. But in the super-relativistic do-your-own-thing, mobile California scene, it is jarring. Yet it is perhaps this absolutism which attracts the blown-out 17-year-old who simply has nothing to do. High school has not prepared him for anything creative or constructive; it has only driven him to drop acid three times a week. Once that's done, it is impossible to be processed through the mind-cannery of a large university for very long. Nor can he go back home to the carport and a bag-boy job in the supermarket. With neither answers nor alternatives, with the visionary acid world of angels and demons his only certainty, the fast-talking, self-confident preacher steps in and puts his big Biblical foot down, taps it in a few familiar rhythms, stamps it in the fervor of his belief and everything falls into place.

The real issue at stake here is that drug-blown, pop-freaked, ego-defenseless kids, who in their innocence, openness and idealism are truly beautiful, can easily become the victims of a desperate evangelism of any kind—that, just as a handful of Hell's Angels can stomp in and take over a pop festival, a small collection of bell-bottomed Baptists and, at worst, Elmer Gantrys, can begin to redirect whole generations into their scripture-lined tents. It is the same with the Scientologists, the chanters, the T-groupies, the occultists and certain of the liberationist bandwagons.

The preacher does not offer a choice between a confusing array of life styles and locations, but rather a choice between eternal salvation and eternal damnation—which isn't a choice at all. Whether the content of his message is hogwash or holy water doesn't make too much difference. Whether these evangelistic Christians are, as Nietzsche accused, predatory birds who swoop down on weak life in distress or, in a more charitable view, fanatical do-gooders with an overly developed, paternal sense, makes little difference. The fact is, these people, and the leaders of other mass movements like them, are bringing freaked-out kids down and placing them in a community situation where roles are assigned and talents encouraged.

Mything-out on Jesus, though, is not too different from spacing-out on drugs; and once Jesus has brought them down from drugs, what's going to bring them down from Jesus? This kind of ultimate-trip carousel will continue to spin as long as, America being what it is now, there is nothing to come down to. So finally, a message to Jesus-boppers: If your apocalypse does not happen on schedule, and if and when you are lemming off in some new direction, realizing the torment and difficulty of true sainthood and that salvation is not just a shot of anything away, spare us one vision: a littered, trampled post-festival shambles with Jesus Christ, a blown-out superstar, back where he started, unplugging the amps and picking up the empty dixie punch cups and sweeping up the cookie crumbs scattered by the marauding packs of crowded, lonely people: no one was saved.

Turn or Burn

Lowell D. Streiker

Lowell D. Streiker (1939–   ) teaches in the department of religion at Temple University.

Certainly the most ecstatic organization I encountered among the Jesus people was Tony and Sue Alamo's Christian Foundation. It was a lovely cool evening after a scorching hot day when I drove to Saugus, nearly thirty miles north of Los Angeles. The area was hard hit by a recent earthquake. But even without the extensive evidence of the quake—fallen overpasses, condemned buildings, unearthed billboards—the region is remote and unappealing. The land is scruffy and barren, laced with steep foothills of hard, rocky soil. When the sun goes down, the countryside is as gaunt and lonely as the surface of the moon.

As I drove the Sierra highway, I wondered if I would ever find the abandoned restaurant the Alamos use as a house of worship and mess hall for their large Christian commune. In Los Angeles I had heard much about Tony and Sue—much of it unfavorable. The word was that they had been run out of L.A. by the police because they harrassed both residents and tourists with their immoderate "turn or burn" street preaching. I knew that they had inaugurated street witnessing and were largely responsible for the birth of the Jesus movement. But finding them seemed difficult. No one was sure where they had moved their operation. The best procedure seemed to be to allow them to find me, so I casually strolled Hollywood Avenue. Sure enough, within a half-block four young zealots had approached me, eager to tell me how they had been saved and hopeful that I would attend a meeting that evening in Saugus.

"What are you doing in such a remote place?" I asked.

Their reply: "The Lord said that in these last days his disciples should flee from the city to the mountains."

My first sensation when I entered their testimony service was severe discomfort. All the doors and windows were closed, and the body heat of two hundred wildly gyrating bodies raised the room temperature to well over one hundred degrees. Here was an old-fashioned revival service with the beloved gospel songs ("What a Friend We Have in Jesus," "Amazing Grace," etc.), a ceaseless stream of personal testimonies (I counted forty), instrumental and vocal solos ("And now Sister Mary Jane will sing 'In the Garden'"), duets, trios, and a frenzied "Hallelujah Chorus" sung by the forty testimony givers (thus revealing that the spontaneity of the service was more apparent than real). Never have I seen such energy, such fervor, such body-and-soul enthusiasm spent on religious worship. They were on the edge of hysteria the entire time. Arms lifted heavenward, feet stamping, all stops pulled, they screeched song lyrics unto God, moaned and groaned, shuddered, and had fits.

After the service I was escorted to the north Hollywood apartment of the Alamos, who were absent from the service. Tony and Sue sat warily at one side of a huge sofa. Sue is the heart of their operation, Tony the brains. She is late fortyish, hard-looking with crooked teeth and peroxided platinum hair. Tony seems younger, an aging crooner in Levis with a thickening waistline. They watched me like foxes until the ice was broken by the appearance of a busload of kids from Saugus. The occasion was a public unveiling of a phonograph record of the very music I had just heard at Saugus (including Sister Mary Jane's "In the Garden"). The ensuing scene was a revelation. Tony and Sue are Mom and Dad. They love each of these kids. And the kids love them and do whatever Tony and Sue ask. And Tony and Sue are no wishy-washy-do-as-you-please parents. They are do-as-you're-told-or-else-get-out parents. And for once in their lives these kids who have had too much too soon, these kids no one has ever loved enough to say no to, these advantaged kids from broken homes, these aimless kids who don't know what to do with themselves, these kids with too much freedom, too many choices, and too little guidance—for once in their lives they have someone who says, "These are the rules. Keep them and we'll love you. Break them and we'll punish you."

"I'm sick of this sentimental slush about a God of love," declared Tony. "'God will understand. God will forgive you.' What nonsense. God is a God of wrath to those who disobey him and a God of love to those who do his will and keep his commandments. And God says, 'Know ye not that the unrighteous shall not inherit the kingdom of God? Be not deceived: neither fornicators, nor idolators, nor adulterers, . . . nor drunkards'—and that includes every kind of drug addict—'shall inherit the kingdom of God.'"

Tony and Sue Alamo are both Jewish Christians. Their real name is Hoffman. Sue has been a Christian since childhood. After she was miraculously cured from a hopeless disease as a girl, her whole family was converted. But it was not until years later when she received the Pentecostal baptism of the Spirit and the gift of tongues that she began her ministry as a preacher. (And a frighteningly powerful preacher she is!) Tony was a vocalist and a recording industry executive when the Lord appeared to him in a vision right in the middle of a business conference and ordered Tony to inform his colleagues of His imminent return. (Both Tony and Arthur Blessitt state that Christ has appeared to them in person.)

Tony and Sue took to the streets five years ago. They have led thousands to "a saving knowledge of Jesus Christ." But the hippie appearance of their followers and their reputation for accosting tourists on the Sunset Strip with their "the world is coming to an end, repent or go to hell" urgency alienated the religious establishment and the Los Angeles police. More than once their meetings have been invaded by club-swinging police. On one occasion the police held the doors so that no one could leave the building and proceeded to lob Mace into the interior.

Sue and I chatted for about thirty minutes while Tony and the kids consumed refreshments on the patio. I mostly listened to this outgoing, strong-willed lady preacher. Before I left, Sue invited me to return to Saugus on Sunday afternoon for interviews with her followers. I was flattered that she had offered. When I drove away, I noticed that the Alamo apartment was ringed with police cruisers. Were they expecting trouble? Were they monitoring the Alamos? Were they in the vicinity for some other reason? I never discovered.

I returned to Saugus on Sunday at one o'clock in the afternoon. As I was explaining my purpose to the overseers—the title given to selected young people who have been with the Alamos for the longest periods of time (at least a year)— I noticed one of the young men lifting the telephone receiver. He was phoning the Alamos for clearance just as someone had done when I had made my earlier visit to Saugus. After I was O.K.'d, perspective interviewees began materializing one or two at a time.

"Tell me your story," I said to each of them.

Larry is a handsome guy with blue eyes and blond hair. He is from Virginia. When Larry was a child, his father's assignments for the Pentagon kept him away from home for up to three years at a time. Larry was third in his high school class, but a month before he was to graduate (June, 1968), Larry dropped out. Thrown out by his mother, he went to Washington, D.C., and became a heavy drug user ("doper"). Finally bored by Washington's slums, he started traveling with a friend. As the result of several bad experiences along the way, Larry soured on mankind and decided to become a hermit. He was headed for Big Sur, where he intended to live alone in nature, when he hit L.A. He had been wandering aimlessly when he met a kid who offered him a free meal at a little church in Hollywood. There he met the Alamos and was saved. He has spent the past two years living at the Alamos' Foundation—praying, reading the Bible, and inviting others to attend services.

Kent is from upper New York state. His family has been active in the Episcopal Church for generations. A rebellious youngster, Kent was packed off to private prep schools, where he went from bad to worse. "I was pretty nuts when I was younger," he confesses with a grin. "I even shot myself once." He hated school and became involved in a SDS underground newspaper. "I didn't want to get an education so I started traveling. I was dealing drugs in Massachusetts." His interest in Far Eastern religions brought him to California, where he stumbled into a meeting. "All these kids were smiling, and their faces were glowing," he recalled. "I didn't know what they believed. I just knew they were genuine and happy. I started going to their services. Man, they really irritated me—all this smiling. But then all at once I felt peaceful. I felt good. I went up to the altar and got saved. And then I wanted to go out and share what I had with everybody. Now all I do is pray, read the Bible, and witness. And I'm never bored. I'm satisfied. There's peace in my heart."

Greg is an intense, high-strung young fellow. He has piercing brown-gray eyes, a moustache, and slim, narrow shoulders. He was born in Rochester, New York, but soon thereafter his mother inherited a large sum of money and moved the family to Spain. She divorced Greg's father, who was a minister, became a social climber, and finally married a BOAC executive. In his midteens, Greg was sent to boarding school in England, where he learned English for the first time. Curious about an America he had never known, Greg enlisted in the U.S. Navy. Completing his hitch, he toured the States. He reported: "I was surprised to see the corruption of this country. I was really shocked by what I saw—loose morals and poverty." He turned to drugs, especially hashish, bummed around Spain and Canada, and eventually headed for New York City, where he unsuccessfully tried to join the Merchant Marine. He drifted around Greenwich Village, experimented with LSD, wandered around the country, marched on the Pentagon, lived for a while in Boulder, Colorado, and drifted to Chicago, where he was arrested and charged with contributing to the sexual delinquency of a minor. He spent months in Cook County Jail awaiting trial, beat the charge, and returned to New York, where he became hooked on "speed" (methamphetamine—a powerful stimulant). Sickened by his rapid degeneration, Greg headed for Florida, got a construction job, and cleaned himself up. "But I got bored," he recalled, "so I headed west—didn't even wait for my paycheck. I hopped a freight train for L.A. Wow! You wouldn't believe those freezing desert nights. When I got to L.A., I tried panhandling and was almost killed by a biker [a motorcyclist]. I became paranoid, confused," Greg paused for a moment.

"God put a thought in my head that Jesus is the light of the world," he blurted. "I just sat there for a long time. I was going to do what Jesus Christ did—the heaviest thing. But where was I going to get the power to do miracles like Jesus did? Just then someone gave me a gospel tract. I went to a meeting, and I felt the Spirit come into my heart. Then I knew where the power comes from. That was over two years ago."

While Greg was still talking, Tom had joined us. Tom has blond hair and gray eyes and was wearing a sweatshirt with the number twenty-five emblazoned on it. Tom is from a Catholic ghetto neighborhood in the nation's capital. His mother divorced Tom's father and married a Marine. The family moved continually from base to base; his stepfather became an alcoholic; his parents fought incessantly. Many times his stepfather would load Tom's two half sisters in his car and go wildly careening around town. Tom never knew if he would see any of them alive again.

As a high school student in Memphis, Tom and his friends went from beer to marijuana to pills. When his stepfather was sent to Camp Pendleton, Tom returned to Memphis to begin life on his own. After a few months he headed for California to join "the love and peace movement." "But instead of beautiful people, I found dopers and bikers and perversion and weird people," Tom recounted. "We had nightly drug parties. We were so stoned we didn't care about anything. We used to get busted, and we'd just laugh and laugh. The next day we'd be out of jail, and there would be plenty of drugs."

Tom continued, "Then my buddy Ed got saved through Tony and Sue, and he told me 'Jesus is coming.' Ed took me to Tony and Sue's. They pulled no punches—heaven or hell. So I got saved. Susie prayed me through. And right then I saw a vision of Jesus. But that was only the start. You've got to get grounded. They were closer to me than my mother or father ever could be. It was like I knew them all my life. I could trust them. They did the *whole* Bible. Not just the 'God is love' part. You know, 'No drunkards shall enter the kingdom of God.'" I knew.

Tony and Sue came to Tom's group—dopers, bikers, revolutionaries. Tom related: "Tony gave his testimony. And Susie preached a real powerful sermon. And all of them were saved. But some of them didn't go the whole way. So Tony and Susie told them, 'If you don't want to serve God, good-bye.' And Tony and Sue took over the dopers' house right across from the Hollywood Presbyterian Church."

Tom went right on. "We started a twenty-four-hour prayer chain. Each of us puts in at least two one-hour shifts a day."

"What else do you do?" I asked. "I mean, do any of you work or raise crops or anything? After all, there are hundreds of kids living here at Saugus. Where does the food come from? It must cost hundreds of dollars a week."

"I don't know," Tom replied. "The Lord provides. You'll have to ask Tony and Sue. None of us work. We just witness." Tom though for a moment and then he said, "If it hadn't been for Tony and Sue we'd all have ended up in a jail cell, on a morgue slab, or in a mental institution. That's all I know."

James, a young black from L.A., joined us. He had been about to graduate from high school in June, 1966, when the lure of the streets proved overwhelming. "I lived the fast life," he told me, "narcotics, hustling on the streets, for about three years. Two years ago, I was walking Sunset Boulevard when I got this gospel tract that said Jesus Christ is coming back to earth again. You know, it told about all those prophecies—vapors of smoke over the city, confusion on earth. Well, God sent out fear and conviction upon me. I went up to Tony after a service and asked him 'What must I do to be saved?' And Sue and Tony prayed me through."

"Are you still in touch with your family?" I asked.

James nodded.

"What do they think?"

"My mother is glad I'm off the street," he answered.

Tony and Sue had entered the building. A crowd was forming for the three o'clock service, which was about to begin. Sue sat next to me and asked what I had discovered. I told her that I was impressed by their success with heavy drug users. It seemed to me that ninety percent of their kids were once addicts. A look of disdain spread over Sue's countenance as she gruffly announced. "Yes. Our kids were dopers. Who else would take care of them? If you O.D.'d [suffered a drug overdose] in church, they'd have you arrested. You know what? There is a revival going on. And every time there has been a revival, the 'God is love' movement has moved in. There's a revival going on, and all the resistance is coming from the churches." Sue was preaching at me. I had heard the same sermon at the Alamos' apartment, but she was fascinating so I listened. "It's always been the same story," she insisted. "The churches and the establishment always stand in the way. And you want to know why?"

I nodded, even though I felt I knew what she would say.

"Money. That's why. The churches have too much to lose. Look at the Bible. The Jews cried out to God for a deliverer. When he came, they didn't like his looks. So they crucified him. Now the churches are crying out for revival. And God sent the hippies! And they want to kill them."

Sue was gathering a full head of steam now. She went on. "Revival—a move of God—has never come through the churches. Look at Moses. He knew nothing about the religion of the Jews. It was Aaron that did. But Moses was raised as a Gentile. He was a fugitive from justice because he had murdered a man. But God used him. Look at John the Baptist. 'Repent,' he said. He dressed odd, so he offended the establishment." Sue took a breath and concluded, "Every prophet of God has been slain by the churches and by the establishment." The service had started. Tony was asking visitors to donate copies of the Bible, "but only the King James Version, God's inspired Word." It was almost time for Sue to preach. As Sue got up to leave, she motioned to a tall, slim girl. "This is Cathy," Sue explained, "our oldest and dearest convert. She's been with us since the beginning. She's like a daughter to us. Talk to her." And Sue was gone.

Cathy, one of the most attractive girls I have ever seen, was apprehensive from the start of our conversation. I remembered her from my earlier visit to the Alamos' apartment. I had observed her washing Sue's dishes and looking after the Alamos' grandchild. Like a daughter indeed! A very rare daughter. Blonde, blue-eyed Cathy with the grace of a cat and the look of a lynx was one of fifteen children from a north California family. She had been on her own since she was fourteen. At eighteen she had come to Los Angeles for a job. She had worked as a dancer for three hundred dollars a week. Cathy seemed worried as she rapidly summarized her story. Not only was she saved through Tony and Sue, but five or six hundred of her friends had been converted also. "Five or six *hundred?*" I queried. "Uh-huh," she responded, nervously glancing over her shoulder.

"Do you plan to stay here forever?" I asked.

"What do you mean?" she said.

"Wouldn't you like to get married or—"

She interrupted. "I've got a husband somewhere. I don't even know where he is. I haven't seen him for years. Listen. I really can't talk to you now. Sue is going to preach and they really don't like us talking during services. I'll see you later." She slipped away.

I sat and wondered about Cathy and all the other kids at the Christian Foundation, all these attractive, joyful, personable youngsters. Something was bothering me. Why did they all seem eighteen years old? Why did I keep visualizing them in my mind as faultless specimens trapped in amber? Just because we find someone to love us, guide us, feed and house us, do we have to sacrifice our wills, our imaginations, our distinctive personalities? Does God want us to be personable teen-agers forever? All right, so Cathy and Larry and Kent and Greg and the rest have found a mother and father in Tony and Sue. But how long can they be Tony and Sue's perfect children? Five years? Ten years? Fifteen years?

Tony and Sue need not worry. As Tony remarked, "There are plenty of hippies for everyone. We'll never run out of kids. Who else wants them?"

In Search of a New Community
Paul Kagan

Paul Kagan (1943–   ) is a photographer, graphic artist, and historian living in Berkeley, California.

Men today have lost the knowledge of when to come together and when not to come together. And with this has been lost the sense of what communication or community means, and why it is necessary. In an age when the details of a military massacre are available in seconds to a public halfway around the globe, when relatives thousands of miles apart can be reunited in hours, the speed and availability of technological communications operate in perverse contrast to the lack of human communication among individuals and groups. What passes for a serious exchange on community affairs today is usually an exposition of random opinions and idle gossip. Little wonder, then, that a response to this unfulfilled but not forgotten need has become the formation of communal families or its obverse, withdrawal into routine days of work and nights of television.

The attraction to communal life can be identified as an attraction to wholeness—it is in the commune that life becomes complete, an encompassing world is formed. But it is also in the commune that the real disunity—the frictions and factions—appears that has resulted in an ever-decreasing lifetime for communal experiments not based on traditional ideals.

Why have people been turning more and more toward non-traditional, ephemeral communes, both today and in the past hundred years of California's relatively short history? The traditional communes—the monasteries—exist, as they have for several thousand years. What is it about the ideas motivating the monasteries that have given them their longevity? Why do monasteries not appeal to the people who found new and autonomous communes?

There is obvious confusion in life. It becomes so unbearable at certain periods of history that some men leave society for the isolation of the desert or the mountains. This extreme rejection of society takes two forms. It can produce the short-lived communities that are catalysts in a changing society. On the other hand, such movement away from the present world may, paradoxically, bring one in touch with a knowledge or understanding of an even earlier world. An increasing awareness of our rejection of the old, and attraction to the new, sometimes leads to the appearance of ideas completely unexpected and unexplored, which often derive from older more harmonious societies that took into account the complex needs in man's nature.

Interest in traditional ways of leaving society is diminishing. Monasteries are regarded as institutions which are too rigidly structured and whose dogma is stale. At the same time, those who flee to the communal life have the burden of making it up as they go along. They are without the formal structure provided by the church. The problems of starting a new community require so much initiative and work that little energy is left to devote to the purposes which first attracted the members and drew them together. This discovery of lack of purpose is compounded by the recognition that the problems that one is escaping are present in the community, intensified by numbers. The old baggage arrives at the new destination.

This problem appears in the commune in various forms. Terms like "authority" and "obedience" are not often used. But the roles implied by these terms are present under different names. The same devotion to work, and adherence to shibboleths and half-truths, that were demanded by the rejected society are demanded by the new.

After Job Harriman's experience at Llano del Rio, he wrote in 1923: "Under a system of private ownership of property one may exclude from his thought and companionship whomsoever he may dislike; . . . in a co-operative community this cannot be done." The community is, after all, a microcosm of the larger world. Here, men's smallest and pettiest habits cannot go undetected; brother is up against brother at every turn."

The surprise of the commune member is not unlike that of the marriage partner who discovers the early dream of going away and building a world together has lost its appeal. So it must be asked: Why doesn't the idea and intention of change work? Perhaps naivete is the answer: naivete concerning what needs to be changed, what can be changed, and what must be done in order to change. Commune members rarely understand their motivations, their contradictory natures, their selfishness, the extent of their involvement in the world outside, or their belief that a physical wall will protect them from the pressures they felt in society.

The life-span of a "successful" California community was about twenty years. The life-span of a monastery often surpasses two thousand years. Why is it, then, that at a time when the monasteries are struggling to survive, non-traditional communities are formed so frequently? Why Holy City and not the Catholic Church? Why Vedanta and not a Hasidic community?

Utopian experiments have been dichotomized as political–religious, soft–hard, static–dynamic, sensate–spiritual, aristocratic–plebian, escape–realization, collectivist–individualist. Why do these dualities exist? It appears that all utopian attempts to overcome conflict have resulted only in more serious strife and division. Perhaps this is why Sir Thomas More's word "utopia" means "nowhere." There is nowhere that man can go to strive toward wholeness without recognizing, and even coming toward, his fragmented nature. Do any utopian experiments take into account both the part of man that wishes to be whole and the part that longs for division?

Which ideas are practical? Some ideas help to perpetuate communities. Other ideas die out. Still others reappear cloaked in new forms. Perhaps this is what is meant by enduring, real ideas—the ones that live on and continue to be practical by altering their forms to meet changing conditions.

In this context is it useful to speak of communities as having a birth, a life, and a death, similar to that of individuals, civilizations, and living systems? There is little doubt that a commune is born and dies. But it lives as part of the world around it. Some of the new communes even rely on support by government food-stamps, welfare, and foundation grants to survive, in spite of their members' skills as gardeners and builders. Conversely, the economically successful Shakers profited from the revenue provided by a society which valued their products. But there is a finer interdependence. A commune may die because the original leader fails to provide a suitable successor, as at Point Loma, or because the members find their utopia reflects the world's strife, as at Kaweah. Sometimes the commune simply comes to the end of its natural life-span; it no longer has any function in itself, although it has probably had some impact on the world around it that will persist.

The Hermetic principle "as above, so below" applies to the question of man's dependence on his fellow man. In a world where "self-sufficiency" is a major value, communal members seek dependence on one another. They may, however, only rarely see the relationship of their experiment to the complex conditions that surround it.

In most communes there is little self-conscious concern with the questions of survival and motivation. Amazingly enough, even the leader rarely knows why his group exists, and for what. The member is often attracted to "a better way of life" and then is satisfied with much less. Why? The type of commune he joins seems to promise the style of life he seeks but when the commune does not meet his expectations, he may remain as a "hanger-on" because he is reluctant to return to society. In religious communes, if a member becomes harmful to the group, the leader may throw him out. In a socio-economic group, the difficulties of the "hangers-on" are reflected in the endless petty "democratic" meetings, filled with elementary "motions" and "decisions," such as the injunction of Llano not to urinate in the stream upriver of the drinking supply. Generally, there was little need for sanctions, because the group shared a common aim. If a person strayed from the accepted intention, he could leave. The question has always been—who is to judge?

In asking what common influences are present in the formation of one communal experiment as opposed to another in the same geographical region, the role of the leader must be questioned. Present-day communes vehemently affirm the principle of non-leadership, yet there is always a leader. In Eastern religious traditions the leader himself serves the same authority as the group he is helping. Why does the cynicism towards this type of relationship, where the leader himself is subservient to a higher power, exist in large measure in the West today? One of the implications may be that the leader's ability to organize is often greater than the knowledge he professes to possess. The leader is a good leader by virtue of his setting the example. Perhaps it is the narrow Western vision of leader and follower that has bred today's prevailing rejection of authority.

The way in which a leader takes part in the activities of the group, and his understanding of his own role, are vital factors in the life of the commune. In a way, the leader is a prisoner of the utopian experiment—could the community continue without his constant presence? The energy that is generated by the concentrated interinvolvement of a group and its leader has to be expressed. It often takes the form of feelings that move from affection to loyalty to disappointment.

There have been several attempts to evaluate the results of communal endeavors. One writer of the 1930's felt that the value of a commune was not in its survival, but in its giving birth to new experiments. Yet, some social scientists today feel that perpetuation is the measure of success; unless children are trained to continue the group's work, the commune may die. Still others look at the effects of the communal group on society in terms of contributions to culture, education, economics, human understanding, social reform, etc. St. Benedict viewed the monastery as a microcosm of a state that could emerge from the new Christian society.

The outside world has a tendency to look at members of communal experiments as stereotypes, rather than as people. Direct contact with various communal experiments, however, creates an appreciation of the efforts of the individuals involved, the fruits of these efforts, and the promise they hold for the future. An example of this is the role played by the Theosophists and Vedantists in making the ideas sacred in the East available to Western culture today. Unfamiliar impulses are generated by groups of people who are trying things that are not a part of the society from which they came. When money and success are not the goal, other goals emerge in their place.

One of the main differences between the traditional and non-traditional communes is in their identification of goals. Both groups understand that the main purpose is to learn by experience—that real knowledge does not come from reading a book or real success from becoming the president of Shell Oil.

But the people who join contemporary communes rarely realize that the long-standing tradition, the knowledge that has built up over centuries, offers the traditional communes at least a better quality of the experience which is sought in non-traditional communes. An even more important distinction between the two is that the traditional monastery offered a different level of experience, while today's commune offers a heightening or improvement of a level of experience already known to those who join.

In contrasting the traditional monasteries to the ephemeral communes we are studying, the role of sex is important. The monasteries required the separation of members from their families. Abstinence from sex was a form of payment much more extreme than anything demanded by the non-traditional communes, where women and children were usually welcome. Those who join today's communes take the conditions of their life with them. Although they may be asked to relinquish privacy and possessions, this does not evidence the same self-denial that was demanded as a spiritual payment by the monasteries.

Abstinence from the drugs, alcohol, and tobacco so commonly used in the outside world is a requirement promulgated in some communes so as not to "artificially heighten the experience." It can also be a rite of purification from past use of these volatile substances in the larger society.

Novitiates enter the monastery with a commitment—they have prepared and have some awareness of the ideals embodied by the institution. They come to perfect these ideals in themselves. Those entering non-traditional communes bring a passive hope for transformation simply through change of environment. Attraction to groups embodying values opposed to society is on the same level as attraction to groups devoted to maintaining society. Monastic aspiration, however, is not passive transformation by the same or opposite conditions of life, but a coming in touch with an entirely different type of experience. Out of the traditional communes of the Middle Ages came cathedrals and Gregorian chants. Out of Llano del Rio came endless bickering about the laziness of its indifferent members.

The distinctions here call for a definition of the term "intentional community." The intentional community is one whose purpose or intention is not solely a reaction to the surrounding society. An intentional community makes room for new ideas which, though occasionally appearing in communes, are entirely unknown to outside society. For example, the current terms "inner space" and "levels of consciousness" are two such new ideas from today's communes.

The idea of intention raises the question of how a group, or an individual, or a culture discovers its identity. A popular theory says that an adolescent arrives at his identity through those influences of his family and his peer group to which he reacts, for whatever reason. But an unknown part of the identity must come from the individual himself.

A trace of an impersonal goal lies in the intention of the "back to the land" communes, where nature has become the teacher. There is an ancient knowledge embodied in the Hopi Indian's respect for "our mother the earth and our father the sun." Communes in New Mexico have learned from the Indians to build with adobe—the earth itself—and their architecture is a manifestation of their intention, perhaps comparable on a smaller scale in some cases to the work of the cathedral builders.

Yesterday it was possible for a college graduate, not wishing to become a bank president, to enter public service with a clear conscience. Increased governmental repression at home and continuing massacre abroad have made the choice of private business or public service less meaningful, and a commune may appear as the only means to maintain one's individuality. Many come to believe in the concept of communal sharing as a means of growth, despite competitive upbringing.

Today's questions of identity are often posed in terms of civil rights, the Vietnam war, drugs, television, the establishment, and ecology. The resolution of reactions to these issues cannot be foreseen, but one could question whether the widening gulf between the establishment and the divergent culture of today's youth might not be the birth-pangs of a new culture. Another aspect of the same process is exemplified by the growth of interest in non-traditional communes.

California's place as the "last frontier" raises the question of a substitute for the frontier. When societies have no room for people, the people go somewhere else. They "light out for the territory," in Huck Finn's words. With little unexplored territory left, the pioneering instinct is being turned inwards and to outer space.

Today's technology more and more restricts the participation of the individual and he becomes a cog in a wheel. The communal wish to see the whole wheel is evidenced by activities that are followed through from start to finish, such as raising a sheep, shearing it, combing, carding, and spinning the yarn, and finally knitting it into a sweater. This reaction was presaged by the reaction of the Romantic Poets to the Industrial Revolution, and later by the Marxist goal of having the worker less separated from the product by having him control the means of production. With the dual problem of the new technology on the one hand, and the need for community on the other, it is possible that automation might actually help to solve the problem. By eliminating "scissors and paper-clip" jobs and automating all functions possible, a new system of goods and services might appear that allows for a more personal relationship of the individual to society.

What, then, is the meaning of the communal movement? Communal experiments on the West Coast today stretch from British Columbia to Peru. Most are small, unpublicized, and, unlike their predecessors, they share an interest in each other's doings and whereabouts. There are inter-community magazines and newsletters, and conferences covering the diverse spectrum of communal endeavor. If the emergence of interest in these non-traditional groups through the past hundred years and through the varied spectrum of today can be seen as the emergence of a newly developing and as yet unknown culture, then the phenomena described by Roszak as the "counter-culture" and by Reich as "consciousness III" are steps in the self-examination necessary for the new culture to be born.

The movement toward utopia highlights not only the increasing schism in society, but also the direction necessary for the birth of a new society. The direction begins with an awareness of the schism, or duality, and the possibility of wholeness through this awareness.

The search for community is generally directed towards someplace "over there." Can the vision of the utopians be pursued in the context of one's life in the world? Need one go to the desert? There is evidence that at times means have existed within the society for bringing together the inner and outer sides of man. Today, man is lacking in knowledge about his needs, motivations, structure, purpose, and place. But the means that provide this knowledge have no external safeguards against degeneration. They change with the times. When they cease to be flexible, all energy goes into preserving the external forms and traditions, a "church" is created, and the essential knowledge is lost.

If the church appears to be hypocritical, society divided, and the communes defined negatively by their reaction to society, where can man turn for real ideas? The need would seem to call for the appearance of a way in life that fulfills both the rational and the mystical needs of men, a way that includes the additional need to come together as part of the other functions and activities of society. How much time would such a society then give to the study of utopia, and how much time to the study of thermodynamics? What would be the right tension between the individual and the community? Perhaps the means for such a study already exist. The question then would not be "How does one form a community?" but rather "How does one find the conditions in the midst of one's life to allow for such a study?"

There has been a gradual movement in history from traditional knowledge to humanist psychology, in which the aim is no longer to understand but, instead, to adapt. On the other hand, people still get together on Sundays. But who knows why they get together?

Is Religion Religion?

INTRODUCTION

Among the important cultural changes that have occurred in the last hundred
  years, we certainly must include the sweep of science. It has spawned a
  pervasive technology; more and more aspects of the world have become
  scientific subject matter, and, with its wholesale introduction into the school
  curriculum, it has shaped the cognitive and emotional consciousness of
  every person in the literate societies. This "scientific" consciousness
  naturally affects other cultural institutions and aspects of life; it has had a
  particularly massive impact on the church and religion.
Reason and revelation have struggled for centuries for authority over men's
  minds. The rise of science as a method of gaining knowledge has tipped
  the balance away from revelation and toward reason. The result has been
  a growing inability of men to believe the statements in sacred texts and the
  reports of mystics; this has weakened the cognitive authority of religion
  and put it on the defensive.
Perhaps even more contributory to the declining status of religion has been
  the tendency to make "religious phenomena" themselves a subject matter
  for science. Religion is something to be "explained." Given that a scientific attitude discredits the cognitive claims of religion, the science-minded
  person finds it difficult to see how anyone could have literally believed
  religious statements to be true. He finds it necessary to give an account,
  an explanation, of how people could have believed something so patently
  false or nonsensical. Surely, he thinks, religion must be a causally produced
  response to some natural conditions. He is curious to identify these conditions, and, in terms of laws from some science, he tries to find the causal
  links between these natural conditions and the phenomenon of religion.
Notice that "science" is not something to be explained. Scientific claims are
  to be examined, evidence looked for, hypotheses tested, experiments
  undertaken, all with the purpose of either validating or invalidating a
  scientific claim. The chief interest in scientific statements is their truth or
  falsity; we are not generally interested in explaining their occurrence. The

most we might do is try to appreciate how someone could have "discovered" his hypothesis or "created" it. Discovery and creation are honorific events; that which needs explanation is reduced to the level of such mundane events as fertilization, internal combustion, and heat transfer.

An anthology on religion that purports to cover the main facets of the study of religion has to include a chapter such as this one, which presents claims that religion can be explained away as not being religion at all but something else. None of the authors, with the possible exception of R. D. Laing, takes the cognitive claims of religion seriously. However, they do see that religion does perform some function—Marx finds that it has a function that is harmful, Dewey that it has a useful function. The assignment of a function to religion is one way of explaining its nature, origin, and continued existence. In the first selection in this chapter, **Sigmund Freud** sees religion as a form of wish-fulfillment; for him, the dogmas of religion are illusions, derived from deep, persistent wishes. Religion is not, therefore, something *sui generis* but an aspect of our psychological life. In terms of his science of psychology, Freud finds laws that connect one of the natural conditions of our life, namely, insecurity, with the characteristic phenomena of religion. For Freud, then, religion is not religion but a psychological manifestation.

In the second selection, **Karl Marx** describes religion as an ideological weapon of the ruling class. Man under capitalism is alienated from himself and from reality; his conditions of earthly existence are miserable. The proletariat everywhere suffers. Religion is a means the ruling class uses to pacify the proletariat and to keep them from revolting. Religion "is the *opium* of the people." Once again, religion is not religion; it is an ideational form of social control and, as such, is simply political. Men will be emancipated from religion when religion is replaced by philosophy.

In the third selection, **Emile Durkheim** finds that religions universally maintain a two-worlds view, of a world of the sacred and a world of the profane. Religion purportedly transports people from the profane to the sacred world. Of course, this is metaphysical nonsense to Durkheim; there is only one world, the natural world, the world that science studies. To understand religion, we must understand how the notion that there is a sacred world ever came into being. Durkheim claims that it is a social phenomenon and tries to isolate the social conditions that make it possible for men to have experiences in which they project an ideal world beyond the mundane, natural one. "The formation of the ideal world is therefore not an irreducible fact which escapes science; it depends upon conditions which observation can touch; it is a natural product of social life." So, once again, religion is not religion, it is a manifestation of man's social existence.

In the fourth selection, **John Dewey** finds that religion cannot claim the loyalty of men as long as it sets itself in competition with science. Religion has a valuable function to perform, and if it surrenders its claims to knowledge while emphasizing its moral function, it can continue to claim man's loyalty. For Dewey, religious faith is "the unification of the self through allegiance to inclusive ideal ends, which imagination presents to us and to which the human will responds as worthy of controlling our desires and choices." Once again, religion is not, or ought not to be, religion as traditionally conceived; for continuing effectiveness, religion must become a dramatic form of morals, reconceiving God as "the unity of all ideal ends arousing us to desire and actions."

In the fifth selection, **I. A. Richards** sees religion as having performed yet another function, namely, having given to life emotional coherence and organization of feelings. It performed that function because the magical view of the universe was simplified and personalized. Science has irrevocably altered that view of the universe and, consequently, stripped away the basis for emotional coherence. Religious knowledge is, for Richards, composed of pseudo-statements; if we are to supply man with emotional coherence, we must supply him with pseudo-statements that do not run afoul of scientific credibility. Poetry consists of pseudo-statements, and, because it does not claim cognitive status, it can replace religion. Religion is not, then, religion any longer, because it cannot do what it once did. Religion, functionally, must become poetry.

In the sixth selection, **Wang Tao-ming** provides a vivid, deeply felt, sincere expression of how political commitment can replace religion as a controlling center for life. When the opium is smoked to ashes, Marx's promised emancipation comes about through Mao's philosophical statements and injunctions.

In the seventh and last selection in this chapter, **R. D. Laing** recognizes that so-called religious experiences seem hopelessly invalid to people enmeshed in the framework that our social, interpersonal mind constructs. The mystic makes deviant claims—deviant, at least, to the "normal," scientific man, who consigns the mystic to madness, and hence to illness. Laing realizes that to many who consider themselves sane because they are able to adapt to the external world as defined by "human collectivities," religion is not religion, but madness. However, Laing believes that our "sane" egoic experience is ontologically relative. Transcendental experiences wherein the self is lost may not be pathological manifestations that need a cure but rather may be illumination from within, a relief from our present age of outer darkness, a mediation of divine powers. Laing promotes the possibility that religion based on transcendental experiences may, indeed, truly be religion and not something else.

A. K. B.

Suggested Readings

Berger, Peter. *Sacred Canopy.* New York: Doubleday, 1967.

Dewey, John. *A Common Faith.* London: H. Milford—Oxford University Press, 1934.

Durkheim, Emile. *Elementary Forms of Religious Life.* Glencoe, Ill.: Free Press, 1954.

Findlay, J. N. "The Phenomenology of Spirit-II." *Hegel: A Re-examination.* New York: Collier Books, 1962. Chapter 5.

Freud, Sigmund. *Civilization and Its Discontents.* Translated by James Strachey. New York: Norton, 1962.

Santayana, George. *Reason in Religion.* New York: Scribner's, 1905.

Yinger, J. Milton. *The Scientific Study of Religion.* New York: Macmillan, 1970.

CAN RELIGION BE EXPLAINED?

Religion as a Psychological Weakness

Sigmund Freud

Sigmund Freud (1856–1939), the founder of psychoanalysis, was the most influential psychologist of modern times.

Wherein lies the peculiar value of religious ideas?

We have spoken of the hostility to culture, produced by the pressure it exercises and the instinctual renunciations that it demands. If one imagined its prohibitions removed, then one could choose any woman who took one's fancy as one's sexual object, one could kill without hesitation one's rival or whoever interfered with one in any other way, and one could seize what one wanted of another man's goods without asking his leave: how splendid, what a succession of delights, life would be! True, one soon finds the first difficulty: everyone else has exactly the same wishes, and will treat one with no more consideration than one will treat him. And so in reality there is only one single person who can be made unrestrictedly happy by abolishing thus the restrictions

From Sigmund Freud, *The Future of an Illusion*, trans. by W. D. Robson-Scott (New York, 1955), pp. 21-32, 41-58. Permission of Liveright, Publishers, N.Y. Acknowledgment is also made to Sigmund Freud Copyrights Ltd., The Institute of Psycho-Analysis, and the Hogarth Press Ltd. for permission to quote from "The Future of an Illusion" in Volume XXI of *The Standard Edition of the Complete Psychological Works of Sigmund Freud*, revised and edited by James Strachey.

imposed by culture, and that is a tyrant or dictator who has monopolized all the means of power; and even he has every reason to want the others to keep at least one cultural commandment: thou shalt not kill.

But how ungrateful, how short-sighted after all, to strive for the abolition of culture! What would then remain would be the state of nature, and that is far harder to endure. It is true that nature does not ask us to restrain our instincts, she lets us do as we like; but she has her peculiarly effective mode of restricting us: she destroys us, coldly, cruelly, callously, as it seems to us, and possibly just through what has caused our satisfaction. It was because of these very dangers with which nature threatens us that we united together and created culture, which, amongst other things, is supposed to make our communal existence possible. Indeed, it is the principal task of culture, its real *raison d'être,* to defend us against nature.

One must confess that in many ways it already does this tolerably well, and clearly as time goes on it will be much more successful. But no one is under the illusion that nature has so far been vanquished; few dare to hope that she will ever be completely under man's subjection. There are the elements, which seem to mock at all human control: the earth, which quakes, is rent asunder, and buries man and all his works; the water, which in tumult floods and submerges all things; the storm, which drives all before it; there are the diseases, which we have only lately recognized as the attacks of other living creatures; and finally there is the painful riddle of death, for which no remedy at all has yet been found, nor probably ever will be. With these forces nature rises up before us, sublime, pitiless, inexorable; thus she brings again to mind our weakness and helplessness, of which we thought the work of civilization had rid us. It is one of the few noble and gratifying spectacles that men can offer, when in the face of an elemental catastrophe they awake from their muddle and confusion, forget all their internal difficulties and animosities, and remember the great common task, the preservation of mankind against the supremacy of nature.

For the individual, as for mankind in general, life is hard to endure. The culture in which he shares imposes on him some measure of privation, and other men occasion him a certain degree of suffering, either in spite of the laws of this culture or because of its imperfections. Add to this the evils that unvanquished nature—he calls it Fate—inflicts on him. One would expect a permanent condition of anxious suspense and a severe injury to his innate narcissism to be the result of this state of affairs. We know already how the individual reacts to the injuries that culture and other men inflict on him: he develops a corresponding degree of resistance against the institutions of this culture, of hostility towards it. But how does he defend himself against the supremacy of nature, of fate, which threatens him, as it threatens all?

Culture relieves him of this task: it performs it in the same way for everyone. (It is also noteworthy that pretty well all cultures are the same in this respect.) It does not cry a halt, as it were, in its task of defending man against nature; it merely pursues it by other methods. This is a complex business; man's seriously menaced self-esteem craves for consolation, life and the universe must be rid of their terrors, and incidentally man's curiosity, reinforced, it is true, by the strongest practical motives, demands an answer.

With the first step, which is the humanization of nature, much is already won. Nothing can be made of impersonal forces and fates; they remain eternally remote. But if the elements have passions that rage like those in our own souls, if death itself is not something spontaneous, but the violent act of an evil Will, if everywhere in nature we have about us beings who resemble those of our own environment, then indeed we can breathe freely, we can feel at home in face of the supernatural, and we can deal psychically with our frantic anxiety. We are perhaps still defenceless, but no longer helplessly paralysed; we can at least react; perhaps indeed we are not even defenceless, we can have recourse to the same methods against these violent supermen of the beyond that we make use of in our own community; we can try to exorcise them, to appease them, to bribe them, and so rob them of part of their power by thus influencing them. Such a substitution of psychology for natural science provides not merely immediate relief, it also points the way to a further mastery of the situation.

For there is nothing new in this situation. It has an infantile prototype, and is really only the continuation of this. For once before one has been in such a state of helplessness: as a little child in one's relationship to one's parents. For one had reason to fear them, especially the father, though at the same time one was sure of his protection against the dangers then known to one. And so it was natural to assimilate and combine the two situations. Here, too, as in dream-life, the wish came into its own. The sleeper is seized by a presentiment of death, which seeks to carry him to the grave. But the dream-work knows how to select a condition that will turn even this dreaded event into a wish-fulfilment: the dreamer sees himself in an ancient Etruscan grave, into which he has descended, happy in the satisfaction it has given to his archaeological interests. Similarly man makes the forces of nature not simply in the image of men with whom he can associate as his equals—that would not do justice to the overpowering impression they make on him—but he gives them the characteristics of the father, makes them into gods, thereby following not only an infantile, but also, as I have tried to show, a phylogenetic prototype.

In the course of time the first observations of law and order in natural phenomena are made, and therewith the forces of nature lose their human traits. But men's helplessness remains, and with it their father-longing and the gods. The gods retain their threefold task: they must exorcise the terrors of nature, they must reconcile one to the cruelty of fate, particularly as shown in death, and they must make amends for the sufferings and privations that the communal life of culture has imposed on man.

But within these there is a gradual shifting of the accent. It is observed that natural phenomena develop of themselves from inward necessity; without doubt the gods are the lords of nature: they have arranged it thus and now they can leave it to itself. Only occasionally, in the so-called miracles, do they intervene in its course, as if to protest that they have surrendered nothing of their original sphere of power. As far as the vicissitudes of fate are concerned, an unpleasant suspicion persists that the perplexity and helplessness of the human race cannot be remedied. This is where the gods are most apt to fail us; if they themselves make fate, then their ways must be deemed inscrutable. The most gifted people of the ancient world dimly surmised that above the gods stands Destiny and that the gods themselves have their destinies. And the more autonomous nature becomes and the more earnestly are all expectations concentrated on the third task assigned to them and the more does morality become their real domain. It now becomes the business of the gods to adjust the defects and evils of culture, to attend to the sufferings that men inflict on each other in their communal life, and to see that the laws of culture, which men obey so ill, are carried out. The laws of culture themselves are claimed to be of divine origin, they are elevated to a position above human society, and they are extended over nature and the universe.

And so a rich store of ideas is formed, born of the need to make tolerable the helplessness of man, and built out of the material offered by memories of the helplessness of his own childhood and the childhood of the human race. It is easy to see that these ideas protect man in two directions; against the dangers of nature and fate, and against the evils of human society itself. What it amounts to is this: life in this world serves a higher purpose; true, it is not easy to guess the nature of this purpose, but certainly a perfecting of human existence is implied. Probably the spiritual part of man, the soul, which in the course of time has so slowly and unwillingly detached itself from the body, is to be regarded as the object of this elevation and exaltation. Everything that takes place in this world expresses the intentions of an Intelligence, superior to us, which in the end, though its devious ways may be difficult to follow, orders everything for good, that is, to our advantage. Over each one of us watches a benevolent, and only apparently severe, Providence, which will not suffer us to become the plaything of the stark and pitiless forces of nature; death itself is not annihilation, not a return to inorganic lifelessness, but the beginning of a new kind of existence, which lies on the road of development to something higher. And to turn to the other side of the question, the moral laws that have formed our culture govern also the whole universe, only they are upheld with incomparably more force and consistency by a supreme judicial court. In the end all good is rewarded, all evil punished, if not actually in this life, then in the further existences that begin after death. And thus all the terrors, the sufferings, and the hardships of life are destined to be obliterated; the life after death, which continues our earthly existence as the invisible part of the spectrum adjoins the visible, brings all the perfection that perhaps we have missed here. And the superior wisdom that directs this issue, the supreme goodness that expresses itself thus, the justice that thus achieves its aim—these are the qualities of the divine beings who have fashioned us and the world in general; or rather of the one divine being into which in our culture all the gods of antiquity have been condensed. The race that first succeeded in thus concentrating the divine qualities was not a little proud of this advance. It had revealed the father nucleus which had always lain hidden behind every divine figure; fundamentally it was a return to the historical beginnings of the idea of God. Now that God was a single person, man's relations to him could recover the intimacy and intensity of the child's relation to the father. If one had done so much for the father, then surely one would be rewarded—at least the only beloved child, the chosen people, would be. More recently, pious America has laid claim to be "God's own country," and for one of the forms under which men worship the deity the claim certainly holds good.

The religious ideas that have just been summarized have of course gone through a long process of development, and have been held in various phases by various cultures. I have singled out one such phase of development, which more or less corresponds to the final form of our contemporary Christian culture in the west. It is easy to see that not all the parts of this whole tally equally well with each other, that not all the questions that press for an answer receive one, and that the contradiction of daily experience can only with difficulty be dismissed. But such as they are, these ideas—religious, in the broadest sense of the word—are prized as the most precious possession of culture, as the most valuable thing it has to offer its members; far more highly prized than all our devices for winnng the treasures of the earth, for providing men with sustenance, or for preventing their diseases, and so forth; men suppose that life would be intolerable if they did not accord these ideas the value that is claimed for them. And now the question arises: what are these ideas in the light of psychology; whence do they derive the esteem in which they are held; and further, in all diffidence, what is their real worth?

. . .

Now to take up again the threads of our enquiry: what is the psychological significance of religious ideas and how can we classify them? The question is at first not at all easy to answer. Having rejected various formulas, I shall take my stand by this one: religion consists of certain dogmas, assertions about facts and conditions of external (or internal) reality, which tell one something that one has not oneself discovered and which claim that one should give them credence. As they give information about what are to us the most interesting and important things in life, they are particularly highly valued. He who knows nothing of them is ignorant indeed, and he who has assimilated them may consider himself enriched.

. . .

. . . If we ask on what their claim to be believed is based, we receive three answers, which accord remarkably ill with one another. They deserve to be believed: firstly, because our primal ancestors already believed them; secondly, because we possess proofs, which have been handed down to us from this very period of antiquity; and thirdly, because it is forbidden to raise the question of their authenticity at all. Formerly this presumptuous act was visited with the very severest penalties, and even to-day society is unwilling to see anyone renew it.

This third point cannot but rouse our strongest suspicions. Such a prohibition can surely have only one motive: that society knows very well the uncertain basis of the claim it makes for its religious doctrines. If it were otherwise, the relevant material would certainly be placed most readily at the disposal of anyone who wished to gain conviction for himself. And so we proceed to test the other two arguments with a feeling of mistrust not easily allayed. We ought to believe because our forefathers believed. But these ancestors of ours were far more ignorant than we; they believed in things we could not possibly accept to-day; so the possibility occurs that religious doctrines may also be in this category. The proofs they have bequeathed to us are deposited in writings that themselves bear every trace of being untrustworthy. They are full of contradictions, revisions, and interpolations; where they speak of actual authentic proofs they are themselves of doubtful authenticity. It does not help much if divine revelation is asserted to be the origin of their text or only of their content, for this assertion is itself already a part of those doctrines whose authenticity is to be examined, and no statement can bear its own proof.

Thus we arrive at the singular conclusion that just what might be of the greatest significance for us in our cultural system, the information which should solve for us the riddles of the universe and reconcile us to the troubles of life, that just this has the weakest possible claim to authenticity. We should not be able to bring ourselves to accept anything of as little concern to us as the fact that whales bear young instead of laying eggs, if it were not capable of better proof than this.

This state of things is in itself a very remarkable psychological problem. Let no one think that the foregoing remarks on the impossibility of proving religious doctrines contain anything new. It has been felt at all times, assuredly even by the ancestors who bequeathed this legacy. Probably many of them nursed the same doubts as we, but the pressure imposed on them was too strong for them to have dared to utter them. And since then countless people have been tortured by the same doubts, which they would fain have suppressed because they held themselves in duty bound to believe, and since then many brilliant intellects have been wrecked upon this conflict and many characters have come to grief through the compromises by which they sought a way out.

.   .   .

One must now mention two attempts to evade the problem, which both convey the impression of frantic effort. One of them, high-handed in its nature, is old; the other is subtle and modern. The first is the *Credo quia absurdum* of the early Fathers. It would imply that religious doctrines are outside reason's jurisdiction; they stand above reason. Their truth must be inwardly felt: one does not need to comprehend them. But this *Credo* is only of interest as a voluntary confession; as a decree it has no binding force. Am I to be obliged to believe every absurdity? And if not, why just this one? There is no appeal beyond reason. And if the truth of religious doctrines is dependent on an inner experience which bears witness to that truth, what is one to make of the many people who do not have that rare experience? One may expect all men to use the gift of reason that they possess, but one cannot set up an obligation that shall apply to all on a basis that only exists for quite a few. Of what significance is it for other people that you have won from a state of ecstasy, which has deeply moved you, an imperturbable conviction of the real truth of the doctrines of religion?

The second attempt is that of the philosophy of "As If." It explains that in our mental activity we assume all manner of things, the groundlessness, indeed the absurdity, of which we fully realize. They are called "fictions," but from a variety of practical motives we are led to behave "as if" we believed in these fictions. This, it is argued, is the case with religious doctrines on account of their unequalled importance for the maintenance of human society. This argument is not far removed from the *Credo quia absurdum*. But I think that the claim of the philosophy of "As If" is such as only a philosopher could make. The man whose thinking is not influenced by the wiles of philosophy will never be able to accept it; with the confession of absurdity, of illogicality, there is no more to be said as far as he is concerned. He cannot be expected to forgo the guarantees he demands for all his usual activities just in the matter of his most important interests. I am reminded of one of my children who was distinguished at an early age by a peculiarly marked sense of reality. When the children were told a fairy tale, to which they listened with rapt attention, he would come forward and ask: Is that a true story? Having been told that it was not, he would turn away with an air of disdain. It is to be expected that men will soon behave in like manner towards the religious fairy tales, despite the advocacy of the philosophy of "As If."

But at present they still behave quite differently, and in past ages, in spite of their incontrovertible lack of authenticity, religious ideas have exercised the very strongest influence on mankind. This is a fresh psychological problem. We must ask where the inherent strength of these doctrines lies and to what circumstance they owe their efficacy, independent, as it is, of the acknowledgement of the reason.

. . .

I think we have sufficiently paved the way for the answer to both these questions. It will be found if we fix our attention on the psychical origin of religious ideas. These, which profess to be dogmas, are not the residue of experience or the final result of reflection; they are illusions, fulfilments of the oldest, strongest and most insistent wishes of mankind; the secret of their strength is the strength of these wishes. We know already that the terrifying effect of infantile helplessness aroused the need for protection—protection through love—which the father relieved, and that the discovery that this helplessness would continue through the whole of life made it necessary to cling to the existence of a father—but this time a more powerful one. Thus the benevolent rule of divine providence allays our anxiety in face of life's dangers, the establishment of a moral world order ensures the fulfilment of the demands of justice, which within human culture have so often remained unfulfilled, and the prolongation of earthly existence by a future life provides in addition the local and temporal setting for these wish-fulfilments. Answers to the questions that tempt human curiosity, such as the origin of the universe and the relation between the body and the soul, are developed in accordance with the underlying assumptions of this system; it betokens a tremendous relief for the individual psyche if it is released from the conflicts of childhood arising out of the father complex, which are never wholly overcome, and if these conflicts are afforded a universally accepted solution.

When I say that they are illusions, I must define the meaning of the word. An illusion is not the same as an error, it is indeed not necessarily an error. Aristotle's belief that vermin are evolved out of dung, to which ignorant people still cling, was an error; so was the belief of a former generation of doctors that *tabes dorsalis* was the result of sexual excess. It would be improper to call these errors illusions. On the other hand, it was an illusion on the part of Columbus that he had discovered a new sea-route to India. The part played by his wish in this error is very clear. One may describe as an illusion the statement of certain nationalists that the Indo-Germanic race is the only one capable of culture, or the belief, which only psycho-analysis destroyed, that the child is a being without sexuality. It is characteristic of the illusion that it is derived from men's wishes; in this respect it approaches the psychiatric delusion, but it is to be distinguished from this, quite apart from the more complicated structure of the latter. In the delusion we emphasize as essential the conflict with reality; the illusion need not be necessarily false, that is to say, unrealizable or incompatible with reality. For instance, a poor girl may have an illusion that a prince will come and fetch her home. It is possible; some such cases have occurred. That the Messiah will come and found a golden age is much less probable; according to one's personal attitude one will classify this belief as an illusion or as analogous to a delusion.

Examples of illusions that have come true are not easy to discover, but the illusion of the alchemists that all metals can be turned into gold may prove to be one. The desire to have lots of gold, as much gold as possible, has been considerably damped by our modern insight into the nature of wealth, yet chemistry no longer considers a transmutation of metals into gold as impossible. Thus we call a belief an illusion when wish-fulfilment is a prominent factor in its motivation, while disregarding its relations to reality, just as the illusion itself does.

If after this survey we turn again to religious doctrines, we may reiterate that they are all illusions, they do not admit of proof, and no one can be compelled to consider them as true or to believe in them. Some of them are so improbable, so very incompatible with everything we have laboriously discovered about the reality of the world, that we may compare them—taking adequately into account the psychological differences—to delusions. Of the reality value of most of them we cannot judge; just as they cannot be proved, neither can they be refuted. We still know too little to approach them critically. The riddles of the universe only reveal themselves slowly to our enquiry, to many questions science can as yet give no answer; but scientific work is our only way to the knowledge of external reality. . . .

.   .   .

It does not lie within the scope of this enquiry to estimate the value of religious doctrines as truth. It suffices that we have recognized them, psychologically considered, as illusions. But we need not conceal the fact that this discovery strongly influences our attitude to what must appear to many the most important of questions. We know approximately at what periods and by what sort of men religious doctrines were formed. If we now learn from what motives this happened, our attitude to the problem of religion will suffer an appreciable change. We say to ourselves: it would indeed be very nice if there were a God, who was both creator of the world and a benevolent providence, if there were a moral world order and a future life, but at the same time it is very odd that this is all just as we should wish it ourselves. And it would be still odder if our poor, ignorant, enslaved ancestors had succeeded in solving all these difficult riddles of the universe.

.   .   .

. . . I know how difficult it is to avoid illusions. But I hold fast to one distinction. My illusions—apart from the fact that no penalty is imposed for not sharing them—are not, like the religious ones, incapable of correction, they have no delusional character. If experience should show—not to me, but to others after me who think as I do—that we are mistaken, then we shall give up our expectations. Take my endeavour for what it is. A psychologist, who does not deceive himself about the difficulty of finding his bearings in this world, strives to review the development of mankind in accord with what insight he has won from studying the mental processes of the individual during his development from childhood to manhood. In this connection the idea forces itself upon him that religion is comparable to a childhood neurosis, and he is optimistic enough to assume that mankind will overcome this neurotic phase, just as so many children grow out of their similar neuroses. . . .

.   .   .

... But science has shown us by numerous and significant successes that it is no illusion. Science has many open, and still more secret, enemies among those who cannot forgive it for having weakened religious belief and for threatening to overthrow it. People reproach it for the small amount it has taught us and the incomparably greater amount it has left in the dark. But then they forget how young it is, how difficult its beginnings, and how infinitesimally small the space of time since the human intellect has been strong enough for the tasks it sets it. Do we not all do wrong in that the periods of time which we make the basis of our judgements are of too short duration? We should take an example from the geologist. People complain of the unreliability of science, that she proclaims as a law to-day what the next generation will recognize to be an error and which will replace by a new law of equally short currency. But that is unjust and in part untrue. The transformation of scientific ideas is a process of development and progress, not of revolution. A law that was at first held to be universally valid proves to be a special case of a more comprehensive law, or else its scope is limited by another law not discovered until later; a rough approximation to the truth is replaced by one more carefully adjusted, which in its turn awaits a further approach to perfection. In several spheres we have not yet surmounted a phase of investigation in which we test hypotheses that have soon to be rejected as inadequate; but in others we have already an assured and almost immutable core of knowledge. Finally an attempt has been made to discredit radically scientific endeavour on the ground that, bound as it is to the conditions of our own organization, it can yield nothing but subjective results, while the real nature of things outside us remains inaccessible to it. But this is to disregard several factors of decisive importance for the understanding of scientific work. Firstly, our organization, *i.e.* our mental apparatus, has been developed actually in the attempt to explore the outer world, and therefore it must have realized in its structure a certain measure of appropriateness; secondly, it itself is a constituent part of that world which we are to investigate, and readily admits of such investigation; thirdly, the task of science is fully circumscribed if we confine it to showing how the world must appear to us in consequence of the particular character of our organization; fourthly, the ultimate findings of science, just because of the way in which they are attained, are conditioned not only by our organization but also by that which has affected this organization; and, finally, the problem of the nature of the world irrespective of our perceptive mental apparatus is an empty abstraction without practical interest.

No, science is no illusion. But it would be an illusion to suppose that we could get anywhere else what it cannot give us.

The Opium of the People
Karl Marx

Karl Marx (1818–1883), collaborated with Friedrich Engels on *The Communist Manifesto* (1848) and is the author of *Das Kapital* (1867–1888). Marx is the most important single figure in the development of the philosophy of modern Communism. Marx rebelled against the Hegelian philosophy, saying "the most important task of the philosopher is not to know the world but to change it."

CONTRIBUTION TO THE CRITIQUE OF HEGEL'S PHILOSOPHY OF RIGHT

Introduction. For Germany, the *criticism of religion* has been largely completed; and the criticism of religion is the premise of all criticism.

The *profane* existence of error is compromised once its *celestial oratio pro aris et focis* has been refuted. Man, who has found in the fantastic reality of heaven, where he sought a supernatural being, only his own reflection, will no longer be tempted to find only the *semblance* of himself—a non-human being—where he seeks and must seek his true reality.

The basis of irreligious criticism is this: *man makes religion;* religion does not make man. Religion is indeed man's self-consciousness and self-awareness so long as he has not found himself or has lost himself again. But *man* is not an abstract being, squatting outside the world. Man is *the human world,* the state, society. This state, this society, produce religion which is an *inverted world consciousness,* because they are an *inverted world.* Religion is the general theory of this world, its encyclopedic compendium, its logic in popular form, its spiritual *point d'honneur,* its enthusiasm, its moral sanction, its solemn complement, its general basis of consolation and justification. It is *the fantastic realization* of the human being inasmuch as the *human being* possesses no true reality. The struggle against religion is, therefore, indirectly a struggle against *that world* whose spiritual *aroma* is religion.

Religious suffering is at the same time an *expression* of real suffering and a *protest* against real suffering. Religion is the sigh of the oppressed creature, the sentiment of a heartless world, and the soul of soulless conditions. It is the *opium* of the people.

The abolition of religion as the *illusory* happiness of men, is a demand for their *real* happiness. The call to abandon their illusions about their condition is a *call to abandon a condition which requires illusions.* The criticism of religion is, therefore, *the embryonic criticism of this vale of tears* of which religion is the *halo.*

Criticism has plucked the imaginary flowers from the chain, not in order that man shall bear the chain without caprice or consolation but so that he shall cast off the chain and pluck the living flower. The criticism of religion disillusions man so that he will think, act and fashion his reality as a man who has lost his illusions and regained his reason; so that he will revolve about himself as his own true sun. Religion is only the illusory sun about which man revolves so long as he does not revolve about himself.

It is the *task of history,* therefore, once the *other-world of truth* has vanished, to establish the *truth of this world.* The immediate *task of philosophy,* which is in the service of history, is to unmask human self-alienation in its *secular form* now that it has been unmasked in its *sacred form.* Thus the criticism of heaven is transformed into the criticism of earth, the *criticism of religion* into the *criticism of law,* and the *criticism of theology* into the *criticism of politics.*

The following exposition[1]—which is a contribution to this undertaking— does not deal directly with the original but with a copy, the German *philosophy* of the state and of right, for the simple reason that it deals with Germany.

.   .   .

It is clear that the arm of criticism cannot replace the criticism of arms. Material force can only be overthrown by material force; but theory itself becomes a material force when it has seized the masses. Theory is capable of seizing the masses when it demonstrates *ad hominem,* and it demonstrates *ad hominem* as soon as it becomes radical. To be radical is to grasp things by the root. But for man the root is man himself. What proves beyond doubt the radicalism of German theory, and thus its practical energy, is that it begins from the resolute *positive* abolition of religion. The criticism of religion ends with the doctrine that *man is the supreme being for man.* It ends, therefore, with the *categorical imperative to overthrow all those conditions* in which man is an abased, enslaved, abandoned, contemptible being—conditions which can hardly be better described than in the exclamation of a Frenchman on the occasion of a proposed tax upon dogs: "Wretched dogs! They want to treat you like men!"

Even from the historical standpoint theoretical emancipation has a specific practical importance for Germany. In fact Germany's *revolutionary* past is theoretical—it is the *Reformation.* In that period the revolution orginated in the brain of a monk, today in the brain of the philosopher.

Luther, without question, overcame servitude through devotion but only by substituting servitude through *conviction.* He shattered the faith in authority by restoring the authority of faith. He transformed the priests into laymen by turning laymen into priests. He liberated man from external religiosity by making religiosity the innermost essence of man. He liberated the body from its chains because he fettered the heart with chains.

But if Protestantism was not the solution it did at least pose the problem correctly. It was no longer a question, thereafter, of the layman's struggle against the priest outside himself, but of his struggle against his *own internal*

---

[1] Marx refers to his intentions to publish a critical study of Hegel's *Philosophy of Right,* to which this essay was an introduction. One of Marx's preliminary manuscripts for such a study has been published entitled "Aus der Kritik der Hegelschen Rechtsphilosophie. Kritik des Hegelschen Staatsrechts." (*MEGA* I11, pp. 403–553.) The "Economic and Philosophical Manuscripts" is another version of this study; *see* Marx's comment. . . . [*Editor's note.*]

priest, against his own *priestly nature.* And if the Protestant metamorphosis of German laymen into priests emancipated the lay popes—the *princes* together with their clergy, the privileged and the philistines—the philosophical meta- morphosis of the priestly Germans into men will emancipate the *people.* But just as emancipation will not be confined to princes, so the *secularization* of property will not be limited to the *confiscation of church property,* which was practised especially by hypocritical Prussia. At that time, the Peasant War, the most radical event in German history, came to grief because of theology.

Today, when theology itself has come to grief, the most unfree phenomenon in German history—our *status quo*—will be shattered by philosophy. . . .

.   .   .

Where is there, then, a *real* possibility of emancipation in Germany?

This is our reply. A class must be formed which has *radical chains,* a class in civil society which is not a class of civil society, a class which is the dissolution of all classes, a sphere of society which has a universal character because its sufferings are universal, and which does not claim a *particular redress* because the wrong which is done to it is not a *particular wrong* but *wrong in general.* There must be formed a sphere of society which claims no *traditional* status but only a *human* status, a sphere which is not opposed to particular consequences but is totally opposed to the assumptions of the German political system; a sphere, finally, which cannot emancipate itself without emancipating itself from all the other spheres of society, without, therefore, emancipating all these other spheres, which is, in short, a *total loss* of humanity and which can only redeem itself by a *total redemption of humanity.* This dissolution of society, as a particular class, is the *proletariat.*

The proletariat is only beginning to form itself in Germany, as a result of the industrial movement. For what constitutes the proletariat is not *naturally existing* poverty, but poverty *artificially produced,* is not the mass of people mechanically oppressed by the weight of society, but the mass resulting from the *disintegration* of society and above all from the disintegration of the middle class. Needless to say, however, the numbers of the proletariat are also increased by the victims of natural poverty and of Christian-Germanic serfdom.

When the proletariat announces the *dissolution of the existing social order*, it only declares the *secret of its* own existence, for it *is* the *effective* dissolution of this order. When the proletariat demands the *negation of private property* it only lays down as a *principle for society* what society has already made a principle *for the proletariat,* and what the *latter* already involuntarily embodies as the negative result of society. Thus the proletarian has the same right, in relation to the new world which is coming into being, as the *German king* has in relation to the existing world when he calls the people *his* people or a horse *his* horse. In calling the people his private property the king simply declares that the owner of private property is king.

Just as philosophy finds its *material* weapons in the proletariat, so the pro- letariat finds its *intellectual* weapons in philosophy. And once the lightning of thought has penetrated deeply into this virgin soil of the people, the *Germans* will emancipate themselves and become *men.*

Let us sum up these results. The emancipation of Germany is only possible *in practice* if one adopts the point of view of that theory according to which man is the highest being for man. Germany will not be able to emancipate itself from the *Middle Ages* unless it emancipates itself at the same time from the *partial* victories over the Middle Ages. In Germany *no* type of enslavement can be abolished unless *all* enslavement is destroyed. Germany, which likes to get to the bottom of things, can only make a revolution which upsets *the whole order* of things. The *emancipation of Germany* will be an *emancipation of man*. *Philosophy* is the *head* of this emancipation and the *proletariat* is its *heart*. Philosophy can only be realized by the abolition of the proletariat, and the proletariat can only be abolished by the realization of philosophy.

Religion as a Product of Social Need

Emile Durkheim

Emile Durkheim (1858–1917) was a pioneer in the field of sociology, strongly influenced by the positivistic social philosophy of Auguste Comte. His major works are *The Elementary Forms of Religious Life, Suicide,* and *Rules of Sociological Method.*

THE SOCIAL FOUNDATION OF RELIGION

All known religious beliefs, whether simple or complex, present one common characteristic: they presuppose a classification of all the things, real and ideal, of which men think, into two classes or opposed groups, generally designated by two distinct terms which are translated well enough by the words *profane* and *sacred* (*profane, sacré*). This division of the world into two domains, the one containing all that is sacred, the other all that is profane, is the distinctive trait of religious thought; the beliefs, myths, dogmas and legends are either representations or systems of representations which express the nature of sacred things, the virtues and powers which are attributed to them, or their relations with each other and with profane things. But by sacred things one must not understand simply those personal beings which are called gods or spirits; a rock, a tree, a spring, a pebble, a piece of wood, a house, in a word, anything can be sacred. A rite can have this character; in fact, the rite does not exist which does not have it to a certain degree. There are words, expressions and formulae which can be pronounced only by the mouths of consecrated persons; there are gestures and movements which everybody cannot perform. If the Vedic sacrifice has had such an efficacy that, according to mythology, it was the

From Emile Durkheim, *The Elementary Forms of Religious Life,* trans. by J. Swain (New York, 1961), pp. 42–54. Copyright © 1915 by Allen & Unwin Ltd. First Free Press Paperback edition 1963. Reprinted with permission of The Macmillan Company and George Allen & Unwin Ltd., publishers.

creator of the gods, and not merely a means of winning their favor, it is because it possessed a virtue comparable to that of the most sacred beings. The circle of sacred objects cannot be determined, then, once for all. Its extent varies infinitely, according to the different religions. That is how Buddhism is a religion: in default of gods, it admits the existence of sacred things, namely, the four noble truths and the practices derived from them.

Up to the present we have confined ourselves to enumerating a certain number of sacred things as examples: we must now show by what general characteristics they are to be distinguished from profane things.

One might be tempted, first of all, to define them by the place they are generally assigned in the hierarchy of things. They are naturally considered superior in dignity and power to profane things, and particularly to man, when he is only a man and has nothing sacred about him. One thinks of himself as occupying an inferior and dependent position in relation to them; and surely this conception is not without some truth. Only there is nothing in it which is really characteristic of the sacred. It is not enough that one thing be subordinated to another for the second to be sacred in regard to the first. Slaves are inferior to their masters, subjects to their king, soldiers to their leaders, the miser to his gold, the man ambitious for power to the hands which keep it from him; but if it is sometimes said of a man that he makes a religion of those beings or things whose eminent value and superiority to himself he thus recognizes, it is clear that in any case the word is taken in a metaphorical sense, and that there is nothing in these relations which is really religious.

On the other hand, it must not be lost to view that there are sacred things of every degree, and that there are some in relation to which a man feels himself relatively at his ease. An amulet has a sacred character, yet the respect which it inspires is nothing exceptional. Even before his gods, a man is not always in such a marked state of inferiority; for it very frequently happens that he exercises a veritable physical constraint upon them to obtain what he desires. He beats the fetish with which he is not contented, but only to reconcile himself with it again, if in the end it shows itself more docile to the wishes of its adorer. To have rain, he throws stones into the spring or sacred lake where the god of rain is thought to reside; he believes that by this means he forces him to come out and show himself. Moreover, if it is true that man depends upon his gods, this dependence is reciprocal. The gods also have need of man; without offerings and sacrifices they would die. We shall even have occasion to show that this dependence of the gods upon their worshippers is maintained even in the most idealistic religions.

But if a purely hierarchic distinction is a criterion at once too general and too imprecise, there is nothing left with which to characterize the sacred in its relation to the profane except their heterogeneity. However, this heterogeneity is sufficient to characterize this classification of things and to distinguish it from all others, because it is very particular: *it is absolute*. In all the history of human thought there exists no other example of two categories of things so profoundly differentiated or so radically opposed to one another. The traditional opposition of good and bad is nothing beside this; for the good and the bad are only two opposed species of the same class, namely morals, just as sickness and health are two different aspects of the same order of facts, life, while the sacred and the profane have always and everywhere been conceived by the human mind as two distinct classes, as two worlds between which there is nothing in common. The forces which play in one are not simply those which are met with in the other, but a little stronger; they are of a different sort. In different religions, this opposition has been conceived in different ways. Here, to separate these two sorts of things, it has seemed sufficient to localize them in different parts of the physical universe; there, the first have been put into an ideal and transcendental world, while the material world is left in full possession of the others. But howsoever much the forms of the contrast may vary,[1] the fact of the contrast is universal.

This is not equivalent to saying that a being can never pass from one of these worlds into the other: but the manner in which this passage is effected, when it does take place, puts into relief the essential duality of the two kingdoms. In fact, it implies a veritable metamorphosis. This is notably demonstrated by the initiation rites, such as they are practised by a multitude of peoples. This initiation is a long series of ceremonies with the object of introducing the young man into the religious life: for the first time, he leaves the purely profane world where he passed his first infancy, and enters into the world of sacred things. Now this change of state is thought of, not as a simple and regular development of pre-existent germs, but as a transformation *totius substantiae*—of the whole being. It is said that at this moment the young man dies, that the person that he was ceases to exist, and that another is instantly substituted for it. He is reborn under a new form. Appropriate ceremonies are felt to bring about this death and rebirth, which are not understood in a merely symbolic sense, but are taken literally.[2] Does this not prove that between the profane being which he was and the religious being which he becomes, there is a break of continuity?

This heterogeneity is even so complete that it frequently degenerates into a veritable antagonism. The two worlds are not only conceived of as separate, but as even hostile and jealous rivals of each other. Since men cannot fully belong to one except on condition of leaving the other completely, they are exhorted to withdraw themselves completely from the profane world, in order to lead an exclusively religious life. Hence comes the monasticism which is artificially organized outside of and apart from the natural environment in which the ordinary man leads the life of this world, in a different one, closed to the first, and nearly its contrary. Hence comes the mystic asceticism whose object is to root out from man all the attachment for the profane world that remains in him. From that come all the forms of religious suicide, the logical working-out of this asceticism; for the only manner of fully escaping the profane life is, after all, to forsake all life.

The opposition of these two classes manifests itself outwardly with a visible

---

[1] The conception according to which the profane is opposed to the sacred, just as the irrational is to the rational, or the intelligible is to the mysterious, is only one of the forms under which this opposition is expressed. Science being once constituted, it has taken a profane character, especially in the eyes of the Christian religions; from that it appears as though it could not be applied to sacred things.

[2] See Frazer, "On some ceremonies of the Central Australian tribes" in *Australian Association for the Advancement of Science*, 1901, pp. 313 ff. This conception is also of an extreme generality. In India, the simple participation in the sacrificial act has the same effects; the sacrificer, by the mere act of entering within the circle of sacred things, changes his personality. (See, Hubert and Mauss, "Essai sur la nature et la fonction du sacrifice" in the *Année Sociologique*, vol. 2, 1899, p. 101.)

sign by which we can easily recognize this very special classification, wherever it exists. Since the idea of the sacred is always and everywhere separated from the idea of the profane in the thought of men, and since we picture a sort of logical chasm between the two, the mind irresistibly refuses to allow the two corresponding things to be confounded, or even to be merely put in contact with each other; for such a promiscuity, or even too direct a contiguity, would contradict too violently the dissociation of these ideas in the mind. The sacred thing is *par excellence* that which the profane should not touch, and cannot touch with impunity. To be sure, this interdiction cannot go so far as to make all communication between the two worlds impossible; for if the profane could in no way enter into relations with the sacred, this latter could be good for nothing. But, in addition to the fact that this establishment of relations is always a delicate operation in itself, demanding great precautions and a more or less complicated initiation, it is quite impossible, unless the profane is to lose its specific characteristics and become sacred after a fashion and to a certain degree itself. The two classes cannot even approach each other and keep their own nature at the same time.

Thus we arrive at the first criterion of religious beliefs. Undoubtedly there are secondary species within these two fundamental classes which, in their turn, are more or less incompatible with each other. But the real characteristic of religious phenomena is that they always suppose a bipartite division of the whole universe, known and knowable, into two classes which embrace all that exists, but which radically exclude each other. Sacred things are those which the interdictions protect and isolate; profane things, those to which these interdictions are applied and which must remain at a distance from the first. Religious beliefs are the representations which express the nature of sacred things and the relations which they sustain, either with each other or with profane things. Finally, rites are the rules of conduct which prescribe how a man should comport himself in the presence of these sacred objects.

... We arrive at the following definition: *a religion is a unified system of beliefs and practices relative to sacred things, that is to say, things set apart and forbidden—beliefs and practices which unite into one single moral community called a Church, all those who adhere to them.* The second element which finds a place in our definition is no less essential than the first; for by showing that the idea of religion is inseparable from that of the Church, it makes it clear that religion should be an eminently collective thing. ...

Our entire study rests upon the postulate that the unanimous sentiment of the believers of all times cannot be purely illusory.[3] Together with an apologist of the faith[4] we admit that these religious beliefs rest upon a specific experience whose demonstrative value is, in one sense, not one bit inferior to that of scientific experiments, though different from them. We, too, think that "a tree is known by its fruits,"[5] and that fertility is the best proof of "what the roots are worth." But from the fact that a "religious experience," if we choose to call it this, does exist and that it has a certain foundation—and, by the way, is there any experience which has none?—it does not follow that the reality

[3] Durkheim refers here and subsequently to the details of his analysis of aboriginal religion in Australia—*Ed.*

[4] William James, *The Varieties of Religious Experience.*

[5] Quoted by James, op. cit., p. 20.

which is its foundation conforms objectively to the idea which believers have of it. The very fact that the fashion in which it has been conceived has varied infinitely in different times is enough to prove that none of these conceptions express it adequately. If a scientist states it as an axiom that the sensations of heat and light which we feel correspond to some objective cause, he does not conclude that this is what it appears to the senses to be. Likewise, even if the impressions which the faithful feel are not imaginary, still they are in no way privileged intuitions; there is no reason for believing that they inform us better upon the nature of their object than do ordinary sensations upon the nature of bodies and their properties. In order to discover what this object consists of, we must submit them to an examination and elaboration analogous to that which has substituted for the sensuous idea of the world another which is scientific and conceptual.

This is precisely what we have tried to do, and we have seen that this reality, which mythologies have represented under so many different forms, but which is the universal and eternal objective cause of these sensations *sui generis* out of which religious experience is made, is society. We have shown what moral forces it develops and how it awakens this sentiment of a refuge, of a shield and of a guardian support which attaches the believer to his cult. It is that which raises him outside himself; it is even that which made him. For that which makes a man is the totality of the intellectual property which constitutes civilization, and civilization is the work of society. This is explained by the preponderating role of the cult in all religions, whichever they may be. This is because society cannot make its influence felt unless it is in action, and it is not in action unless the individuals who compose it are assembled together and act in common. It is by common action that it takes consciousness of itself and realizes its position; it is before all else an active cooperation. The collective ideas and sentiments are even possible only owing to these exterior movements which symbolize them, as we have established. Then it is action which dominates the religious life, because of the mere fact that it is society which is its source.

In addition to all the reasons which have been given to justify this conception, a final one may be added here, which is the result of our whole work. As we have progressed, we have established the fact that the fundamental categories of thought, and consequently of science, are of religious origin. We have seen that the same is true for magic and consequently for the different processes which have issued from it. On the other hand, it has long been known that up until a relatively advanced moment of evolution, moral and legal rules have been indistinguishable from ritual prescriptions. In summing up, then, it may be said that nearly all the great social institutions have been born in religion. Now in order that these principal aspects of the collective life may have commenced by being only varied aspects of the religious life, it is obviously necessary that the religious life be the eminent form and, as it were, the concentrated expression of the whole collective life. If religion has given birth to all that is essential in society, it is because the idea of society is the soul of religion.

Religious forces are therefore human forces, moral forces. It is true that since collective sentiments can become conscious of themselves only by fixing themselves upon external objects, they have not been able to take form without adopting some of their characteristics from other things: they have thus acquired a sort of physical nature; in this way they have come to mix themselves with the life of the material world, and then have considered themselves capable of explaining what passes there. But when they are considered only from this point of view and in this role, only their most superficial aspect is seen. In reality, the essential elements of which these collective sentiments are made have been borrowed by the understanding. It ordinarily seems that they should have a human character only when they are conceived under human forms;[6] but even the most impersonal and the most anonymous are nothing else than objectified sentiments.

It is only by regarding religion from this angle that it is possible to see its real significance. If we stick closely to appearances, rites often give the effect of purely manual operations: they are anointings, washings, meals. To consecrate something, it is put in contact with a source of religious energy, just as today a body is put in contact with a source of heat or electricity to warm or electrize it; the two processes employed are not essentially different. Thus understood, religious technique seems to be a sort of mystic mechanics. But these material maneuvers are only the external envelope under which the mental operations are hidden. Finally, there is no question of exercising a physical constraint upon blind and, incidentally, imaginary forces, but rather of reaching individual consciousnesses of giving them a direction and of disciplining them. It is sometimes said that inferior religions are materialistic. Such an expression is inexact. All religions, even the crudest, are in a sense spiritualistic: for the powers they put in play are before all spiritual, and also their principal object is to act upon the moral life. Thus it is seen that whatever has been done in the name of religion cannot have been done in vain: for it is necessarily the society that did it, and it is humanity that has reaped the fruits.

But, it is said, what society is it that has thus made the basis of religion? Is it the real society, such as it is and acts before our very eyes, with the legal and moral organization which it has laboriously fashioned during the course of history? This is full of defects and imperfections. In it, evil goes beside the good, injustice often reigns supreme, and the truth is often obscured by error. How could anything so crudely organized inspire the sentiments of love, the ardent enthusiasm and the spirit of abnegation which all religions claim of their followers? These perfect beings which are gods could not have taken their traits from so mediocre, and sometimes even so base a reality.

But, on the other hand, does someone think of a perfect society, where justice and truth would be sovereign, and from which evil in all its forms would be banished for ever? No one would deny that this is in close relations with the religious sentiment; for, they would say, it is towards the realization of this that all religions strive. But that society is not an empirical fact, definite and observable; it is a fancy, a dream with which men have lightened their sufferings, but in which they have never really lived. It is merely an idea which comes to express our more or less obscure aspirations towards the good, the beautiful and the ideal. Now these aspirations have their roots in us; they come from the very depths of our being; then there is nothing outside of us which can

---

[6] It is for this reason that Frazer and even Preuss set impersonal religious forces outside of, or at least on the threshold of religion, to attach them to magic.

account for them. Moreover, they are already religious in themselves; thus it would seem that the ideal society presupposes religion, far from being able to explain it.

But, in the first place, things are arbitrarily simplified when religion is seen only on its idealistic side: in its way, it is realistic. There is no physical or moral ugliness, there are no vices or evils which do not have a special divinity. There are gods of theft and trickery, of lust and war, of sickness and of death. Christianity itself, howsoever high the idea which it has made of the divinity may be, has been obliged to give the spirit of evil a place in its mythology. Satan is an essential piece of the Christian system; even if he is an impure being, he is not a profane one. The anti-god is a god, inferior and subordinated, it is true, but nevertheless endowed with extended powers; he is even the object of rites, at least of negative ones. Thus religion, far from ignoring the real society and making abstraction of it, is in its image; it reflects all its aspects, even the most vulgar and the most repulsive. All is to be found there, and if in the majority of cases we see the good victorious over evil, life over death, the powers of light over the powers of darkness, it is because reality is not otherwise. If the relation between these two contrary forces were reversed, life would be impossible; but, as a matter of fact, it maintains itself and even tends to develop.

But if, in the midst of these mythologies and theologies we see reality clearly appearing, it is none the less true that it is found there only in an enlarged, transformed and idealized form. In this respect, the most primitive religions do not differ from the most recent and the most refined. For example, we have seen how the Arunta place at the beginning of time a mythical society whose organization exactly reproduces that which still exists today; it includes the same clans and phratries, it is under the same matrimonial rules and it practises the same rites. But the personages who compose it are ideal beings, gifted with powers and virtues to which common mortals cannot pretend. Their nature is not only higher, but it is different, since it is at once animal and human. The evil powers there undergo a similar metamorphosis: evil itself is, as it were, made sublime and idealized. The question now raises itself of whence this idealization comes.

Some reply that men have a natural faculty for idealizing, that is to say, of substituting for the real world another different one, to which they transport themselves by thought. But that is merely changing the terms of the problem; it is not resolving it or even advancing it. This systematic idealization is an essential characteristic of religions. Explaining them by an innate power of idealization is simply replacing one word by another which is the equivalent of the first; it is as if they said that men have made religions because they have a religious nature. Animals know only one world, the one which they perceive by experience, internal as well as external. Men alone have the faculty of conceiving the ideal, of adding something to the real. Now where does this singular privilege come from? Before making it an initial fact or a mysterious virtue which escapes science, we must be sure that it does not depend upon empirically determinable conditions.

The explanation of religion which we have proposed has precisely this advantage, that it gives an answer to this question. For our definition of the sacred is that it is something added to and above the real; now the ideal answers to this same definition; we cannot explain one without explaining the other. In fact, we have seen that if collective life awakens religious thought on reaching a certain degree of intensity, it is because it brings about a state of effervescence which changes the conditions of psychic activity. Vital energies are over-excited, passions more active, sensations stronger; there are even some which are produced only at this moment. A man does not recognize himself; he feels himself transformed and consequently he transforms the environment which surrounds him. In order to account for the very particular impressions which he receives, he attributes to the things with which he is in most direct contact properties which they have not, exceptional powers and virtues which the objects of everyday experience do not possess. In a word, above the real world where his profane life passes he has placed another which, in one sense, does not exist except in thought, but to which he attributes a higher sort of dignity than to the first. Thus, from a double point of view it is an ideal world.

The formation of the ideal world is therefore not an irreducible fact which escapes science; it depends upon conditions which observation can touch; it is a natural product of social life. For a society to become conscious of itself and maintain at the necessary degree of intensity the sentiments which it thus attains, it must assemble and concentrate itself. Now this concentration brings about an exaltation of the mental life which takes form in a group of ideal conceptions where is portrayed the new life thus awakened; they correspond to this new set of psychical forces which is added to those which we have at our disposition for the daily tasks of existence. A society can neither create itself nor recreate itself without at the same time creating an ideal. This creation is not a sort of work of supererogation for it, by which it would complete itself, being already formed; it is the act by which it is periodically made and remade. Therefore when some oppose the ideal society to the real society, like two antagonists which would lead us in opposite directions, they materialize and oppose abstractions. The ideal society is not outside of the real society; it is a part of it. Far from being divided between them as between two poles which mutually repel each other, we cannot hold to one without holding to the other. For a society is not made up merely of the mass of individuals who compose it, the ground which they occupy, the things which they use and the movements which they perform, but above all is the idea which it forms of itself. It is undoubtedly true that it hesitates over the manner in which it ought to conceive itself; it feels itself drawn in divergent directions. But these conflicts which break forth are not between the ideal and reality, but between two different ideals, that of yesterday and that of today, that which has the authority of tradition and that which has the hope of the future. There is surely a place for investigating whence these ideals evolve; but whatever solution may be given to this problem, it still remains that all passes in the world of the ideal.

Thus the collective ideal which religion expresses is far from being due to a vague innate power of the individual, but it is rather at the school of collective life that the individual has learned to idealize. It is in assimilating the ideals elaborated by society that he has become capable of conceiving the ideal. It is society which, by leading him within its sphere of action, has made him acquire the need of raising himself above the world of experience and has at the same time furnished him with the means of conceiving another. For society has constructed this new world in constructing itself, since it is society which this expresses. Thus both with the individual and in the group, the faculty of idealizing has nothing mysterious about it. It is not a sort of luxury which a man could get along without, but a condition of his very existence. He could not be a social being, that is to say, he could not be man, if he had not acquired it. It is true that in incarnating themselves in individuals, collective ideals tend to individualize themselves. Each understands them after his own fashion and marks them with his own stamp; he suppresses certain elements and adds others. Thus the personal ideal disengages itself from the social ideal in proportion as the individual personality develops itself and becomes an autonomous source of action. But if we wish to understand this aptitude, so singular in appearance, of living outside of reality, it is enough to connect it with the social conditions upon which it depends.

Therefore it is necessary to avoid seeing in this theory of religion a simple restatement of historical materialism: that would be misunderstanding our thought to an extreme degree. In showing that religion is something essentially social, we do not mean to say that it confines itself to translating into another language the material forms of society and its immediate vital necessities. It is true that we take it as evident that social life depends upon its material foundation and bears its mark, just as the mental life of an individual depends upon his nervous system and in fact his whole organism. But collective consciousness is something more than a mere epiphenomenon of its morphological basis, just as individual consciousness is something more than a simple efflorescence of the nervous system. In order that the former may appear, a synthesis *sui generis* of particular consciousness is required. Now this synthesis has the effect of disengaging a whole world of sentiments, ideas and images which, once born, obey laws all their own. They attract each other, repel each other, unite, divide themselves and multiply, though these combinations are not commanded and necessitated by the condition of the underlying reality. The life thus brought into being even enjoys so great an independence that it sometimes indulges in manifestations with no purpose or utility of any sort, for the mere pleasure of affirming itself. We have shown that this is often precisely the case with ritual activity and mythological thought.

Religion as an Ethical Ideal

John Dewey

John Dewey (1859–1952) has had a greater influence on the world of practical affairs in the United States than any other professor of philosophy. This is not accidental, for in all his writings Dewey regards philosophy as a human activity whose value lies in its social impact. Greatly influenced by C. S. Pierce and William James, Dewey developed his own type of pragmatism that has become known as instrumentalism, and wielded his instrumentalism to create new approaches to and new insights into all branches of philosophy, psychology, and educational theory.

All religions . . . involve specific intellectual beliefs, and they attach—some greater, some less—importance to assent to these doctrines as true, true in the intellectual sense. They have literatures held especially sacred, containing historical material with which the validity of the religions is connected. They have developed a doctrinal apparatus it is incumbent upon "believers" (with varying degrees of strictness in different religions) to accept. They also insist that there is some special and isolated channel of access to the truths they hold.

No one will deny, I suppose, that the present crisis in religion is intimately bound up with these claims. The skepticism and agnosticism that are rife and that from the standpoint of the religionist are fatal to the religious spirit are directly bound up with the intellectual contents, historical, cosmological, ethical, and theological, asserted to be indispensable in everything religious. There is no need for me here to go with any minuteness into the causes that have generated doubt and disbelief, uncertainty and rejection, as to these contents. It is enough to point out that all the beliefs and ideas in question, whether having to do with historical and literary matters, or with astronomy, geology and biology, or with the creation and structure of the world and man, are connected with the supernatural, and that this connection is the factor that has brought doubt upon them; the factor that from the standpoint of historic and institutional religions is sapping the religious life itself.

The obvious and simple facts of the case are that some views about the origin and constitution of the world and man, some views about the course of human history and personages and incidents in that history, have become so interwoven with religion as to be identified with it. On the other hand, the growth of knowledge and of its methods and tests has been such as to make acceptance of these beliefs increasingly onerous and even impossible for large numbers of cultivated men and women. With such persons, the result is that the more these ideas are used as the basis and justification of a religion, the more dubious that religion becomes.

From John Dewey, "Faith and Its Object," in *A Common Faith* (New Haven, Conn., 1934). Copyright © 1934 by Yale University Press. Reprinted by permission.

Protestant denominations have largely abandoned the idea that particular ecclesiastic sources can authoritatively determine cosmic, historic and theological beliefs. The more liberal among them have at least mitigated the older belief that individual hardness and corruption of heart are the causes of intellectual rejection of the intellectual apparatus of the Christian religion. But these denominations have also, with exceptions numerically insignificant, retained a certain indispensable minimum of intellectual content. They ascribe peculiar religious force to certain literary documents and certain historic personages. Even when they have greatly reduced the bulk of intellectual content to be accepted, they have insisted at least upon theism and the immortality of the individual.

It is no part of my intention to rehearse in any detail the weighty facts that collectively go by the name of the conflict of science and religion—a conflict that is not done away with by calling it a conflict of science with theology, as long as even a minimum of intellectual assent is prescribed as essential. The impact of astronomy not merely upon the older cosmogony of religion but upon elements of creeds dealing with historic events—witness the idea of ascent into heaven— is familiar. Geological discoveries have displaced creation myths which once bulked large. Biology has revolutionized conceptions of soul and mind which once occupied a central place in religious beliefs and ideas, and this science has made a profound impression upon ideas of sin, redemption, and immortality. Anthropology, history and literary criticism have furnished a radically different version of the historic events and personages upon which Christian religions have built. Psychology is already opening to us natural explanations of phenomena so extraordinary that once their supernatural origin was, so to say, the natural explanation.

The significant bearing for my purpose of all this is that new methods of inquiry and reflection have become for the educated man today the final arbiter of all questions of fact, existence, and intellectual assent. Nothing less than a revolution in the "seat of intellectual authority" has taken place. This revolution, rather than any particular aspect of its impact upon this and that religious belief, is the central thing. In this revolution, every defeat is a stimulus to renewed inquiry; every victory won is the open door to more discoveries, and every discovery is a new seed planted in the soil of intelligence, from which grow fresh plants with new fruits. The mind of man is being habituated to a new method and ideal: There is but one sure road of access to truth—the road of patient, cooperative inquiry operating by means of observation, experiment, record and controlled reflection.

The scope of the change is well illustrated by the fact that whenever a particular outpost is surrendered it is usually met by the remark from a liberal theologian that the particular doctrine or supposed historic or literary tenet surrendered was never, after all, an intrinsic part of religious belief, and that without it the true nature of religion stands out more clearly than before. Equally significant is the growing gulf between fundamentalists and liberals in the churches. What is not realized—although perhaps it is more definitely seen by fundamentalists than by liberals—is that the issue does not concern this and that piecemeal *item* of belief, but centers in the question of the method by which any and every item of intellectual belief is to be arrived at and justified.

The positive lesson is that religious qualities and values if they are real at all are not bound up with any single item of intellectual assent, not even that of the existence of the God of theism; and that, under existing conditions, the religious function in experience can be emancipated only through surrender of the whole notion of special truths that are religious by their own nature, together with the idea of peculiar avenues of access to such truths. For were we to admit that there is but one method for ascertaining fact and truth—that conveyed by the word "scientific" in its most general and generous sense—no discovery in any branch of knowledge and inquiry could then disturb the faith that is religious. I should describe this faith as the unification of the self through allegiance to inclusive ideal ends, which imagination presents to us and to which the human will responds as worthy of controlling our desires and choices.

It is probably impossible to imagine the amount of intellectual energy that has been diverted from normal processes of arriving at intellectual conclusions because it has gone into rationalization of the doctrines entertained by historic religions. The set that has thus been given the general mind is much more harmful, to my mind, than are the consequences of any one particular item of belief, serious as have been those flowing from acceptance of some of them. The modern liberal version of the intellectual content of Christianity seems to the modern mind to be more rational than some of the earlier doctrines that have been reacted against. Such is not the case in fact. The theological philosophers of the Middle Ages had no greater difficulty in giving rational form to all the doctrines of the Roman church than has the liberal theologian of today in formulating and justifying intellectually the doctrines he entertains. This statement is as applicable to the doctrine of continuing miracles, penance, indulgences, saints and angels, etc., as to the trinity, incarnation, atonement, and the sacraments. The fundamental question, I repeat, is not of this and that article of intellectual belief but of intellectual habit, method and criterion.

One method of swerving aside the impact of changed knowledge and method upon the intellectual content of religion is the method of division of territory and jurisdiction into two parts. Formerly these were called the realm of nature and the realm of grace. They are now often known as those of revelation and natural knowledge. Modern religious liberalism has no definite names for them, save, perhaps, the division . . . between scientific and religious experience. The implication is that in one territory the supremacy of scientific knowledge must be acknowledged, while there is another region, not very precisely defined, of intimate personal experience wherein other methods and criteria hold sway.

This method of justifying the peculiar and legitimate claim of certain elements of belief is always open to the objection that a positive conclusion is drawn from a negative fact. Existing ignorance or backwardness is employed to assert the existence of a division in the nature of the subject-matter dealt with. Yet the gap may only reflect, at most, a limitation now existing but in the future to be done away with. The argument that because some province or aspect of experience has not yet been "invaded" by scientific methods, it is not subject to them, is as old as it is dangerous. Time and time again, in some particular reserved field, it has been invalidated. Psychology is still in its infancy. He is bold to the point of rashness who asserts that intimate personal experience will never come within the ken of natural knowledge.

It is more to the present point, however, to consider the region that is claimed by religionists as a special reserve. It is mystical experience. The difference, however, between mystic experience and the theory about it that is offered to us must be noted. The experience is a fact to be inquired into. The theory, like any theory, is an interpretation of the fact. The idea that by its very nature the experience is a veridical realization of the direct presence of God does not rest so much upon examination of the facts as it does upon importing into their interpretation a conception that is formed outside them. In its dependence upon a prior conception of the supernatural, which is the thing to be proved, it begs the question.

History exhibits many types of mystic experience, and each of these types is contemporaneously explained by the concepts that prevail in the culture and the circle in which the phenomena occur. There are mystic crises that arise, as among some North American Indian tribes, induced by fasting. They are accompanied by trances and semi-hysteria. Their purpose is to gain some special power, such perhaps as locating a person who is lost or finding objects that have been secreted. There is the mysticism of Hindoo practice now enjoying some vogue in Western countries. There is the mystic ecstasy of Neoplatonism with its complete abrogation of the self and absorption into an impersonal whole of Being. There is the mysticism of intense esthetic experience independent of any theological or metaphysical interpretation. There is the heretical mysticism of William Blake. There is the mysticism of sudden unreasoning fear in which the very foundations seem shaken beneath one—to mention but a few of the types that may be found.

What common element is there between, say, the Neoplatonic conception of a super-divine Being wholly apart from human needs and conditions and the medieval theory of an immediate union that is fostered through attention to the sacraments or through concentration upon the heart of Jesus? The contemporary emphasis of some Protestant theologians upon the sense of inner personal communion with God, found in religious experience, is almost as far away from medieval Christianity as it is from Neoplatonism or Yoga. Interpretations of the experience have not grown from the experience itself with the aid of such scientific resources as may be available. They have been imported by borrowing without criticism from ideas that are current in the surrounding culture.

The mystic states of the shaman and of some North American Indians are frankly techniques for gaining a special power—the power as it is conceived by some revivalist sects. There is no especial intellectual objectification accompanying the experience. The knowledge that is said to be gained is not that of Being but of particular secrets and occult modes of operation. The aim is not to gain knowledge of superior divine power, but to get advice, cures for the sick, prestige, etc. The conception that mystic experience is a normal mode of religious experience by which we may acquire knowledge of God and divine things is a nineteenth-century interpretation that has gained vogue in direct ratio to the decline of older methods of religious apologetics.

There is no reason for denying the existence of experiences that are called mystical. On the contrary, there is every reason to suppose that, in some degree of intensity, they occur so frequently that they may be regarded as normal manifestations that take place at certain rhythmic points in the movement of experience. The assumption that denial of a particular interpretation of their objective content proves that those who make the denial do not have the experience in question, so that if they had it they would be equally persuaded of its objective source in the presence of God, has no foundation in fact. As with every empirical phenomenon, the occurrence of the state called mystical is simply an occasion for inquiry into its mode of causation. There is no more reason for converting the experience itself into an immediate knowledge of its cause than in the case of an experience of lightning or any other natural occurrence.

My purpose, then, in this brief reference to mysticism is not to throw doubt upon the existence of particular experiences called mystical. Nor is it to propound any theory to account for them. I have referred to the matter merely as an illustration of the general tendency to mark off two distinct realms in one of which science has jurisdiction, while in the other, special modes of immediate knowledge of religious objects have authority. This dualism as it operates in contemporary interpretation of mystic experience in order to validate certain beliefs is but a reinstatement of the old dualism between the natural and the supernatural, in terms better adapted to the cultural conditions of the present time. Since it is the conception of the supernatural that science calls in question, the circular nature of this type of reasoning is obvious.

Apologists for a religion often point to the shift that goes on in scientific ideas and materials as evidence of the unreliability of science as a mode of knowledge. They often seem peculiarly elated by the great, almost revolutionary, change in fundamental physical conceptions that has taken place in science during the present generation. Even if the alleged unreliability were as great as they assume (or even greater), the question would remain: Have we any other recourse for knowledge? But in fact they miss the point. Science is not constituted by any particular body of subject-matter. It is constituted by a method, a method of changing beliefs by means of tested inquiry as well as of arriving at them. It is its glory, not its condemnation, that its subject-matter develops as the method is improved. There is no special subject-matter of belief that is sacrosanct. The identification of science with a particular set of beliefs and ideas is itself a holdover of ancient and still current dogmatic habits of thought which are opposed to science in its actuality and which science is undermining.

For scientific method is adverse not only to dogma but to doctrine as well, provided we take "doctrine" in its usual meaning—a body of definite beliefs that need only to be taught and learned as true. This negative attitude of science to doctrine does not indicate indifference to truth. It signifies supreme loyalty to the method by which truth is attained. The scientific-religious conflict ultimately is a conflict between allegiance to this method and allegiance to even an irreducible minimum of belief so fixed in advance that it can never be modified.

The method of intelligence is open and public. The doctrinal method is limited and private. This limitation persists even when knowledge of the truth that is religious is said to be arrived at by a special mode of experience, that termed "religious." For the latter is assumed to be a very special kind of experience. To be sure it is asserted to be open to all who obey certain conditions. Yet the mystic experience yields, as we have seen, various results in the way of belief to different persons, depending upon the surrounding culture of those who undergo it. As a method, it lacks the public character belonging to the method of intelligence. Moreover, when the experience in question does not yield consciousness of the presence of God, in the sense that is alleged to exist, the retort is always at hand that it is not a genuine religious experience. For by definition, only that experience *is* religious which arrives at this particular result. The argument is circular. The traditional position is that some hardness or corruption of heart prevents one from having the experience. Liberal religionists are now more humane. But their logic does not differ.

It is sometimes held that beliefs about religious matters are symbolic, like rites and ceremonies. This view may be an advance upon that which holds to their literal objective validity. But as usually put forward it suffers from an ambiguity. Of what are the beliefs symbols? Are they symbols of things experienced in other modes than those set apart as religious, so that the things symbolized have an independent standing? Or are they symbols in the sense of standing for some transcendental reality—transcendental because not being the subject-matter of experience generally? Even the fundamentalist admits a certain quality and degree of symbolism in the latter sense in objects of religious belief. For he holds that the objects of these beliefs are so far beyond finite human capacity that our beliefs must be couched in more or less metaphorical terms. The conception that faith is the best available substitute for knowledge in our present estate still attaches to the notion of the symbolic character of the materials of faith; unless by ascribing to them a symbolic nature we mean that these materials stand for something that is verifiable in general and public experience.

Were we to adopt the latter point of view, it would be evident not only that the intellectual articles of a creed must be understood to be symbolic of moral and other ideal values, but that the facts taken to be historic and used as concrete evidence of the intellectual articles are themselves symbolic. These articles of a creed present events and persons that have been made over by the idealizing imagination in the interest, at their best, of moral ideals. Historic personages in their divine attributes are materializations of the ends that enlist devotion and inspire endeavor. They are symbolic of the reality of ends moving us in many forms of experience. The ideal values that are thus symbolized also mark human experience in science and art and the various modes of human association: they mark almost everything in life that rises from the level of manipulation of conditions as they exist. It is admitted that the objects of religion are ideal in contrast with our present state. What would be lost if it were also admitted that they have authoritative claim upon conduct just because they are ideal? The assumption that these objects of religion exist already in some realm of Being seems to add nothing to their force, while it weakens their claim over us as ideals, in so far as it bases that claim upon matters that are intellectually dubious. The question narrows itself to this: Are the ideals that move us genuinely ideal or are they ideal only in contrast with our present estate?

The import of the question extends far. It determines the meaning given to the word "God." On one score, the word can mean only a particular Being. On the other score, it denotes the unity of all ideal ends arousing us to desire and actions. Does the unification have a claim upon our attitude and conduct because it is already, apart from us, in realized existence, or because of its own inherent meaning and value? Suppose for the moment that the word "God" means the ideal ends that at a given time and place one acknowledges as having authority over his volition and emotion, the values to which one is supremely devoted, as far as these ends, through imagination, take on unity. If we make this supposition, the issue will stand out clearly in contrast with the doctrine of religions that "God" designates some kind of Being having prior and therefore non-ideal existence.

The word "non-ideal" is to be taken literally in regard to some religions that have historically existed, to all of them as far as they are neglectful of moral qualities in their divine beings. It does not apply in the same *literal* way to Judaism and Christianity. For they have asserted that the Supreme Being has moral and spiritual attributes. But it applies to them none the less in that these moral and spiritual characters are thought of as properties of a particular existence and are thought to be of religious value for us because of this embodiment in such an existence. Here, as far as I can see, is the ultimate issue as to the difference between *a* religion and the religious as a function of experience.

The idea that "God" represents a unification of ideal values that is essentially imaginative in origin when the imagination supervenes in conduct is attended with verbal difficulties owing to our frequent use of the word "imagination" to denote fantasy and doubtful reality. But the reality of ideal ends as ideals is vouched for by their undeniable power in action. An ideal is not an illusion because imagination is the organ through which it is apprehended. For *all* possibilities reach us through the imagination. In a definite sense the only meaning that can be assigned the term "imagination" is that things unrealized in fact come home to us and have power to stir us. The unification effected through imagination is not fanciful, for it is the reflex of the unification of practical and emotional attitudes. The unity signifies not a single Being, but the unity of loyalty and effort evoked by the fact that many ends are one in the power of their ideal, or imaginative, quality to stir and hold us.

We may well ask whether the power and significance in life of the traditional conceptions of God are not due to the ideal qualities referred to by them, the hypostatization of them into an existence being due to a conflux of tendencies in human nature that converts the object of desire into an antecedent reality . . . with beliefs that have prevailed in the cultures of the past. For in the older cultures the idea of the supernatural was "natural," in the sense in which "natural" signifies something customary and familiar. It seems more credible that religious persons have been supported and consoled by the reality with which ideal values appeal to them than that they have been upborne by sheer matter of fact existence. That, when once men are inured to the idea of the union of the ideal and the physical, the two should be so bound together in emotion that it is difficult to institute a separation, agrees with all we know of human psychology.

The benefits that will accrue, however, from making the separation are evident. The dislocation frees the religious values of experience once for all from matters that are continually becoming more dubious. With that release there comes emancipation from the necessity of resort to apologetics. The reality of ideal ends and values in their authority over us is an undoubted fact. The validity of justice, affection, and that intellectual correspondence of our ideas with realities that we call truth, is so assured in its hold upon humanity that it is unnecessary for the religious attitude to encumber itself with the apparatus of dogma and doctrine. Any other conception of the religious attitude, when it is adequately analysed, means that those who hold it care more for force than for ideal values—since all that an Existence can add is force to establish, to punish, and to reward. There are, indeed, some persons who frankly say that their own faith does not require any guarantee that moral values are backed up by physical force, but who hold that the masses are so backward that ideal values will not affect their conduct unless in the popular belief these values have the sanction of a power that can enforce them and can execute justice upon those who fail to comply.

There are some persons, deserving of more respect, who say: "We agree that the beginning must be made with the primacy of the ideal. But why stop at this point? Why not search with the utmost eagerness and vigor for all the evidence we can find, such as is supplied by history, by presence of design in nature, which may lead on to the belief that the ideal is already extant in a Personality having objective existence?"

One answer to the question is that we are involved by this search in all the problems of the existence of evil that have haunted theology in the past and that the most ingenious apologetics have not faced, much less met. If these apologists had not identified the existence of ideal goods with that of a Person supposed to originate and support them—a Being, moreover, to whom omnipotent power is attributed—the problem of the occurrence of evil would be gratuitous. The significance of ideal ends and meanings is, indeed, closely connected with the fact that there are in life all sorts of things that are evil to us because we would have them otherwise. Were existing conditions wholly good, the notion of possibilities to be realized would never emerge.

But the more basic answer is that while if the search is conducted upon a strictly empirical basis there is no reason why it should not take place, as a matter of fact it is always undertaken in the interest of the supernatural. Thus it diverts attention and energy from ideal values and from the exploration of actual conditions by means of which they may be promoted. History is testimony to this fact. Men have never fully used the powers they possess to advance the good in life, because they have waited upon some power external to themselves and to nature to do the work they are responsible for doing. Dependence upon an external power is the counterpart of surrender of human endeavor. Nor is emphasis on exercising our own powers for good an egoistical or a sentimentally optimistic recourse. It is not the first, for it does not isolate man, either individually or collectively, from nature. It is not the second, because it makes no assumption beyond that of the need and responsibility for human endeavor, and beyond the conviction that, if human desire and endeavor were enlisted in behalf of natural ends, conditions would be bettered. It involves no expectation of a millennium of good.

Belief in the supernatural as a necessary power for apprehension of the ideal and for practical attachment to it has for its counterpart a pessimistic belief in the corruption and impotency of natural means. That is axiomatic in Christian dogma. But this apparent pessimism has a way of suddenly changing into an exaggerated optimism. For according to the terms of the doctrine, if the faith in the supernatural is of the required order, regeneration at once takes place. Goodness, in all essentials, is thereby established; if not, there is proof that the established relation to the supernatural has been vitiated. This romantic optimism is one cause for the excessive attention to individual salvation characteristic of traditional Christianity. Belief in a sudden and complete transmutation through conversion and in the objective efficacy of prayer, is too easy a way out of difficulties. It leaves matters in general just about as they were before; that is, sufficiently bad so that there is additional support for the idea that only supernatural aid can better them. The position of natural intelligence is that there exists a *mixture* of good and evil, and that reconstruction in the direction of the good which is indicated by ideal ends, must take place, if at all, through continued cooperative effort. There is at least enough impulse toward justice, kindliness, and order so that if it were mobilized for action, not expecting abrupt and complete transformation to occur, the disorder, cruelty, and oppression that exist would be reduced.

The discussion has arrived at a point where a more fundamental objection to the position I am taking needs consideration. The misunderstanding upon which this objection rests should be pointed out. The view I have advanced is sometimes treated as if the identification of the divine with ideal ends left the ideal wholly without roots in existence and without support from existence. The objection implies that my view commits one to such a separation of the ideal and the existent that the ideal has no chance to find lodgment even as a seed that might grow and bear fruit. On the contrary, what I have been criticizing is the *identification* of the ideal with a particular Being, especially when that identification makes necessary the conclusion that this Being is outside of nature, and what I have tried to show is that the ideal itself has its roots in natural conditions; it emerges when the imagination idealizes existence by laying hold of the possibilities offered to thought and action. There are values, goods, actually realized upon a natural basis—the goods of human association, of art and knowledge. The idealizing imagination seizes upon the most precious things found in the climacteric moments of experience and projects them. We need no external criterion and guarantee for their goodness. They are had, they exist as good, and out of them we frame our ideal ends.

Moreover, the ends that result from our projection of experienced goods into objects of thought, desire and effort exist, only they exist *as* ends. Ends, purposes, exercise determining power in human conduct. The aims of philanthropists, of Florence Nightingale, of Howard, of Wilberforce, of Peabody, have not been ideal dreams. They have modified institutions. Aims, ideals, do not exist simply in "mind"; they exist in character, in personality and action. One might call the roll of artists, intellectual inquirers, parents, friends, citizens who are neighbors, to show that purposes exist in an *operative* way. What I have been objecting to, I repeat, is not the idea that ideals are linked with existence and that they themselves exist, through human embodiment, as forces, but the idea that their authority and value depend upon some prior complete embodiment—as if the efforts of human beings in behalf of justice, or knowledge or beauty, depended for their effectiveness and validity upon assurance that there already existed in some supernal region a place where criminals are humanely treated, where there is no serfdom or slavery, where all facts and truths are already discovered and possessed, and all beauty is eternally displayed in actualized form.

The aims and ideals that move us are generated through imagination. But they are not made out of imaginary stuff. They are made out of the hard stuff of the world of physical and social experience. The locomotive did not exist before Stevenson, nor the telegraph before the time of Morse. But the conditions for their existence were there in physical material and energies and in human capacity. Imagination seized hold upon the idea of a rearrangement of existing things that would evolve new objects. The same thing is true of a painter, a musician, a poet, a philanthropist, a moral prophet. The new vision does not arise out of nothing, but emerges through seeing, in terms of possibilities, that is, of imagination, old things in new relations serving a new end which the new end aids in creating.

Moreover the process of creation is experimental and continuous. The artist, scientific man, or good citizen, depends upon what others have done before him and are doing around him. The sense of new values that become ends to be realized arises first in dim and uncertain form. As the values are dwelt upon and carried forward in action they grow in definiteness and coherence. Interaction between aim and existent conditions improves and tests the ideal; and conditions are at the same time modified. Ideals change as they are applied in existent conditions. The process endures and advances with the life of humanity. What one person and one group accomplish becomes the standing ground and starting point of those who succeed them. When the vital factors in this natural process are generally acknowledged in emotion, thought and action, the process will be both accelerated and purified through elimination of that irrelevant element that culminates in the idea of the supernatural. When the vital factors attain the religious force that has been drafted into supernatural religions, the resulting reinforcement will be incalculable.

These considerations may be applied to the idea of God, or, to avoid misleading conceptions, to the idea of the divine. This idea is, as I have said, one of ideal possibilities unified through imaginative realization and projection. But this idea of God, or of the divine, is also connected with all the natural forces and conditions—including man and human association—that promote the growth of the ideal and that further its realization. We are in the presence neither of ideals completely embodied in existence nor yet of ideals that are mere rootless ideals, fantasies, utopias. For there are forces in nature and society that generate and support the ideals. They are further unified by the action that gives them coherence and solidity. It is this *active* relation between ideal and actual to which I would give the name "God." I would not insist that the name *must* be given. There are those who hold that the associations of the term with the supernatural are so numerous and close that any use of the word "God" is sure to give rise to misconception and be taken as a concession to traditional ideas.

They may be correct in this view. But the facts to which I have referred are there and they need to be brought out with all possible clearness and force. There exist concretely and experimentally goods—the values of art in all its forms, of knowledge, of effort and of rest after striving, of education and fellowship, of friendship and love, of growth in mind and body. These goods are there and yet they are relatively embryonic. Many persons are shut out from generous participation in them; there are forces at work that threaten and sap existent goods as well as prevent their expansion. A clear and intense conception of a union of ideal ends with actual conditions is capable of arousing steady emotion. It may be fed by every experience, no matter what its material.

In a distracted age, the need for such an idea is urgent. It can unify interests and energies now dispersed; it can direct action and generate the heat of emotion and the light of intelligence. Whether one gives the name "God" to this union, operative in thought and action, is a matter for individual decision. But the *function* of such a working union of the ideal and actual seems to me to be identical with the force that has in fact been attached to the conception of God in all the religions that have a spiritual content; and a clear idea of that function seems to me urgently needed at the present time.

The sense of this union may, with some persons, be furthered by mystical experiences, using the term "mystical" in its broadest sense. That result depends largely upon temperament. But there is a marked difference between the union associated with mysticism and the union which I had in mind. There is nothing mystical about the latter; it is natural and moral. Nor is there anything mystical about the perception or consciousness of such union. Imagination of ideal ends pertinent to actual conditions represents the fruition of a disciplined mind. There is, indeed, even danger that resort to mystical experiences will be an escape, and that its result will be the passive feeling that the union of actual and ideal is already accomplished. But in fact this union is active and practical; it is a *uniting*, not something given.

One reason why personally I think it fitting to use the word "God" to denote that uniting of the ideal and actual which has been spoken of, lies in the fact that aggressive atheism seems to me to have something in common with traditional supernaturalism. I do not mean merely that the former is mainly so negative that it fails to give positive direction to thought, though that fact is pertinent. What I have in mind especially is the exclusive preoccupation of both militant atheism and supernaturalism with man in isolation. For in spite of supernaturalism's reference to something beyond nature, it conceives of this earth as the moral center of the universe and of man as the apex of the whole scheme of things. It regards the drama of sin and redemption enacted within the isolated and lonely soul of man as the one thing of ultimate importance. Apart from man, nature is held either accursed or negligible. Militant atheism is also affected by lack of natural piety. The ties binding man to nature that poets have always celebrated are passed over lightly. The attitude taken is often that of man living in an indifferent and hostile world and issuing blasts of defiance. A religious attitude, however, needs the sense of a connection of man, in the way of both dependence and support, with the enveloping world that the imagination feels is a universe. Use of the words "God" or "divine" to convey the union of actual with ideal may protect man from a sense of isolation and from consequent despair or defiance.

In any case, whatever the name, the meaning is selective. For it involves no miscellaneous worship of everything in general. It selects those factors in existence that generate and support our idea of good as an end to be striven for. It excludes a multitude of forces that at any time are irrelevant to this function. Nature produces whatever gives reinforcement and direction but also what occasions discord and confusion. The "divine" is thus a term of human choice and aspiration. A humanistic religion, if it excludes our relation to nature, is pale and thin, as it is presumptuous, when it takes humanity as an object of worship. Matthew Arnold's conception of a "power not ourselves" is too narrow in its reference to operative and sustaining conditions. While it is selective, it is too narrow in its basis of selection—righteousness. The conception thus needs to be widened in two ways. The powers that generate and support the good as experienced and as ideal, work *within* as well as without. There seems to be a reminiscence of an external Jehovah in Arnold's statement. And the powers work to enforce other values and ideals than righteousness. Arnold's sense of an opposition between Hellenism and Hebraism resulted in exclusion of beauty, truth, and friendship from the list of the consequences toward which powers work within and without.

In the relation between nature and human ends and endeavors, recent science has broken down the older dualism. It has been engaged in this task for three centuries. But as long as the conceptions of science were strictly mechanical (mechanical in the sense of assuming separate things acting upon one another purely externally by push and pull), religious apologists had a standing ground in pointing out the differences between man and physical nature. The differences could be used for arguing that something supernatural had intervened in the case of man. The recent acclaim, however, by apologists for religion of the surrender by science of the classic type of mechanicalism[1] seems ill-advised from their own point of view. For the change in the modern scientific view of nature simply brings man and nature nearer together. We are no longer compelled to choose between explaining away what is distinctive in man through reducing him to another form of a mechanical model and the doctrine that something literally supernatural marks him off from nature. The less mechanical—in its older sense—physical nature is found to be, the closer is man to nature.

In his fascinating book, *The Dawn of Conscience,* James Henry Breasted refers to Haeckel as saying that the question he would most wish to have answered is this: Is the universe friendly to man? The question is an ambiguous one. Friendly to man in what respect? With respect to ease and comfort, to material success, to egoistic ambitions? Or to his aspiration to inquire and discover, to invent and create, to build a more secure order for human existence? In whatever form the question be put, the answer cannot in all honesty be an unqualified and absolute one. Mr. Breasted's answer, as a historian, is that nature has been friendly to the emergence and development of conscience and character. Those who will have all or nothing cannot be satisfied with this answer. Emergence and growth are not enough for them. They want something more than growth accompanied by toil and pain. They want final achievement. Others who are less absolutist may be content to think that, morally speaking, growth is a higher value and ideal than is sheer attainment. They will remember also that growth has not been confined to conscience and character; that it extends also to discovery, learning and knowledge, to creation in the arts, to furtherance of ties that hold men together in mutual aid and affection. These persons at least will be satisfied with an intellectual view of the religious function that is based on continuing choice directed toward ideal ends.

For, I would remind readers in conclusion, it is the intellectual side of the religious attitude that I have been considering. I have suggested that the religious element in life has been hampered by conceptions of the supernatural that were imbedded in those cultures wherein man had little control over outer nature and little in the way of sure method of inquiry and test. The crisis today as to the intellectual content of religious belief has been caused by the change in the intellectual climate due to the increase of our knowledge and our means of understanding. I have tried to show that this change is not fatal to the religious values in our common experience, however adverse its impact may be upon historic religions. Rather, provided that the methods and results of intelligence at work are frankly adopted, the change is liberating.

It clarifies our ideals, rendering them less subject to illusion and fantasy. It relieves us of the incubus of thinking of them as fixed, as without power of growth. It discloses that they develop in coherence and pertinency with increase of

---

[1] I use this term because science has not abandoned its beliefs in working mechanisms in giving up the idea that they are of the nature of a strictly mechanical contact of discrete things.

natural intelligence. The change gives aspiration for natural knowledge a definitely religious character, since growth in understanding of nature is seen to be organically related to the formation of ideal ends. The same change enables man to select those elements in natural conditions that may be organized to support and extend the sway of ideals. All purpose is selective, and all intelligent action includes deliberate choice. In the degree in which we cease to depend upon belief in the supernatural, selection is enlightened and choice can be made in behalf of ideals whose inherent relations to conditions and consequences are understood. Were the naturalistic foundations and bearings of religion grasped, the religious element in life would emerge from the throes of the crisis in religion. Religion would then be found to have its natural place in every aspect of human experience that is concerned with estimate of possibilities, with emotional stir by possibilities as yet unrealized, and with all action in behalf of their realization. All that is significant in human experience falls within this frame.

IS THERE A SUBSTITUTE FOR RELIGION?

Poetry as the Religion of the Twentieth Century

I. A. Richards

Ivor Armstrong Richards (1893–   ), literary critic, educator, poet, and playwright, is the author of a large body of literature and literary criticism. His works include *The Meaning of Meaning, Mencius on the Mind,* and a notable translation of Plato's *Republic.*

The future of poetry is immense, because in poetry, where it is worthy of its high destinies, our race, as time goes on, will find an ever surer and surer stay. There is not a creed which is not shaken, not an accredited dogma which is not shown to be questionable, not a received tradition which does not threaten to dissolve. Our religion has materialised itself in the fact, in the supposed fact; it has attached its emotion to the fact, and now the fact is failing it. But for poetry the idea is everything.
— *Matthew Arnold*

THE NEUTRALIZATION OF NATURE

The poets are failing us, or we them, if after reading them we do not find ourselves changed; not with a temporary change, such as luncheon or slumber will produce, from which we inevitably work back to the *status quo ante,* but with a permanent alteration of our possibilities as responsive individuals in good or bad adjustment to an all but overwhelming concourse of stimulations. How many living poets have the power to make such deep changes? Let us set aside youthful enthusiasms; there is a time in most lives when, rightly enough, Mr. Masefield, Mr. Kipling, Mr. Drinkwater, or even Mr. Noyes or Mr. Studdert Kennedy may profoundly affect the awakening mind; it is being introduced to poetry. Later on, looking back, we can see that any one of a hundred other poets would have served as well or better. Let us consider only the experienced, the fairly hardened reader, who is familiar with a great deal of the poetry of the past.

Contemporary poetry which will, accidents apart, modify the attitudes of this reader must be such as could not have been written in another age than our

From I. A. Richards. *Poetries and Sciences* (New York, 1970), pp. 47–82. Copyright © 1970 by W. W. Norton & Company, Inc.–Reprinted by permission of W. W. Norton & Company, Inc.

own. It must have sprung in part from the contemporary situation. It must correspond to needs, impulses, attitudes, which did not arise in the same fashion for poets in the past, and criticism also must take notice of the contemporary situation. Our attitudes to man, to nature, and to the universe change with every generation, and have changed with unusual violence in recent years. We cannot leave these changes out of account in judging modern poetry. When attitudes are changing, neither criticism nor poetry can remain stationary. To those who realize what the poet is this will be obvious; but all literary history bears it out.

It would be of little use to give a list of the chief recent intellectual revolutions and to attempt to deduce therefrom what must be happening to poetry. The effects upon our attitudes of changes of opinion are too complex to be calculated so. What we have to consider is not men's current opinions but their attitudes—how they feel about this or that as part of the world; what relative importance its different aspects have for them; what they are prepared to sacrifice for what; what they trust, what they are frightened by, what they desire. To discover these things we must go to the poets. Unless they are failing us, they will show us just these things.

They will *show* them, but, of course, they will not state them. Their poetry will not be *about* their attitudes in the sense in which a treatise on anatomy is about the structure of the body. Their poetry will arise out of their attitudes and will evoke them in an adequate reader, but, as a rule, it will not mention any attitudes. We must, of course, expect occasional essays in verse upon psychological topics, but these should not mislead us. Most of the attitudes with which poetry is concerned are indescribable—because psychology is still in a primitive stage—and can only be named or spoken about as the attitude of this poem or that. The poem, the actual experience as it forms itself in the mind of the fit reader, controlling his responses to the world and ordering his impulses, is our best evidence as to how other men feel about things; and we read it, if we are serious, partly to discover how life seems to another, partly to try how his attitudes suit us, engaged as we also are in the same enterprise.

Although we cannot—for lack of a sufficient psychology—describe attitudes in terms which do not apply also to others which we are not considering, and although we cannot deduce a poet's attitudes from the general intellectual background, none the less, after reading his poetry, when his experience has become our own, we can sometimes profitably look round us to see why these attitudes should be so very different, in some ways, from those we find in the poetry of one hundred or one thousand years ago. In so doing we gain a means of indicating what these attitudes are, useful both for those who are constitutionally unable to read poetry (an increasing number), and for those victims of education who neglect modern poetry because they "don't know what to make of it."

What, then, has been happening to the intellectual background, to the world-picture, and in what ways may changes here have caused a reorganization of our attitudes?

The central dominant change may be described as the *Neutralization of Nature*, the transference from the Magical View of the world to the scientific, a change so great that it is perhaps only paralleled historically by the change, from whatever adumbration of a world-picture preceded the Magical View, to the Magical View itself. By the Magical View I mean, roughly, the belief in a world of Spirits and Powers which control events, and which can be evoked and, to some extent, controlled themselves by human practices. The belief in Inspiration and the beliefs underlying Ritual are representative parts of this view. It has been decaying slowly for some three hundred years, but its definite overthrow has taken place only in the last sixty. Vestiges and survivals of it prompt and direct a great part of our daily affairs, but it is no longer the world-picture which an informed mind most easily accepts. There is some evidence that Poetry, together with the other Arts, arose with this Magical View. It is a possibility to be seriously considered that Poetry may pass away with it.

The reasons for the downfall of the Magical View are familiar. It seems to have arisen as a consequence of an increase in man's knowledge of and command over nature (the discovery of agriculture). It fell through the extension of that knowledge of and command over nature. Throughout its (10,000 years?) reign its stability has been due to its capacity for satisfying men's emotional needs through its adequacy as an object for their attitudes. We must remember that human attitudes have developed always *inside* the social group; they are what a man feels, the mainsprings of his behavior towards his fellow-men, and they have only a limited field of applicability. Thus the Magical View, being an interpretation of nature in terms of man's own most intimate and most important affairs, very soon came to suit man's emotional make-up better than any other view possibly could. The attraction of the Magical View lay very little in the actual command over nature which it gave. That Galton was the first person to test the efficacy of prayer experimentally is an indication of this. What did give the Magical View its standing was the ease and adequacy with which the universe therein presented could be emotionally handled, the scope offered for man's love and hatred, for his terror as well as for his hope and his despair. It gave life a sharpness, and a coherence that no other means could so easily secure.

In its place we have the universe of the mathematician, a field for the tracing out of ever wider and more general uniformities. A field in which intellectual certainty is, almost for the first time, available, and on an unlimited scale. Also the despondencies, the emotional excitements accompanying research and discovery, again on an unprecedented scale. Thus a number of men who might in other times have been poets are to-day in bio-chemical laboratories—a fact of which we might avail ourselves, did we feel the need, in defense of an alleged present poverty in poetry. But apart from these thrills, what has the world-picture of science to do with human emotions? A god voluntarily or involuntarily subjected to the General Theory of Relativity does not make an emotional appeal. So this form of compromise fails. Various emergent deities have been suggested—by Mr. Wells, by Professors Alexander and Lloyd Morgan—but, alas! the reasons for suggesting them have become too clear and conscious. They are there to meet a demand, not to make one; they do not do the work for which they were invented.

The revolution brought about by science is, in short, too drastic to be met by any such half-measures. It touches the central principle by which the Mind has been deliberately organized in the past, and no alteration in beliefs, however great, will restore equilibrium while that principle is retained. I come now to the main purport of these remarks.

Ever since man first grew self-conscious and reflective he has supposed that his feelings, his attitudes, and his conduct spring from his knowledge. That as far as he could it would be wise for him to organize himself in this way, with knowledge[1] as the foundation on which should rest feeling, attitude, and behavior. In point of fact, he never has been so organized, knowledge having been until recently too scarce; but he has constantly been persuaded that he was built on this plan, and has endeavored to carry the structure further on these lines. He has sought for knowledge, supposing that it would itself *directly* excite a right orientation to existence, supposing that, if he only knew what the world was like, this knowledge in itself would show him how to feel towards it, what attitudes to adopt, and with what aims to live. He has constantly called what he found in this quest, "knowledge," unaware that it was hardly ever pure, unaware that his feelings, attitudes, and behavior were *already* orientated by his physiological and social needs, and were themselves, for the most part, the sources of whatever it was that he supposed himself to be knowing.

Suddenly, not long ago, he began to get genuine knowledge on a large scale. The process went faster and faster; it snowballed. Now he has to face the fact that the edifices of supposed knowledge, with which he has for so long buttressed and supported his attitudes, will no longer stand up, and at the same time, he has to recognize that pure knowledge is irrelevant to his aims, that it has no *direct* bearing upon what he should feel, or what he should attempt to do.

For science, which is simply our most elaborate way of *pointing* to things systematically, tells us and can tell us nothing about the nature of things in any *ultimate* sense. It can never answer any question of the form: *What* is so and so? It can only tell us *how* so and so behaves. And it does not attempt to do more than this. Nor, indeed, can more than this be done. Those ancient, deeply troubling formulations that begin with "What" and "Why" prove, when we examine them, to be not questions at all; but requests—for emotional satisfaction. They indicate our desire not for knowledge but for assurance,[2] a point which appears clearly when we look into the "How" of questions and requests, of knowledge and desire. Science can tell us about man's place in the universe and his chances; that the place is precarious, and the chances problematical. It can enormously increase our chances if we can make wise use of it. But it cannot tell us what we are or what this world is; not because these are in any sense insoluble questions, but because they are not questions at all.[3] And if science cannot answer these pesudo-questions no more can philosophy or religion. So that all the varied answers which have for ages been regarded as the keys of wisdom are dissolving together.

The result is a biological crisis which is not likely to be decided without trouble. It is one which we can, perhaps, decide for ourselves, partly by thinking partly by reorganizing our minds in other ways; if we do not it may be decided

---

[1] *I.e.*, thoughts which are both true and evidenced, in the narrower, stricter senses. For a discussion of some relevant senses of "truth" and "knowledge" see *Principles of Literary Criticism*, Chapters xxxiii and xxxiv, and *Mencius on the Mind*, Chapter iv, also *The Meaning of Meaning*, Chapters vii and x.

[2] On this point the study of the child's questions included in *The Language and Thought of the Child* by J. Piaget (Kegan Paul, 1926) is illuminating.

[3] The remarks of Wittgenstein (*Tractatus Logico-Philosophicus*, 6.5, 6.52), which superficially resemble this, should be consulted, if only to show how important the *context* of a statement may be; for what is said above should lead not towards but away from all forms of mysticism.

for us, not in the way we should choose. While it lasts it puts a strain on each individual and upon society, which is part of the explanation of many modern difficulties, the difficulties of the poet in particular. . . .

POETRY AND BELIEFS

The business of the poet . . . is to give order and coherence, and so freedom, to a body of experience. To do so through words which act as its skeleton, as a structure by which the impulses which make up the experience are adjusted to one another and act together. The means by which words do this are many and varied. To work them out is a problem for psychology. A beginning has been indicated above, but only a beginning. What little can be done shows already that most critical dogmas of the past are either false or nonsense. A little knowledge is not here a danger, but clears the air in a remarkable way.

Roughly and inadequately, even in the light of our present knowledge, we can say that words work in the poem in two main fashions. As sensory stimuli and as (in the *widest* sense) symbols. We must refrain from considering the sensory side of the poem, remarking only that it is *not* in the least independent of the other side, and that it has for definite reasons prior importance in most poetry. We must confine ourselves to the other function of words in the poem, or rather, omitting much that is of secondary relevance, to one form of that function, let me call it *pseudo-statement*.

It will be admitted—by those who distinguish between scientific statement, where truth is ultimately a matter of verification as this is understood in the laboratory, and emotive utterance, where "truth" is primarily acceptability *by* some attitude, and more remotely is the acceptability *of* this attitude itself— that it is *not* the poet's business to make true statements. Yet poetry has constantly the air of making statements, and important ones; which is one reason why some mathematicians cannot read it. They find the alleged statements to be *false*. It will be agreed that their approach to poetry and their expectations from it are mistaken. But what exactly is the other, the right, the poetic, approach and how does it differ from the mathematical?

The poetic approach evidently limits the framework of possible consequences into which the pesudo-statement is taken. For the scientific approach this framework is unlimited. Any and every consequence is relevant. If any of the consequences of a statement conflicts with acknowledged fact then so much the worse for the statement. Not so with the pesudo-statement when poetically approached. The problem is—just how does the limitation work? The usual account is in terms of a supposed universe of discourse, a world of make-believe, of imagination, of recognized fictions common to the poet and his readers. A pseudo-statement which fits into this system of assumptions would be regarded as "poetically true"; one which does not, as "poetically false." This attempt to treat "poetic truth" on the model of general "coherence theories" is very natural for certain schools of logicians; but is inadequate, on the wrong lines from the outset. To mention two objections out of many; there is no means of discovering what the "universe of discourse" is on any occasion, and the kind of coherence which must hold within it, supposing it to be discoverable, is not an affair of logical relations. Attempt to define the system of propositions into which

O Rose, thou art sick!

must fit, and the logical relations which must hold between them if it is to be "poetically true"; the absurdity of the theory becomes evident.

We must look further. In the poetic approach the relevant consequences are not logical or to be arrived at by a partial relaxation of logic. Except occasionally and by accident logic does not enter at all. They are the consequences which arise through our emotional organization. The acceptance which a pesudo-statement receives is entirely governed by its effects upon our feelings and attitudes. Logic only comes in, if at all, in subordination, as a servant to our emotional response. It is an unruly servant, however, as poets and readers are constantly discovering. A pseudo-statement is "true" if it suits and serves some attitude or links together attitudes which on other grounds are desirable. This kind of truth is so opposed to scientific truth that it is a pity to use so similar a word, but at present it is difficult to avoid the malpractice.[4]

This brief analysis may be sufficient to indicate the fundamental disparity and opposition between pseudo-statements as they occur in poetry and statements as they occur in science. A pesudo-statement is a form of words which is justified entirely by its effect in releasing or organizing our impulses and attitudes (due regard being had for the better or worse organizations of these *inter se*); a statement, on the other hand, is justified by its truth, *i.e.,* its correspondence, in a highly technical sense, with the fact to which it points.

Statements true and false alike do of course constantly touch off attitudes and action. Our daily practical existence is largely guided by them. On the whole true statements are of more service to us than false ones. None the less we do not and, at present, cannot order our emotions and attitudes by true statements alone. Nor is there any probability that we ever shall contrive to do so. This is one of the great new dangers to which civilization is exposed. Countless pseudo-statements—about God, about the universe, about human nature, the relations of mind to mind, about the soul, its rank and destiny—pseudo-statements which are pivotal points in the organization of the mind, vital to its well-being, have suddenly become, for sincere, honest, and informed minds, impossible to believe.[5] For centuries they have been believed; now they are gone, irrecoverably; and the knowledge which has killed them is not of a kind upon which an equally fine organization of the mind can be based.

[4] A pseudo-statement, as I use the term, is not necessarily false in any sense. It is merely a form of words whose scientific truth or falsity is irrelevant to the purpose at hand.

"Logic" in this paragraph is, of course, being used in a limited and conventional, or popular, sense.

[5] The accustomed incidences of the modes of believing are changed irrevocably. See Appendix. For the mind I am considering here, the question "Do I believe x?" is no longer the same. Not only the "What" that is to be believed but the "How" of the believing has changed—through the segregation of science and its clarification of the techniques of proof. This is the danger; and the remedy suggested is a further differentiation of the "Hows." To these differences correspond differences in the senses of "is so" and "being" where, as is commonly the case, "is so" and "being" assert believings. As we admit this, the world that "is" divides into worlds incommensurable in respect of so-called "degrees of reality." Yet, and this is all-important, these worlds have an order, with regard to one another, which is the order of the mind; and interference between them imperils sanity.

This is the contemporary situation. The remedy, since there is no prospect of our gaining adequate knowledge, and since indeed it is fairly clear that genuine knowledge cannot serve us here and can only increase our practical control of Nature, is to cut our pseudo-statements free from belief, and yet retain them, in this released state, as the main instruments by which we order our attitudes to one another and to the world. Not so desperate a remedy as may appear, for poetry conclusively shows that even the most important among our attitudes can be aroused and maintained without any belief entering in at all. Those of Tragedy, for example. We need no beliefs, and indeed we must have none, if we are to read *King Lear*. Pseudo-statements to which we attach no belief and statements proper such as science provides cannot conflict. It is only when we introduce illicit beliefs into poetry that danger arises. To do so is from this point of view a profanation of poetry.

Yet an important branch of criticism which has attracted the best talents from prehistoric times until to-day consists of the endeavor to persuade men that the functions of science and poetry are identical, or that the one is a "higher form" of the other, or that they conflict and we must choose between them.

The root of this persistent endeavor has still to be mentioned; it is the same as that from which the Magical View of the world arose. If we give to a pseudo-statement the kind of unqualified acceptance which belongs by right only to certified scientific statements, if we can contrive to do this, the impulses and attitudes with which we respond to it gain a notable stability and vigor. Briefly, if we can contrive to believe poetry, then the world *seems,* while we do so, to be transfigured. It used to be comparatively easy to do this, and the habit has become well established. With the extension of science and the neutralization of nature it has become difficult as well as dangerous. Yet it is still alluring; it has many analogies with drug-taking. Hence the endeavors of the critics referred to. Various subterfuges have been devised along the lines of regarding Poetic Truth as figurative, symbolic; or as more immediate, as a truth of Intuition, not of reason; or as a higher form of the same truth as reason yields. Such attempts to use poetry as a denial or as a corrective of science are very common. One point can be made against them all: they are never worked out in detail. There is no equivalent to Mill's *Logic* expounding any such view. The language in which they are framed is usually a blend of obsolete psychology and emotive exclamations.

The long-established and much-encouraged habit of giving to emotive utterances—whether pseudo-statements simple, or looser and larger wholes taken as saying something figuratively—the kind of assent which we give to established facts, has for most people debilitated a wide range of their responses. A few scientists, caught young and brought up in the laboratory, are free from it; but then, as a rule, they pay no *serious* attention to poetry. For most men the recognition of the neutrality of nature brings about—through this habit—a divorce from poetry. They are so used to having their responses propped up by beliefs, however vague, that when these shadowy supports are removed they are no longer able to respond. Their attitudes to so many things have been forced in the past, over-encouraged. And when the world-picture ceases to assist there is a collapse. Over whole tracts of natural emotional response we are to-day like a bed of dahlias whose sticks have been removed. And this effect of the neutralization of nature is only in its beginnings. Consider the probable effects upon love-poetry in the near future of the kind of enquiry into basic human constitution exemplified by psychoanalysis.

A sense of desolation, of uncertainty, of futility, of the groundlessness of aspirations, of the vanity of endeavor, and a thirst for a life-giving water which seems suddenly to have failed, are the signs in consciousness of this necessary reorganization of our lives.[6] Our attitudes and impulses are being compelled to become self-supporting; they are being driven back upon their biological justification, made once again sufficient to themselves. And the only impulses which seem strong enough to continue unflagging are commonly so crude that, to more finely developed individuals, they hardly seem worth having. Such people cannot live by warmth, food, fighting, drink, and sex alone. Those who are least affected by the change are those who are emotionally least removed from the animals. . . .

It is important to diagnose the disease correctly and to put the blame in the right quarter. Usually it is some alleged "materialism" of science which is denounced. This mistake is due partly to clumsy thinking, but chiefly to relics of the Magical View. For even if the Universe were "spiritual" all through (whatever that assertion might mean; all such assertions are probably nonsense), that would not make it any more accordant to human attitudes. It is not what the universe is made of but how it works, the law it follows, which makes knowledge of it incapable of spurring on our emotional responses, and, further, the nature of knowledge itself makes it inadequate. The contact with things which we therein establish is too sketchy and indirect to help us. We are beginning to know too much about the bond which unites the mind to its object in knowledge[7] for that old dream of a perfect knowledge which would guarantee perfect life to retain its sanction. What was thought to be pure knowledge, we see now to have been shot through with hope and desire, with fear and wonder, and these intrusive elements indeed gave it all its power to support our lives. In knowledge, in the "How?" of events, we can find hints by which to take advantage of circumstances in our favor and avoid mischances. But we cannot get from it a *raison d'être* or a justification of more than a relatively lowly kind of life.

The justification, or the reverse, of any attitude lies, not in the object, but in itself, in its serviceableness to the whole personality. Upon its place in the whole

---

[6] My debt to *The Waste Land* here will be evident. The original footnote seems to have puzzled Mr. Eliot and some other readers. Well it might! In saying, though, that he "had effected a complete severance between his poetry and all beliefs" I was referring not to the poet's own history, but to the technical detachment of the poetry. And the way in which he then seemed to me to have "realized what might otherwise have remained a speculative possibility" was by finding a new order through the contemplation and exhibition of disorder.

"Yes! Very funny this terrible thing is. A man that is born falls into a dream like a man who falls into the sea. If he tries to climb out into the air as inexperienced people endeavour to do, he drowns—*nicht wahr?* . . . No! I tell you! The way is to the destructive element submit yourself, and with the exertions of your hands and feet in the water make the deep, deep sea keep you up. So if you ask me how to be? In the destructive element immerse . . . that was the way." *Lord Jim*, p. 216. Mr. Eliot's later verse has sometimes shown still less "dread of the unknown depths." That, at least, seems in part to explain to me why *Ash Wednesday* is better poetry than even the best sections of *The Waste Land*.

[7] Verifiable scientific knowledge, of course. Shift the sense of "knowledge" to include hope and desire and fear as well as reference, and what I am saying would no longer be true. But then the relevant sense of "true" would have changed too. Its sanction would no longer be verifiability.

system of attitudes, which is the personality, all its worth depends. This is true equally for the subtle, finely compounded attitudes of the civilized individual as for the simpler attitudes of the child.

In brief, experience is its own justification; and this fact must be faced, although sometimes—by a lover, for example—it may be very difficult to accept. Once it is faced, it is apparent that all the attitudes to other human beings and to the world in all its aspects, which have been serviceable to humanity, remain as they were, as valuable as ever. Hesitation felt in admitting this is a measure of the strength of the evil habit we have described. But many of these attitudes, valuable as ever, are now that they are being set free, more difficult to maintain, because we still hunger after a basis in belief.

· · ·

We must distinguish here, however. There are many feelings and attitudes which, though in the past supported by beliefs now untenable, can survive their removal because they have other, more natural, supports and spring directly from the necessities of existence. To the extent to which they have been undistorted by the beliefs which have gathered round them they will remain as before. But there are other attitudes which are very largely the product of belief and have no other support. These will lapse if the changes here forecast continue. With their disappearance some forms of poetry—much minor devotional verse, for example—will become obsolete. And with the unraveling of the intellect *versus* emotion entanglement, there will be cases where even literature to which immense value has been assigned—the speculative portions of the work of Dostoevsky may be instanced—will lose much of its interest, except for the history of the mind. It was because he belonged to our age that Dostoevsky had to wrestle so terribly in these toils. A poet to-day, whose integrity is equal to that of the greater poets of the past, is inevitably plagued by the problem of thought and feeling as poets have never been plagued before.

A pioneer in modern research upon the origins of culture was asked recently whether his work had any bearing upon religion. He replied that it had, but that at present he was engaged merely in "getting the guns into position." The same answer might be given with regard to the probable consequences of recent progress in psychology, not only for religion but for the whole fabric of our traditional beliefs about ourselves. In many quarters there is a tendency to suppose that the series of attacks upon received ideas which began, shall we say, with Galileo and rose to a climax with Darwinism, has over-reached itself with Einstein and Eddington, and that the battle is now due to die down. This view seems to be too optimistic. The most dangerous of the sciences is only now beginning to come into action. I am thinking less of Psychoanalysis or of Behaviorism than of the whole subject which includes them.

The Hindenburg Line to which the defense of our traditions retired as the result of the onslaughts of the last century may still be officially held (in the schools, for example), but it is really abandoned as worth neither defense nor attack. The struggle is elsewhere, and it is no longer over matters suited to intellectual debate. "What to believe?"—which could be argued—has given place to "With what different kinds of believings must we order the different ranks of our myths?"[8] and that is decided not by arguing but in living. The

---

[8] Not necessarily a derogatory word; see *Coleridge on Imagination*, Chapter VII.

lowest rank and the least challengeable or optional or dispensable—that routine of perception which guards the safety of our every bodily step, that order of expectations or of assumptions in virtue of which we catch or miss our trains—has unequalled authority over its own members. It lends this authority to the sciences which derive from it—though not, of course, to their optional, speculative aspects. And these sciences progressively invade every province of our thought. They meet nothing with equal authority, or that can resist them, which does not take its power from the same source in verifiable happenings.

In so far as any question comes within their peculiar authority they decide it; and a peculiar believing or acceptance there belongs. Challenge from myths of other ranks is suicidal. They challenge by mistake as to their own rank (which would, if they kept it, be higher, as concerned with more inclusive interests) and thus degrade the kinds of believing they embody. The danger is that science, as it has more to tell us about ourselves, may more and more invite this mistake and so provoke other myths to defy it and then force them to surrender. But their work is not that of science; as they do not give us what science gives, so science cannot give us what they give.

If a conflict which should never have arisen extends much further, a moral chaos such as man has never experienced may be expected. Our protection, as Matthew Arnold, in my epigraph, insisted, is in poetry. It is capable of saving us, or, since some have found a scandal in this word, of preserving us or rescuing us from confusion and frustration. The poetic function is the source, and the tradition of poetry is the guardian, of the supra-scientific myths. "The poetry of a people takes its life from the people's speech and in turn gives life to it; and represents its highest point of consciousness, its greatest power and its most delicate sensibility." So wrote the best poet of my generation recently.[9] That we should consider further what this power is, what it has given us, and what threatens it, is all my argument.

APPENDIX

Two chief words seem likely occasions of misunderstanding in the above; and they have in fact misled some readers. One is *Nature*, the other is *Belief*.

Nature is evidently as variable a word as can be used. Its senses range from the mere inclusive THAT, in which we live and of which we are a part, to whatever would correspond to the most detailed and interconnected account we could attain of this. Or we omit ourselves (and other minds) and make Nature *either* what influences us (in which case we should not forget our metabolism), *or* an object we apprehend (in which case there are as many Natures as there are types of apprehension we care to distinguish). And what is "natural" to one culture is strange and artificial to another. (See *Mencius on the Mind*, Chap. III.) More deceptively, the view here being inseparable from the eye, and this being a matter of habitual speculation, we may talk, as we think, the same language and yet put very different things into Nature; and what we then find will not be unconnected with what we have put in. I have attempted some further discussion of these questions in Chapters VI and VII of *Coleridge on Imagination*.

[9] T. S. Eliot, *The Use of Poetry*, p. 15.

Belief. Two "beliefs" may differ from one another: (1) In their objects, (2) In their statements or expressions, (3) In their modes, (4) In their grounds, (5) In their occasions, (6) In their connections with other "beliefs," (7) In their links with possible action, (8) And in other ways. Our chief evidence usually for the beliefs of other people (and often for our own) must be some statement or other expression. But very different beliefs may fittingly receive the same expression. Most words used in stating any speculative opinion are as ambiguous as "Belief"; and yet by such words belief-objects must be distinguished.

But in the case of "belief" there is an additional difficulty. Neither it nor its partial synonyms suggest the great variety of the attitudes (3) that are commonly covered (and confused) by the term. They are often treated as though they were mere variations in degree. Of what? Of belief, it would be said. But this is no better than the parallel trick of treating all varieties of love as a mere more or less only further differentiated by their objects. Such crude oversimplifications distort the structure of the mind and, although favorite suasive devices with some well-intentioned preachers, are disastrous.

There is an ample field here awaiting a type of dispassionate inquiry which it has seldom received. A world threatened with ever more and more leisure should not be too impatient of important and explorable subtleties.

Meanwhile, as with "Nature," misunderstandings should neither provoke nor surprise. I should not be much less at my reader's mercy if I were to add notes doubling the length of this little book. On so vast a matter, even the largest book could contain no more than a sketch of how things have seemed to be sometimes to the writer.

Political Ideology as Religion

Wang Tao-ming

Wang Tao-ming is a deputy political instructor in a unit of the Red Chinese People's Liberation Army.

TO REMOULD MY WORLD OUTLOOK WITH MAO TSE-TUNG'S THOUGHT

Under the guidance of the Party and with the help of my comrades, I have been studying and applying Chairman Mao's works in a practical way in order to remould my ideology and as a result I have made some progress in class consciousness and theoretical understanding of revolution in the last few years.

From *Mao Tse-tung's Thought Is the Invincible Weapon* (Peking: Foreign Languages Press, 1968).

Following are some of my experiences in remoulding my thinking by studying and applying Chairman Mao's "Three Good Old Articles" and other articles in a positive way.

THERE IS NO "BORN RED"

I did not understand the importance of ideological remoulding before enlisting and was just not interested in the idea. I thought, "Our generation studies in the schools run by the Party, reads the books published in the new society, receives the Party's education from childhood and grows up with the song *The East Is Red* on the lips and the Young Pioneer's tie around the neck. Our thinking has been revolutionary since childhood. Because I am of a poor peasant family and my father is a revolutionary cadre, I have absorbed no undesirable ideas and there is no need for me to undergo any remoulding. I am a 'born red' youth and a 'born' revolutionary successor. My taking the revolutionary road is not in question at all." So when my father told me to work hard on Chairman Mao's works and remould my thinking earnestly or I would commit errors and would degenerate, I thought what he said was exaggerated to scare me.

After enlisting, I heard the leadership speaking of ideological remoulding and again doubted the necessity of it. I thought to myself: I am determined to become a good fighter, I have the desire to improve myself ideologically and I am doing well in work, drill and production and have been often singled out for praise. What is there to be remoulded?

But some later happenings caused contradictions in my mind and I sensed there was something wrong. For instance, I thought the uniform of our Army was not "tastefully" designed and the toe-cap of the padded shoes was too large to be attractive. In spite of the coldness of winter, I would rather put on the rubber shoes than the "big toe-capped shoes" when going out on the street. But the officers and veterans of our unit seemed to be quite satisfied with the uniform and the padded shoes. The officers often told us what a scarcity of clothes and shoes there had been in the revolutionary war periods and reminded us never to forget the hard and difficult life of the old days and never to forget the people. Why did the officers and veterans like the things which I did not like? What lay at the root of this difference? It was from these trifles that I began to feel that there *was* something in my mind which needed remoulding. It seemed that it was not enough to rely on the little class consciousness I had acquired in the "sugar-pot of socialism" in my boyhood.

But it was only after Chairman Mao issued the call "Learn from Comrade Lei Feng"[1] that I really and truly realized the importance of ideological remoulding and began conscientiously to remould myself with Mao Tse-tung's

---

[1] Lei Feng was a squad leader in a transportation company of the P.L.A. stationed in Shenyang. He worked very hard on Chairman Mao's works and put special emphasis on applying what he had learnt. As a result he attained a high political consciousness, a firm proletarian stand and the noble quality of serving the people whole-heartedly. He received distinction three times for meritorious service and was cited as a model Communist Youth Leaguer. He joined the Party in November 1960 and died in August 1962 while performing his duty. Chairman Mao wrote the inscription "Learn from Comrade Lei Feng!"

thought. I came to see that the reason why Comrade Lei Feng could perform great deeds in everyday life and become a communist fighter lies basically in the fact that by studying and applying Chairman Mao's works in a vital way, he understood the significance of life, knew whom he should serve and formed the world outlook of serving the people whole-heartedly. I had also studied the "Three Good Old Articles" and done a few good things. But I was far from being devoted utterly to the people without any thought of self as Lei Feng had done. Nor had I paid enough attention to tying up everything I did with ideological remoulding as he had done, and had not conscientiously followed his advice: "Live to better the lives of others." In learning from Lei Feng, I understood that to be able to devote oneself utterly to the people it is imperative to dig out selfishness from one's mind by the roots. A revolutionary must fight not only with the class enemies in society, but also with the class enemy in his mind—selfishness. He must resist all kinds of non-proletarian ideas, build up revolutionary quality with the thought of Mao Tse-tung and permeate his thinking with Chairman Mao's teaching of serving the people whole-heartedly.

Later, using the form of a small-scale rectification movement, the company leadership organized us to study Chairman Mao's teachings on class and class struggle. In the course of this study I examined myself and realized that I was far from being immune from non-proletarian influences and the force of old habits. For instance, there were such sayings as "Once you master mathematics, physics and chemistry, you don't have to worry about your livelihood anywhere!" I had thought that there was some reality behind such catch-phrases. I absorbed quite a few bad influences in school and the old idea of seeking personal fame and furthering my own interests had also left its imprint on my mind. This shows that there does exist acute and complicated class struggle in socialist society. Confronting our generation are two kinds of teachers: the proletariat, our teacher by positive example, and the bourgeoisie, our teacher by negative example. Unless we arm ourselves consciously with proletarian thinking, we will surely be influenced by bourgeois thinking.

With these problems in mind I studied the following quotation in Chairman Mao's "On the Correct Handling of Contradictions Among the People":

In the building of a socialist society, everybody needs remoulding. . . . It [the working class] must ceaselessly learn in the course of its work and overcome its shortcomings step by step, and must never stop doing so.

Chairman Mao says everybody needs remoulding. Young men like myself who have grown up under the Red Banner should of course be included. What were my shortcomings? From the many problems posed, I felt the first I should overcome was the idea that because I was "born red" there was no need for me to undergo any remoulding.

Can the young people in socialist society be "born red"? I realized that what I considered as a sound ideology is just a simple class feeling. This feeling is born out of the understanding that socialism brings happiness to us and out of our thankfulness to the Party and Chairman Mao. This simple class feeling enables us to embrace Mao Tse-tung's thought more readily. However, it is not yet the full understanding that socialism is by no means for the happiness of just some individuals but for the well-being of the entire proletariat and labouring people. If we do not raise it to the stage of conscious class awareness we cannot resist the assault of bourgeois ideology and will not be able to stand the test if circumstances require us to sacrifice our personal interests for the interests of the majority of the people. One should never rest content with his simple class feeling, but should raise it to a conscious class awareness, to the height of Mao Tse-tung's thought. To achieve this, one has to study and apply Chairman Mao's works in a living way and remould his ideology. There is no such thing as being "born red," one must learn to be red. I am now in the prime of life. I must study Chairman Mao's works earnestly and give myself a correct answer to the question of what I live for and whom should I serve. I must consciously arm myself with Mao Tse-tung's thought and lay a good foundation for my following the revolutionary road all my life.

REMOULD MYSELF IN ACCORDANCE WITH THE STANDARDS OF THE COMMUNIST NEW MAN

Once the need for conscientious self-remoulding became clear, I began in real earnest to study and apply in a positive way Chairman Mao's "Three Good Old Articles" and other works and, with Mao Tse-tung's thought as a weapon, to make a painstaking effort to change my old thinking and alter my world outlook. After pin-pointing the problems uppermost in my mind at the different times, I successively solved some over the past several years.

Personal Interest and the Needs of the Revolution. A lover of painting since childhood, I took a drawing board with me when I joined the army after graduating from the middle school attached to the College of Fine Arts. I was immediately attracted by the exciting life of the army. I congratulated myself on having found the richest source of inspiration for my artistic efforts and hoped to do some real painting. I suggested to the officers that I should paint the history of the regiment and received a highly encouraging reply. But just as I was about to start the pictures, I got instructions to go to another camp for further training. I felt disconcerted and asked whether I could be allowed to stay behind. Seeing my reluctance, the deputy political commissar of the regiment sent for me and told me of his personal experience. He had been a turner before he joined the revolution. Though highly skilled, a poverty-stricken worker like him could not make a living in the old society and he joined the revolution. He had hoped to do some technical work after joining the revolution. However, what the revolution most needed then was men to take up arms and destroy the enemy. He did what was required of him. "Had all of us thought only of our own inclinations and skills and not followed the need of the revolution," he said to me, "where would the victory be that we see today?" He concluded by asking me to study hard the "Three Good Old Articles." I studied these articles and thought to myself, "Comrade Bethune was a very good surgeon, yet he never cared about his personal fame and position. He always served the needs of the revolution and finally he gave his life for the Chinese revolution. Why cannot I subordinate my petty interest in painting to the needs of the revolution?"

This ideological knot untied, I went off happily to the training camp. But the old idea could not be suppressed once and for all and it returned from time to time. It needs repeated ideological struggle to subordinate entirely one's personal inclinations to the needs of the revolution. For instance, when I heard some schoolmates had done some good painting or had been sent to a college for further studies, I would waver. On these occasions, I would study "In Memory of Norman Bethune" and Chairman Mao's teachings on serving the people heart and soul, to replace personal preference with the needs of the revolution. Finally I came to see that in our country there is room enough for each to cultivate his own interests and tastes. But this does not mean that we should develop our interests and tastes regardless of the needs of the Party and the goal of serving the people; instead, we should acquire skills and techniques in order to serve the people. If we develop our interests and pursuits regardless of the needs of the revolution, we will become bourgeois individualists. This understanding enables me to bear situations like this with a calmness of mind and to do whatever my superiors want me to do and do it well. But I did not lay aside my brushes. I took an active part in preparing the blackboard newspaper in my company. I painted pictures to commend fine deeds of my comrades and copied slogans. From this I realized that when needed by the revolution, one's personal interests can play their fullest role and serve the revolution. When divorced from the needs of the revolution, one's personal interests can only serve oneself, or may even serve the enemy.

Planting the Trees and Enjoying the Shade. I used to think that I was born at a good time, the time of socialism. As an old adage goes, "The fathers plant the trees, the sons enjoy the cool shade." Our predecessors in the revolution had endured so much suffering, had conquered and taken over the country, to let later generations enjoy a happy life. That is why I would not wear any mended clothes at home and did not even want to wear a coat my mother had made out of an old one of my father's. Over a period of time after my enlisting, I felt that life in the army was not as good as at home.

One Sunday, I was sent with a letter to the regimental commander at his living quarters. As soon as I stepped in I saw him mending shoes there, first his children's and then his own, with his own tools. I thought to myself: The leading officers like the regimental commander risked their lives for the revolution. Their revolutionary spirit is just as good as in the old days. They lead a frugal and simple life, work hard and often drill with the fighters. They go to great pains to bring up the revolutionary young generation. When later I saw a picture of Chairman Mao in patched padded-trousers taken in northern Shensi, I was greatly moved. Gradually I came to see that my former ideas were very wrong. At my age, the revolutionary predecessors had already taken up the burden of revolution and were struggling and shedding blood for it. What they had in mind was the great cause of the liberation of the oppressed classes and the nation. What they have in mind now is how to carry the revolutionary cause of the proletariat through to the end. They still maintain the style of hard work and simple living, while I think of nothing but personal comforts.

Why did I think of only "enjoying the shade" and not "planting the trees"? With this question in mind, I studied Chairman Mao's works. He said:

Because of their lack of political and social experience, quite a number of young people are unable to see the contrast between the old China and the new, and it is not easy for them thoroughly to comprehend the hardships our people went through in the struggle to free themselves from the oppression of the imperialists and Kuomintang reactionaries, or the long period of arduous work needed before a happy socialist society can be established.

These words had a great impact on me. I had forgotten that the happiness we enjoy today is the fruit of bloodshed and the sacrifices of many people and that our country is still "poor and blank"; I had forgotten my responsibility. This realization made me see that I had no reason whatsoever to indulge in comforts and relax my will to fight. I asked myself further—what is happiness? Different classes have different views on this question. The proletarian concept of happiness is struggle, revolution, work and serving the people. Comrades Norman Bethune, Chang Szu-teh and Lei Feng set the finest examples. I felt I ought to be like them and regard serving the people whole-heartedly as the greatest pleasure and the greatest happiness.

Since then I have endeavoured to turn myself in practice into such a person, one who puts the interests of the public and the collective before those of his own and who is the first to bear hardship, the last to enjoy comforts. Sometimes I wanted to send some money home by post. But when I found some other comrades' families needed it more urgently, I sent the money to them instead. At meals, I would first take food made of coarse grains. In the night marches, I would walk in front to find the road. For the good of the others, I preferred to risk more stumblings and falls myself. After repeated ideological struggle and tempering in practice, a change in feeling is gradually effected. I have come to see that a man can be really happy only when he understands thoroughly what is bitterness and what is happiness, only when he has come to a proletarian view-point on happiness, whereas those who are fettered by bourgeois individualism, who are obsessed by selfishness can never have their desires satisfied and can never be happy. We are indeed enjoying the happy life our predecessors in the revolution have won for us at the cost of bloodshed and sacrifice and we are indeed enjoying the "cool shade." But we must not be people who just make use of the shade. First of all we should become tree-planters so that people throughout the world may enjoy the cool shade of socialism and communism.

The Defence of the Country and the Making of Revolution. I enlisted in August 1962 when the Chiang Kai-shek reactionaries were trying to invade the mainland. I thought, "I am of a poor peasant family and the son of a revolutionary cadre. It is my unshirkable duty to enlist and defend our motherland and the happy life of the people. I will never allow these cannibals to ride roughshod over us again." Day in and day out I dreamed about fighting the enemy and was always asking when we would set out for the front. When it turned out that the Chiang Kai-shek reactionaries did not dare to come, I went to the commander of my unit and said, "I'll now go home since there is no war for the time being. But I'll come back as soon as the war starts." The commander asked me, "What did you enlist for?" I replied, "To defend the country." The commander persisted, "And what else?" I was at a loss. "What else could there be?" I said to myself. "Our predecessors in revolution have liberated the country and the task of our generation is to defend it. What else are we to do?" The commander seemed able to read my thought and said, "There are still many oppressed and exploited labouring people in the world. We must not only defend our motherland, but should also support the world revolution. We should not just safeguard the country our predecessors have gained for us, but must make it function as the bastion of the revolution. War is inevitable as long as imperialism exists. There will be plenty of chances to fight in your generation. And to fight well, it is very important for us to bear in mind always the oppressed and the not yet liberated people, to bear in mind always imperialism and the reactionaries in various countries. We must learn from Norman Bethune."

After this talk, I read the article "In Memory of Norman Bethune." Chairman Mao says:

We must unite with the proletariat of all the capitalist countries . . . to liberate our nation and people and to liberate the other nations and peoples of the world.

He also enjoins us to learn from Comrade Norman Bethune, who selflessly adopted the cause of the Chinese people's liberation as his own, and to learn from him the spirit of internationalism and spirit of communism. From these teachings of Chairman Mao, I came to see that the cause of the liberation of the proletariat is internationalist from beginning to end.

Later the company leadership organized activity for the purposes of recalling the grievances the labouring people suffered in the past. I thought again and again, "Why did the landlords and capitalists dare to exploit and oppress the workers and peasants so ferociously in the old society?" I studied Chairman Mao's works and realized that the landlords and capitalists were protected by the Kuomintang reactionaries, who in turn were backed by U.S. imperialism. U.S. imperialism had backed the Chiang Kai-shek reactionaries in their killing of the Chinese people, and today it is slaughtering the people of Vietnam, aiding and abetting the reactionaries in various countries in their massacres. Why does it do that? The reason is that U.S. imperialism and the reactionaries of various countries all protect the interests of the landlords and the capitalists. Therefore, they work hand in glove to bully and exploit the people, and to prevent them from making revolution and seeking liberation. U.S. imperialism is the general root-cause of the sufferings of the people of the world. Till it is wiped out the people of the world will never gain final liberation and we can never consider our victory as consolidated. The task resting on the shoulders of our generation is not only to defend the socialist land of China, but also to support the revolution of the people of the world, to bring about communism. We must emulate Norman Bethune and become internationalist fighters.

With the idea of making revolution for the world's people strongly in my mind, I set higher demands on myself and plunge into my work with greater enthusiasm. In daily life, I struggle hard against any manifestation of selfishness in me and sometimes while I am eating my meal I will ask myself whether I really put others before myself. While practising bayonet fighting last year, some comrades thought this method of fighting amounted to very little in modern warfare. I organized my comrades to study Chairman Mao's teachings on people's war and built up our belief in the importance of bayonet fighting. We arrived at the conclusion that "we can defeat atom bombs by bayonet fighting." We are ready at any time to support the revolutionary struggles of the people of the world.

Sunshine and Rice Shoot. Last year, after my articles "On Bayonet Practice" and "How Our Squad Tackle Ideological Problems" were published in the newspaper, many officers and comrades wrote to encourage me. I was confronted with the problem of how to treat the honours that were bestowed on me. What was uppermost in my mind was that people might think me conceited. I weighed every word I spoke, lest I might make some blunder and cause people to think that the honours had gone to my head. But I was also aware that if I went on like this, I would become a timid and overcautious man. So I felt I must speak whatever was right and proper. Another thing I feared was that people might discover my shortcomings. At the end of last year, a commander wanted to see the bayonet practice between Squad Eight and Squad Three and asked me to take part in it. I was then reporting my experience in the corps and had not practised bayonet fighting for a long time. I did not want to go for fear that I might disgrace myself. But on second thoughts, I saw it was very wrong of me to think of that and finally went as I was required. The fact that I should have such wrong ideas at all made me repeatedly ask myself why I was always thinking of myself since I had received some honours. I found it was "fear," engendered by honours, the root of which was "selfishness." It was precisely when I did not fear to expose my own shortcomings that I was able to get help from the comrades and make progress. My fear of having my shortcomings discovered was essentially a reflection of my vanity. This manifestation of selfishness must be resolutely repudiated.

At the beginning of this year in the Great Hall of the People in the capital I made a report on how I had studied Chairman Mao's works. I put the ticket in my notebook. On returning, many comrades in my unit wanted to have a look at it. This drew my attention. When I had gone out to make my report in the past, I never kept any momento. Why did I keep the ticket this time? Was it not that I wanted the comrades to know that I had made a report in the Great Hall of the People? Yes, that was what was at the back of my mind. I therefore cut the printed half off the ticket and wrote on the remaining blank part "Wage a bayonet fight against my selfish thinking" to warn myself against allowing undesirable ideas to creep into my mind.

The above-mentioned event set me thinking for a long time. I realized that it is most essential to adopt a correct view on the achievements of my study and the honours bestowed on me by the Party if I am to be able to have a correct attitude towards them. When I first took up Chairman Mao's works, I did not know how to study them in order to resolve problems, how to apply what I had learnt and how to summarize my experience. It was the officers and comrades who helped me to learn all this. I was encouraged when I made some progress and criticized when I had shortcomings. Just like the tender seedlings which cannot grow without sunshine, I cannot make an iota of progress without learning from Mao Tse-tung's thought. In a bumper harvest, people often say how strong the plants are. When I have made some progress in study, people tend to see only my good points and give me encouragement. But I myself know very well that I am just a very tender seedling. It is entirely due to Mao Tse-tung's thought that I have been able to grow at all. Mao Tse-tung's thought is the unsetting red sun in my heart and I will forever consider myself a seedling which cannot do without the sunshine even for a single moment.

With this realization, I have been more conscientious in dealing with problems. For instance, when I go out on business and return late the cooks often want to prepare a special meal for me. But I insist on having just what is left. The cooks know that I like onions and often want to give me some. But I refuse to accept any. It is out of their concern for me that they want to do these things. But if I accept these favours, I will put myself in a privileged position and become different from the masses. Another example, when some comrades have made some progress and say that this is due to my help, I will strictly examine myself to see whether I have given too much prominence to my personal role in the work and will organize the core members to talk with these comrades so that they will not only tell their ideological problems to me but also to the leader of the Party group and other Party members. It will never do to overemphasize one's own role in work and seek to win personal fame.

Chairman Mao has said:

Even if we achieve gigantic successes in our work, there is no reason whatsoever to feel conceited and arrogant. Modesty helps one to go forward, whereas conceit makes one lag behind. This is a truth we must always bear in mind.

He has also said, "It is not hard for one to do a bit of good. What is hard is to do good all one's life and never do anything bad. . . ." He teaches us to engage in arduous struggle for decades on end. I think that I have made some progress in studying Chairman Mao's works. Nevertheless I should not try to live on what I have achieved for the rest of my life. The road of revolution and the road of life still stretch out a long way ahead. As long as I am alive, I will go on making revolution, remoulding myself, and studying and applying Chairman Mao's works in a living way. I'll follow Mao Tse-tung's thought and be a revolutionary all my life. To persons with heads full of bourgeois individualism, achievements and honours are signboards painted in golden letters, are "capital" with which to gain personal position and comfort and at that point they come to the dead end of progress. But proletarian fighters never rest content because of achievements and honours. In their view, achievements and honours are a kind of encouragement and stimulant, prompting them to achieve still greater successes for the Party, setting new tasks for them, and setting still higher demands for revolutionizing their ideology; they are the point of departure for new progress.

USING MAO TSE-TUNG'S THOUGHT TO WAGE A "BAYONET FIGHT" AGAINST SELFISHNESS

I have come to understand that it is of paramount importance to use Mao Tse-tung's thought to struggle against the bourgeois thinking within oneself, if one is to study and apply well Chairman Mao's works and to plant Mao Tse-tung's thought firmly in the mind. He must study, apply Chairman Mao's works in struggle, remould himself and grow up in struggle. Only through repeated struggle, can he raise his understanding about Chairman Mao's works, strengthen his class feelings for them and gain real understanding of his teachings. Otherwise, he won't be able to learn much and he will have difficulty in consolidating what he has learnt. "Using Mao Tse-tung's thought to wage a 'bayonet fight' against selfishness!" has long been the motto of Squad Eight in ideological remoulding. According to my experience, there are eight points we should pay attention to in this respect:

1. It is essential to memorize Chairman Mao's teachings, especially many of his basic concepts and important statements. Only when we have memorized them, can we think of what his precepts are when confronted with problems. When I first studied his works, I could not find any quotations, or could not find the right ones, to solve the problem I had in mind and therefore could not deal with my problems in a proper way. Later as I often studied and applied his teachings, I have managed to learn quite a few by heart with the passage of time. Of course, we do not memorize these teachings just to remember them, but to apply them in action. Only when we have memorized his teachings, can we study and apply them at any time and become more conscientious in our thinking and action.

2. It is necessary to set up "models," examples for ideological remoulding, for ourselves. That is to say, we must have a clear-cut view of what sort of a person we want to train and temper ourselves into becoming, we must have a future "image" of ourselves in our mind. I began to have "models" after studying the "Three Good Old Articles." Later I learnt from Lei Feng and had another "model" who handles correctly the relation between public and private affairs. After listening to Chen Chin-yuan's report, I had one more "model" who takes great care to make his comrades lifelong revolutionaries. Every time I learn from a hero or an advanced person, I will add one more standard for my ideological remoulding. I also have "models" in my own company: the company commander who has a high sense of responsibility and an eager desire to learn, the political instructor who is highly-principled and persists in the struggle against anything undesirable, and a comrade who was wronged but still works very hard. In fact everyone has certain "models" in his mind. Everyone is learning from and is modelling himself on one or several persons. We must consciously model ourselves on and learn from the revolutionaries who are armed with the thought of Mao Tse-tung. We must wage struggle against any bad concept, squeeze it out, and firmly establish the concept of a communist fighter in our mind.

3. It is important to be able to grasp the ideas flashing through one's mind. The things we have seen, heard and smelt are bound to give rise to some ideas in the mind. We must be good at grasping these ideas in our daily life to see whether they are correct and whether they correspond to Mao Tse-tung's thought. To be able to study Chairman Mao's works with certain problems in mind, one must be able to grasp these problems. For instance, I once this year went with some comrades to a certain unit to report our experience in studying and later held a discussion there with the activists on learning from Chairman Mao's works. At the beginning, everybody said something to praise us and I felt quite at home. But when the comrade in charge of our party asked for comments and criticism, my heart missed a beat and I hardly dared raise my head, fearing

that I might be criticized. Immediately I sensed that it was a very bad idea and made a self-criticism at this very meeting.

4. Develop an "ideological film" every night. The ears, eyes, nose and other sense organs of a person are comparable to the diaphragm of a camera. The things reflected through these sense organs will leave their impressions in one's mind. When I lay in bed at night, I would recall the day's life to see what is on the "ideological film." I will keep what is good and eliminate what is bad in accordance with Chairman Mao's teachings. On the points I cannot see clearly, I would ask others to "magnify" them for me. If I had not done this con-scientiously, some bad thinking would have formed and grown before I knew what was happening.

5. Hold every pass. At the beginning of this year, I once went out on busi-ness. When I came back I went to the political instructor to report my recent thinking. By the time I finished, it was past ten o'clock. The political instructor asked me to stay in the company headquarters for the night and already had had the bed made. My first reflection was that though I was a platoon leader, it would not matter if I stayed in the company headquarters for a night, since I had been away from my platoon for some time. But on second thoughts, I found this was only making an excuse for myself. If I got into such a habit, I would be treating myself as someone different from others and become divorced from the masses. Instead of excusing myself with "It doesn't matter!," I should set a high ideological standard for myself and not do anything, not even once, which is not beneficial to the revolutionization of my ideology. So I went back to the platoon that night. I came to understand that mistaken and bad patterns are often formed through one's doing the first wrong thing. We must hold the first pass so that there would not be an opening, a point of breakthrough for the first mistaken, bad ideas. The occasion when a man finds excuses for himself is the time he lowers the standard of ideological revolutionization and takes the downward road ideologically. One should never permit oneself any excuse to explain away one's mistaken ideas.

On the other hand good ideas, good style of work are formed bit by bit through tempering over long years. One should never refuse to do the first good thing and at the same time should never rest content with doing only one good thing. Good ideas cannot be developed and good style of work cannot be formed overnight. One must be good at "accumulating ideological sparks." When he has accumulated enough of such sparks, a leap will take place and there will be a qualitative change in his ideology.

6. It is important to have an unflinching revolutionary will. In order to make revolution and remould and temper ourselves into a new, communist generation, we must have an unflinching revolutionary will. When I was guided by such a will, I gave way to no undesirable thought or action, and I struggled hard under the direction of Mao Tse-tung's thought against any selfish thinking in my mind and "compelled" myself to do good deeds. I would then think more of Chair-man Mao's teachings, the heroes and models and the example I should follow in the future. In my opinion this revolutionary will is an essential thing. Chair-man Mao has said:

We the Chinese nation have the spirit to fight the enemy to the last drop of our blood, the determina-tion to recover our lost territory by our own efforts, and the ability to stand on our own feet in the family of nations.

We must have the spirit, determination and ability referred to by Chairman Mao, to fight to the very end the enemy in our own minds, in order to train ourselves to be staunch fighters for communism.

Madness as Religious Experience
R. D. Laing

R. D. Laing (1927–   ) is a British psychologist whose controversial theories have lately attracted world-wide attention. Among his books are *The Self and Others, The Divided Self,* and *Knots.*

TRANSCENDENTAL EXPERIENCE

Certain *transcendental experiences* seem to me to be the original wellspring of all religions. Some psychotic people have transcendental experiences. Often (to the best of their recollection), they have never had such experiences before, and frequently they will never have them again. I am not saying, however, that psychotic experience necessarily contains this element more manifestly than sane experience.

We experience in different modes. We perceive external realities, we dream, imagine, have semi-conscious reveries. Some people have visions, hallucinations, experience faces transfigured, see auras and so on. Most people most of the time experience themselves and others in one or another way that I shall call *egoic.* That is, centrally or peripherally, they experience the world and themselves in terms of a consistent identity, a me-here over against a you-there, within a framework of certain ground structures of space and time shared with other members of their society.

This identity-anchored, space-and-time-bound experience has been studied philosophically by Kant, and later by the phenomenologists, e.g. Husserl, Merleau-Ponty. Its historical and ontological relativity should be fully realized by any contemporary student of the human scene. Its cultural, socioeconomic relativity has become a commonplace among anthropologists and a platitude to the Marxists and neo-Marxists. And yet, with the consensual and inter-personal confirmation it offers, it gives us a sense of ontological security, whose validity we *experience* as self-validating, although metaphysically-historically-ontologically-socioeconomically-culturally we know its apparent absolute validity as an illusion.

From R. D. Laing, *The Politics of Experience* (New York, 1967), pp. 137–145. Copyright © R. D. Laing, 1967. Reprinted by permission of Penguin Books Ltd.

In fact all religious and all existential philosophies have agreed that such *egoic experience* is a preliminary illusion, a veil, a film of *maya*—a dream to Heraclitus, and to Lao Tzu, the fundamental illusion of all Buddhism, a state of sleep, of death, of socially accepted madness, a womb state to which one has to die, from which one has to be born.

The person going through ego-loss or transcendental experiences may or may not become in different ways confused. Then he might legitimately be regarded as mad. But to be mad is not necessarily to be ill, notwithstanding that in our culture the two categories have become confused. It is assumed that if a person is mad (whatever that means) then *ipso facto* he is ill (whatever that means). The experience that a person may be absorbed in, while to others he appears simply ill-mad, may be for him veritable manna from heaven. The person's whole life may be changed, but it is difficult not to doubt the validity of such vision. Also, not everyone comes back to us again.

Are these experiences simply the effulgence of a pathological process or of a particular alienation? I do not think they are.

In certain cases, a man blind from birth may have an operation performed which gives him his sight. The result—frequently misery, confusion, disorientation. The light that illumines the madman is an unearthly light. It is not always a distorted refraction of his mundane life situation. He may be irradiated by light from other worlds. It may burn him out.

This "other" world is not essentially a battlefield wherein psychological forces, derived or diverted, displaced or sublimated from their original object-cathexes, are engaged in an illusionary fight—although such forces may obscure these realities, just as they may obscure so-called external realities. When Ivan in *The Brothers Karamazov* says, "If God does not exist, everything is permissible," he is *not* saying, "If my super-ego, in projected form, can be abolished, I can do anything with a good conscience." He *is* saying, "If there is *only* my conscience, then there is no ultimate validity for my will."

Among physicians and priests there should be some who are guides, who can educt the person from this world and induct him to the other. To guide him in it and to lead him back again.

One enters the other world by breaking a shell: or through a door: through a partition: the curtains part or rise: a veil is lifted. Seven veils: seven seals, seven heavens.

The "ego" is the instrument for living in *this* world. If the "ego" is broken up or destroyed (by the insurmountable contradictions of certain life situations, by toxins, chemical changes, etc.), then the person may be exposed to other worlds, "real" in different ways from the more familiar territory of dreams, imagination, perception or fantasy.

The world that one enters, one's capacity to experience it, seem to be partly conditional on the state of one's "ego."

Our time has been distinguished, more than by anything else, by a drive to control the external world, and by an almost total forgetfulness of the internal world. If one estimates human evolution from the point of view of knowledge of the external world, then we are in many respects progressing.

If our estimate is from the point of view of the internal world and of oneness of internal and external, then the judgement must be very different.

Phenomenologically the terms "internal" and "external" have little validity.

But in this whole realm one is reduced to mere verbal expedients—words are simply the finger pointing at the moon. One of the difficulties of talking in the present day of these matters is that the very existence of inner realities is now called in question.

By "inner" I mean our way of seeing the external world and all those realities that have no "external," "objective" presence—imagination, dreams, fantasies, trances, the realities of contemplative and meditative states, realities of which modern man, for the most part, has not the slightest direct awareness.

For example, nowhere in the Bible is there any argument about the *existence* of gods, demons, angels. People did not first "believe in" God: they experienced His presence, as was true of other spiritual agencies. The question was not whether God existed, but whether this particular God was the greatest god of all, or the only God; and what was the relation of the various spiritual agencies to each other. Today, there is a public debate, not as to the trustworthiness of God, the particular place in the spiritual hierarchy of different spirits, etc., but whether God or such spirits *even* exist or ever have existed.

Sanity today appears to rest very largely on a capacity to adapt to the external world—the interpersonal world, and the realm of human collectivities.

As this external human world is almost completely and totally estranged from the inner, any personal direct awareness of the inner world already has grave risks.

But since society, without knowing it, is *starving* for the inner, the demands on people to evoke its presence in a "safe" way, in a way that need not be taken seriously, etc., is tremendous—while the ambivalence is equally intense. Small wonder that the list of artists, in say the last 150 years, who have become ship-wrecked on these reefs is so long—Hölderlin, John Clare, Rimbaud, Van Gogh, Nietzsche, Antonin Artaud. . . .

Those who survived have had exceptional qualities—a capacity for secrecy, slyness, cunning—a thoroughly realistic appraisal of the risks they run, not only from the spiritual realms they frequent, but from the hatred of their fellows for anyone engaged in this pursuit.

Let us *cure* them. The poet who mistakes a real woman for his Muse and acts accordingly. . . . The young man who sets off in a yacht in search of God. . . .

The outer divorced from any illumination from the inner is in a state of darkness. We are in an age of darkness. The state of outer darkness is a state of sin—i.e., alienation or estrangement from the *inner light*.[1] Certain actions lead to greater estrangement; certain others help one not to be so far removed. The former used to be called sinful.

The ways of losing one's way are legion. Madness is certainly not the least unambiguous. The countermadness of Kraepelinian psychiatry is the exact counterpart of "official" psychosis. Literally, and absolutely seriously, it is as *mad*, if by madness we mean any radical estrangement from the totality of what is the case. Remember Kierkegaard's objective madness.

As we experience the world, so we act. We conduct ourselves in the light of our view of what is the case and what is not the case. That is, each person is a more or less naïve ontologist. Each person has views of what is and what is not.

There is no doubt, it seems to me, that there have been profound changes

[1] M. Eliade, *The Two and the One* (London: Harvill Press, 1965), especially Chapter I.

in the experience of man in the last thousand years. In some ways this is more evident than changes in the patterns of his behavior. There is everything to suggest that man experienced God. Faith was never a matter of believing. He existed, but of trusting, in the presence that was experienced and known to exist as a self-validating datum. It seems likely that far more people in our time experience neither the presence of God, nor the presence of his absence, but the absence of his presence.

We require a history of phenomena, not simply more phenomena of history.

As it is, the secular psychotherapist is often in the role of the blind leading the half-blind.

The fountain has not played itself out, the frame still shines, the river still flows, the spring still bubbles forth, the light has not faded. But between *us* and It, there is a veil which is more like fifty feet of solid concrete. *Deus absconditus*. Or we have absconded.

Already everything in our time is directed to categorizing and segregating this reality from objective facts. This is precisely the concrete wall. Intellectually, emotionally, interpersonally, organizationally, intuitively, theoretically, we have to blast our way through the solid wall, even if at the risk of chaos, madness and death. For from *this* side of the wall, this is the risk. There are no assurances, no guarantees.

Many people are prepared to have faith in the sense of scientifically indefensible belief in an untested hypothesis. Few have trust enough to test it. Many people make-believe what they experience. Few are made to believe by their experience. Paul of Tarsus was picked up by the scruff of the neck, thrown to the ground and blinded for three days. This direct experience was self-validating.

We live in a secular world. To adapt to this world the child abdicates its esctasy. ("*L'enfant abdique son extase*": Malarmé.) Having lost our experience of the spirit, we are expected to have faith. But this faith comes to be a belief in a reality which is not evident. There is a prophecy in Amos that a time will come when there will be a famine in the land, "not a famine for bread, nor a thirst for water, but of *hearing* the words of the Lord." That time has now come to pass. It is the present age.

From the alienated starting point of our pseudo-sanity, everything is equivocal. Our sanity is not "true" sanity. Their madness is not "true" madness. The madness of our patients is an artifact of the destruction wreaked on them by us and by them on themselves. Let no one suppose that we meet "true" madness any more than that we are truly sane. The madness that we encounter in "patients" is a gross travesty, a mockery, a grotesque caricature of what the natural healing of that estranged integration we call sanity might be. True sanity entails in one way or another the dissolution of the normal ego, that false self competently adjusted to our alienated social reality; the emergence of the "inner" archetypal mediators of divine power, and through this death a rebirth, and the eventual re-establishment of a new kind of ego-functioning, the ego now being the servant of the divine, no longer its betrayer.

Religion and the Current Crisis

INTRODUCTION

The current crisis in man's earthly tenure has been limned by war, racism, pollution, suppression of women, excess of sexual liberty, social oppression, conflict between self and society, and the griefs of ambition. They are great rocks hanging around the neck of man's hope. Evil stalks the world, its bag full of stones with which to weight us into despair. We have all long left the Garden of Eden to wander cursed on the face of the earth. Deliver us.

Religions have maintained their relevancy to most of humanity throughout history because they have not blinked the omnipresence of evil. We have included the selections in this chapter in this book because they show the historical continuity of contemporary religious thinkers with past thinkers; these contemporary religious thinkers, like their predecessors, do not blink the presence of evil—they face the current forms that evil takes, and they try to show how we can contend with evil in religious terms. For example, in the fifteenth selection in this chapter, **Harvey Cox** addresses himself to the continual manifestations of sex in such a magazine as *Playboy* and in such a fleshly display as the Miss America contest, and he finds that these stimuli, linked with the emphasis on romantic love, have placed young people in a troubling moral situation. By formulating an interpretation of Christian ethics, he tries to show that the Christian religion can help to identify what is really evil and what is sheer puritanism in the current sexual scene; further, he wishes to show that religion can give meaningful answers to questions young people have about the morality of sex.

Another example of contemporary religious thinkers' willingness to contend with evil is the effort of **Major T. Jones**, in the second selection in this chapter, to find a theology of hope for black people, many of whom take hope only from revolution. Because revolutions generally entail violence, the course of revolution runs counter to the traditional Christian ethic of nonviolence. If this ethic is to be maintained, and if one wants to maintain that there is hope elsewhere than in revolution, the religious thinker must replace revolution with a theology of hope or be useless to oppressed black people.

There are several ways to contend with evil. As Albert Camus reminded us, suicide is a form of deliverance from our absurd existence. It is not a popular form of deliverance, however. Literature has more popularly suggested that deliverance is to be found by taking certain attitudes toward evil. Philosophers have recommended insouciance or indifference, but Rasselas* discovered that the philosopher soon lost the insouciance he advocated when his daughter died. Defiance is an admirable attitude, but it implies expectation of defeat. Going down with a curse and fistshake is still going down. Captain Ahab went down defiantly, but, nevertheless, down, before Moby Dick. ("Towards thee I roll, thou all-destroying but unconquering whale; ... from hell's heart I stab at thee; for hate's sake I spit my last breath at thee ... thou damned whale!") And for all Sancho Panza's drollery, Don Quixote could not be saved from evil in the end; humor is an attitude that provides relief but does not provide a cure for evil, any more than morphine cures cancer.

Religious thinkers have proposed more ambitious deliverance schemes. Consider a cosmological deliverance. Man may, indeed, be subject to unremitting evil in this world, but suppose that there is some divine intelligence who conceived a grand purpose with man as ingredient. The evil that man suffers may be no accidental, provincial affair of his kin on this small planet. The plot may be of massive, cosmological proportions. In fact, the plot may be so massive that it involves two universes, one in which there is evil and another in which there is no evil. Perhaps this divine intelligence, who also bears the virtue of divine mercy, has placed us temporarily in the evil cosmos so that when he delivers us into the cosmos without evil we can live in the blessed knowledge of a goodness that we could not have known without the experience of evil.

Metaphysical deliverances also have been proposed by religious thinkers. These often turn on the distinction between appearance and reality. Suppose that all evil is traceable to the body's desires, lusts, greed, excesses, and needs. Now, suppose that man were shown not to be identical with his body but with a spiritual soul, and suppose, further, that by careful metaphysical argument we could show that matter is only appearance, that it has no reality; then the evil that originates in the body would also be unreal, mere appearance. This is a metaphysical deliverance from evil.

We have reviewed four forms of deliverance: suicidal, attitudinal, cosmological, and metaphysical. There is a fifth form of deliverance that characterizes the thrust of this chapter. This is the way of action, the attempt to defeat the forces of evil here and now in this world.

Even for those religious seers who hold that deliverance from evil comes finally in another universe than this one, the believers and followers are here and now in this world. They are impatient for deliverance. These believers

* Rasselas was a fictional character in Ben Jonson's play "Rasselas, Prince of Abyssinia." Rasselas left the happy valley of Amahra to venture into the outer world, found it a miserable place, and returned to that valley only to discover that its happiness was an illusion of youth.

are organized typically into a churchly institution. Such institutions can press a struggle against evil. Being temporally organized, institutional religion is a political affair. The decisions and pronouncements of religious leaders are of this world; they are born out of politically structured councils, conventions, struggles, and power conflicts. True, leaders seek the sanction of sacred texts for their decisions and pronouncements, but that claim, too, is temporal, as temporal as a judge's who claims the sanction of statute or precedent for his decision.

In this chapter, then, the essays belong to a category we might call "religious politics."

The idea of religious politics may offend the pious, because the juncture of temporal politics with the eternal verities of religion seems to them a breach of the sacred by the profane. But to take offense would betray a certain naiveté about the relation between sacred texts and the ethical foundations of a righteous political struggle with evil. There is nothing either strange or strained about the juncture of politics and religion. Some reflections on a question Socrates asked will help us to see that the juncture is a fitting one. A form of Socrates' question, one he put to Euthyphro, is this: "Is something right because God said it or did God say it because it was right?"

Suppose a religious-minded policeman justifies making an arrest of a seller of pornographic books by citing a sacred text, perhaps something from St. Paul. Supposing the St. Paul text to be divinely inspired, we may inquire now, as Socrates did, why the cited text is supposed to justify the action. If God's saying it alone makes it right, then the sacred text itself is the justification, but if God says it because it is right, then He must have grounds or reasons that we intelligent, temporal beings can share. This sharing means that a rational bridge between sacred texts and temporal, political decisions exists and that, consequently, the notion of religious politics is not impious.

The view that something is right merely because God says so makes the distinction between good and evil purely arbitrary; the distinction would not, then, be based on a difference in the nature of good and evil. Additionally, if God's arbitrarily saying something makes it right, we would have to acknowledge that he could just as reasonably have said the opposite of what he said. In that case, today the pious should be encouraging the pornographers, the cursers of God, the rapists of little children, and the defilers of the temple. If this seems ridiculous to you, there must be a basis for God's saying that something is right, and since we and God can divine the basis and say something because it is right, politics and religion may reasonably be fused into religious politics.

The fusion should not be cause for concern. It only implies that the day of prophets is not over. Didn't Isaiah come after Abraham? The fact that he came later didn't nullify his being a prophet. Deny not the fullness of time. There may be prophets in this chapter.

A. K. B.

Suggested Readings

Boisen, A. T. "Religion and Hard Times. A Study of Holy Rollers." *Social Action*, March 15, 1939, pp. 8–35.

Campbell, Ernst Q. and T. F. Pettigrew. *Christians in Racial Crisis. A Study of Little Rock's Ministry*. Washington D.C.: Public Affairs Press, 1959.

Cohn, Norman. *Pursuit of the Millenium*. 2nd ed. New York: Harper & Row, 1961.

Gish, Arthur, G. *The New Left and Christian Radicalism*. Grand Rapids, Mich.: Wm. B. Eerdmans Publishing Co., 1970.

Glock, Charles, and Stark, Rodney, *Religion and Society in Tension*. Chicago: Rand McNally, 1965. Chapters 9–13.

Glock, Charles, Ringer, Benjamin, and Babbie, Earl. *To Comfort, and to Challenge*. Berkeley, Calif.: University of California Press, 1967.

Gray, Francine du Plessix. *Divine Disobedience: Profiles in Catholic Radicalism*. New York: Knopf, 1970.

Hadden, Jeffrey K. *The Gathering Storm in the Churches*. Garden City, N.Y.: Doubleday, 1970.

———. *Religion in Radical Transition*. Chicago: Aldine, 1971.

King, Martin Luther Jr. *Stride Toward Freedom: The Montgomery Story*. New York: Harper & Row, 1958.

———. *The Trumpet of Conscience*. New York: Harper & Row, 1968.

———. *Why We Can't Wait*. New York: Harper & Row, 1963.

Lanternari, Vittorio. *The Religions of the Oppressed. A Study of Modern Messianic Cults*. New York: Knopf, 1963.

Lenin, V. I. *Religion*. New York: International Publishers, 1933.

Lincoln, C. Eric. *The Black Muslims in America*. Boston: Beacon Press, 1961.

Marx, Gary. *Protest and Prejudice*. New York: Harper & Row, 1967.

May, Henry F. *Protestant Churches and Industrial America*. New York: Harper & Row, 1949.

Pope, Liston. *Millhands and Preachers*. New Haven, Conn.: Yale University Press, 1942.

Smith, Donald E. *Religion and Political Development*. Boston: Little, Brown, 1970.

Solt, Leo. *Saints in Arms. Puritanism and Democracy in Cromwell's Army*. Stanford, Calif.: Stanford University Press, 1959.

Washington, Joseph R. Jr. *The Politics of God. The Future of the Black Churches*. Boston: Beacon Press, 1967.

Willems, Emilio. *Followers of the New Faith. Culture Change and the Rise of Protestantism in Brazil and Chile*. Nashville, Tenn.: Vanderbilt University Press, 1967.

Williams, George H. *The Radical Transformation*. London: Weidenfeld and Nicolson, 1962.

Yinger, J. Milton. *Religion in the Struggle for Power*. Durham, N.C.: Duke University Press, 1946 (reprinted: Russell & Russell, 1961).

WAR AND THE NATIONS

The "Just War" Justifies Too Much

Donald A. Wells

Donald A. Wells (1917–   ), who teaches philosophy at the University of Hawaii at Hilo, is the author of *The War Myth* and *God, Man and the Thinker*.

"Justification" is not an unambiguous term. In the context of logical justification, the defense of a claim is a function of a given system, where consistency with axioms is a necessary, if not sufficient, criterion of proof. In normative discourse, however, justification takes on an honorific and emotion-laden aura. In addition to both consistency and truth claims, moral justification entails some notion of "rightness" or "goodness." The problem of the "Just War" is, in this latter sense, more than a matter of consistency with some given axioms, more than a question of the truth of some factual claims, more than a matter of what is permissible legally, and surely more than an exercise in the possible limits of an hypothetical ethics.

In a very ordinary sense of the term "justify" we commonly seek an explanation of why a war was waged in the first place. "Why did Athens war against Sparta?" is in this sense "justified" by giving the antecedent reasons prompting the declaration. But more has been involved than this in traditional dispute over the justice of some war. Commonly the dispute sounds more like the defense of an appellant before a judge, and the "justification" consists in part in showing that some acts of war were consistent with the legal rules under which we have agreed to operate. In a further sense, the justification of war is like the famous "justification of induction," and its resolution involves us in a metalinguistic search for some frame of reference that transcends both politics and morals.

More pertinently, however, the attempts to justify war constitute a recognition that the terms "just" and "war" are, if not contradictions, at least of doubtful conjunction. Since the kind of havoc which war entails is normally classed with immoral actions, the concept of the "just war" aims to show the circumstances under which it would be proper to perform otherwise immoral acts and to

From Donald A. Wells, "How Much Can 'the Just War' Justify?" *Journal of Philosophy*, LXVI (December 1969), 819–829. Reprinted by permission.

contribute to evil consequences. The first century of the Christian church, with its pacifist rejection of war altogether, did not produce any theorizers of the just war, while by the time Christianity was adopted as the official religion of the Roman Empire, war had lost its aura of absolute evil, and men now proposed conditions under which it would be appropriate to kill in war. While the post-Constantine church accepted war as a defensible method, it never quite lost its first-century suspicion that killing was still evil. Thus the defenses of the "just war" exhibited a friction or tension between the ethical ideal of non-killing and the political practice of killing in the service of the state.

In his essay "Politics As A Vocation" Max Weber distinguished these two basically contrary concerns. He formulated them in two maxims: (1) the ethics of ultimate ends, and (2) the ethics of responsibility. In the case of the first position the Christians act rightly and leave the outcome to God. The Christian commitment to the sacredness of human life led them to posit limits to the means a person can rightly perform in the support of any other end. The end of human life precluded, in this sense, the acceptance of any alternative end which might destroy this prior humanistic one. In the case of the second position, the politician or head of state accepts the survival of the state as the supreme goal, and he rejects, therefore, the idea that there are limits to permissible action. While he did not intend that the statesman be given carte blanche to do any act whatsoever, he did mean to grant to the statesman the right to perform absolutely any act needed to preserve the state. While Weber's essay suggests that the problem is basically one of ends versus means, this is surely not what differentiates the traditional or modern conflict between moralists and statesmen over the use of war. What is, for the Christian of the first century, the summum bonum of human life, is for the statesman of the Empire replaced by the summum bonum of national survival. The former could scarcely adopt a means that destroyed human life, while the latter could sacrifice human lives since he did not value them above the life of the state. Put in very simple terms, the problem of the just war became one of reconciling early Christian compunction with later political necessity.

Historically the medieval thesis of the just war was to set limits to the so-called "reasons of state" without at the same time denying that right of the state to survive, apparently at any cost. The just war criteria set hypothetical limits, but at no point was it intended to require states to surrender their sovereignty. In operation the criteria of the just war established the rules by which states ought to defend themselves. These rules aimed to curb excessively inhumane war practices, where they were not really needed, to reduce the number of reasons that could justify a war, to assure that the means of war bore some proportional relation to the ends of war, and generally to reduce the number of wars that actually occurred. There was no doubt in the middle ages that the concept functioned as a defense of national sovereignty, and of the right of nations to defend themselves by war in a basically lawless world. It made national survival feasible, while making international organization unlikely. If the rules for just wars seemed counsels of perfection, it was clear enough in practice that they set no serious limits to the aspiration of Princes.

Since the notion of the just war has been revived after nearly two centuries of silence on the issue, it is appropriate to look again at the general principles of the medieval position to determine whether, if they had a defense then, they have any defense now. The entire case for the medieval thinker rested, of course, on a concession which itself needs reassessment: namely, that war has a place in the moral scheme. Traditional questions about war were prudential, and the discussion centered on such questions as to time, place, and cause. Wars were presumed to be neutral means which could be given moral properties under the appropriate conditions. Wars were criticised, if at all, in practice rather than in principle. In this regard, medieval discussion of capital punishment shared common predicates. It wasn't the fact of killing that was the determinant, but rather the reasons given for the acts of killing that were decisive. How did the medieval thinker develop this notion?

THE CRITERIA OF SAINT THOMAS

In order for a war to be just three general conditions had to be met: (1) an authoritative sovereign must declare the war, (2) a just cause is required, and (3) the men who wage the war must have noble intentions and moderate means so that some good actually results. Furthermore, the good that results should be greater by some magnitude than the evil that must be produced by waging war. In the application of these criteria very few criticisms of war emerged, suggesting that Princes were remarkably wise and beneficent, or else that the criteria of the just war were too vague to be discriminating. In addition to the paucity of critique against wars, what protest there was came from persons not officially in government so that their objection was a kind of baying at the moon. George Fox, for example, challenged the wars of Cromwell, but then Fox was a pacifist who rejected all wars and could thus be dismisssd as unrealistic. Franciscus de Victoria, a theological professor at the University of Salamanca in the 16th century, chastised his Spanish superiors for their wars against the American Indians.[1] University professors, however, were no more influential in effecting changes in foreign policy in the 16th century than they appear to be now, and thus such remarks as these constituted a kind of irrelevant campus protest.

More recently, Joseph McKenna[2] has revived the just war doctrine with an expanded list of seven conditions. They are: (1) the war must be declared by the duly constituted authority, (2) the seriousness of the injury inflicted on the enemy must be proportional to the damage suffered by the virtuous, (3) the injury to the aggressor must be real and immediate, (4) there must be a reasonable chance of winning the war, (5) the use of war must be a last resort, (6) the participants must have right intentions, and (7) the means used must be moral. The problem before us is whether such criteria can be made applicable to modern war. To put the issue this way suggests that the methodology of war is a datum entailing its justice, and it insinuates that the weapons of war determine to some degree the morality of war. This brings us back to the medieval position that it is not so much a question of killing as it is the manner of the killing that really counts.

[1] Franciscus de Victoria, *On The Law Of War*. Washington, D.C. The Carnegie Institute, 1917. Section 22.

[2] "Ethics and War: A Catholic View." *American Political Science Review*. September, 1960. pp. 647–658.

JUST WAR IS ONE DECLARED BY THE DULY CONSTITUTED AUTHORITY

For a theologian like Saint Augustine or Saint Thomas, who presumed some ameliorating influence from Christian prelates, such a criterion might be considered to constitute a limitation on careless heathen scoundrels. Since both worthy Saints accepted heathen Princes as duly constituted, it was not obvious how this influence was supposed to work. By the 16th century, however, with the proliferation of Princes, and the fading away of Christian prelates, a radically new situation had emerged. By this time the "reasons of state" as Machiavelli elaborated them, permitted every Prince to wage war whenever he deemed it fit. Since by the 18th century war had become the sport of kings, it was clear that authorities had no special claim to sensitivity or good sense.

The rise of nationalism made this first criterion undifferentiating. It became increasingly obvious that to grant to any Prince the privilege of judging his neighboring prelates posed an odd situation. Every Prince judged every other Prince and was in turn judged by them, and there appeared to be a kind of gentleman's agreement not to be too critical of each other. It was this anomaly that led Grotius and Victoria to insist that while only one side of a war should properly be considered to be just, in fact persons on both sides could, in good conscience, presume that they had justice on their respective sides. In the absence of any international judge, no one was in a position to assess the claims of the national judges.

If rulers were saints or scholars there might be some reason to suppose that their judgements on war were adequate, and that they would not declare war for scurrilous reasons. At least two obstacles lay in the way of such a likelihood occurring. In the first place, the permissible reasons for waging war were so inclusive that virtually any conceivable princely aim could get support. Even wars of vindictive justice were permitted. In the second place, there were no plausible reasons to suppose that secular leaders had intentions that would meet even minimal standards of humaneness. It is not necessary to have in mind leaders like Hitler, Mussolini, Tojo, or Thieu to see that this is so. There is nothing in the nature of the process by which leaders are selected to give assurance that the leaders of France, England, or America have moral insights that are even as good as the average, let alone sufficiently discerning to be used as the criteria for a just war. We do not imagine our Princes to be especially gifted in domestic policy. Why should we imagine that they are wise as Solomon in foreign affairs?

Even clerics have had a rather poor reputation for sound moral judgement. Witness, for example, the stand of Archbishop Groeber of Freiburg-im-Breisgau who rejected Christian pacifism for German Catholics on the grounds that Hitler was the duly constituted authority. Pope Pius XII was no more reassuring on this point when he rejected the right of conscientious objection for German Catholics at the time of the formation of NATO. This first criterion of the duly constituted authority seems, therefore, to serve no distinguishing function at all. Indeed it is so ambiguous that applied to the present conflict in Vietnam both Ho Chi Minh and Thieu would satisfy the condition since they have declared war, while the American part in the war would be unjust since no war declaration has been made by the duly constituted authority.

A JUST WAR USES MEANS PROPORTIONAL TO THE ENDS

Franciscus de Victoria (1480–1546) observed that if to retake a piece of territory would expose a people to "intolerable ills and heavy woes,"[3] then it would not be just to retake it. We must be sure, he continued, that the evils we commit in war do not exceed the evils we claim to be averting. This was appropriate general advice, but in the absence of any specific suggestions as to how to make such measurement of relative ills, it was not even a helpful counsel of perfection, let alone a practical guide in the concrete situation. How do we measure proportionality? This was the problem of the hedonic calculus on which Mill's system first foundered. Since Victoria granted to Princes the right to despoil innocent children, if military necessity required it, it ceased to be apparent what proportionality meant at all. When this was combined with an equal vagueness on what constituted military necessity, the net contribution amounted to zero.

In a recent paper on this issue Father John A. Connery[4] stated that the morality of the violence depends on the proportionality of this violence to that of the aggression. Here again, what is required is some calculus to make this measurement. The latitude with which conscientious persons have interpreted what is proportional as a response suggests, what was clear enough to Mill, that we possess neither the quantitative nor the qualitative yardstick for such a decision. Pope Pius XII believed that the annihilation of vast numbers of persons was impermissible. Did he then intend for nations to surrender if the only price for success was such annihilation? Since the Pope was not explicit on this matter, John Courtney Murray[5] assumed that the papal prohibition was a conditional one. It was merely that large numbers of persons ought not to be slaughtered needlessly. Such a view, however, makes Pope Pius XII appear like a fool, for either he did not mean what he appeared to be saying, or he had not thought through the implications of what he appeared to be saying.

Proportionality is a slippery term unless there is some measure. Herbert Hoover thought in 1939 that the aerial bombing of cities was beyond moral proportion, although he did urge the U.S. to build bombing planes to perform this banned action. Jacques Maritain also put bombing from the air in the category of an absolutely proscribed act.[6] But how is such a determination made? In the early period of World War II "saturation bombing" was considered to be too inhumane for the American citizens to accept. Our military practiced instead what was euphemistically called "precision bombing." But even here where measurement would seem most plausible, the distinction was empty. This was illustrated when the Air Force announced at the time of the first test shot of the Atlas missile, that a bomb that lands within fifty miles of its target is considered accurate.[7]

---

[3] Victoria, op. cit., Sections 33, 37.

[4] "Morality and Nuclear Armament." in William J. Nagle (Ed.) Morality and Modern Warfare. Baltimore: Helicon, 1960. p. 92.

[5] Morality and Modern War. New York: The Council on Religion and International Affairs, 1959. p. 9.

[6] "War and the Bombardment of Cities." Commonweal. September 2, 1938.

[7] Nagle, op. cit., p. 107.

In the concept of proportionality the medieval theorist introduced a distinction that made no difference. It is all very well to insist that actions be proportional, but if there are no criteria for the determination of proportionality, then the advice is not even a helpful counsel of perfection, let alone a useful curb to military excesses. Here again history reports the vacuity of the criterion. In the days of the cross-bow it was deemed necessary to remind military men of proportionality in relation to the ends to be preserved. If this was needful then, what about proportionality in the use of guns, fragmentation bombs, germ and chemical weapons, and thermonuclear explosives. Since the ends to be preserved by the cross-bow are essentially the same as those to be preserved by the H-bomb, one would expect that if there could have been an excessive use of the bow, then modern weapons could have no proportional use at all.

During World War II the English writer, Vera Brittain, attacked both Britain and America for the bombing of civilians in her book, *Massacre by Bombing*. Here was an opportunity to see whether proportionality was still alive. Mrs. Brittain said that the bombing of civilians was not proportional to the threat or to the goal to be achieved. The Protestant journal, *The Christian Century*, editorialized in support of the bombing of civilians. The American Bar Association defeated a resolution calling for a condemnation of the bombing of civilians.[8] *The Saturday Evening Post* suggested that it was a sign of "instability" to question the need for the bombing of civilians. Orthodox clergy like the Reverend Carl McIntyre and the Reverend H. J. Ockenga called Mrs. Brittain's position "un-American and pro-Fascist." Can such positions be defended on the basis of proportionality? Whether they can or not, the fact is that they were not so defended.

Proportionality, in use, appears to have been a justification for increasing escalation, rather than a curb to ascending violence. John Courtney Murray, in an essay on "Morality and Modern War,"[9] defended the survival of American culture as well as of the American state on the grounds that it was without peer in any moral system. Furthermore, he saw Communism as a kind of Anti-Christ, so evil and so destructive of the values of his personal national outlook, that he defended any means necessary to their preservation. The possibility of the loss of the pure and noble Western capitalist, democratic, and Christian culture was so unpleasant to him that he was able to tolerate the intolerable, think the unthinkable, and admit a cosmic amount of human destruction as quite proportional to the ends and the threat. Is there, indeed, any measure for such an assessment? The medieval concern with misplaced sword-thrusts is qualitatively unrelated to the contemporary calculation with the mega-death of civilians. Unless some case could be made that the modern values are infinitely more worthy than medieval values, the immense increase in human destruction that our wars now involve makes proportionality absolutely inapplicable.

In the medieval calculation, wars for religion were considered to be unsupportable. Waging wars for religious reasons, such as the goal of conversion to Christianity or of abolishing heathenism, was classed as simply disproportional to war's havoc. Part of the medieval rejection of religious war, at least in principle, rested on their objection to wars against ideas or abstractions. Such

[8] *New York Times*. July 15, 1939, p. 3.
[9] Murray, *op cit.*, p. 6.

an antipathy may be supported from a variety of bases. Conversion to an idea is normally considered a function of education, not of war. The method of war is simply not suited to changing opinion. In addition, false opinion or even heretical doctrine is not so cosmic an evil that war could be considered the lesser of two so-called evils. Much of the modern just war theorizing presumes that wars for politics are proportionally defensible, and it would seem that the medieval reasons against wars for religion hold here with equal cogency. Our twentieth century wars to save democracy, freedom, or to banish fascism, communism, or socialism have failed signally to alter opinion or to establish new thinking on such generalities. War is, in this regard, not a form of debate or of mental persuasion. As a matter of fact persons live well under a variety of economic and political systems—communist, socialist, capitalist, monarchic, democratic, or republican, even fascist. They can equally live poorly under these same systems—the Jews in Germany, the Blacks in the United States, and the Orientals in Australia. Wars for ideology not only misunderstand the sources of human ills, but they are, in part because of this misunderstanding, all out of proportion. Even our most callous storm-trooper does not recommend the bomb on Selma, Little Rock, or Chicago, while some of our most sensitive leaders propose simple genocide on Vietnam for putative ideological reasons.

Consideration of the current discussion of what is called "rational nuclear armament" suggests that the criterion calling for just means or for proportionality in our actions of war is only a verbal genuflection. Dr. Kahn, famous for his ability to think the unthinkable, has recommended in the interests of proportionality that bombs be limited to the one-half megaton class. Since this is fifty times greater than the bomb dropped on Hiroshima proportionality has obviously become a rather loose term. This is the same conclusion we reach in the context of the language of "overkill" or "megakill." If we have enough bombs to kill every person in a country twice, or in effect twice as many bombs as we actually need to exterminate the population, then it makes no moral sense to speak of the reduction of bombs to the precise amount needed as illustrating any degree of humane or ethical proportion. To be sure there is a mathematical difference, and from the point of view of the military-educational-industrial complex there is a production difference. From the point of view of moral distinctions, however, there is no difference at all. The use of too much "firepower" is an economic waste, not a superfluity of immorality.

WAR MAY JUSTLY BE TAKEN ONLY AS A LAST RESORT

In conventional discourse the notion of a "last resort" presupposes some notion of "first resort." Thus, unless a nation could show that it had indeed exhausted first resorts, it would make no sense for that nation to claim any right to use the last resort. First resorts might be such alternatives as economic, social, or political boycott, negotiations through the U.N. or through some unilateral means, and, of course, surrender is a first resort. Now let us assume that the first resorts have all been attempted, and that there appear to be no non-violent alternatives nor any violent options less destructive than war. We would still need to show that the last resort of war ought to be taken in this case. To permit war as a last resort is not the same as requiring that the last resort be taken. To say that war is a last resort is not the same as granting the right to go to war. It is possible that the last resort that can morally be defended is the first resort that is taken. This is clearer in a case like that of the Nazi treatment of the Jews than it is usually seen to be in actions of our own nation like our treatment of the Blacks or of the Vietnamese. Could the Germans have defended the statement: "Having exhausted every other resort to remove the threat of the Jews to Aryan supremacy, may we now as a last resort, open the gas chambers?"

What confuses the case in war is the presumption that war is a proper resort at all, while domestically we assume citizens deserve better treatment. Somehow we contemporaries have retained the legitimacy of the means of war in spite of the escalation of its instruments and the scope of its use. In domestic gas chambers, on the contrary, we draw the line at excess. Some American states still use gas chambers on offenders, but these same defenders of local gas chambers were offended by the German use of them. It was as if they were saying that gas chambers as methods are proper or proportional as a last resort, provided that they are not used too widely. Or that the use of gas chambers was an appropriate last resort provided that the offense was of a certain magnitude. If all the German Jews had been culpable by American standards of offenses that in America would have sent them to the gas chambers, then, the conjecture seems to be, it would have been a proper last resort for the German Nazis to administer Belsen, Buchenwald, and the rest.

Most contemporary defense of the just war doctrine bypasses an important decisional matter: is the expression "just war" different in kind from the expressions "just murder," "just torture," "just genocide," or even "just annihilation of innocents." Since the words "murder," "torture," and "genocide" are pejorative, and communicate a clear moral condemnation as to their practice, we surely need to show that "war" is not also this kind of pejorative term. If war were shown to be a kind of murder, would just war theorists now wish to speak of just murder? At least a part of the implication of the War Crimes Trials in Nuremberg was that if war did become murder or genocide then it could not be justified. Thus in some cases, at least, war could not be considered as even a viable or justifiable last resort.

In this day of massive retaliation and mega-kill, the justification of war as any resort at all requires a defense that medieval concepts are unable to support. If persons are of the value that medieval theology assigned to them, then the sheer scope and devastation of modern war makes it impossible to find another value so over-riding that an Hiroshima becomes the lesser of two evils, and that war becomes a proper resort at all. The military claim that Ben Tre was destroyed to save Ben Tre makes no sense in the language of resorts. That vacuous maxim "military necessity" has led us to endorse unbelievable slaughter on the inference that what is militarily necessary must be morally approvable. There has never been a clear explication of what is militarily necessary, and furthermore, there has been no argument to show that morality should take its cue from generals. Paul Ramsey, the distinguished Protestant advocate of the just war thesis, endorses the use of thermonuclear bombs on civilians if military necessity requires it.[10] Obviously the only way to answer his claim that this is not too

[10] "Just War and Reasons of State," in Robert W. Tucker, *Just War and Vatican Council II: A Critique*. New York: The Council on Religion and International Affairs, 1966, pp. 68f.

great a price to pay is to consult the living, but equally the only way for him to defend his thesis is for him to consult the dead.

Since the doctrine of the just war has become the verbal tool of military theologians or moral tacticians of war, no one seriously considers that surrender might be the most moral option, making it additionally clear that the discussants are speaking only for nations that win wars. Indeed, if the just war has any credence at all, there should be situations where the wise Prince surrenders rather than declare war. Politicians and military strategists argue from premises of national sovereignty and a proper power struggle, not from a concern with virtue, and this is further reason why modern carnage turns out to be just. That there is a blind spot on this forbidden notion of surrender was illustrated by the spectacle in August, 1958, when the Senate of the United States voted 82 to 2 to deny government funds to any person or institution that proposes or actually conducts any study regarding the possible results of the surrender of the U.S. as an alternative to war. Since nations with arms are loth to succumb to their national neighbors, and moreover to do so over concern with whether first resorts still remain, about all the theory of last resort tells us is that war is a resort that nations are bound to take.

A JUST WAR MUST BE WAGED BY MEN WITH RIGHT INTENTIONS

This issue has a direct relation to the question of whether war is an appropriate resort, first or last. Both what we intend to do and what we intend to preserve are related to whether it can be said that our intentions in war are actually just. Vatican II spoke to this matter when it reported: "As long as the danger of war remains and there is no competent and sufficiently powerful authority at the international level, governments cannot be denied the right to legitimate defense once every means of peaceful settlement has been exhausted."[11] But are there no limits on any governments? Isn't it conceivable that Nazi Germany did not deserve to survive, any more than the government of Thieu in South Vietnam? Is the preservation of the state so incontrovertibly significant that the resort to war to save it is always an act of right intention?

Much of the medieval controversy over intentionality revolved around the doctrine of the "double-effect." A just belligerent intended only as much killing as was proportional to the threat, and he was responsible only for the deaths he intended to cause. It was, of course, assumed that he did not intend to kill noncombatants. That this was the ideal, not always implemented in practice, was borne out by the concessions of men from Saint Thomas to Victoria that military necessity might justify even the despoiling of innocents. Still the medieval concern with the death of the by-stander was one that could be implemented. Their weapons made such a concern practical. Although an archer might shoot his arrow into the air and not be too clear as to where it landed, he was not in doubt as to whether he was aiming it at combatants. He might miss a small barn, but he did hit the right city. Modern weapons make such a concern with the

---

[11] *Pastoral Constitution on the Church in the Modern World.* Part II, Chapter V. National Catholic Welfare Conference, 1966.

innocents inoperable and unfeasible. In addition, the fact that so many non-combatants are killed in modern war, a number commonly exceeding that of the soldiers, suggests that something is awry. Instead of proper regret for the scope of modern weapons of destruction on the civilians, contemporaries have theorized that the class of non-combatants is now a null class. The limited war of the past has been replaced by the total war of the present—total in the sense that military necessity now justifies the death of all without exception. The medieval man might pardonably weep for the accidentally slain civilians, but modern man cannot afford to weep since he knows that he intends the death of every person slain.

This problem of unwanted or unintended death has always been an harassing one. In 1076 at a Council in Winchester, England the cases were considered of men who had fought with William the Conqueror at the Battle of Hastings. Many of the soldiers were troubled by the memory of the men they had slain, and in the case of archers, with the thought that they had slain some unknowingly. Archers were assigned the penance of daily prayers for the rest of their lives for the unknown deaths they may have caused. No comparable cleric or council concern has emerged in the twentieth century. Now when our weapons make our intentions to no avail, we cling to the weapons and adjust our intentions to our moral yardstick. If military necessity now requires the mega-death of civilians, then modern theorists will show that such intended deaths are consistent with the doctrine of right intentions. If medieval men suffered pangs of guilt for ricocheting arrows, modern men exhibit no comparable concern for Dresden, Tokyo, Hiroshima, Nagasaki, or Ben Tre. When we realize, in addition, that "double-effect" is not something that plays a role in military tactics or political strategy, it is apparent that moral concerns at this point are rather ivory tower ephemera.

A further problem with intentionality is that of showing that the means of war are appropriate even for those persons considered to be fair game because they are combatants. Nowhere has the ingenuity of man been more exercised than in the enterprise of developing "humane" ways to exterminate his fellows. In 1041 the Bishop of Arles and the Abbot of Cluny established the "truce of God" which limited the times when war could properly be carried out. Initially, war was permitted only between Monday morning and Wednesday evening, and holy days could further delimit this range. The "peace of God" decreed at the Council of Narbonne in 1054 limited the kinds of persons who could properly be attacked. By the sixteenth century Pierino Belli[12] while urging that war remain a conflict only of armed soldiers concluded that the rules of the "peaces" may safely be ignored.

In every age the attempt was made anew to proscribe some war weapons even against combatants. William Paley eschewed poison and assassination.[13] J. G. Fichte considered the use of snipers to be "downright illegal."[14] Pope Pius XII added his anathema against poison gas.[15] By the time Hitler declaimed against attack from the air as too inhumane to be tolerated,[16] it should have occurred to all that this discussion left something to be desired. The Hague Declarations of

[12] Pierino Belli, *A Treatise On Military Matters*. Oxford: Clarendon Press, 1936. p. 81.
[13] William Paley, *Moral Philosophy*, *Volume IV*. London: C. and J. Rivington, 1825. p. 531.
[14] J. G. Fichte, *The Science of Rights*. Philadelphia: J. B. Lippincott, 1869. p. 484.
[15] "C'est une Vive Satisfaction." September 14, 1939.
[16] Adolf Hitler, *My New Order*. New York: Reynal and Hitchcock, 1941. p. 951.

1899 and 1907 made "prohibited" the discharge of projectiles from the air, the use of asphyxiating gases, expanding bullets, contact mines, and torpedoes which remain dangerous after they have missed their mark.[17] Little remained for soldiers to do save to joust in the knightly fashion of the middle ages. The absurdity of such an exercise was sharpened by the remarks of a doctor to the Berlin Military Medical Society in 1885 on the discovery of a high-speed, non-expanding bullet. "I welcome the new bullet with great joy and believe that if it were generally adopted by international consent, all humanity would have cause to rejoice."[18] He called this new type bullet "humane." Haven't we lost something of the medieval sense of humane intention if we can talk seriously in this fashion? Yet the mandate against expanding bullets so impressed Hiram Maxim (1840–1916) that he considered his machine gun to be "the greatest life-saving instrument ever invented."[19]

Serious discussion among just war theorists today about the limits of just intention rarely begins until thermonuclear weapons. The whole range of "lesser" evils has been reconciled into the moral scheme. Only new tools of destruction pose any problem. Thus Richard J. Krickus[20] believed that chemical bombs were moral while biological bombs were not. Part of his reasoning rested on the thesis that control was more possible with the former than with the latter, but also that there has been a long religious-physic association between germs and evil. Still napalm, anti-personnel shrapnel, and expanding bullets posed no moral dilemmas.

The Gas Chamber has been a disturbing symbol in modern times of a possible limit to how man can justly treat his fellows. Since we in America use gas chambers for domestic offenders, it must have been something other than the tool itself that led to the War Crimes Trials against the Nazis. Perhaps it was that the Germans gassed the wrong persons. Would the deed have been palatable if they had killed only soldiers, and had left the women, children, and civilian men alone? Was it that the Nazis killed the Jews for the wrong reasons? If the Nazis were being exterminated in Belsen would there be no moral problem? Is there a way to calculate that the death of twenty civilians poses a different moral problem from the death of twenty soldiers? Is it worse to kill twenty children than to kill twenty adults? Perhaps there is no way to calculate the relative horrors in these alternatives, but it is precisely this kind of question that the just war theorists must answer.

Our problem here is one of calculating the relative evil of war with the relative evil of any alternative. And surely part of the relevant variables includes the magnitude of the weapons, and the scope of their application to various persons normally considered to be innocent or at least non-combatant. Since it is unlikely that the values now claimed to be the justification for war are any better, let alone any different, from those in the middle ages, the increased destruction of war must surely be germane to the question whether war as a means can be made just at all any more. If in the middle ages some wars were conceivably less tragic

---

[17] Carnegie Endowment for International Peace. Pamphlets 1–22.

[18] I. S. Bloch, *The Future of War*. New York: Doubleday, 1902. p. 150.

[19] Hiram Maxim, *Defenseless America*. New York: Hearst, 1915. p. 83.

[20] Richard J. Krickus, "On the Morality of Chemical/Biological War." *Journal of Conflict Resolution*. June, 1965. pp. 200–210.

than the alternatives, although live illustrations would be hard to find, modern wars are so ghastly and so much more destructive of the humane virtues than the alternatives, that to justify war now seems to justify too much.

CONCLUSION

We are back to our starting point and the problem, as yet unpersuasively resolved, is to show that war is a potentially moral means at all. While we know the legal distinction between killing done by private citizens (called murder) and the killing done by soldiers in the name of the state (called war) and the killing done by the state to its criminals (called capital punishment), the moral indictment against taking life once applied equally to every instance. Surely it made no difference to the person slain what the circumstances of his death were, or by what name the deed was called. "Thou shalt not kill" once had an absolute ring to it. Since human life was the supreme value, taking it was a supreme disvalue, and extenuating circumstances did not alter this assessment. Furthermore, the question of self-defense posed an apparent dilemma to the matter of human life. If each person has a right to self-defense, at the price of the death of the opponent, hasn't there occurred a radical reorganization of relative values? Or isn't it rather that self-defense, while a ubiquitous political right renowned in oratory, is not a moral right at all. Nor, doubtless, is the supposed right of national defense any more rooted in moral axioms. In fact, for rather evident reasons national survival is less important than personal survival. The former can be revived should it be thought a good idea, while dead citizens are irrevocably gone.

What has not yet been demonstrated by the just war theorist is the radical distinction he draws between killing in war and killing under any other circumstance. The following illustration is not resolved by any just war dogmas yet devised. Suppose we are the Aryans, genuinely confronted by "mongrelization" by the Jews, and we approach our problem with the concepts and axioms of the medieval theologian. Our problem is that of the "just pogrom." Aryans may, of course, exterminate the Jews provided that the duly constituted leader declares the pogrom. Furthermore, the "death camps" need to be administered with means proportional to the threat, taking special care not to kill non-Jews. With this minimum presumption the citizens may kill the Jews if the Prince commands it with reasons as good as outlined. Cultural defense, like national defense, once granted as a supreme good, will allow all the gas chambers needed to preserve it. This is what military necessity justifies. The citizens would, in addition, be expected to implement the State Department policy of the "containment of Judaism" and to seek to rid by every means creeping Jews from the world. With no more intellectual effort than the just war theory requires we would be able to conduct the pogrom in accordance of the "laws of pogroms." Our means would naturally be humane gas chambers and sanitary ovens. With pure hearts we could march to Armageddon, with "just war" or "just pogrom" emblazoned on our banners. But isn't this to justify too much?

There are several presuppositions in conventional just war theory that make any resolution, short of ultimate annihilation under a mushroom-shaped cloud, unlikely.

(1) Given a world of sovereign nation states, and without any adjudicating power, and given that such nations deserve to survive ultimately and unquestionably, then no moral doctrine can take away the right of states to do whatever is needful for their continuation.

(2) Given war as a proper method, at worst neutral in quality and at best endowed with virtue, then no moral doctrine can attack war because it contains both the weapons and the deeds that destroy human life. It would be comparable to condemning the surgeon and his scalpel since there is a risk that the patient may die. Obviously the analogy is not quite appropriate here since the successful soldier kills his "patient," while the successful surgeon saves his patient.

(3) Given that the state is more important than the individual, indeed, that the state is more important than an infinite number of individuals, mere human death will never be a significant argument against war.

But, if this much be "given" then what is left for just war theory to adjudicate? Generally, it will be able to resolve what the medieval theorists claimed, namely:

(1) It can resolve that the war was properly announced.

(2) It can assess reasons, other than national defense, for their appropriateness. It must, of course, be recognized that national defense is the only reason theorists give any more, and thus there really isn't any assessment called for.

(3) It can determine that the means are proportional to the end of national defense. But unless it is clearly stated how long it is proper to wage a war, how great a human price it is proper to pay, what subsidiary losses in property, culture, or manner of living it is moral to suffer—this is, what "military necessity" consists of—then there really isn't anything save an hypothetical exercise in casuistry that can engage the effort of the just war spokesman.

With these limitations, discussion of the just war can raise merely questions of consistency within the set of given axioms, and engage in a kind of aesthetic or psychological exercise in sensitivity. In the context of the presuppositions with which theories of the just war must operate, the "just war" justifies too much.

Man, God, and Atomic War

Samuel H. Dresner

Rabbi Samuel H. Dresner (1925–   ) is the spiritual leader of the North Suburban Synagogue Beth El, Highland Park, Illinois. A past editor of *Conservative Judaism*, he is the author of many books, including *Man, God and Atomic War*, *The Sabbath*, and *Between the Generations*.

Religious View.

There are those who assert that if human might and mind—military defense and international agreement—cannot prevent atomic destruction, there is One who can, One higher than all men, wiser than all human minds, more powerful than all human might—*God*! Surely He will not permit the creature that He fashioned and placed upon this earth, who was made in His image, to whom He gave lordship over the entire earth, to be destroyed. This is an argument that many of us toy with in the back of our minds when all else begins to crumble. We like to consider it, rest upon it, embrace it—because it is reassuring.

But are we so sure that God wants to save us, even if He could? Are we so confident that we deserve being saved at all? Who dares declare that he knows the will of God? Perhaps it is all quite different. Perhaps God has had enough of the human race. Perhaps He is fed up with us, disgusted with our killing, our hating, our wars, our treachery, our intrigue, our concentration camps and gas chambers, our Bergen-Belsens and Treblinkas, our Cains and Hamans, our Genghis Khans and Attilas, our Hitlers and Stalins, our miserable struggle for money and power and ego-satisfaction, with the filth and rottenness of our world and our lives. Perhaps He thought that the human race might learn in time from the suffering and tragedy which it encountered in the world and would, thereby—in a hundred years, a thousand years, three thousand years—become faithful to Him. But we did not. Every generation repeated the same errors of the generation before. Indeed, as time passes the errors seem to grow larger.

From the very beginning the creation of man was a doubtful venture. This is the verdict of more than a few of the ancient sages of Israel. According to rabbinic parable of creation (Breshit Rabbah 8), God created and destroyed many worlds before He created ours. When He was about to make man, we are told great consternation arose in heaven. The forces of truth and justice arose to oppose the creation of man. For if the truth were known and pure justice were exercised, man could never be created, since he could not survive God's justice. Therefore, according to the rabbis, God cast truth away and put aside justice for mercy and, while the angels were weighing the merits of the case—whether or not man should be created—God created him.

Has man been able to justify God's hope? We are told in the Talmud that the schools of Hillel and Shammai disputed two and a half years whether it would have been better if man had or had not been created. Finally they agreed that it would have been better had he not been created, but since he had been created, let him examine his past deeds and take care in what he was about to do. (Eruvin 13b.)

What the ancients expressed through Biblical exegesis and fanciful fable, we would put differently today. The Bible taught them that man exists through God's grace and not by His justice. This is fundamental. For if pure justice were to prevail, man would be destroyed. But God tempers His justice with mercy and thus man survives. Man's continued existence is by no means guaranteed; it is, on the contrary, tenuous and dependent. There is no stability or certainty to man's existence. The angels opposed the creation of man; the forces of truth and justice opposed the creation of man. The creation of man was opposed because the evil that would come forth from him was foreseen. The creation of man was opposed because man's power to hurt, his will to destroy, was foreseen. Notwithstanding, God created man (according to the rabbis) in the hope that the good would conquer the evil, the power to love would conquer the power to hurt, and the will to obey His will would conquer the will to destroy. The history of man, however, has been the history of God's disappointment with man.

Indeed the Bible may be described as God's search for the righteous man and His repeated disappointment. God regretted that He had made man, Scripture tells us, and was about to destroy him, but He offered him a second opportunity through Noah, who seemed to be a righteous man, at least in comparison with his generation. So all the rest of mankind was swept away in the flood, and it was as if Noah were again the first man. But Noah too disappointed God. He was a drunkard, and his descendants in their rebellious pride built a great tower reaching up to the heavens, so that they might know the mysteries of God and themselves become gods. God punished them by confounding their language so that "they would not understand one another's speech," and "scattered them abroad from thence upon the face of all the earth."

Once more the Almighty was about to bring an end to the human experiment when He offered mankind another hope, perhaps its last. But this time He would place His hope in one family and in the people that would come from it—Abraham, Isaac and Jacob, the children of Israel. They were a small people crushed by slavery and open, perhaps, to His word. He revealed His will to this people at Sinai, transforming them into a kingdom of priests and a holy nation, that through them the world might come to know the Lord and follow His ways. If mankind will accept the Torah, the rabbis taught, the world will survive; but if they will not, it will be turned back into chaos.

Adam failed, Cain failed, Noah failed, the generations of the Tower of Babel failed. Is it so utterly inconceivable that man's last chance was given with the covenant at Sinai? Is it inconceivable to believe that if Judaism and Christianity fail, there will be an end? Ludicrous as this may have sounded a century ago, it does not sound ludicrous at all today. Man has known the teachings of the Bible for more than three thousand years. How much progress has the world made in understanding and obeying that book? Perhaps our Earth will take its place among the others which God was said to have created and destroyed. Perhaps the time of reckoning has come and God is abandoning us to ourselves.

See! the Lord's hand is not too short to save.
Nor His ear too dull to hear;
But your iniquities have been a barrier
Between you and your God.
And your sins have hidden His face,

So that He could not hear you.
For your hands are stained with blood,
And your fingers with iniquity;
Your lips have spoken lies,
And your tongue utters untruths.
There is none who sues honestly,
None who pleads his case truthfully.
But each one trusts in vanity and speaks lies,
Conceives wrong, and brings forth mischief.

Therefore is justice far from us,
And righteousness does not reach us;
We look for light, but lo! darkness,
For rays of dawn, but we walk in gloom.
We grope like blind men along a wall,
Like men without eyes we grope;
We stumble at noonday as in the twilight,
In the strength of manhood we are like the dead.
We growl like bears,
And moan like doves,
And look for redress, but it comes not,
For salvation, but it remains far from us.[1]

What the prophets feared most was God's abandonment of man, the silencing of His voice, the withdrawal of His presence. Perhaps this is the meaning of our time. If man wants to destroy himself, God seems to say, "Let him. I have had enough. I shall try again elsewhere." There is no guarantee that God will intervene to save our world from disaster.

Neither military defense, international agreement or God's miraculous intervention is the solution we are seeking. But this does not mean that there is no solution. There *is* a solution to the problem of nuclear war and the possible end of human life. But it is a radical solution. It must be so. It can only be so. A radical situation demands a radical solution. Nothing short of that will avail. It is in the roots of the human being and the human situation that the solution lies. It is not a political formula, a diplomatic theory, a gospel of economics or a master plan for world government, but something which, on the one hand, reaches beyond them all and, on the other hand, is their foundation, the only real hope for their fulfillment. It goes to the root of them all.

Perhaps the clearest expression of our solution is found in this passage of the Bible:

"I call heaven and earth to witness against you this day, that I have set before thee life and death, and blessing and the curse; therefore choose life, that thou mayest live, thou and thy seed; to love the Lord thy God, to hearken to His voice, and to cleave unto Him; for that is thy life and the length of thy days . . .

[1] Isa. 50:1–11.

" If you obey the commandment of the Lord thy God which I command you this day by loving the Lord thy God, by walking in His ways, and by keeping His commandments . . . , then you shall live and multiply and the Lord thy God will bless you . . .

" But if your heart turns away and you will not hear, but are drawn away to worship other gods and serve them, I declare unto you this day, that you shall surely perish . . ."[2]

These ancient words, hoary with time and memory, were written down in an ancient book by an ancient people who claimed that they were confronted by God and found the truth about man for all time. These simple yet profound words contain the answer we seek. Their meaning is evident. We are placed on earth with freedom of will to choose the evil way or the good way, the blessing or the curse. God urges us to choose the good way, to love the Lord and walk in His ways. For in that way lies life, length of days and blessing. But there is the other way, too, and it is a tempting way, the worship of false gods as the true God, the idols of nature, society and the ego, of man himself. In that way lies the curse and death, for the idol becomes a demon which ultimately destroys those who worship it.

Moses has been right all these years, but the truth of his words has been ignored by the majority of mankind. It seemed perfectly possible in all the ages gone by to swindle, to cheat, to fight, to wage war, to break treaties, to seek power, to deny every law of God and man—and still get along, even to flourish. By and large, in the past, the man who loved God and obeyed His law was rewarded with a joyous life, and, by and large, those who violated God's law inherited misery. But that was only "by and large," and even the lesson of "by and large" did not impress many people, because it seemed easier and more tempting to be one's own god, live for one's own interests and serve one's own welfare. There were also history's Jobs to consider, those whose innocence did not prevent the wrath of sickness, poverty and anguish from reaching them; and the kings and princes and merchants and generals and pirates and gangsters and criminals of all ages to consider, those whose evil deeds, far from bringing them misery, rewarded them with untold wealth, power and pleasure. The world, in the past, has been able to tolerate vast amounts of evil and still maintain itself. But today it has reached the saturation point. This is the unending chasm that divides all that has gone before us from today.

In the past, loving God, walking in His ways and obeying His Commandments, was looked upon as desirable, the proper thing to do. Some even took it seriously and devoted their lives to the service of God; many more took it less seriously, but at least allowed it to play some role in their lives. Still, if there were people who did not walk in God's ways—who defiled, corrupted and oppressed—the world would survive. Today it is quite a different matter. Whether or not men walk in God's ways—whether or not men are criminals or responsible citizens, tyrants or dedicated leaders, corrupt or decent, depraved or exalted—is literally a matter of life and death, of the very survival of the world. Either there will be a change in man's heart or there will be no man nor heart to change!

It almost seems as if the premodern concept of divine reward and punishment for human deeds, which was one of the strongest forces in days gone by to encourage good deeds and prevent evil deeds, has now become reinstated.

[2] Deut. 30:19, 20:15–18.

The fiery threat of Hell which motivated so much of the lives of our ancestors, now, ironically, takes on a new form. There are two differences, however. In the past, the fear of punishment was largely relegated to a future world and, in the opinion of scoffers, was nothing but superstition. Today, fear of physical punishment for man's deeds is moved ahead to our own world, and is a fear that, far from being argued by religious fanatics, is a demonstrated fact in the minds of Nobel-prize-winning physicists.

Nevertheless, I am not arguing that men should love God and obey His Commandments out of fear of punishment alone. This would return us to the argument for preventing war by mutual fear or retaliation. Rather must it awaken us to the terrible relevancy of man's inner life to our outer situation. Indeed nothing—*nothing*—is more relevant to the problem we face than the condition of the human spirit.

It is not as if, down through the ages, man had not endeavored to solve the problems of our world. Man's error was repeated again and over again in a thousand different forms, but in essence it was the same error. It was the error of making relative truths absolute. And each time this happened something fallible and finite, the product of man's mind and hands, was raised to the throne of God Himself and worshipped as God, as absolute. But when a relative good is turned into an absolute, it becomes a demon that carries us away with it. This is the lesson of history.

There is only one way to remember that everything human is dependent or relative, and that is by accepting the Lord of justice and mercy, the Creator of heaven and earth, as our God and our absolute. Then there can be no other gods, and all else is constantly judged in terms of the one absolute.

What gives meaning and usefulness is the simple command of the Bible to love God and walk in His ways. We can exist without skyscrapers and air conditioning, without gas chambers and H-bombs. But we cannot get along without the spiritual source of our existence. The problem is not how to escape civilization—that is impossible—but how to surpass it. It is not enough to say, as is said again and again, that our spiritual progress has not kept up with our technological progress, but rather that our *technological advance has finally reached such a point that virtual spiritual perfection is demanded to harness it to good purposes and prevent it from being used for evil purposes.* This is a dreadful prospect, but it clearly defines our position. Scientific progress has brought us to the spiritual saturation point. And we are not at all ready.

In such a context a strange thing happens. The Bible becomes what it always has been—the most relevant of all books. If man walks in the ways of God, he will have peace and blessing. If man rebels against Him and worships gods of his own—the state, power, the ego—he will have death and the end of the world.

The simple fact is that the ultimate questions of the universe are no longer for the philosopher or the saint. They have become peculiarly relevant to the day-to-day life of every single one of us and to the future of our world. The truth is, of course, that they have always been relevant to our life and our world. But this relevancy, the relevancy of revering God and walking in His ways—rarely apparent in the course of history—has now assumed tremendous significance to millions of minds, and must of necessity become apparent to millions more. It is only a question of time. *Ultimate* issues—good and evil, justice and mercy, the love and law of God—are now *necessary* issues. *Ultimate* concerns are now *immediate* concerns. They are now, perhaps, for the first time in the history of mankind, seen in a new light and from the most practical of vantage points.

What the inescapable facts of our situation are forcing man to understand with merciless pressure is the very meaning of life itself. He soon comes to the solemn and frightening conclusion that life is not simply a game without rules, created solely for his pleasure. He understands that life must be taken *seriously*. That man's actions have *consequences*. That man may be *called to account* for his actions, by overwhelming disaster. That *man himself is only an experiment*, a possibility in time, a colossal gamble in joining the holy and the profane, heaven and earth, angel and animal, infinite and finite, a *divine experiment* with no guarantee of success; and it is precisely this experimental nature of man's existence, which the Bible has always taught, that men everywhere have suddenly become aware of.

What the prophets ranted and raved about some twenty-five hundred years ago—that the murder of the innocent would bring destruction upon nations, that the persecution of a stranger could lead to catastrophe, that hurting an orphan was a crime of cosmic proportions, that despising the poor could cause the heavens to shake, that lies and robbery and crime might shatter the very foundations of the world—was almost always taken by readers to indicate some manner of ecstatic hysteria which was responsible for the cataclysmic conclusions they drew from such insignificant causes. After all, how could good or evil affect the natural order? How could doing wrong jeopardize the existence of the world?

Few people understood in the past that loving God and walking in His ways meant life, while following after the idols of our own creation meant death; that the existence of the world depends on goodness and not steel, on justice and not iron, on mercy and not power. The scientist would no doubt claim that the world stands upon natural law, the philosopher upon reason, the tyrant upon power, the businessman upon profit. But these are not the real foundations of the world; they cannot guarantee the stability and permanence of our society. They are weak, fallible and deceitful. We are now suddenly awakened to the supreme fact: the true foundations of the world are the foundations of the human spirit.

And if there is no change in the heart of man, then it seems as if an end may come to our world as we know it. Does that sound fantastic? It is the plain, simple truth, without embellishment or fancy. How is it possible that we go about our ways so blissfully complacent, so incredibly oblivious to the reality of the age in which we live? Perhaps it is because it is incredible. It is an either-or age. *Either* we transform our inner life—*or* we may perish. Either we get us a new heart—or we may be turned into ashes. Either we destroy the idols we worship—or the end may be upon us. It is a time of such extremes, an eschatological age.

Between man and his world stands that power, peace, and plenty which is the will of God and the presence of God. It is this sense of God's will and God's presence that modern man has lost, sundering himself from the very roots of his existence. The ultimate must once again become real, so that it possesses the strength to transform, interpenetrating the disciplines of our society with new power and new perspective.

To revere God and walk in His ways is, of course, no easy solution. I am not saying that it is, holding a simple formula aloft as the magic removal for all our ills. Far from it. I am only making one claim: that the material world is dependent, in the last analysis, upon the spiritual world, that ultimate realities have become immediate realities, and that our world may be annihilated unless we awake. This is what we face, and these are its consequences:

1. The machinery for instant death for all mankind is now in men's hands.
2. There is no defense.
3. Only the creation of a new society can prevent the use of the bomb and outlaw war.
4. A new society requires a new man who can only become so by revering God and walking in His ways.

THE CRISIS OF RACE

A Theology of Hope for the Black Community

Major J. Jones

Major J. Jones (1920–   ) is president-director of Gammon Theological Seminary, active in numerous academic, church, and community organizations.

THE FUSED CONCEPTS OF HOPE AND REVOLUTION

The current development in the movement toward black awareness has been characterized by a kind of learned hope that presses its adherents, as Christians, to acknowledge the ontological priority of a kind of future mode of black being which has not yet revealed itself in the fullness of maturity. . . . However, it should be made clearer that this hope is currently at the very heart of the mood of black existence.

This is made more true because this hope is akin to the black revolution, whether violent or nonviolent, and it also seeks to make itself known to the nonblack world. Further, hope and revolution are sometimes fused concepts for black people for the simple reason that so many black people do not feel that the two concepts can be separated in a complex, inflexible, fixed, and unchangeable social structure such as ours. Meaningful change is so hard to come by that many have about lost faith in a hope unrelated to violence, revolution, or extreme social pressure.

.   .   .

Above all, it must be said that a black theology of hope, based on the black awareness movement, is not theological in a Moltmann or a Bloch sense of a theology of hope. This is so because the traditional language of theology is not very intelligible to the man in the street, and especially to the current black man of hope. An intelligible black theology of hope has been almost nonexistent, and yet for some time now black Christians have needed to take a look at the problems that might confront any attempts to develop an adequate theology of hope. This is not surprising when we recall that for too long white theologians have been producing systems in which the alien virtues of harmony, order, and stability have been stressed.

It may well be that black people have come to a time when, if the black theologian is to speak to their current conditions, he must at least develop a theology of hope that will embrace in some sense the concept of revolution in its fullest implications. Harvey Cox has seen this problem, which is faced not only by the black Christian in America, but by all Christians. He contends that "we are trying to live in a period of revolution without a theology of revolution. The development of such a theology should be the first item on the theological agenda today."[1] But the average Christian, black or white, might well venture the question of just why do we need a theology of revolution. For many minds such a thought is a terrifying mixture of categories or a confusion of horizons. Indeed, they ask, how can we define a theology of revolution as a theology related to an earthly eschatological hope within the context of our present society?

Within the black community, especially outside the church, there is too little time for the reflective type of theologizing of the past. We have come to a point where there is a tendency to fuse the concepts of hope and revolution. For the average black man in the ghetto, for any theology to be meaningful it must speak to only those factors or actions which are going to help him realize a better day within his lifetime; he would insist that the only time he has is now. In this light, then, there is a very practical reason for the urgent need for a theology of hope that is closely related to revolution. Without such hope, it would seem, the black churchman will be at a total loss about what to do with the concept of revolution for a long time to come. It may be that this is the reason there is such a cry against the black church, the black college, and many other black institutions—they simply have not found adequate words to articulate what they think of the future. It may well be because, as has been said, they have not seen hope as a viable possibility without revolutionary actions that are totally alien to their present mode of thought. Indeed, did the black theologians

---

[1] Harvey Cox, *The Secular City* (New York: Macmillan, 1965), p. 107.

really mean it when they asserted with Eldridge Cleaver: "We shall have our manhood. We shall have it or the earth will be leveled by our efforts to gain it?"[2] One is moved to ask of them whether they are at one with Hannah Arendt in her book *On Revolution*, when she predicts that even though mankind has the good sense to set aside war as an international political instrument, revolutions will continue into the foreseeable future to make this a century of revolution. Then she says that "in the contests which divide the world today, and in which so much is at stake, those will probably win who understand revolution."[3] Black Christians must at least understand revolution, not with the intent to win a political revolution as such, but rather because, if it takes place, they cannot escape accepting or acquiring some responsibility for its outcome. The stakes are always high in revolutionary times—the future of mankind, the scale of justice, the quality of freedom; and ultimately there is at stake the shape of society beyond revolution. Indeed, the ultimate concern of the Christian, black or white, does not lie outside these secular interests; it rather relates to the problem of finding a formative expression through them. No matter what the context, the religious relationship between man and God does run alongside the relationship of both to the world. The commandment to love God has no substance at all apart from love of neighbor. Love of neighbor is always at stake in a revolution.

Though the church is to a large degree responsible for the revolutionary consciousness that is emerging around the world today, the people who seem now to be talking revolution, especially in the black community, are largely nontheological in their views. Thus, their view of revolution has very little of the content of a theology of hope. And yet in many ways whether violent or nonviolent, a theology of hope must be related to a theology of revolution.

In the chapter "The Revolutionary West," in his book *Christianity in World History*, A. T. Van Leeuwen ascribes the revolutionary impulse in the West to the revolutionizing impact of the gospel of the coming kingdom of God.[4] Indirectly the church has sponsored the revolutionary process by preaching a message that sets things in motion by stirring up the imagination, arousing new expectations, and stimulating a crusading zeal to translate hopes—whose realization some would postpone for heaven above—into the social structures of this world. The simple fact of preaching the gospel is itself like putting sticks of explosives into the social structure. The church is indeed responsible for having planted the seed within the beloved structures that it, at the same time, had no desire to explode, since its own privileges were beholden to them. The church has too long preached a gospel of revolution without meaning to do so, and, more than that, without knowing clearly what it was talking about when it mentioned some of the revolutionary themes of the Bible and the Christian faith.

A theology of revolution is made all the more urgent by the additional fact that the Christian churches must repent of the inglorious role they have played in most modern revolutionary situations. While the gospel they preached pointed the way to hope for the future, the institutions they built impeded its coming.

---

[2] Produced by the Committee of Theological Prospectus, June 13, 1969, at the Interdenominational Theological Center, Atlanta, Georgia.

[3] Hannah Arendt, *On Revolution* (New York: Viking Press, 1963), p. 8.

[4] Arend Th. Van Leeuwen, *Christianity in World History*, trans. by H. H. Hoskins (New York: Scribner's, 1966), p. 344.

The white church and the black church have, at times, been at one in proclaiming a revolutionary gospel of equality. Neither one, however, has fully adhered to the reality in the area of race relations. If they had, both now would be more deeply engaged in the black liberation struggle of our time. Hope and revolution must be brought into some kind of understandable relationship.

When we speak specifically of the black church and a theology of hope, we must take a hard look at what revolution means for the black community, for this is where the issue is in such sharp current focus.

First of all, it must be understood that there is a sharp distinction between rebellion and revolution. The aim of a rebellion is to restore what has been lost; the aim of revolution is to create something new. The vision of the radically new, inherent in revolution, is what links revolutionary action to eschatological hope. Revolution is a relevant concept within the context of the black community.

Second, when revolution is mentioned in the black community, it is not confined, and many times not even related, to current theological expressions of hope; it is rather an expression related only to despair and hopelessness. This is why revolution should now be related to a theology of hope, lest we end up with despair and hopelessness.

.   .   .

THE CONFLICTING IDEOLOGIES OF VIOLENCE AND NONVIOLENCE

The black or white Christian theologians who attempt to construct a theology of revolution must face the ultimate risk of whether violence can produce enough good to justify the means. Without exception, any theology of revolution has to face the question whether under any condition, circumstances, or occasion it could ever support theologically or ethically the act of killing a neighbor. For when one enters the political arena, especially the revolutionary political arena, in any way at all, he must cope with the possibility that violence will ensue. Whether the call for revolution be a first or a last resort, the question the black Christian faces, in relation to violence, is whether he can, as a Christian, kill another person. Does killing ever become right in any war, even a "just" war? Whether the killing is intentional or unintentional, the problem is the same for the Christian. Even in contextual or situational ethics, if one is committed to act under the mandate of love for neighbor, the necessity of killing another person is problematic for the Christian. If one is committed to the love of neighbor, then it would seem impossible to reconcile the act of killing the neighbor that one is committed to love. Indeed, is it ever possible to kill a person one is committed by God to love? Is it at all possible for one to give adherence to the concept of the sacredness of persons, and at the same time will the destruction of a person? It would seem that it is impossible for the Christian to answer such questions in the affirmative.

Within this context there has been no attempt to deal with conditions that may, under certain circumstances, make killing necessary. Granted that some wars or revolutions may be just and even necessary. When such action becomes necessary, and the Christian feels that he must not or cannot remain neutral, he must at that point adopt what Paul Ricoeur has called the "ethics of distress,"[5] admitting to himself and to God that his actions beyond this point are not Christian. Such a stance would, it seems, prevent all impossible attempts to construct blanket theological justifications for so much that is wrong with war in general and killing in particular. Violence is necessarily contrary to love.

Indeed, to a black theologian, what is troubling is not that the opinions of Christians, black or white, are changing, or that their opinions are shaped by the current problems of a time—on the contrary, this is as it should be. What is more troubling is that too many Christians conform to the trend of the moment without introducing into it anything specifically Christian. Their ethical convictions are too often determined by their social milieu, not by faith in Christian revelation; they too often lack the uniqueness that ought to be more expressive of their religious faith. Thus, theologies, especially the newer expressions, tend too often to become mere mechanical exercises that justify the positions adopted on grounds that are absolutely not Christian. Much of what is now called theological justification for revolution would bespeak such a trend. Currently black churchmen and black theologians increasingly are finding it hard to resist offering theological justification for views akin to the black racism current within much of the black community. This is not to say that some counter-racism is probably not needed in the black community; it is rather to contend that black theology should not extend justification for it. Yet it is strange how far theologians will go in their attempt to be all things to all kinds of people.

THE HUMANE PRINCIPLE OF REVOLUTION

One finds it hard to disagree that

the humane principle of revolution is this way: the slave revolts against his master. He denies him as a master, but not as a man. For his protest is directed against the master's refusal to treat him as a man. As master and slave, neither is a true man and neither can relate to the other in a humane way. If the denial of the master were total, the slave's revolt would bring nothing new into the world but would exchange the roles of inhumanity. The humane revolution, however, is not out to turn slaves into masters but to abolish the whole master-slave relationship so that in the future men will be able to treat one another as men. If the revolution loses sight of this goal, it becomes nihilistic and forfeits its fascination.[6]

In addition to this interesting exposition of Albert Camus's concept of a humane principle of revolution, Moltmann further contends that under certain conditions the use of revolutionary violence can be justified by humane goals. However, he is not too sure that such justification can be assured, and so he concludes that unless it is possible and assured, "revolutionary violence cannot be made meaningful or appropriate. Unless every possible means is put to use, the revolutionary future is not worth committing oneself to."[7] However, one

[5] See Ricoeur's *History and Truth* (Evanston: Northwestern University Press, 1965), p. 243. Martin E. Marty concurs with this view in *The Search for a Usable Future* (New York: Harper, 1969), p. 115.

[6] Jürgen Moltmann, *Religion, Revolution and the Future*, p. 142.

[7] *Ibid.*, p. 143.

wonders if black theology can embrace Moltmann's position when he advises that "people must be able to combine what they desire with what is objectively possible and what they can subjectively accomplish."[8]

Indeed, if a revolution can be this rational and if the aims can be preconceived, then one wonders if some more rational approach cannot be found than a violent revolution. It would seem that Moltmann is nearer right when he reminds us that

if the revolutionary goal is a more fully realized humanity, then revolutionaries cannot afford to be inhuman during the so-called transitional period. Already, on the way, we must directly begin with the future and make life truly human during the transitional period....

It follows, therefore, that a revolution of the present for the benefit of a better and more humane future must not mold itself after the strategies of the world to be overthrown. Only with great restraint can revolutionaries enter the diabolical circle of violence and counter-violence if they are ever to conquer and abolish it as a whole.... How are we to bring about the kingdom of non-violent brotherhood with the help of violent action?[9]

These words of Moltmann cannot be read without recalling the teachings of Martin Luther King, Jr., for it was he who, perhaps more than many people who talk of revolution today, thought and acted out of a deep dimension of truth which was not dependent on political power and the rules of its games. Too many people could not accept this fact—that his frame of reference was theological, and he was, to a great extent, immune from anxiety and the seduction of political power. Precisely for that reason alone he became more and more in disfavor, and a greater threat to people in positions of great power than even the prophets of violence themselves. In a very real sense, the true revolutionary must not allow the law of the opposition to prescribe his own course of action or response, otherwise he cannot become a part of the new humanity. Any means may be appropriate, but they must be different and better than those of the opposition if they would bewilder the opposition.

TOWARD AN "ETHICS OF DISTRESS"

...There has been little attempt to discuss whether the present social or political systems of the world can or cannot be altered without violence. My main concern has been over the trend of modern theologians to attempt to extend theological or ethical justifications for violent revolution, thus further confusing persons into believing that they are being Christian when indeed they are not. Colin Morris, in his book *Unyoung, Uncolored, Unpoor*, has made a cogent plea for such an unconditional justification, so it might be helpful to assess his basic thesis within this context. He contends that "Christians have both the right and the responsibility to take part in revolution," be it violent or nonviolent in nature. He is right in his assertion that

we weep with pride in the story of Dietrich Bonhoeffer's triumphant death at the hands of the Flossenberg hangman, and pore over his last writings with an eagerness that could not be greater had he handed them out personally to us from the other side of the Beyond. But we scurry quickly away from the tougher truth that he was a justly condemned accessory to murder. Hitler, the main

[8] *Ibid.*, p. 144.
[9] *Ibid.*

target of the plot, indeed survived Stauffenberg's bomb, but others in that map room were destroyed, some of them honorable soldiers. If only Bonhoeffer had lived, we lament, to tell us more about the line of thought sketched out in the startling epigrams of Letters and Papers from Prison. I, for one, believe that his explanation of the theology behind the bomb plot might have more to say to our time. The new theology for which the Church is searching may be hidden in that violent deed of Bonhoeffer's which misfired and not in his musings about God without religion. Any Christian, tasting the sulphur which hangs in the air of our time, could wish for a theology of violence from the pen of a great theologian who dared to strike and paid for his temerity with his life.[10]

In his further contention, Dr. Morris talks about the timing of the Christian's action as being problematic because he has to delay long enough to make sure that the extent of the evil justifies the radical action. The problem is, how long should one delay doing what one feels that he has to do? Hitler should have been cut down sooner, and the six million Jews would have been spared, and the world would not have suffered so greatly at his hands. This is rightly a concern of the Christian. "Bonhoeffer, Stauffenberg, and the rest indeed died to rid the world of a fount of evil. Yet if they had struck ten years earlier, before the smoke and the gas chambers had blackened the sky and Europe's cities were aflame, who knows how history might have been changed?"[11]

One might well accept the actions of Bonhoeffer, one might have agreed with those who plotted Hitler's death, one might also have accepted the fact that Hitler was indeed a "fount of evil"; but to say that even such a great theologian as Bonhoeffer was acting like a Christian is a much deeper question and a much more serious problem. Indeed, it would seem that maybe had he lived he would have admitted that when the group gathered to plot Hitler's death they were not attempting to find theological justification for their actions, because there could be none. But they were honest Christians fully realizing that they were acting without any theological or ethical justification; and had they survived they would have been in need of deep forgiveness for actions that they might well have admitted were not Christian. But nevertheless, theirs were actions which they thought needed to be taken. Are there not times when Christian man

has not to decide simply between right and wrong and between good and evil, but between right and right and between wrong and wrong.... Precisely in this respect responsible action is a free venture; it is not justified by any law; it is performed without any claim to a valid self-justification, and therefore also without any claim to an ultimate valid knowledge of good and evil. Good, as what is responsible, is performed in ignorance of good and in the surrender to God of the deed which has become necessary and which is nevertheless, or for that very reason, free.[12]

It matters not how frustrating the situation may become, it would seem that any lasting solution must be found, especially for the black man, in some approach other than violence, for violence is the very language of the enemy, and against violence he seems to have an adequate response that would assure all rational thinkers that liberation cannot come by the way of violence.

This is not to withdraw from those actions which are necessary to counter the evils of racism, and this is not to rule out the fact that some of these actions may even be violent. It is just to argue that any actions against the enemy should further the cause of freedom, rather than restrict it.

[10] Colin Morris, *Unyoung, Uncolored, Unpoor* (Nashville: Abingdon Press, 1969), p. 24.
[11] *Ibid.*, p. 25.
[12] Dietrich Bonhoeffer, *Ethics*, ed. by Eberhard Bethge and trans. by N. H. Smith (New York: Macmillan, 1955), p. 249.

So the concern here is not with a lack of action, it is rather that actions be seen rationally and honestly for what they are and not justified for what they are not. Thus, an "ethics of distress" is more honest to both self and God. And the lack of success, while engaging in actions that are ill advised, will not commit God to failures for which he may or may not be totally responsible.

Paul Ricoeur, in his book *History and Truth*, has described the violent moment as a time when an ethics of distress is invoked, and such an ethics would suggest that conditions are such that remedies cannot be justified theologically. His contention is that such honesty is better than an ethics or a theology which anticipates the legitimacy either of killing or of a pure passivism and the victim role. There are times, one must agree, when conventional ethical norms cannot be applied, especially in the black community. Indeed, there are situations in which one must do what one must do and then say one's prayers.

The current problem facing the black community is one of change, which will make life bearable for many black people in white America. For the oppressed and for those who appear now to have no hope, there seems to be no way except to embrace violence as a means of social change. To tell them it is futile and that it will bring no real change is an impossible position. They have tried other ways.

They saw the way of nonviolence suffer a bitter blow in the death of Dr. King. They also recall that Stokely Carmichael and H. Rap Brown both were once adherents to the nonviolent way of protest. In later years, they contended on many occasions that nonviolent protest was always met with violence from the white community, which resisted any change whatsoever. Intellectual guerrilla warfare, properly located spokesmen for change, the government, the police forces, all have failed in their support of any great and meaningful change for the vast majority of the black community.

The one question that faces the black community is still whether there are yet more effective nonviolent means for perfecting social change. There are many who still think that all the means have not been exhausted. Vincent Harding contends that massive nonviolent means have not been fully tried, and his is still a strong voice for further exploration of nonviolent means of protest for social change. But there are others, for instance the Black Panthers, who have come to feel that there is no hope short of violent revolution for changing current social structures; it is for them that hope is needed. But, while black Christian radicalism, even if it takes love seriously, forbids participation in violence of any kind, it cannot ever give counsel to the oppressed to be submissive and accepting. Too often in history Christians have betrayed their faith by preaching resignation to the oppressed without giving due attention to the oppressor.

NONVIOLENCE AS A REVOLUTIONARY METHOD

Adherents of the way of nonviolence, whether it be conceived as a methodology or as a way of life, root their actions in a strong Christian belief that one should absorb hatred and transform it through love, that one should endure rather than inflict violence. This basic faith in the nonviolent way leads to two approaches. First, centering on persons, the proponents of nonviolence contend that nonviolence cannot be an external attitude; it must be internalized. It is in being himself at peace that a person becomes peaceful; it is in living by the law and mandate of love that a person becomes capable of manifesting that love; it is through the practice of it in one's personal life that nonviolence spreads to others. Second, it must be recalled that the whole problem of nonviolence comes down to two conclusions: (a) the state must be divested of its instruments of violence, and (b) for their part, proponents of nonviolence must respond to other people's use of violence by nonviolent actions—sacrifice, noncooperation, civil disobedience, etc. Nonviolence has not been tried on a wide scale since Gandhi. No hope for the future, whether with or without violence, can adequately speak to the black community unless it takes seriously the oppressed people's contentions against the oppressors.

On the assumption that the Christian cannot choose the way of violence, the ethics of revolutionary involvement is particularly problematic for those who advocate a nonviolent approach. Especially is it so if they do not believe that military action solves as much as it purports to achieve, and if they further contend that a man does not have a right to arrogate to himself the decision concerning who should live and who should die. The Christian who gives adherence to violence always must run the risk that violence will demand the end to the potentiality of another person, a person who may himself have been able to contribute to the world's good. The black Christian cannot propose to live by any other standard than those ethical principles, or the unconditional mandate of love, if he lives by any principle at all. It would seem that no ethical frame of reference which makes the development rather than the destruction of the person one of its central concerns can adhere to any concept of violent revolution. When the black Christian thinks otherwise, then he must embrace an ethics of distress, admitting that he has passed beyond Christian action. However, for nonviolence, as a method or as a way of life, to work, it would have to be adopted with the belief that: (1) a government can maintain itself without ever using violence against its citizens; (2) there is such a thing as a "just state" that would be sufficient unto itself; (3) the structures of society are still flexible enough for there to be a deep moral ethos that makes society receptive.

Few people of the black community would now accept such a basic presupposition. Most black people with whom one talks are more ready to believe that most levels of white society are ready for what Lerone Bennett calls "confrontation"[13] between the races, and that the majority of the black people know this will mean violence against the black community. Thus, there seems to be little hope for the black man ever retrogressing to the way of nonviolence as a means of protest or revolution.

There is no suggestion in this context that violence should be the methodology now adopted; it is rather to suggest that the "black mood" has created a new man who is through with humiliation, and he is seeking rescue through whatever means necessary, even revolution. This type of revolution is not, and cannot be, a strategy consciously devised. It will grow out of the deep, instinctive expression of human being denied individuality. Such expressions of revolution, violent or nonviolent, can be liberating. Or as Lerone Bennett puts it: "The boundary of freedom is man's power to say 'No!' and whoever refuses to say 'No' involves

---

[13] Lerone Bennett, *Confrontation: Black and White* (Baltimore: Penguin Books, 1966). See also Bennett's *Negro Mood*, p. 95.

himself tragically in his own degradation."[14] From all levels of the black community there will increasingly come the answer "No!" to any type of degrading actions on the part of the white community.

The basic thesis of this book is that such a "No!" does not have to be violent if it is a collective "No!" and if it comes from the lips of a liberated people who really mean "No!" Such an ethos is collecting within the black community; it is the "now" and the "not-yet" facet of the hope that is inherent in the black awareness movement.

The hope within the black awareness movement is theological, because it is, as one can conceive it, under God. . . .

.   .   .

Any Christian hope, current in such a world of despair, must be a hope that has been internalized to the point where it makes of the adherent a new being in the fullest ontological sense. By and large, such a hope must be positive if it is to prove adequate as a foundation for authentic selfhood. While black awareness, as a movement, has not reached its fullest potential, it still is a sufficient concept upon which to build the hope of a people. But too much of the black experience of the past has been articulated in a totally negative literature, while it should have taken on a positive potential. To become a concept of hope, it would seem, the concept of black selfhood must become a forward concept, divesting itself of much of the personal doubts and uncertainties of the past. It must get beyond the bitterness of the past; it must fix on the intentions and possibilities of the future. Black theology, to become a theology of hope, must fix on the forward intentions of the black man. Indeed, is it not true that "whoever does not meet a man at this level of his being knows nothing deeply significant about him. Having met him 'there' everything else about him is stamped with the unique quality of his own transcendence. He is seen no longer as a simple prolongment of his background, but rather is known in his possible surpassingness."[15]

Christian hope is futuristic, then, in the sense that it fixes on the forwardness of selfhood. Heraclitus was right when he reminded us that "he who does not hope for the unexpected, will not find it." Hope alone is called realistic for the simple reason that it alone takes seriously the possibilities with which all reality is fraught. It takes things not as they happen to be, but rather as progressive, moving things with possibilities of change. Only as long as racism exists and peoples of different skins are in a fragmented and, at times, experimental state that is not yet resolved, is there any sense in earthly hope? Black awareness, in its truest sense, anticipates what is possible to reality; historic and moving as it is, those who adhere to the concept are under mandate to use their influence to help decide the processes of the future. Thus the hopes and the anticipations of the future are not a transfiguring glow superimposed upon a darkened existence, as some current black theologians would have us believe, but are realistic ways of perceiving the scope of our possibilities; and as such they set everything in motion and keep it in a state of change. Black people can achieve change. They have a right to hope only if in their eyes the world is full of all kinds of possibilities, namely all the possibilities ordained by the God of hope. Black people

[14] *Ibid.*, p. 256.
[15] Ray L. Hart, *Unfinished Man and the Imagination* (New York: Herder and Herder, 1968), pp. 143–44.

have a right to hope only if they see reality and mankind, white and black, in the hands of him whose voice calls into history from its end, saying, "Behold, I make all things new," and only if, from hearing this word of promise, they acquire the freedom to renew life here and change the face of the earth.

It is true, as Moltmann has suggested, that "the most serious objection to a theology of hope springs not from presumption or despair, for these two basic attitudes of human existence presuppose hope, but the objection to hope arises from the religion of humble acquiescence in the present."[16]

Too much of the literature of the religion of black power, black awareness, and even black theology is void of hope; it is so bogged down in attempting to articulate what is wrong with the lot of the black peoples of the pro-white world that it may forget to ask the question:

Is it not always in the present alone that man is truly existent, real, contemporary with himself, acquiescent and certain? Memory binds him to the past that no longer is. Hope casts him upon the future that is not yet. He remembers having lived, but he does not live. He remembers having loved, but he does not love. He remembers the thoughts of others, but he does not think. It seems to be the same with him in hope. He hopes to live, but he does not live. He expects to be happy one day, and this expectation causes him to pass over the happiness of the present. He is never, in memory and hope, wholly himself and wholly in his present. Always he either limps behind it or hastens ahead of it. Memories and hopes appear to cheat him of the happiness of being undividedly present. They rob him of his present and drag him into times that no longer exist or do not yet exist. They surrender him to the non-existent and abandon him to vanity. For these times subject him to the stream of transience—the stream that sweeps him to annihilation.[17]

Faith in God brings a new dimension to life, a result of the fact that one has tuned in to the nearness of God, for living amid the simple everyday things of today is, of course, living in the fullness of time and in the nearness of God. However, to know the fullness of God is to grasp the never-returning moment, to be wholly at one with oneself, wholly self-possessed and on the mark. He is, as Paul says, the God who raises the dead and calls into being the things that are not (Rom. 4-17). This God is present where we wait in hope upon his prom-ises and transformation. When we have faith in a God who calls into being things that are not, then the things that are not yet, that are the future, become "thinkable" because they can be hoped for.

Under God, there is possible such a positive, forward thrust in black awareness for many reasons. This is what is meant by "being-toward." Man in general, and especially black man now, has his being vouchsafed to him not as a possession but only as a being-toward, which is a positive commitment to what Carl E. Braaten calls "the power of the future."[18]

Christian hope, as it is inherent in black awareness, gives the movement a teleological dimension because of its tendency of being-toward and because of the prospects that such a tendency creates for further actions. Such a tendency, if it is a part of the mind-set of the black mood of thinking, enables the adherent to anticipate the possibilities that the future holds, avoiding either false optimism or premature despair.

[16] Moltmann, *Theology of Hope*, p. 26.
[17] *Ibid.*
[18] See his *Future of God* (New York: Harper, 1969), pp. 59 ff.

Having spoken of the possibilities of black awareness, as a concept that commits its adherents to a teleological future, we must admit that there are certain characteristics that have to be related and explained, if they are to be understood as facets of a theology of hope.

1. First of all, black awareness is humanistic in the Ernst Bloch sense of a theology of hope, and yet it is more than mere humanism or naturalism in relation to the black man's hope under God. While no black theologian knowledgeable of the current aspirations of the black community would ignore the "this-world" concerns of black people's hopes, he could not agree with Bloch when he contends that religion can well be conceived of as mere "meta-religion," inherited and void of a "God-reference" which transcends mere hope or human aspirations.[19] Even in the "religion of black power," as Vincent Harding characterizes it in *The Religious Situation 1968*, there is a strong God-Entity implicit, even if not admitted by many exponents of the ideology.

.   .   .

2. Second, under the mandate of hope, black awareness literature has a strong sense of messianic mission. Whether it is theological or nontheological in nature, there is a sense in which black men think they are called of God to deliver black America from its bondage and white America from its lethal folly. The Marcus Garvey movement seemingly has taken on new life in our time, and it may well be that Ronald Fair is not too far wrong when he contends that "every black man in this country is aware that our time has come." Indeed there is a new wind of freedom astir within the black community so that this current period in history is the fullness of time in many black minds. . . .

.   .   .

3. Third, black awareness is characterized by the lack of a centralized programmatic thrust. At the moment there are many who would offer some type of program under the general label of protest, but there is no one overall civil rights program that now unites all black people and commits them to one way of achieving the white man's acceptance of the black man's full personhood. Even a black theology of hope can but ask, Is this part of the process of coming of age? Is this a part of a coming of age when the black man's struggle must reveal itself in many, many facets, each a part of one total overall thrust of human blackness struggling to be recognized within the context of the family of God? For the black awareness movement, rightly interpreted the emergence of black selfhood—is not to be taken or conceived as a thing in itself; rather it is to be viewed against the background of an emergent community. The Judeo-Christian faith, considering that man, black or white, finds himself in history and on a pilgrimage toward selfhood and community, gives some hints about how men ought to learn to live together while they are realizing that promise. It is never a mandate to self alone; it is always an openness toward others. Selfhood is not self-evidence; in other words, one can be himself only when he has the benefit of a community of judgment. The Christian ethic, when it confers selfhood upon a man, should insist that a realistic self-judgment, the marrow of divine judgment, be part of that selfhood.

.   .   .

[19] See Moltmann's *Religion, Revolution and the Future*, pp. 148 ff.

In the last section on "hopes," in his book *Public Ethics*, James Sellers gives two theological points concerning short-term prospects for the current black theology of hope which should be seen in the light of the tendency toward despair. The first is that history does bring the really new, but never the Kingdom of God in its fullness. "Part of the realization of the promise is in the struggle. Put this way, this is not a sentiment that revolutionaries have usually wanted to reckon with,"[20] and who could blame them. Indeed, history, Sellers further contends, will never change men so much that they are not finite any more, so much that they are not tempted to want more, so much that they can really get interested in the destinies of other men besides themselves. Is that too harsh, one would ask? Sellers thinks not; he cites four great political revolutions of the modern world—the American, the English, the French, and the Russian. He contends that none of them brought enough change, none of them failed to bring some change, but none brought the whole vision to reality. Certainly none of them, according to Sellers, left its beneficiaries able to love one another. . . .

Here is the test to which Christianity and the Christian ethics are put in our time. "If the concept of God has any validity or any use," says Baldwin, "it can only be to make us larger, freer, and more loving. If God cannot do this, then it is time we get rid of Him."[21] That is also to be said of religion itself—this force that seems to be not too far from the heart of every revolution—even the religion of black power, which is especially close to the black revolution. However, sadly, religion is also to be seen at the center of every resistance to the emergence of man, more certain if that which is emerging is new.

4. Finally, no black theologian can miss the fact that we move, as if we were indeed under some power of the future, toward some larger context wherein every person, race, or ethnic group shall take comfort in the fact of separateness and difference. Identity will be no problem, for identity will have been achieved within a climate wherein it will be fully recognized, fully accepted, and fully respected. There will be a pluralism of ideologies, interests, aims and aspirations, and personhood; and no one will for any purpose be denied opportunity to achieve, or be excluded from community.

Such a climate, however, will not exclude the emergence of new concerns, new struggles, new aspirations, and a yearning for even newer levels of maturity. Let this tomorrow, this future day, be nearer the ideal of the Creator of the hope that compels such a dream.

[20] James Sellers, *Public Ethics: American Morals and Manners* (New York: Harper, 1970), p. 309.
[21] Baldwin, *The Fire Next Time* (New York: Dial Press, 1963), p. 119.

Racism as a Form of Idolatry

George D. Kelsey

George D. Kelsey (1910–   ) is an American theologian. He received his Ph.D. at Yale University. He teaches at Drew University Theological School.

Racism is a faith. It is a form of idolatry. It is an abortive search for meaning. In its early modern beginnings, racism was a justficatory device. It did not emerge as a faith. It arose as an ideological justification for the constellations of political and economic power which were expressed in colonialism and slavery. But gradually the idea of the superior race was heightened and deepened in meaning and value so that it pointed beyond the historical structures of relation, in which it emerged, to human existence itself. The alleged superior race became and now persists as a center of value and an object of devotion. Multitudes of men gain their sense of the "power of being" from their membership in the superior race. Accordingly, the most deprived white man, culturally and economically, is able to think of himself as "better'n any nigger."

The purpose of this book is to provide a Christian criticism of racism as a faith system in all of its facets and tendencies. By and large, Christians have failed to recognize racism as an idolatrous faith, even though it poses the problem of idolatry among Christians in a way that no other tendency does. Racism is especially problematical not only because of the peculiar nature of the racist faith, but because it is a "Trojan horse" within organized Christianity and Christian civic communities.

The procedure which is followed ... [here] is that of correlating the questions implied in the racist situation with the relevant answers of the Christian message. The search for meaning is first pursued from the side of racism. This is followed by the elaboration of Christian answers which are related to the situation. The use of the expression "the Christian" ... is done in full acknowledgment that a particular theological point of view is represented.

The Christian faith is brought into dialogue with racism for two reasons. First, I am convinced that Christian faith provides authentic answers to the questions which racism poses but to which racism is able to provide only false answers. Second, racism is a phenomenon of modern Christian civilization. By and large, the people who have been the racists of the modern world have also been Christians or the heirs of Christian civilization. Among large numbers of Christians, racism has been the other faith or one of the other faiths. . . .

The phrase "in-race" refers to the race of the speaker who makes the racist pronouncements or the actor who implements racist aims. The "out-race" is the ethnic group which is vilified, discriminated against, segregated, exterminated, or is to be exterminated in the great "eschatological event." The terms "aggressive racism" or "imperialistic racism" are used to describe white racism or racism in power. Black racism or Black Muslimism is referred to as "counter-racism" because it arises as a racist answer to white "imperialistic racism."

Racism has the character of faith in both its imperialistic and counter-racist forms, but an important distinction between the two must be noted. Imperialistic racism is full-bodied. It can walk on its feet and strike with its fists because its spirit permeates the institutions of power. A race as such lacks centeredness. The racist faith must therefore find its life through the use of political, military, economic, and cultural institutions. White men control the political, military, economic, and cultural institutions. Black men do not. Racism among the former is accordingly imperialistic and aggressive. They are able to project and imple-ment concrete programs of political action while the Black Muslims must substitute eschatology for political action. Black Muslimism is racism out of power.

This difference is important to the analysis found in this book. The form of racism is a naturalistic ontology, but its vital principle is the will to power expres-sed in a political plan of action. Since Black Muslimism lacks power, it is not full-bodied racism. It lacks feet to walk on and fists with which to strike. The spirit is present; the hope is compelling; but the will to power cannot find the institutions of power through which it can express itself. The result of this distinction for this book is the fact that Black Muslimism provides no illustrative material for the study of racism in its most important facet—the plan of political action. ...

RACISM—MODERN PHENOMENON

Racism is a modern phenomenon. It is a product of modern world conditions. It is a system of meaning and value that could only have arisen out of the peculiar conjunction of modern ideas and values with the political, economic, and tech-nological realities of colonialism and slavery. Various forms of groupism appeared on the stage of history prior to the modern period, but none of them was racist.[1] In the late 1880's, the French racist philosopher Vacher de Lapouge wrote, "I am convinced that in the next century millions will cut each other's throats because of one or two degrees more or less of cephalic index."[2] In this statement, Lapouge gave a strictly modern reason for the mutual slaughter of men.

It is often said that racism has been a perennial problem in human history. But those who make this claim employ the concept of race erroneously. They loosely identify the idea of race with tribal, territorial, national, religious, and cultural groups. It is true that ethnocentrism—the belief in the unique value and rightness of one's own group—is universal as well as perennial. But ethno-centrism does not always take the form of racism....

While the late medieval and early modern Church granted the right of

[1] The Hindu caste system of India is frequently identified with the caste practices of modern racism because it maintains itself primarily by direct blood relationship. But the Indian caste order is not based on color or physical characteristics in the sense that its objective is "purity of blood." The aim of the caste order is to preserve the sacred style of life. Sacred duties and ritualistic requirements are correlated with status and rank, and the community is accordingly preserved.

[2] Quoted in Ruth Benedict, *Race: Science and Politics* (rev. ed.; New York, 1947), p. 3.

conquest and enslavement of the heathen, it nevertheless imposed a responsibility with that right. In the fifteenth century Nicholas V issued a papal bull
authorizing the Portuguese "to attack, subject, and reduce to perpetual slavery
the Saracens, pagans, and other enemies of Christ southward of Cape Bojador
and Non, including all the coast of Guinea."[3] The condition attached to this
authorization was that the captives must be converted to Christianity, and
conversion must be followed by manumission. About a century after the bull of
Nicholas V, a memorial of the Archbishop of Valencia was issued to Philip III
of Spain. This memorial reaffirms the "Christian justification for conquest and
enslavement," but it also reflects a new motive. The memorial explicitly affirms
the economic motive in addition to that of conversion to Christianity as a
justification for slavery.

*... Your majesty may, without any scruple of conscience, make slaves of all the Moriscos and may
put them into your own galleys or mines, or sell them to strangers. And as to their children they may
be all sold at good rates here in Spain, which will be so far from being a punishment, that it will be
a mercy to them; since by that means they will all become Christians.... By the holy execution of
which piece of Justice, a great sum of money will flow into your majesty's treasury.[4]...*

Since men are never willing to justify their behavior on the simple claim that
might makes right or that their conduct satisfies their interests and desires, a
new justification for colonialism and slavery was necessary. A ready-made
explanation was at hand. The conquered and enslaved people were dark-skinned.
The conquerors were white. Since the white people possessed a superior economic
and military technology and were therefore able to conquer and enslave the
people of color, it was a simple matter to explain the superiority of the cultural
apparatus in terms of a superior human endowment. In other words, the exploiters
read from right to left—from a cultural effect to a natural or congenital cause.
Thus modern racism emerged as a sort of afterthought, a by-product of the
ideological justification of European political and economic power arrangements
over colored peoples—the justification of a set of advantages that medieval
religious sanctions could no longer sustain.

For this reason, and because racial hostility is most potently manifest on the
political and economic planes, many observers mistakenly assume that racism is
nothing more than a device by which political, economic, and cultural interests
are defended and expanded. Although racism did have its beginnings in a particular constellation of political and economic events in the early modern world, it
has developed into an independent phenomenon, possessing meaning and value
in itself and giving character to all the institutions of some societies. The
cultural phenomenon that made its appearance in modern history as a form of
self-justification and a defense of political and economic interests eventually
became a complete system of meaning, value, and loyalty.

The fact that racism exists alongside other faiths does not make it any less a
faith. Rather, this fact is testimony to the reality of polytheism in the modern age.
In its maturity, racism is not a mere ideology that a political demagogue may be
expected to affirm or deny, depending upon the political situation in which he

[3] Quoted in Ina Corinne Brown, *Race Relations in a Democracy* (New York, 1949), p. 41.
[4] *Ibid.*, p. 42.

finds himself. Racism is a search for meaning. The devotee of the racist faith is as certainly seeking self-identity in his acts of self-exaltation and his self-deifying pronouncements as he is seeking to nullify the selfhood of members of out-races by acts of deprivation and words of vilification.

HUMAN ALIENATION PURELY AND SIMPLY

It is this faith character of racism which makes it the final and complete form of human alienation. Racism is human alienation purely and simply; it is the proto-type of all human alienation. It is the one form of human conflict that divides human beings as human beings. That which the racist glorifies in himself is his being. And that which he scorns and rejects in members of out-races is precisely their human being. Although the racist line of demarcation and hostility in-evitably finds expression through the institutions of society, it is not primarily a cultural, political, or economic boundary. Rather, it is a boundary of estrange-ment in the order of human being as such.

Accordingly, the basic racist affirmation of superiority, on the one hand, and inferiority, on the other, is not an empirical generalization as is commonly supposed. Rather, it is an affirmation concerning the fundamental nature of human beings. It is a declaration of faith that is neither supported nor weakened by any objective body of fact. Racism is an expression of the will to believe. The fundamental racist affirmation is that the in-race is glorious and pure as to its being, and out-races are defective and depraved as to their being. Any statement the racist makes concerning the cultural and political achievement, or potential, of the in-race or the out-races is based on this prior judgment concerning human being.

The claim of the racist that he studies the facts of history and arrives inductively at his generalizations is contradicted by his consistently negative response to contrasting situations. For example, when the racist asserts that Negroes cannot learn to operate complicated machinery or that all Jews are dishonest, instances to the contrary do not disturb his confidence in the truth of these generalizations. His confidence is not disturbed because his assertions are not empirical general-izations. The "facts" which the racist claims to be reading from Negro and Jewish character and behavior are in reality "faith" facts. Declarations of faith do not need to be proved from evidences in the objective world of facts. They do not need to be proved because the devotee of a faith is convinced that his faith assertions are reflections of the fundamental order of reality.

Thus when the racist sees Negroes actually operating complicated machinery he dismisses the meaning of what he sees by pointing out that these particular Negroes are "different." He believes that the place of the Negro is fixed in the fundamental order of reality: his status is not a matter of the accidents of history. And when the racist sees Jews who are honest by every objectively discernible standard available, he is still convinced that Jews are dishonest because the honesty of the Jew is Jewish honesty. To the anti-Semitic consciousness, the honesty of the Jew is not the same as the honesty of the Christian or non-Jew. The honesty of the Jew inheres in the Jewish being. Even the virtue of the Jew is therefore vice because it is his—because it inheres in defective being.

The claim that racism is human alienation purely and simply may be clarified by comparing racial alienation with other forms of human conflict. All other forms of collective hostility are expressions of conflict over some value or interest that exists *between* men. Human groups contend with each other because they cannot agree on the appropriate relationship each has to some value or values. For example, capital and labor struggle over the definition of their respective shares in the distribution of income from a product or a service. They also contend over their respective rights to power of decision in certain areas of economic process. The nations compete and contend against each other for land, minerals, markets, spheres of influence, and political hegemony. Organized religious bodies struggle with each other over the issues of who possesses the truth, of the proper means for its communication, and of the right to propagate it. Racial alienation stands alone among the forms of human conflict as the one form of collective hostility founded in the question of human being as such. A particular conflict among races may involve political or economic interests, but it is not the political or economic interests that make the conflict racial. The conflict is racial because of the racist faith present in the society involved. Numerous political and economic conflicts occur in one and the same society, but they have a racial character only when two or more racially related groups of that society are in contention. Furthermore, racial antipathy exists and persists in the hearts of men who have no contact whatsoever with the objects of their hostility. A popular saying in many suburbs and small towns of America is, "We do not have the problem because we do not have any of them here." The damaging nature of this claim to the very people who utter it is completely overlooked. It means that if any of *them* do show up, we are ready spiritually and politically to send them reeling back where they came from.

CHRISTIAN RACISM IMPLIES A PEJORATIVE JUDGMENT CONCERNING THE ACTION OF GOD

Since racism assumes some segments of humanity to be defective in essential being, and since for Christians all being is from the hand of God, racism alone among the idolatries calls into question the divine creative action. The central claim of the racist is fundamentally a proposition concerning the nature of creation and the action of God rather than a doctrine concerning the nature of man. By implication, one part of the primary racist affirmation is the idea that God has made a creative error in bringing out-races into being. For Christians, the only possible theological alternative to the implication that God has made a creative error is the doctrine that out-races are the victims of a double fall. If the doctrine of the Demiurge had triumphed in Christianity, a third theological ground for explaining the existence of out-races would be available. But in the Gnostic controversies of the early Church the concept of the Demiurge was relegated to the limbo of heresy. In accounting for the origin of out-races, the Black Muslims enjoy a decided advantage over Christian racists. The creation mythology of the Black Muslims contains a Demiurge as the creator of the white man.

While Christian racists never appeal to the notion of the Demiurge to account for the nature of the existence of out-races, the doctrine of a second fall is explicitly enunciated in some naïve and obscurantist circles. The usual form of this theological proposition is the assertion that God himself has condemned Negroes to be "the hewers of the wood and drawers of the water now henceforth and forever" under the curse of Ham. A variation of the doctrine is the notion that Negroes are the descendants of Cain's union with an ape whom Cain, the first criminal, saw fit to marry "in the land of Nod."[5] This means that while the Negro shares the universal condemnation of the human race in Adam, he also bears the added condemnation of God in a special, racial fall. Since no promise of renewal and redemption is ever correlated with this second, special, racial fall, the Negro is a permanent victim of history and ultimately without hope. Whether the defectiveness in the humanity of out-races be an implication of the nature of creation or an explicit affirmation concerning a special, racial fall, the conclusion cannot be avoided that the action of God is the primary point of reference for Christian racists.

THE FAITH CHARACTER OF RACISM

As a doctrine concerning the fundamental nature of human beings and a way of life elaborated on that doctrine, racism is a faith. H. Richard Niebuhr defines faith as "trust in that which gives value to the self," on the one hand; and on the other, "it is loyalty to what the self values."[6] It is in this sense that we speak of the racist faith.

In the experience of faith, the devotee has a double relation to the object of faith. He trusts in it as the source of his personal value, and at the same time he is loyal to the object of his faith for the value it possesses independent of himself. Niebuhr illustrates this double relation in the life of the patriot whose faith is nationalism. The experience of the racist corresponds to that of the patriot, with the difference that the racist deifies his own being rather than an objective historic structure. The racist relies on the race as the source of his personal value. His life has meaning and worth because it is a part of the racial context. It fits into and merges with a valuable whole, the race. As the value-center, the race is the source of value, and it is at the same time the object of value. No questions can be raised about the rightness or wrongness of the race; it is the value-center which throws light on all other value. Criminals, degenerates, and even enemies have worth and goodness if they are members of the in-race. They have a goodness and worth which is not found in the most noble character of members of out-races, for goodness and worth are only secondarily qualities of behavior and character. Primarily they are qualities of being. Goodness and worth inhere in being that is worthy. If noble character inheres in a racially defective being, that person of noble character is nonetheless depraved, for the nobility he has achieved inheres in his unalterably corrupt humanity....

When the racist is also a Christian, which is often the case in America, he is frequently a polytheist. Historically, in polytheistic faiths, various gods have controlled various spheres of authority. Thus a Christian racist may think he

[5] The idea of a racial fall is also ascribed to the Jews. It is the view, held by some Christians, that since the Jews are the chosen people, God has punished them and will continue to punish them until they acknowledge the Messiah. Thus the persecutions of Jews by Christians are preordained.

[6] H. Richard Niebuhr, *Radical Monotheism and Western Culture* (New York, 1960), p. 16.

lives under the requirements of the God of biblical faith in most areas of his life, but whenever matters of race impinge on his life, in every area so affected, the idol of race determines his attitude, decision, and action.

Polytheistic faith has been nowhere more evident than in that sizable group of Christians who take the position that racial traditions and practices in America are in no sense a religious matter. These people assert that the whole field of race relations is an area with which religion has nothing to do. When pressed for a positive statement of the matter, they say that segregationist racial practices are merely amoral expressions of private preference. They completely overlook the fact that race relations are structured as a system which is not only enforced by the social mores but by institutional policy over all the country, and in some sections of the country, by law and public policy as well. The judgment that race relations involve amoral forms of behavior means in effect that interracial attitudes and practices are beyond the reach of Christian moral ideas and norms. The presence of polytheism among the adherents of the greatest monotheistic religion is not shocking in view of the insights of that very religion concerning original sin. The Old Testament provides ample historical evidence of man's continuous effort to restrict the Covenant of the Lord so that he may pursue certain interests and values as he sees fit. The prophetic tradition makes it equally clear that the only alternative to the worship of and obedience to the Lord God Jehovah is devotion to the Baals of the Canaanites.

It is an anomaly that morally concerned Christian leaders have rarely understood racism for what it really is. For a long time racist ideas and practices were viewed by morally sensitive Christians as nothing more than expressions of cultural lag and as products of ignorance. Since racial hostility is one of the forms of human conflict, many Christians have sought to understand racism wholly in terms of political, economic, and cultural factors. They have not seen the faith character of racist devotion and commitment, nor that racial antipathy is conflict in the order of humanity. A probable explanation of this peculiar state of affairs is that modern Christianity and Christian civilization have domesticated racism so thoroughly that most Christians stand too close to assess it properly.

THE MEANING OF RACISM

The faith character of racism may be fully disclosed by an analysis of its various facets. In her *Race: Science and Politics*, Ruth Benedict defines racism as

the dogma that one ethnic group is condemned by Nature to hereditary inferiority and another group is destined to hereditary superiority. It is the dogma that the hope of civilization depends upon eliminating some races and keeping others pure. It is the dogma that one race has carried progress throughout human history and can alone ensure future progress.[7]

From this definition, it may be seen first of all that racism is a form of naturalism. Man owes his existence to nature and nature controls his destiny. Nature has condemned inferior races and blessed the superior race. This means that the fundamental thing about a man is his body, specifically his genetic

[7] Benedict, *op. cit.*, p. 98.

structure. Mental and spiritual qualities depend upon the natural quality, and are, in fact, but expressions of it.

This naturalistic view of man is diametrically opposed to the biblical doctrine of the creation of man in the image of God; it is also opposed to the main tendencies in the development of Western philosophy. One of the great anomalies of our time is the fact that the racist ideology has taken so firm a grasp upon the heirs of both traditions, and has emerged in the modern world which is precisely that world wherein philosophy and theology broke their esoteric bonds, and became widely available, at least in their main ideas, through popular education.

It must be observed that not all people who understand man naturalistically in the context of race relations subscribe to the naturalistic doctrine in general. Some Christians would be horrified to discover that they really believe in a naturalistic view of man when race relations call for decision and action. If told that this is the case, they will vigorously deny it. Many of them are quite orthodox in their theology and even literalistic in their approach to the Bible. In the abstract, they constantly repeat the phrase that God has created all men in His own image. In the abstract, they believe that the essence of man is spirit. But when they actually view the races in relation to each other, or make social and political decisions concerning race, they bring judgments to bear upon the situation which clearly indicate their belief that the races are poles apart in the order of humanity and that the ground of the great human differences lies in the genes.

The fact that racist claims are affirmations concerning the fundamental nature of humanity, rather than empirical generalizations as they are popularly thought to be, may be made more evident by a few illustrations. During the last war, General J. L. DeWitt was in charge of the evacuation of naturalized Japanese from California. General DeWitt made the following statement concerning Japanese Americans: "A Jap's a Jap.... It makes no difference whether he is an American citizen or not.... I don't want any of them here.... They are a dangerous element.... There is no way to determine their loyalty."[8] In another statement, General DeWitt made it unqualifiedly clear that the element which he regarded as evil within the Japanese character is incorrigible because it is rooted in the genetic structure. "The Japanese race is an enemy race and while many second and third generation Japanese born on United States soil, possessed of United States citizenship, have been 'Americanized' the racial strains are undiluted."[9] ...

KNOWLEDGE OF THE SELF IN ANTITHETICAL RELATION TO THE OTHER

The racist consciousness operates in what Martin Buber has called "the World of It."[10] The World of It is the world of objects and things. In this world there is a single center of consciousness. This single subject, the "I," experiences, arranges, and appropriates. It does not enter into relationship with other, differ-

[8] U.S. Army, Western Defense Command and Fourth Army, Final Report, Japanese Evacuation from the West Coast, 1942 (Washington, D.C., Government Printing Office, 1943), p. 34; quoted in Charles Abrams, *Forbidden Neighbors* (New York, 1955), p. 41.
[9] *Ibid.*
[10] Martin Buber, *I and Thou*, trans. Ronald Gregor Smith (New York, 1937).

ent beings. It experiences human beings racially different from itself only as "the other," as antithetical to the self in the order of humanity. The "I" self "knows" itself as pure being while it "knows" the other as depraved being. The "I" self does not enter into communion with the other, for the other is not known as "Thou." The other is first, last, and always "It." The other is an object to be used, manipulated, or eliminated. But since the other in fact belongs to the order of human being, and not merely to the animal kingdom, the relation of the self to the other is on a different plane than the relation of the self to the worlds of animality and nature. The self is aware that the other is in some sense a center of consciousness. The fact that the other in some way belongs on the same plane with the self will not down. The radical contrast between the self and the other can therefore be expressed only in polar terms. The racist consciousness knows itself in contrast, in polarity with and opposition to the racially contemptible object. This means that in the racial context, the racist cannot know himself until he first knows the other. The racist is completely dependent upon the antithetical correlation. When the other is properly experienced, appropriated, and arranged, the racist consciousness can know itself as the other pole in a structure of human contrasts.

The idea that the Negro appears in the anti-Negro consciousness as a contrast conception was ably presented by Lewis Copeland about a generation ago, but very little has been made of this notion in the literature of race relations. Copeland found the social opposition between Negroes and whites so sharp as to give rise to a conceptual dichotomy "somewhat analogous to that between God and the devil in popular religion."[11] And just as in popular religion the contrast between God and the devil introduces a dichotomy which is conceived as running through the whole universe, dividing both the natural world and the social order, the counterconcepts of the racist consciousness "form the basis for the interpretation of human nature and society."[12]

The idea of the contrast conception as a basic constituent of the racist self-consciousness seems to have originated with Erich Voegelin. In his *Rasse und Staat*, Voegelin develops the thesis that Judaism in Christian Germany is a counterconception. Likewise, Jean-Paul Sartre, writing on French anti-Semitism, designates the Jew as a contrast conception. When the anti-Semite speaks of Jewish avarice, says Sartre, he means there is a "Jewish" avarice, an avarice determined by that synthetic whole, the Jewish person. This avarice is different from Christian avarice. It is not the universal, human trait of avarice, but an avarice which emerges from a unique synthesis, the Jewish being.

In popular thought in America, black and white have become conceptual opposites.

The black man and his appurtenances stand at the antithesis of the character and properties of the white man. The conception makes of the Negro a counter-race. The black race serves as a foil for the white race, by which the character of the latter is made all the more impressive.[13]

The antipodal positions of the two races are often verbalized in the phrase "the opposite race." In its fullest meaning, the word "opposite" is a reference to more

[11] Lewis C. Copeland, "The Negro as a Contrast Conception," in Edgar T. Thompson, ed., *Race Relations and the Race Problem* (Durham, N.C., 1939), p. 152.
[12] *Ibid.*
[13] Copeland, *op. cit.*, p. 153.

than the extremes of color. It suggests the two opposites of human being. An examination of the counter-racist consciousness discloses the same element. Eric Lincoln writes:

> To a great extent the Muslims define their movement by negative contrast to their most important audiences; Negroes, Jews, the orthodox Moslems in America and the hated whites. They assert their strength and purity by castigating the weakness and depravity they claim to see among these strangers.[14]

To the Black Muslim, knowledge of the self has its corollary in "the truth about the white man."[15] The Black Muslim therefore cannot "know" himself until he first "knows" the white man. Knowledge of "the truth about the white man" produces knowledge of the self as the opposite in the order of human being....

THE CHRISTIAN DOCTRINE OF EQUALITY

The Christian doctrine of equality is an affirmation of faith. It is not a perception of sight. It is an affirmation of faith because it relates solely to the action of God, and not to the achievements of men or to any intrinsic quality which men may possess. Men are equal because God has created them in His own image and called them to sonship. The Christian doctrine of equality does not draw at all upon measurements of talent and merit. It is a doctrine concerning the creative gift of God.

There is ample evidence in history that men are unequal in knowledge, skill, power, and cultural achievements in general. Most of life is organized and proceeds on the assumption of these inequalities. Men of sight, rather than faith, are obviously much more impressed and influenced by historically conditioned and structured inequalities than by any doctrines of equality, philosophical or theological. But the conviction that men are equal in some fundamental sense has not been destroyed in the West, despite the ideological claims to the contrary or widespread practices that belie the idea. The Western democracies have developed a relatively high degree of political equalitarianism at the very moment in history when disproportions of power, wealth, knowledge, and skill are great and numerous as never before. An important influence in this development has been Christian teachings concerning man.

When Christian faith speaks of equality, it refers to the action and purpose of God. God has created all men in His own image and called all men to the same destiny. The decision as to whether or not men are equal cannot be made by looking at men; he who would decide must look at God. God alone is the source of human dignity. All men are equal because God has bestowed upon all the very same dignity. He has created them in His own image and herein lies their dignity. Human dignity is not an achievement, nor is it an intrinsic quality; it is a gift, a bestowal. Christian faith asserts that men are equally human; all are creatures and all are potentially spiritual sons of God. Variations in the talents and skills of culture rest upon this fundamental humanness.

[14] Eric Lincoln, *The Black Muslims in America* (Boston, 1961), p. 135.
[15] *Ibid.*, p. 190.

Thus Christian faith affirms the unity of mankind. The idea of the unity of mankind is another way of expressing the essential likeness of man. Modern science supports the claim of biblical faith that mankind is a unity, but it is not upon empirical evidence that the biblical conviction is based. The conviction of faith is independent of all scientific results because creation stands above the historical and empirical planes.

The religious belief in the unity of the human race through the Creation, in and for the Divine image, is completely independent of all biological, palaeontological, scientific results. The story of Adam in Genesis expresses, in historical form, it is true, a fact which in itself is super-empirical and super-historical; the biological genealogical question has very little to do with belief in the unity of the creation.... The unity of the divine creation of man lies upon a quite different plane. Humanity is not necessarily a unity from a zoological point of view; it may indeed be composed of different species of differing origin or it may not. It is, however, beyond all doubt a unity, a humanitas, "through" the humanum, its one origin and its one destiny in God's creative Word and plan of salvation, spiritually given to man by God himself.[16]

It is upon the foundation of the equal humanness of men that democratic rights are established. The American Declaration of Independence asserts that "all men are created equal." This proposition was never intended to mean that all men are equal in capacity, knowledge, and skill. Yet it does have concrete political significance. It means that there are some rights that belong to persons as persons, as creatures of God. These rights are said to be inalienable for the very reason that they belong to every person as a person. They can no more be transferred from one person to another than personhood itself can be transferred. And to deny these rights is identical with denying the reality of the person. Inalienable rights are primal. They exist prior to the performance of any function, and are the foundation upon which all secondary and derived rights are elaborated. The rights of the individual as man are primary and unique. All particularized rights are secondary and derived. They derive from the social organization of life and belong to persons only in the exercise of their particular technical, professional, and institutional functions.

Not only does the idea of equal human dignity place the stress on the likeness and unity of mankind and thus constitute the foundation for all assessment of human rights; it also combines harmoniously with unlikeness and inequality. The essential rights of the individual are primary and universal; but individual rights combine harmoniously with derived and differentiated rights relating to historic function because individuality and community are equally original in God's creative act. Man is the covenant-partner of God and of man from the creation. But each man is also created a unique being, with his own individuality. Thus equal dignity and likeness are united with individuality and unlikeness in the Christian doctrine of creation.

The Christian doctrine of individuality and unlikeness is radically opposed to racist particularism. In the Christian idea, individuality means unlikeness and inequality in community. But in the racist idea, individuality does not exist: the individual is made faceless in a homogeneized collectivity. Unlikeness and inequality are alleged to be characteristics of racial collectivities rather than individuals. While even the racist is obliged to admit the reality of inequality and

[16] Emil Brunner, *Man in Revolt*, trans. Olive Wyon (London, 1939), p. 333.

unlikeness within races, it is only the alleged inequalities between races that have significance for him. Christian faith knows of unlikeness and inequality only as between individuals. But since individuality is always related to community which is also original in God's plan for man, inequality and equality are harmoniously combined.

The Christian conception of equality is inseparable from the idea of person in community. The two elements of equality and inequality, of equal dignity and different function, are both fully expressed. They are brought together in the Christian idea of communion. The fact that men are different from each other means that they are dependent on each other. In a Christian community, men will to serve each other in their mutual dependence. The one recognizes his dependence upon the other, no matter how lowly the occupation of the other may be in the eyes of the world. There are so many respects in which one man may be superior or inferior to another that there is probably no man who is superior or inferior to another in every respect. The unity of mankind is made the more manifest by the inequalities which have their basis in individuality.

The Christian idea of the unity of mankind finds concrete expression in societies of mutual cooperation and helpfulness. Differences of function create of necessity variations in status and role in institutional structures. But the roles and statuses in these institutions are assigned on the strength of real individual differences. They are not, as in racism, based upon hostile power arrangements, upon the results of previous discriminations, or upon invidious comparisons that falsify the nature of man as a creature of God....

DESEGREGATION AND INTEGRATION

In the field of race relations, American society is in a state of flux. Within the last decade, social change in this field has reached revolutionary proportions. Since American society is, and has been to a great degree, a color-caste society, the terms "desegregation" and "integration" are now in constant use. These terms belong together, but they do not mean the same thing. Desegregation refers to a process—the elimination of compulsory segregation. Desegregation may be voluntary or involuntary. It is voluntary when those who administer and make the policies in an institution freely decide to change its policy from one of racial exclusivism to one of racial inclusivism. It is involuntary when law, judicial decision, or public pressure requires such a change. Integration refers to a realized condition of community, involving mutuality, reciprocity, and respect among persons. Integration is voluntary and spiritual. The two terms belong together because in a racially segregated society, by and large, people of different racial groups lack the simple conditions and experience of togetherness upon which integration can exist without the prior process of desegregation.

Desegregation is referred to as a prior process because the mere "mixing" of the races is not integration. There is much desegregation in the United States outside the South but little integration. Integration requires more of persons than the mere removal of the external barriers and distances that separate them. But the transition from a segregated to an integrated society cannot be made without the process of removing the external barriers. The simple experiences of doing things together, such as working, playing, learning, etc., provide the foundation upon which genuine community can grow.

A society may be referred to as integrated when it has become a community of persons.

In the deepest sense, integration has taken place only when those of another race or class are accepted as full and equal partners in a common task. It is based on mutual respect and on a sense of the dignity and worth of the human person.[17]

An integrated society is one in which there is both a sense of and a will toward the common good. The common good is received through and communicated by persons. This means that an integrated society is one in which the individual person comes alive. It is not really the group which accepts or respects another group; it is, rather, a community of persons who accept and respect each other. In such a society, all definitions of function and opportunity presuppose the equal dignity of persons. Men are thus able in defining tasks to focus on those qualities of the individual person which are really related to performance; namely talent, training, knowledge, and skill. Extraneous issues, such as the question, "Who is your mother?" do not enter into the decision as to whether a man shall be permitted to study law in the state university. His admission to the law school rests on such criteria as his individual character, ability, and the quality of his prelegal training. And these are precisely the same criteria which every other person must individually meet in the society.

An integrated society in no sense reduces the individual. It is the one society in which a person can at all times be a person. In racially segregated society, parochialism and prideful separation are normative values. Lest some people fail to interiorize these values, they are forced by law and custom to "keep step" in their external behavior. Thus a white man is required by law to relate to a Negro as a white man; he is not permitted to relate to him as a creature of God or as a religiously committed person. Obviously, the same law regulates the goings, comings, and doings of the Negro, except that it specifies that he remain "outside" or "beneath," in all matters, pertaining to the larger society. To dare to act in a legally segregated society as a member of a more universal community of love than a racial community can provide is often to court imprisonment. An integrated society is, on the contrary, a community in which persons have become persons. They remain persons in all their relationships, for even professional and technical functions are exercised by persons.

The objection may rightly be raised that an authentic community of persons does not exist anywhere on a large scale; and accordingly, a truly integrated society, with or without a history of racial alienation, is an ideal. But to say this is not to dismiss such a society as a human and Christian requirement. Man never fully achieves any of his ideals that have the quality of the transcendent, but they are nevertheless incumbent upon him. In truth, an authentic community of persons would be a society of pure persons in which "the good of society and the good of each person would be one and the same good."[18] Although such a society is never fully realized, nevertheless it can be in process of realization if its ideal of the common good is informed and urged by that which transcends itself.

A society is integrated and is a genuine community of persons when it exists

---

[17] Maston, *op. cit.*, p. 63.
[18] Jacques Maritain, *The Person and the Common Good* (New York, 1947), p. 50.

under God in fact. The community of persons is found in the common bond of the Spirit. The common good of society escapes every form of particularism—racial, class, religious, or otherwise—because the center of meaning and value transcends the society.

THE CRISIS OF ECOLOGY

Ecology and Man
Paul Shepard

Paul Shepard (1925–   ) is on the faculty at Williams College, Williamstown, Massachusetts. He is author of *Man in the Landscape*.

Ecology is sometimes characterized as the study of a natural "web of life." It would follow that man is somewhere in the web or that he in fact manipulates its strands, exemplifying what Thomas Huxley called "man's place in nature." But the image of a web is too meager and simple for the reality. A web is flat and finished and has the mortal frailty of the individual spider. Although elastic, it has insufficient depth. However solid to the touch of the spider, for us it fails to denote the *eikos*—the habitation—and to suggest the enduring integration of the primitive Greek domicile with its sacred hearth, bonding the earth to all aspects of society.

Ecology deals with organisms in an environment and with the processes that link organism and place. But ecology as such cannot be studied, only organisms, earth, air, and sea can be studied. It is not a discipline: there is no body of thought and technique which frames an ecology of man.[1] It must be therefore a scope or a way of seeing. Such a *perspective* on the human situation is very old and has been part of philosophy and art for thousands of years. It badly needs attention and revival.

Man is in the world and his ecology is the nature of that *inness*. He is in the world as in a room, and in transcience, as in the belly of a tiger or in love. What

From Paul Shepard, "Ecology and Man—A Viewpoint," in *The Subversive Science: Essays Toward an Ecology of Man,* ed. by Paul Shepard and Daniel McKinley (Boston, 1969), pp. 1–10. Reprinted by permission of the publisher, Houghton Mifflin Company.

[1] There is a branch of sociology called Human Ecology, but it is mostly about urban geography.

does he do there in nature? What does nature do there *in him*? What is the nature of the transaction? Biology tells us that the transaction is always circular, always a mutual feedback. Human ecology cannot be limited strictly to biological concepts, but it cannot ignore them. It cannot even transcend them. It emerges from biological reality and grows from the fact of interconnection as a general principle of life. It must take a long view of human life and nature as they form a mesh or pattern going beyond historical time and beyond the conceptual bounds of other humane studies. As a natural history of what it means to be human, ecology might proceed the same way one would define a stomach, for example, by attention to its nervous and circulatory connections as well as its entrance, exit, and muscular walls.

Many educated people today believe that only what is unique to the individual is important or creative, and turn away from talk of populations and species as they would from talk of the masses. I once knew a director of a wealthy conservation foundation who had misgivings about the approach of ecology to urgent environmental problems in America because its concepts of communities and systems seemed to discount the individual. Communities to him suggested only followers, gray masses without the tradition of the individual. He looked instead—or in reaction—to the profit motive and capitalistic formulas, in terms of efficiency, investment, and production. It seemed to me that he had missed a singular opportunity. He had shied from the very aspect of the world now beginning to interest industry, business, and technology as the biological basis of their —and our—affluence, and which his foundation could have shown to be the ultimate basis of all economics.

Individual man *has* his particular integrity, to be sure. Oak trees, even mountains, have selves or integrities too (a poor word for my meaning, but it will have to do). To our knowledge, those other forms are not troubled by seeing themselves in more than one way, as man is. In one aspect the self is an arrangement of organs, feelings, and thoughts—a "me"—surrounded by a hard body boundary: skin, clothes, and insular habits. This idea needs no defense. It is conferred on us by the whole history of our civilization. Its virtue is verified by our affluence. The alternative is a self as a center of organization, constantly drawing on and influencing the surroundings, whose skin and behavior are soft zones contacting the world instead of excluding it. Both views are real and their reciprocity significant. We need them both to have a healthy social and human maturity.

The second view—that of relatedness of the self—has been given short shrift. Attitudes toward ourselves do not change easily. The conventional image of a man, like that of the heraldic lion, is iconographic; its outlines are stylized to fit the fixed curves of our vision. We are hidden from ourselves by habits of perception. Because we learn to talk at the same time we learn to think, our language, for example, encourages us to see ourselves—or a plant or animal— as an isolated sack, a thing, a contained self. Ecological thinking, on the other hand, requires a kind of vision across boundaries. The epidermis of the skin is ecologically like a pond surface or a forest soil, not a shell so much as a delicate interpenetration. It reveals the self ennobled and extended rather than threatened as part of the landscape and the ecosystem, because the beauty and complexity of nature are continuous with ourselves.

And so ecology as applied to man faces the task of renewing a balanced view where now there is man-centeredness, even pathology of isolation and fear. It implies that we must find room in "our" world for all plants and animals, even for their otherness and their opposition. It further implies exploration and openness across an inner boundary—an ego boundary—and appreciative understanding of the animal in ourselves which our heritage of Platonism, Christian morbidity, duality, and mechanism has long held repellent and degrading. The older counter-currents—relics of pagan myth, the universal application of Christian compassion, philosophical naturalism, nature romanticism and pantheism—have been swept away, leaving only odd bits of wreckage. Now we find ourselves in a deteriorating environment which breeds aggressiveness and hostility toward ourselves and our world.

How simple our relationship to nature would be if we only had to choose between protecting our natural home and destroying it. Most of our efforts to provide for the natural in our philosophy have failed—run aground on their own determination to work out a peace at arm's length. Our harsh reaction against the peaceable kingdom of sentimental romanticism was evoked partly by the tone of its dulcet façade but also by the disillusion to which it led. Natural dependence and contingency suggest togetherness and emotional surrender to mass behavior and other lowest common denominators. The environmentalists matching culture and geography provoke outrage for their over-simple theories of cause and effect, against the sciences which sponsor them and even against a natural world in which the theories may or may not be true. Our historical disappointment in the nature of nature has created a cold climate for ecologists who assert once again that we are limited and obligated. Somehow they must manage in spite of the chill to reach the centers of humanism and technology, to convey there a sense of our place in a universal vascular system without depriving us of our self-esteem and confidence.

Their message is not, after all, all bad news. Our natural affiliations define and illumine freedom instead of denying it. They demonstrate it better than any dialectic. Being more enduring than we individuals, ecological patterns—spatial distributions, symbioses, the streams of energy and matter and communication —create among individuals the tensions and polarities so different from dichotomy and separateness. The responses, or what theologians call "the sensibilities" of creatures (including ourselves) to such arrangements grow in part from a healthy union of the two kinds of self already mentioned, one emphasizing integrity, the other relatedness. But it goes beyond that to something better known to 12th century Europeans or Paleolithic hunters than to ourselves. If nature is not a prison and earth a shoddy way-station, we must find the faith and force to affirm its metabolism as our own—or rather, our own as part of it. To do so means nothing less than a shift in our whole frame of reference and our attitude towards life itself, a wider perception of the landscape as a creative, harmonious being where relationships of things are as real as the things. Without losing our sense of a great human destiny and without intellectual surrender, we must affirm that the world is a being, a part of our own body.[2]

Such a being may be called an ecosystem or simply a forest or landscape. Its members are engaged in a kind of choreography of materials and energy and

[2] See Alan Watts, "The World is Your Body," in *The Book on the Taboo Against Knowing Who You Are* (New York: Pantheon Books, 1966).

information, the creation of order and organization. (Analogy to corporate organization here is misleading, for the distinction between social (one species) and ecological (many species) is fundamental.) The pond is an example. Its ecology includes all events: the conversion of sunlight to food and the food-chains within and around it, man drinking, bathing, fishing, plowing the slopes of the watershed, drawing a picture of it, and formulating theories about the world based on what he sees in the pond. He and all the other organisms at and in the pond act upon one another, engage the earth and atmosphere, and are linked to other ponds by a network of connections like the threads of protoplasm connecting cells in living tissues.

The elegance of such systems and delicacy of equilibrium are the outcome of a long evolution of interdependence. Even society, mind and culture are parts of that evolution. There is an essential relationship between them and the natural habitat: that is, between the emergence of higher primates and flowering plants, pollinating insects, seeds, humus, and arboreal life. It is unlikely that a man-like creature could arise by any other means than a long arboreal sojourn following and followed by a time of terrestriality. The fruit's complex construction and the mammalian brain are twin offspring of the maturing earth, impossible, even meaningless, without the deepening soil and the mutual development of savannas and their faunas in the last geological epoch. Internal complexity, as the mind of a primate, is an extension of natural complexity, measured by the variety of plants and animals and the variety of nerve cells—organic extensions of each other.

The exuberance of kinds as the setting in which a good mind could evolve (to deal with a complex world) was not only a past condition. Man did not arrive in the world as though disembarking from a train in the city. He continues to arrive, somewhat like the birth of art, a train in Roger Fry's definition, passing through many stations, none of which is wholly left behind. This idea of natural complexity as a counterpart to human intricacy is central to an ecology of man. The creation of order, of which man is an example, is realized also in the number of species and habitats, an abundance of landscapes, lush and poor. Even deserts and tundras increase the planetary opulence. Curiously, only man and possibly a few birds can appreciate this opulence, being the world's travelers. Reduction of this variegation would, by extension then, be an amputation of man. To convert all "wastes"—all deserts, estuaries, tundras, ice-fields, marshes, steppes and moors—into cultivated fields and cities would impoverish rather than enrich life esthetically as well as ecologically. By esthetically, I do not mean that weasel term connoting the pleasure of baubles. We have diverted ourselves with litter-bug campaigns and greenbelts in the name of esthetics while the fabric of our very environment is unravelling. In the name of conservation, too, such things are done, so that conservation becomes ambiguous. Nature is a funda-mental "resource" to be sustained for our own well-being. But it loses in the translation into usable energy and commodities. Ecology may testify as often against our uses of the world, even against conservation techniques of control and management for sustained yield, as it does for them. Although ecology may be treated as a science, its greater and overriding wisdom is universal.

That wisdom can be approached mathematically, chemically, or it can be danced or told as a myth. It has been embodied in widely scattered economically different cultures. It is manifest, for example, among pre-Classical Greeks, in

Navajo religion and social orientation, in Romantic poetry of the 18th and 19th centuries, in Chinese landscape painting of the 11th century, in current White-headian philosophy, in Zen Buddhism, in the world view of the cult of the Cretan Great Mother, in the ceremonials of Bushman hunters, and in the medieval Christian metaphysics of light. What is common among all of them is a deep sense of engagement with the landscape, with profound connections to sur-roundings and to natural processes central to all life.

It is difficult in our language even to describe that sense. English becomes imprecise or mystical—and therefore suspicious—as it struggles with "process" thought. Its noun and verb organization shapes a divided world of static doers separate from the doing. It belongs to an idiom of social hierarchy in which all nature is made to mimic man. The living world is perceived in that idiom as an upright ladder, a "great chain of being," an image which seems at first ecological but is basically rigid, linear, condescending, lacking humility and love of otherness.

We are all familiar from childhood with its classifications of everything on a scale from the lowest to the highest: inanimate matter/vegetative life/lower animals/higher animals/men/angels/gods. It ranks animals themselves in categories of increasing good: the vicious and lowly parasites, pathogens and predators/the filthy decay and scavenging organisms/indifferent wild or merely useless forms/good time creatures/and virtuous beasts domesticated for human service. It shadows the great man-centered political scheme upon the world, derived from the ordered ascendency from parishioners to clerics to bishops to cardinals to popes, or in a secular form from criminals to proletarians to aldermen to mayors to senators to presidents.

And so is nature pigeonholed. The sardonic phrase, "the place of nature in man's world," offers, tongue-in-cheek, a clever footing for confronting a world made in man's image and conforming to words. It satirizes the prevailing philos-ophy of anti-nature and human omniscience. It is possible because of an attitude which—like ecology—has ancient roots, and whose modern form was shaped when Aquinas reconciled Aristotelian homocentrism with Judeo-Christian dogma. In a later setting of machine technology, puritanical capitalism, and an urban ethos it carves its own version of reality into the landscape like a schoolboy initialing a tree. For such a philosophy nothing in nature has inherent merit. As one professor recently put it, "The only reason anything is done on this earth is for people. Did the rivers, winds, animals, rocks, or dust ever consider my wishes or needs? Surely, we do all our acts in an earthy environment, but I have never had a tree, valley, mountain, or flower thank me for preserving it."[3] This view carries great force, epitomized in history by Bacon, Descartes, Hegel, Hobbes, and Marx.

Some other post-Renaissance thinkers are wrongly accused of undermining our assurance of natural order. The theories of the heliocentric solar system, of biological evolution, and of the unconscious mind are held to have deprived the universe of the beneficence and purpose to which man was a special heir and to have evoked feelings of separation, of antipathy towards a meaningless existence in a neutral cosmos. Modern despair, the arts of anxiety, the politics of patho-logical individualism and predatory socialism were not, however, the results of Copernicus, Darwin and Freud. If man was not the center of the universe, was

[3] Clare A. Gunn in *Landscape Architecture*, July 1966, p. 260.

not created by a single stroke of Providence, and is not ruled solely by rational intelligence, it does not follow therefore that nature is defective where we thought it perfect. The astronomer, biologist and psychiatrist each achieved for mankind corrections in sensibility. Each showed the interpenetration of human life and the universe to be richer and more mysterious than had been thought.

Darwin's theory of evolution has been crucial to ecology. Indeed, it might have helped rather than aggravated the growing sense of human alienation had its interpreters emphasized predation and competition less (and, for this reason, one is tempted to add, had Thomas Huxley, Herbert Spencer, Samuel Butler and G. B. Shaw had less to say about it). Its bases of universal kinship and common bonds of function, experience and value among organisms were obscured by pre-existing ideas of animal depravity. Evolutionary theory was exploited to justify the worst in men and was misused in defense of social and economic injustice. Nor was it better used by humanitarians. They opposed the degradation of men in the service of industrial progress, the slaughter of American Indians, and child labor, because each treated men "like animals." That is to say, men were not animals, and the temper of social reform was to find good only in attributes separating men from animals. Kindness both towards and among animals was still a rare idea in the 19th century, so that using men as animals could mean only cruelty.

Since Thomas Huxley's day the nonanimal forces have developed a more subtle dictum to the effect that, "Man may be an animal, but he is more than an animal, too!" The *more* is really what is important. This appealing aphorism is a kind of anesthetic. The truth is that we are ignorant of what it is like or what it means to be any other kind of creature than we are. If we are unable to truly define the animal's experience of life or "being an animal" how can we isolate our animal part?

The rejection of animality is a rejection of nature as a whole. As a teacher, I see students develop in their humanities studies a proper distrust of science and technology. What concerns me is that the stigma spreads to the natural world itself. C. P. Snow's *Two Cultures*, setting the sciences against the humanities, can be misunderstood as placing nature against art. The idea that the current destruction of people and environment is scientific and would be corrected by more communication with the arts neglects the hatred for this world carried by our whole culture. Yet science as it is now taught does not promote a respect for nature. Western civilization breeds no more ecology in Western science than in Western philosophy. Snow's two cultures cannot explain the antithesis that splits the world, nor is the division ideological, economic or political in the strict sense. The antidote he proposes is roughly equivalent to a liberal education, the traditional prescription for making broad and well-rounded men. Unfortunately, there is little even in the liberal education of ecology-and-man. Nature is usually synonymous with either natural resources or scenery, the great stereotypes in the minds of middle class, college-educated Americans.

One might suppose that the study of biology would mitigate the humanistic—largely literary—confusion between materialism and a concern for nature. But biology made the mistake at the end of the 17th century of adopting a *modus operandi* or life style from physics, in which the question why was not to be asked, only the question how. Biology succumbed to its own image as an esoteric prologue to technics and encouraged the whole society to mistrust naturalists.

When scholars realized what the sciences were about it is not surprising that they threw out the babies with the bathwater: the information content and naturalistic lore with the rest of it. This is the setting in which academia and intellectual America undertook the single-minded pursuit of human uniqueness, and uncovered a great mass of pseudo distinctions such as language, tradition, culture, love, consciousness, history and awe of the supernatural. Only men were found to be capable of escape from predictability, determinism, environmental control, instincts and other mechanisms which "imprison" other life. Even biologists, such as Julian Huxley, announced that the purpose of the world was to produce man, whose social evolution excused him forever from biological evolution. Such a view incorporated three important presumptions: that nature is a power structure shaped after human political hierarchies; that man has a monopoly of immortal souls; and omnipotence will come through technology. It seems to me that all of these foster a failure of responsible behavior in what Paul Sears calls "the living landscape" except within the limits of immediate self-interest.

What ecology must communicate to the humanities—indeed, as a humanity —is that such an image of the world and the society so conceived are incomplete. There is overwhelming evidence of likeness, from molecular to mental, between men and animals. But the dispersal of this information is not necessarily a solution. The Two Culture idea that the problem is an information bottleneck is only partly true; advances in biochemistry, genetics, ethology, paleoanthropology, comparative physiology and the psychobiology are not self-evidently unifying. They need a unifying principle not found in any of them, a wisdom in the sense that Walter B. Cannon used the word in his book *Wisdom of the Body*,[4] about the community of self-regulating systems within the organism. If the ecological extension of that perspective is correct, societies and ecosystems as well as cells have a physiology, and insight into it is built into organisms, including man. What was intuitively apparent last year—whether aesthetically or romantically—is a find of this year's inductive analysis. It seems to me that there is an ecological instinct which probes deeper and more comprehensively than science, and which anticipates every scientific confirmation of the natural history of man.

It is not surprising, therefore, to find substantial ecological insight in art. Of course there is nothing wrong with a poem or dance which is ecologically neutral; its merit may have nothing to do with the transaction of man and nature. It is my impression, however, that students of the arts no longer feel that the subject of a work of art—what it "represents"—is without importance, as was said about 40 years ago. But there are poems and dances as there are prayers and laws attending to ecology. Some are more than mere comments on it. Such creations become part of all life. Essays on nature are an element of a functional or feedback system influencing men's reactions to their environment, messages projected by men to themselves through some act of design, the manipulation of paints or written words. They are natural objects, like bird nests. The essay is as real a part of the community—in both the one-species sociological and many-species ecological senses—as are the songs of choirs or crickets. An essay is an Orphic sound, words that make knowing possible, for it was Orpheus as Adam who named and thus made intelligible all creatures.

[4] Walter B. Cannon, *Wisdom of the Body* (New York: W. W. Norton, 1932).

What is the conflict of Two Cultures if it is not between science and art or between national ideologies? The distinction rather divides science and art within themselves. An example within science was the controversy over the atmospheric testing of nuclear bombs and the effect of radioactive fallout from the explosions. Opposing views were widely published and personified when Linus Pauling, a biochemist, and Edward Teller, a physicist, disagreed. Teller, one of the "fathers" of the bomb, pictured the fallout as a small factor in a world-wide struggle, the possible damage to life in tiny fractions of a percent, and even noted that evolutionary progress comes from mutations. Pauling, an expert on the hereditary material, knowing that most mutations are detrimental, argued that a large absolute number of people might be injured, as well as other life in the world's biosphere.

The humanness of ecology is that the dilemma of our emerging world ecological crises (overpopulation, environmental pollution, etc.) is at least in part a matter of values and ideas. It does not divide men as much by their trades as by the complex of personality and experience shaping their feelings towards other people and the world at large. I have mentioned the disillusion generated by the collapse of unsound nature philosophies. The anti-nature position today is often associated with the focusing of general fears and hostilities on the natural world. It can be seen in the behavior of control-obsessed engineers, corporation people selling consumption itself, academic superhumanists and media professionals fixated on political and economic crisis, neurotics working out psychic problems in the realm of power over men or nature, artistic symbol-manipulators disgusted by anything organic. It includes many normal, earnest people who are unconsciously defending themselves or their families against a vaguely threatening universe. The dangerous eruption of humanity in a deteriorating environment does not show itself as such in the daily experience of most people, but is felt as general tension and anxiety. We feel the pressure of events not as direct causes but more like omens. A kind of madness arises from the prevailing nature-conquering, nature-hating and self- and world-denial. Although in many ways most Americans live comfortable, satiated lives, there is a nameless frustration born of an increasing nullity. The aseptic home and society are progressively cut off from direct organic sources of health and increasingly isolated from the means of altering the course of events. Success, where its price is the misuse of landscapes, the deterioration of air and water and the loss of wild things, becomes a pointless glut, experience one-sided, time on our hands an unlocalized ache.

The unrest can be exploited to perpetuate itself. One familiar prescription for our sick society and its loss of environmental equilibrium is an increase in the intangible Good Things: more Culture, more Security, and more Escape from pressures and tempo. The "search for identity" is not only a social but an ecological problem having to do with a sense of place and time in the context of all life. The pain of that search can be cleverly manipulated to keep the *status quo* by urging that what we need is only improved forms and more energetic expressions of what now occupy us: engrossment with ideological struggle and military power, with productivity and consumption as public and private goals, with commerce and urban growth, with amusements, with fixation on one's navel, with those tokens of escape or success already belabored by so many idealists and social critics so ineffectually.

To come back to those Good Things: the need for culture, security and escape is just near enough to the truth to take us in. But the real cultural deficiency is the absence of a true *cultus* with its significant ceremony, relevant mythical cosmos, and artifacts. The real failure in security is the disappearance from our personal lives of the small human group as the functional unit of society and the web of other creatures, domestic and wild, which are part of our humanity. As for escape, the idea of simple remission and avoidance fails to provide for the value of solitude, to integrate leisure and natural encounter. Instead of these, what are foisted on the puzzled and troubled soul as Culture, Security and Escape are more art museums, more psychiatry, and more automobiles.

The ideological status of ecology is that of a resistance movement. Its Rachel Carsons and Aldo Leopolds are subversive (as Sears recently called ecology itself [5]). They challenge the public or private right to pollute the environment, to systematically destroy predatory animals, to spread chemical pesticides indiscriminately, to meddle chemically with food and water, to appropriate without hindrance space and surface for technological and military ends; they oppose the uninhibited growth of human populations, some forms of "aid" to "underdeveloped" peoples, the needless addition of radioactivity to the landscape, the extinction of species of plants and animals, the domestication of all wild places, large-scale manipulation of the atmosphere or the sea, and most other purely engineering solutions to problems of and intrusions into the organic world.

If naturalists seem always to be *against* something it is because they feel a responsibility to share their understanding, and their opposition constitutes a defense of the natural systems to which man is committed as an organic being. Sometimes naturalists propose projects too, but the project approach is itself partly the fault, the need for projects a consequence of linear, compartmental thinking, of machine-like units to be controlled and manipulated. If the ecological crisis were merely a matter of alternative techniques, the issue would belong among the technicians and developers (where most schools and departments of conservation have put it).

Truly ecological thinking need not be incompatible with our place and time. It does have an element of humility which is foreign to our thought, which moves us to silent wonder and glad affirmation. But it offers an essential factor, like a necessary vitamin, to all our engineering and social planning, to our poetry and our understanding. There is only one ecology, not a human ecology on one hand and another for the subhuman. No one school or theory or project or agency controls it. For us it means seeing the world mosaic from the human vantage without being man-fanatic. We must use it to confront the great philosophical problems of man—transience, meaning, and limitation—without fear. Affirmation of its own organic essence will be the ultimate test of the human mind.

---

[5] Paul B. Sears, "Ecology—a subversive subject," *BioScience*, Vol. 14, No. 7 (July 1964), p. 11.

Man Against Nature

Thomas Sieger Derr

Thomas Sieger Derr (1931–   ) is chairman of the department of religion, Smith College, and author of *The Political Thought of the Ecumenical Movement, 1900–1939*. He has written numerous articles in the area of social ethics and has served as college chaplain at Stanford University and Smith College.

HIDDEN ASSUMPTIONS IN THE ARGUMENT OVER ENVIRONMENTAL CONTROL

Ever since the demise of the civil rights movement in the mid-1960's, there has been, particularly on college campuses, a lot of restless righteousness looking for a new home. The peace movement has been a little too complex and divisive to fill the vacuum, and the course of its current "Cambodian renaissance" is hard to predict. But at last the long-sought morally unambiguous cause seems to have come along: ecology, or environmental control. The issues are, indeed, of vital importance to absolutely everyone; and insofar as the new movement's goal is life and health, no one can possibly quarrel with its aims. The villains are few and easily isolated, yet of sufficient stature to provide rather satisfying targets. One of my students quite matter-of-factly summed up the new movement as "a confrontation between industrialists and conservationists." Manufacturers are, of course, by now rather traditional enemies for the young, a point which suggests another benefit of the ecology crusade: It is continuous with, and gives new voice to, existing student contempt of "the system," the wasteful, consumption-oriented, production-minded, capitalist society. Life attuned to the natural values would be simpler, purer, more "human" than one oriented to gadgets and profits. This latest cause can even be easily exploited for generation-gap purposes, the pollution of the environment being the ultimate betrayal of youth by their forebears.

But all is not well, despite these useful features. In the world of student activism, where causes succeed one another like summer thunderstorms, the new deluge is regarded with disfavor by those who retain their prior commitments. They resent the ephemeral faddism illustrated in the story of the young man who went west after his role in the Chicago riots "looking for new causes," stumbled upon the Sierra Club, and "realized that ecology would be my thing for a while." The war and the draft can hardly lose their primary place for those who would be their victims. And among black militants ecological enthusiasm is widely regarded as the white activists' cop-out, diverting consciences, and drawing energy and resources away from what blacks understandably see as the primary social issue of our times. For the poor and the relatively poor, black and white alike, the anti-consumption language of environmental control sounds like an

From Thomas Sieger Derr, "Man Against Nature." *Cross Currents* (Summer 1970). Reprinted by permission.

attempt on the part of the comfortable to restrict the spread of homes, cars, and industrial services at the expense of those who currently lack them.

The portrait of the ecologists' enemy, moreover, is a caricature. He is that rapacious man who is despoiling the planet, heedless of the cost to our own and future generations. He scars hillsides, cuts redwoods, dumps oil into the sea, pours garbage into rivers, pumps noxious gases into the air. His destructiveness is compounded by his faulty knowledge of the ecological consequences of his acts, and by a mischievous mythology we have all inherited, consciously or unconsciously, from the western religious tradition which tells us that man is meant to dominate nature. But mainly the fault is his overweening pride and simple greed. The enemy is, in short, a grasping lout, an aesthetic Philistine who wouldn't know the difference between the Grand Canyon and lower Broadway. In the acid description of David Brower, formerly executive director of the Sierra Club and certainly one of the most outspoken conservationists alive, "The implicit assumption is that Man is the Master of Nature, and that losing a wild place or species of plant is of no great importance to us, and never mind the aesthetics."[1]

This character sketch was applied on many an editorial page to Walter Hickel when he was first designated as Secretary of the Interior. (He has since shown some ability to charm the conservationists.) At the height of the controversy over his nomination the *New York Times* commented,

It is already clear that [Mr. Hickel] is not a conservative in the sense of having a reverence for nature's balance, a skepticism about technology's marvels, and a respect for posterity's claims. If he were, he would probably be a conservationist and his confirmation would not be in doubt.[2]

Now, "a respect for posterity's claims" belongs to the heart of the argument, and of course a Secretary of the Interior would have to show such respect. But "reverence" for the natural and "skepticism" about modern technology are something else again; and there is no demonstrable reason why these attributes should have been prerequisites for the Secretary's confirmation by the Senate. Their inclusion in an otherwise judicious editorial points to what may be the least noticed yet most fundamental fault in the renewed interest in ecology, namely, a romanticism that distorts the issues, needlessly arouses opposition, and is positively inimical to wise, deliberate control of the environment. The programs of many of the new ecological action groups display this romanticism, embodying an attitude toward the relation of man to nature which I can only call a theology.

The word "theology" is advisedly chosen. The false assumptions that are distorting the discussion originate in a theology, namely, deism. The deists, whose height of popularity was two hundred years ago but whose ideas many find continually appealing, thought, or think, that the order of the natural world exhibits such a marvelous perfection or harmony as to demonstrate a supreme mind behind its creation. Here is the famous argument for the existence of God from the evidence of design in the universe. This is a "natural theology," where the natural world mirrors, or testifies to, the transcendent God. The deists were impressed with the regularity, the reliability, of the laws of nature. The movement was strongest in England in the seventeenth and eighteenth centuries, for it was

[1] From a Sierra Club advertisement in the *New York Times*, 14 January 1969, p. 31.
[2] Editorial, *New York Times*, 14 January 1969, p. 44.

there and then that Isaac Newton lived and wrote. Newton's formulations of the laws of the behavior of matter were impressive not only to the physicist but to the theologian, and Newton was both. The mechanistic Newtonian universe became the chief prop and exhibit of deism. Its perfection was built in. God became for many the Great Clockmaker, who had constructed the universe with its immutable laws like a fine timepiece, set it going, and left it to run forever in the perfection for which He had designed it. The universe was thus invested with moral quality. One could call it "good," the moral judgment. In its laws one read virtue. The fact that the laws were unchangeable meant there were absolute standards for ethics, and that one could somehow read these standards, by the light of one's natural reason, in the book of nature which the Creator had authored. This is a philosophy of timelessness that talks of Absolute Being, a static theology whose God is an Unmoved Mover.

If nature thus becomes the revelation of God, man will find the divine wisdom by contemplating nature as it comes, so to speak, fresh from the Creator's hand —that is, in its pristine condition, before man has worked on it, or, to use the conservationists' characteristic phrase, "*unspoiled* nature." Its revelatory capacity is diminished after man has altered it. Nature which man has touched is literally spoiled; it is no longer the mirror of the divine will. It becomes important, then, if man is to learn the eternal verities, to keep some portion of the natural world "unspoiled," "forever wild." In such a place, a laboratory of both physical and moral laws, the meaning, the truth of life is available to us. This idea can be expressed very finely, as in these words of Wallace Stegner:

Something will have gone out of us as a people if we ever let the remaining wilderness be destroyed.... Without any ... wilderness we are committed ... to a headlong drive into our technological termite-life, the Brave New World of a completely man-controlled environment.... We simply need that wild country available to us, even if we never do more than drive to its edge and look in ... (as) part of the geography of hope.[3]

In humbler ways men less gifted with words pay tribute to the same thought when they denominate some beautiful place as "inspiration point," or the "cathedral of the pines." They are saying that in pure nature one draws near to God, or, if you like, to the ultimate meaning of existence. Some years ago when someone wanted to build a chapel on the rim of the Grand Canyon conservationists protested vigorously, pointing out that the Canyon itself was already in effect a house of worship, to which man's works, however well-intentioned, could add nothing.

Note, by the way, that there is a peculiarly American component to this general deistic appreciation of virgin nature. We want to keep parts of our country as they were "when the first white men saw them." Blended with our intention here (the racial connotation aside) is the thought that our land was perhaps purer in its early days, actually "holier," before the settlements spread across the face of the American earth. Sometimes we have used the existence of wilderness as the occasion for a national boast, implying that it makes us better, in a truly moral sense "better," than Europeans, whose land has been worked by man for centuries. Of course, in many of those past ages Europeans were given to building

[3] Quoted in Roderick Nash, *Wilderness and the American Mind*, New Haven, 1967, p. 226.

chapels on remote and dramatic pieces of natural scenery, as *their* way of expressing the marriage of heaven and earth, the sacredness of the world of nature.

Such, then, is one component of the conservationist theology: a deism that reads holiness in untouched nature. I have no special wish to attack the ideological descendants of Isaac Newton; indeed, I come from a family of scientists who admired Newton as a kind of demigod of his day. A large portrait of Sir Isaac hung in my grandfather's house, and in later years came to my parents' house, where his stern and thoughtful gaze accosts the visitor to this day. It was my grandmother who taught me Pope's proposed epitaph for him:

> Nature and Nature's laws lay hid in night;
> God said, "Let Newton be!" and all was light.

Nevertheless, despite the affection that filial piety may inspire, I shall have to say that there are problems with deism, and problems for its view of nature, which I want, in the end, to reject.

Before I come to my critique, however, there is a further development of the deistic attitude toward nature to be noted. That is romanticism. In some theoretical ways the romantic attitude is different from deism. What the deists love in nature is its order, harmony, symmetry, while the romantics exalt nature for its own sake. That is, the deist sees the divine mirrored in nature. Nature is a way into the mind of God, who is Himself above His handiwork. The theology of the romantic, however, is more likely to be pantheistic than deistic: nature, instead of *revealing* God, becomes divine itself. God is not transcendent, but identified with the universe. It becomes possible to worship nature itself, as God, rather than seeking through nature to find a way beyond to the Creator. Whereas the deist is a rationalist, who believes he can use his reason to read the rational mind of the Maker in the design of the universe, the pantheist, the romantic, tends to be a mystic, who yearns for union with divine nature.

Thus my Smith colleague Paul Shepard, himself an ecologist of distinction, appeals in his recent book for "a deep sense of engagement with the landscape, with profound connections to surroundings and to natural processes central to all life"; and he finds this deep sense historically manifested in a variety of cultural episodes involving the mystical union of man and nature, including significantly both an early Cretan cult of the Great Mother and the Romantic poetry of the 18th and 19th centuries.[4] (I hope to make it clear before I finish that I am in agreement with his practical goals, even if his language makes me uneasy.) Romantic language, when it appears in conservationist writing, is apt to personify nature, to treat nature as sentient being whom we men offend and wound by our thoughtless cruelty to the natural world. Thus David Brower speculates about the earth after men have made themselves extinct by poisoning the environment, "As humbling a thought as it may be, Nature might scarcely miss the people."[5] (Note the capital N.)

Despite these theoretical differences between the deists and the romantics, the practical effect of their thought on the conservation movement is roughly comparable. The two are in many ways blended in American Transcendentalism, which has eighteenth century deism for its theological ancestor and nineteenth

---

[4] Paul Shepard and Daniel McKinley, eds., *The Subversive Science*, Boston, 1967, p. 5.
[5] Sierra Club advertisement.

century romanticism for its operating mood. Like deism, Transcendentalism saw divinity *through* nature, nature in its "wild" state. The realm of the divine, to which man might aspire, was transcendent. But like the romantics the transcendentalists located the power to transcend this world, via communion with nature, not in man's reason, but in his intuition or imagination, the faculties by which the soul reached spiritual truth. Still, the differences between deist and pantheist are perhaps not of great practical importance at this point. Their convergence shows in the German astronomer Johann Kepler, whose work preceded Newton's by a lifetime. Kepler was both a sophisticated scientist and a pantheist mystic, who is said to have exclaimed, on his discovery of the laws of planetary motion, "O God, I think thy thoughts after Thee!" Here, apparently, God *is* the universe, in all its wonderful precision; and Kepler's worshipful attitude toward it is clear.

In any event, the transcendentalists in marrying romanticism to deism simply reinforced the respect, really the *reverence*, due to unspoiled nature. They feared the spread of industrial civilization would destroy this pure nature, and so destroy the source of virtue, strength, and freedom. Hence Emerson's famous epigrammatic lament, "Things are in the saddle, and ride mankind." Or there is Thoreau's plea, "In wildness is the preservation of the world," which, not surprisingly, has been used by the Sierra Club as the title of a book matching quotations from Thoreau's *Walden* with photographs of unspoiled nature.

It belongs to this romanticized deism to think of man himself in terms of nature. Man's ideal condition is a union with nature just because he is really part of nature. In thinking of himself as somehow apart from nature, superior to it, he violates the deepest laws of his own being. A young woman associated with the Berkeley-based group Ecology Action speaks quite accurately for this group when she says of a camping trip, "It is really a new religion.... It did fantastic things for my head. I had a really mystical feeling about being part of a total living community."[6]

The attitude of separation, of superiority, is alleged to be at the root of our ecological crisis. What we call civilization is thus really a source of corruption. True man, the natural man, is the "noble savage." Wilderness is a source of virtue; and the closer one lives to it the more virtuous one is, the less spoiled by urban man's violations of nature. The city is destructive of man as he was meant to be. In the mythology of this position the countryman is the bearer of true humanity. His relative "innocence," that is, his lack of "civilization," meaning "citifying," makes him the model of civic virtue around which the ideal society is to be created. In our folk literature the "city slicker" is the crook, the cheat, the deceiver; and if the country rube, the "hayseed," should have the last laugh, we are to consider that only justice. The city is the spoiler of morals and vigor, the antithesis of the purity and strength of true nature. To recover the virtue of the natural, to find one's true being again, we are to turn away from the city and go towards the wild. We are to "rough it," return to the wilderness, to learn what man really is, to become one with the divinity of the universe. This romantic protest against the works of civilization appears again in Brower's words, "The wild places are where we began. When they end,

---

[6] Steven V. Roberts, "The Better Earth," *New York Times Magazine*, 29 March 1970, p. 56.

so do we."[7] "There is need to think of the organic wholeness of nature, not man apart from that. . . ." The world must be thought of as "a wildlife preserve, where *we* are the wildlife."[8]

Against the claim of the romanticized deist that nature is the locus of final truth, I should want to argue that nature is neutral with respect to ultimate wisdom or rationality, and also neutral with respect to virtue or goodness. If a value system were reflected in nature, we should have to say it is very different from ours, at least from the one we profess. Men have observed for ages that nature is a realm of struggle, often savage, brutal struggle, where the big fish eat the little ones. When an ecologist describes nature's balance, he is talking of mutually predatory relationships, of suffering and decay. A friend of mine once read a book on the ecology of a summer pond and concluded that what was therein described was "systematic murder." When our scarred family tomcat returns from his nightly prowl, he is often in a rather battered condition. By day friendly and lovable, a pet to romanticize, he becomes at night a hunter and a killer, faithful to his nature.

There is a vast difference between knowing the truths of nature as useful facts, and taking them as signs of divine virtue. Knowledge of the facts about the natural world does not bestow meaning on the process nor dictate ethical priorities and proprieties. Meaning, and meaningful, responsible choice, that is, ethics, belongs to another order entirely, to a vision of the *place* of this scientific data in the history and purpose of the whole, a vision of the destiny of the cosmos, and of man within it. Science does not dictate an ethic, and strictly speaking, nature is not "wise." A scientist certainly has an ethic, but it is one he brings *to* his work, not one which follows directly *from* his work. The work is in itself morally neutral. It acquires moral meaning only in terms of the uses to which man may put it, the place to which he assigns it in his scheme of purposes. Morality, and ultimate wisdom of any sort, does not belong to the study of natural phenomena, though that study is necessary to define the possible limits of certain kinds of human action. Morality is a function of man's goals, of his understanding of the meaning of his life.

We can see the problem more clearly if we find an example where an attempt to derive the divine will, ethical wisdom, from the facts of nature has evidently led to disaster. Such an illustration lies ready to hand in the famous and fearful population problem, where a papal encyclical has derived a prohibition on artificial, i.e., non-natural, means of contraception from the observable "laws of nature." The argument, which goes back to St. Thomas Aquinas, is not actually a deist one, but in this respect very much like it. The "laws of nature" which we read by our reason in the natural world are the reflection in created things of the "eternal law," the mind of God. An earlier pope, whose decision was reaffirmed by the present pope just two years ago, had put the theory this way: "No reason, however grave, may be put forward by which anything intrinsically against nature may become conformable to nature and morally good."[9] There it is: What is against nature is against the mind of God, sinful. Nature is

[7] "A Time for Sarsaparilla," from Foreword to *Summer Island: Penobscot Country*, by Eliot Porter, Sierra Club, 1966; in Garrett De Bell, *The Environmental Handbook*, New York, 1970, p. 11.

[8] Sierra Club advertisement.

[9] Pius XI, "Casti Connubii," 31 December 1930, paragraph 54.

actually glorified religiously. Letting things take their natural course becomes equivalent to saying that it was or wasn't the will of God, that it was wholly "providential" that children came or didn't come.

The consequences of this viewpoint are obvious. If nature is indeed allowed to take its course, the population will eventually thin itself by starvation or other catastrophe. That is, starvation will be a perfectly "natural" result of the ecological problem, which is not exactly a catastrophe for *nature*. But that is my argument: mass starvation is called "catastrophic," a value word, only when looked at from the point of view of man, as if he were not wholly bound to nature. His moral judgment is here separated from nature, and is set against nature. If we follow the logic of natural wisdom we should eventually give in to the simple fatalism of "What is, must be," a fatalism that is, I think, the temptation and tendency of any view which uncritically regards nature as wise, moral, or divine.

This brings me to my second quarrel with romanticized deism and its relatives —namely, the characterization of man as belonging wholly to the natural world. Now, no one will deny that man has biological limits. There are certain environments in which he simply cannot live, and he is finally mortal in any event. The whole field of space medicine is a fascinating and dramatic object lesson in the limits of human biology. Some people have further worried that given the rapid changes in various areas of contemporary life, we may find that man himself has been left behind, that as an organism he will be unable to adapt rapidly enough to survive in the new environment being created about him, ironically by his own technological capacities.

That may be true; but most men have regarded technology not as the devil which has seduced the race from its oneness with the natural, but as the liberator. When people lose their capacity for surmounting nature, we say they "vegetate." The word aptly describes the return to oneness with nature, but we understand it deploringly. One of my summer neighbors, out in his boat one day, came upon a canoe which at a distance appeared to be adrift empty. He investigated and found a man slouched down in the bottom, hat over his eyes, untended fishing line over the edge. Apologetically the man sat up, saying that he was really all right, but that when he came up to the lake for his vacation it took him just about a day to become a vegetable. He understood this to be a subhuman pose, and he retained a vestige of his normal dominance over nature by ostensibly preying on the fish, even while he vegetated. In fact we do regard people who have, almost truly, become vegetable-like as dead. The brain which has made possible their mastery over their environment has failed them, and they have become in consequence not truly human. They are, as nature is, comparatively mindless. But *man* cannot be mindless and be truly alive, truly man.

I would guess that most serious students of the impact of technology on man do not waste time lamenting the simple existence of technological skills. The problem is not to roll back the ages to the state of nature, but to exercise more careful human control over technology so that it does really serve as liberator. Our technical power does sometimes seem to increase faster than our ability to understand it or use it well. But that does not alter its inner character as extension of humanity. One man who has spent a lot of his professional time with this problem is Emmanuel Mesthene of Harvard, who says man's aim is "to be free of the tyranny of physical nature that has plagued him since his beginnings."

Physical nature was brute, recalcitrant, limiting, indifferent or hostile. But finally we have escaped, and we can make matter serve our own purposes. We are more free, and can be more human.[10] The French philosopher and historian Jacques Ellul, to whom Mesthene seems too optimistic, nevertheless agrees on this essential point, that man must use technology, make it the servant of his values, and not reject it; for man can never be fully integrated with nature. He is different from it, and his indifference shows in his capacity to make conscious choices, ethical decisions, regarding his use of nature through technology.[11]

Man is not so constituted that he can be wholly at one with nature. He has a non-natural dimension, call it "spirit" or whatever you will, which he cannot shed, and which ever reminds him of his separateness from his own biology. There is something fraudulent, even comic, about his attempts to return to nature even for a brief period. The annual camping trip is accompanied by aerosol insect bombs and Coleman stoves, air mattresses and trailers, even electricity—a rolling bit of city running through nature's hostile territory on the pretext of enjoying it, but really scarcely able to wait for the next motel and its hot shower. Man seems to sense at all times that descent to nature is a *danger* to his humanity, not a recovery of it, as the romantic would say. The animal in us represents a threat. Man is continually *made* human by asserting his distinction from the animal. Philosophers are always working over that distinction. Paul Tillich put it this way: "In all nature the existence of things is a necessary result of their essence. In man existence is opposed to his essence."[12] Nature has no freedom, so it has no history, strictly speaking. Nature is "mere becoming." Man alone has a history.

Let me try now to be a little more constructive, to build up the thesis implicit in these criticisms of romanticism as an alternative way of viewing the relation between man and nature. The starting point is the view of man just suggested, as both nature *and* spirit, but neither exclusively. This means that man's capacity for altering the circumstances of his life is not entirely limited to the normal processes of nature, yet never completely free from what nature will permit. Man's ability to transcend nature is unique in the world we know, and it makes him in a real sense a non-natural creature. But this is not an unmixed blessing. Man's spiritual dimension is used not just to gain a humanizing freedom *from* nature, but also to *destroy* nature and gain the mastery over other men as well as nature. While I can appreciate Emmanuel Mesthene's celebration of technology as the liberator, his optimistic attitude toward the peril of technology's misuse is more than I can presently share. He says, simply, that we shall have to become wiser about its use. The celebrated biologist René Dubos seems to me to offer a corrective when he reminds us that man for all his freedom in the realm of culture never escapes the clutches of biology. Perhaps we may say that man evolves along with the nature of which he is part, yet ever more as himself the controlling factor in that evolutionary process, so that the story becomes one mainly of the evolution of *man*. Man is part of nature, and yet he is not; and in that tension he finds his existence. The tension is illustrated in a curiously

[10] Address at the World Conference on Church and Society, Geneva, 1966.
[11] Address at the World Conference on Church and Society, Geneva, 1966.
[12] Essay in *The Kingdom of God and History*, Chicago, 1938, p. 110.

memorable passage from Francis Parkman's classic personal narrative, *The Oregon Trail*. Hunting for food, he shot an antelope, and went to fetch his kill:

When I stood by his side, the antelope turned his expiring eye upward. It was like a beautiful woman's, dark and bright. "Fortunate that I am in a hurry," thought I; "I might be troubled with remorse, if I had time for it."[13]

The human connection with the natural shows in the romantic comparison, the mystic lure of the dark, bright eye. But the man's gun has shown the impassible barrier between him and nature; he must have his way with it, and hurry on.

This appraisal of man as in a special relation to nature, different from the other creatures, finds its expression in the religious mythology of the western tradition in a familiar passage from Genesis which has probably had a considerable effect on the shaping of our attitudes:

Then God said, "Let us make man in our image ... and let them have dominion over the fish of the sea, and over the birds of the air, and over the cattle, and over all the earth, and over every creeping thing that creeps upon the earth." So God created man, ... male and female created he them.... And God said to them, "Be fruitful and multiply, and fill the earth and subdue it; and have dominion over the fish of the sea and over the birds of the air and over every living thing that moves upon the earth." (Genesis 1:26–28)

Notice that the central point is reservation of "dominion" to man among all the creatures. This claim is, of course, the despair of romantics, but I want openly to accept its implications as far more realistic and useful than romanticism. Western man has treated this passage as his charter to subdue nature, to conquer the wilderness and bend it to man's purpose. Let it be said at once that it is crucial to know just how this dominion is exercised, how this conquest is accomplished. Nature is not to be for the sole use of the first man to come upon a particular piece of it, but for all men for all generations. So this is not a charter for wanton destruction, but for planned and constructive use. No one knows better than the Biblical writers how rapacious man can be, and he is sternly admonished to a right use of the gift of the earth. He does not enjoy absolute right of disposition over it, but is the steward of nature, both using it and preserving its usefulness to future generations.

But nature is not the standard of virtue or goodness. Its value is in its usefulness to mankind. In fact, nature in itself is capricious, ambivalent, in need of healing. Man is right to view nature as half friend, half enemy. So he distinguishes himself from nature, and makes "dominion" over it his peculiar task. It is that separation that makes him man. He rises out of nature. The word we use for this process of human ascent is *civilization*. To be civilized is to be free of nature's strictures, to escape from the "mere becoming" of natural change into the freedom of true history. Biblical thought, and western religious thought which follows it, is anti-romantic, desacralizing nature completely, making God the Lord of nature, not part of it nor bound to its processes. He is involved not in the cyclical patterns of nature, but in the directional course of human history. I like Eric Hoffer's remark that the Genesis story makes Jacob the father of the

[13] *The Oregon Trail*, New York, 1931, quoted in Sidney Mead, *The Lively Experiment*, New York, 1963, p. 4.

race, not his brother Esau, the man of nature. The man of nature is not the noble savage, in this way of thinking. He is more likely to be called a barbarian. The wild land where he dwells, or where no man dwells, is not the fount of virtue, but the place of rudeness, danger, the enemy of civilization. The Biblical wilderness is uninhabitable land, desert no doubt, where the tempter appears to Jesus, where in earlier centuries the wandering Israelites fought grimly for survival, dreaming of a promised land of milk and honey ahead. Or perhaps the wilderness is the wild sea, the ancient symbol for chaos and darkness, the home of unknown monsters. Always, the wilderness is hostile to man, beyond his dominion, the antithesis of civilization.

In our folk tales the forest is dark and dangerous, the place where the innocents Hansel and Gretel encounter the wicked witch who seeks to devour them. Our image of ourselves as Americans is as the wilderness conquerors, makers of civilization in a forbidding and empty land. Ours was a divinely-ordered subjugation of nature, which means a mission to civilize. We sing this theme in "America the Beautiful," which may yet become our national anthem:

> O beautiful for pilgrim feet, whose stern impassioned stress
> A thoroughfare for freedom beat across the wilderness!

Conversely, Americans, and western man more generally, associate the decline of civilization with a return to the wild. My favorite passage describing the decline of civilization is from Ruskin's *Stones of Venice:*

Thenceforward, year after year, the nation drank with deeper thirst from the fountains of forbidden pleasure, and dug for springs, hitherto unknown, in the dark places of the earth. In the ingenuity of indulgence, in the varieties of vanity, Venice surpassed the cities of Christendom, as of old she had surpassed them in fortitude and devotion. ... It is as needless as it is painful to trace the steps of her final ruin. That ancient curse was upon her, the curse of the cities of the plain, "Pride, fulness of bread, and abundance of idleness." By the inner burning of her own passions, as fatal as the fiery rain of Gomorrah, she was consumed from her place among the nations; and her ashes are choking the channels of the dead salt sea.[14]

The passage equates immorality with decadence, morality with a sense of purpose and direction; "immoral" with the dehumanizing and brutal, "moral" with the humanizing element. Morality, the ability of man to respond to felt obligation against his "natural" or slothful inclination, is basic not only to his escape from primitivism into civilization, but to his maintenance of that civilization as a trans-natural, historical reality, vibrant with purpose and direction.

What I have sketched here is a rather different theology from romanticized deism. Not surprisingly, the romantics in the new ecology action groups often consciously reject these ideas of the western tradition for other theologies satisfying their mystic, pantheist bent. The superimposed "o" and "e" adopted by Environmental Teach-In as its insignia for its April 22 action day comes complete with explanatory symbol-words redolent of primitive and eastern religions ("oneness, om, orgasm, enlightenment, eros, ecstasy"), but is remarkably innocent of ideas drawn from the western religious tradition. This latter is clearly an embarrassment to advocates of mystic union between man and nature.

[14] *Stones of Venice*, Boston, n.d., Vol. III, p. 165.

I have no special label for my alternative, but since it stresses man in his distinction from nature it is clearly some kind of humanism. Qualifying adjectives might identify it as Biblical, western, and historical. Whatever we call it, it says that man is emancipated *from* nature *for* history, that he creates civilization as a work with an historical dimension, a conscious shaping of the environment in accord with human purposes. Instead of depending on a cyclical, ultimately static pattern of nature, it is a theology radically open to the future, a theology which does not find its God in nature's patterns, but in human destiny. Insofar as it understands that man is also a *natural* being, inescapably biological, this theology recognizes that man can alter his own biology, in principle and increasingly in fact. Man's "natural" dimension then also becomes amenable to human purposes, and we can say that all existence participates in human evolution.

This theology is at one with the type of conservationism which advocates our seizing conscious, intelligent control of our environment and thus of our destiny. There is, in fact, substantial agreement between this approach and much modern conservationist writing. The only difficulty is that the romantic language has often been mixed in with the more realistic, practical, and thoughtful historical humanism, to sow confusion and breed trouble by suggesting, falsely, I argue, that nature's inviolability is due to its *inherent* sacredness. Actually, directly adjacent to the passages already cited from conservationists are such observations as, "Nature is a fundamental resource to be sustained for *our own* well-being" (Paul Shepard),[15] and,

"Our motives are selfish; they are on behalf of our very own lives and the lives of our children.... (We strive for) environmental conditions that are necessary constituents of our survival and happiness." (David Brower)[16]

The theme here is that the spoiling of nature is immoral because that ruins *man's* capacity to use it, now and in the future—and, note well, to arrange and preserve nature so as to enjoy it is to use it.

To sum up, then, the romanticized deist wants man to live in harmony with nature, on nature's given immutable terms, forgetting that existence is a struggle, forgetting what is at best the essential neutrality of nature toward man, in favor of reading metaphysical propositions into the physical environment. The historical humanist, on the other hand, knows that the expansion of the human spirit involves the conquest of the natural, a sense of triumph over adversity in an environment unfriendly to man. The contract between these two shows vividly in the case of space exploration. The trip to the moon requires the use of very sophisticated technology to expand man into an extremely hostile environment, where no one can pretend he is meant to live "in harmony with nature." Wouldn't the romantic have to say that man should stay home in the natural environment which bred him? But then, would he be *man*? The historical humanist would answer *no*. Think of the exultation we felt when the astronauts set foot on the moon. This was not an emotion to occasion guilt, but a genuine and worthy celebration of the triumph of the spirit.

[15] Shepard and McKinley, p. 4. Shepard makes it clear that we must not lose "our sense of a great human destiny," even while he says, "We must affirm that the world is a being, a part of our own body," (p. 3) and, "The rejection of (our human) animality is a rejection of nature as a whole." (p. 6)
[16] Sierra Club advertisement.

The vision of the historical humanist is of perpetual human achievement, evolving toward an open future for both man and nature. That vision is not very different from the religious mythology which has dominated western civilization, the Biblical idea that the whole of creation awaits its transformation, or to use the theological word, its redemption. And in the evolution toward "new creation" man is to be the priest of the transformation—man as scientist and statesman, moral philosopher and citizen.

THE CRISIS OF SEXUALITY: WOMAN AND GOD

Statement on the Proposed Ordination of Women to the 122nd Diocesan Convention, October 1971

C. Kilmer Myers

Chauncie Kilmer Myers (1916–   ) is bishop of California (Episcopalian) and resides in San Francisco. He is especially concerned with the social aspects of the church. His works include *Light in Dark Streets* and *Behold the Church*.

I would like to make a statement with respect to the ordination of women to the Sacred Priesthood.

This question is basically a theological question pertaining to the Christian doctrine of God. Under this general statement may I make the following observations:

1.) A priest is a "God symbol" whether he likes it or not. In the imagery of both the Old and New Testaments God is represented in masculine imagery.

Open letter by the Rt. Rev. C. Kilmer Myers, Bishop of California, distributed to the public.

The Father begets the Son. This is essential to the *givingness* of the Christian Faith and to tamper with this imagery is to change that Faith into something else.

Of course, this does not mean that God is a male. The biblical language is the language of analogy. It is imperfect even as all human imagery of God must be imperfect. Nevertheless, it has meaning. The male image about God pertains to the divine initiative in creation. Initiative is in itself a male rather than a female attribute. This is *not* an assertion of male superiority. In the Christian doctrine of the Trinity of God, the priority of the Father does not constitute His superiority. The Father is the source of the Godhead, but the Son Whom He begets is His equal as also is the Holy spirit. This is the language of giving, of love, not the language of domination.

The Priest acts as the commissioned agent of Christ. His priesthood partakes of Christ's Priesthood which is generative, initiating, giving. This generative function is plainly a masculine kind of imagery making Priesthood a masculine conception.

2.) Christ is The Source of Priesthood. The sexuality of Christ is no accident nor is His masculinity incidental. This is the divine choice. Jesus continued that choice in His selection of men to be His Apostles. And to this day whoever receives them receives Him. The masculinity of commissioned ministry is consistently present in the New Testament even though the early Church knew that there is no inequality between male and female in Christ. The Young Church went out into a world which had a ready acceptance of priestesses. And even though it often appropriated for its own enrichment the religions, language and customs of the Mediterranean world, it never departed from the maleness of the apostolic ministry. It is my conviction that in a day characterized by a destructive confusion in sexuality, it is necessary for the Church to maintain and cherish the apostolic tradition. It is required of the Church that she again protest that sexual equality is not sexual identity.

3.) The overwhelming majority of Christians cannot tolerate the idea of the ordination of women to the priesthood. For Anglicans to ordain them would produce a painful ecumenical tension.

We must not be swayed by the apparent willingness of some Roman Catholics to proceed in this direction. Those Roman Catholics who speak in favor of the ordination of women to the priesthood do not represent the mainstream of that Church's tradition. At this moment in history the Roman Church is experiencing a crisis of identity which makes it very difficult for *that* Church to be a guide for the rest of us.

4.) Lastly, and most importantly, the Church has not adequately provided for the ministry of women. This the Church must do creatively and joyfully. But it will not be done if in seeking reparation for the past failures we act suddenly and in confusion. We will not compensate for our failure in the ministry of women by giving them the ministry of men.

The prototype of the ministry of women is the ministry of the seers and prophetesses of both the Old and New Testaments. But above all their ministry is rooted in that of Mary the Mother of Jesus. Could it be that our Anglican lack of veneration for her as Theotokos (God bearer) is at the root of much of our confusion?

We call her by the name Blessed—Blessed Mary, the Mother of Christ our

Saviour—because she heard the Word of God and in obedience bore within her body that Word which enlightens the cosmos. She therefore is the First among humans and to use a papal phrase spoken of approvingly by our Anglican Theologian, John MacQuarrie, "The Mother of the Church."

After the Death of God the Father
Mary Daly

Mary Daly (1928–   ) is associate professor of theology at Boston College and author of *The Church and the Second Sex*.

WOMEN'S LIBERATION AND THE TRANSFORMATION OF CHRISTIAN CONSCIOUSNESS

The women's liberation movement has produced a deluge of books and articles. Their major task has been exposition and criticism of our male-centered heritage. In order to reveal and drive home to readers the oppressive character of our cultural institutions, it was necessary to do careful research, to trot out passages from leading philosophers, psychologists, statesmen, poets, historians, saints and theologians which make the reader's hair stand on end by the blatancy of their misogynism. Part of the task also has been the tracing of the subtle psychological mechanisms by which society has held men up and women down. This method of exposition and analysis reached its crescendo within this past year when Kate Millet's *Sexual Politics* rocketed her into the role of American counterpart to Simone de Beauvoir.

As far as the level of creative research is concerned, that phase of the work is finished. The skeletons in our cultural closet have been hauled out for inspection. I do not mean to imply that there are not countless more of the same to be uncovered (just the other day I noticed for the first time that Berdyaev blandly affirms there is "something base and sinister in the female element." Etcetera). Nor do I mean that the task of communicating the message is over. Millions have yet to hear the news, let alone to grasp its import. Certainly it would be a mistake and a betrayal to trivialize the fact that our culture is so diseased. That has always been a major tactic in the fine art of suppressing the rage of women. No, what I am saying is that Phase One of critical research and writing in the movement has opened the way for the logical next step in creative thinking. We now have to ask how the women's revolution can and should change our whole vision of reality. What I intend to do here is to sketch some of the ways in which it can influence Western religious thought.

From Mary Daly, "After the Death of God the Father," *Commonweal*, March 12, 1971, pp. 7–11. Reprinted by permission.

The Judaic-Christian tradition has served to legitimate sexually imbalanced patriarchal society. Thus, for example, the image of the Father God, spawned in the human imagination and sustained as plausible by patriarchy, has in turn rendered service to this type of society by making its mechanisms for the oppression of women appear right and fitting. If God in "his" heaven is a father ruling "his" people, then it is in the "nature" of things and according to divine plan and the order of the universe that society be male-dominated. Theologian Karl Barth found it appropriate to write that woman is "ontologically" subordinate to man. Within this context a mystification of roles takes place: the husband dominating his wife represents God himself. What is happening, of course, is the familiar mechanism by which the images and values of a given society are projected into a realm of beliefs, which in turn justify the social infrastructure. The belief system becomes hardened and objectified, seeming to have an unchangeable independent existence and validity of its own. It resists social change which would rob it of its plausibility. Nevertheless, despite the vicious circle, change does occur in society, and ideologies die, though they die hard.

As the women's revolution begins to have its effect upon the fabric of society, transforming it from patriarchy into something that never existed before—into a diarchal situation that is radically new—it will, I believe, become the greatest single potential challenge to Christianity to rid itself of its oppressive tendencies or go out of business. Beliefs and values that have held sway for thousands of years will be questioned as never before. It is also very possibly the greatest single hope for survival of religious consciousness in the West.

At this point it is important to consider the objection that the liberation of women will only mean that new characters will assume the same old roles, but that nothing will change essentially in regard to structure, ideology, or values. This objection is often based upon the observation that the very few women in "masculine" occupations seem to behave very much as men do. This is really not to the point for it fails to recognize that the effect of tokenism is not to change stereotypes or social systems but to preserve these. What I am discussing here is an emergence of women such as has never taken place before. It is naive to assume that the coming of women into equal power in society generally and in the church in particular will simply mean uncritical acceptance of values formerly given priority by men. Rather, I suggest that it will be a catalyst for transformation of our culture.

The roles and structures of patriarchy have been developed and sustained in accordance with an artificial polarization of human qualities into the traditional sexual stereotypes. The image of the person in authority and the accepted understanding of "his" role have corresponded to the eternal masculine stereotype, which implies hyper-rationality, "objectivity," aggressivity, the possession of dominating and manipulative attitudes toward persons and environment and the tendency to construct boundaries between the self (and those identified with the self) and "the other." The caricature of a human being which is represented by this stereotype depends for its existence upon the opposite caricature—the eternal feminine (hyper-emotional, passive, self-abasing, etc.). By becoming whole persons women can generate a counterforce to the stereotype of the leader as they challenge the artificial polarization of human characteristics. There is no reason to assume that women who have the support of their sisters to criticize the masculine stereotype will simply adopt it as a model for themselves. More likely they will develop a wider range of qualities and skills in themselves and thereby encourage men to engage in a comparably liberating procedure (a phenomenon we are beginning to witness already in men's liberation groups). This becoming of *whole* human beings will affect the values of our society, for it will involve a change in the fabric of human consciousness.

Accordingly, it is reasonable to anticipate that this change will affect the symbols which reflect the values of our society, including religious symbols. Since some of these have functioned to justify oppression, women and men would do well to welcome this change. Religious symbols die when the cultural situation that supported them ceases to give them plausibility. This should pose no problem to authentic faith, which accepts the relativity of all symbols and recognizes that fixation upon any of them as absolute in itself is idolatrous.

The becoming of new symbols is not a matter than can arbitrarily be decided around a conference table. Rather, they grow out of a changing communal situation and experience. This does not mean that theologically we are consigned to the role of passive spectators. We are called upon to be attentive to what the new experience of the becoming of women is revealing to us, and to foster the evolution of consciousness beyond the oppressiveness and imbalance reflected and justified by symbols and doctrines throughout the millennia of patriarchy.

This imbalance is apparent first of all in the biblical and popular image of the great patriarch in heaven who rewards and punishes according to his mysterious and arbitrary will. The fact that the effects of this image have not always been humanizing is evident to any perceptive reader of history. The often cruel behavior of Christians toward unbelievers and even toward dissenters among themselves is shocking evidence of the function of that image in relation to values and behavior.

Sophisticated thinkers, of course, have never intellectually identified God with an elderly parent in heaven. Nevertheless it is important to recognize that even when very abstract conceptualizations of God are formulated in the mind, images have a way of surviving in the imagination in such a way that a person can function on two different and even apparently contradictory levels at the same time. Thus one can speak of God as spirit and at the same time imagine "him" as belonging to the male sex. Such primitive images can profoundly affect conceptualizations which appear to be very refined and abstract. Even the Yahweh of the future, so cherished by the theology of hope, comes through on an imaginative level as exclusively a He-God, and it is perhaps consistent with this that theologians of hope have attempted to develop a political theology which takes no explicit cognizance of the devastation wrought by sexual politics.

The widespread conception of the "Supreme Being" as an entity distinct from this world but controlling it according to plan and keeping human beings in a state of infantile subjection has been a not too subtle mask of the divine patriarch. The Supreme Being's plausibility, and that of the static worldview which accompanies this projection has, of course, declined. This was a projection grounded in specifically patriarchal infrastructures and sustained as subjectively real by the usual processes of generating plausibility. The sustaining power of the social infrastructures has been eroded by a number of developments in recent history, including the general trend toward democratization of society and the emergence of technology with the accompanying sense of mastery over the world and man's destiny. However, it is the women's movement which appears destined to play the key-role in the overthrow of such oppressive elements in traditional theism, precisely because it strikes at the source of the imbalance reflected in traditional beliefs.

The women's movement will present a growing threat to patriarchal religion less by attacking it than by simply leaving it behind. Few of the leaders in the movement evince an interest in institutional religion, having recognized it as an instrument of their betrayal. Those who see their commitment to the movement as consonant with concern for the religious heritage are aware that the Christian tradition is by no means bereft of elements which foster genuine experiences and intimations of transcendence. The problem is that their liberating potential is choked off in the surrounding atmosphere of the images, ideas, values, and structures of patriarchy. What will, I think, become possible through the social change coming from radical feminism is a more acute and widespread perception of qualitative differences between those conceptualizations of God and of the human relationship to God which are oppressive in their implications, and those which encourage self-actualization and social commitment.

The various theologies that hypostatize transcendence invariably use this "God" to legitimate oppression, particularly that of women. These are irredeemably antifeminine and therefore antihuman. In contrast to this, a more authentic language of transcendence does not hypostatize or objectify God and consequently does not lend itself to such use. So for example, Tillich's way of speaking about God as ground and power of being would be very difficult to use for the legitimation of any sort of oppression. It grows out of awareness of that reality which is both transcendent and immanent, not reducible to or adequately represented by such expressions as person, father, supreme being. Awareness of this reality is not achieved by playing theological games but by existential courage. I am not saying that a liberated consciousness necessarily will use Tillich's language of transcendence. That of Whitehead, James, Jaspers, to mention a few—or an entirely new language—may do as well or better. But it remains true that the driving revelatory force which will make possible an authenticity of religious consciousness is courage in the face of anxiety.

Since the projections of patriarchal religion have been blocking the dynamics of existential courage by offering the false security of alienation—that is, of self-reduction to stereotyped roles—there is reason to see hope for the emergence of genuine religious consciousness in the massive challenge to patriarchy which is now in its initial stages. The becoming of women may be not only the doorway to deliverance from the omnipotent Father in all of his disguises—a deliverance which secular humanism has passionately fought for—but also a doorway to something, that is, the beginning for many of a more authentic search for transcendence, that is, for God.

The imbalance in Christian ideology resulting from sexual hierarchy is manifested not only in the doctrine of God but also in the notion of Jesus as the unique God-man. A great deal of Christian doctrine concerning Jesus has been docetic, that is, it has not really seriously accepted the fact that Jesus was a human being. An effect of the liberation of women will very likely be the loss of plausibility of Christological formulas which come close to reflecting a kind of idolatry in regard to the person of Jesus. As it becomes better understood that God is transcendent and unobjectifiable—or else not at all—it will become less plausible to speak of Jesus as the Second Person of the Trinity who "assumed" a human nature. Indeed, the prevalent emphasis upon the total uniqueness and supereminence of Jesus will, I think, become less meaningful. To say this is not at all to deny his extraordinary character and mission. The point is to attempt a realistic assessment of certain ways of using his image (which in all likelihood he himself would repudiate). It is still not uncommon for priests and ministers, when confronted with the issue of women's liberation, to assert that God became incarnate uniquely as a male, and then to draw arguments for male supremacy from this. Indeed, the tradition itself tends to justify such assertions. The underlying—and often explicit—assumption in the minds of theologians down through the centuries has been that the divinity could not have deigned to become incarnate in the "inferior" sex, and the "fact" that "he" did not do so reinforces the belief in masculine superiority. The transformation of society by the erosion of male dominance will generate serious challenges to such assumptions of the Christological tradition.

It will, I think, become increasingly evident that exclusively masculine symbols for the ideal of "incarnation" will not do. As a uniquely masculine divinity loses credibility, so also the idea of a unique divine incarnation in a human being of the male sex may give way in the religious consciousness to an increased awareness of the divine presence in all human beings, understood as expressing and in a real sense incarnating—although always inadequately—the power of being. The seeds of this awareness are already present, of course, in the traditional doctrine that all human beings are made to the image of God and in a less than adequate way in the doctrine of grace. Now it should become possible to work out with increasing realism the implication in both of these doctrines that human beings are called to self-actualization and to the creation of a community that fosters the becoming of women and men. This means that no completely adequate models can be taken from the past. It may be that we will witness a remythologizing of Western religion. Certainly, if the need for parental symbols for God persists, something like the Father-Mother God proposed by Mary Baker Eddy will be more acceptable to the new woman and the new man than the Father God of the past. A symbolism for incarnation of the divine in human beings may continue to be needed in the future, but it is highly unlikely that women or men will continue to find plausible that symbolism which is epitomized in the image of the Virgin kneeling in adoration before her own son. Perhaps this will be replaced by the emergence of bisexual imagery which is not hierarchical. The experience of the past brought forth a new Adam and a new Eve. Perhaps the future will bring a new Christ and a new Mary. For the present, it would appear that we are being called upon to recognize the poverty of all symbols and the fact of our past idolatry regarding them, and to turn to our own resources for bringing about the radically new in our own lives.

The manifestation of God in Jesus was an eschatological event whose fulfilled reality lies in the future. The Jesus of the Gospels was a free person who challenged ossified beliefs and laws. Since he was remarkably free of prejudice against women and treated them as equals insofar as the limitations of his culture would allow, it is certain that he would be working with them for their liberation today. This awakening of women to their human potentiality by creative action as they assume equal partnership with men in society can bring about a manifestation of God in themselves which will be the Second Coming of God incarnate, fulfilling the latent promise in the original revelation that men and women are made to the image of God.

BEHIND THE MASK

It should be evident, then, that women's liberation is an event that can challenge authoritarian, exclusive and non-existential notions of faith and revelation. Since women have been extra-environmentals, to use a McLuhanish term, that is, since they have not been part of the authority structure which uses "faith" and "revelation" to reinforce the mechanisms of alienation, their emergence can effect a more widespread criticalness of idolatry which is often masked by these ideas. There could result from this a more general understanding of faith as a state of ultimate concern and commitment and a heightened sense of relativity concerning the symbols it uses to express this commitment. An awareness might also emerge—not merely in the minds of a theological elite, but in the general consciousness—that revelation is an ongoing experience.

The becoming of women implies also a transvaluation of values in Christian morality. As the old order is challenged and as men and women become freed to experience a wholeness of personality which the old polarizations impeded, the potentiality will be awakened for a change in moral consciousness which will go far beyond Nietzsche's merely reactionary rejection of Christian values.

Much of the traditional theory of Christian virtue appears to be the product of reactions on the part of men—perhaps guilty reactions—to the behavioral excesses of the stereotypic male. There has been theoretical emphasis upon charity, meekness, obedience, humility, self-abnegation, sacrifice, service. Part of the problem with this moral ideology is that it became generally accepted not by men but by women, who have hardly been helped by an ethic which reinforced their abject situation. This emphasis upon the passive virtues, of course, has not challenged exploitativeness but supported it. Part of the syndrome is the prevailing notion of sin as an offense against those in power, or against "God" (the two are often equated). Within the perspective of such a privatized morality the structures themselves of oppression are not seen as sinful.

Consistent with all of this is the fact that the traditional Christian moral consciousness has been fixated upon the problems of reproductive activity in a manner totally disproportionate to its feeble political concern. This was summed up several years ago in Archbishop Roberts' remark that "if contraceptives had been dropped over Japan instead of bombs which merely killed, maimed and shriveled up thousands alive there would have been a squeal of outraged protest from the Vatican to the remotest Mass center in Asia." Pertinent also is Simone de Beauvoir's remark that the church has reserved its uncompromising humanitarianism for man in the fetal condition. Although theologians today acknowledge that this privatized morality has failed to cope with the structures of oppression, few seriously face the possibility that the roots of this distortion are deeply buried in the fundamental and all-pervasive sexual alienation which the women's movement is seeking to overcome.

It is well-known that Christians under the spell of the jealous God who represents the collective power of his chosen people can use religion to justify that "us and them" attitude which is disastrous in its consequences for the powerless. It is less widely understood that the projection of "the other"—easily adaptable to national, racial and class differences—has basically and primordially been directed against women. Even the rhetoric of racism finds its model in sexism.

The consciousness-raising which is beginning among women is evoking a qualitatively new understanding of the subtle mechanisms which produce and destroy "the other," and a consequent empathy with all of the oppressed. This gives grounds for the hope that their emergence can generate a counterforce to the exploitative mentality which is destroying persons and the environment. Since the way men and women are seen in society is a prime determinant in the whole social system and ideology, radical women refuse to see their movement as simply one among others. What I am suggesting is that it might be the only chance for the turning of human beings from a course leading to the deterioration and perhaps the end of life on this planet.

Those who see their concern for women's liberation as consonant with an evolving Christianity would be unrealistic to expect much comprehension from the majority of male ecclesiastics. Such writers as Gordon Rattrey Taylor (*The Biological Time Bomb*), Robert Francoeur (*Utopian Motherhood*), and others keep beeping out the message that we are moving into a world in which human sexuality is no longer merely oriented to reproduction of the species—which means that the masculine and feminine mystiques are doomed to evaporate. Within the theological community, however, the predictable and almost universal response has been what one might call the ostrich syndrome. Whereas the old theology justified sexual oppression, the new theology for the most part simply ignores it and goes on in comfortable compatibility with it, failing to recognize its deep connection with such other major problems as war, racism and environmental pollution. The work of fostering religious consciousness which is explicitly incompatible with sexism will require an extraordinary degree of creative rage, love and hope.

Status of Indian Women
Ananda K. Coomaraswamy

Ananda Kentish Coomaraswamy (1877–1947) was born in Ceylon and educated in London to be a scientist. He soon afterward became interested in the religious philosophy of both East and West, especially as it was embodied in sacred art. In this area, he was one of the greatest art historians of modern times, and one of the most penetrating students of comparative religion. He was also active in Indian politics. Among his many works are *Hinduism and Buddhism*, *Buddha and the Gospel of Buddhism*, and *Am I My Brother's Keeper?*

In the *Mahabharata* there is reported a conversation between Shiva and Uma. The Great God asks her to describe the duties of women, addressing her, in so doing, in terms which acknowledge her perfect attainment of the highest wisdom possible to man or god—terms which it would be hard to parallel anywhere in western literature. He says:

"Thou that dost know the Self and the not-Self, expert in every work: endowed with self-restraint and perfect same-sightedness towards every creature: free from the sense of I and my—thy power and energy are equal to my own, and thou hast practised the most severe discipline. O Daughter of Himalaya, of fairest eyebrows, and whose hair ends in the fairest curls, expound to me the duties of women in full."

Then She, who is queen of heaven, and yet so sweetly human, answers:

"The duties of woman are created in the rites of wedding, when in presence of the nuptial fire she becomes the associate of her Lord, for the performance of all righteous deeds. She should be beautiful and gentle, considering her husband as her god and serving him as such in fortune and misfortune, health and sickness, obedient even if commanded to unrighteous deeds or acts that may lead to her own destruction. She should rise early, serving the gods, always keeping her house clean, tending to the domestic sacred fire, eating only after the needs of gods and guests and servants have been satisfied, devoted to her father and mother and the father and mother of her husband. Devotion to her Lord is woman's honor, it is her heaven; and O Maheshvara,"

she adds, with a most touching human cry,

"I desire not paradise itself if thou are not satisfied with me!"

"She is a true wife who gladdens her husband," says Rajashekhara in the *Karpura Manjari*. The extract following is from the Laws of Manu:

Though destitute of virtue, or seeking pleasure elsewhere, or devoid of good qualities, a husband must be constantly worshipped as a god by a faithful wife ... If a wife obeys her husband, she will for that reason alone be exalted in heaven.

The production of children, the nurture of those born, and the daily life of men, of these matters woman is visibly the cause.

She who controlling her thoughts, speech and acts, violates not her duty to her Lord, dwells with him after death in heaven, and in this world is called by the virtuous a faithful wife.

Similar texts from a variety of Indian sources could be indefinitely multiplied.

If such are the duties of women, women are accorded corresponding honor, and exert a corresponding influence upon society. This power and influence do not so much belong to the merely young and beautiful, nor to the wealthy, as to those who have lived—mothers and grandmothers—or who follow a religious discipline—widows or nuns. According to Manu: "A master exceedeth ten tutors in claim to honour; the father a hundred masters; but the mother a thousand fathers in right to reverence and in the function of teacher." When Rama accepted Kaikeyi's decree of banishment, it was because "a mother should be as much regarded by a son as is a father." Even at the present day it would be impossible to over-emphasize the influence of Indian mothers not only upon their children and in all household affairs, but upon their grown-up sons to whom their word is law. According to my observation, it is only those sons who have received an "English" education in India who no longer honour their fathers *and* mothers.

No story is more appropriate than that of Madalasa and her son Vikranta to illustrate the position of the Indian mother as teacher. As Vikranta grew up day by day, the *Markandeya Purana* relates, Madalasa "taught him knowledge of the Self[1] by ministering to him in sickness; and as he grew in strength and there waxed in him his father's heart, he attained to knowledge of the Self by his mother's words." And these were Madalasa's words, spoken to the baby crying on her lap:

"My child, thou art without a name or form, and it is but in fantasy that thou has been given a name. This thy body, framed of the five elements, is not thine in sooth, nor art thou of it. Why dost thou weep? Or, maybe, thou weepest not; it is a sound self-born that cometh forth from the king's son. . . . In the body dwells another self, and therewith abideth not the thought that 'This is mine,' which appertaineth to the flesh. Shame that man is so deceived!"

Even in recent times, in families where the men have received an English education unrelated to Indian life and thought, the inheritance of Indian modes of thought and feeling rests in the main with women; for a definite philosophy of life is bound up with household ritual and traditional etiquette and finds expression equally in folktale and cradle-song and popular poetry, and in those pauranic and epic stories which constitute the household Bible literature of India. Under these conditions it is often the case that Indian women, with all their faults of sentimentality and ignorance, have remained the guardians of a spiritual culture which is of greater worth than the efficiency and information of the educated.

It is according to the Tantrik scriptures, devoted to the cult of the Mother of the World, that women, who partake of her nature more essentially than other living beings, are especially honoured; here the woman may be a spiritual teacher (*guru*), and the initiation of a son by a mother is more fruitful than any other. One doubts how far this may be of universal application, believing with Paracelsus that woman is nearer to the world than man, of which the evidence

---

[1] "Knowledge of the Self"—the *Adhyatmavidya*.

appears in her always more personal point of view. But all things are possible to women such as Madalasa.

The claim of the Buddhist nun—"How should the woman's nature hinder us?"—has never been systematically denied in India. It would have been contrary to the spirit of Indian culture to deny to individual women the opportunity of saintship or learning in the sense of closing to them the schools of divinity or science after the fashion of the Western academies in the nineteenth century. But where the social norm is found in marriage and parenthood for men and women alike, it could only have been in exceptional cases and under exceptional circumstances that the latter specialised, whether in divinity, like Auvvai, Mira Bai, or the Buddhist nuns, in science, like Lilavati, or in war, like Chand Bibi or the Rani of Jhansi. Those set free to cultivate expert knowledge of science or to follow with undivided allegiance either religion of any art, could only be the *sannyasini* or devotee, the widow, and the courtesan. A majority of women have always, and naturally, preferred marriage and motherhood to either of these conditions. But those who felt the call of religion, those from whom a husband's death removed the central motif of their life, and those trained from childhood as expert artists, have always maintained a great tradition in various branches of cultural activity, such as social service or music. What we have to observe is that Hindu sociologists have always regarded these specializations as more or less incompatible with wifehood and motherhood; life is not long enough for the achievement of many different things.

Hinduism justifies no cult of ego-expression, but aims consistently at spiritual freedom. Those who are conscious of a sufficient inner life become the more indifferent to outward expression of their own or any changing personality. The ultimate purposes of Hindu social discipline are that men should unify their individuality with a wider and deeper than individual life, should fulfil appointed tasks regardless of failure or success, distinguish the timeless from its shifting forms, and escape the all-too-narrow prison of the "I and mine."

Anonymity is thus in accordance with the truth; and it is one of the proudest distinctions of the Hindu culture. The names of the "authors" of the epics are but shadows, and in later ages it was a constant practise of writers to suppress their own names and ascribe their work to a mythical or famous poet, thereby to gain a better attention for the truth that they would rather claim to have "heard" than to have "made." Similarly, scarcely a single Hindu painter or sculptor is known by name; and the entire range of Sanskrit literature cannot exhibit a single autobiography and but little history. Why should women have sought for modes of self-advertisement that held no lure even for men? The governing concept of Hindu ethics is vocation (*dharma*); the highest merit consists in the fulfilment of "one's own duty," in other words, in dedication to one's calling. Indian society was highly organized; and where it was considered wrong for a man to fulfil the duties of another man rather than his own, how much more must a confusion of function as between woman and man have seemed wrong, where differentiation is so much more evident. In the words of Manu: "To be mothers were women created, and to be fathers men"; and he added significantly "therefore are religious sacraments ordained in the Veda to be observed by the husband together with the wife."[2]

---

[2] Jahangir observes in his "*Memoirs*" that the Hindu woman "is the half of a man, and his companion in religious ceremonies." Cf. the *Prema Sagara*, ch. xxiv: "without a wife a sacrifice is not fruitful."

The Asiatic theory of marriage, which would have been perfectly comprehensible in the Middle Ages, before the European woman had become an economic parasite, and which is still very little removed from that of Roman or Greek Christianity, is not readily intelligible to the industrial democratic consciousness of Europe and America, which is so much more concerned for rights than for duties, and desires more than anything else to be released from responsibilities—regarding such release as freedom. It is thus that Western reformers would awaken a divine discontent in the hearts of Oriental women, forgetting that the way of ego-assertion cannot be a royal road to realization of the Self. The industrial mind is primarily sentimental, and therefore cannot reason clearly upon love and marriage; but the Asiatic analysis is philosophic, religious and practical.

Current Western theory seeks to establish marriage on a basis of romantic love and free choice; marriage thus depends on the accident of "falling in love." Those who are "crossed in love" or do not love are not required to marry. This individualistic position, however, is only logically defensible if at the same time it is recognized that to fall out of love must end the marriage. It is a high and religious ideal which justifies sexual relations only as the outward expression demanded by passionate love and regards an intimacy continued or begun for mere pleasure, or for reasons of prudence, or even as a duty, as essentially immoral; it is an ideal which isolated individuals and groups have constantly upheld; and it may be that the ultimate development of idealistic individualism will tend to a nearer realisation of it. But do not let us deceive ourselves that because the Western marriage is nominally founded upon free choice, it therefore secures a permanent unity of spiritual and physical passion. On the contrary, perhaps in a majority of cases, it holds together those are are no longer "in love"; habit, considerations of prudence, or, if there are children, a sense of duty often compel the passionless continuance of a marriage for the initiation of which romantic love was felt to be a *sine qua non*. Those who now live side by side upon a basis of affection and common interest would not have entered upon marriage on this basis alone.

If the home is worth preserving under modern conditions—and in India at any rate, the family is still the central element of social organization, then probably the "best solution" will always be found in some such compromise as is implied in a more or less permanent marriage; though greater tolerance than is now usual must be accorded to exceptions above and below the norm. What are we going to regard as the constructive basis of the normal marriage?

For Hindu sociologists marriage is a social and ethical relationship, and the begetting of children the payment of a debt. Romantic love is a brief experience of timeless freedom, essentially religious and ecstatic, in itself as purely antisocial as every glimpse of Union is a denial of the Relative; it is the way of Mary. It is true the glamour of this experience may persist for weeks and months, when the whole of life is illumined by the partial merging of the consciousness of the lover and beloved; but sooner or later in almost every case there must follow a return to the world of unreality, and that insight which once endowed the beloved with innumerable perfections fades in the light of commonsense. The lovers are fortunate if there remains to them a basis of common interest and common duty and a mutuality of temperament adequate for friendship, affection and forbearance; upon this chance depends the possibility of happiness during the greater part of almost every married life. The Hindu marriage differs from the marriage of sentiment mainly in putting these considerations first. Here, as elsewhere, happiness will arise from the fulfilment of vocation, far more than when immediate satisfaction is made the primary end. I use the term vocation advisedly; for the Oriental marriage, like the Oriental actor's art, is the fulfilment of a traditional design, and does not depend upon the accidents of sensibility. To be such a man as Rama, such a wife as Sita, rather than to express "oneself," is the aim. The formula is predetermined; husband and wife alike have parts to play; and it is from this point of view that we can best understand the meaning of Manu's law, that a wife should look on her husband as a god, regardless of his personal merit or demerits—it would be beneath her dignity to deviate from a woman's norm merely because of the failure of a man. It is for her own sake and for the sake of the community, rather than for his alone, that life must be attuned to the eternal unity of Purusha and Prakriti.

Whatever the ultimate possibilities of Western individualism, Hindu society was established on a basis of group morality. It is true that no absolute ethic is held binding on all classes alike; but within a given class the freedom of the individual is subordinated to the interest of the group, the concept of duty is paramount. How far this concept of duty trenches on the liberty of the individual may be seen in Rama's repudiation of Sita, subsequent to the victory in Lanka and the coronation at Ayodhya; although convinced of her perfect fidelity, Rama, who stands in epic history as the mirror of social ethics, consents to banish his wife, because the people murmur against her. The argument is that if the king should receive back a wife who had been living in another man's house, albeit faithful, popular morality would be endangered, since others might be moved by love and partiality to a like rehabilitation but with less justification. Thus the social order is placed before the happiness of the individual, whether man or woman. This is the explanation of the greater peace which distinguishes the arranged marriage of the East from the self-chosen marriage of the West; where there is no deception there can be no disappointment. And since the conditions on which it is founded do not change, it is logical that Hindu marriage should be indissoluble; only when social duties have been fulfilled and social debts paid, is it permissible for the householder to relinquish simultaneously the duties and the rights of the social individual. It is also logical that when the marriage is childless, it is permissible to take a second wife with the consent— and often at the wish—of the first.

It is sometimes asked, what opportunities are open to the Oriental woman? How can she express herself? The answer is that life is so designed that she is given the opportunity to be a woman—in other words, to realise, rather than to express herself. It is possible that modern Europe errs in the opposite direction. We must also remember that very much which passes for education nowadays is superficial; some of it amounts to little more than parlor tricks, and nothing is gained by communicating this condition to Asia, where I have heard of modern parents who desired that their daughters should be taught "a little French" or "a few strokes of the violin." The arts in India are professional and vocational, demanding undivided service; nothing is taught to the amateur by way of social accomplishment or studied superficially. And women represents the continuity of the racial life, an energy which cannot be divided or diverted without a corresponding loss of racial vitality; she can no more desire to be something other than herself, than the Vaishya could wish to be known as a Kshattriya, or the Kshattriya, as a Brahman.

It has been shown in fact, some seventy-five percent of Western graduate women do not marry; and apart from these, if it be true that five-sixths of a child's tendencies and activities are already determined before it reaches school age, and that the habits then deeply rooted cannot be greatly modified, if it be true that so much depends on deliberate training while the instincts of the child are still potential and habits unformed, can we say that women whose social duties or pleasures, or self-elected careers or unavoidable wage slavery draw them into the outer world, are fulfilling their duty to the race, or as we should say, the debt of the ancestors? The modern suffragist declares that the state has no right to demand of woman, whether directly or indirectly, by bribe or pressure of opinion, that she consider herself under any obligation, in return for the protection afforded her, to produce its future citizens. But we are hardly likely to see this point of view accepted in these days when the right of society to conscript the bodies of men is almost universally conceded. It is true that many who do not acquiesce in the existing industrial order are prepared to resist conscription in the military sense, that is to say, conscription for destruction; but we are becoming accustomed to the idea of another kind of conscription, or rather co-operation, based on service, and indeed, according to the two dynamic theories of a future society—the syndicalist and the individualistic—it must appear that without the fulfilment of function there can exist no *rights*. From the co-operative point of view society has an absolute right to compel its members to fulfil the functions that are necessary to it; and only those who, like the anchorite, voluntarily and entirely renounce the advantages of society and the protection of law have a right to ignore the claims of society.[3] From the individualist point of view, on the other hand, the fulfilment of function is regarded as a spontaneous activity, as is even now true in the cases of the thinker and the artist; but even the individualist does not expect to get something for nothing, and the last idea he has is to compel the service of others.

I doubt if anyone will deny that it is the function or nature of women, as a group—not necessarily in every individual case—in general, to be mothers, alike in spiritual and physical senses. What we have to do then, is not to assert the liberty of women to deny the duty or right of motherhood, however we regard it, but to accord this function a higher protection and honor than it now receives. And here, perhaps, there is still something to be learnt in Asia. There the pregnant woman is auspicious, and receives the highest respect; whereas in many industrial and secular Western societies she is an object of more or less open ridicule, she is ashamed to be seen abroad, and tries to conceal her condition, sometimes even by means that are injurious to her own and the child's health. That this was not the case in a more vital period of European civilization may be seen in all the literature and art of the Middle Ages, and particularly in the status of the Virgin Mary, whose motherhood endeared her to the folk so much more nearly than her virginity.

[3] A vigorous society can well afford to support, and in the interests of spiritual values will gladly support, so far as support is necessary, not only thinkers and artists, whose function is obvious, but also a certain number of thorough-going rebels who to all appearances are mere idlers. But the idler, whether anchorite or courtezan, must not *demand* to be supported in luxury, and must recognize that whatever he or she receives is given in *love*, and not according to *law*.

To avoid misunderstanding, let me say in passing, that in depicting the life of Hindu women as fulfilling a great ideal, I do not mean to indicate the Hindu social formula as a thing to be repeated or imitated. This would be a view as futile as that of the Gothic revival in architecture; the reproduction of period furniture does not belong to life. A perfection that has been can never be a perfection for us.

Marriage was made for man, not man for marriage. One would gladly accept for Europe very soon, and for Asia in due time, temporary marriage, the endowment of motherhood, and matriarchal succession, or whatever other forms our own spiritual and economic necessity may determine for us—not because such forms may be absolutely better than the Asiatic or mediaeval European institutions, but because they correspond more nearly to *our* inner life. In comparing one social order with another, I have no faith in any millennium past or future, but only in the best attainable adaptation of means to ends; and, "let the ends determine the means," should be the evidence of our idealism.

Let us now return to the Indian Sati and try to understand her better. The root meaning of the word is essential being, and we have so far taken it only in the wide sense. But she who refuses to live when her husband is dead is called Sati in a more special sense, and it is only so that the word (suttee) is well-known to Europeans. This last proof of the perfect unity of body and soul, this devotion beyond the grave, has been chosen by many Western critics as our reproach; we differ from them in thinking of our "suttees" not with pity, but with understanding, respect, and love. So far from being ashamed of our "suttees" we take a pride in them; that is even true of the most "progressive" amongst us. It is very much like the tenderness which our children's children may some day feel for those of their race who were willing to throw away their lives for "their country right or wong," though the point of view may seem to us then, as it seems to so many already, evidence rather of generosity than balanced judgment.

The criticism we make on the institution of Sati and woman's blind devotion is similar to the final judgment we are about to pass on patriotism. We do no not, as pragmatists may, resent the denial of the ego for the sake of an absolute, or attach an undue importance to mere life; on the contrary we see clearly that the reckless and useless sacrifice of the "suttee" and the patriot is spiritually significant. And what remains perpetually clear is the superiority of the reckless sacrifice to the calculating assertion of rights. Criticism of the position of the Indian woman from the ground of assertive feminism, therefore, leaves us entirely unmoved: precisely as the patriot must be unmoved by an appeal to self-interest or a merely utilitarian demonstration of futility. We do not object to dying for an idea as "suttees" and patriots have died; but we see that there may be other and greater ideas we can better serve by living for them.

For some reason it has come to be believed that Sati must have been a man-made institution imposed on women by men for reasons of their own, that it is associated with feminine servility, and that it is peculiar to India. We shall see that these views are historically unsound. It is true that in aristocratic circles Sati became to some degree a social convention,[4] and pressure was put on unwilling individuals, precisely as conscripts are even now forced to suffer or

---

[4] "Social conventions" are rarely "*man*-made laws" alone.

die for other people's ideas; and from this point of view we cannot but be glad that it was prohibited by law in 1829 on the initiative of Raja Rammohun Roy. But now that nearly a century has passed it should not be difficult to review the history and significance of Sati more dispassionately than was possible in the hour of controversy and the atmosphere of religious prejudice.

It is not surprising that the idea of Sati occupies a considerable place in Indian literature. Parvati herself, who could not endure the insults levelled against her husband by her father, is the prototype of all others. In the early Tamil lyrics we read of an earthly bride whom the Brahmans seek to dissuade from the sacrifice; but she answers that since her lord is dead, the cool waters of the lotus pool and the flames of the funeral pyre are alike to her. Another pleads to share her hero's grave, telling the potter that she had fared with her lord over many a desert plain, and asking him to make the funeral urn large enough for both. Later in history we read of the widowed mother of Harsha that she replied to her son's remonstrances:

"I am the lady of a great house; have you forgotten that I am the lioness-mate of a great spirit, who, like a lion, had his delight in a hundred battles?"

A man of such towering genius and spirituality as Kabir so takes for granted the authenticity of the impulse to Sati that he constantly uses it as an image of surrender of the ego to God; and indeed, in all Indian mystical literature the love-relation of woman to man is taken unhesitatingly as an immediate reflection of spiritual experience. This is most conspicuous in all the Radha-Krishna literature. But here let us notice more particularly the beautiful and very interesting poem of Muhammad Riza Nau'i, written in the reign of Akbar upon the "suttee" of a Hindu girl whose betrothed was killed on the very day of the marriage. This Musulman poet, to whom the Hindus were "idolaters," does not relate his story in any spirit of religious intolerance or ethical condescension; he is simply amazed "that after the death of men, the woman shows forth her marvellous passion." He does not wonder at the wickedness of men, but at the generosity of women; how different from the modern critic who can see no motive but self-interest behind a social phenomenon that passes his comprehension!

This Hindu bride refused to be comforted and wished to be burnt on the pyre of her dead betrothed. When Akbar was informed of this, he called the girl before him and offered wealth and protection, but she rejected all his persuasion as well as the counsel of the Brahmans, and would neither speak nor hear of anything but the Fire.

Akbar was forced, though reluctantly, to give his consent to the sacrifice, but sent with her his son Prince Daniyal who continued to dissuade her. Even from amidst the flames, she replied to his remonstrances, "Do not annoy, do not annoy, do not annoy." "Ah," exclaims the poet:

Let those whose hearts are ablaze with the Fire of
Love learn courage from this pure maid!
Teach me, O God, the Way of Love, and enflame my
heart with this maiden's Fire.

Thus he prays for himself; and for her:

Do Thou, O God, exalt the head of that rare hidden
virgin, whose purity exceeded that of the Houris,
Do Thou endear her to the first kissing of her King,
and graciously accept her sacrifice.

Matter of fact accounts of more modern "suttees" are given by Englishmen who have witnessed them. One which took place in Baroda in 1825 is described by R. Hartley Kennedy, the widow persisting in her intention in spite of "several fruitless endeavors to dissuade her." A more remarkable case is described by Sir Frederick Halliday. Here also a widow resisted all dissuasion, and finally proved her determination by asking for a lamp, and holding her finger in the flame until it was burnt and twisted like a quill pen held in the flame of a candle; all this time she gave no sign of fear or pain whatever. Sir F. Halliday had therefore to grant her wish, even as Akbar had had to do three centuries earlier.

It is sometimes said by Indian apologists that at certain times or places in India—amongst the Buddhists, or the Marathas, or in the epics—there was no purdah; or that certain historic or mythic individual women were not secluded. Such statements ignore the fact that there are other kinds of seclusion than those afforded by palace walls. For example, though Rama, Lakshman and Sita had lived together in forest exile for many years in closest affection, it is expressly stated that Lakshman had never raised his eyes above his brother's wife's feet, so that he did not even know her appearance. To speak more generally, it is customary for Hindus, when occasion arises for them to address an unknown woman, to call her "mother" irrespective of her age or condition. These unseen walls are a seclusion equally absolute with any purdah. One result is that the streets of an Indian city by night are far safer for a woman than those of any city in Europe. I have known more than one European woman, acquainted with India, express her strong conviction of this.

Western critics have often asserted that the Oriental woman is a slave, and that we have made her what she is. We can only reply that we do not identify freedom with self-assertion, and that the Oriental woman is what she is, only because our social and religious culture has permitted her to be and to remain essentially feminine. Exquisite as she may be in literature and art, we dare not claim for ourselves as men the whole honor of creating such a type, however persistently the industrious industrial critic would thrust it upon us.

The Eastern woman is not, at least we do not claim that she is, superior to other women in her innermost nature; she is perhaps an older, purer and more specialised type, but certainly an universal type, and it is precisely here that the industrial woman departs from type. Nobility in women does not depend upon race, but upon ideals; it is the outcome of a certain view of life.

Savitri, Padmavati, Sita, Radha, Uma, Lilavati, Tara—our divine and human heroines—have an universal fellowship, for everything feminine is of the Mother. Who could have been more wholly devoted than Alcestis, more patient than Griselda, more loving than Deirdre, more soldier than Joan of Arc, more Amazon than Brynhild?

When the Titanic sank, there were many women who refused—perhaps mistakenly, perhaps quite rightly—that was their own affair—to be rescued without their husbands, or were only torn from them by force; dramatic confirmation of the conviction that love-heroism is always and everywhere the same, and not only in India, nor only in ages past, may be stronger than death.

I do not think that the Indian ideal has ever been the exclusive treasure of any one race or time, but rather, it reappears wherever woman is set free to be truly herself, that is wherever a sufficiently religious, heroic and æsthetic culture has afforded her the necessary protection. Even the freedom which she seeks in modern self-assertion—which I would grant from the standpoint of one who will not govern—is merely an inverted concept of protection, and it may be that the more she is freed the more she will reveal the very type we have most adored in those who seemed to be slaves. Either way would be happier for men than the necessity of protecting women from themselves, and the tyranny of those who are not capable of friendship, being neither bound nor free.

The cry of our Indian Sati, "Do not annoy, do not annoy," and "No one has any right over the life of another; is not that my own affair?" is no cry for protection from a fate she does not seek; it is passionate, and it has been uttered by every woman in the world who has followed love beyond the grave. Deirdre refused every offer of care and protection from Conchubar: "It is not land or earth or food I am wanting," she said, "or gold or silver or horses, but leave to go to the grave where the sons of Usnach are lying." Emer called to Cuchullain slain: "Love of my life, my friend, my sweetheart, my one choice of the men of the world, many is the women, wed or unwed, envied me until to-day, and now I will not stay living after you."

Irish women were free, but we are used even more to look on the old Teutonic type as representative of free and even amazonian womanhood. We do not think of Brynhild, Shield-may and Victory-wafter, as compelled by men to any action against her will, or as weakly submissive. Yet when Sigurd was slain she became "suttee"; the prayers of Gunnar availed as little as those of Conchubar with Deirdre. He "laid his arms about her neck, and besought her to live and have wealth from him; and all others in like wise letter her from dying; but she thrust them all from her, and said that it was not the part of any to let her in that which was her will." And the second heroic woman figured in the saga, wedded to Sigurd, though she did not die, yet cried when he was betrayed:

> Now am I as little
> As the leaf may be
> Amid wind-swept wood,
> Now when dead he lieth.

"She who is courteous in her mind," says the *Shacktafelsk*, "with shyness shall her face be bright; of all the beauties of the body, none is more shining than shyness." This theory of courtesy, of supreme gentleness—"full sweetly bowing down her head," says the English Merlin, "as she that was shamefast," runs also through all mediæval chivalry. Yet it is about this shy quiet being, a mystery to men, that the whole mediæval world turns; "first reserve the honor to God," says Malory, "and secondly, the quarrel must come of thy lady." Like Uma and Sita, Virgin Mary is the image of a perfect being—

> For in this rose conteined was
> Heaven and earth in litel space—

and for a little while, in poetry and architecture, we glimpse an idealisation of woman and woman's love akin to the praise of Radha in the contemporary songs of Chandidas and Vidyapati.

But for our purpose even more significant than the religious and knightly culture, the product of less quickly changing conditions, and impressive too in its naïveté, is the picture of the woman of the people which we can gather from folk-song and lyric. Here was a being obviously strong and sensible, not without knowledge of life, and by no means economically a parasite. If we study the folk speech anywhere in the world we shall see that it reveals woman, and not the man, as typically the lover; when her shyness allows, it is she who would pray for man's love, and will serve him to the utmost. Industrialism reverses this relation, making man the suppliant and the servant, a condition as unnatural as any other of its characteristic perversions.

The woman of the folk does not bear resentment. Fair Helen, who followed Child Waters on foot, and bore his child in a stable, is overheard singing:

> *Lullaby, my owne deere child!*
> *I wold thy father were a king,*
> *Thy mother layed on a beere.*

Is she not like the Bengali Malanchamala, whose husband had married a second wife, and left her unloved and forgotten—who says, "though I die now, and become a bird or a lesser creature or whatever befall me, I care not, for I have seen my darling happy?"

If woman under industrialism is unsatisfied, it would be difficult to say how much man also loses. For woman is naturally the lover, the bestower of life:

> *Conjunction with me renders life long.*
> *I give youth when I enter upon amorousness.* [5]

Her complaint is not that man demands too much, but that he will accept too little.

> *Long time have I been waiting for the coming of my dear;*
> *Sometimes I am uneasy and troubled in my mind,*
> *Sometimes I think I'll go to my lover and tell him my mind.*
> *But if I should go to my lover, my lover he will say me nay,*
> *If I show to him my boldness, he'll ne'er love me again.* [6]

And it is to serve him, not to seek service from him that she desires:

> *In the cold stormy weather, when the winds are a-blowing,*
> *My dear, I shall be willing to wait on you then.* [7]

The Oriental woman, perhaps is not Oriental at all, but simply woman. If the modern woman could accept this thought, perhaps she would seek a new way of escape, not an escape from love, but a way out of industrialism. Could we not undertake this quest together?

[5] Nizami.
[6] Eastern Counties folk-song.
[7] Somerset folksong.

It is true that the modern woman is justified in her discontent. For of what has she not been robbed? The organization of society for competition and exploitation has made possible for the few, and only the very few, more physical comfort and greater security of life; but even these it has robbed of all poise, of the power to walk or to dress or to marry wisely, or to desire children or lovers, or to believe in any power not legally exteriorised. From faith in herself to a belief in votes, what a descent!

Decade after decade since the fourteenth century has seen her influence reduced. It was paramount in religion, in poetry, in music, in architecture and in all life. But men, when they reformed the church and taught you that love was not a sacrament without the seal of clerical approval; when they forced your music into modes of equal temperament; when they substituted knowledge for feeling and wisdom in education,[8] when they asked you to pinch your shoes and your waists, and persuaded you to think this a refinement, and the language of Elizabethan poetry coarse; when at last they taught you to become Imperialists, and went away alone to colonise and civilise the rest of the world, leaving you in England with nothing particular to do; when, if you have the chance to marry at all, it is ten or fifteen years too late—who can wonder that you are dissatisfied, and claim the right to a career of your own "not merely to earn your livelihood, but to provide yourself with an object in life?"[9] How many women have only discovered an object in life since the energies of men have been employed in activities of pure destruction? What a confession! To receive the franchise would be but a small compensation for all you have suffered, if it did not happen that we have now seen enough of representative government and the tyranny of majorities to understand their futility. Let women as well as men, turn away their eyes from the delusions of government, and begin to understand direct action, finding enough to do in solving the problems of their own lives, without attempting to regulate those of other people. No man of real power has either time or strength for any other man's work than his own, and this should be equally true for women. Aside from all questions of mere lust for power or demand for rights, untold evils have resulted from the conviction that it is our God-given duty to regulate other people's lives—the effects of the current theories of "uplift," and of the "white man's burden" are only single examples of this; and even if the intentions are good, we need not overlook the fact that the way to hell is often paved with good intentions.

Meanwhile there lies an essential weakness in the propaganda of emancipation, inasmuch as the argument is based on an unquestioning acceptance of male values. The so-called feminist is as much enslaved by masculine ideals as the so-called Indian nationalist is enslaved by European ideals. Like industrial man, the modern woman values industry more than leisure, she seeks in every way to externalise her life, to achieve success in men's professions, she feigns to be ashamed of her sexual nature, she claims to be as reasonable, as learned, as expert as any man, and her best men friends make the same claims on her behalf. But just in proportion as she lacks a genuine feminine idealism, inasmuch as she wishes to be something other than herself, she lacks power.

The claim of women to share the loaves and fishes with industrial man may

[8] Cf. *The Great State*, p. 127.
[9] From an advertisement in the *Englishwoman's Year Book*, 1911.

be as just as those of Indian politicians. But the argument that women can do what men can do ("we take all labor for our province," says Olive Schreiner) like the argument that Indians can be prepared to govern themselves by a course of studies in democracy, implies a profound self-distrust. The claim to equality with men, or with Englishmen—what an honor! That men, or Englishmen, as the case may be, should grant the claim—what a condescension!

If there is one profound intuition of the non-industrial consciousness, it is that the qualities of men and women are incommensurable. "The sexes are differently entertained," says Novalis, "man demands the sensational in intellectual form, woman the intellectual in sensational form. What is secondary to the man is paramount to the woman. Do they not resemble the Infinite, since it is impossible to square (*quadriren*) them, and they can only be approached through approximation?" Is not the Hindu point of view possibly right; not that men and woman should approach an identity of temperament and function, but that for the greatest abundance of life, there is requisite the greatest possible sexual differentiation?

What is it that great men—poets and creators, not men of analysis—demand of women? It is, surely, the requirements of the prolific, rather than of the devourers, which are of most significance for the human race, which advances under the guidance of leaders, and not by accident. The one thing they have demanded of women is Life.

To one thing at least the greatest men have been always indifferent, that is, the amount of knowledge a woman may possess. It was not by her learning that Beatrice inspired Dante, or the washerwoman Chandidas. When Cuchullain chose a wife, it was Emer, because she had the six gifts of beauty, voice, sweet speech, needlework, wisdom and charity. We know only of Helen that "strangely like she was to some immortal spirit"; in other words, she was radiant. Radha's shining made the ground she stood on bright as gold. The old English poet wrote of one like her

> *Hire lure lumes liht*
> *As a launterne a nyht.*

It is this radiance in women, more than any other quality, that urges men to every sort of heroism, be it martial or poetic.

Everyone understands the heroism of war; we are not surprised at Lady Hamilton's adoration of Nelson. But the activity of war is atavistic, and highly civilized people such as the Chinese regard it with open contempt. What nevertheless we do not yet understand is the heroism of art, that exhausting and perpetual demand which all creative labor makes alike on body and soul. The artist must fight a continual battle for mastery of himself and his environment; his work must usually be achieved in the teeth of violent, ignorant and often well-organised opposition, or against still more wearing apathy, and in any case, even at the best, against the intense resistance which matter opposes to the moulding force of ideas, the tamasic quality in things. The ardent love of women is not too great a reward for those who are faithful. But it is far more than the reward of action, it is the energy without which action may be impossible. As pure male, the Great God is inert, and his "power" is always feminine, and it is she who leads the hosts of heaven against the demons.

When man of necessity spent his life in war or in hunting, when women needed a personal physical as well as a Spiritual protection, then she could not do enough for him in personal service; we have seen in the record of folk-song and epic how it is part of woman's innermost nature to worship man. In the words of another Indian scripture, her husband is for her a place of pilgrimage, the giving of alms, the performance of vows, and he is her spiritual teacher—this according to the same school which makes the initiation of son by mother eight times more efficacious than any other. What we have not yet learnt is that like relations are needed for the finest quality of life, even under conditions of perpetual peace; the tenderness of women is as necessary to man now, as ever it was when his first duty was that of physical warfare, and few men can achieve greatness, and then scarcely without the danger of a one-sided development, whose environment lacks this atmosphere of tenderness. Woman possesses the power of perpetually creating in man the qualities she desires, and this is for her an infinitely greater power than the possession of those special qualities could ever confer upon her directly.

Far be it from us, however, to suggest the forcing of any preconceived development upon the modern individualist. We shall accomplish nothing by pressing anything in moulds. What I have tried to explain is that notwithstanding that the formula of woman's status in Oriental society may have ere now crystallised—as the formulae of classic art have become academic—nevertheless this formula represented once, and still essentially represents, although "unfelt" in realisation, a veritable expression of woman's own nature. If not so, then the formula stands self-condemned. I do not know if through our modern idealistic individualism it may be possible to renounce all forms and formulae for ever—I fear that it is only in heaven that there shall be neither marrying nor giving in marriage—but were that the case, and every creature free to find itself, and to behave according to its own nature, then it is possible, at least, that the "natural" relation of woman to man would after all involve the same conditions of magic that are implied in the soon-to-be-discarded conventional and calculated forms of mediæval art and Oriental society. If not, we must accept things as they really are—however they may be.

Meanwhile, it would be worth while to pause before we make haste to emancipate, that is to say, reform and industralize the Oriental woman. For it is not for Asia alone that she preserves a great tradition, in an age that is otherwise preoccupied. If she too should be persuaded to expend her power upon externals, there might come a time on earth when it could not be believed that such women had ever lived, as the ancient poets describe; it would be forgotten that woman had ever been unselfish, sensuous and shy. Deirdre, Brynhild, Alcestis, Sita, Radha, would then be empty names. And that would be a loss, for already it has been felt in Western schools that we "are not furnished with adequate womanly ideals in history and literature."[10]

The industrial revolution in India is of external and very recent origin; there is no lack of men, and it is the sacred duty of parents to arrange a marriage for every daughter: there is no divergence of what is spiritual and what is sensuous: Indian women do not deform their bodies in the interests of fashion: they are more concerned about service than rights: they consider barrenness the greatest

[10] Stanley Hall, *Youth*, ed. 1909, p. 286.

possible misfortune, after widowhood. In a word, it has never happend in India that women have been judged by or have accepted purely male standards. What possible service then, except in few externals, can the Western world render to Eastern women? Though it may be able to teach us much of the means of life, it has everything yet to relearn about life itself. And what we still remember there, we would not forget before we must.

THE CRISIS OF SEXUALITY: RELIGION AND EROS

Sex and Secularization

Harvey Cox

Harvey G. Cox (1929–   ) is associate professor of church and society at Harvard Divinity School. He is also author of *Feast of Fools* and *On Not Leaving It to the Snake*.

No aspect of human life seethes with so many unexorcised demons as does sex. No human activity is so hexed by superstition, so haunted by residual tribal lore, and so harassed by socially induced fear. Within the breast of urban-secular man, a toe-to-toe struggle still rages between his savage and his bourgeois forebears. Like everything else, the images of sex which informed tribal and town society are expiring along with the eras in which they arose. The erosion of traditional values and the disappearance of accepted modes of behavior have left contemporary man free, but somewhat rudderless. Abhoring a vacuum, the mass media have rushed in to supply a new code and a new set of behavioral prototypes. They appeal to the unexorcised demons. Nowhere is the persistence of mythical and metalogical denizens more obvious than in sex, and the shamans of sales do their best to nourish them. Nowhere is the humanization of life more frustrated. Nowhere is a clear word of exorcism more needed.

From Harvey G. Cox, *The Secular City* (New York, 1965), pp. 192–216. Copyright © 1965 by Harvey G. Cox. Reprinted with permission of The Macmillan Company.

How is the humanization of sex impeded? First it is thwarted by the parading of cultural-identity images for the sexually dispossessed, to make money. These images become the tyrant gods of the secular society, undercutting its liberation from religion and transforming it into a kind of neotribal culture. Second, the authentic secularization of sex is checkmated by an anxious clinging to the sexual standards of the town, an era so recent and yet so different from ours that simply to transplant its sexual ethos into our situation is to invite hypocrisy of the worst degree.

Let us look first at the spurious sexual models conjured up for our anxious society by the sorcerers of the mass media and the advertising guild. Like all pagan deities, these come in pairs—the god and his consort. For our purposes they are best symbolized by The Playboy and Miss America, the Adonis and Aphrodite of a leisure-consumer society which still seems unready to venture into full postreligious maturity and freedom. The Playboy and Miss America represent The Boy and The Girl. They incorporate a vision of life. They function as religious phenomena and shoud be exorcised and exposed.

THE RESIDUE OF TRIBALISM

Let us begin with Miss America. In the first century B.C., Lucretius wrote this description of the pageant of Cybele:

Adorned with emblem and crown . . . she is carried in awe-inspiring state. Tight-stretched tambourines and hollow cymbals thunder all round to the stroke of open hands, hollow pipes stir with Phrygian strain.... She rides in procession through great cities and mutely enriches mortals with a blessing not expressed in words. They straw all her path with brass and silver, presenting her with bounteous alms, and scatter over her a snow-shower of roses.[1]

Now compare this with the annual twentieth-century Miss America pageant in Atlantic City, New Jersey. Spotlights probe the dimness like votive tapers, banks of flowers exude their varied aromas, the orchestra blends feminine strings and regal trumpets. There is a hushed moment of tortured suspense, a drumroll, then the climax—a young woman with carefully prescribed anatomical proportions and exemplary "personality" parades serenely with scepter and crown to her throne. At TV sets across the nation throats tighten and eyes moisten. "There she goes, Miss America—" sings the crooner. "There she goes, your ideal." A new queen in America's emerging cult of The Girl has been crowned.

Is it merely illusory or anachronistic to discern in the multiplying pageants of the Miss America, Miss Universe, Miss College Queen type a residuum of the cults of the pre-Christian fertility goddesses? Perhaps, but students of the history of religions have become less prone in recent years to dismiss the possibility that the cultural behavior of modern man may be significantly illuminated by studying it in the perspective of the mythologies of bygone ages. After all, did not Freud initiate a revolution in social science by utilizing the venerable myth of Oedipus to help make sense out of the strange behavior of his Viennese

[1] This is quoted from Lucretius ii, 608f. in T. R. Glover, *The Conflict of Religions in the Early Roman Empire* (Boston: Beacon, 1960), p. 20. It was originally published in 1909 by Methuen & Co. Ltd.

contemporaries? Contemporary man carries with him, like his appendix and his finger-nails, vestiges of his tribal and pagan past.

In light of this fertile combination of insights from modern social science and the history of religions, it is no longer possible to see in the Miss America pageant merely an overpublicized prank foisted on us by the advertising industry. It certainly is this, but it is also much more. It represents the mass cultic celebration, complete with a rich variety of ancient ritual embellishments, of the growing place of The Girl in the collective soul of America.

This young woman—though she is no doubt totally ignorant of the fact—symbolizes something beyond herself. She symbolizes The Girl, the primal image, the One behind the many. Just as the Virgin appears in many guises—as our Lady of Lourdes or of Fatima or of Guadalupe—but is always recognizably the Virgin, so with the Girl.

The Girl is also the omnipresent icon of consumer society. Selling beer, she is folksy and jolly. Selling gems, she is chic and distant. But behind her various theophanies she remains recognizably The Girl. In Miss America's glowingly healthy smile, her openly sexual but officially virginal figure, and in the name-brand gadgets around her, she personifies the stunted aspirations and ambivalent fears of her culture. "There she goes, your ideal."

Miss America stands in a long line of queens going back to Isis, Ceres, and Aphrodite. Everything from the elaborate sexual taboos surrounding her person to the symbolic gifts at her coronation hints at her ancient ancestry. But the real proof comes when we find that the function served by The Girl in our culture is just as much a "religious" one as that served by Cybele in hers. The functions are identical—to provide a secure personal "identity" for initiates and to sanctify a particular value structure.

Let us look first at the way in which The Girl confers a kind of identity on her initiates. Simone de Beauvoir says in *The Second Sex* that "no one is *born* a woman."[2] One is merely born a female, and "*becomes* a woman" according to the models and meanings provided by the civilization. During the classical Christian centuries, it might be argued, the Virgin Mary served in part as this model. With the Reformation and especially with the Puritans, the place of Mary within the symbol system of the Protestant countries was reduced or eliminated. There are those who claim that this excision constituted an excess of zeal that greatly impoverished Western culture, an impoverishment from which it has never recovered. Some would even claim that the alleged failure of American novelists to produce a single great heroine (we have no Phaedra, no Anna Karenina) stems from this self-imposed lack of a central feminine ideal.

Without entering into this fascinating discussion, we can certainly be sure that, even within modern American Roman Catholicism, the Virgin Mary provides an identity image for few American girls. Where then do they look for the "model" Simone de Beauvoir convincingly contends they need? For most, the prototype of femininity seen in their mothers, their friends, and in the multitudinous images to which they are exposed on the mass media is what we have called The Girl.

In his significant monograph *Identity and the Life Cycle*, Erik Erikson reminds us that the child's identity is not modeled simply on the parent but on the

[2] Simone de Beauvoir, *The Second Sex* (New York: Knopf, 1953; London: Cape), p. 41.

parent's "super-ego."[3] Thus in seeking to forge her own identity the young girl is led beyond her mother to her mother's ideal image, and it is here that what Freud called "the ideologies of the superego . . . the traditions of the race and the people" become formative. It is here also that The Girl functions, conferring identity on those for whom she is—perhaps never completely consciously—the tangible incarnation of womanhood.

To describe the mechanics of this complex psychological process by which the fledgling American girl participates in the life of The Girl and thus attains a woman's identity would require a thorough description of American adolescence. There is little doubt, however, that such an analysis would reveal certain striking parallels to the "savage" practices by which initiates in the mystery cults shared in the magical life of their god.

For those inured to the process, the tortuous nightly fetish by which the young American female pulls her hair into tight bunches secured by metal clips may bear little resemblance to the incisions made on their arms by certain African tribesmen to make them resemble their totem, the tiger. But to an anthropologist comparing two ways of attempting to resemble the holy one, the only difference might appear to be that with the Africans the torture is over after initiation, while with the American it has to be repeated every night, a luxury only a culture with abundant leisure can afford.

In turning now to an examination of the second function of The Girl—supporting and portraying a value system—a comparison with the role of the Virgin in the twelfth and thirteenth centuries may be helpful. Just as the Virgin exhibited and sustained the ideals of the age that fashioned Chartres Cathedral, as Henry Adams saw, so The Girl symbolizes the values and aspirations of a consumer society. (She is crowned not in the political capital, remember, but in Atlantic City or Miami Beach, centers associated with leisure and consumption.) And she is not entirely incapable of exploitation. If men sometimes sought to buy with gold the Virgin's blessings on their questionable causes, so The Girl now dispenses her charismatic favor on watches, refrigerators, and razor blades—for a price. Though The Girl has built no cathedrals, without her the colossal edifice of mass persuasion would crumble. Her sharply stylized face and figure beckon us from every magazine and TV channel, luring us toward the beatific vision of a consumer's paradise.

The Girl is *not* the Virgin. In fact she is a kind of anti-Madonna. She reverses most of the values traditionally associated with the Virgin—poverty, humility, sacrifice. In startling contrast, particularly, to the biblical portrait of Mary in Luke 1:46–55, The Girl has nothing to do with filling the hungry with "good things," hawking instead an endless proliferation of trivia on TV spot commercials. The Girl exalts the mighty, extols the rich, and brings nothing to the hungry but added despair. So The Girl does buttress and bring into personal focus a value system, such as it is. In both social and psychological terms, The Girl, whether or not she is really a goddess, certainly acts that way.

Perhaps the most ironic element in the rise of the cult of The Girl is that Protestantism has almost completely failed to notice it, while Roman Catholics have at least given some evidence of sensing its significance. In some places, for

[3] Erik Erikson, *Identity and the Life Cycle* (New York: International University Press, 1959).

instance, Catholics are forbidden to participate in beauty pageants, a ruling not entirely inspired by prudery. It is ironic that Protestants have traditionally been most opposed to lady cults while Catholics have managed to assimilate more than one at various points in history.

If we are correct in assuming that The Girl *functions* in many ways as a goddess, then the cult of The Girl demands careful Protestant theological criticism. Anything that functions, even in part, as a god when it is in fact not God, is an idol. When the Reformers and their Puritan offspring criticized the cult of Mary it was not because they were antifeminist. They opposed anything—man, woman, or beast (or dogma or institution)—that usurped in the slightest the prerogatives that belonged alone to God Almighty. As Max Weber has insisted, when the prophets of Israel railed against fertility cults, they had nothing against fertility. It is not against sexuality but against a cult that protest is needed. Not, as it were, against the beauty but against the pageant.

Thus the Protestant objection to the present cult of The Girl must be based on the realization that The Girl is an *idol*. She functions as the source of value, the giver of personal identity. But the values she mediates and the identity she confers are both spurious. Like every idol she is ultimately a creation of our own hands and cannot save us. The values she represents as ultimate satisfactions—mechanical comfort, sexual success, unencumbered leisure—have no ultimacy. They lead only to endless upward mobility, competitive consumption, and anxious cynicism. The devilish social insecurities from which she promises to deliver us are, alas, still there, even after we have purified our breaths, our skins, and our armpits by applying her sacred oils. She is a merciless goddess who draws us farther and farther into the net of accelerated ordeals of obeisance. As the queen of commodities in an expanding economy, the fulfillment she promises must always remain just beyond the tips of our fingers.

Why has Protestantism kept its attention obsessively fastened on the development of Mariolatry in Catholicism and not noticed the sinister rise of this vampirelike cult of The Girl in our society? Unfortunately, it is due to the continuing incapacity of theological critics to recognize the religious significance of cultural phenomena outside the formal religious system itself. But the rise of this new cult reminds us that the work of the reformer is never done. Man's mind is indeed—as Luther said—a factory busy making idols. The Girl is a far more pervasive and destructive influence than the Virgin, and it is to her and her omnipresent altars that we should be directing our criticism.

Besides sanctifying a set of phony values, The Girl compounds her noxiousness by maiming her victims in a Procrustean bed of uniformity. This is the empty "identity" she panders. Take the Miss America pageant, for example. Are these virtually indistinguishable specimens of white, middle-class post-adolescence really the best we can do? Do they not mirror the ethos of a mass-production society, in which genuine individualism somehow mars the clean, precision-tooled effect? Like their sisters, the finely calibrated Rockettes, these meticulously measured and pretested "beauties" lined up on the Boardwalk bear an ominous similarity to the faceless retinues of goose-steppers and the interchangeable mass exercisers of explicitly totalitarian societies. In short, *who* says this is beauty?

The caricature becomes complete in the Miss Universe contest, when Miss Rhodesia is a blonde, Miss South Africa is white, and Oriental girls with a totally different tradition of feminine beauty are forced to display their thighs and appear in spike heels and Catalina swim suits. Miss Universe is as universal as an American adman's stereotype of what beauty should be.

The truth is that The Girl can*not* bestow the identity she promises. She forces her initiates to torture themselves with starvation diets and beauty-parlor ordeals, but still cannot deliver the satisfactions she holds out. She is young, but what happens when her followers, despite added hours in the boudoir, can no longer appear young? She is happy and smiling and loved. What happens when, despite all the potions and incantations, her disciples still feel the human pangs of rejection and loneliness? Or what about all the girls whose statistics, or "personality" (or color) do not match the authoritative "ideal"?

After all, it is God—not The Girl—who is God. He is the center and source of value. He liberates men and women from the bland uniformity of cultural deities so that they may feast on the luxurious diversity of life He has provided. The identity He confers frees men from all pseudo-identities to be themselves, to fulfill their human destinies regardless whether their faces or figures match some predetermined abstract "ideal." As His gift, sex is freed from both fertility cults and commercial exploitation to become the thoroughly human thing He intended. And since it is one of the last items we have left that is neither pre-packaged nor standardized, let us not sacrifice it too hastily on the omnivorous altar of Cybele.

The Playboy, illustrated by the monthly magazine of that name, does for the boys what Miss America does for the girls. Despite accusations to the contrary, the immense popularity of this magazine is not solely attributable to pin-up girls. For sheer nudity its pictorial art cannot compete with such would-be competitors as *Dude* and *Escapade*. *Playboy* appeals to a highly mobile, increasingly affluent group of young readers, mostly between eighteen and thirty, who want much more from their drugstore reading than bosoms and thighs. They need a total image of what it means to be a man. And Mr. Hefner's *Playboy* has no hesitation in telling them.

Why should such a need arise? David Riesman has argued that the responsibility for character formation in our society has shifted from the family to the peer group and to the mass-media peer-group surrogates.[4] Things are changing so rapidly that one who is equipped by his family with inflexible, highly internalized values becomes unable to deal with the accelerated pace of change and with the varying contexts in which he is called upon to function. This is especially true in the area of consumer values toward which the "other-directed person" is increasingly oriented.

Within the confusing plethora of mass media signals and peer-group values, *Playboy* fills a special need. For the insecure young man with newly acquired free time and money who still feels uncertain about his consumer skills, *Playboy* supplies a comprehensive and authoritative guidebook to this forbidding new world to which he now has access. It tells him not only who to be; it tells him *how* to be it, and even provides consolation outlets for those who secretly feel that they have not quite made it.

[4] David Riesman, *The Lonely Crowd* (New Haven: Yale University Press, 1950; Harmondsworth, Middlesex: Penguin).

In supplying for the other-directed consumer of leisure both the normative identity image and the means for achieving it, *Playboy* relies on a careful integration of copy and advertising material. The comic book that appeals to a younger generation with an analogous problem skillfully intersperses illustrations of incredibly muscled men and excessively mammalian women with advertisements for body-building gimmicks and foam-rubber brassière supplements. Thus the thin-chested comic-book readers of both sexes are thoughtfully supplied with both the ends and the means for attaining a spurious brand of maturity. *Playboy* merely continues the comic-book tactic for the next age group. Since within every identity crisis, whether in teens or twenties, there is usually a sexual-identity problem, *Playboy* speaks to those who desperately want to know what it means to be a man, and more specifically a *male*, in today's world.

Both the image of man and the means for its attainment exhibit a remarkable consistency in *Playboy*. The skilled consumer is cool and unruffled. He savors sports cars, liquor, high fidelity, and book-club selections with a casual, unhurried aplomb. Though he must certainly *have* and *use* the latest consumption item, he must not permit himself to get too attached to it. The style will change and he must always be ready to adjust. His persistent anxiety that he may mix a drink incorrectly, enjoy a jazz group that is passé, or wear last year's necktie style is comforted by an authoritative tone in *Playboy* beside which papal encyclicals sound irresolute.

"Don't hesitate," he is told, "this assertive, self-assured weskit is what every man of taste wants for the fall season." Lingering doubts about his masculinity are extirpated by the firm assurance that "real men demand this ruggedly masculine smoke" (cigar ad). Though "the ladies will swoon for you, no matter what they promise, don't give them a puff. This cigar is for men only." A fur-lined canvas field jacket is described as "the most masculine thing since the cave man." What to be and how to be it are both made unambiguously clear.

Since being a male necessitates some kind of relationship to females, *Playboy* fearlessly confronts this problem too, and solves it by the consistent application of the same formula. Sex becomes one of the items of leisure activity that the knowledgeable consumer of leisure handles with his characteristic skill and detachment. The girl becomes a desirable—indeed an indispensable—"Playboy accessory."

In a question-answering column entitled "The Playboy Adviser," queries about smoking equipment (how to break in a meerschaum pipe), cocktail preparation (how to mix a Yellow Fever), and whether or not to wear suspenders with a vest alternate with questions about what to do with girls who complicate the cardinal principal of casualness either by suggesting marriage or by some other impulsive gesture toward a permanent relationship. The infallible answer from the oracle never varies: sex must be contained, at all costs, within the entertainment-recreation area. Don't let her get "serious."

After all, the most famous feature of the magazine is its monthly fold-out photo of a *play*mate. She is the symbol par excellence of recreational sex. When playtime is over, the playmate's function ceases, so she must be made to understand the rules of the game. As the crew-cut young man in a *Playboy* cartoon says to the rumpled and disarrayed girl he is passionately embracing, "Why speak of love at a time like this?"

The magazine's fiction purveys the same kind of severely departmentalized sex. Although the editors have recently dressed up the *Playboy* contents with contributions by Hemingway, Bemelmans, and even a Chekhov translation, the regular run of stories relies on a repetitious and predictable formula. A successful young man, either single or somewhat less than ideally married—a figure with whom readers have no difficulty identifying—encounters a gorgeous and seductive woman who makes no demands on him except sex. She is the prose duplication of the cool-eyed but hot-blooded playmate of the fold-out.

Drawing heavily on the fantasy life of all young Americans, the writers utilize for their stereotyped heroines the hero's schoolteacher, his secretary, an old girl friend, or the girl who brings her car into the garage where he works. The happy issue is always a casual but satisfying sexual experience with no entangling alliances whatever. Unlike the women he knows in real life, the *Playboy* reader's fictional girl friends know their place and ask for nothing more. They present no danger of permanent involvement. Like any good accessory, they are detachable and disposable.

Many of the advertisements reinforce the sex-accessory identification in another way—by attributing female characteristics to the items they sell. Thus a full-page ad for the MG assures us that this car is not only "the smoothest pleasure machine" on the road and that having one is a "love-affair," but most important, "you drive it—it doesn't drive you." The ad ends with the equivocal question "Is it a date?"[5]

Playboy insists that its message is one of liberation. Its gospel frees us from captivity to the puritanical "hatpin brigade." It solemnly crusades for "frankness" and publishes scores of letters congratulating it for its unblushing "candor." Yet the whole phenomenon of which *Playboy* is only a part vividly illustrates the awful fact of a new kind of tyranny.

Those liberated by technology and increased prosperity to new worlds of leisure now become the anxious slaves of dictatorial tastemakers. Obsequiously waiting for the latest signal on what is cool and what is awkward, they are paralyzed by the fear that they may hear pronounced on them that dread sentence occasionally intoned by "The Playboy Adviser": "You goofed!" Leisure is thus swallowed up in apprehensive competitiveness, its liberating potential transformed into a self-destructive compulsion to consume only what is *à la mode*. *Playboy* mediates the Word of the most high into one section of the consumer world, but it is a word of bondage, not of freedom.

Nor will *Playboy*'s synthetic doctrine of man stand the test of scrutiny. Psychoanalysts constantly remind us how deep-seated sexuality is in the human being. But if they didn't remind us, we would soon discover it ourselves anyway. Much as the human male might like to terminate his relationship with a woman as he would snap off the stereo, or store her for special purposes like a camel's-hair jacket, it really can't be done. And anyone with a modicum of experience with women knows it can't be done. Perhaps this is the reason *Playboy*'s readership drops off so sharply after the age of thirty.

Playboy really feeds on the existence of a repressed fear of involvement with women, which for various reasons is still present in many otherwise adult Americans. So *Playboy*'s version of sexuality grows increasingly irrelevant as authentic sexual maturity is achieved.

---

[5] This whole fusing of sex and machine symbols in contemporary mass media was once brilliantly explored by Marshall McLuhan in *The Mechanical Bride*, now out of print.

The male identity crisis to which *Playboy* speaks has at its roots a deep-set fear of sex, a fear that is uncomfortably combined with fascination. *Playboy* strives to resolve this antinomy by reducing the proportions of sexuality, its power and its passion, to a packageable consumption item. Thus in *Playboy's* iconography the nude woman symbolizes total sexual accessibility but demands nothing from the observer. "You drive it—it doesn't drive you." The terror of sex, which cannot be separated from its ecstasy, is dissolved. But this futile attempt to reduce the *mysterium tremendum* of the sexual fails to solve the problem of being a man. For sexuality is the basic form of all human relationship, and therein lies its terror and its power.

Karl Barth has called this basic relational form of man's life *Mitmensch,* co-humanity.[6] This means that becoming fully human, in this case a human male, requires not having the other totally exposed to me and my purposes— while I remain uncommitted—but exposing myself to the risk of encounter with the other by reciprocal self-exposure. The story of man's refusal so to be exposed goes back to the story of Eden and is expressed by man's desire to control the other rather than to *be with* the other. It is basically the fear to be one's self, a lack of the "courage to be."

Thus any theological critique of *Playboy* that focuses on its "lewdness" will misfire completely. *Playboy* and its less successful imitators are not "sex magazines" at all. They are basically antisexual. They dilute and dissipate authentic sexuality by reducing it to an accessory, by keeping it at a safe distance.

It is precisely because these magazines are antisexual that they deserve the most searching kind of theological criticism. They foster a heretical doctrine of man, one at radical variance with the biblical view. For *Playboy's* man, others— especially women—are *for* him. They are his leisure accessories, his playthings. For the Bible, man only becomes fully man by being *for* the other.

Moralistic criticisms of *Playboy* fail because its antimoralism is one of the few places in which *Playboy* is right. But if Christians bear the name of One who was truly man because He was totally *for* the other, and if it is in Him that we know who God is and what human life is for, then we must see in *Playboy* the latest and slickest episode in man's continuing refusal to be fully human.

Freedom for mature sexuality comes to man only when he is freed from the despotic powers which crowd and cower him into fixed patterns of behavior. Both Miss America and The Playboy illustrate such powers. When they determine man's sexual life, they hold him in captivity. They prevent him from achieving maturity. They represent the constant danger of relapsing into tribal thralldom which always haunts the secular society, a threat from which the liberating, secularizing word of the Gospel repeatedly recalls it.

REMNANTS OF TOWN VIRTUES

Equally hazardous for sexual maturity, however, is the lure of town culture, the period we have most recently left behind, at least in most respects. In the area of sexual ethics, this period speaks to us through the traditional sexual practices of our Puritan and Victorian pasts. Since the melody of this ethic

[6] Karl Barth, *Church Dogmatics* (Edinburgh: T & T Clark, 1957), II/2.

lingers on today, our sexual ethics are caught in the crossfire of contradiction and confusion. To illustrate this tension, let us take the traditional ideal of premarital chastity.

I choose this not because of any belief that it is really the key issue. It does seem clear, however, that for many young adults today "to bed or not to bed" *seems* to be the Big Question, and I believe the reasons they press it so vigorously merit exploration. Three aspects of the problem require particular attention: (1) why the yes or no of premarital chastity is more critical for young adults today than in the past; (2) why the answers we usually give to this question are either not heard or provide little guidance; and (3) what, if anything, we should be saying about the matter.

Let us reject at the outset any Kinseyian inference that what *is* being done should determine what *ought* to be done. But let us candidly admit that our culture has undergone drastic changes. Though our Puritan style of life has vanished almost completely, the Puritan sex ethic remains, at least on paper. We have exchanged ankle-length dresses for bikinis. We hold blanket parties instead of bobbing for apples. But the people caught up in these epochal changes are still taught, albeit with winks and evasions, the selfsame code of total premarital abstinence that was instilled into Priscilla Alden.

We have thus fashioned for unmarried young adults a particularly unfortunate combination of emotional environments. They are constantly bombarded —through clothing styles, entertainment, advertising, and courtship mores— with perhaps the most skillfully contrived array of erotic stimulants ever amassed. Their sexual fears and fantasies are studied by motivational researchers and then ruthlessly exploited by mass-media hucksters. Elizabeth Taylor's Brobdingnagian bosom decorates billboards, and throaty songstresses hum their hoarse invitations from transistors.

Yet we pass on to our youth, unaltered, a set of behavioral taboos that, in a sex-saturated society, seem diabolically created to produce a high level of duplicity and desperation.

Why have we deliberately constructed such a bizarre imbalance in our moral and psychological milieu? Obviously because we want to have our cake and eat it too. We want to gorge ourselves at the table of an affluent society whose continued prosperity, we are told, necessitates a constantly expanding market. And sex sells anything. At the same time we want to cherish our national memories of Pilgrims and piety, including the sexual code of Massachusetts Bay. The inherent contradiction comes home to roost in the already tormented psyche of the unmarried young adult.

The essential contradictions of any society, as the Marxists say, are concentrated in its proletariat. In a sexually exploitative society, youth subculture becomes the psychological proletariat. It picks up the tab for our hypocrisy. Exposed to all the stimulants married people are, young people are forbidden the socially acceptable form of fulfillment. The refusal is expressed both in the laws of the realm and in the official taboos of the culture. Enforcement, however, is sporadic, and, because the signals are so confused and contradictory, adolescents suspect that it is all one vast dissimulation.

No wonder the beatnik, who rejects *both* the signals of the mass media and the sexual mores, becomes the secret hero of many young adults.

To make matters just a bit more trying, we have thoughtfully provided Jane and Joe more privacy and permissiveness in dating than ever before. This extends far beyond Harvard dormitory rooms. I wonder if Henry Ford ever realized that his invention would be viewed by many not primarily as a means of transportation but as the urban society's substitute for Keats' "elfin grot."

Remember also that dating (and with it various types of petting) now reaches down to the sixth grade. Youngsters are thus exposed for a longer period and much more intensely to the mutual exploration of erogenous regions, which is the American courtship pattern. The only advice they get is "Don't go too far," and it is usually the girl who is expected to draw the line.

By the time a girl who begins petting at thirteen has reached marriageable age, she has drawn an awful lot of lines. If she is especially impressed with her religious duty to avoid sexual intercourse, she will probably have mastered, by twenty-one, all the stratagems for achieving a kind of sexual climax while simultaneously preventing herself and her partner from crossing the sacrosanct line.

What this border-skirting approach does to inhibit her chances for a successful adjustment in marriage is a question now engaging the attention of psychologists and marriage counselors. One psychologist who specializes in sexual behavior remarked recently that if Americans had consciously set out to think up a system that would produce maximal marital and premarital strife for both sexes, we could scarcely have invented a sexually more sabotaging set of dating procedures than we have today. This may be an overstatement, but I suspect the inherent hypocrisy of the cultural taboo and the patterns of behavior it engenders must have considerable negative influence on marriage.

Add to this the fact that penicillin and oral contraceptives will soon remove the last built-in deterrents to premarital coitus, and the reason for the recent rumblings of discontent with traditional standards becomes clearer. Not that the young adults themselves are guiltless. They share the blame for perpetuating the same values. But they also consider themselves the victims of a kind of cultural charade. They are shown one thing, told another, and they never know when the society will wink and when it will whip them. Their suspicion that they are the fall guys in a giant collusion is expressed in their growing demand that we come clean on this matter.

Now we can turn to the question of why, amid this schizophrenic carnival of prurience and prudery, the Christian Gospel seems to offer so little positive guidance. I believe the answer to this question is that most young adults do not perceive Christian sexual ethics as "evangelical," that is, as *good news*. They are not hearing the Gospel as good news and therefore they are not hearing the Gospel at all, but something else.

The German theologian Friedrich Gogarten states that the two most serious dangers from which the Gospel must be protected are (a) its being dissolved into a myth and (b) its being hardened into a religion of Law.[7] In either case it ceases to be the Gospel. When we examine what has happened to the Gospel as it touches the area of sex, it is evident that both of these distortions have set in.

The Gospel comes to the sexual puzzlement of most young adults not as a liberating *yes*, not as God's Good News freeing them for personhood and community. It comes rather as a remnant of cultural Christendom and an

[7] Friedrich Gogarten, *Der Mensch zwischen Gott und Welt* (Stuttgart: F. Vorwerk Verlag, 1956), p. 34.

assortment of confused conventions. To be heard once again as the Gospel it must be demythologized and delegalized.

Let us turn first to the task of demythologizing it from odd bits of sexual folklore with which it has been confused. I shall refer to only two of the many mythical motifs that obfuscate the Gospel in its bearing on sexual conduct. First the ideal of romantic love, which Denis de Rougement has traced to paganism and which is almost always fused with any young American's ideas about sex.[8] Second, the Western obsession with coital intercourse as normative sexuality and hence as that which defines the content of chastity and virginity. The identification is now so complete that, as Theodor W. Adorno recently pointed out, intercourse now *means* coitus.[9]

Both the romantic ideal and the identification of intercourse with coitus are cultural accretions that have been coalesced with the rule of premarital chastity. The combination has so beclouded the liberating power of the Gospel that it can scarcely be heard because of them, and the Gospel is frequently perceived to be saying almost the opposite of what is intended.

The ideal of romantic love is the most obvious mythical excrescence. It leads often to the belief, especially among girls, that certain forms of intimacy become progressively less objectionable the more you "love" the boy. The snares in this curious amalgam of Our Gal Sunday and Saint Teresa are manifold. Among adolescents of all ages, *love* has come to mean nothing more than a vague emotional glow. It's "that ol' black magic, ... those icy fingers up and down my spine."

The belief that love is the only honest basis for sex forces countless maidens into anguished efforts to justify their sexual inconstancy by falling in and out of love with a passing parade of partners. Naturally, opportunities for self-deception are almost endless, and the outcome is often an acid cynicism about the possibility of ever really loving anyone.

Furthermore, the sex-and-romantic-love equation sets up an inevitable collision course. The conflict occurs because, although girls tend to "go the limit" only with a boy they believe they "love," many boys, as sociologist Winston Ehrmann shows in his *Premarital Dating Behavior,*[10] will stop short of intercourse with girls they "love" or "respect," though they will go as far as possible with another girl. Thus girls associate sex with romantic love far more than boys do, and emotional scars emerging from this built-in contradiction often last far into married life.

Since girls feel they must be swept into sexual experience by something "bigger than both of us," they often fail to take the precautions against pregnancy they might otherwise. Somehow it doesn't seem romantic to go out with a boy, having prepared in advance to be swept off one's feet. Consequently, many instances of intercourse are not "planned," but occur more or less spontaneously at the end of an evening of progressively heavier necking. Unwanted pregnancies, abortions, shattered family relations, and forfeited careers are the inevitable result.

---

[8] Denis de Rougement, *Love in the Western World* (New York: Pantheon, 1956).
[9] Theodor W. Adorno, *Neun Kritische Modelle* (Frankfurt: Suhrkamp Verlag, 1963), pp. 99ff.
[10] Winston Ehrmann, *Premarital Dating Behavior* (New York: Holt, 1959).

One solution is to admonish everybody to avoid any physical contact that could spiral toward intercourse. But how sane or compassionate is this advice in a society where various types of petting are the only socially approved way of handling tensions exacerbated by a sexually saturated culture? Petting does sometimes lead to intercourse, but not always. Most of the time it does not. To try to abolish it while still retaining our prosperity and our aphrodisiac advertising would be even less honest than the preach-and-wink pharisaism.

Another antidote is simply to deromanticize sex. This would mean urging young people who are going to have intercourse anyway (and who, under layers of unsuccessful self-deception, know they will) to accept the full responsibility for their behavior and to take the necessary steps to avoid pregnancy.

Such a solution, although more realistic, has almost as little chance of acceptance as the first. It would necessitate dispelling the illusions of romantic love and suggesting that young people ponder soberly in the light of day what they are really doing. But it would also require our society to face up to the cant and flimflam of its sexual folkways, and this no one really wants to do. So the black magic, petting, and pregnancies will probably continue.

A more stubborn and deceptive segment of folklore that has been equated with the doctrine of premarital chastity is one that is rarely discussed openly: the curious presumption that a person who has not experienced coital intercourse remains a virgin—no matter what else he or she has done. This popular piece of legerdemain explains in part the discovery by Kinsey that, although the incidence of premarital intercourse among women has merely mounted steadily, premarital petting of all varieties has skyrocketed.

Kinsey's finding could be substantiated by the most casual observer of the American college scene. The number of students who do not pet at all is negligible. An increasing number regularly carry their necking to the point of heavy sex play and orgasm. A pert young graduate of a denominational college assured me recently that although she had necked to orgasm every week-end for two years, she had never "gone all the way." Her premarital chastity was intact.

Or was it? Only, I submit, by the most technical definition of what is meant by preserving virginity. True, some writers actually advocate such noncoital orgasm as the "safest" way for unmarried people to achieve sexual climax. However distasteful this idea may seem to some, it is extremely important to realize that the church's traditional teaching actually functions in such a fashion as to give considerable support to this view.

The ideal of premarital chastity is generally understood to mean that, although necking is somewhat questionable, the fragile gem of virginity remains intact so long as coitus is avoided. This myth has helped open the floodgate to a tidal wave of noncoital promiscuity.

Here the demythologizing process might be helped if we note Saint Paul's insistence (in I Corinthians 6:15–16) that liaisons intended to be highly casual, for example with prostitutes, nevertheless involve us in a relationship that is inevitably much deeper than we bargained for. We "become one flesh." D. S. Bailey calls this "a psychological insight ... altogether exceptional by first-century standards."[11]

[11] D. S. Bailey, *Sexual Relations in Christian Thought* (New York: Harper, 1959; London: Longmans, Green).

Saint Paul saw the striking fact that as human beings we both *have* and *are* bodies. This is an issue that has been explored at length by such contemporary philosophers as Gabriel Marcel and Maurice Merleau-Ponty. Paul saw that sex—unlike excretion, for example—is not simply a physiological but also a "bodily" (somatic) activity. It involves us at the deepest levels of our personal identity.

But why limit Saint Paul's insight to coital intercourse alone, or to contacts with prostitutes? The mere avoidance of coitus does not exempt anyone from becoming "one flesh" with another. All "virgins" who are promiscuous neckers should know that. Nor can the "one flesh" phenomenon be restricted to the bordello.

Saint Paul knew that no sexual relationship could be kept merely physical without ceasing to be really sexual in the fully human sense of the word. This is why the playmate-of-the-month domestication of sex as a purely recreational pursuit just doesn't work. Paul really appreciated sex more than Hugh Hefner does. He expected more from it. Sex is certainly fun, but to make it *simply* fun is to eviscerate and enfeeble it. Then it eventually ceases even to be fun.

When it is demythologized, the evangelical sexual ethic turns out to be an invitation to life together in a community of personal selves. The Gospel frees us from the need to cling to romantic self-deception and the works righteousness by which we clothe our promiscuity in the costume of technical virginity. By delivering us from mythology into history, Jesus Christ allows us to see that the marvelous skein of privileges and responsibilities in which we find ourselves as human beings is something for which we are responsible. But how do we exercise this responsibility?

At this point the going becomes more difficult. Any effort to arrest the degeneration of the Gospel into some form of Law will be viewed in some quarters as antinomianism, the belief that the precepts of the Law are not binding for Christians. A Gospel ethic, however, demands more maturity and more discipline than a Law ethic. Evangelical ethics are by nature riskier. This risk must be run since the New Testament insists unequivocally that it is the Gospel and not the Law that saves. How then can we begin to "delegalize" the Gospel when sexual behavior is the question at issue?

The Gospel is addressed to persons; the Law sees acts. One weakness of the traditional ethical formulation on premarital chastity is its sweeping inclusiveness and total lack of discrimination. Reduced to a precept, the ideal of premarital chastity permits no distinction between intercourse by engaged couples, for example, and the chilling exploitation of high school girls at fraternity parties. Both are transgressions of the Law, and there is no middle ground between virginity and nonvirginity.

Consequently there emerges alongside the technical virgin her shadowy counterpart, the technically fallen woman—the girl who, because she once consented to intercourse, now feels she is permanently pastured among the goats. She has crossed the sexual Styx and there is no way back. Because she can no longer present herself to her husband in purity on the wedding night anyway, why shouldn't anything go?

Her self-condemnation arises in part because she has not heard the *good* news. She has perceived the traditional teaching as a *law*. Law without Gospel is arbitrary and abstract. It cannot discriminate among cases. And it has nothing helpful to say to the transgressor. Consequently, for the increasing proportion of young people who have already had sexual intercourse, the rule of premarital chastity is simply irrelevant. And since for many it appears to be the only record the church ever plays on this subject, they conclude the church has nothing to say to them.

But preaching the Gospel also entails preaching the Law—exposing the false absolutes from which one is liberated. Negatively this means making clear the distorted images of sex from which the Gospel delivers us. Positively it entails protecting sex as a fully human activity against all the principalities and powers that seek to dehumanize it. In our day these include the forces, both within and without, that pervert sex into a merchandising technique, a means of self-aggrandizement, a weapon for rebelling against parents, a recreational pursuit, a way to gain entrance into the right clique, or—let the reader beware—a devotional act with some sort of religious significance.

To be freed from the "bondage of the Law" means to be freed from these dehumanizing powers. It also means to be freed from those diabolical pressures toward subcultural conformity that push so many adolescents into whatever is "in" at the moment. Sexual freedom in Christ, in one concrete case, means that a harried co-ed can say *no* to a cloying Romeo without feeling she is being hopelessly square.

Evangelical ethics cease to be Law and once again become Gospel when the Word liberates people from cultural conventions and social pressures, when persons discover their sexuality as a delightful gift of God that links them in freedom and concern to their fellows. But how do we make *this* Gospel heard by young adults in today's sexually rapacious society?

Before answering this question we must admit that we have created a set of cultural conditions in which sexual responsibility is made exceedingly difficult. In our American Xanadu, exhortations to individual continence are almost as useless as urging businessmen to eschew the profit motive.

It is strange how even people who see most clearly that crime, illegitimacy, narcotics addiction, and poverty are largely structural problems still interpret the increase in premarital sexual experience as a breakdown in personal morals.

But the jig is nearly up. Our feverish effort to paper over a society propelled by drives for sex and status with a set of Victorian courtship mores is breaking down badly. We must direct our fire more toward the "feminine mystique" and the cynical misutilization of sex by the public-relations culture than toward the hapless individual offender.

This may involve some searching questions about limiting the deliberate use of sexual stimulation in selling or, even more radically, about the merit of an economic system that seems to require a constant perversion of sexuality in order to survive. Commercial exploitation of sex drives—not the call girls—is our most serious form of prostitution today.

When we do turn from the society to the individual, especially to the unmarried young adult, we must avoid giving a simple yes-or-no answer to the question of premarital chastity. Of course, this will sound like evasion, but any simple answer panders to the cheap attempt to oversimplify the issue, to reduce all the intricacies of premarital sexuality to one decision. And churchmen, by allowing the Gospel to deteriorate into folklore and fiat, have contributed to this fatal oversimplification.

I do not believe that an evangelical ethic of premarital sex can be chopped down to a flat answer to this weighted question without impoverishing and distorting it. Instead of registering an answer, the Gospel poses a question of its own (as Jesus himself frequently did with such questions). It asks how I can best nourish the maturity of those with whom I share the torments and transports of human existence.

The Gospel liberates men from mythical taboos and rigid concepts for a purpose: so that the full and untrammeled resources of the human imagination can be exercised in responsibility for others within the patterns of public and private life. In the freedom of the Gospel, we arrive at decisions by utilizing norms that themselves must always be open to criticism and transformation and are therefore never final. Traditional Christian sexual norms are no exception. They do not stand above history. They have arisen as Christians attempted to live faithfully through constantly changing social systems. Like all human codes they stand in continuous need of revision so they will help rather than hinder God's maturation of man.

Christians believe God is at work in history bringing man to adulthood and responsibility. Within this framework the norms by which we make our decisions are fashioned and discarded in a continuing conversation with the Bible and with the culture, a conversation that is never completed. The Christian knows he is free only as a partner in this conversation and as a member of this community. This means, among other things, that his decisions about sexual conduct inevitably involve more people than he would sometimes like to involve. Sex is never simply a private matter.

To refuse to deliver a prepared answer whenever the question of premarital intercourse pops up will have a healthy influence on the continuing conversation that is Christian ethics. It moves the axis of the discussion away from the arid stereotypes by which we oversimplify intricate human issues. It gets us off dead-end arguments about virginity and chastity, forces us to think about fidelity to persons. It exposes the promiscuity of sexual pharisees and the subtle exploitation that poisons even the most immaculate Platonic relationships.

By definition, premarital refers to people who plan to marry someone someday. Premarital sexual conduct should therefore serve to strengthen the chances of sexual success and fidelity in marriage, and we must face the real question of whether avoidance of intercourse beforehand is always the best preparation.

This question includes consideration of the appropriate degree of sexual intimacy during increasingly extended engagement periods. The reason it cannot be answered once and for all is that circumstances vary from couple to couple. Guidance must be given with specific persons rather than with general conventions in view.

Admittedly, this approach requires more resourcefulness and imagination than relying on universally applicable axioms. Principles are useful, perhaps indispensable in ethical thinking, but all too often "sticking to principles" can become just another way to avoid seeing persons. It can signify a relapse from Gospel into Law.

Perhaps one day we in America will put away childish things and become mature men and women who do not have to rely on the male and female deities of the mass media to tell us who to be. Perhaps one day we will outgrow our ridiculous obsession with sex, of which our fixation on chastity and virginity is just the other side of the coin. Until that time, however, we should rejoice that in Jesus Christ we are freed from myth and from Law. We are placed in a community of selves, free to the extent that we live for each other, free to develop whatever styles of life will contribute to the maturation of persons in a society where persons are often overlooked as we scamper to pursue profits and piety all at once.

The Problem of Sex
Meher Baba

Merwan Sheriar Irani (1894–1969), later known as Meher Baba, was born in Poona, India, of Persian parents and grew up mainly in the ambience of the Sufi tradition. His mission as a spiritual leader began in India in 1921. He traveled to the West in the early 1930s and by the time of his death had attracted large numbers of followers in America. Although he took a vow of silence in 1925, he dictated many books by means of hand signals. Among them: *Discourses*, *Listen Humanity*, *God Speaks*, and *The Everything and the Nothing*.

THE PROBLEM OF SEX

Sex is decidedly one of the most important problems with which the human mind is confronted in the domain of duality. It is one of the "givens" in the make-up of human nature with which one has to deal. Like everything else in human life, sex comes to be considered through the opposites which are the necessary creations of the limited mind. Just as the mind tries to fit life into a scheme of alternatives such as joy or pain, good or bad, solitude or company, attraction or repulsion, so in relation to sex it tends to think of indulgence and repression as alternatives from which there is no escape. It seems as if man must accept the one alternative or the other. Yet he cannot whole-heartedly accept either, for when he tries repression he is dissatisfied with his lot and longingly thinks of indulgence. When he tries indulgence he becomes conscious of his bondage to the senses and seeks freedom by going back to mechanical repression. The mind remains dissatisfied with *both* alternatives and there thus arises one of the most vital and complicated problems of human life.

In order to solve the problem of sex, the mind must first understand that both alternatives are equally the creation of imagination working under the deluding influence of craving. Craving is implicitly present in the repression of sex as well as in its gratification. Both result in the vitiation of consciousness through lust or the desire for sensations. The mind is therefore inevitably restless

From Meher Baba, *Discourses*, Vol. I (San Francisco, 1967), pp. 142–164. Reprinted by permission of Sufism Reoriented, Inc.

in either alternative. Just as when there are clouds in the sky, there is gloom and lack of sunshine, whether it rains or not; so when the human mind is shrouded by craving there is diminution of being and lack of true happiness, whether this craving is gratified or not. The mind when restless with desire creates an illusory idea of happiness in the gratification of desire, and then knowing that the soul remains dissatisfied even after gratification of desire, seeks freedom through repression. Thus *searching for happiness and freedom, the mind gets caught up in the opposites of indulgence and repression which it finds equally disappointing.* Since it does not try to go *beyond* these opposites, its movement is always from one opposite to the other and consequently from one disappointment to another.

Thus craving falsifies the operation of imagination and presents the mind with the option between the alternatives of indulgence and repression which prove to be equally deceptive in their promise of happiness. However, in spite of alternate and repeated disappointment in indulgence as well as in repression, the mind usually does not renounce the root cause of unhappiness which is craving, because, while experiencing disappointment in repression, it is easily susceptible to the false promise of gratification, and while experiencing disappointment in gratification, it is easily susceptible to the false promise of purely mechanical repression.

This is like moving within a cage. The gateway to the spiritual Path of internal and spontaneous renunciation of craving remains closed for those who have not the good fortune to be awakened by a Master. But true awakening is the entering into the path of wisdom which, in course of time, surely leads to the freedom and abiding happiness of life eternal. Internal and spontaneous renunciation of craving is as different from mechanical repression as it is from indulgence. *Mind turns to the mechanical repression of craving because of disappointment, but it turns to internal and spontaneous renunciation of craving because of disillusionment or awakening.*

The need for indulgence or mechanical repression arises only when the nature of craving is not clearly grasped. When the aspirant becomes fully awake to the inevitable bondage and suffering entailed by craving, he begins voluntarily to disburden himself of craving through intelligent understanding. *The question of indulgence or repression arises only when there is craving. The need for both vanishes with the complete disappearance of craving.* When the mind is free from craving, the mind can no longer be moved by the false promises of indulgence or mechanical repression.

However, it should be borne in mind that *the life of freedom is nearer to the life of restraint than to the life of indulgence* (though in quality it is essentially different from both). Hence for the aspirant a life of strict celibacy is preferable to married life, if restraint comes to him easily without undue sense of self-repression. Such restraint is difficult for most persons and sometimes impossible, and for them married life is decidedly more helpful than a life of celibacy. For ordinary persons, married life is undoubtedly advisable unless they have a special aptitude for celibacy.

Just as the life of celibacy requires and calls forth the development of many virtues, married life in turn also nourishes the growth of many spiritual qualities of utmost importance. *The value of celibacy lies in the habit of restraint and the sense of detachment and independence which it gives.* But as long as the mind is not altogether free from craving there is no true freedom. In the same way, *the value of marriage lies in lessons of mutual adjustment and the sense of unity with the other.* True union or dissolution of duality is possible, however, only through Divine Love which can never dawn as long as there is the slightest shadow of lust or craving in the mind. Only by treading the path of inner and spontaneous renunciation of craving is it possible to attain true freedom and unity.

For the celibate as well as for the married person the path of inner life is the same. When the aspirant is drawn by the Truth he longs for nothing else, and as the Truth increasingly comes within his ken, he gradually *disburdens* himself of craving. Whether in celibacy or in marriage, he is no longer swayed by the deceptive promises of indulgence or mechanical repression, and he practises internal and spontaneous renunciation of craving until he is freed from the deceptive opposites. The path of perfection is open to the aspirant whether in celibacy or in marriage, and *whether he begins from celibacy or from marriage will depend upon his sanskaras and karmic ties.* He cheerfully accepts the conditions which his past life has determined for him and utilises them towards his spiritual advancement in the light of the ideal which he has come to perceive.

The aspirant must choose one of the two courses which are open to him. He must take to the life of celibacy or to the married life, and he must avoid at all costs a cheap compromise between the two. *Promiscuity in sex gratification is bound to land the aspirant in a most pitiful and dangerous chaos of ungovernable lust.* As such diffused and undirected lust veils the higher values, it perpetuates entanglement and creates in the spiritual path insuperable difficulties to the internal and spontaneous renunciation of craving. Sex in marriage is entirely different from sex outside marriage. In marriage the *sanskaras* of lust are much lighter and are capable of being removed more easily. When sex-companionship is accompanied by a sense of responsibility, love and spiritual idealism, conditions for the sublimation of sex are much more favourable than when it is cheap and promiscuous.

In promiscuity the temptation to explore the possibilities of mere sex contact is formidable. It is only by the maximum restriction of the scope of mere sex that the aspirant can arrive at any real understanding of the values attainable through the gradual transformation of sex into love. If the mind tries to understand sex through increasing the scope of sex, there is no end to the delusions to which it is a prey, for there is no end to the enlarging of its scope. In promiscuity the suggestions of lust are necessarily the first to present themselves to the mind, and the individual is *doomed to react to people within the limitation of this initial perversion* and thus close the door to deeper experiences.

Truth cannot be grasped by skipping over the surface of life and multiplying superficial contacts. It requires the preparedness of mind which can centre its capacities upon selected experiences and free itself from its limiting features. This process of discrimination between the higher and the lower, and the transcendence of the lower in favour of the higher, is made possible through *wholehearted concentration and a real and earnest interest in life.* Such whole-hearted concentration and real interest is necessarily precluded when the mind becomes a slave to the habit of running at a tangent and wandering between many possible objects of similar experience. In married life the range of experience to be had in the company of the partner is so wide that the suggestions of lust are not necessarily the first to present themselves to the mind. There is therefore a real opportunity for the aspirant *to recognise and annul the limiting factors in experience*. By the gradual elimination of lust and the progression through a series of increasingly richer experiences of love and sacrifice, he can finally arrive at Infinity.

THE SANCTIFICATION OF MARRIED LIFE

Most persons enter into married life as a matter of course, but marriage will become a help or a hindrance according to the manner in which it is handled. There is no doubt that some of the immense spiritual possibilities are accessible through a married life, but all this depends upon having the right attitude. From the spiritual point of view, married life will be a success only if it is thoroughly determined by the vision of Truth. It cannot offer much if it is based upon nothing more than the limited motives of mere sex, or if it is inspired by considerations which usually prevail in business partnership. It has to be undertaken as *a real spiritual enterprise which is intended to discover what life can be at its best*. When the two partners launch together upon the spiritual adventure of exploring the higher possibilities of spirit, they cannot at the outset limit their experiment by any nice calculations concerning the nature and amount of *individual gain*.

Married life almost always makes many demands upon both partners for mutual adjustment and understanding, and creates many problems which were not originally expected. Though this might in a sense be true of life in general it is particularly true of married life. In married life two souls get linked in many ways, with the result that they are called upon to *tackle the whole complex problem of personality rather than any simple problem created by some isolated desire*. This is precisely why married life is utterly different from promiscuous sex relations. Promiscuous sex attempts to separate the problem of sex from *other* needs of the developing personality and seeks to solve it in isolation from them. Although this kind of solution might seem to be easy, it turns out to be very superficial and has the further disadvantage of *side-tracking* the aspirant from attempting the real solution.

The relative values of the various sides of the limited personality can best be appreciated when they become intertwined and appear in varied settings and perspectives. It is difficult to discriminate between them if they appear fitfully in a disconnected series. In married life there is ample room for varied experience, with the result that the different tendencies latent in the mind begin to organise around the crystallised scheme of married life. This organisation of varied purposes *not only provides an unlimited field for discrimination between the higher and lower values but also creates between them a necessary tension which requires and calls forth effective and intelligent sublimation*.

In one sense married life may be looked upon as the intensification of most human problems. As such it becomes *the rallying ground for the forces of bondage as well as for the forces of freedom,* the factors of ignorance as well as the factors of light. As the married life of ordinary persons is determined by mixed motives and considerations, it inevitably invites an uncompromising opposition between the higher and the lower self. Such opposition is necessary for the wearing out of the lower self and the dawning of the true Divine Self. Married life develops so many points of contact between two souls that severance of all connection would mean the unsettlement and derangement of practically the whole tenor of life. Since this difficulty of breaking away from one another invites and precipitates inner readjustment, marriage is really a disguised opportunity for the souls to establish a real and lasting understanding which can cope with the most complex and delicate situations.

The spiritual value of married life is directly related to the nature of the preponderating factors which determine its daily course. If it is based upon shallow considerations, it can deteriorate into a partnership in selfishness aimed against the rest of the world. If it is inspired by lofty idealism, it can rise to a fellowship which not only requires and calls forth increasingly greater sacrifices for each other, but actually *becomes a medium through which the two souls can offer their united love and service to the whole family of humanity.* When married life is thus brought into direct line with the Divine Plan for the evolution of the individual, it becomes a pure blessing for the children who are the fruit of the marriage, for they have the advantage of absorbing a spiritual atmosphere from the very beginning of their earthly career.

Though the children are thus the beneficiaries of the married life of the parents, *the married life of the parents is in its turn enriched by the presence of the children.* Children give to parents an opportunity for expressing and developing a real and spontaneous love in which sacrifice becomes easy and delightful, and the part played by children in the life of parents is of tremendous importance for the spiritual advancement of parents themselves. It therefore follows that when children make their appearance in married life they ought to be whole-heartedly welcomed by the parents.

In view of the claims which children have on married lives the present birth control movement deserves careful attention and critical examination. The question must not be considered from the point of view of any one special or limited interest but from the point of view of the *ultimate* well-being of the individual and society. The right opinion in this respect, as in all respects, must above everything be based upon spiritual considerations. The attitude which most persons have towards birth control is oscillating and confused because it contains a queer admixture of good and bad elements. *While birth control is right in its aim of securing the regulation of population, it is disastrously unfortunate in the choice of its means.* There can be no doubt that the regulation of child-bearing is often desirable for personal and social reasons. Uncontrolled breeding intensifies the struggle for existence and may bring about a social order where ruthless competition becomes inevitable. Apart from creating a responsibility for parents which they may be unable to adequately discharge, it becomes an indirect and contributory cause of crime, war and poverty. Though humane and rational considerations demand and justify all serious attempts to regulate the birth of children, the use of physical means for securing this purpose remains fundamentally indefensible and unjustifiable.

The purely physical means which are generally advocated by the supporters of birth control are most objectionable from the spiritual point of view. Although the physical means of birth control are advocated on humanitarian grounds, they are almost always used by the generality of people to serve their own selfish ends and to avoid the responsibility of bearing and bringing up children. Since the physical consequences of yielding to lust can be so successfully avoided through the use of these means, those who have not begun to awaken to the higher values have no incentive to moderation in the gratification of passion. They thus become victims of excessive indulgence and bring about their own physical, moral and spiritual ruin by neglecting mental control and becoming slaves to animal passion.

The easy use of the physical means obscures the spiritual side of the question and is far from being contributory to the awakening of man to his real dignity and freedom as a spiritual being. Thoughtless and uncontrolled indulgence must inevitably lead to reaction and spiritual bondage. For spiritual aspirants in particular, but also for all human beings (because they are all potentially spiritual aspirants), it is extremely inadvisable to rely upon physical means for the regulation of child-bearing. *For such regulation the individual must rely upon nothing but mental control.* Mental control secures the humanitarian purposes which inspire birth control and keeps clear of the spiritual disasters entailed by the use of physical means. Mental control is not only useful for regulating the number of children but is also indispensable for restoring to man his divine dignity and spiritual well-being. *Only through the wise exercise of mental control is it possible for man to rise from passion to peace, from bondage to freedom and from animality to purity.* In the minds of thoughtful persons the much ignored spiritual side of this question must assume the importance which it deserves.

Since woman has to undertake the troubles and the responsibility of bearing and rearing children she may seem to be affected more seriously by any possible failure in mental control than man. In fact it does not mean any real unfairness to woman. While it is true that woman has to undertake the troubles and the responsibility of bearing and rearing children, she also has the compensating joy of feeding and fondling them. Thus motherhood is much greater than the joy of fatherhood. Further, the man must also face and shoulder the economic and educational responsibility towards the children. In a properly adjusted marriage there need not be any injustice in the distribution of parental responsibility to be shared between man and woman. If both are truly conscious of their mutual responsibility, *inconsiderateness will give way to active and co-operative endeavour to attain full mental control.* In the event there is any failure in mental control they will cheerfully and willingly discharge the joint responsibility of parenthood.

If a person is not prepared to undertake the responsibility of children there is only one course left to him. He must remain celibate and practise strict mental control, for though such mental control is extemely difficult to attain, it is not impossible. From the purely spiritual point of view strict celibacy is best, but since it is so difficult, few can practise it. For those who cannot practise it, the next best course is to marry rather than fall a prey to promiscuity. Within married life one can learn to control animal passion. It is bound to be a gradual process, and *in cases of failure in practising control, the couple must allow nature to take its own course rather than interfere with it through artificial means.* They must cheerfully welcome the consequences and be prepared to shoulder the responsibility of bringing up the children.

From the spiritual point of view, birth control must essentially be effected through mental control and nothing else. Physical means are under no circumstances advisable *even when a person seeks to use them merely as a provisional and secondary aid, without intending to ignore the ideal of developing mental control.* While using physical means he can never arrive at real mental control, though he might want it in real earnest. On the contrary he becomes addicted to the use of physical means and even begins to justify them. To explain still more clearly, what happens in the use of physical means is that while the individual thinks that he is using them merely as a preliminary step before mental control is fully developed, he actually gets addicted to their use and becomes a slave to the habit. Though he may remain for some time under the delusion that he is trying to develop mental control (side by side with the use of physical means), he is actually losing it gradually. In short, *mental power is necessarily undermined by reliance on physical means.* Thus the use of physical means is detrimental to the development of self-control and is positively disastrous for spiritual advancement. It is therefore entirely inadvisable even for the best of motives.

In the beginning of married life the partners are drawn to each other by lust as well as love, but with conscious and deliberate co-operation they can gradually lessen the element of lust and increase the element of love. Through this process of sublimation lust ultimately gives place to deep love. By the mutual sharing of joys and sorrows the partners march on from one spiritual triumph to another, from deep love to ever deeper love, till *the possessive and jealous love of the initial period is entirely replaced by a self-giving and expansive love.* In fact, through the intelligent handling of marriage a person may traverse so much of the spiritual path that it needs only a touch by the Master to raise him into the sanctuary of eternal life.

LOVE

Life and love are inseparable from each other. Where there is life, there is love. Even the most rudimentary consciousness is always trying to burst out of its limitations and experience some kind of unity with other forms. Though each form is separate from other forms, in *reality* they are all forms of the same unity of life. The latent sense for this hidden inner reality indirectly makes itself felt even in the world of illusion through the attraction which one form has for another form.

The law of *gravitation,* to which all the planets and the stars are subject, is in its own way a dim reflection of the love which pervades every part of the universe. Even the forces of repulsion are in truth expressions of love, since things are repelled from each other because they are more powerfully attracted to some other things. Repulsion is a negative consequence of positive attraction. The forces of *cohesion* and *affinity* which prevail in the very constitution of matter are positive expressions of love. A striking example of love at this level is found in attraction which the magnet exercises for iron. All these forms of love are of the lowest type, since they are necessarily conditioned by the rudimentary consciousness in which they appear.

In the animal world love becomes more explicit in the form of *conscious impulses* which are directed towards different objects in the surroundings. *This love is instinctive* and it takes the form of gratifying different desires through the appropriation of suitable objects. When the tiger seeks to devour the deer he is in a very real sense in love with the deer. Sex-attraction is another form of love at this level. All the expressions of love at this stage have one thing in common, *viz., they all seek to satisfy some bodily impulse or desire* through the object of love.

Human love is much higher than all these lower forms of love because human beings have the fully developed form of consciousness. Though human love is continuous with the lower sub-human forms of love, in a way, it is different from them, for henceforth its operations have to be carried on side by side with a new factor which is *reason*. Sometimes human love manifests itself as a force which is *divorced* from reason and runs parallel to it. Sometimes it manifests itself as a force which gets *mixed up* with reason and comes into *conflict* with it. Lastly, it expresses itself as a constituent of the harmonised whole where *love and reason have been balanced and fused into an integral unity*.

Thus human love can enter into three types of combination with reason. In the first type, the sphere of thought and the sphere of love are kept as separate as possible, *i.e.*, the sphere of love is practically inaccessible to the operation of reason, and love is allowed little or no access to the objects of thought. Complete separation between these two aspects of the spirit is of course never possible, but when there is an alternate functioning of love and reason (oscillating in their predominance) we have *a love which is unillumined by reason or a reason which is unenlivened by love.* In the second type, love and reason are both simultaneously operative but they *do not work in harmony with each other.* Though this conflict creates confusion, it is a necessary phase in the evolution of the higher state where there is a real synthesis of love and reason. In the third type of love this synthesis between love and reason is an accomplished fact with the result that *both love as well as reason are so completely transformed that they precipitate the emergence of a new level of consciousness* which, compared to the normal human consciousness, is best described as *super-consciousness*.

Human love makes its appearance in the matrix of ego-consciousness which has countless desires. Love is coloured by these factors in many ways. Just as we get an ever changing variety of designs in a kaleidoscope by the various combinations of simpler elements, we find an almost limitless qualitative variety in the range of love owing to novel combinations of psychic factors. And just as there are infinite shades of colour in different flowers, so there are diverse delicate differences in human love.

Human love is encircled by a number of obstructive factors such as infatuation, lust, greed, anger and jealousy. In one sense, even these obstructive factors are either *forms* of lower love or the inevitable *side-results* of these lower forms of love. Infatuation, lust and greed might be looked upon as perverted and lower forms of love. In infatuation a person is *enamoured* of a sensual object; in lust he develops a *craving* for sensations in relation to it; and in greed he desires to *possess* it. Of these three forms of lower love, greed has a tendency to extend from the original object to the *means* of obtaining it. Thus persons become greedy for money or power or fame, which can be instruments for possessing the different objects that are craved. Anger and jealousy come into existence when these lower forms of love are thwarted or threatened to be thwarted.

These lower forms of love obstruct the release of pure love. The stream of love can never become clear and steady until it is disentangled from these limiting and perverting forms of lower love. *The lower is the enemy of the higher.* If consciousness is caught in the rhythm of the lower it cannot emancipate itself from its self-created ruts, finding it difficult to get out of them and advance further. Thus the lower form of love continues to interfere with the development of the higher form, and has to be given up in order to allow for the untramelled appearance of the higher form of love.

The emergence of higher love from the shell of lower love is helped by the constant exercise of *discrimination*. Therefore, love has to be carefully distinguished from the obstructive factors of infatuation, lust, greed and anger. In infatuation, the person is a *passive victim* of the spell of conceived attraction for the object. In love there is an *active appreciation* of the intrinsic worth of the object of love.

Love is also different from lust. In lust there is reliance upon the *object of sense* and consequent spiritual *subordination* of the soul to it, but love puts the soul into direct and *co-ordinate* relation with the *reality* which is behind the form. Therefore lust is experienced as being *heavy* and love is experienced as being *light*. In lust there is a *narrowing down* of life and in love there is an *expansion* in being. *To have loved one soul is like adding its life to your own.* Your life is, as it were, multiplied and you virtually live in two centres. If you love the whole world you vicariously live in the whole world, but in lust there is an ebbing down of life and a general sense of hopeless dependence upon a form which is regarded as *another*. Thus, in lust there is the *accentuation of separateness and suffering,* but in love there is the *feeling of unity and joy.* Lust is dissipation, love is recreation. Lust is a craving of the senses, love is the expression of the spirit. Lust *seeks* fulfillment but love *experiences* fulfillment. In lust there is *excitement,* but in love there is *tranquility.*

Love is equally different from greed. Greed is possessiveness in all its gross and subtle forms. It seeks to appropriate gross things and persons as well as such abstract and intangible things as fame and power. In love, the annexation of the other person to your individual life is out of the question, and there is a free and creative outpouring that enlivens and replenishes the psychic being of the beloved independently of any expectations for the self. We have the paradox that *greed, which seeks for the appropriation of another object, in fact leads to the opposite result of bringing the self under the tutelage of the object; and love, which aims at giving away the self to the object, in fact leads to a spiritual incorporation of the beloved in the very being of the lover. In greed the self tries to possess the object, but is itself possessed by the object. In love the self offers itself to the beloved without any reservations, but in that very act it finds that it has included the beloved in its own being.*

Infatuation, lust and greed constitute a spiritual malady which is often rendered more virulent by the aggravating symptoms of anger and jealousy. Pure love, in sharp contradistinction, is the bloom of spiritual perfection. Human love is so tethered by these limiting conditions that the spontaneous appearance of pure love from within becomes impossible. So, when such pure love arises in the aspirant it is always a *gift. Pure love arises in the heart of the aspirant in response to the descent of grace from the Master.* When pure love is first received as a gift of the Master it becomes lodged in the consciousness of the aspirant like a seed in favourable soil, and in the course of time the seed develops into a plant and then into a full-grown tree.

The descent of the grace of the Master is conditioned, however, by the preliminary spiritual preparation of the aspirant. This preliminary spiritual preparation for grace is never complete until the aspirant has built into his psychic make-up some divine attributes. When a person avoids backbiting and thinks more of the good points in others than of their bad points, and when he can practise supreme tolerance, and desires the good of others even at the cost of his own self, he is ready to receive the grace of the Master. One of the greatest obstacles hindering this spiritual preparation of the aspirant is *worry*. When, with supreme effort, this obstacle of worry is overcome, a way is paved for the cultivation of the divine attributes which constitute the spiritual preparation of the disciple. *As soon as the disciple is ready the grace of the Master descends, for the Master, who is the ocean of divine love, is always on the look-out for the soul in whom his grace will fructify.*

The kind of love which is awakened by the grace of the Master is a rare privilege. The mother who is willing to sacrifice all and to die for her child, and the martyr who is prepared to give up his very life for his country are indeed supremely noble, but they have not necessarily tasted this pure love which is born through the grace of the Master. Even the great *yogis* with long beards who, sitting in caves and mountains, are completely absorbed in deep *samadhi*, do not necessarily have this precious love.

Pure love awakened through the grace of the Master is more valuable than any other stimulus which may be utilised by the aspirant. Such love not only combines in itself the merits of all the disciplines but excels them all in its efficacy to lead the aspirant to his goal. When this love is born the aspirant has only one desire, and that is to be united with the Divine Beloved. Such withdrawal of consciousness from all other desires leads to infinite purity; therefore nothing purifies the aspirant more completely than this love. The aspirant is always willing to offer everything for the Divine Beloved, and no sacrifice is too difficult for him. All his thoughts are turned away from the self and come to be exclusively centred on the Divine Beloved. *Through the intensity of this ever-growing love he eventually breaks through the shackles of the self and becomes united with the Beloved.* This is the consummation of love. When love has thus found its fruition it has become *divine*.

Divine love is qualitatively different from human love. Human love is for the *many in the One* and divine love is for the *One in the many*. Human love leads to innumerable complications and tangles, but divine love leads to integration and freedom. *In divine love the personal and the impersonal aspects are equally balanced, but in human love the two aspects are in alternating ascendency.* When the personal note is predominant in human love it leads to utter blindness to the intrinsic worth of other forms. When, as in sense of duty, love is predominantly impersonal, it often makes one cold, rigid and mechanical. Sense of duty comes to the individual as an external *constraint* on behaviour, but in divine love there is *unrestrained freedom and unbounded spontaneity*. Human love in its personal and impersonal aspects is limited, but divine love with its fusion of the personal and the impersonal aspects is *infinite* in being and expression.

Even the highest type of human love is subject to the limitation of individual nature which persists till the seventh plane. *Divine love arises after the disappearance of the individual mind and is free from the trammels of individual nature.* In human love the duality of the lover and the beloved persists, but in divine love *the lover and the Beloved become one.* At this stage the aspirant has stepped out of the domain of duality and become one with God, for divine love *is* God. *When the lover and the Beloved are one, that is the end and the beginning.*

It is for love that the whole universe sprang into existence and it is for the sake of love that it is kept going. God descends into the realm of illusion because the apparent duality of the Beloved and the lover is eventually contributory to His conscious enjoyment of His own divinity. *The development of love is conditioned and sustained by the tension of duality*. God has to suffer apparent differentiation into a multiplicity of souls in order to carry on the game of love. They are His own forms, and in relation to them He at once assumes the role of the Divine Lover and the Divine Beloved. As the Beloved, He is the real and the ultimate object of their appreciation. As the Divine Lover, He is their real and ultimate saviour drawing them back to Himself. Thus though the whole world of duality is only an illusion, that illusion has come into being for a *significant purpose*.

Love is the reflection of God's unity in the world of duality. It constitutes the entire significance of creation. If love is excluded from life, all the souls in the world assume complete externality to each other and the only possible relations and contacts in such a loveless world are superficial and mechanical. It is because of love that the contacts and relations between individual souls become significant. It is love which gives meaning and value to all the happenings in the world of duality. But, *while love gives meaning to the world of duality, it is at the same time a standing challenge to duality*. As love gathers strength, it generates *creative restlessness* and becomes the main driving power of that *spiritual dynamic* which ultimately succeeds in *restoring to consciousness the original unity of being*.

RELIGION AND SOCIAL ACTION

Letter from Birmingham Jail

Martin Luther King, Jr.

Martin Luther King, Jr. (1929–1968), Southern Baptist minister, was the most influential and famous civil rights leader in America during the 1960s. His works include *Stride Toward Freedom* and *Strength to Love*.

April 12, 1963

We the undersigned clergymen are among those who, in January, issued "An Appeal for Law and Order and Common Sense," in dealing with racial problems in Alabama. We expressed understanding that honest convictions in racial matters could properly be pursued in the courts, but urged that decisions of those courts should in the meantime be peacefully obeyed.

Since that time there had been some evidence of increased forbearance and a willingness to face facts. Responsible citizens have undertaken to work on various problems which cause racial friction and unrest. In Birmingham, recent public events have given indication that we all have opportunity for a new constructive and realistic approach to racial problems.

However, we are now confronted by a series of demonstrations by some of our Negro citizens, directed and led in part by outsiders. We recognize the natural impatience of people who feel that their hopes are slow in being realized. But we are convinced that these demonstrations are unwise and untimely.

We agree rather with certain local Negro leadership which has called for honest and open negotiation of racial issues in our area. And we believe this kind of facing of issues can best be accomplished by citizens of our own metropolitan area, white and Negro, meeting with their knowledge and experience of the local situation. All of us need to face that responsibility and find proper channels for its accomplishment.

Just as we formerly pointed out that "hatred and violence have no sanction in our religious and political traditions," we also point out that such actions as incite to hatred and violence, however technically peaceful those actions may be, have not contributed to the resolution of our local problems. We do not believe that these days of new hope are days when extreme measures are justified in Birmingham.

We commend the community as a whole, and the local news media and law enforcement officials in particular, on the calm manner in which these demonstrations have been handled. We urge the public to continue to show restraint should the demonstrations continue, and the law enforcement officials to remain calm and continue to protect our city from violence.

We further strongly urge our own Negro community to withdraw support from these demonstrations, and to unite locally in working peacefully for a better Birmingham. When rights are consistently denied, a cause should be pressed in the courts and in negotiations among local leaders, and not in the streets. We appeal to both our white and Negro citizenry to observe the principles of law and order and common sense.

C. C. J. CARPENTER, *D.D., LL.D., Bishop of Alabama;* JOSEPH A. DURICK, *D.D., Auxiliary Bishop, Diocese of Mobile-Birmingham;* RABBI MILTON L. GRAFMAN, *Temple Emanu-El, Birmingham, Alabama;* BISHOP PAUL HARDIN, *Bishop of the Alabama-West Florida Conference of the Methodist Church;* BISHOP NOLAN B. HARMON, *Bishop of the North Alabama Conference of the Methodist Church;* GEORGE M. MURRAY, *D.D. LL.D., Bishop Coadjutor, Episcopal Diocese of Alabama;* EDWARD V. RAMAGE, *Moderator, Synod of the Alabama Presbyterian Curch in the United States;* EARL STALLINGS, *Pastor, First Baptist Church, Birmingham, Alabama.*

April 16, 1963

MY DEAR FELLOW CLERGYMEN:

While confined here in the Birmingham city jail, I came across your recent statement calling my present activities "unwise and untimely." Seldom do I pause to answer criticism of my work and ideas. If I sought to answer all the criticisms that cross my desk, my secretaries would have little time for anything other than such correspondence in the course of the day, and I would have no time for constructive work. But since I feel that you are men of genuine good will and that your criticisms are sincerely set forth, I want to try to answer your statement in what I hope will be patient and reasonable terms.

I think I should indicate why I am here in Birmingham, since you have been influenced by the view which argues against "outsiders coming in." I have the honor of serving as president of the Southern Christian Leadership Conference, an organization operating in every southern state, with headquarters in Atlanta, Georgia. We have some eighty-five affiliated organizations across the South, and one of them is the Alabama Christian Movement for Human Rights. Frequently we share staff, educational and financial resources with our affiliates. Several months ago the affiliate here in Birmingham asked us to be on call to engage in a nonviolent direct-action program if such were deemed necessary. We readily consented, and when the hour came we lived up to our promise. So I, along with several members of my staff, am here because I was invited here. I am here because I have organizational ties here.

But more basically, I am in Birmingham because injustice is here. Just as the prophets of the eighth century B.C. left their villages and carried their "thus saith the Lord" far beyond the boundaries of their home towns, and just as the Apostle Paul left his village of Tarsus and carried the gospel of Jesus Christ to the far corners of the Greco-Roman world, so am I compelled to carry the gospel of freedom beyond my own home town. Like Paul, I must constantly respond to the Macedonian call for aid.

Moreover, I am cognizant of the interrelatedness of all communities and states. I cannot sit idly by in Atlanta and not be concerned about what happens in Birmingham. Injustice anywhere is a threat to justice everywhere. We are caught in an inescapable network of mutuality, tied in a single garment of destiny. Whatever affects one directly, affects all indirectly. Never again can we afford to live with the narrow, provincial "outside agitator" idea. Anyone who lives inside the United States can never be considered an outsider anywhere within its bounds.

You deplore the demonstrations taking place in Birmingham. But your statement, I am sorry to say, fails to express a similar concern for the conditions that brought about the demonstrations. I am sure that none of you would want to rest content with the superficial kind of social analysis that deals merely with effects and does not grapple with underlying causes. It is unfortunate that demonstrations are taking place in Birmingham, but it is even more unfortunate that the city's white power structure left the Negro community with no alternative.

In any nonviolent campaign there are four basic steps: collection of the facts to determine whether injustices exist; negotiation; self-purification; and direct action. We have gone through all these steps in Birmingham. There can be no gainsaying the fact that racial injustice engulfs this community. Birmingham is probably the most thoroughly segregated city in the United States. Its ugly record of brutality is widely known. Negroes have experienced grossly unjust treatment in the courts. There have been more unsolved bombings of Negro homes and churches in Birmingham than in any other city in the nation. These are the hard, brutal facts of the case. On the basis of these conditions, Negro leaders sought to negotiate with the city fathers. But the latter consistently refused to engage in good-faith negotiation....

[Omitted here are three paragraphs describing unsuccessful negotiations with merchants to remove racial signs from stores, and strategies for timing the direct action campaign which followed.]

You may well ask: "Why direct action? Why sit-ins, marches and so forth? Isn't negotiation a better path?" You are quite right in calling for negotiation. Indeed, this is the very purpose of direct action. Nonviolent direct action seeks to create such a crisis and foster such a tension that a community which has constantly refused to negotiate is forced to confront the issue. It seeks so to dramatize the issue that it can no longer be ignored. My citing the creation of tension as part of the work of the nonviolent-resister may sound rather shocking. But I must confess that I am not afraid of the word "tension." I have earnestly opposed violent tension, but there is a type of constructive, nonviolent tension which is necessary for growth. Just as Socrates felt that it was necessary to create a tension in the mind so that individuals could rise from the bondage of myths and half-truths to the unfettered realm of creative analysis and objective appraisal, so must we see the need for nonviolent gadflies to create the kind of tension in society that will help men rise from the dark depths of prejudice and racism to the majestic heights of understanding and brotherhood.

The purpose of our direct-action program is to create a situation so crisis-packed that it will inevitably open the door to negotiation. I therefore concur with you in your call for negotiation. Too long has our beloved Southland been bogged down in a tragic effort to live in monologue rather than dialogue.

One of the basic points in your statement is that the action that I and my associates have taken in Birmingham is untimely.... My friends, I must say to you that we have not made a single gain in civil rights without determined legal and nonviolent pressure. Lamentably, it is an historical fact that privileged groups seldom give up their privileges voluntarily. Individuals may see the moral light and voluntarily give up their unjust posture; but, as Reinhold Niebuhr has reminded us, groups tend to be more immoral than individuals.

We know through painful experience that freedom is never voluntarily given by the oppressor; it must be demanded by the oppressed. Frankly, I have yet to engage in a direct-action campaign that was "well timed" in the view of those who have not suffered unduly from the disease of segregation. For years now I have heard the word "Wait!" It rings in the ear of every Negro with piercing familiarity. This "Wait" has almost always meant "Never." We must come to see, with one of our distinguished jurists, that "justice too long delayed is justice denied."

We have waited for more than 340 years for our constitutional and God-given rights. The nations of Asia and Africa are moving with jetlike speed toward gaining political independence, but we still creep at horse-and-buggy pace toward gaining a cup of coffee at a lunch counter. Perhaps it is easy for those who have never felt the stinging darts of segregation to say, "Wait." But when you have seen vicious mobs lynch your mothers and fathers at will and drown your sisters and brothers at whim; when you have seen hate-filled policemen curse, kick and even kill your black brothers and sisters; when you see the vast majority of your twenty million Negro brothers smothering in an airtight cage of poverty in the midst of an affluent society; when you suddenly find your tongue twisted and your speech stammering as you seek to explain to your six-year-old daughter why she can't go to the public amusement park that has just been advertised on television, and see tears welling up in her eyes when she is told that Funtown is closed to colored children, and see ominous clouds of inferiority beginning to form in her little mental sky, and see her beginning to distort her personality by developing an unconscious bitterness toward white people; when you have to concoct an answer for a five-year-old son who is asking: "Daddy, why do white people treat colored people so mean?"; when you take a cross-country drive and find it necessary to sleep night after night in the uncomfortable corners of your automobile because no motel will accept you; when you are humiliated day in and day out by nagging signs reading "white" and "colored"; when your first name becomes "nigger," your middle name becomes "boy" (however old you are) and your last name becomes "John," and your wife and mother are never given the respected title "Mrs."; when you are harried by day and haunted by night by the fact that you are a Negro, living constantly at tiptoe stance, never quite knowing what to expect next, and are plagued with inner fears and outer resentments; when you are forever fighting a degenerating sense of "nobodiness"—then you will understand why we find it difficult to wait. There comes a time when the cup of endurance runs over, and men are no longer willing to be plunged into the abyss of despair. I hope, sirs, you can understand our legitimate and unavoidable impatience.

You express a great deal of anxiety over our willingness to break laws. This is certainly a legitimate concern. Since we so diligently urge people to obey the Supreme Court's decision of 1954 outlawing segregation in the public schools, at first glance it may seem rather paradoxical for us consciously to break laws. One may well ask: "How can you advocate breaking some laws and obeying others?" The answer lies in the fact that there are two types of laws: just and unjust. I would be the first to advocate obeying just laws. One has not only a legal but a moral responsibility to obey just laws. Conversely, one has a moral responsibility to disobey unjust laws. I would agree with St. Augustine that "an unjust law is no law at all."

Now, what is the difference between the two? How does one determine whether a law is just or unjust? A just law is a man-made code that squares with the moral law or the law of God. An unjust law is a code that is out of harmony with the moral law. To put it in the terms of St. Thomas Aquinas: An unjust law is a human law that is not rooted in eternal law and natural law. Any law that uplifts human personality is just. Any law that degrades human personality is unjust. All segregation statutes are unjust because segregation distorts the soul and damages the personality. It gives the segregator a false sense of superiority and the segregated a false sense of inferiority. Segregation, to use the terminology of the Jewish philosopher Martin Buber, substitutes an "I–it" relationship for an "I–thou" relationship and ends up relegating persons to the status of things. Hence segregation is not only politically, economically and sociologically unsound, it is morally wrong and sinful. Paul Tillich has said that sin is separation. Is not segregation an existential expression of man's tragic separation, his awful estrangement, his terrible sinfulness? Thus it is that I can urge men to obey the 1954 decision of the Supreme Court, for it is morally right; and I can urge them to disobey segregation ordinances, for they are morally wrong.

Let us consider a more concrete example of just and unjust laws. An unjust law is a code that a numerical or power majority group compels a minority group to obey but does not make binding on itself. This is *difference* made legal. By the same token, a just law is a code that a majority compels a minority to follow and that it is willing to follow itself. This is *sameness* made legal.

Let me give another explanation. A law is unjust if it is inflicted on a minority that, as a result of being denied the right to vote, had no part in enacting or devising the law. Who can say that the legislature of Alabama which set up that state's segregation laws was democratically elected? Throughout Alabama all sorts of devious methods are used to prevent Negroes from becoming registered voters, and there are some counties in which, even though Negroes constitute a majority of the population, not a single Negro is registered. Can any law enacted under such circumstances be considered democratically structured?

Sometimes a law is just on its face and unjust in its application. For instance, I have been arrested on a charge of parading without a permit. Now, there is nothing wrong in having an ordinance which requires a permit for a parade. But such an ordinance becomes unjust when it is used to maintain segregation and to deny citizens the First-Amendment privilege of peaceful assembly and protest.

I hope you are able to see the distinction I am trying to point out. In no sense do I advocate evading or defying the law, as would the rabid segregationist. That would lead to anarchy. One who breaks an unjust law must do so openly, lovingly, and with a willingness to accept the penalty. I submit that an individual who breaks a law that conscience tells him is unjust, and who willingly accepts the penalty of imprisonment in order to arouse the conscience of the community over its injustice, is in reality expressing the highest respect for law.

Of course, there is nothing new about this kind of civil disobedience. It was evidenced sublimely in the refusal of Shadrach, Meshach and Abednego to obey the laws of Nebuchadnezzar, on the ground that a higher moral law was at stake. It was practiced superbly by the early Christians, who were willing to face hungry lions and the excruciating pain of chopping blocks rather than submit to certain unjust laws of the Roman Empire. To a degree, academic freedom is a reality today because Socrates practiced civil disobedience. In our own nation, the Boston Tea Party represented a massive act of civil disobedience.

We should never forget that everything Adolf Hitler did in Germany was "legal" and everything the Hungarian freedom fighters did in Hungary was "illegal." It was "illegal" to aid and comfort a Jew in Hitler's Germany. Even so, I am sure that, had I lived in Germany at the time, I would have aided and comforted my Jewish brothers. If today I lived in a Communist country where certain principles dear to the Christian faith are suppressed, I would openly advocate disobeying that country's antireligious laws.

I must make two honest confessions to you, my Christian and Jewish brothers. First, I must confess that over the past few years I have been gravely disappointed with the white moderate. I have almost reached the regrettable conclusion that the Negro's great stumbling block in his stride toward freedom is not the White Citizen's Councilor or the Ku Klux Klanner, but the white moderate, who is more devoted to "order" than to justice; who prefers a negative peace which is the absence of tension to a positive peace which is the presence of justice; who constantly says: "I agree with you in the goal you seek, but I cannot agree with your methods of direct action"; who paternalistically believes he can set the timetable for another man's freedom; who lives by a mythical concept of time and who constantly advises the Negro to wait for a "more convenient season." Shallow understanding from people of good will is more frustrating than absolute misunderstanding from people of ill will. Lukewarm acceptance is much more bewildering than outright rejection.

I had hoped that the white moderate would understand that law and order exist for the purpose of establishing justice and that when they fail in this purpose they become the dangerously structured dams that block the flow of social progress. I had hoped that the white moderate would understand that the present tension in the South is a necessary phase of the transition from an obnoxious negative peace, in which the Negro passively accepted his unjust plight, to a substantive and positive peace, in which all men will respect the dignity and worth of human personality. Actually, we who engage in nonviolent direct action are not the creators of tension. We merely bring to the surface the hidden tension that is already alive. We bring it out in the open, where it can be seen and dealt with. Like a boil that can never be cured so long as it is covered up but must be opened with all its ugliness to the natural medicines of air and light, injustice must be exposed, with all the tension its exposure creates, to the light of human conscience and the air of national opinion before it can be cured.

In your statement you assert that our actions, even though peaceful, must be condemned because they precipitate violence. But is this a logical assertion? Isn't this like condemning a robbed man because his possession of money precipitated the evil act of robbery? Isn't this like condemning Socrates because his unswerving commitment to truth and his philosophical inquiries precipitated the act by the misguided populace in which they made him drink hemlock? Isn't this like condemning Jesus because his unique God-consciousness and never-ceasing devotion to God's will precipitated the evil act of crucifixion? We must come to see that, as the federal courts have consistently affirmed, it is wrong to urge an individual to cease his efforts to gain his basic constitutional rights because the quest may precipitate violence. Society must protect the robbed and punish the robber....

[Omitted here is one paragraph expressing disappointed hope "that the white moderate would reject the myth of time "—i.e., the idea that man's lot inevitably improves, irrespective of actions performed for good or evil.]

You speak of our activity in Birmingham as extreme. At first I was rather disappointed that fellow clergymen would see my nonviolent efforts as those of an extremist. I began thinking about the fact that I stand in the middle of two opposing forces in the Negro community. One is a force of complacency, made up in part of Negroes who, as a result of long years of oppression, are so drained of self-respect and a sense of "somebodiness" that they have adjusted to segregation; and in part of a few middle-class Negroes who, because of a degree of academic and economic security and because in some ways they profit by segregation, have become insensitive to the problems of the masses. The other force is one of bitterness and hatred, and it comes perilously close to advocating violence. It is expressed in the various black nationalist groups that are springing up across the nation, the largest and best-known being Elijah Muhammad's Muslim movement. Nourished by the Negro's frustration over the continued existence of racial discrimination, this movement is made up of people who have lost faith in America, who have absolutely repudiated Christianity, and who have concluded that the white man is an incorrigible "devil."

I have tried to stand between these two forces, saying that we need emulate neither the "do-nothingism" of the complacent nor the hatred and despair of the black nationalist. For there is the more excellent way of love and nonviolent protest. I am grateful to God that, through the influence of the Negro church, the way of nonviolence became an integral part of our struggle.

If this philosophy had not emerged, by now many streets of the South would, I am convinced, be flowing with blood. And I am further convinced that if our white brothers dismiss as "rabble-rousers" and "outside agitators" those of us who employ nonviolent direct action, and if they refuse to support our non-violent efforts, millions of Negroes will, out of frustration and despair, seek solace and security in black-nationalist ideologies—a development that would inevitably lead to a frightening racial nightmare.

Oppressed people cannot remain oppressed forever. The yearning for freedom eventually manifests itself, and that is what has happened to the American Negro. Something within has reminded him of his birthright of freedom, and something without has reminded him that it can be gained. Consciously or unconsciously, he has been caught up by the *Zeitgeist,* and with his black brothers of Africa and his brown and yellow brothers of Asia, South America and the Caribbean, the United States Negro is moving with a sense of great urgency toward the promised land of racial justice. If one recognizes this vital urge that has engulfed the Negro community, one should readily understand why public demonstrations are taking place. The Negro has many pent-up resentments and latent frustrations, and he must release them. So let him march; let him make prayer pilgrimages to the city hall; let him go on freedom rides—and try to understand why he must do so. If his repressed emotions are not released in nonviolent ways, they will seek expression through violence; this is not a threat but a fact of history. So I have not said to my people: "Get rid of your discontent." Rather, I have tried to say that this normal and healthy discontent can be channeled into the creative outlet of nonviolent direct action. And now this approach is being termed extremist.

But though I was initially disappointed at being categorized as an extremist, as I continued to think about the matter I gradually gained a measure of satisfaction from the label. Was not Jesus an extremist for love: "Love your enemies, bless them that curse you, do good to them that hate you, and pray for them which despitefully use you, and persecute you." Was not Amos an extremist for justice: "Let justice roll down like waters and righteousness like an ever-flowing stream." Was not Paul an extremist for the Christian gospel: "I bear in my body the marks of the Lord Jesus." Was not Martin Luther an extremist: "Here I stand; I cannot do otherwise, so help me God." And John Bunyan: "I will stay in jail to the end of my days before I make a butchery of my conscience." And Abraham Lincoln: "This nation cannot survive half slave and half free." And Thomas Jefferson: "We hold these truths to be self-evident, that all men are created equal...." So the question is not whether we will be extremists, but what kind of extremists we will be. Will we be extremists for hate or for love? Will we be extremists for the preservation of injustice or for the extension of justice? In that dramatic scene on Calvary's hill three men were crucified. We must never forget that all three were crucified for the same crime—the crime of extremism. Two were extremists for immorality, and thus fell below their environment. The other, Jesus Christ, was an extremist for love, truth and goodness, and thereby rose above his environment. Perhaps the South, the nation and the world are in dire need of creative extremists.

I had hoped that the white moderate would see this need. Perhaps I was too optimistic; perhaps I expected too much. I suppose I should have realized that few members of the oppressor race can understand the deep groans and passionate yearnings of the oppressed race, and still fewer have the vision to see that injustice must be rooted out by strong, persistent and determined action. I am thankful, however, that some of our white brothers in the South have grasped the meaning of this social revolution and committed themselves to it. They are still all too few in quantity, but they are big in quality. Some—such as Ralph McGill, Lillian Smith, Harry Golden, James McBride Dabbs, Ann Braden and Sarah Patton Boyle—have written about our struggle in eloquent and prophetic terms. Others have marched with us down nameless streets of the South. They have languished in filthy, roach-infested jails, suffering the abuse and brutality of policemen who view them as "dirty nigger-lovers." Unlike so many of their moderate brothers and sisters, they have recognized the urgency of the moment and sensed the need for powerful "action" antidotes to combat the disease of segregation....

[Omitted here is King's second confession ...; eleven paragraphs expressing his dissatisfaction "with the white Church and its leadership."]

But even if the church does not come to the aid of justice, I have no despair about the future. I have no fear about the outcome of our struggle in Birmingham, even if our motives are at present misunderstood. We will reach the goal of freedom in Birmingham and all over the nation, because the goal of America is freedom. Abused and scorned though we may be, our destiny is tied up with America's destiny. Before the pilgrims landed at Plymouth, we were here. Before the pen of Jefferson etched the majestic words of the Declaration of Independence across the pages of history, we were here. For more than two centuries our fore-bears labored in this country without wages; they made cotton king; they built the homes of their masters while suffering gross injustice and shameful humiliation—and yet out of a bottomless vitality they continued to thrive and develop. If the inexpressible cruelties of slavery could not stop us, the opposition we now face will surely fail. We will win our freedom because the sacred heritage of our nation and the eternal will of God are embodied in our echoing demands.

Before closing I feel impelled to mention one other point in your statement that has troubled me profoundly. You warmly commended the Birmingham police force for keeping "order" and "preventing violence." I doubt that you would have so warmly commended the police force if you had seen its dogs sinking their teeth into unarmed, nonviolent Negroes. I doubt that you would so quickly commend the policemen if you were to observe their ugly and inhumane treatment of Negroes here in the city jail; if you were to watch them push and curse old Negro women and young Negro girls; if you were to see them slap and kick old Negro men and young boys; if you were to observe them, as they did on two occasions, refuse to give us food because we wanted to sing our grace together. I cannot join you in your praise of the Birmingham police department.

It is true that the police have exercised a degree of discipline in handling the demonstrators. In this sense they have conducted themselves rather "nonviolently" in public. But for what purpose? To preserve the evil system of segregation. Over the past few years I have consistently preached that nonviolence demands that the means we use must be as pure as the ends we seek. I have tried to make clear that it is wrong to use immoral means to attain moral ends. But now I must affirm that it is just as wrong, or perhaps even more so, to use moral means to preserve immoral ends.... As T. S. Eliot has said: "The last temptation is the greatest treason: To do the right deed for the wrong reason."

I wish you had commended the Negro sit-inners and demonstrators of Birmingham for their sublime courage, their willingness to suffer and their amazing discipline in the midst of great provocation. One day the South will recognize its real heroes. They will be the James Merediths, with the noble sense of purpose that enables them to face jeering and hostile mobs, and with the agonizing loneliness that characterizes the life of the pioneer. They will be old, oppressed, battered Negro women, symbolized in a seventy-two-year-old woman in Montgomery, Alabama, who rose up with a sense of dignity and with her people decided not to ride segregated buses, and who responded with ungrammatical profundity to one who inquired about her weariness: "My feets is tired, but my soul is at rest." They will be the young high school and college students, the young ministers of the gospel and a host of their elders, courageously and nonviolently stitting in at lunch counters and willingly going to jail for conscience' sake. One day the South will know that when these disinherited children of God sat down at lunch counters, they were in reality standing up for what is best in the American dream and for the most sacred values in our Judaeo-Christian heritage, thereby bringing our nation back to those great wells of democracy which were dug deep by the founding fathers in their formulation of the Constitution and the Declaration of Independence.

Never before have I written so long a letter. I'm afraid it is much too long to take your precious time. I can assure you that it would have been much shorter if I had been writing from a comfortable desk, but what else can one do when he is alone in a narrow jail cell, other than write long letters, think long thoughts and pray long prayers?

If I have said anything in this letter that overstates the truth and indicates an unreasonable impatience, I beg you to forgive me. If I have said anything that understates the truth and indicates my having a patience that allows me to settle for anything less than brotherhood, I beg God to forgive me.

I hope this letter finds you strong in the faith. I also hope that circumstances will soon make it possible for me to meet each of you, not as an integrationist or a civil-rights leader but as a fellow clergyman and a Christian brother. Let us all hope that the dark clouds of racial prejudice will soon pass away and the deep fog of misunderstanding will be lifted from our fear-drenched communities, and in some not too distant tomorrow the radiant stars of love and brotherhood will shine over our great nation with all their scintillating beauty.

Yours for the cause of Peace and Brotherhood,

MARTIN LUTHER KING, JR.

Poems
Daniel Berrigan

Daniel Berrigan (1921–   ) is an American Jesuit priest, who recently served a jail sentence for burning draft records in a protest against the war in Southeast Asia. He is the author of many books, including *They Call Us Dead Men* and *Consequences: Truth And ....*

SEMINAR

One speaker
an impeccable
Californian
impelled to explain

The Chinese Belong In China
The Russians In Russia.
we however—
messiah, oversoul
a pink   muscled   clear-eyed
Texan dream
fumigating
Hanoi privies
from above—
napalm   jigger bombs   gas
God's saniflush, in sum—

The gentleman was
four square as State
or the pentateuch;
sans beard, rope sandals, foul talk, pot—
a fire extinguisher
on Pentecost day;
exuding good will
like a mortician's convention
in a plague year.

Indeed yes.
There is nothing sick
(the corpse said)
about death.
Come in.

THERE MUST BE A GOD

I thought I heard
my own life say it
and the crumbling streets
and alkys mumbling, and the shot landscape
of my youth; gone—
trees, sweetness, euphoria

Yet in someone's hair or hand
a rose, blown and ragged,
a victory somewhere
like a torch in the hands of a runner
beat, dying, but on his feet.

Let there be a God
is man's big news;
let Him show as much heart
as a good man musters;
leave us alone
to make do, fumble about, fret through;
He must leave us our sins
to learn and ravel;
sweat, start false, feint, dissimulate.

Let Him be a dying vine, a back door
marked "colored only"
day old bread, wino's wine.
Let Him "stand with the fate
of the majority of men."
A shepherd, if He like folklore,
like the Roman gypsies
at Christmas time

blowing their big sheep bladders
like an ass's brag
crying, not Christmas
but their own sores and rags.

A CIVIL RIGHTS DEMONSTRATION

That morning I weighed
like a Dickens brat
no expectations. Would I march
capped in bells like Christ's fool, or Christ?

who walked with us
borne on what wind?
driven Jews, sere in vein and eye?
Sharpeville's seventy, brave in red ribbons?

O who will turn
dust to a man on march? I taste in mouth
the dust of Jews, the *durst not kill* of prophets
a taste that kills.

Bread loaf king
shelved, mouldering; a churchmice clergy start

cut, flee for cover. See how they run
like field mice under the teeth or scythe. Like men.

TO THE PRISONERS (Mexico City)

I saw the iron rings about the necks
of tortured prisoners
in frescoes by Rivera, in the National Palace.
Above, monkey-faced monks
held to the dying, the lying crucifix.

Behold, the iron on other necks now!
the cleric's collar, like a spiked mastiff
warns; *keep off*
color, music, sexual sweetness, spontaneity
passionate use of the world!
a black coverall
begins at wrists and ankles
like sacking on the dolls
that in my childhood, began to be true
at neck, hands and feet; all between
homunculus of straw, alas!

When they had locked the prisoners' irons
(the guide book says)
the executioners came forward
a line of purposeful apes
Platonic, implacable...

it is our history. In the mercado
you choose from a basket;
doll's head, hands, feet
and in another booth
sacking and shredded straw
to fashion
that five-pointed rustling star
sew it to limbs
that walk, gesticulate—
a blank-eyed verisimilitude,
Tissot's still born first born.

Madame's son?
we will never know; the crotch
is decently stitched
sterile as an armpit.

Our testament forbids
(despite the bloody hands
that stain the text)
torture, murder, the bloody curriculum taken like rare meat.
I am so apart from the fresco,
at the same time
I lie within it!
A friend, a psychologist
half serious, called me
his "troubled adolescent."
I had not sought him out; he found me
lightheaded in Mexican air
weeping
for organized madness
a half starved dog
guarding the dead flesh of my brother.
Better, I thought, among men, a dog
than among dogs, a killer.

Every day, every day for three years
efficient as a madman's
three-year plan
for renewal of the earth
the bombers go out
renewing the earth.

You may say; the descent of the beast
if it be motivated, moral, compassionate,
ensures
the survival of all.

It is indeed to the advantage
of the king of beasts
to weave analogies
from the lives of beasts.
Bear with me. I am
neither sawdust doll nor brutish monk.
I wear
foolish collar, sacking
the circus pie
of a clown whose passionate will
persuades him to be useless,
whose death
sheriffs, cardinals, generals
conspire, in the old moralities
to bring to pass—
a providence, a use.

O church and state
my church, O mausoleum;
state
the stated clerk of death
I take in my two hands
the tortured mother, the blighted child
the prisoner's face
lax as a wax work—
Christ's tears have dulled
the sheriff's rage, sharpened
the doll's dead eyes.
Surprise!
(we have his word)
we burst like straw
our sexual death
we sow like autumn fools
hope in the leprous furrow.

Revolutionary Faithfulness
R. W. Tucker

R. W. Tucker is an editor in the trade journal field and is a member of the Friends Meeting in Springfield, Pennsylvania.

Revolution has become the world's most important social fact. In the advanced nations, revolutionary change is imposed upon us by technology, and we are profoundly unsettled. In the backward nations, the Marxists have taught millions to think of revolution as their only hope for material gain within their lifetimes. In Vietnam as in our city slums, dissent hardens into resistance, apocalypse is in the air. This is the environment in which official Quaker thinkers are so busily asking themselves if our faith can be made "relevant." What they really ask is whether Quakerism can be relevant to revolution.

We Quakers were born during an earlier revolution, and we were born relevant to it. That is, we were part of it.

Every great religious awakening works by revolutionizing men's hearts. But Quakerism, along with its Puritan antecedents, belonged to a more select category. Theology and exterior events were such as to turn inward energies outward and apply them to the social fabric.

The first Friends were changed men who were ardently concerned to change their world in fundamental ways. The social and doctrinal causes they thought up were extraordinarily advanced; many of them are still far from victory. Because we are loyal to one and another inherited cause, we rank today as first-rate reformers. The founders of our faith were not reformers. They were revolutionists in the sense in which that term is commonly used today. Like today's political revolutionists, they possessed revolutionary vision, revolutionary program, revolutionary discipline, and revolutionary organization.

Yet, unlike today's political revolutionsists, they were not primarily political people. Their fervor was not for social change, but for faithfulness. What was revolutionary about them was their understanding of the obligations of faithfulness.

That is, it is clear what early Quaker social radicalism was not. It was not an admixture of Christian belief and radical ideology. This makes it sharply different from most current forms of Christian social radicalism.

Earlier in this century, the socialist movement in America produced revolutionists who tried to rethink their native Protestantism in the light of their

From R. W. Tucker, "Revolutionary Faithfulness," in *New Theology No. 6*, ed. by Martin E. Marty and Dean G. Peerman (New York, 1969), pp. 199–227. The article first appeared in *Quaker Religious Thought*, Vol. 9, No. 2 (Winter 1967–1968), Rio Grande College, Rio Grande, Ohio 45674. Reprinted by permission of the author and the Quaker Theological Discussion Group.

Marxism. On one level this produced a rather engaging cult of "Comrade Jesus." On another level it produced the social gospel movement, which has attracted many modern Friends. Social gospel theology occupied itself in adapting Christian tradition to humanist social goals; it is being revived today within many Christian groups as they, too, look for relevance. They are right in seeing that Christians must come to terms with contemporary revolutionary ideologies. But Friends can approach this task with an enormous initial advantage, because we can start from an authentic revolutionary dynamic of our own. . . .

. . . Friends represented, historically, a new quickening of revolutionary life within the Puritan revolution, and "Puritanism" to most of us is merely a bad word describing attitudes which were, at most, a minor element in authentic Puritanism.

Let us begin, then, by reminding ourselves that the Puritans were the bolsheviks of their time. They fought and won a long and bloody civil war. They cut off the head of a king, after holding what C. V. Wedgwood calls "history's first great show trial." They established a viable regime. They instituted new social and political and economic patterns. They worked hard to export their revolution and subvert neighboring governments. The religious historians produce long studies that barely mention these facts; likewise the political historians pay little attention to Puritan theology. But to the Puritans, politics and religion were one.

They had, like all revolutionists, an opposition on the left—people who felt they had not gone far enough in either social or ecclesiastical change; people who dissented from their subordination of means to ends. The Society of Friends arose among these opponents.

The first revolutionizing element in Puritanism was its understanding of the Christian's function in history. In those pre-Wesleyan times, Christians laid less stress on the notion that "Christ came to save sinners"; they *did* emphasize that Christ came "because God so loved the world." That meant what it said—the world as a social entity; institutions as well as individuals. Like medieval Catholics, and unlike modern American Protestants, they assumed that government should reflect religion and serve its purposes.

The great theological discovery of Puritanism, "the marrow of Puritan divinity" (as Perry Miller has labelled it), was covenant theology. God is concerned to save the world. He elects to do this by gathering a people to Himself through which to do His work of salvation. The Old Testament records his covenant with the Jews, in which He promised to be their God and they agreed to be His people. According to His grand design for human history, the old covenant with the Jews paved the way for, and was a model for, the new covenant through Christ, which superseded it. The Puritans thought of themselves as the exclusive people of God, expressly gathered for the purpose of doing His work in history.

The Puritans came out of the first generation of Englishmen to be biblically literate. They discovered covenant theology by reading Scripture in the light of Calvin's *Institutes;* it was, they insisted, plainly the theology of the writers of the New Testament, the one viewpoint that makes the entire Bible into an understandable whole. They discovered in the Bible a total blueprint for organizing church and state. They also discovered, or thought they discovered, a directive to themselves to go forth and rearrange church and state in accordance with that blueprint.

For early Friends, the revolutionary break with Puritanism came in their rejection of Calvinism. But it did not involve a rejection of covenant theology, certainly not of its political applications. If they rarely wrote about it, this is because they didn't have to; it was in the air they breathed; anyway, they were too busy writing about the things they *did* reject. One way of explaining Quakerism is to say that in the context of Puritan covenantism, the first Friends were teaching a radically new and deeper understanding of the nature of the new covenant. Christ had come to lead His people Himself. The new covenant was a living "dialogic" *relationship*.

The people of God were to be gathered into communities of discipleship; the model for any Christian community was the twelve original disciples. Like the original disciples, the community of discipleship engaged itself continually in hearing and obeying its divine leader; Christ sat at the head of Meeting. Leadership in the new covenant was prophetic, as it had been in the old covenant.

Exactly how did this set of beliefs produce revolutionary social purpose? It is instructive to make a list of specific revolutionary ingredients in original Quakerism:

1. Early Friends knew that what they were doing really mattered in world history. God does not gather a people to Himself just to have a people; history *is* God-in-history. To early Friends, *they* were the whole point of history. A belief in the importance of one's role in history is a key part of any revolutionist's make-up; it is a major ingredient in Marxism.

2. They possessed a revolutionary vision. For any revolutionary movement, the revolutionary vision is its explicit and detailed understanding of how the world could and should work. It continually produces criticisms of the existing social order. People who take up these criticisms for their own sake, however militantly they do it, are merely reformers; the revolutionist sees immediate social reform as a step toward a new order. We must take care not to see the first Friends as reformers. They started with the general Puritan vision of a new world, and drastically improved upon it; they envisioned a Christian world radically different from the actual world; this was the source of their social creativity. Early American socialism was socially creative for a similar reason; it compares closely with early Quakerism, as a minority movement whose revolutionary vision evolved into other people's reforms.

3. Early Friends were not class-bound. They were not comfortable in their environment; they felt alienated from their society; they were outsiders. Revolutions are always made by people who at least inwardly are outsiders. After Friends became prosperous and comfortable, through some left-over revolutionary impulse, for generations we artificially maintained our sense of outsiderness by practices of deliberate peculiarity. Have we abandoned plainness for the positive reasons we like to cite, or because we no longer have a sense of ourselves as creatively different?

4. Early Friends understood that revolutionists need the support of revolutionary communities. When today we read the accounts of men like James Naylor or Marmaduke Stevenson, we are struck first by their total faithfulness, second by their readiness to abandon family duties in the cause of faithfulness.

These were people over 30 who yet could be trusted, because they had behind them Meetings which, in endorsing their concerns, automatically took over their private responsibilities for them.

We still produce our Stevensons, but nowadays they are highly unusual and cause controversy among us. In the beginning it was their Meetings that made them what they were. The original Friends Meeting was a community of revolutionary faithfulness, revolutionary in a collective sense even more than in its individuals. The intense corporateness of early Quakerism is its most alien characteristic to us today, yet the one perhaps most needed by Friends, because it offers so much to a world afflicted by the dissipation of community.

5. Early Friends had a revolutionary discipline, summarized in the word "faithfulness." They had a divine Leader; the whole work of their lives was to be faithful to Him; members helped one another in the task of learning and doing the things faithfulness required; corporate faithfulness made private faithfulness easier. Discipline, that is, was understood dynamically in terms of loyalty to a leader, rather than statically in terms of obeying rules. The indiscipline so rampant among modern Friends, painful though it often is, in part represents an effort to smash outdated norms and clear the way to get back to the original sense of discipline.

6. Finally, early Friends built a revolutionary apparatus through which to do the work of overturning the old and instituting the new. Of this, more later. But it is worth noting that Quaker organization even to this day succeeds, surprisingly often, in producing and following prophetic leadership; the community is wiser and holier than the sum of its parts. Revisionist versions of Quakerism have inherited a revolutionary organizational structure that tends to push them toward stances more radical than most members want.

A sense of historical role; revolutionary vision; estrangement from the status quo; revolutionary corporateness; revolutionary apparatus and discipline— these are the ingredients that make any revolutionary movement work, whether Gandhi's in India or Castro's in Cuba. Revolutionary ideologies—violent or nonviolent, religious or secular—produce much the same sociology. This list shows that early Quakerism had a great deal in common with every other revolutionary movement. We should not fail to see it that way.

For all that, there is a fundamental difference between religiously motivated revolution, and revolution in terms of a secular ideology. This, too, we must not fail to see. The difference is eschatological. In the final analysis, Christians understand that the Kingdom comes as a gift from God, not at the end of a human struggle.

This insight has been misapplied by many Christian groups in a way that removes them from social struggle. Not so with Friends; our doctrine has always been, "the Kingdom of God is within." We are to practice "realized eschatology"—living *now* as though the Kingdom were already realized, because for us it is.

Among early Friends that meant a provocative innocency which was the lifestyle not only of individuals, but of Christian communities, Meetings. This was the immediate cause of their tension with the world around them. It also defines the methodological differences between early Friends and other revolutionists: They didn't just envision an ideal social order; so far as the world let them, they *lived* it. This was their mode of social confrontation. Marxists, like all politicians, are eternally calculating the effects of their actions. Early Friends were deeply interested in effects, but they sought first the Kingdom.

As we examine contemporary revolutionary ideologies, we must hold clearly in mind both the many points they have in common with early Quakerism, and this key point of difference.

THE LESSONS OF MARXISM

With contrite hearts we must acknowledge that Marxist successes are a measure of Christian failure. If the churches of Europe had been less committed, a century ago, to property and the status quo, they might have responded to the urgent need for distributive justice, and Marxism might never have arisen.

On this particular point Friends threw away their chance for relevance. "The trimmings of the vain world would clothe the naked one," said William Penn; and for generations, long before Thorstein Veblen, Friends wore plain dress first of all as a testimony against conspicuous consumption. We saw early that social and economic inequalities are the wellspring of vanity. This is to our credit. But we applied this insight only in terms of private witness, when what was also needed was political organizing.

For Friends, of course, insights so advanced did not flow from rigorous development of ideological presuppositions, but from lives lived obediently, in the Power that brings the world under judgment. The fact remains that our insights were badly needed by the world, and after our first generation we treated them as private property. We retained our revolutionary vision, but we lost heart for the actual work of revolution.

There are many other Marxist insights that parallel Quaker thinking and condemn Quaker behavior. As a conspicuous current example, it is the Marxist intellectuals who worry themselves sick about mass culture and what it's doing to people. This corresponds to the traditional Friendly concern about worldliness. Revolutionary Quakerism should be busy updating its tradition on worldliness to a meaningful testimony on mass culture. Instead we are quietly abandoning our ancient witness to an inner-directed cultural life. We become indistinguishable from the world's people not only in our dress and speech, which hardly matters—but also in our television-watching and in our politics, which matters a lot.

This parallelism of social insight suggests a fascinating vision of what might have been. Rufus Jones and his successors "modernized" the Quaker social vision by making it coterminous with ideological pacifism, which was then in very primitive form. A generation or so earlier, they might just as readily, and just as legitimately, have turned instead to early Marxism. Had they done so, it would be the job of this essay to debunk Marxism, and to urge the lessons of pacifism, instead of vice versa.

Coming to terms with Marxism means coming to terms with humanism, since Marxism is humanism in revolutionary guise. "Man is the measure of all things" is a phrase the Marxists have borrowed from Protagoras. They interpret it to mean that the purpose of revolution is to put man in control of his own fate. It is impossible to overstate how basic this concept is to Marxist thinking.

An example may help. Marxism's labor theory of value starts as a moral assertion: The very economy can and should be organized around the belief that human ingenuity and human labor are the most valuable things there are; the value of every commodity is to be reckoned in terms of the human effort that went into its designing, its manufacture, its marketing. Thus man is to be the measure of all things in the most literal sense.

Christians must say "Yes, and no" to this sort of humanist concern. Man is *not* the measure of all things. *Sanctified* man is the measure of all things. That is, Christ is the measure. And it is Christ whom we seek to put in control of our fate.

But Christ said, "So far as ye have done it unto the least of these, ye have done it unto me." The second great commandment, to love one another, is, He said, "like unto" the first, to love God. Loving God entails loving people; inwardly it is the same process. So the Christian fully shares the humanist's concern for the condition of man. Indeed, his concern is more radical and his vision brighter, because it is Christ who defines his hope for all men.

In practice, Christianity has responded to humanism either with blind hostility, or, among Christian "liberals," by swallowing it whole. Social gospel Christianity, for instance, agrees with humanism in treating the human social struggle as an end in itself. Revolutionary Quakerism must respond instead with extensive agreement coupled with friendly criticism from the left. Our attitude must be, "You're right as far as you go, but you don't go far enough."

The real problem facing us all is not to oppose the humanist vision, in which man is the measure of all things, with the vision of a nobler world in which Christ is the measure of all things—but the prior difficulty of undoing a world in which things are the measure of man. Focussing on this, we are set free to put the so-called humanist challenge to Christianity in proper perspective, as a quarrel over theory among people who are allies in practice. It is an important quarrel, but in many ways it need not be a divisive one.

Few revolutionary movements have been as self-analytical as Marxism. What it has learned about itself may be applied broadly to Christianity viewed as a revolutionary movement.

Historically, Marxists have perverted their own principles in three different ways, which they label "utopianism," "reformism," and "bolshevism."

The utopian goes apart from the world to build his own revolutionary community. The reformist lowers his sights in the interest of immediate minor reform in his own lifetime, and lapses into liberalism. The bolshevik accepts any means to achieve his revolutionary end, so of course ends up with something quite different from the ideal social order originally envisioned. All three suffer from the same disease—impatience.

All three patterns may readily be found in Christian history. In fact, most Christians, like most Marxists, have ended up on one or another of these three sidetracks.

The problem is that people cannot readily reconcile themselves to a role of eternal struggle for goals eternally unreached. Yet this is precisely what is required. Even for the Marxist, a mature understanding must teach that perfection recedes infinitely—if you create the society you thought you wanted, by then you will see a need for still further change. For Christians the theoretical social goal is nothing less than universal sainthood and a social order that reflects, serves, and nurtures it. This goal is so lofty that it may never exist except in the Christian imagination as a standard by which to measure reality. It imposes upon Christianity a doctrine of permanent revolution.

The Christian, then, must reconcile himself to a revolutionary role that may bear no visible fruit at all in his lifetime. He must understand the need for constant revision of proximate goals. Somehow he must also maintain his revolutionary fervor. It is an extremely difficult balance to maintain.

Yet here is where the Christian revolutionist has an enormous advantage over the Marxist. He has already learned to live with receding perfection in his inward life; it is our common experience that the nearer we get to holiness, the more acute our awareness of how far we yet must go. And on the social plane, Christians are concerned for revolution as an aspect of their concern for inward spiritual revolution. Their inward satisfaction comes from being faithful, only secondarily from success in the outward goals that faithfulness directs them to labor for. The Marxist has only his outward success to sustain him; frustration in worldly goals is far more painful to him than to the Christian. No doubt revolutionary movements are inherently unstable, but the Christian revolution is markedly less so than the Marxist.

Most people do not think of history as something they need to have an attitude toward. Marxists do. They see history as process. Changes are taking place; they can be analyzed. The *method* of the revolutionist is to work in terms of historic trends, and bend them to his purpose.

Thus early Marxists saw labor unions as an instrument of the new class of industrial workers that history was bringing into being. The function of unions was to express the aspirations of the dispossessed. Therefore Marxists were active from the start in organizing unions and in bending them to explicit revolutionary purpose. Today the civil rights movement is seen as another potential vehicle for revolution, for the same reason. The Marxist, in short, studies history to find the motors that may get revolution moving.

Marxism is commonly misunderstood as seeking to collectivize mankind. It does not. Rather, Marxist analysis of economic history leads to the conclusion that collectivization is taking place willy-nilly, as a byproduct of an integrating economy. The Marxists then tackle the question of how to rationalize the process into community and brotherhood. Again, Marxism does not think of itself as favoring the bureaucratization of mankind. Rather, it concludes that huge bureaucracies are necessary for modern government and modern corporations and, indeed, for modern living standards. Then it tackles the question of how to return to people some measure of control over the decisions that affect our lives. Pacifists, Friends, and other well-intentioned people resist the assumption that collectivism and bureaucracy are inevitable, since both of these are rather unpleasant things; and therefore we are not equipped to influence their evolution, which is a principle reason why they are unpleasant things. The moral here is that relevance begins with the capacity to see reality as it is, even when we don't like it.

Reconstructionist Quaker thinkers stress the need for Friends to see history as drama, the eternal drama of God's way with man. God works constantly in history; He raises up prophets; He gathers a people to Himself.

What is hard to understand is the belief of some of these Friends that this view of history and the Marxist view are incompatible. Cannot the divine drama take place within a human history that is in process? The Marxist view of history is not necessarily a dogma; it is an analytical tool, a guide to action; anyone can use it. Granted, prophetic witness is motivated by inward urgency, not by analysis of social process. Granted, the Lord may use His prophets to produce changes that the Marxists can prove are not yet possible. Yet at the same time, an awareness of social process may help the witnessing Christian apply his witness more effectively. It may help him see the need for witness in the first place. We are not so rich in our understanding of the world we would be relevant to as to be able to throw away any tool that may increase our understanding.

Finally, Friends need to understand something of the Marxist view of class.

A few years back, a Quaker committee rejected a manuscript on the dilemmas of middle-class pacifism, on grounds that "class" is an un-Friendly concept. One is obliged to reply (echoing Galileo): *Nevertheless, class exists.* It's even mentioned in the Seventh (Philadelphia) Query. High-minded religious people cannot wish it out of existence. The very desire to do so is itself a class phenomenon, as any Marxist can easily explain. People who are dispossessed do not need to be taught about class; only the comfortable and self-satisfied can ignore it.

Marxists define class economically; it is a function of one's relationship to the means of production. They have discovered that people who own a part of the economy, or have economic reason for identifying with the owning class, are inclined to see the world in a different way from those who are alienated from ownership. They see the world as manipulable, themselves as capable of individual influence. Nonowners see their world as hostile and themselves as impotent, except when they can be educated and led (by Marxists) to act collectively as a class.

Moreover, to justify their position, the upper classes are obliged to think of the lower classes as less than fully human. They end by making themselves unable to identify with the viewpoint of the dispossessed.

Christians, of course, have always understood hard-heartedness. They have always striven to open their hearts to the condition of all other men. This is the basic radicalizing element in Christianity.

But opening one's heart to the condition of others is not easy. Here is where the Marxist insights about class are helpful. They show us how our attitudes are hard-hearted, rooted in self-interest, where we may not be aware of it. Middle-class people grow up class-blind, but class-blindness is one of the few traits people can surmount by thinking about it. Marxism itself proves this; its leadership has come mainly from the upper classes.

Surmounting class-blindness is Quakerism's most urgent need today. Especially in Britain and the eastern United States, the Society of Friends is almost exclusively a middle-class organization, with disastrous effects upon its inner life and social potential.

Anarchic individualism, the characteristic that most separates us from our forefathers, is a class trait by Marxist analysis. The first Friends developed a tightly disciplined collective radicalism, but as we became more prosperous, we developed bourgeois beliefs in individual significance, until finally discipline collapsed and we started going off in all directions at once in both theological and social witness.

Working-class people just don't feel comfortable in most Friends Meetings, because of the kind of people we are. We export service to the slums, but, virtually alone among Christian bodies in America today, we offer no ministry there at all. Our Meetings there are declining Meetings, peopled by nonresidents. Other Christian bodies have found new congregations when their neighborhoods ran down, deepening their vision and broadening their horizons along the way. We, to our shame, instead have developed subterranean elitist theories about ourselves.

Thus there is a widespread view that Quakerism is a "special" faith for "spiritual aristocrats," and not for the ordinary run of people. Yet original Quakerism was emphatically a movement of farmers, workingmen, and artisans. We honor the memory of martyrs who were employed as menial servants, whom we would not know how to welcome in our Meetings today.

Thus there is a general opinion that Quaker worship is too sophisticated for children, who should instead go to First-day schools. Yet children went to Meeting for 250 years; this was how they grew up to know about their faith. In one early Meeting, when all the adults were jailed, the children maintained public worship. In the unlikely event that any modern Meeting should be that faithful, could it possibly rely upon its children to keep things going? Children tend to be what we expect them to be—and we expect them to be something that makes us feel our worship is superior, something that excuses us from the need to widen our class basis.

THE CULT OF NONVIOLENCE

The class character of Quakerism explains the peculiar nature of our pacifism these days. Our revolutionary inheritance, our truer instinct, leads us to seek out a revolutionary viewpoint. Yet we are estranged from our own revolutionary origin, even as we are influenced by it. Rampant individualism has reduced our sense of corporateness, leaving us free to look outside our own inheritance. So we discover a secular ideological system, pacifism, and make it one of our norms. Pacifism can be radical and sometimes revolutionary—but to a large extent we are capable of using it only in its nonrevolutionary and middle-class variant. That is, we use it cultishly.

Cultishness is the first and most conspicuous face of Quaker pacifism today. A prospective new Friend is likely to meet Quaker pacifism first in the shape of the dear old lady who rises in Meeting for Worship to speak to the children about why they ought to be pacifists. She tells homely little stories about pacifists who won through to victory in some worldly dilemma.

Such cult pacifism is pretty easy to debunk. It is false doctrine in obvious ways. It discounts the Cross, and the whole bloody history of martyrdom. Pacifist behavior may lead to great suffering and total worldly failure. Even when it does work as a tactic, religious people are not pacifists for that reason. Sophisticated pacifists are, of course, often the first to point this out. Still, there is a sense in which any ideology can be seen most clearly in caricature. Our old lady is interesting because her cultism is so evident.

The word "cult," when used pejoratively as it is here, is meant to suggest such grouplets as the Rosicrucians in religion, or the Trotskyists in politics—cliques of initiates, adhering to an esoteric doctrine which they are forever narrowing and defining, which they think gives them a special POWER. Just as the Rosicrucians claim they have special mental powers, so many pacifists believe they have special spiritual powers; pacifism makes them permanently one-up. Like the Trotskyists they think they are a vanguard, the experts to whom the world must someday turn.

There is a valid basis for such attitudes. The methodology of nonviolence often works by one-upping those who think more conventionally. And in a world in which violence has become impossibly dangerous, nonviolence may yet become the last resort of aggressors, as Nehru foreshadowed when he non-violently invaded Goa. The point to be emphasized is that purely as a method-ology, nonviolence need not necessarily have anything to do with religion, or even with peaceseeking. It can just as readily be used for power-seeking.

This is not to suggest that the methodology, or the so-called Philosophy of Nonviolence, which is its usual ideological companion, are without value for Christian revolutionists. It is extremely helpful to have available an arsenal of techniques which offer real hope in confronting and confounding violence. Pacifist insights can be as instructive to the religious radical as Marxist insights; perhaps more so. The trouble is that middle-class, respectable, very nonrevolu-tionary Friends have come to equate this modern methodology with their tradi-tional Peace Testimony, with some very strange results.

What makes a cultist is not the truth discoverable in his position, but his vulgarizing of truth. Nonrevolutionary Friends vulgarize the Philosophy of Nonviolence when they religify it and try to make it inoffensive. Likewise, if the Philosophy of Nonviolence is to be equated with a Christian principle of loving others, then it must be defined as a vulgarization of Christian truth.

For one thing, there is a sense in which it is unseemly to speak of a Christian "principle" of loving others. Rather, there is an inward experience and growth to which Christ summons us, one of whose consequences is that we find ourselves responding lovingly to others, or at least trying to. Christian experience may very properly be summarized into general rules; in some measure, Jesus did so Himself; but Friends, above all others, have always emphasized that it is the experience that lies at the heart of Christian faith and practice, which alone can give spiritual validity to rule-following by individual or community.

The Philosophy of Nonviolence begins by assuming that love can replace violence as a practical social force. Christian experience impels one to live as though that assumption were valid, but we are given no assurance at all that it really is valid. On the contrary: "As they have hated me, so will they hate you." Quaker commitment to love as a social principle was historically a matter of faith—faith held onto sometimes desperately, in the face of overwhelming evidence that the world does not work that way.

A Christian, as Friends have understood the word, is someone who elects *now* to live as though the world were Christian. He will remain a committed person though the heavens fall, because his inward condition demands it of him. He ardently hopes to end war—a political change—but he would continue a pacifist though certain his efforts would never bear any fruit at all. The purely secular pacifist, if such a creature exists, starts by being concerned with consequences. He is a pacifist because he wants to end war. His motivation is pragmatic, teleological, and political.

What happens when an act of faith is turned into a political creed? Secular pacifist ideology, so far as it *is* secular, cannot demand that its adherents remain faithful regardless of whether it works. So the ideologues of pacifism are obliged to figure out a methodology which they can say will probably work, or at least work better in the long run than any other method of social change. Where violence seems to work—when race riots get anti-poverty funds for urban Negro ghettoes—pacifists have to assert that their way would have worked better. Possibly they are right. But along the way, they have to make certain assumptions about human nature and human motivation—and presto! a new theology.

When Friends begin to be pacifists not out of direct faithfulness to the Lord, but out of faithfulness to an ideological system, one effect is scrupulosity, the sin of the Pharisees. Scrupulosity consists in making up a code, an "ism," and living by it instead of living in the Life. Corporately, the effect is to take our most difficult social testimony, divorce it from our other beliefs, and make it a detailed system complete in itself, with its own burden of doctrinal assumptions. We give varying degrees of allegiance to it, while still thinking we give whole-hearted allegiance to our several kinds of Quakerism.

What are some of the narrower pacifist notions which are now so often taught as part of Quaker belief? Let us start with these two:

Nonviolent principles apply equally in personal and international relationships. Cultists of nonviolence do not simply oppose war and other forms of socially organized violence. They also eschew violence on a personal level. They teach that we ought not to spank our children, or permit schoolboy fights, or give a neighbor a piece of our mind, or *ever* admit to ourselves that we may not like someone. They assume that valid conscientious objection to war presupposes these attitudes.

And: *There is no significant moral difference between the violence of policy and the violence of passion.* There is the case of the man who cold-bloodedly, as an act of will, commits himself to a course of violence, for instance by going to war. Then there is the case of someone who loses his temper for a moment, in spite of his general desire to avoid violence and to treat lovingly with the world. By any standard of reason the first (moral error) is incomparably worse than the second (moral lapse). But in practice it is the second that shocks and upsets the cultists, because it happens in front of them and because it violates middle-class behavior norms. In almost any Friends Meeting, the mild-mannered nonpacifist is likely to be weightier than the impatient, short-tempered Friend who tries and tries to be a pacifist.

Most people believe that "It's human nature to succumb to violence now and then." Pacifists could reply, "So what? We're talking about ending war. That's a social problem, not a problem of personal ethics." Instead, they urge that human nature should not be violent. This does profound disservice to their cause. Pacifism's failure as a popular movement in America, more than anything else, is because most people just do not believe that men are good enough to be pacifists.

Granted, a Christian hopes to respond lovingly to all who come his way. He has discovered that this has something to do with his ability to worship, with his capacity to love God. He knows that hatred stultifies inward growth, so he is determined not to let it take root in him. Granted, if we never got angry, if all men were tender at all times toward others, many evils would vanish. But, assuming everybody is not that good, we can still oppose social evils. The abolition of slavery certainly did not end man's exploitation of man, nor abolish our tendency toward the sin of using one another; it was nevertheless a cause worth working for, and Friends did work for it at great cost, both personal and corporate.

Quakerism is an "optimistic" faith, in that Friends have always insisted that man *can* be good. This was the great cry of early Friends against the Calvinists. But this is not to say that men *are* good. Early Friends knew, with Fox, that there is an ocean of darkness as well as an ocean of light. To come out of the darkness into the light is a work of total regeneration. It can occur in anyone, but few *will* it.

To the degree that we become regenerate, we see that we cannot take part in war, and that the ending of war is a political change we favor. But if we tie this political demand to the insistence that all who accept it become regenerate, we subvert the political aspect of our own cause. If on the other hand our real interest is in regeneration, why not foster it in terms of all the truth we know about the inward life, and let pacifism take care of itself? "Seek first the Kingdom."

And whether teaching politics or regeneration, let us beware of embodying our teaching within a specific view of human nature. The pacifist cultist's view of human nature is probably not true, but in any event, it excludes those who cannot accept it. By committing ourselves to it, we depart from the catholicity that ought to characterize any Christian body, and condemn ourselves to sectarianism.

A related cultist dogma is this: *Communication is a warm puppy.* Pacifists are hung up on communication, to the point of often resisting verbal confrontation. All problems can be solved, they tend to insist, if only people will communicate; and we can establish communication unilaterally if we are just pacifist enough. Offensive people with obnoxious doctrines will be our friends if only we will "understand" them. Behind this attitude is an assumption produced by class-blindness: *Anglo-American middle-class nice-guyism is a universal principle of behavior.*

George Fox was not a "nice guy." He could never have been hired as a Y.M.C.A. secretary. He said to a critic, "Thou art a dog," because that was what the man needed to have said to him. Gandhi, in the same spirit, said, "You are a fool," not to a heckler, but to an admirer. There was nothing genteel in "speaking to the condition" of others, and not much that was polite. Frequently the purpose of communicating was to disturb. As for "understanding" the people they were disturbing, "that of God" in early Friends really did respond to "that of God" in others, and so they understood all too well.

In the real world, some people *are* offensive and some doctrines *are* obnoxious, and the more one understands them, the more evident this becomes. Seeing such people as sick rather than evil, or as evil because they are sick, or because they had an unfortunate childhood environment, may help us not to hate them. It may also help us see how to shake them up. It is not much use in countering their influence, except as a debater's ploy. Some pacifists are like the girl in the *New Yorker* cartoon, tied to a railroad track by a mustachioed villain and saying to him earnestly, "You're sick, Murgatroyd, and I feel sorry for you," while the train approaches around a bend.

In the real world, some people who are not offensive, and whose doctrines are not obnoxious, may have good reasons for reacting to pacifists in hostile ways. The cultists who are so dismayed by verbal confrontation also seem able to conceal from themselves how extremely provocative of violence their tactics sometimes are.

A few years ago, some pacifists organized a sit-down in front of trucks at a missile construction site. After a while, an exasperated truck driver drove over one of them and all but killed him. A cry of protest went up from pacifists in all corners of the land, which was politically the thing to do—but the burden of their cry was "unfair!" How shocked they were! Yet surely the one thing they could not legitimately say was "unfair." Their sit-down was right and good—but they did ask for what they got.

Pacifist Friends are inclined to understand nonviolence as a gimmick for making the world respond to us in a genteel way. Our shock, when the world does not respond that way, is a measure of how sheltered our lives are.

American pacifists are not numbered among that segment of the population which has learned to expect to be pushed around. Yet we have the arrogance to go to American Negroes, for instance, and instruct them in nonviolence. How we grieve when they decide, after bitter experience, that it no longer fits their needs.

American pacifists cannot speak to the condition of lower-income working-class neighborhoods, where people are not hopeless but do live on the verge of hopelessness, and life is an unending struggle to maintain order in the face of chaos. For psychological reasons as well as because of outside pressures, these people exist in a highly authoritarian environment—in the education they get, in their families, in jobs and unions, in church life and all the other forms of community available to them. They can be led by indigenous, charismatic, authoritarian leaders into insurrectionary behavior over issues that seem close to them, i.e., violent labor struggles over bread-and-butter questions. Their young men detest the army and will play the corrupt system all they can to keep from being conscripted; those who cheat the medical examiners are regarded as lucky or clever. But confronting the system head-on seems idiotic to them at best, and may arouse extreme and irrational hostility. Pacifist attitudes and especially pacifist demonstrations are a threat to them on the deepest psychological level. These are an offense against order, and seem to them less than totally necessary. And the nonauthoritarian mode of middle-class pacifism is an attack against all the defenses working-class people have erected to preserve some measure of dignity in their lives.

American pacifists seem equally unable to feel the inwardness of life among the desperate poor, those who have no grasp on hope at all. With the rest of the middle classes, we were appalled by teen-age gang violence in New York City, and applauded when the gangs were broken up. It was then, and consequently, that teen-age drug addiction in the slums reached epidemic proportions. In an environment that was sick from past violence done to those who dwell in it, the gangs had provided an instrument for social cohesion that was desperately needed. In such an environment, perhaps no response is worse than a violent response.

At any rate, we don't know, because it is not our environment. Have we the right to assume that violence can never be chosen as a course of action by a person of conscience and intelligence? To weigh our personal commitment to refuse to accept a lesser evil, against someone's belief that involvement and participation is for him a more important value? Our tolerance is curiously one-sided—we easily tolerate nonpacifism among other Friends, who are our own kind and whose backsliding is in the direction of standard middle-class patrio-tism, while we condemn nonpacifism in the desperate poor.

If we are going to ask the world to accept pacifism as more than an occasional tactic, then we had better find a form of pacifism that is not tied to middle-class values. When we assume that humans are good, that evil is unreal, that with love we can get our adversaries to be nice, we cannot expect to be taken seriously by those whose whole life has taught them that men are always self-serving and often cruel, and that the haves will do anything to keep down the have-nots. A class-limited pacifism is incapable, by definition, of relevance in a time of revolution.

There are, of course, pacifists who understand all these things. Some of them have combined their pacifism with Marxist or anarchist insights. Some have made heroic efforts to get inside the life of the poor; the Catholic Worker move-ment, for example. The ideology of pacifism does offer useful insights from which Quakerism has benefited; individuals among us have adopted it in its revolution-ary variant in ways that usefully force all of us to confront ourselves. But even if a secular ideology does hold the key to revolutionary relevance for the Society of Friends, it will not be this ideology, so long as its comfortable variant is so ready to hand.

THE LAMB'S WAR

According to the cultists of nonviolence, the secret of revolutionary relevance for the first Friends *was* pacifism. They teach, for instance, that the Quaker struggle for tolerance in Stuart England is a glowing early example of nonviolent tactics.

Like so many pacifist notions, this just isn't so. It assigns to early Friends an understanding of what they were doing that would not be invented for another 250 years. It puts them in a light that makes them seem attractive to twentieth-century middle-class American liberals. In fact, the first Friends were not engaged in a struggle for tolerance. They were engaged in what they called the "Lamb's War." When they filled the jails in London for openly violating the Conventicle Act, what they hoped for was the Quakerization of England. The live-and-let-live compromise of toleration was an accident, their acceptance of it a retreat.

According to Marxists, the Puritan revolution (including Quakerism) was a struggle between late feudalism and early capitalism. It succeeded because it was in tune, as its opponents were not, with the needs of its time. This may well be true as far as it goes, and it is suggestive to us in our present situation. But, equally with the pacifist view, it doesn't begin to touch the internal dynamic of early Quakerism.

The power to which the Bible and George Fox bear witness is not the power of a technique for getting people to do what we want them to do, nor is it the power of historical necessity. What they bear witness to is the power of the Cross. In very practical ways, the Cross is the most revolutionary fact in history. Relevance to it *is* relevance to revolution; this is the great lesson our forebears can teach us.

The lesson is almost inaccessible to us because we have let the Bible-thumpers spoil evangelical language for us. They use it individualistically, by teaching that the church is a byproduct of personal faith. When early Friends spoke of Christ's saving grace and the need to respond to it, they meant not only that individuals should be reborn, but that Christian community should be reborn to perform a revolutionary function in history, through day-to-day immediate corporate faithfulness to its divine Leader. We cannot readily grasp this even when we try, some of us because we have adopted Protestant piety, others because we are rebelling against it.

. . .

Today, with urbanization, mass culture, collectivization, bureaucratization, men become strangers to one another. The whole world longs for community. This is one of the great problems Marxism proposes to answer. Friends could make a contribution. A Meeting in the full spirit of authentic Quakerism would fully satisfy its members' need for community. It would also satisfy their need for an ideology that copes with change, and for an instrument to mold it.

Only, many of our Meetings are too large to be communities, if only for the mechanical reason that members are strangers to one another. Instead of subdividing, they turn into institutions and grow on that basis. Their unity is shallow, organizational rather than organic, founded at best on "love" in its more amorphous sense, at worst on burial-ground housekeeping. Even in small Meetings, where community is mechanically possible and often seems to exist, it is not overtly grounded in discipleship.

The Meeting structure was designed to be a flexible instrument in the hands of Christian revolutionists, and a new generation of revolutionary Friends can be expected to use it in exciting new ways. Can't a Meeting function as a housing co-op? Or a workers' co-op? A repertory theatre, perhaps? Job and neighborhood are the two areas where community is most natural, where its dissipation is most acutely felt. There is a gap here that could be filled by Meetings that are also semivoluntary communities performing an economic role. A few of our school Meetings already approximate this function.

. . .

The number of possible concerns to serve as a focus for a Meeting is limitless. I can even envision a Meeting that is also a political club. Like a local in a radical political party, it would dispatch its members into neighborhood organizations, hold public meetings, arrange educational seminars, hire organizers, plan agitational activity. Bizarre? The original Meetings did all these things and more.

How do we get from here to there? The Marxist method is to look for tendencies toward the desired goal, and, finding them, to exacerbate them and inform them with revolutionary purpose. Are there trends within Quakerism today that potentially will free us to recover our revolutionary heritage?

Fortunately, there are. The Society of Friends is going through a period when many of its non-basic beliefs are being shaken to their roots.

One cherished Quaker belief has been that we can bring holiness into our lives in the business world. Our prosperity and respectability as a people have been founded upon our discovery that it's good business to be a Christian businessman. Yet each year sees fewer and fewer young Friends seeking careers in the business world. There seems to be an unarticulated but growing conviction that in more and more areas of business life, it's no longer possible to be both a good Christian and a good businessman.

We have taught that the retailer must sell in a spirit of concern for his customer. But in a time of mass merchandising, the good salesman is the man who can move customers "up the line" from the advertised price leader to the higher-priced, more profitable merchandise. In many fields the retailer who scruples at victimizing the poor may shortly go out of business. We have maintained that the Christian businessman is "prompt in the payment of debts." But today in America the sharp businessman pays his debts as late as he can, so he can have the use of the money. Businessmen who refuse to play this game suffer competitively for their refusal. We have proclaimed the virtues of thrift and frugality, but most businessmen find it is bad business to practice either, and worse business if one's customers practice these ancient Protestant virtues. The small businessman, in short, must more and more weigh principle against competitive advantage. And of course, more and more of our commerce and manufacture is in the hands not of small businessmen, but of giant corporations; the Friend who works for them finds his ethical decisions have been made for him.

It is time we started generalizing from this situation. In the United States today, "affluence" depends on the manipulation of consent, the consent of human beings to pink telephones and electric manicures and other things commercially profitable, rather than to what is socially needed. We have created a new category of poor, people impoverished by lack of sales resistance; this is the proper significance of Cadillacs in Harlem. All these things the Marxists have been saying for some time. Can't the Quaker businessman say them with equal fervor?

It is leftists who have insisted that men are not things to be used by the hucksters, and have tried to organize consumer resistance. It is Marxists who have understood that advertising, as it is now generally practiced, is of itself an evil. And what have the Christians done? They have used huckster methods themselves, with ads about putting Christ back in Christmas, about how the family that prays together stays together. Friends, to our credit, instinctively avoid sloganistic religion (though partly for snob reasons). We believe "that of God" in one man can speak to "that of God" in another—can we adapt this principle to modern tasks of commercial and political persuasion? Have we really tried? We have a strong consumer testimony on funerals, but we have not expanded it into an understanding that one function of the Christian community is to act generally as an organizing center for consumer rebellion.

Here are major areas of life in which Friends have strong traditional positions, which events are asking us to reexamine. By doing so we may take a large step toward revolutionary relevance.

Another cherished Quaker belief is that the dissenter is the best citizen of all. This notion, too, is quietly fading. Quaker bodies recently have not felt it necessary to proclaim their patriotism in the process of declaring their dissent. We are not as sanctimonious these days in our conscientious objection as we used to be. Many of us have reached the point of advocating draft-dodging. That is, we maintain our ancient witness against war, but we also acknowledge that opposition to the Vietnam war in any form is preferable to non-opposition, and deserves our encouragement.

A number of Yearly Meetings are sending money through Canada illegally to help both sides in the Vietnam war. This is in our full tradition; we have always tried to act as neutrals and reconcilers. What is not at all traditional is the readiness of many Friends to admit that their attitudes are treasonable. We are so alienated from our government that increasingly we feel "treason" is an honorable word.

We seem to have concluded that we can no longer realistically hope to influence government by love and by Friendly persuasion. So in all types of dissent, many Friends turn more and more to civil disobedience. The theory here is that if social dislocation through protest can make the power structure uncomfortable enough, the power structure may make changes in order to regain its comfort. This is an outrightly revolutionary theory.

In short, events are more and more forcing us to think of ourselves as outsiders. Our social posture becomes steadily more radical. We lose members who are not ready to go along with this, but find a new constituency among concerned radical young people who feel a need for faith and religious fellowship. This change in membership makes it easier for us to assume a yet more radical posture, and so forth around again.

. . .

There is a real possibility that we will in fact become once more revolutionary, not of our own accord but because we are forced to. This raises a question: When most of our members are conscious revolutionists, will they be revolutionists in their capacity as Friends? Or will they be revolutionists in terms of secular ideologies, who just happen to be Friends? Will we find an organic corporate relevance to revolution, or will we just be swept along?

The attitudes that gave our forebears corporate relevance are available to us today if we want to use them. We can try to direct our own future, or we can let it happen to us. It is certain to happen anyway. Those of us who believe revolutionary faithfulness can make a contribution to it had better get busy contributing.

THE FUNDAMENTAL QUESTION: TO CHANGE MAN OR SOCIETY?

The New Man

Ernesto "Che" Guevara

Ernesto "Che" Guevara (1928–1967) was trained in medicine and took a leading part in the Cuban revolution in 1959. Afterward, he held high government posts under Fidel Castro. He left Cuba to become a guerilla leader in South America, where he was killed. He is the author of *Reminiscences of the Cuban Revolutionary War*.

Dear Comrade:

I am finishing these notes while traveling through Africa, moved by the desire to keep my promise, although after some delay. I should like to do so by dealing with the topic that appears in the title. I believe it might be of interest to Uruguayan readers.

It is common to hear how capitalist spokesmen use as an argument in the ideological struggle against socialism the assertion that such a social system, or the period of building socialism upon which we have embarked, is characterized by the extinction of the individual for the sake of the state. I will make no attempt to refute this assertion on a merely theoretical basis, but will instead establish the facts of the Cuban experience and add commentaries of a general nature. I shall first broadly sketch the history of our revolutionary struggle both before and after taking of power.

As we know, the exact date of the beginning of the revolutionary actions which were to culminate on January 1, 1959, was July 26, 1953. A group of men led by Fidel Castro attacked the Moncada military garrison in the province of Oriente, in the early hours of the morning of that day. The attack was a failure. The failure became a disaster and the survivors were imprisoned, only to begin the revolutionary struggle all over again, once they were amnestied.

During this process, which contained only the first seeds of socialism, man was a basic factor. Man—individualized, specific, named—was trusted and the

From Ernesto "Che" Guevara, "The New Man," letter to Carlos Quijano, editor-publisher of the Uraguayan weekly *Marcha*, written in 1965 and published in Cuba as "El Socialismo y el Hombre en Cuba" (Havana: Ediciones R). Official government translation by Margarita Zimmerman.

triumph or failure of the task entrusted to him depended on his capacity for action.

Then came the stage of guerrilla warfare. It was carried out in two different environments: the people, an as yet unawakened mass that had to be mobilized, and its vanguard, the guerrilla, the thrusting engine of mobilization, the generator of revolutionary awareness and militant enthusiasm. This vanguard was the catalyst which created the subjective condition necessary for victory. The individual was also the basic factor in the guerrilla, in the framework of the gradual proletarianization of our thinking, in the revolution taking place in our habits and in our minds. Each and every one of the Sierra Maestra fighters who achieved a high rank in the revolutionary forces has to his credit a list of noteworthy deeds. It was on the basis of such deeds that they earned their rank.

It was the first heroic period in which men strove to earn posts of greater responsibility, of greater danger, with the fulfillment of their duty as the only satisfaction. In our revolutionary educational work we often return to this instructive topic. The man of the future could be glimpsed in the attitude of our fighters.

At other times of our history there have been repetitions of this utter devotion to the revolutionary cause. During the October Crisis and at the time of the hurricane Flora, we witnessed deeds of exceptional valor and self-sacrifice carried out by an entire people. One of our fundamental tasks from the ideological standpoint is to find the way to perpetuate such heroic attitudes in everyday life.

The revolutionary government was established in 1959 with the participation of several members of the "sell-out" bourgeoisie. The presence of the rebel army constituted the guarantee of power as the fundamental factor of strength.

Serious contradictions arose which were solved in the first instance in February 1959, when Fidel Castro assumed the leadership of the government in the post of Prime Minister. This process culminated in July of the same year with the resignation of President Urrutia in the face of mass pressure.

With clearly defined features, there now appeared in the history of the Cuban Revolution a personage which will systematically repeat itself: the masses.

This multifacetic being is not, as it is claimed, the sum total of elements of the same category (and moreover, reduced to the same category by the system imposed upon them) and which acts as a tame herd. It is true that the mass follows its leaders, especially Fidel Castro, without hesitation, but the degree to which he has earned such confidence is due precisely to the consummate interpretation of the people's desires and aspirations, and to the sincere struggle to keep the promises made.

The mass participated in the agrarian reform and in the difficult undertaking of the management of the state enterprises; it underwent the heroic experience of Playa Girón; it was tempered in the struggle against the groups of bandits armed by the CIA; during the October Crisis it lived one of the most important definitions of modern times, and today it continues the work to build socialism.

Looking at things from a superficial standpoint, it might seem that those who speak of the submission of the individual to the state are right; with incomparable enthusiasm and discipline, the mass carries out the tasks set by the government whatever their nature: economic, cultural, defense, sports, etc. The initiative generally comes from Fidel or the high command of the revolution: it is explained to the people, who make it their own. At times local experiences are taken up by the party and the government and are thereby generalized, following the same procedure.

However, the state at times makes mistakes. When this occurs, the collective enthusiasm diminishes palpably as a result of a quantitative diminishing that takes place in each of the elements that make up the collective, and work becomes paralyzed until it finally shrinks to insignificant proportions; this is the time to rectify.

This was what happened in March 1962 in the presence of the sectarian policy imposed on the party by Anibal Escalante.

This mechanism is obviously not sufficient to ensure a sequence of sensible measures; what is missing is a more structured relationship with the mass. We must improve this connection in the years to come, but for now, in the case of the initiatives arising on the top levels of government, we are using the almost intuitive method of keeping our ears open to the general reactions in the face of the problems that are posed.

Fidel is a past master at this; his particular mode of integration with the people can only be appreciated by seeing him in action. In the big public meetings one can observe something like the dialogue of two tuning forks whose vibrations summon forth new vibrations each in the other. Fidel and the mass begin to vibrate in a dialogue of growing intensity which reaches its culminating point in an abrupt ending crowned by our victorious battle cry.

What is hard to understand for anyone who has not lived the revolutionary experience is that close dialectical unity which exists between the individual and the mass, in which both are interrelated, and the mass, as a whole composed of individuals, is in turn interrelated with the leader.

Under capitalism certain phenomena of this nature can be observed with the appearance on the scene of politicians capable of mobilizing the public, but if it is not an authentic social movement, in which case it is not completely accurate to speak of capitalism, the movement will have the same life span as its promoter or until the rigors of capitalist society put an end to popular illusions. Under capitalism man is guided by a cold ordinance which is usually beyond his comprehension. The alienated human individual is bound to society as a whole by an invisible umbilical cord: the law of value. It acts upon all facets of his life, shaping his road and his destiny.

The laws of capitalism, invisible and blind for most people, act upon the individual without his awareness. He sees only the broadness of horizon that appears infinite. Capitalist propaganda presents it in just this way, and attempts to use the Rockefeller case (true or not) as a lesson in the prospects for success. The misery that must be accumulated for such an example to arise and the sum total of baseness contributing to the formation of a fortune of such magnitude do not appear in the picture, and the popular forces are not always able to make these concepts clear. (It would be fitting at this point to study how the workers of the imperialist countries gradually lose their international class spirit under the influence of a certain complicity in the exploitation of the dependent countries and how this fact at the same time wears away the militant spirit of the masses within their own national context, but this topic is outside the framework of the present note.)

In any case we can see the obstacle course which may apparently be overcome by an individual with the necessary qualities to arrive at the finish line. The reward is glimpsed in the distance and the road is solitary. Furthermore, it is a race of wolves: He who arrives does so only at the expense of the failure of others.

I shall now attempt to define the individual, the actor in this strange and moving drama that is the building of socialism, in his twofold existence as a unique being and a member of the community.

I believe that the simplest approach is to recognize his unmade quality: he is an unfinished product. The flaws of the past are translated into the present in the individual consciousness and constant efforts must be made to eradicate them. The process is twofold: On the one hand society acts upon the individual by means of direct and indirect education, while on the other hand the individual undergoes a conscious phase of self-education.

The new society in process of formation has to compete very hard with the past. This makes itself felt not only in the individual consciousness, weighed down by the residues of an education and an upbringing systematically oriented toward the isolation of the individual, but also by the very nature of this transition period, with the persistence of commodity relations. The commodity is the economic cell of capitalist society: As long as it exists, its effects will make themselves felt in the organization of production and therefore in man's consciousness.

Marx's scheme conceived of the transition period as the result of the explosive transformation of the capitalist system torn apart by its inner contradictions: Subsequent reality has shown how some countries, the weak limbs, detach themselves from the imperialist tree, a phenomenon foreseen by Lenin. In those countries capitalism has developed sufficiently to make its effects felt upon the people in one way or another, but it is not its own inner contradictions that explode the system after exhausting all of its possibilities. The struggle for liberation against an external oppressor, the misery which has its origin in foreign causes, such as war, whose consequences make the privileged classes fall upon the exploited, the liberation movements aimed at overthrowing neocolonial regimes, are the customary factors in this process. Conscious action does the rest.

In these countries there still has not been achieved a complete education for the work of society, and wealth is far from being within the reach of the masses through the simple process of appropriation. Underdevelopment and the customary flight of capital to "civilized" countries make impossible a rapid change without sacrifices. There still remains a long stretch to be covered in the building of the economic base, and the temptation to follow the beaten paths of material interest as the lever of speedy development is very great.

There is a danger of not seeing the forest because of the trees. Pursuing the chimera of achieving socialism with the aid of the blunted weapons left to us by capitalism (the commodity as the economic cell, profitability and individual material interest as levers, etc.), it is possible to come to a blind alley. And the arrival there comes about after covering a long distance where there are many crossroads and where it is difficult to realize just when the wrong turn was taken. Meanwhile, the adapted economic base has undermined the development of consciousness. To build communism, a new man must be created simultaneously with the material base.

That is why it is so important to choose correctly the instrument of mass mobilization. That instrument must be fundamentally of a moral character, without forgetting the correct use of material incentives, especially those of a social nature.

As I already said, in moments of extreme danger it is easy to activate moral incentives: To maintain their effectiveness, it is necessary to develop a consciousness in which values acquire new categories. Society as a whole must become a huge school.

The broad characteristics of the phenomenon are similar to the process of formation of capitalist consciousness in the system's first stage. Capitalism resorts to force, but it also educates people in the system. Direct propaganda is carried out by those who are entrusted with the task of explaining the inevitability of a class regime, whether it be of divine origin or due to the imposition of nature as a mechanical entity. This placates the masses, who see themselves oppressed by an evil against which it is not possible to struggle.

This is followed by hope, which differentiates capitalism from the previous caste regimes that offered no way out. For some the caste formula continues in force: The obedient are rewarded by the *post mortem* arrival in other wonderful worlds where the good are requited, and the old tradition is continued. For others, innovation: The division in classes is a matter of fate, but individuals can leave the class to which they belong through work, initiative, etc. This process, and that of self-education for success, must be deeply hypocritical: It is the interested demonstration that a lie is true.

In our case, direct education acquires much greater importance. Explanations are convenient because they are genuine; subterfuges are not needed. It is carried out through the State's educational apparatus in the form of general, technical, and ideological culture, by means of bodies such as the Ministry of Education and the party's information apparatus. Education takes among the masses, and the new attitude that is praised tends to become habit; the mass gradually takes it over and exerts pressure on those who have still not become educated. This is the indirect way of educating the masses, as powerful as the other, structured, one.

But the process is a conscious one: The individual receives the impact of the new social power and perceives that he is not completely adequate to it. Under the influence of the pressure implied in indirect education, he tries to adjust to a situation that he feels to be just and whose lack of development has kept him from doing so thus far. He is educating himself.

We can see the new man who begins to emerge in this period of the building of socialism. His image is as yet unfinished. In fact it will never be finished, since the process advances parallel to the development of new economic forms. Discounting those whose lack of education makes them tend toward the solitary road, toward the satisfaction of their ambitions, there are others who, even within this new picture of over-all advances, tend to march in isolation from the accompanying mass. What is important is that people become more aware every day of the need to incorporate themselves into society and of their own importance as motors of that society.

The institutionality of the Revolution has still not been achieved. We are seeking something new that will allow a perfect identification between the government and the community as a whole, adapted to the special conditions of the building of socialism and avoiding to the utmost the commonplaces of bourgeois democracy transplanted to the society in formation (such as legislative houses, for example). Some experiments have been carried out with the aim of gradually creating the institutionalization of the Revolution, but without too much hurry. We have been greatly restrained by the fear that any formal aspect might make us lose sight of the ultimate and most important revolutionary aspiration: to see man freed from alienation.

Notwithstanding the lack of institutions, which must be overcome gradually, the masses now make history as a conscious aggregate of individuals who struggle for the same cause. In spite of the apparent standardization of man in socialism, he is more complete; his possibilities for expressing himself and making himself heard in the social apparatus are infinitely greater, in spite of the lack of a perfect mechanism to do so.

It is still necessary to accentuate his conscious, individual and collective, participation in all the mechanisms of direction and production and associate it with the idea of the need for technical and ideological education, so that the individual will realize that these processes are closely interdependent and their advances are parallel. He will thus achieve total awareness of his social being, which is equivalent to his full realization as a human being, having broken the chains of alienation.

This will be translated concretely into the reappropriation of his nature through freed work and the expression of his own human condition in culture and art.

In order for it to develop in culture, work must acquire a new condition; man as commodity ceases to exist, and a system is established that grants a quota for the fulfillment of social duty. The means of production belong to society, and the machine is only the front line where duty is performed. Man begins to free his thought from the bothersome fact that presupposed the need to satisfy his animal needs by working. He begins to see himself portrayed in his work and to understand its human magnitude through the created object, through the work carried out. This no longer involves leaving a part of his being in the form of labor power sold, which no longer belongs to him; rather it signifies an emanation from himself, a contribution to the life of society in which he is reflected, the fulfillment of his social duty.

We are doing everything possible to give work this new category of social duty and to join it to the development of technology, on the one hand, which will provide the conditions for greater freedom, and to voluntary work on the other, based on the Marxist concept that man truly achieves his full human condition when he produces without being compelled by the physical necessity of selling himself as a commodity.

It is clear that work still has coercive aspects, even when it is voluntary: Man has still not transformed all the coercion surrounding him into conditioned reflexes of a social nature, and in many cases he still produces under the pressure of the environment (Fidel calls this moral compulsion). He is still to achieve complete spiritual recreation in the presence of his own work, without the direct pressure of the social environment but bound to it by new habits. That will be communism.

The change in consciousness does not come about automatically, just as it does not come about automatically in the economy. The variations are slow and not rhythmic; there are periods of acceleration, others are measured and some even involve a retreat.

We must also consider as we have pointed out previously, that we are not before a pure transition period such as that envisioned by Marx in the "Critique of the Gotha Program," but rather a new phase not foreseen by him: the first period in the transition to communism or in the building of socialism.

Elements of capitalism are present within this process, which takes place in the midst of violent class struggle. These elements obscure the complete understanding of the essence of the process.

If to this be added the scholasticism that has held back the development of Marxist philosophy and impeded the systematic treatment of the period, whose political economy has still not been developed, we must agree that we are still in diapers. We must study all the primordial features of the period before elaborating a more far-reaching economic and political theory.

The resulting theory will necessarily give preeminence to the two pillars of socialist construction: the formation of the new human being and the development of technology. We still have a great deal to accomplish in both aspects, but the delay is less justifiable as far as the conception of technology as the basis is concerned: Here, it is not a matter of advancing blindly, but rather of following for a sizable stretch the road opened up by the most advanced countries of the world. This is why Fidel harps so insistently on the necessity of the technological and scientific formation of all of our people and especially of the vanguard.

In the field of ideas that lead to nonproductive activities, it is easier to see the division between material and spiritual needs. For a long time man has been trying to free himself from alienation through culture and art. He dies daily in the eight and more hours during which he performs as a commodity to resuscitate in his spiritual creation. But this remedy itself bears the germs of the same disease: He is a solitary being who seeks communion with nature. He defends his environment-oppressed individuality and reacts to esthetic ideas as a unique being whose aspiration is to remain immaculate.

It is only an attempt at flight. The law of value is no longer a mere reflection of production relations; the monopoly capitalists have surrounded it with a complicated scaffolding which makes of it a docile servant, even when the methods used are purely empirical. The artist must be educated in the kind of art imposed by the superstructure. The rebels are overcome by the apparatus, and only exceptional talents are able to create their own work. The others become shamefaced wage-workers, or they are crushed.

Artistic experimentation is invented and is taken as the definition of freedom, but this "experimentation" has limits which are imperceptible until they are clashed with, that is, when the real problems of man and his alienated condition are dealt with. Senseless anguish or vulgar pastimes are comfortable safety valves for human uneasiness; the idea of making art a weapon of denunciation and accusation is combatted.

If the rules of the game are respected, all honors are obtained—the honors that might be granted to a pirouette-creating monkey. The condition is not attempting to escape from the invisible cage.

When the Revolution took power, the exodus of the totally domesticated took place; the others, revolutionaries or not, saw a new road. Artistic experimentation took on new force. However, the routes were more or less traced, and the concept of flight was the hidden meaning behind the word freedom. This attitude, a reflection in consciousness of bourgeois idealism, was frequently maintained in the revolutionaries themselves.

In countries that have gone through a similar process, endeavors were made to combat these tendencies with an exaggerated dogmatism. General culture became something like a taboo, and a formally exact representation of nature was proclaimed as the height of cultural aspiration. This later became a mechanical representation of social reality created by wishful thinking: the ideal society, almost without conflict or contradictions, that man was seeking to create.

Socialism is young and makes mistakes. We revolutionaries often lack the knowledge and the intellectual audacity to face the task of the development of the new human being by methods different from the conventional ones, and the conventional methods suffer from the influence of the society that created them (once again the topic of the relation between form and content appears). Disorientation is great and the problems of material construction absorb us. There are no artists of great authority who also have great revolutionary authority.

The men of the party must take this task upon themselves and seek the achievement of the principal aim: to educate the people.

What is then sought is simplification, what everyone understands, that is, what the functionaries understand. True artistic experimentation is obliterated and the problem of general culture is reduced to the assimilation of the socialist present and the dead (and therefore not dangerous) past. Socialist realism is thus born on the foundation of the art of the last century.

But the realistic art of the nineteenth century is also class art, perhaps more purely capitalist than the decadent art of the twentieth century, where the anguish of alienated man shows through. In culture, capitalism has given all that it had to give and all that remains of it is the foretaste of a bad-smelling corpse; in art, its present decadence. But why endeavor to seek in the frozen forms of socialist realism the only valid recipe? "Freedom" cannot be set against socialist realism because the former does not yet exist: It will not come into being until the complete development of the new society. But let us not attempt to condemn all post-midnineteenth-century art forms from the pontifical throne of realism-at-all-costs. That would mean committing the Proudhonian error of the return to the past, and straitjacketing the artistic expression of the man who is born and being formed today.

An ideological and cultural mechanism must be developed which will permit experimentation and clear out the weeds that shoot up so easily in the fertilized soil of state subsidization.

The error of mechanical realism has not appeared (in Cuba), but rather the contrary. This is so because of the lack of understanding of the need to create a new human being who will represent neither nineteenth-century ideas nor those of our decadent and morbid century. It is the twenty-first-century man whom we must create, although this is still a subjective and unsystematic aspiration. This is precisely one of the basic points of our studies and work; to the extent that we make concrete achievements on a theoretical base or vice versa, that we come to broad theoretical conclusions on the basis of our concrete studies, we will have made a valuable contribution to Marxism-Leninism, to the cause of mankind.

The reaction against nineteenth-century man has brought a recurrence of twentieth-century decadence. It is not a very serious error, but we must overcome it so as not to leave the doors open to revisionism.

The large multitudes of people are developing themselves, the new ideas are acquiring an adequate impetus within society, the material possibilities of the integral development of each and every one of its members make the task ever more fruitful. The present is one of struggle; the future is ours.

To sum up, the fault of many of our intellectuals and artists is to be found in their "original sin": They are not authentically revolutionary. We can attempt to graft elm trees so they bear pears, but at the same time we must plant pear trees. The new generations will arrive free of "original sin." The likelihood that exceptional artists will arise will be that much greater because of the enlargement of the cultural field and the possibilities for expression. Our job is to keep the present generation, maladjusted by its conflicts, from becoming perverted and perverting the new generations. We do not want to create salaried workers docile to official thinking or "fellows" who live under the wing of the budget, exercising freedom in quotation marks. Revolutionaries will come to sing the song of the new man with the authentic voice of the people. It is a process that requires time.

In our society the youth and the party play a big role. The former is particularly important because it is the malleable clay with which the new man, without any of the previous defects, can be formed.

Youth receives treatment in consonance with our aspirations. Education is increasingly integral, and we do not neglect the incorporation of the students into work from the very beginning. Our scholarship students do physical work during vacation or together with their studies. In some cases work is a prize, while in others it is an educational tool; it is never a punishment. A new generation is being born.

The party is a vanguard organization. The best workers are proposed by their comrades for membership. The party is a minority, but the quality of its cadres gives it great authority. Our aspiration is that the party become a mass one, but only when the masses reach the level of development of the vanguard, that is, when they are educated for communism. Our work is aimed at providing that education. The party is the living example; its cadres must be full professors of assiduity and sacrifice; with their acts they must lead the masses to the end of the revolutionary task, which means years of struggle against the difficulties of construction, the class enemies, the defects of the past, imperialism.

I should now like to explain the role played by the personality, the man as the individual who leads the masses that make history. This is our experience, and not a recipe.

Fidel gave impulse to the Revolution in its first years, he has always given it leadership and set the tone, but there is a good group of revolutionaries developing in the same direction as Fidel and a large mass that follows its leaders because it has faith in them. It has faith in them because these leaders have known how to interpret the longings of the masses.

It is not a question of how many kilograms of meat are eaten or how many times a year someone may go on holiday to the seashore or how many pretty imported things can be bought with present wages. It is rather that the individual feels greater fulfillment, that he has greater inner wealth and many more responsibilities. In our country the individual knows that the glorious period in which it has fallen to him to live is one of sacrifice; he is familiar with sacrifice.

The first came to know it in the Sierra Maestra and wherever there was fighting; later we have known it in all Cuba. Cuba is the vanguard of America and must make sacrifices because it occupies the advance position, because it points out to the Latin American masses the road to full freedom.

Within the country, the leaders have to fulfill their vanguard role; and it must be said with complete sincerity that in a true revolution, to which you give yourself completely without any thought for material retribution, the task of the vanguard revolutionary is both magnificent and anguishing.

Let me say, with the risk of appearing ridiculous, that the true revolutionary is guided by strong feelings of love. It is impossible to think of an authentic revolutionary without this quality. This is perhaps one of the great dramas of a leader; he must combine an impassioned spirit with a cold mind and make painful decisions without flinching. Our vanguard revolutionaries must idealize their love for the people, for the most hallowed causes, and make it one and indivisible. They cannot descend, with small doses of daily affection, to the terrain where ordinary men put their love into practice.

The leaders of the Revolution have children who do not learn to call their father with their first faltering words; they have wives who must be part of the general sacrifice of their lives to carry the Revolution to its destination; their friends are strictly limited to their comrades in revolution. There is no life outside the Revolution.

In these conditions the revolutionary leaders must have a large dose of humanity, a large dose of a sense of justice and truth, to avoid falling into dogmatic extremes, into cold scholasticism, into isolation from the masses. They must struggle every day so that their love of living humanity is transformed into concrete deeds, into acts that will serve as an example, as a mobilizing factor.

The revolutionary, ideological motor of the Revolution within his party, is consumed by this uninterrupted activity that ends only with death, unless construction be achieved on a worldwide scale. If his revolutionary eagerness becomes dulled when the most urgent tasks are carried on a local scale, and if he forgets about proletarian internationalism, the revolution that he leads ceases to be a driving force and it sinks into a comfortable drowsiness which is taken advantage of by imperialism, our irreconcilable enemy, to gain ground. Proletarian internationalism is a duty, but it is also a revolutionary need. This is how we educate our people.

That immense multitude is ordering itself; its order responds to an awareness of the need for order; it is no longer a dispersed force, divisible in thousands of fractions shot into space like the fragments of a grenade, trying by any and all means, in a fierce struggle with their equals, to achieve a position that would give them support in the face of an uncertain future.

We know that we have sacrifices ahead of us and that we must pay a price for the heroic fact of constituting a vanguard as a nation. We, the leaders, know that we must pay a price for having the right to say that we are at the head of the people that is at the head of America.

Each and every one of us punctually pays his share of sacrifice, aware of being rewarded by the satisfaction of fulfilling our duty, aware of advancing with everyone toward the new human being who is to be glimpsed on the horizon.

Allow me to attempt to come to some conclusions:

We socialists are more free because we are more fulfilled: We are more fulfilled because we are more free.

The skeleton of our complete freedom is formed, but it lacks the protein substance and the draperies. We will create them.

Our freedom and its daily sustenance are the color of blood and swollen with sacrifice.

Our sacrifice is a conscious one: It is in payment for the freedom we are building.

The road is long and in part unknown; we are aware of our limitations. We will make the twenty-first-century man; we ourselves.

We will be tempered in daily actions, creating a new human being with a new technology.

The personality plays the role of mobilization and leadership in so far as it incarnates the highest virtues and aspirations of the people and does not become detoured.

The road is opened up by the vanguard group, the best among the good, the party.

The basic raw material of our work is the youth: In it we place our hopes and we are preparing it to take the banner from our hands.

If this faltering letter has made some things clear, it will have fulfilled my purpose in sending it.

Accept our ritual greetings, as a handshake or an "Ave María Purísima."

Patria o muerte

Individual and Society
J. Krishnamurti

Jiddu Krishnamurti (1897–   ) was born at Madanapalle in Southern India. At a very early age, he was introduced by the Theosophists as the avatar of the age and as such was worshipped by thousands until his late twenties. At that time, he renounced this position and became one of this century's most penetrating critics of organized religion. For the past 45 years he has toured the world speaking to millions.

INDIVIDUAL AND SOCIETY

The problem that confronts most of us is whether the individual is merely the instrument of society or the end of society. Are you and I as individuals to be used, directed, educated, controlled, shaped to a certain pattern by society and government; or does society, the State, exist for the individual? Is the individual the end of society; or is he merely a puppet to be taught, exploited, butchered as an instrument of war? That is the problem that is confronting most of us. That is the problem of the world; whether the individual is a mere instrument of society, a plaything of influences to be moulded; or whether society exists for the individual.

How are you going to find this out? It is a serious problem, isn't it? If the individual is merely an instrument of society, then society is much more important than the individual. If that is true, then we must give up individuality and work for society; our whole educational system must be entirely revolutionized and the individual turned into an instrument to be used and destroyed, liquidated, got rid of. But if society exists for the individual, then the function of society is not to make him conform to any pattern but to give him the feel, the urge of freedom. So we have to find out which is false.

How would you inquire into this problem? It is a vital problem, isn't it? It is not dependent on any ideology, either of the left or of the right; and if it *is* dependent on an ideology, then it is merely a matter of opinion. Ideas always breed enmity, confusion, conflict. If you depend on books of the left or of the right or on sacred books, then you depend on mere opinion, whether of Buddha, of Christ, of capitalism, communism or what you will. They are ideas, not truth. A fact can never be denied. Opinion *about* fact can be denied. If we can discover what the truth of the matter is, we shall be able to act independently of opinion. Is it not, therefore, necessary to discard what others have said? The opinion of the leftist or other leaders is the outcome of their conditioning, so if you depend for your discovery on what is found in books, you are merely bound by opinion. It is not a matter of knowledge.

How is one to discover the truth of this? On that we will act. To find the truth of this, there must be freedom from all propaganda, which means you are capable of looking at the problem independently of opinion. The whole task of education is to awaken the individual. To see the truth of this, you will have to be very clear, which means you cannot depend on a leader. When you choose a leader you do so out of confusion, and so your leaders are also confused, and that is what is happening in the world. Therefore you cannot look to your leader for guidance or help.

A mind that wishes to understand a problem must not only understand the problem completely, wholly, but must be able to follow it swiftly, because the problem is never static. The problem is always new, whether it is a problem of starvation, a psychological problem, or any problem. Any crisis is always new; therefore, to understand it, a mind must always be fresh, clear, swift in its pursuit. I think most of us realize the urgency of an inward revolution, which alone can bring about a radical transformation of the outer, of society. This is the problem with which I myself and all seriously-intentioned people are occupied. How to bring about a fundamental, a radical transformation in society, is our problem; and this transformation of the outer cannot take place without inner revolution. Since society is always static, any action, any reform which is accomplished without this inward revolution becomes equally static; so there is no hope without this constant inward revolution, because, without it, outer action becomes repetitive, habitual. The action of relationship between you and another, between you and me, is society; and that society becomes static, it has no life-giving quality, so long as there is not this constant inward revolution, a creative, psychological transformation; and it is because there is not this constant inward revolution that society is always becoming static, crystallized, and has therefore constantly to be broken up.

What is the relationship between yourself and the misery, the confusion, in and around you? Surely this confusion, this misery, did not come into being by itself. You and I have created it, not a capitalist nor a communist nor a fascist society, but you and I have created it in our relationship with each other. What you are within has been projected without, on to the world; what you are, what you think and what you feel, what you do in your everyday existence, is projected outwardly, and that constitutes the world. If we are miserable, confused, chaotic within, by projection that becomes the world, that becomes society, because the relationship between yourself and myself, between myself and another is society—society is the product of our relationship—and if our relationship is confused, egocentric, narrow, limited, national, we project that and bring chaos into the world.

What you are, the world is. So your problem is the world's problem. Surely, this is a simple and basic fact, is it not? In our relationship with the one or the many we seem somehow to overlook this point all the time. We want to bring about alteration through a system or through a revolution in ideas or values based on a system, forgetting that it is you and I who create society, who bring about confusion or order by the way in which we live. So we must begin near, that is we must concern ourselves with our daily existence, with our daily thoughts and feelings and actions which are revealed in the manner of earning our livelihood and in our relationship with ideas or beliefs. This is our daily existence, is it not? We are concerned with livelihood, getting jobs, earning money; we are concerned with the relationship with our family or with our neighbours, and we are concerned with ideas and with beliefs. Now, if you examine our occupation, it is fundamentally based on envy, it is not just a means of earning a livelihood. Society is so constructed that it is a process of constant conflict, constant becoming; it is based on greed, on envy, envy of your superior; the clerk wanting to become the manager, which shows that he is not just concerned with earning a livelihood, a means of subsistence, but with acquiring position and prestige. This attitude naturally creates havoc in society, in relationship, but if you and I were only concerned with livelihood we should find out the right means of earning it, a means not based on envy. Envy is one of the most destructive factors in relationship because envy indicates the desire for power, for position, and it ultimately leads to politics; both are closely related. The clerk, when he seeks to become a manager, becomes a factor in the creation of power-politics which produce war; so he is directly responsible for war.

What is our relationship based on? The relationship between yourself and myself, between yourself and another—which is society—what is it based on? Surely not on love, though we talk about it. It is not based on love, because if there were love there would be order, there would be peace, happiness between you and me. But in that relationship between you and me there is a great deal of ill will which assumes the form of respect. If we were both equal in thought, in feeling, there would be no respect, there would be no ill-will, because we would be two individuals meeting, not as disciple and teacher, nor as the husband dominating the wife, nor as the wife dominating the husband. When there is ill-will there is a desire to dominate which arouses jealousy, anger, passion, all of which in our relationship create constant conflict from which we try to escape, and this produces further chaos, further misery.

Now as regards ideas which are part of our daily existence, beliefs and formulations, are they not distorting our minds? For what is stupidity? Stupidity is the giving of wrong values to those things which the mind creates, or to those things which the hands produce. Most of our thoughts spring from the self-protective instinct, do they not? Our ideas, oh, so many of them, do they not receive the wrong significance, one which they have not in themselves? Therefore when we believe in any form, whether religious, economic or social, when we believe in God, in ideas, in a social system which separates man from man, in nationalism and so on, surely we are giving a wrong significance to belief, which indicates stupidity, for belief divides people, doesn't unite people. So we see that by the way we live we can produce order or chaos, peace or conflict, happiness or misery.

So our problem, is it not?, is whether there can be a society which is static, and at the same time an individual in whom this constant revolution is taking place. That is, revolution in society must begin with the inner, psychological transformation of the individual. Most of us want to see a radical transformation in the social structure. That is the whole battle that is going on in the world—to bring about a social revolution through communistic or any other means. Now if there is a social revolution, that is an action with regard to the outer structure of man, however radical that social revolution may be its very nature is static if there is no inward revolution of the individual, no psychological transformation. Therefore to bring about a society that is not repetitive, nor static, not disintegrating, a society that is constantly alive, it is imperative that there should be a revolution in the psychological structure of the individual, for without inward, psychological revolution, mere transformation of the outer has very little significance. That is society is always becoming crystallized, static, and is therefore always disintegrating. However much and however wisely legislation may be promulgated, society is always in the process of decay because revolution must take place within, not merely outwardly.

I think it is important to understand this and not slur over it. Outward action, when accomplished, is over, is static; if the relationship between individuals, which is society, is not the outcome of inward revolution, then the social structure, being static, absorbs the individual and therefore makes him equally static, repetitive. Realizing this, realizing the extraordinary significance of this fact, there can be no question of agreement or disagreement. It is a fact that society is always crystallizing and absorbing the individual and that constant, creative revolution can only be in the individual, not in society, not in the outer. That is creative revolution can take place only in individual relationship, which is society. We see how the structure of the present society in India, in Europe, in America, in every part of the world, is rapidly disintegrating; and we know it within our own lives. We can observe it as we go down the streets. We do not need great historians to tell us the fact that our society is crumbling; and there must be new architects, new builders, to create a new society. The structure must be built on a new foundation, on newly discovered facts and values. Such architects do not yet exist. There are no builders, none who, observing, becoming aware of the fact that the structure is collapsing, are transforming themselves into architects. That is our problem. We see society crumbling, disintegrating;

and it is we, you and I, who have to be the architects. You and I have to rediscover the values and build on a more fundamental, lasting foundation; because if
we look to the professional architects, the political and religious builders, we shall
be precisely in the same position as before.

Because you and I are not creative, we have reduced society to this chaos, so
you and I have to be creative because the problem is urgent; you and I must be
aware of the causes of the collapse of society and create a new structure based
not on mere imitation but on our creative understanding. Now this implies, does
it not?, negative thinking. Negative thinking is the highest form of understanding. That is in order to understand what is creative thinking, we must approach
the problem negatively, because a positive approach to the problem—which is
that you and I must become creative in order to build a new structure of society—
will be imitative. To understand that which is crumbling, we must investigate it,
examine it negatively—not with a positive system, a positive formula, a positive
conclusion.

Why is society crumbling, collapsing, as it surely is? One of the fundamental
reasons is that the individual, you, has ceased to be creative. I will explain what I
mean. You and I have become imitative, we are copying, outwardly and inwardly. Outwardly, when learning a technique, when communicating with each
other on the verbal level, naturally there must be some imitation, copy. I copy
words. To become an engineer, I must first learn the technique, then use the
technique to build a bridge. There must be a certain amount of imitation, copying, in outward technique, but when there is inward, psychological imitation
surely we cease to be creative. Our education, our social structure, our so-called
religious life are all based on imitation; that is I fit into a particular social or
religious formula. I have ceased to be a real individual; psychologically, I have
become a mere repetitive machine with certain conditioned responses, whether
those of the Hindu, the Christian, the Buddhist, the German or the Englishman.
Our responses are conditioned according to the pattern of society, whether it is
eastern or western, religious or materialistic. So one of the fundamental causes of
the disintegration of society is imitation, and one of the disintegrating factors is
the leader, whose very essence is imitation.

In order to understand the nature of disintegrating society is it not important
to inquire whether you and I, the individual, can be creative? We can see that
when there is imitation there must be disintegration; when there is authority
there must be copying. And since our whole mental, psychological make-up is
based on authority, there must be freedom from authority, to be creative. Have
you not noticed that in moments of creativeness, those rather happy moments of
vital interest, there is no sense of repetition, no sense of copying? Such moments
are always new, fresh, creative, happy. So we see that one of the fundamental
causes of the disintegration of society is copying, which is the worship of authority.

SELF-KNOWLEDGE

The problems of the world are so colossal, so very complex, that to understand
and so to resolve them one must approach them in a very simple and direct
manner; and simplicity, directness do not depend on outward circumstances nor

on our particular prejudices and moods. As I was pointing out, the solution is not to be found through conferences, blue-prints, or through the substitution of new leaders for old, and so on. The solution obviously lies in the creator of the problem, in the creator of the mischief, of the hate and of the enormous misunderstanding that exists between human beings. The creator of this mischief, the creator of these problems, is the individual, you and I, not the world as we think of it. The world is your relationship with another. The world is not something separate from you and me; the world, society, is the relationship that we establish or seek to establish between each other.

So you and I are the problem, and not the world, because the world is the projection of ourselves and to understand the world we must understand ourselves. The world is not separate from us; we are the world, and our problems are the world's problems. This cannot be repeated too often, because we are so sluggish in our mentality that we think the world's problems are not our business, that they have to be resolved by the United Nations or by substituting new leaders for the old. It is a very dull mentality that thinks like that, because we are responsible for this frightful misery and confusion in the world, this ever-impending war. To transform the world, we must begin with ourselves; and what is important in beginning with ourselves is the intention. The intention must be to understand ourselves and not to leave it to others to transform themselves or to bring about a modified change through revolution, either of the left or of the right. It is important to understand that this is our responsibility, yours and mine; because, however small may be the world we live in, if we can transform ourselves, bring about a radically different point of view in our daily existence, then perhaps we shall affect the world at large, the extended relationship with others.

As I said, we are going to try and find out the process of understanding ourselves, which is not an isolating process. It is not withdrawal from the world, because you cannot live in isolation. To be is to be related, and there is no such thing as living in isolation. It is the lack of right relationship that brings about conflicts, misery and strife; however small our world may be, if we can transform our relationship in that narrow world, it will be like a wave extending outward all the time. I think it is important to see that point, that the world is our relationship, however narrow; and if we can bring a transformation there, not a superficial but a radical transformation, then we shall begin actively to transform the world. Real revolution is not according to any particular pattern, either of the left or of the right, but it is a revolution of values, a revolution from sensate values to the values that are not sensate or created by environmental influences. To find these true values which will bring about a radical revolution, a transformation or a regeneration, it is essential to understand oneself. Self-knowledge is the beginning of wisdom, and therefore the beginning of transformation or regeneration. To understand oneself there must be the intention to understand—and that is where our difficulty comes in. Although most of us are discontented, we desire to bring about a sudden change, our discontent is canalized merely to achieve a certain result; being discontented, we either seek a different job or merely succumb to environment. Discontent, instead of setting us aflame, causing us to question life, the whole process of existence, is canalized, and thereby we become mediocre, losing that drive, that intensity to find out the whole significance of existence. Therefore it is important to discover these things for ourselves, because self-knowledge cannot be given to us by another, it is not to be found through any book. We must discover, and to discover there must be the intention, the search, the inquiry. So long as that intention to find out, to inquire deeply, is weak or does not exist, mere assertion or a casual wish to find out about oneself is of very little significance.

Thus the transformation of the world is brought about by the transformation of oneself, because the self is the product and a part of the total process of human existence. To transform oneself, self-knowledge is essential; without knowing what you are, there is no basis for right thought, and without knowing yourself there cannot be transformation. One must know oneself as one is, not as one wishes to be which is merely an ideal and therefore fictitious, unreal; it is only that which *is* that can be transformed, not that which you wish to be. To know oneself as one is requires an extraordinary alertness of mind, because what *is* is constantly undergoing transformation, change, and to follow it swiftly the mind must not be tethered to any particular dogma or belief, to any particular pattern of action. If you would follow anything it is not good being tethered. To know yourself, there must be the awareness, the alertness of mind in which there is freedom from all beliefs, from all idealization because beliefs and ideals only give you a colour, perverting true perception. If you want to know what you are you cannot imagine or have belief in something which you are not. If I am greedy, envious, violent, merely having an ideal of non-violence, of non-greed, is of little value. But to know that one is greedy or violent, to know and understand it, requires an extraordinary perception, does it not? It demands honesty, clarity of thought, whereas to pursue an ideal away from what *is* is an escape; it prevents you from discovering and acting directly upon what you are.

The understanding of what you are, whatever it be—ugly or beautiful, wicked or mischievous—the understanding of what you are, without distortion, is the beginning of virtue. Virtue is essential, for it gives freedom. It is only in virtue that you can discover, that you can live—not in the *cultivation* of a virtue, which merely brings about respectability, not understanding and freedom. There is a difference between being virtuous and becoming virtuous. Being virtuous comes through the understanding of what *is,* whereas becoming virtuous is postponement, the covering up of what *is* with what you would like to be. Therefore in becoming virtuous you are avoiding action directly upon what *is.* This process of avoiding what *is* through the cultivation of the ideal is considered virtuous; but if you look at it closely and directly you will see that it is nothing of the kind. It is merely a postponement of coming face to face with what *is.* Virtue is not the becoming of what is not; virtue is the understanding of what *is* and therefore the freedom from what *is.* Virtue is essential in a society that is rapidly disintegrating. In order to create a new world, a new structure away from the old, there must be freedom to discover; and to be free, there must be virtue, for without virtue there is no freedom. Can the immoral man who is striving to become virtuous ever know virtue? The man who is not moral can never be free, and therefore he can never find out what reality is. Reality can be found only in understanding what *is;* and to understand what *is,* there must be freedom, freedom from the fear of what *is.*

To understand that process there must be the intention to know what *is,* to follow every thought, feeling and action; and to understand what *is* is extremely difficult, because what *is* is never still, never static, it is always in movement. The what *is* is what you are, not what you would like to be; it is not the ideal, because the ideal is fictitious, but it is actually what you are doing, thinking and feeling from moment to moment. What *is* is the actual, and to understand the actual requires awareness, a very alert, swift mind. But if we begin to condemn what *is,* if we begin to blame or resist it, then we shall not understand its movement. If I want to understand somebody, I cannot condemn him: I must observe, study him. I must love the very thing I am studying. If you want to understand a child, you must love and not condemn him. You must play with him, watch his movements, his idiosyncrasies, his ways of behaviour; but if you merely condemn, resist or blame him, there is no comprehension of the child. Similarly, to understand what *is,* one must observe what one thinks, feels and does from moment to moment. That is the actual. Any other action, any ideal or ideological action, is not the actual; it is merely a wish, a fictitious desire to be something other than what *is.*

To understand what *is* requires a state of mind in which there is no identification or condemnation, which means a mind that is alert and yet passive. We are in that state when we really desire to understand something; when the intensity of interest is there, that state of mind comes into being. When one is interested in understanding what *is,* the actual state of the mind, one does not need to force, discipline, or control it; on the contrary, there is passive alertness, watchfulness. This state of awareness comes when there is interest, the intention to understand.

The fundamental understanding of oneself does not come through knowledge or through the accumulation of experiences, which is merely the cultivation of memory. The understanding of oneself is from moment to moment; if we merely accumulate knowledge of the self, that very knowledge prevents further understanding, because accumulated knowledge and experience becomes the centre through which thought focuses and has its being. The world is not different from us and our activities because it is what we are which creates the problems of the world; the difficulty with the majority of us is that we do not know ourselves directly, but seek a system, method, a means of operation by which to solve the many human problems.

Now is there a means, a system, of knowing oneself? Any clever person, any philosopher, can invent a system, a method; but surely the following of a system will merely produce a result created by that system, will it not? If I follow a particular method of knowing myself, then I shall have the result which that system necessitates; but the result will obviously not be the understanding of myself. That is by following a method, a system, a means through which to know myself, I shape my thinking, my activities, according to a pattern; but the following of a pattern is not the understanding of oneself.

Therefore there is no method for self-knowledge. Seeking a method invariably implies the desire to attain some result—and that is what we all want. We follow authority—if not that of a person, then of a system, of an ideology—because we want a result which will be satisfactory, which will give us security. We really do not want to understand ourselves, our impulses and reactions, the whole process of our thinking, the conscious as well as the unconscious; we would rather pursue a system which assures us of a result. But the pursuit of a system is invariably the outcome of our desire for security, for certainty, and the result is obviously not the understanding of oneself. When we follow a method, we must have authorities—the teacher, the *guru,* the saviour, the Master—who will guarantee us what we desire; and surely that is not the way to self-knowledge.

Authority prevents the understanding of oneself, does it not? Under the shelter of an authority, a guide, you may have temporarily a sense of security, a sense of well-being, but that is not the understanding of the total process of oneself. Authority in its very nature prevents the full awareness of oneself and therefore ultimately destroys freedom; in freedom alone can there be creativeness. There can be creativeness only through self-knowledge. Most of us are not creative; we are repetitive machines, mere gramophone records playing over and over again certain songs of experience, certain conclusions and memories, either our own or those of another. Such repetition is not creative being—but it is what we want. Because we want to be inwardly secure, we are constantly seeking methods and means for this security, and thereby we create authority, the worship of another, which destroys comprehension, that spontaneous tranquillity of mind in which alone there can be a state of creativeness.

Surely our difficulty is that most of us have lost this sense of creativeness. To be creative does not mean that we must paint pictures or write poems and become famous. That is not creativeness—it is merely the capacity to express an idea, which the public applauds or disregards. Capacity and creativeness should not be confused. Capacity is not creativeness. Creativeness is quite a different state of being, is it not? It is a state in which the self is absent, in which the mind is no longer a focus of our experiences, our ambitions, our pursuits and our desires. Creativeness is not a continuous state, it is new from moment to moment, it is a movement in which there is not the "me," the "mine," in which the thought is not focused on any particular experience, ambition, achievement, purpose and motive. It is only when the self is not that there is creativeness—that state of being in which alone there can be reality, the creator of all things. But that state cannot be conceived or imagined, it cannot be formulated or copied, it cannot be attained through any system, through any philosophy, through any discipline; on the contrary, it comes into being only through understanding the total process of oneself.

The understanding of oneself is not a result, a culmination; it is seeing oneself from moment to moment in the mirror of relationship—one's relationship to property, to things, to people and to ideas. But we find it difficult to be alert, to be aware, and we prefer to dull our minds by following a method, by accepting authorities, superstitions and gratifying theories; so our minds become weary, exhausted and insensitive. Such a mind cannot be in a state of creativeness. That state of creativeness comes only when the self, which is the process of recognition and accumulation, ceases to be; because, after all, consciousness as the "me" is the centre of recognition, and recognition is merely the process of the accumulation of experience. But we are all afraid to be nothing, because we all want to be something. The little man wants to be a big man, the unvirtuous wants to be virtuous, the weak and obscure crave power, position and authority. This is the incessant activity of the mind. Such a mind cannot be quiet and therefore can never understand the state of creativeness.

In order to transform the world about us, with its misery, wars, unemployment, starvation, class divisions and utter confusion, there must be a transformation in ourselves. The revolution must begin within oneself—but not according to any belief or ideology, because revolution based on an idea, or in conformity to a particular pattern, is obviously no revolution at all. To bring about a fundamental revolution in oneself, one must understand the whole process of one's thought and feeling in relationship. That is the only solution to all our problems —not to have more disciplines, more beliefs, more ideologies and more teachers. If we can understand ourselves as we are from moment to moment without the process of accumulation, then we shall see how there comes a tranquillity that is not a product of the mind, a tranquillity that is neither imagined nor cultivated; and only in that state of tranquillity can there be creativeness.

Arjuna in the Field of Life
Bhagavad-Gita

The *Bhagavad-Gita*, or Song of God, is the most popular work in all the religious literature of India, where its influence has been comparable to that of the Bible in the West. The text occurs as part of the great epic *The Mahabharata*, which is dated by scholars between the fifth and second centuries before Christ. *The Mahabharata* relates the story of the struggle among the descendants of King Bharata, one of whom is the warrior Arjuna. The *Bhagavad-Gita* opens as Arjuna is about to engage in final battle against his enemies, and is seized with fear at having to shed blood. He questions his chariot-companion, Krishna, an incarnation of God. The reply of Krishna to Arjuna touches on every aspect of spiritual life and cosmic law, and forms the content of the poem.

1

Dhrita-Rashtra
1. On the field of Truth, on the battle-field of life, what came to pass, Sanjaya, when my sons and their warriors faced those of my brother Pandu?

Sanjaya
2. When your son Duryodhana saw the armies of the sons of Pandu he went to his master in the art of war and spoke to him these words:

3. See there, master, the vast army of the Pandavas well set in order of battle by the son of Drupada, your own wise pupil.

4. There can we see heroic warriors, powerful archers, as great as Bhima and Arjuna in battle: Yuyudhana and Virata and king Drupada of the great chariot of war.

5. And Dhrishta-ketu of the steadfast banner, and Chekitana, the king of the Chedis. We see the heroic king of Kasi, and Purujit the conqueror, and his brother Kunti-bhoja, and Saibya mighty among men.

6. And victorious Yudhamanyu, and powerful Uttamaujas; and Saubhadra, the son of Arjuna, and the five princes of queen Draupadi. See them all in their chariots of war.

. . .

12. To encourage Duryodhana, Bhishma, the glorious old warrior of the Kurus, sounded loud his war-cry like the roar of a lion, and then blew his far-sounding conch-shell.

13. Then the rumbling of war drums, the stirring sound of cymbals and trumpets, and the roaring of conch-shells and horns filled the sky with a fearful thunder.

14. Thereupon Krishna of Madhava and Arjuna, the son of Pandu, standing in their glorious chariot drawn by white horses, answered the challenge and blew their divine conch-shells.

15. Krishna, the Lord of the soul, blew his conch-shell Pancha-janya. Arjuna, the winner of treasure, sounded forth his own Deva-datta. His brother Bhima, of tremendous feats, blew his great conch-shell the Paundra.

. . .

19. At that fearful sound the earth and the heavens trembled, and also trembled the hearts of Duryodhana and his warriors.

20. The flight of arrows was now to begin and Arjuna, on whose banner was the symbol of an ape, saw Duryodhana and his warriors drawn up in their lines of battle. He thereupon took up his bow.

21. And spoke these words to Krishna:

Arjuna

Drive my chariot, Krishna immortal, and place it between the two armies.

22. That I may see those warriors who stand there eager for battle, with whom I must now fight at the beginning of this war.

23. That I may see those who have come here eager and ready to fight, in their desire to do the will of the evil son of Dhirita-rashtra.

Sanjaya

24. When Krishna heard the words of Arjuna he drove their glorious chariot and placed it between the two armies.

25. And facing Bhishma and Drona and other royal rulers he said: "See, Arjuna, the armies of the Kurus, gathered here on this field of battle."

26. Then Arjuna saw in both armies fathers, grandfathers,

27. sons, grandsons; fathers of wives, uncles, masters;

28. brothers, companions and friends.

When Arjuna thus saw his kinsmen face to face in both lines of battle, he was overcome by grief and despair and thus he spoke with a sinking heart.

Arjuna
When I see all my kinsmen, Krishna, who have come here on this field of battle,

29. Life goes from my limbs and they sink, and my mouth is sear and dry; a trembling overcomes my body, and my hair shudders in horror;

30. My great bow Gandiva falls from my hands, and the skin over my flesh is burning; I am no longer able to stand, because my mind is whirling and wandering.

31. And I see forebodings of evil, Krishna. I cannot foresee any glory if I kill my own kinsmen in the sacrifice of battle.

32. Because I have no wish for victory, Krishna, nor for a kingdom, nor for its pleasures. How can we want a kingdom, Govinda, or its pleasures or even life.

33. When those for whom we want a kingdom, and its pleasures, and the joys of life, are here in this field of battle about to give up their wealth and their life?

34. Facing us in the field of battle are teachers, fathers and sons; grandsons, grandfathers, wives' brothers; mothers' brothers and fathers of wives.

35. These I do not wish to slay, even if I myself am slain. Not even for the kingdom of the three worlds: how much less for a kingdom of the earth!

36. If we kill these evil men, evil shall fall upon us: what joy in their death could we have, O Janardana, mover of souls?

37. I cannot therefore kill my own kinsmen, the sons of king Dhrita-rashtra, the brother of my own father. What happiness could we ever enjoy, if we killed our own kinsmen in battle?

38. Even if they, with minds overcome by greed, see no evil in the destruction of a family, see no sin in the treachery to friends;

39. Shall we not, who see the evil of destruction, shall we not refrain from this terrible deed?

40. The destruction of a family destroys its rituals of righteousness, and when the righteous rituals are no more, unrighteousness overcomes the whole family.

41. When unrighteous disorder prevails, the women sin and are impure; and when women are not pure, Krishna, there is disorder of castes, social confusion.

42. This disorder carries down to hell the family and the destroyers of the family. The spirits of their dead suffer in pain when deprived of the ritual offerings.

43. Those evil deeds of the destroyers of a family, which cause this social disorder, destroy the righteousness of birth and the ancestral rituals of righteousness.

44. And have we not heard that hell is waiting for those whose familiar rituals of righteousness are no more?

45. O day of darkness! What evil spirit moved our minds when for the sake of an earthly kingdom we came to this field of battle ready to kill our own people?

46. Better for me indeed if the sons of Dhrita-rashtra, with arms in hand, found me unarmed, unresisting, and killed me in the struggle of war.

Sanjaya
47. Thus spoke Arjuna in the field of battle, and letting fall his bow and arrows he sank down in his chariot, his soul overcome by despair and grief.

2

Sanjaya
1. Then arose the Spirit of Krishna and spoke to Arjuna, his friend, who with eyes filled with tears, thus had sunk into despair and grief.

Krishna
2. Whence this lifeless dejection, Arjuna, in this hour, the hour of trial? Strong men know not despair, Arjuna, for this wins neither heaven nor earth.

3. Fall not into degrading weakness, for this becomes not a man who is a man. Throw off this ignoble discouragement, and arise like a fire that burns all before it.

Arjuna
4. I owe veneration to Bhishma and Drona. Shall I kill with my arrows my grandfather's brother, great Bhishma? Shall my arrows in battle slay Drona, my teacher?

5. Shall I kill my own masters who, though greedy of my kingdom, are yet my sacred teachers? I would rather eat in this life the food of a beggar than eat royal food tasting of their blood.

6. And we know not whether their victory or ours be better for us. The sons of my uncle and king, Dhirita-rashtra, are here before us: after their death, should we wish to live?

7. In the dark night of my soul I feel desolation. In my self-pity I see not the way of righteousness. I am thy disciple, come to thee in supplication: be a light unto me on the path of my duty.

8. For neither the kingdom of the earth, nor the kingdom of the gods in heaven, could give me peace from the fire of sorrow which thus burns my life.

Sanjaya
9. When Arjuna the great warrior had thus unburdened his heart, "I will not fight, Krishna," he said, and then fell silent.

10. Krishna smiled and spoke to Arjuna—there between the two armies the voice of God spoke these words:

Krishna
11. Thy tears are for those beyond tears; and are thy words words of widsom? The wise grieve not for those who live; and they grieve not for those who die —for life and death shall pass away.

12. Because we all have been for all time; I, and thou, and those kings of men. And we all shall be for all time, we all for ever and ever.

13. As the Spirit of our mortal body wanders on in childhood, and youth and old age, the Spirit wanders on to a new body: of this the sage has no doubts.

14. From the world of the senses, Arjuna, comes heat and comes cold, and pleasure and pain. They come and they go: they are transient. Arise above them, strong soul.

15. The man whom these cannot move, whose soul is one, beyond pleasure and pain, is worthy of life in Eternity.

16. The unreal never is: the Real never is not. This truth indeed has been seen by those who can see the true.

17. Interwoven in his creation, the Spirit is beyond destruction. No one can bring to an end the Spirit which is everlasting.

18. For beyond time he dwells in these bodies, though these bodies have an end in their time; but he remains immeasurable, immortal. Therefore, great warrior, carry on thy fight.

19. If any man thinks he slays, and if another thinks he is slain, neither knows the ways of truth. The Eternal in man cannot kill: the Eternal in man cannot die.

20. He is never born, and he never dies. He is in Eternity: he is for evermore. Never-born and eternal, beyond times gone or to come, he does not die when the body dies.

21. When a man knows him as never-born, everlasting, never-changing, beyond all destruction, how can that man kill a man, or cause another to kill?

22. As a man leaves an old garment and puts on one that is new, the Spirit leaves his mortal body and wanders on to one that is new.

23. Weapons cannot hurt the Spirit and fire can never burn him. Untouched is he by drenching waters, untouched is he by parching winds.

24. Beyond the power of sword and fire, beyond the power of waters and winds, the Spirit is everlasting, omnipresent, never-changing, never-moving, ever One.

25. Invisible is he to mortal eyes, beyond thought and beyond change. Know that he is, and cease from sorrow.

26. But if he were born again and again, and again and again he were to die, even then, victorious man, cease thou from sorrow.

27. For all things born in truth must die, and out of death in truth comes life. Face to face with what must be, cease thou from sorrow.

28. Invisible before birth are all beings and after death invisible again. They are seen between two unseens. Why in this truth find sorrow?

29. One sees him in a vision of wonder, and another gives us words of his wonder. There is one who hears of his wonder; but he hears and knows him not.

30. The Spirit that is all beings is immortal in them all: for the death of what cannot die, cease thou to sorrow.

31. Think thou also of thy duty and do not waver. There is no greater good for a warrior than to fight in righteous war.

32. There is a war that opens the doors of heaven, Arjuna! Happy the warriors whose fate is to fight such war.

33. But to forgo this fight for righteousness is to forgo thy duty and honor: is to fall into transgression.

34. Men will tell of thy dishonour both now and in times to come. And to a man who is in honour, dishonour is more than death.

35. The great warriors will say that thou hast run from the battle through fear; and those who thought great things of thee will speak of thee in scorn.

36. And thine enemies will speak of thee in contemptuous words of ill-will and derision, pouring scorn upon thy courage. Can there be for a warrior a more shameful fate?

37. In death thy glory in heaven, in victory thy glory on earth. Arise therefore, Arjuna, with thy soul ready to fight.

38. Prepare for war with peace in thy soul. Be in peace in pleasure and pain, in gain and in loss, in victory or in the loss of a battle. In this peace there is no sin.

39. This is the wisdom of Sankhya—the vision of the Eternal. Hear now the wisdom of Yoga, path of the Eternal and freedom from bondage.

40. No step is lost on this path, and no dangers are found. And even a little progress is freedom from fear.

41. The follower of this path has one thought, and this is the End of his determination. But many-branched and endless are the thoughts of the man who lacks determination.

42. There are men who have no vision, and yet they speak many words. They follow the letter of the Vedas, and they say: "there is nothing but this."

43. Their soul is warped with selfish desires, and their heaven is a selfish desire. They have prayers for pleasures and power, the reward of which is earthly rebirth.

44. Those who love pleasure and power hear and follow their words: they have not the determination ever to be one with the One.

45. The three Gunas of Nature are the world of the Vedas. Arise beyond the three Gunas, Arjuna! Be in Truth eternal, beyond earthly opposites. Beyond gains and possessions, possess thine own soul.

46. As is the use of a well of water where water everywhere overflows, such is the use of all the Vedas to the seer of the Supreme.

47. Set thy heart upon thy work, but never on its reward. Work not for a reward; but never cease to do thy work.

48. Do thy work in the peace of Yoga and, free from selfish desires, be not moved in success or in failure. Yoga is evenness of mind—a peace that is ever the same.

49. Work done for a reward is much lower than work done in the Yoga of wisdom. Seek salvation in the wisdom of reason. How poor those who work for a reward!

50. In this wisdom a man goes beyond what is well done and what is not well done. Go thou therefore to wisdom: Yoga is wisdom in work.

51. Seers in union with wisdom forsake the rewards of their work, and free from the bonds of birth they go to the abode of salvation.

52. When thy mind leaves behind its dark forest of delusion, thou shalt go beyond the scriptures of times past and still to come.

53. When thy mind, that may be wavering in the contradictions of many scriptures, shall rest unshaken in divine contemplation, then the goal of Yoga is thine.

Arjuna
54. How is the man of tranquil wisdom, who abides in divine contemplation? What are his words? What is his silence? What is his work?

Krishna
55. When a man surrenders all desires that come to the heart and by the grace of God finds the joy of God, then his soul has indeed found peace.

56. He whose mind is untroubled by sorrows, and for pleasures he has no longings, beyond passion, and fear and anger, he is the sage of unwavering mind.

57. Who everywhere is free from all ties, who neither rejoices nor sorrows if fortune is good or is ill, his is a serene wisdom.

58. When in recollection he withdraws all his senses from the attractions of the pleasures of sense, even as a tortoise withdraws all its limbs, then his is a serene wisdom.

59. Pleasures of sense, but not desires, disappear from the austere soul. Even desires disappear when the soul has seen the Supreme.

60. The restless violence of the senses impetuously carries away the mind of even a wise man striving towards perfection.

61. Bringing them all into the harmony of recollection, let him sit in devotion and union, his soul finding rest in me. For when his senses are in harmony, then his is a serene wisdom.

62. When a man dwells on the pleasures of sense, attraction for them arises in him. From attraction arises desire, the lust of possession, and this leads to passion, to anger.

63. From passion comes confusion of mind, then loss of remembrance, the forgetting of duty. From this loss comes the ruin of reason, and the ruin of reason leads man to destruction.

64. But the soul that moves in the world of the senses and yet keeps the senses in harmony, free from attraction and aversion, finds rest in quietness.

65. In this quietness falls down the burden of all her sorrows, for when the heart has found quietness, wisdom has also found peace.

66. There is no wisdom for a man without harmony, and without harmony there is no contemplation. Without contemplation there cannot be peace, and without peace can there be joy?

67. For when the mind becomes bound to a passion of the wandering senses, this passion carries away man's wisdom, even as the wind drives a vessel on the waves.

68. The man who therefore in recollection withdraws his senses from the pleasures of sense, his is a serene wisdom.

69. In the dark night of all beings awakes to Light the tranquil man. But what is day to other beings is night for the sage who sees.

70. Even as all waters flow into the ocean, but the ocean never overflows, even so the sage feels desires, but he is ever one in his infinite peace.

71. For the man who forsakes all desires and abandons all pride of possession and of self reaches the goal of peace supreme.

72. This is the Eternal in man, O Arjuna. Reaching him all delusion is gone. Even in the last hour of his life upon earth, man can reach the Nirvana of Brahman —man can find peace in the peace of his God.

3

Arjuna

1. If thy thought is that vision is greater than action, why dost thou enjoin upon me the terrible action of war?

2. My mind is in confusion because in thy words I find contradictions. Tell me in truth therefore by what path may I attain the Supreme.

Krishna

3. In this world there are two roads of perfection, as I told thee before, O prince without sin: Jñana Yoga, the path of wisdom of the Sankhyas, and Karma Yoga, the path of action of the Yogis.

4. Not by refraining from action does man attain freedom from action. Not by mere renunciation does he attain supreme perfection.

5. For not even for a moment can a man be without action. Helplessly are all driven to action by the forces born of Nature.

6. He who withdraws himself from actions, but ponders on their pleasures in his heart, he is under a delusion and is a false follower of the Path.

7. But great is the man who, free from attachments, and with a mind ruling its powers in harmony, works on the path of Karma Yoga, the path of consecrated action.

8. Action is greater than inaction: perform therefore thy task in life. Even the life of the body could not be if there were no action.

9. The world is in the bonds of action, unless the action is consecration. Let thy actions then be pure, free from the bonds of desire.

10. Thus spoke the Lord of Creation when he made both man and sacrifice: "By sacrifice thou shalt multiply and obtain all thy desires.

11. By sacrifice shalt thou honour the gods and the gods will then love thee. And thus in harmony with them shalt thou attain the supreme good.

12. For pleased with thy sacrifice, the gods will grant to thee the joy of all thy desires. Only a thief would enjoy their gifts and not offer them in sacrifice."

13. Holy men who take as food the remains of sacrifice become free from all their sins; but the unholy who have feasts for themselves eat food that is in truth sin.

14. Food is the life of all beings, and all food comes from rain above. Sacrifice brings the rain from heaven, and sacrifice is sacred action.

15. Sacred action is described in the Vedas and these come from the Eternal, and therefore is the Eternal everpresent in a sacrifice.

16. Thus was the Wheel of the Law set in motion, and that man lives indeed in vain who in a sinful life of pleasures helps not in its revolutions.

17. But the man who has found the joy of the Spirit and in the Spirit has satisfaction, who in the Spirit has found his peace, that man is beyond the law of action.

18. He is beyond what is done and beyond what is not done, and in all his works he is beyond the help of mortal beings.

19. In liberty from the bonds of attachment, do thou therefore the work to be done: for the man whose work is pure attains indeed the Supreme.

20. King Janaka and other warriors reached perfection by the path of action: let thy aim be the good of all, and then carry on thy task in life.

21. In the actions of the best men others find their rule of action. The path that a great man follows becomes a guide to the world.

22. I have no work to do in all the worlds, Arjuna—for these are mine. I have nothing to obtain, because I have all. And yet I work.

23. If I was not bound to action, never-tiring, everlastingly, men that follow many paths would follow my path of inaction.

24. If ever my work had an end, these worlds would end in destruction, confusion would reign within all: this would be the death of all beings.

25. Even as the unwise work selfishly in the bondage of selfish works, let the wise man work unselfishly for the good of all the world.

26. Let not the wise disturb the mind of the unwise in their selfish work. Let him, working with devotion, show them the joy of good work.

27. All actions take place in time by the interweaving of the forces of Nature; but the man lost in selfish delusion thinks that he himself is the actor.

28. But the man who knows the relation between the forces of Nature and actions, sees how some forces of Nature work upon other forces of Nature, and becomes not their slave.

29. Those who are under the delusion of the forces of Nature bind themselves to the work of these forces. Let not the wise man who sees the All disturb the unwise who sees not the All.

30. Offer to me all thy works and rest thy mind on the Supreme. Be free from vain hopes and selfish thoughts, and with inner peace fight thou thy fight.

31. Those who ever follow my doctrine and who have faith, and have a good will, find through pure work their freedom.

32. But those who follow not my doctrine, and who have ill-will, are men blind to all wisdom, confused in mind: they are lost.

33. "Even a wise man acts under the impulse of his nature: all beings follow nature. Of what use is restraint?"

34. Hate and lust for things of nature have their roots in man's lower nature. Let him not fall under their power: they are the two enemies in his path.

35. And do thy duty, even if it be humble, rather than another's, even if it be great. To die in one's duty is life: to live in another's is death.

Arjuna

36. What power is it, Krishna, that drives man to act sinfully, even unwillingly, as if powerlessly?

Krishna

37. It is greedy desire and wrath, born of passion, the great evil, the sum of destruction: this is the enemy of the soul.

38. All is clouded by desire: as fire by smoke, as a mirror by dust, as an unborn babe by its covering.

39. Wisdom is clouded by desire, the everpresent enemy of the wise, desire in its innumerable forms, which like a fire cannot find satisfaction.

40. Desire has found a place in man's senses and mind and reason. Through these it blinds the soul, after having overclouded wisdom.

41. Set thou, therefore, thy senses in harmony, and then slay thou sinful desire, the destroyer of vision and wisdom.

42. They say that the power of the senses is great. But greater than the senses is the mind. Greater than the mind is Buddhi, reason; and greater than reason is He—the Spirit in man and in all.

43. Know Him therefore who is above reason; and let his peace give thee peace. Be a warrior and kill desire, the powerful enemy of the soul.

The Religious Diagnosis of Man

INTRODUCTION

We have now seen in some detail how the torments of the modern world-situation inevitably lead us back again and again to the question: who is man? But now it no longer appears as a question to be contemplated when the smoke of battle clears and the external problems of life are relatively eased. It appears that the "battle" itself, the pattern of human suffering and disillusionment and the all-too-fleeting glimpses of joy and communion, is to some extent an expression of man's nature. The selections in this chapter argue, each in its own way, that man cannot wait for the smoke to clear before solving the problem of his inner structure, its possibilities for transcendence and its inclinations to failure.

If there are any lingering doubts that great religious thought is at least as "tough-minded" and unsentimental as anything modern psychology has brought forth, the opening selection of this chapter, by **W. Rahula**, should erase these doubts once and for all. Here we are given an exceptionally clear and balanced presentation of the Buddhist idea that man has no real self and that his sorrow is caused by his attachment to an illusion about his own nature. According to the Buddha, all human enterprise that is based on the effort to affirm the ego is doomed and can only perpetuate the general round of misery. To feel the cutting edge of the Buddha's diagnosis, we need only ask ourselves to what extent such an enterprise defines the present society of man.

In the second selection of this chapter, **Thomas Merton**, writing from a contemplative understanding of Christianity, casts this problem in terms of the Western religious genius. Man falls, he writes, not only because of an illusion about himself but because of a love for this illusion, a passion for an unreal picture of himself. In this way, Merton connects the sin of pride, which defines the Christian diagnosis of man, to the error of self-affirmation, which characterizes the Oriental view. Through Merton's brilliant psychospiritual analysis of pride, we are given a glimpse of why it has been so difficult for man to accept the Christian understanding of divine love.

In both of these selections, the negative side of man is emphasized and the positive—man's possibility for transcendence—is there more or less between the lines. Our third selection, by **Karl Barth**, lays forth both sides of man's nature with unmistakable force. In his epoch-making commentary on *Romans*, Barth defines the place of religious man as the place of suffering in between his two natures, caught between Spirit and nature, inward and outward, unable to resolve them without the energies of grace.

We conclude this chapter with a famous selection from **Friedrich Nietzsche's** *The Antichrist*, in which he attempts to tear limb from limb the accepted body of Christian values. Why do we include this here? Perhaps the reader can decide why himself by seriously asking what Nietzsche is really attacking. How much would Barth or Merton or the Buddha agree with Nietzsche? In what sense of the word "religion" is Nietzsche antireligious and anti-Christian? And to what extent is he as passionately religious a thinker as we can find in modern philosophy?

J. N.

Suggested Readings

Attar, Farid Ud-Din. *The Conference of the Birds*. Berkeley, Calif.: Shambala, 1971.

Bultmann, Rudolph. "Man Prior to Faith." *Theology of the New Testament*. Vol. 1. New York: Scribner's, 1951. Chapter III.

Burckhardt, Titus. "The Seven Deadly Sins." *The Sword of Gnosis*. New York: Penguin Books, 1973.

Guenon, Rene. *The Crisis of the Modern World*. London: Luzac & Co. 1962.

Guenther, Herbert V. *Treasures on the Tibetan Middle Way*. Berkeley, Calif.: Shambala, 1969.

Kierkegaard, S. *The Sickness Unto Death*. Translated by Walter Lowrie. Princeton, N.J.: Princeton University Press, 1941.

Krishnamurti, J. *The Flight of the Eagle*. New York: Harper & Row, 1971.

Merton, Thomas. *The New Man*. New York: Mentor-Omega, 1963.

Niebuhr, Reinhold. *The Nature and Destiny of Man*. New York: Scribner's, 1951.

The Delusion of Selfhood According to the Buddha

W. Rahula

Walpola Rahula is on the faculty of the Sorbonne in Paris. He received the traditional training and education of a Buddhist monk in Ceylon and, prior to coming to the West, held an eminent position in one of Ceylon's leading monastic institutes. He is also author of *History of Buddhism in Ceylon* and *The Heritage of the Bhikshu.*

THE DOCTRINE OF NO-SOUL: ANATTA

What in general is suggested by Soul, Self, Ego, or to use the Sanskrit expression *Ātman,* is that in man there is a permanent, everlasting and absolute entity, which is the unchanging substance behind the changing phenomenal world. According to some religions, each individual has such a separate soul which is created by God, and which, finally after death, lives eternally either in hell or heaven, its destiny depending on the judgment of its creator. According to others, it goes through many lives till it is completely purified and becomes finally united with God or Brahman, Universal Soul or *Ātman,* from which it originally emanated. This soul or self in man is the thinker of thoughts, feeler of sensations, and receiver of rewards and punishments for all its actions good and bad. Such a conception is called the idea of self.

Buddhism stands unique in the history of human thought in denying the existence of such a Soul, Self, or *Ātman.* According to the teaching of the Buddha, the idea of self is an imaginary, false belief which has no corresponding reality, and it produces harmful thoughts of "me" and "mine," selfish desire, craving, attachment, hatred, ill-will, conceit, pride, egoism, and other defilements, impurities, and problems. It is the source of all the troubles in the world from personal conflicts to wars between nations. In short, to this false view can be traced all the evil in the world.

Two ideas are psychologically deep-rooted in man: self-protection and self-preservation. For self-protection man has created God, on whom he depends for his own protection, safety and security, just as a child depends on its parent. For self-preservation man has conceived the idea of an immortal Soul or *Ātman,* which will live eternally. In his ignorance, weakness, fear, and desire, man needs these two things to console himself. Hence he clings to them deeply and fanatically.

The Buddha's teaching does not support this ignorance, weakness, fear, and desire, but aims at making man enlightened by removing and destroying them, striking at their very root. According to Buddhism, our ideas of God and Soul are false and empty. Though highly developed as theories, they are all the same extremely subtle mental projections, garbed in an intricate metaphysical and philosophical phraseology. These ideas are so deep-rooted in man, and so near and dear to him, that he does not wish to hear, nor does he want to understand, any teaching against them.

The Buddha knew this quite well. In fact, he said that his teaching was "against the current" (*paṭisotagāmi*), against man's selfish desires. Just four weeks after his Enlightenment, seated under a banyan tree, he thought to himself: "I have realized this Truth which is deep, difficult to see, difficult to understand . . . comprehensible only by the wise . . . Men who are overpowered by passions and surrounded by a mass of darkness cannot see this Truth, which is against the current, which is lofty, deep, subtle and hard to comprehend."

With these thoughts in his mind, the Buddha hesitated for a moment, whether it would not be in vain if he tried to explain to the world the Truth he had just realized. Then he compared the world to a lotus pond: In a lotus pond there are some lotuses still under water; there are others which have risen only up to the water level; there are still others which stand above water and are untouched by it. In the same way in this world, there are men at different levels of development. Some would understand the Truth. So the Buddha decided to teach it.

The doctrine of *Anatta* or No-Soul is the natural result of, or the corollary to, the analysis of the Five Aggregates* and the teaching of Conditioned Genesis (*Paṭicca-samuppāda*).

. . . What we call a being or an individual is composed of the Five Aggregates, and . . . when these are analysed and examined, there is nothing behind them which can be taken as "I," *Ātman,* or Self, or any unchanging abiding substance. That is the analytical method. The same result is arrived at through the doctrine of Conditioned Genesis which is the synthetical method, and according to this nothing in the world is absolute. Everything is conditioned, relative, and interdependent. This is the Buddhist theory of relativity.

Before we go into the question of *Anatta* proper, it is useful to have a brief idea of the Conditioned Genesis. The principle of this doctrine is given in a short formula of four lines:

When this is, that is (*Imasmiṃ sati idaṃ hoti*);
This arising, that arises (*Imassuppāda idaṃ uppajjati*);
When this is not, that is not (*Imasmiṃ asati idaṃ na hoti*);
This ceasing, that ceases (*Imassa nirodhā idaṃ nirujjhati*).

On this principle of conditionality, relativity, and interdependence, the whole existence and continuity of life and its cessation are explained in a detailed formula which is called *Paṭicca-samuppāda* "Conditioned Genesis," consisting of twelve factors:

1. Through ignorance are conditioned volitional actions or karma-formations (*Avijjāpaccayā saṃkhārā*).

* [According to Buddhist philosophy what we call a "being," or an "individual," or "I" is only a combination of ever-changing physical and mental energies that may be divided into five groups or aggregates: matter, sensation, perception, mental formations, and consciousness—Eds.]

2. Through volitional actions is conditioned consciousness (*Saṃkhārapaccayā viññāṇaṃ*).
3. Through consciousness are conditioned mental and physical phenomena (*Viññāṇapaccayā nāmarūpaṃ*).
4. Through mental and physical phenomena are conditioned the six faculties (i.e., five physical sense-organs and mind) (*Nāmarūpapaccayā saḷāyatanaṃ*).
5. Through the six faculties is conditioned (sensorial and mental) contact (*Saḷāyatanapaccayā phasso*).
6. Through (sensorial and mental) contact is conditioned sensation *Phas* (*sapaccayā vedanā*).
7. Through sensation is conditioned desire, "thirst" (*Vedanāpaccayā taṇhā*).
8. Through desire ("thirst") is conditioned clinging (*Taṇhāpaccayā upādānaṃ*).
9. Through clinging is conditioned the process of becoming (*Upādānapaccayā bhavo*).
10. Through the process of becoming is conditioned birth (*Bhavapaccayā jāti*).
11. Through birth are conditioned (12) decay, death, lamentation, pain, etc. (*Jātipaccayā jarāmaraṇaṃ . . .*).

This is how life arises, exists and continues. If we take this formula in its reverse order, we come to the cessation of the process:

Through the complete cessation of ignorance, volitional activities or karma-formations cease; through the cessation of volitional activities, consciousness ceases; . . . through the cessation of birth, decay, death, sorrow, etc., cease.

It should be clearly remembered that each of these factors is conditioned (*paṭiccasamuppanna*) as well as conditioning (*paṭiccasamuppāda*). Therefore they are all relative, interdependent, and interconnected, and nothing is absolute or independent; hence no first cause is accepted by Buddhism. . . . Conditioned Genesis should be considered as a circle, and not as a chain.

The question of Free Will has occupied an important place in Western thought and philosophy. But according to Conditioned Genesis, this question does not and cannot arise in Buddhist philosophy. If the whole of existence is relative, conditioned and interdependent, how can will alone be free? Will, like any other thought, is conditioned. So-called "freedom" itself is conditioned and relative. There can be nothing absolutely free, physical or mental, as everything is interdependent and relative. Free Will implies a will independent of conditions, independent of cause and effect. How can a will, or anything for that matter, arise without conditions, away from cause and effect, when the whole of existence is conditioned and relative, and is within the law of cause and effect? Here again, the idea of Free Will is basically connected with the ideas of God, Soul, justice, reward, and punishment. Not only is so-called free will not free, but even the very idea of Free Will is not free from conditions.

According to the doctrine of Conditioned Genesis, as well as according to the analysis of being into Five Aggregates, the idea of an abiding, immortal substance in man or outside, whether it is called *Ātman*, "I," Soul, Self, or Ego, is considered only a false belief, a mental projection. This is the Buddhist doctrine of *Anatta*, No-Soul or No-Self.

In order to avoid a confusion it should be mentioned here that there are two kinds of truths: conventional truth (*sammuti-sacca*, Skt. *saṃvṛti-satya*) and ultimate truth (*paramattha-sacca*, Skt. *paramārtha-satya*). When we use such expressions in our daily life as "I," "you," "being," "individual," etc., we do not lie because there is no self or being as such, but we speak a truth conforming to the convention of the world. But the ultimate truth is that there is no "I" or "being" in reality. As the *Mahāyāna-sūtrālaṅkāra* says: "A person (*pudgala*) should be mentioned as existing only in designation (*prajñapti*) (i.e., conventionally there is a being), but not in reality (or substance *dravya*)."

"The negation of an imperishable *Ātman* is the common characteristic of all dogmatic systems of the Lesser as well as the Great Vehicle, and, there is, therefore, no reason to assume that Buddhist tradition which is in complete agreement on this point has deviated from the Buddha's original teaching."

. . .

People become nervous at the idea that through the Buddha's teaching of *Anatta,* the self they imagine they have is going to be destroyed. The Buddha was not unaware of this.

A bhikkhu once asked him: "Sir, is there a case where one is tormented when something permanent within oneself is not found?"

"Yes, bhikkhu, there is," answered the Buddha. "A man has the following view: 'The universe is that *Ātman,* I shall be that after death, permanent, abiding, ever-lasting, unchanging, and I shall exist as such for eternity.' He hears the Tathāgata or a disciple of his, preaching the doctrine aiming at the complete destruction of all speculative views . . . aiming at the extinction of 'thirst,' aiming at detachment, cessation, Nirvāṇa. Then that man thinks: 'I will be annihilated, I will be destroyed, I will be no more.' So he mourns, worries himself, laments, weeps, beating his breast, and becomes bewildered. Thus, O bhikkhu, there is a case where one is tormented when something permanent within oneself is not found."

Elsewhere the Buddha says: "O bhikkhus, this idea that I may not be, I may not have, is frightening to the uninstructed worldling."

Those who want to find a "Self" in Buddhism argue as follows: It is true that the Buddha analyses being into matter, sensation, perception, mental formations, and consciousness, and says that none of these things is self. But he does not say that there is no self at all in man or anywhere else, apart from these aggregates.

This position is untenable for two reasons:

One is that, according to the Buddha's teaching, a being is composed only of these Five Aggregates, and nothing more. Nowhere has he said that there was anything more than these Five Aggregates in a being.

The second reason is that the Buddha denied categorically, in unequivocal terms, in more than one place, the existence of *Ātman,* Soul, Self, or Ego within man or without, or anywhere else in the universe. Let us take some examples.

. . .

In the *Alagaddūpama-sutta* of the *Majjhima-nikāya,* addressing his disciples, the Buddha said: "O bhikkhus, accept a soul-theory (*Attavāda*) in the acceptance of which there would not arise grief, lamentation, suffering, distress, and tribulation. But, do you see, O bhikkhus, such a soul-theory in the acceptance of which there would not arise grief, lamentation, suffering, distress, and tribulation?"

"Certainly not, Sir."

"Good, O bhikkhus. I, too, O bhikkhus, do not see a soul-theory, in the acceptance of which there would not arise grief, lamentation, suffering, distress and tribulation."

If there had been any soul-theory which the Buddha had accepted, he would certainly have explained it here, because he asked the bhikkhus to accept that soul-theory which did not produce suffering. But in the Buddha's view, there is no such soul-theory, and any soul-theory, whatever it may be, however subtle and sublime, is false and imaginary, creating all kinds of problems, producing in its train grief, lamentation, suffering, distress, tribulation, and trouble.

Continuing the discourse the Buddha said in the same *sutta:*

"O bhikkhus, when neither self nor anything pertaining to self can truly and really be found, this speculative view: 'The universe is that *Ātman* (Soul); I shall be that after death, permanent, abiding, ever-lasting, unchanging, and I shall exist as such for eternity'—is it not wholly and completely foolish?"

Here the Buddha explicitly states that an *Ātman,* or Soul, or Self, is nowhere to be found in reality, and it is foolish to believe that there is such a thing.

Those who seek a self in the Buddha's teaching quote a few examples which they first translate wrongly, and then misinterpret. One of them is the well-known line *Attā hi attano nātho* from the *Dhammapada* (XII, 4, or verse 160), which is translated as "Self is the lord of self," and then interpreted to mean that the big Self is the lord of the small self.

First of all, this translation is incorrect. *Attā* here does not mean self in the sense of soul. In Pali the word *attā* is generally used as a reflexive or indefinite pronoun, except in a few cases where it specifically and philosophically refers to the soul-theory, as we have seen above. But in general usage, as in the XII chapter in the *Dhammapada* where this line occurs, and in many other places, it is used as a reflexive or indefinite pronoun meaning "myself," "yourself," "himself," "one," "oneself," etc.

Next, the word *nātho* does not mean "lord," but "refuge," "support," "help," "protection." Therefore, *Attā hi attano nātho* really means "One is one's own refuge" or "One is one's own help" or "support." It has nothing to do with any metaphysical soul or self. It simply means that you have to rely on yourself, and not on others.

Another example of the attempt to introduce the idea of self into the Buddha's teaching is in the well-known words *Attadīpā viharatha, attasaraṇā anaññasaraṇā*, which are taken out of context in the *Mahāparinibbāna-sutta*. This phrase literally means: "Dwell making yourselves your island (support), making yourselves your refuge, and not anyone else as your refuge." Those who wish to see a self in Buddhism interpret the words *attadīpā* and *attasaraṇā* "taking self as a lamp," "taking self as a refuge."

We cannot understand the full meaning and significance of the advice of the Buddha to Ānanda, unless we take into consideration the background and the context in which these words were spoken.

The Buddha was at the time staying at a village called Beluva. It was just three months before his death, *Parinirvāṇa.* At this time he was eighty years old, and was suffering from a very serious illness, almost dying (*māraṇantika*). But he thought it was not proper for him to die without breaking it to his disciples who were near and dear to him. So with courage and determination he bore all his pains, got the better of his illness, and recovered. But his health was still poor. After his recovery, he was seated one day in the shade outside his residence. Ānanda, the most devoted attendant of the Buddha, went to his beloved Master, sat near him, and said: "Sir, I have looked after the health of the Blessed One, I have looked after him in his illness. But at the sight of the illness of the Blessed One the horizon became dim to me, and my faculties were no longer clear. Yet there was one little consolation: I thought that the Blessed One would not pass away until he had left instructions touching the Order of the Sangha."

Then the Buddha, full of compassion and human feeling, gently spoke to his devoted and beloved attendant. "Ānanda, what does the Order of the Sangha expect from me? I have taught the *Dhamma* (Truth) without making any distinction as exoteric and esoteric. With regard to the truth, the Tathāgata has nothing like the closed fist of a teacher (*ācariya-muṭṭhi*). Surely, Ānanda, if there is anyone who thinks that he will lead the Sangha, and that the Sangha should depend on him, let him set down his instructions. But the Tathāgata has no such idea. Why should he then leave instructions concerning the Sangha? I am now old, Ānanda, eighty years old. As a worn-out cart has to be kept going by repairs, so, it seems to me, the body of the Tathāgata can only be kept going by repairs. *Therefore, Ānanda, dwell making yourselves your island (support), making yourselves, not anyone else, your refuge; making the Dhamma your island (support), the Dhamma your refuge, nothing else your refuge.*"

What the Buddha wanted to convey to Ānanda is quite clear. The latter was sad and depressed. He thought that they would all be lonely, helpless, without a refuge, without a leader after their great Teacher's death. So the Buddha gave him consolation, courage, and confidence, saying that they should depend on themselves, and on the *Dhamma* he taught, and not on anyone else, or on anything else. Here the question of a metaphysical *Ātman,* or Self, is quite beside the point.

Further, the Buddha explained to Ānanda how one could be one's own island or refuge, how one could make the *Dhamma* one's own island or refuge: through the cultivation of mindfulness or awareness of the body, sensations, mind, and mind-objects (the four *Satipaṭṭhānas*). There is no talk at all here about an *Ātman* or Self.

Another reference, oft-quoted, is used by those who try to find *Ātman* in the Buddha's teaching. The Buddha was once seated under a tree in a forest on the way to Uruvelā from Benares. On that day, thirty friends, all of them young princes, went out on a picnic with their young wives into the same forest. One of the princes who was unmarried brought a prostitute with him. While the others were amusing themselves, she purloined some objects of value and disappeared. In their search for her in the forest, they saw the Buddha seated under a tree and asked him whether he had seen a woman. He enquired what was the matter. When they explained, the Buddha asked them: "What do you think, young men? Which is better for you? To search after a woman, or to search after yourselves?"

Here again it is a simple and natural question, and there is no justification for introducing far-fetched ideas of a metaphysical *Ātman* or Self into the business. They answered that it was better for them to search after themselves. The Buddha then asked them to sit down and explained the *Dhamma* to them. In the available account, in the original text of what he preached to them, not a word is mentioned about an *Ātman*.

Much has been written on the subject of the Buddha's silence when a certain Parivrājakā (Wanderer) named Vacchagotta asked him whether there was an *Ātman* or not. The story is as follows:

Vacchagotta comes to the Buddha and asks:

"Venerable Gotama, is there an *Ātman?*"

The Buddha is silent.

"Then Venerable Gotama, is there no *Ātman?*"

Again the Buddha is silent.

Vacchagotta gets up and goes away.

After the Parivrājakā had left, Ānanda asks the Buddha why he did not answer Vacchagotta's question. The Buddha explains his position:

"Ānanda, when asked by Vacchagotta the Wanderer: 'Is there a self?,' if I had answered: 'There is a self,' then, Ānanda, that would be siding with those recluses and brāhmaṇas who hold the eternalist theory (*sassata-vāda*).

"And, Ānanda, when asked by the Wanderer: 'Is there no self?' if I had answered: "There is no self," then that would be siding with those recluses and brāhmaṇas who hold the annihilationist theory (*uccheda-vāda*).

"Again, Ānanda, when asked by Vacchagotta: 'Is there a self?,' if I had answered: 'There is a self,' would that be in accordance with my knowledge that all *dhammas* are without self?"

"Surely not, Sir."

"And again, Ānanda, when asked by the Wanderer: 'Is there no self?,' if I had answered: 'There is no self,' then that would have been a greater confusion to the already confused Vacchagotta. For he would have thought: Formerly indeed I had an *Ātman* (self), but now I haven't got one."

It should now be quite clear why the Buddha was silent. But it will be still clearer if we take into consideration the whole background, and the way the Buddha treated questions and questioners—which is altogether ignored by those who have discussed this problem.

The Buddha was not a computing machine giving answers to whatever questions were put to him by anyone at all, without any consideration. He was a practical teacher, full of compassion and wisdom. He did not answer questions to show his knowledge and intelligence, but to help the questioner on the way to realization. He always spoke to people bearing in mind their standard of development, their tendencies, their mental make-up, their character, their capacity to understand a particular question.

According to the Buddha, there are four ways of treating questions: (1) Some should be answered directly; (2) others should be answered by way of analysing them; (3) yet others should be answered by counter-questions; (4) and lastly, there are questions which should be put aside.

There may be several ways of putting aside a question. One is to say that a particular question is not answered or explained, as the Buddha had told this very same Vacchagotta on more than one occasion, when those famous questions whether the universe is eternal or not, etc., were put to him. In the same way he had replied to Māluṅkyaputta and others. But he could not say the same thing with regard to the question whether there is an *Ātman* (Self) or not, because he had always discussed and explained it. He could not say "there is self," because it is contrary to his knowledge that "all *dhammas* are without self." Then he did not want to say "there is no self," because that would unnecessarily, without any purpose, have confused and disturbed poor Vacchagotta who was already confused on a similar question, as he had himself admitted earlier. He was not yet in a position to understand the idea of *Anatta*. Therefore, to put aside this question by silence was the wisest thing in this particular case.

We must not forget too that the Buddha had known Vacchagotta quite well for a long time. This was not the first occasion on which this inquiring Wanderer had come to see him. The wise and compassionate Teacher gave much thought and showed great consideration for this confused seeker. There are many references in the Pali texts to this same Vacchagotta the Wanderer, his going round quite often to see the Buddha and his disciples and putting the same kind of question again and again, evidently very much worried, almost obsessed by these problems. The Buddha's silence seems to have had much more effect on Vacchagotta than any eloquent answer or discussion.

Some people take "self" to mean what is generally known as "mind" or "consciousness." But the Buddha says that it is better for a man to take his physical body as self rather than mind, thought, or consciousness, because the former seems to be more solid than the latter, because mind, thought, or consciousness (*citta, mano, viññāṇa*) changes constantly day and night even faster than the body (*kāya*).

It is the vague feeling "I AM" that creates the idea of self which has no corresponding reality, and to see this truth is to realize Nirvāṇa, which is not very easy. In the *Saṃyutta-nikāya* there is an enlightening conversation on this point between a bhikkhu named Khemaka and a group of bhikkhus.

These bhikkhus ask Khemaka whether he sees in the Five Aggregates any self or anything pertaining to a self. Khemaka replies "No." Then the bhikkhus say that, if so, he should be an Arahant free from all impurities. But Khemaka confesses that though he does not find in the Five Aggregates a self, or anything pertaining to a self, "I am not an Arahant free from all impurities. O friends, with regard to the Five Aggregates of Attachment, I have a feeling 'I AM,' but I do not clearly see 'This is I AM.'" Then Khemaka explains that what he calls "I AM" is neither matter, sensation, perception, mental formations, nor consciousness, nor anything without them. But he has the feeling "I AM" with regard to the Five Aggregates, though he could not see clearly "This is I AM."

He says it is like the smell of a flower: it is neither the smell of the petals, nor of the colour, nor of the pollen, but the smell of the flower.

Khemaka further explains that even a person who has attained the early stages of realization still retains this feeling "I AM." But later on, when he progresses further, this feeling of "I AM" altogether disappears, just as the chemical smell of a freshly washed cloth disappears after a time when it is kept in a box.

This discussion was so useful and enlightening to them that at the end of it, the text says, all of them, including Khemaka himself, became Arahants free from all impurities, thus finally getting rid of "I AM."

According to the Buddha's teaching, it is as wrong to hold the opinion "I have no self" (which is the annihilationist theory) as to hold the opinion "I have self" (which is the eternalist theory), because both are fetters, both arising out of the false idea "I AM." The correct position with regard to the question of *Anatta* is not to take hold of any opinions or views, but to try to see things objectively as they are without mental projections, to see that what we call "I," or "being," is only a combination of physical and mental aggregates, which are working together interdependently in a flux of momentary change within the law of cause and effect, and that there is nothing permanent, everlasting, unchanging, and eternal in the whole of existence.

Here naturally a question arises: If there is no *Ātman* or Self, who gets the results of karma (actions)? No one can answer this question better than the Buddha himself. When this question was raised by a bhikkhu the Buddha said: "I have taught you, O bhikkhus, to see conditionally everywhere in all things."

The Buddha's teaching on *Anatta*, No-Soul, or No-Self, should not be considered as negative or annihilistic. Like Nirvāṇa, it is Truth, Reality; and Reality cannot be negative. It is the false belief in a non-existing imaginary self that is negative. The teaching on *Anatta* dispels the darkness of false beliefs, and produces the light of wisdom. It is not negative: as Asanga very aptly says: "There is the fact of No-selfness" (*nairātmyāstitā*).

Spirit in Bondage
Thomas Merton

Thomas Merton (1915–1968) was born in Prades, in Southern France. In 1941, he entered the Trappist Monastery at Gethsemani, Kentucky. Among his numerous and influential books are *The Seven Storey Mountain, Seeds of Contemplation,* and *Mystics and Zen Masters.* He died while visiting Bangkok in December 1968.

The *parrhesia** which gave Adam free access to God in Paradise and which also gives us access to Him in the new Paradise opened to the world by the Passion of Christ, was based on confidence in the truth of God's mercy. But the sin of Adam which robbed him and us of paradise was due to a false confidence, a confidence which deliberately willed to make the option and experiment of believing in a lie. There was nothing in Adam's perfect peace that warranted this playing with unreality. There was no difficulty in the precept that had to be kept, to avoid falling into illusion. There was no weakness, no passion in his flesh, that drove him to an irrational fulfillment in spite of his better judgment. All these things would only be the consequence of his preferences for what "was not." Even the natural and healthy self-love by which Adam's nature rejoiced in its own full realization could gain nothing by adding unreality to the real. On the contrary, he could only become less himself by being other than what he already was.

* [*Parrhesia* : Greek term meaning "freedom of speech" and referring here to Adam's freedom to converse with God.—Eds.]

All this can be summed up in the one word: pride. For pride is a stubborn insistence on being what we are not and never were intended to be. Pride is a deep, insatiable need for unreality, an exorbitant demand that others believe the lie we have made ourselves believe about ourselves. It infects at once man's person and the whole society he lives in. It has infected all men in the original pride of Adam. It has, as a secondary effect, what theologians call concupiscence: the convergence of all passion and all sense upon the self. Pride and selfishness then react upon one another in a vicious circle, each one greatly enlarging the other's capacity to destroy our life. In a sense, pride is simply a form of supreme and absolute subjectivity. It sees all things from the viewpoint of a limited, individual self that is constituted as the center of the universe. Now everybody knows that subjectively we see and feel as if we were at the center of things, since that is the way we are made. Pride however comes and elevates this subjective feeling into metaphysical absolute. The self must be treated as if, not merely in feeling but in actual fact, the whole universe revolved around it. Concupiscence is then enlisted in the service of pride, to prove this one obsessive metaphysical thesis. If I am the center of the universe, then everything belongs to me. I can claim, as my due, all the good things of the earth. I can rob and cheat and bully other people. I can help myself to anything I like, and no one can resist me. Yet at the same time all must respect and love me as a benefactor, a sage, a leader, a king. They must let me bully them and take away all that they have and on top of it all they must bown down, kiss my feet and treat me as god.

Humility, therefore, is absolutely necessary if man is to avoid acting like a baby all his life. To grow up means, in fact, to become humble, to throw away the illusion that I am the center of everything and that other people only exist to provide me with comfort and pleasure. Unfortunately, pride is so deeply embedded in human society that instead of educating one another for humility and maturity, we bring each other up in selfishness and pride. The attitudes that ought to make us "mature" too often only give us a kind of poise, a kind of veneer, that make our pride all the more suave and effective. For social life, in the end, is too often simply a convenient compromise by which your pride and mine are able to get along together without too much friction.

That is why it is a dangerous illusion to trust in society to make us "balanced," "realistic" and "humble." Very often the humility demanded of us by our society is simply an acquiescence in the pride of the collectivity and of those in power. Worse still, while we learn to be humble and virtuous as individuals, we allow ourselves to commit the worst crimes in the name of "society." We are gentle in our private life in order to be murderers as a collective group. For murder, committed by an individual, is a great crime. But when it becomes war or revolution, it is represented as the summit of heroism and virtue.

One would almost think that the great benefit modern man seeks in collective living is the avoidance of guilt by the simple expedient of having the state, the party, or the class command us to do the evil that lies hidden in our heart. Thus we are no longer responsible for it, we imagine. Better still, we can satisfy all our worst instincts in the service of collective barbarism, and in the end we will be praised for it. We will be heroes, chiefs of police, and maybe even dictators.

The psychological finesse with which the Fathers of the Church investigate the inter-relation of pride, compulsive drives, anxiety and all the rest of the elements that evolve from the original act by which Adam wrecked the human spirit, is of great importance to ourselves.

Without going into too great detail, let us sketch out some of the broad outlines of the picture freely, following the thought of St. Bernard.[1]

The act which was the source of all man's spiritual deordination was an act by which Adam cut himself off from God, from himself, and from the reality around him. It was the free rupture of the existential communion that not only made Adam fully real, but which gave him a part in all the reality that existed together with him. By an act of pure pride, untainted by the slightest sensuality, passion, weakness, fleshiness, or fear, Adam put an abyss between himself and God and other men. He became a little universe enclosed within himself, communicating feebly, hesitantly and fearfully with the other universes around him. The young worlds that came forth from him and Eve were wild, unpredictable and destructive worlds—beings like Cain that would have to be specially marked by God lest they be killed.

What was this sin? It was first of all an attitude of mind. No doubt there was some overt act which reached forth to eat the fruit of the "forbidden tree." But before the act was done, the attitude was there. It was a way of looking at reality that condemned man, by its very nature, to become unreal. What was the attitude? It was simply this: that Adam, who possessed an existential, an experimental knowledge of all that was good and all that was real, and who was mystically united with God, the infinite source of all actual and possible reality, wanted to improve on this by knowing something else, which, he thought, would be something more. In desiring to eat of the fruit of the tree of the knowledge of good and evil, he wanted, in fact, to add to the knowledge of good, which he already had, the knowledge of evil.[2] To be more precise he wanted to have an experience, an existential knowledge of evil. He wanted not only to know evil by theoretical inference from good (which he could well have done without sin) but he wanted to know evil in a way in which it was not even known by God: that is to say, by *experience*. Now it was metaphysically impossible for him to increase his experience of the good by adding to it an experience of evil. In desiring what seemed to him to be more, he reached out for what was, in fact, disastrously less. In finding "two" he had less, not more, than the original "one." And he lost his inheritance, which was the free possession of all good, as a son of God. He tasted and saw that evil was terrible. And he hated himself for it.

It does not seem to me, however, that this act alone would have sufficed by itself to ruin Adam's spirit and destroy his union with God. That damage was done by all that was actually *implied* in the attitude leading to his sin. What was implied? I think something of a Promethean exploit was secretly implicit in the outlook that led Adam to eat of the one bad tree in the garden.[3] The fact that he was induced to "steal" the experience of evil by an act of disobedience clearly indicates, it seems to me, that he felt that all the good that had come to him could, if it were lost, be stolen back.

---

[1] *Sermons 81 and 82 in Cantica.*
[2] Cf. St. Bernard, *De Duodecim Gradibus Superbiae*, c. 10.
[3] It should be remarked that this was objectively a "bad tree" and not simply a good one which Adam was arbitrarily forbidden to touch in order that God's supremacy might be recognized.

Adam's pride was a kind of Promethean blindness to the true nature of love. He did not understand that the gifts which had been given to him could only be possessed as long as they were received as gifts. They were not and never could be won by right of conquest for that was impossible. To think otherwise was, in fact, completely to misunderstand the true nature of God.

Remember what we said above about Prometheus: thinking that the fire could be stolen, and not knowing it would be freely given, he unavoidably knew only false gods, not the living God. These false gods were beings only a little more strong than man, only a little more spiritual, only a little more wise. They needed fire, in the end, as much as man. They would resent the theft of fire. They would defend themselves jealously against any invasion of their Olympus. They did not want man to have what was theirs, for they could not afford to see themselves weakened and man strengthened. All these concepts imply a narrow, jealous, weak, fearful kind of god.

Now in stretching forth his hand to the bad fruit, that he might know evil by his own taste of it instead of merely by inference, Adam implied that the taste of evil was something God also might possibly be wanting. It was, perhaps, something God feared to let him have, lest man be made too strong and become His equal. (And yet Adam was already the equal of God in the fullest sense possible to mere man short of union with Him in the eternal beatific vision which was to be the reward of his probation.) Such a thought was only possible in one who already ceased to know the true God.

Now St. Bernard puts this *sapor mortis,* this taste for death, at the very heart of original sin. It is the exact opposite of the wisdom, the *sapida scientia* or existential ("tasting") knowledge of the divine good. The two are incompatible with one another. They cannot exist together. Consequently, having acquired the one, Adam necessarily lost the other.

The existential knowledge of the goodness of God is only possible when we experience the goodness of God in God Himself, that is to say, as He Himself "experiences" it. Our experience of His goodness is therefore an experience of infinite freedom, of infinite giving, infinite selflessness. It is invested, however, in our own case, with one modality that differentiates this love as it is in us and as it is in Him. In Him, the love is *experienced as given* with infinite freedom. In us, it is *experienced as received* into the arms of our own finite and contingent freedom. But this modality, this sense of receiving is tremendously important. For there is no full and total experience of God that is not at the same time an exercise of man's fundamental freedom (of spontaneity) and of God's mercy. It is a free consent in an act of mutual giving and receiving that takes place between two wills, two "persons,"[4] finite and Infinite. Finally, the only way in which we can possibly receive the fullness of divine love is to imitate His act of giving by surrendering ourselves completely to His love.

All these elements enter into the very nature of the *sapientia,* the supreme wisdom which is an experience of God, an existential communion in His own intimate life which is Love Itself.

---

[4] Actually, in the full Christian expansion of this experience, there is an awareness of the Three Divine Persons, distinct in their own personalities each, communicating to us that infinite Love which is the Divine Nature.

Adam, by his proud act, his insistence on "improving" his wisdom and science by adding to it the knowledge of evil, inevitably lost the full experience of goodness that was freely given to him by God. But he lost more than an experience. He lost his immortality, his contemplation, his power over himself and over irrational creation and finally even his status as a son of God. Along with all this he lost his immunity from disordered passion, his freedom from ignorance, his incapacity to suffer. These deprivations were not merely the revenge of an irate God—they were inherent in the very attitude and act which constituted Adam's sin. He lost his immortality: why? Because for him, life consisted precisely in his union with God the source of life. Breaking the contact between his soul and the source of life, and left to his own contingency, he himself became his own source of life. But he was a deficient source that soon ran dry.

He lost his freedom: not his freedom of choice, but his freedom from sin, his freedom to attain without obstacle to that love for which he had been created. He exchanged the spontaneity of a perfectly ordered nature elevated by the highest gifts of mystical grace, for the compulsions and anxieties and weaknesses of a will left to itself, a will which does what it does not want to do, hates what it ought to love and avoids what it ought to seek with its whole being.

Since he decided to depend on himself without contact with God, Adam had to become his own poor fallible little god. Everything now had to serve him, since he no longer served the Creator. But precisely, since he no longer fitted perfectly into the order in which they had all been established together, all creatures rebelled against Adam, and he found himself surrounded not with supports but with so many reasons for anxiety, insecurity, and fear. He was no longer able to control even his own body, which became to some extent the master of his soul. His mind, now, since it no longer served God, toiled in the service of the body, wearing itself out in schemes to clothe and feed and gratify the flesh and protect its frail existence against the constant menace of death.

The desire of earthly things, which are all destined for death, surrounded him with thicker and thicker shadows, and soul that thus lived could see nothing around about itself but the pale face of death appearing like a spectre everywhere. . . . By enjoying perishable things as though they were its last end, the soul has put on mortality like a garment. The garment of immortality remains underneath, not cast off, but discolored by the overcast garment of death.[5]

If in the original fall, we had simply been reduced to our own natural level, our condition would not have been so bad. We would indeed have been mortal, subject to ignorance and suffering and the rest: but we would have been able to resign ourselves to our fate and in some sense to adjust ourselves to it. For after all, human nature in its essence was not ruined, only weakened, by original sin. St. Bernard sees the fall not as a descent from the supernatural to the natural, but as a collapse into ambivalence in which the historical "nature" in which man was actually created for supernatural union with God is turned upside down and inside out, and yet *still retains its innate capacity and "need" for divine union.*[6]

[5] St. Bernard, *Sermon 82 in Cantica*, n. 3.
[6] That we have a natural need for union with God does not imply that our nature can demand that union as its fulfillment. But, as St. Augustine says, God has made us for Himself and our souls cannot rest until they rest in him.

The human soul is still the image of God, and no matter how far it travels away from Him into the regions of unreality, it never becomes so completely unreal that its original destiny can cease to torment it with a need to return to itself in God, and become, once again, real.

There is a special anguish in the concrete concept of man that we find in the Bible, where man is never regarded as the embodiment of a pure, abstract human essence. When man is seen as an abstraction, his difficulties are easier to solve, his tragic dilemma can be spirited away, his anguish can be made to disappear. For if man is nothing but a rational animal, all he has to do is live reasonably and keep his animality under the control of his reason. He will thus be able to arrive at a certain natural tranquillity. He will be able to "find himself" at least in his natural dignity as a human being. He may perhaps even arrive at a knowledge of his remote Creator, knowing God as the cause of the effects that surround us on all sides. He may perhaps even "experience" God as the Absolute justification for the ontological sense of being which sometimes springs up from the depths of our own soul. But, that, alas, is not enough. The inner recesses of our conscience, where the image of God is branded in the very depths of our being, ceaselessly remind us that we are born for a far higher freedom and for a far more spiritual fulfillment. Although there is no "natural" bridge between the natural and the supernatural, the concrete situation in which man finds himself, as a nature created for a supernatural end, makes anguish inevitable. He cannot rest unless he rests in God: not merely the God of nature, but the Living God, not the God that can be objectified in a few abstract notions, but the God Who is above all concept. Not the God of a mere notional or moral union, but the God Who becomes One Spirit with our own soul! This alone is the reality for which we are made. Here alone do we finally "find ourselves"—not in our natural selves but out of ourselves in God. For our destiny is to be infinitely greater than our own poor selves: "I said: You are gods, all of you sons of the Most High." [Psalm 81:6.]

The spiritual *anguish of man* has no cure but mysticism.

Adam's sin was a double movement of intraversion and extraversion. He withdraw from God into himself and then, unable to remain centered in himself, he fell beneath himself into the multiplicity and confusion of exterior things; this is St. Augustine's view of the fall.[7] Adam turned human nature inside out and passed it on in this condition to all his children. Each one of us has the task of turning the thing right side out for himself, and the task is by no means easy. Whereas Adam started with his spirit centered in God and everything ordered to that supreme union, he first withdrew spiritually from God into his own soul, as if he could live in his spirit privately and alone, referring everything to himself instead of to God.

The practical consequence of this was that fallen Adam lived as if there were no common good in the world. His existential knowledge of evil involved him in a complete reorientation of his whole being upon a private good of his own which had to be first restricted to itself, entrenched within itself, and then defended against every rival. The fort in which he entrenched himself was his own

---

[7] *De Trinitate*, Bk. 12, ch. 8–10.

body. No longer "spiritual" the body dominated his spirit. Henceforth his only contact with reality was through the openings in the wall of the fort—the five senses. But the senses only directly attain to material things. Hence Adam's spirit, submerged in the flesh, by that very fact became subject to and dependent upon matter. Now matter is in no sense evil of itself. Matter, like everything else made by God, including the body and its passions, is essentially good. But it is evil for spirit to be completely subjected to matter, for reason to be swayed and dominated by passion, and for the flesh to rule the whole man. Why? Because the flesh and the passions, of themselves, tend to anarchy, being at the mercy of sense stimulation, and hence responding blindly and automatically to every stimulus that presents itself. Spirit that is immersed in matter which it cannot fully control is therefore something like the captain of a ship that has lost its rudder and is carried away by the waves of a storm. The ship may well be a good ship, but it is lost.

The human soul in its fallen condition is worse, however, than the captain of a rudderless ship, because the captain can at least see that the ship is in danger. Our spirit, left to itself, is only dimly aware that it has been the victim of a disaster. It thinks, at first, that its condition is tolerably good. It feels to some extent at home in its own little universe—the body. It sets about its task of governing this universe with its own laws. Gradually it comes to find how little control it actually has: and how much it is actually governed by the blind needs and compulsive demands of passion. If it has doubted this for long centuries, psychoanalysis has made it no longer possible to doubt the tyranny that subconscious drives and compulsions exercise over the fallen human spirit.

Rationalizing and excusing the lusts and ambitions of a selfish and fleshly ego, camouflaging its own defects and magnifying the sins of others, evading its countless fears, forcing itself to believe its own lies, the psyche of man struggles in a thousand ways to silence the secret voice of anxiety.

Having lost his realization of his true identity, man has exchanged the peace of innocent self-realization for the agony of guilt-ridden self-awareness. Instead of being perfectly actualized in spirit, integrated and unified in the selfless ecstasy of a contemplation that goes out entirely to the "other," man is literally "distracted"—pulled apart—by an almost infinite number of awarenesses. He is conscious of everything trivial, remembers everything except what is most necessary, feels everything that he should not feel, yields to demands that he should never even hear, looks everywhere, pays attention to every creaking board and rattling shutter in his haunted house. For his soul and body, created to be a temple of God, cannot help but seem a haunted place after the desecration that has evicted its only rightful dweller. It is of no avail to try to exorcise the accusing silence by turning the place into a den of thieves. No amount of business prosperity and luxury can hide the abomination of desolation within us.

After Adam had passed through the center of himself and emerged on the other side to escape from God by putting himself between himself and God, he had mentally reconstructed the whole universe in his own image and likeness. That is the painful and useless labor which has been inherited by his descendants —the labor of science without wisdom; the mental toil that pieces together fragments that never manage to coalesce in one completely integrated whole:

the labor of action without contemplation, that never ends in peace or satisfaction since no task is finished without opening the way to ten more tasks that have to be done. How few of us have the honesty to cry out, with Ecclesiastes: "Therefore I loathed life, since for me the work that is done under the sun is evil: for all his vanity and a chase after wind. And I detested all the fruits of my labor under the sun . . . "[Ecclesiastes 2:17, 18.]

Those are terrible words, we will not listen to them because they sound too much like despair, and despair is precisely the specter we would like to keep buried in oblivion by our ceaseless activity. For in fallen man action is the desperate anodyne, assuaging the pain of a soul that instinctively knows that it was made for contemplation—a soul that knows that action, which is itself necessary, is only a means to that end.

If we would return to God, and find ourselves in Him, we must reverse Adam's journey, we must go back by the way he came. The path lies through the center of our own soul. Adam withdrew into himself from God and then passed through himself and went forth into creation. We must withdraw ourselves (in the right and Christian sense) from exterior things, and pass through the center of our souls to find God. We must recover possession of our true selves by liberation from anxiety and fear and inordinate desire. And when we have gained possession of our souls, we must learn to "go out" of ourselves to God and to others by supernatural charity.

The first step in all this is to recognize our true condition. Before we can ever hope to find ourselves in God, we must clearly recognize the fact that we are far from Him. Before we can realize who we really are, we must become conscious of the fact that the person we think we are, here and now, is at best an impostor and a stranger. We must constantly question his motives and penetrate his disguises. Otherwise our attempts at self-knowledge are bound to fail, for if we fully and complacently acquiesce in our own illusion of who we are, our "self-knowledge" will only strive to reinforce our identification of ourselves with this impostor.

Nevertheless, even the natural man is able, if he is honest, to make a beginning in the work of self-knowledge. Socrates used to go around Athens confounding the "right-thinking" citizens, the magistrates who assumed they knew who they were, the philosophers who imagined they knew the secret of words and of this power. In the end they killed him because he told them, too clearly, that they did not dare to face such questions. The judicial murder was committed in the name of the gods. But that was precisely the most eloquent admission of the fact that these people feared to face their own unreality, which they defended in the projected "reality" of gods in whom they could not really believe.

It is a spiritual disaster for a man to rest content with his exterior identity, with his passport picture of himself. Is his life merely in his fingerprints? Does he really exist because his name has been inscribed in *Who's Who?* Is his picture in the Sunday paper any safe indication that he is not a zombie? If that is who he thinks he is, then he is already done for, because he is no longer alive, even though he may seem to exist. Actually he is only pushing the responsibility for his existence on to society. Instead of facing the question of who he is, he assumes he is a person because there appear to be other persons who recognize him when he walks down the street.

Since we are made in the image and likeness of God, there is no other way for us to find out who we are than by finding in ourselves the divine image. Now this image, which is present in every one of us by nature, can indeed be known by rational inference. But that is not enough to give us a real experience of our own identity. It is hardly better than inferring that we exist because other people act as if we existed.

Just as some men have to struggle to recover a natural, spontaneous realization of their own capacity for life and movement and physical enjoyment, so all men have to struggle to regain the spontaneous and vital awareness of their *spirituality,* of the fact that they have a soul that is capable of coming to life and experiencing profound and hidden values which the flesh and its senses can never discover alone. And this spirituality in man is identified with the divine image in our soul.

St. Thomas gives us a concrete and thoroughly existential intuition of the divine image when he says that it is not only a static "representation" of something in the divine essence, but a *dynamic tendency* that carries us toward union with God. It is a kind of gravitational sensitivity to the things of God. "The image of God is seen in the soul in so far as the soul is carried, or is able to be carried, towards God."[8]

Now if we are to recognize this image in ourselves, it is not sufficient for us to enter into ourselves. It is not enough for us to realize that the spirituality of our nature makes us potentially god-like. The potentiality must be actualized. How? By knowledge and love: or, more precisely, by a knowledge of God that is inseparable from an experience of love. As St. Thomas says, in the context of the words quoted above: "The image of God is in the soul according to the knowledge it conceives of God and according to the love that flows from that knowledge."

Self-realization in this true religious sense is then less an awareness of ourselves than an awareness of the God to whom we are drawn in the depths of our being. We become real, and experience our actuality, not when we pause to reflect upon our own self as an isolated individual entity, but rather when, transcending ourselves and passing beyond reflection, we center our whole soul upon the God Who is our life. That is to say we fully "realize" ourselves when we cease to be conscious of ourselves in separateness and know nothing but the one God Who is above all knowledge.

We fully realize ourselves when all our awareness is of another—of Him Who is utterly "Other" than all beings because He is infinitely above them. The image of God is brought to life in us when it breaks free from the shroud and the tomb in which our self-consciousness had kept it prisoner, and loses itself in a total consciousness of Him Who is Holy. This is one of the main ways in which "he that would save his life will lose it." [Luke 9:24.]

What this means in practice is fidelity and attentiveness to the Words of God. "He that is of God hears the words of God." To be "aware" of God is to enter into contact with One, Who, infinitely hidden and transcendent, cannot be known as He is in Himself unless He reveals Himself to us. But God speaks to

---

[8] *Imago Dei attenditur in anima secundum quod ferter vel nata est ferri in Deum.* [*Summa Theologica*, I, Q. 93, a.8.]

us, in His Scriptures, and has given Himself to us in his Son—our whole life of faith is a life of attentiveness, of "listening" in order to receive the word of God into our hearts. *Fides ex auditu.* And we listen to God in the Liturgy, in the Scriptures, in meditation, in every expression of His Will for us. "Not by bread alone doth man live but by every word that proceeds from the mouth of God." It is this listening and obedience to the word of God that restores the Divine likeness in our souls, and brings us the truth that makes us free.

The recovery of the divine image in our souls, in so far as it is experienced by us at all, is an experience of a totally new manner of being. We become "new men" in Christ, and we are able to verify the fact by the change in the object of our knowledge and in our manner of knowing. Indeed, when God is known in this sense, He is not known as an "object" since He is not contained in a concept. On the contrary, the mystical knowledge of God, actualized in the mirror of His image within us, mysteriously coincides with His knowledge of us: "I shall know," says St. Paul, "even as I have been known." [I Corinthians 13:12.] We apprehend Him by the love which identifies itself, within us, with His love for us. What will be fully realized in the beatific vision is realized inchoatively in contemplation even in this present life.

The recognition of our true self, in the divine image, is then a recognition of the fact that we are known and loved by God. As such it is utterly different from any self-awareness, no matter how deeply spiritual it may seem. It is utterly different from any other kind of spiritual awakening, except perhaps the awakening of life that takes place within a man when he suddenly discovers that he is indeed loved by another human being. Yet this human awakening is only a faint analogue of the divine awakening that takes place when the "image" in our spirit comes to itself and realizes that it has been "seen" and "called" by God, and that its destiny is to be carried towards Him.

Without this inner awakening, which springs from the realization of God's merciful love for us, the image remains a mere potential likeness, buried and obscured, unappreciated because unseen. The image springs to life when, at the touch of God's ineffable mercy it begins to take on its lost likeness to Him Who is Love. The presence of God in us is the presence of His likeness in our own spirit—a likeness which is more than a representation, it is the Word of God Himself, united to our soul by the action of His Spirit. The sense of being "carried" and "drawn" by love into the infinite space of a sublime and unthinkable freedom is the expression of our spiritual union with the Father, in the Son, and by the Holy Ghost, which constitutes us in our true identity as sons of God.

It is quite usual, when a man comes into intimate spiritual contact with God, that he should feel himself entirely changed from within. Our spirit undergoes a conversion, a *metanoia,* which reorientates our whole being after raising it to a new level, and even seems to change our whole nature itself. And then, "self-realization" becomes an awareness that we are quite different from our normal empirical selves. At the same time we are vividly conscious of the fact that this new mode of being is truly more "normal" than our own ordinary existence. It is more "natural" for us to be "out of ourselves" and carried freely and entirely towards the "Other"—towards God in Himself or in other men—than it is for us to be centered and enclosed in ourselves. We find ourselves to be most truly human when we are raised to the level of the divine. We transcend ourselves, we see ourselves in a new light, by losing sight of ourselves and no longer seeing ourselves but God. Thus in a single act we accomplish the double movement of entering into oursevles and going out of ourselves which brings us back to the paradisiacal state for which we were originally created.

It is a pity that this *metanoia* is so rare, often so completely unknown, in the lives of men. True, no natural power, no human ingenuity, no extreme of courage and generosity can suffice, by itself, to bring about this change of heart. It must be done by the work of God, the work of grace. It is a divine gift. But if the gift be rare, it is not because of any niggardliness on the part of an infinitely liberal God. It is because of our fear, our blindness, our ignorance, our hatred of risk. For after all, in order to make this leap out of ourselves we have to be willing to let go of everything that is our own—all our own plans, all our own hesitations, all our own judgments. That does not mean that we give up thinking and acting: but that we are ready for any change that God's action may make in our lives.

On this readiness to change depends our whole supernatural destiny. There are few true contemplatives in the world because there are few men who are completely lost to themselves and entirely available to love. That is to say there are few who are able to renounce their own methods of self-support in the spiritual journey towards God. This is as much to say that there is too little faith, even among religious men. Perhaps especially in them. For when a man comes close to God and begins to find out that the Lord is hidden in the clouds of an infinite and inexorable transcendency, he begins to be afraid of One Who is completely Other.

God will not reduce the distance between ourselves and Him by any compromise with our own weakness and imperfection. With Him there is and there can be no compromise. The mercy, which is a total giving of His love to us, is anything but compromise, since it demands, in return, the total gift of ourselves to Him, and this gift of ourselves is obstructed, within ourselves, by our own self-alienation.

When the light of God's truth begins to find its way through the mists of illusion and self-deception with which we have unconsciously surrounded ourselves, and when the image of God within us begins to return to itself, the false self which we inherited from Adam begins to experience the strange panic that Adam felt when, after his sin, he hid in the trees of the garden because he heard the voice of the Lord God in the afternoon.

If we are to recover our own identity, and return to God by the way Adam came in his fall, we must learn to stop saying : "I heard you in the garden, and I was afraid, because I was naked. And I hid." [Genesis 2:10.] We must cast away the "aprons of leaves" and the "garments of skins" which the Fathers of the Church variously interpret as passions, and attachments to earthly things, and fixation in our own rigid determination to be someone other than our true selves.

The Two Natures of Man

Karl Barth

Karl Barth (1886–1968) was modern Protestantism's most powerful representative of orthodox thought. He taught in Germany until he was forced by
the Nazis to leave in 1935. From Germany, he returned to Basel, Switzerland,
the city of his birth, and taught there until his death. A vastly prolific writer,
he is best known for his monumental *Church Dogmatics* and *The Epistle
to the Romans.*

The first piece of evidence is: vv. 14–17. *For I know that the law is spiritual:
but I am carnal, sold under sin. For that which I do know not: for not what I
would, that do I practise: but what I hate, that I do. But if what I would not, that
I do, I consent unto the law that it is good. So now it is no more I that do it, but
sin which dwelleth in me.**

I know that the law is spiritual. To know this is the first requirement of a
religious man. Whence does he come? And whither does he go? He comes from
the realm of the Spirit; he passes relentlessly to death. When, therefore, he
stands under the compelling impression of the Spirit, an intolerable tension is
introduced into his life. He is engaged inevitably and hopefully in a conflict
from which there is no escape, because it is the battle for his very existence. A
demand is made upon him which he is bound to accept, because the vast inadequacy of his life in this world means that the demand is not only right but
necessary. A question is asked him, to which he must find an answer. A call is
given him, which he is bound to obey. The existence of God rises up in the midst
of his life, like an immense boundary-wall shutting out some poor neighbour's
view; or like a fortress occupied by the enemy; or like a boxer's closed fist.
Yet he must stand up to it, come to terms with it, and live with it. Paul knows
its meaning, when he calls himself elsewhere *a prisoner in bonds* (Eph. iii. I, iv.I;
2 Tim.i.8; Philem. 9). *O Lord thou hast persuaded me, and I was persuaded:
thou art stronger than I, and hast prevailed* (Jer. xx. 7).

But I am carnal, sold under sin. The tension becomes acute. If God be God,
who then am I? If my human relation to Him be bondage and captivity, who
then am I? The answer of experience to such questioning is quickly made. I
see that the law which proceeds from the Spirit, compelling, necessary, and
inevitable though it be, is excluded from my existence as a man. What form of
human existence is competent to receive THIS impress, to arrange itself according
to THIS misery and hope, and to accept THIS demand? Surely no human existence
of which I have experience. What answer can I give? How can I obey a call which
has emerged from beyond the boundary of my existence? *I am carnal:* never can

From Karl Barth, *The Epistle to the Romans,* trans. by E. C. Hoskyns (London, 1957), pp. 259–270
Reprinted by permission of Oxford University Press.

* [All quotes in this essay are from St. Paul's Epistle to the Romans, Chapter 7.—Eds.]

flesh become spirit, for that would mean the resurrection of the flesh. *I am sold under sin:* a transaction which may not be undone, save by the forgiveness of sin. I am a man: and no emotion or enthusiasm of religion can obscure what this means. Only a new man, only a victory over my humanity, only eternal life, can release me from the enigma of my being. What, then, doth the Spirit profit me? What advantage does the law which proceeds from the Spirit afford me? Of what use is my piety to me? How does the persuasive and prevailing power of God affect me? Is it not only too evident that I have no strength to bring forth? *Depart from me; for I am a sinful man, O Lord* (Luke v. 8). There is no bond of union between me, as I am, and God.

For that which I do I know not: for not what I would, that do I practice; but what I hate, that I do. Yes, this is clearly the case. If the law of my religious being and having, were itself Spirit; if sensitive "apprehension of the absolute" —"feeling and taste for eternity" (Schleiermacher)—could seriously be regarded as lying within the realm of human competence; if God and such a man as I am could be treated as co-partners; I should be in a proper position to contemplate and comprehend my words and acts and deeds from the point of view of eternity, or, at least, to think of them as the first stages of a movement in conformity with the movement of the Spirit of God. Then I should be led on to describe and comprehend myself quite properly as the answer to the problem of life, as obedient to the demand of God, and therefore as the new divinely inspired reality in the midst of other realities. I may, of course, be sufficiently humble and simple-minded only to make this claim occasionally. But facts are hard, and it is difficult for me to retain even this confidence for long. The more luminously clear it becomes that the demand requires my actual obedience to the will of God, and that His commandments are not grievous, the more luminously clear it becomes to me that, even in the simplest occurrences of my life, His will has not been done, is not done, and never will be done. For not even at the most exalted moments of my life do I fulfill His commands. Does any single thought of mine express the all-compelling power of the Spirit? Does one single word of mine formulate the Word after which I am striving and which I long to utter in my great misery and hope? Does not each sentence I frame require another to dissolve its meaning? And are my actions any better? Does my lack of fidelity in little things make amends for my great infidelity, or vice versa? Take the case of any reputable and serious-minded philosopher, poet, statesman, or artist. Does he ever suppose his actual achievement to be identical with what he wished to achieve? When my piece of work is done, do I not take leave of it sorrowfully? Woe is me, if I have unduly celebrated what I have accomplished. If, then, my thoughts and words and actions are of such sort as this, can I seek refuge in the the restless sea of my emotions? Can I find in the witches' cauldron of my unconscious achievements an adequate substitute for the failure of my conscious attainments? None but those who are past reclaiming really believe in the eternal significance of their emotions. No! there is no achievement of mine which I can recognize as legitimate. All my products are foreign bodies testifying to my inadequacy. I have no affection for them, no comprehension of them. If I could, I would deny them. They appear before me as hideous, evil-looking changelings. Fragmentary is our knowledge, and partial our understanding (1 Cor. xiii. 9). I am unable to apprehend what I have done. What I would, I do not; what I hate, that I do. Who then am I? for I stand betwixt and between, dragged hither by my desires and by my hates, and thither by my inability to do what I desire and by my ability to practise what I hate.

If what I would not, that I do, I consent unto the law that it is good. We have just said: *what I hate, that I do.* It would seem, therefore, that a point of contact has been established between myself and the incomprehensible, unapproachable, incommunicable, world of the Spirit. Surely, my hatred of my life as it is, my protesting against it, my dislike of my own behaviour, the disturbance which accompanies my passage through time, are points of contact. Is not such negation the means by which I am brought into harmony with myself? Am I not a doer of the law, at least in so far as I am aware of my deep-seated sinfulness and disgusted at it? Can I not console myself with my own disconsolateness? "If thou dost discover in thyself the conflict between the Spirit and the flesh, if thou doest often what thou willest not, thou dost declare thereby thy heart to be faithful. So long as a man maintains this conflict, he is not under the dominion of sin; so long as he struggles against sin and disapproves of it, sin is not reckoned unto him" (Joh. Arnd). These are perilous opinions. Who does not know this sunset glow, this quiet and secluded nook of pious dialectic? Who does not recognize here that middle way of compromise and resignation, where conscience is soothed by contemplating a conflict accepted and embraced?

So now it is no more I that do it, but sin which dwelleth in me. What, then, is the meaning of my protesting hatred of myself and my actions? It has clearly no further meaning than that an abyss is disclosed between myself and—myself. Can this really be regarded as a satisfactory starting-point for answering the question: "If God be God, who then am I?" The EGO which *practises* what I— the other EGO—contemplate with evident horror, cannot be an EGO capable of surviving the question. May not, however, the other EGO, that horrified, dissatisfied, ever-protesting EGO, survive the question? But what is this other EGO? Can this impotent outsider, this poor innocent, who merely shakes his head and disclaims what I am actually doing and practising, saying it is contrary to his will,—can such an EGO, with all his powers usurped, really survive the question? Can my justification rest upon the claim that it is not I who am doing what I am doing, that another rules in my house, that I am no longer master of it, and that this other thinks, speaks, acts, feels, whilst I merely protest? This, surely, is no justification at all; my agreement with the law is simply my own condemnation of myself—the recognition that *sin dwelleth in me.* Faced by so vast a condemnation, I have no ground upon which I can stand; for who is able to entice me to the opinion that my EGO which acts as it wills is to be distinguished from my other EGO, in spite of its expressed disapproval? Is my onslaught upon myself more than a Münchhausen adventure,[1] which never gets beyond the four walls of that house of sin, which is my EGO? Then it is that religion is never competent to speak of that EGO whose existence lies beyond the boundary of the realm of sin. Religion speaks only of dissension: I practise perpetually what I do not will, and I will what I do not practise. Religion merely exposes the disunion of human knowledge and human life; for it speaks of one reality only—the reality of sin.

The second piece of evidence: vv. 18–20. *For I know that in me, that is, in my flesh, dwelleth no good thing: for to will is present with me, but to perform that*

---

[1] *The Original Travels and Surprising Adventures of Baron Münchhausen* appeared first in England under the title of *Gulliver Revived; or, the Vice of Lying Exposed* (London: Printed for C. & G. Kearsley, 46 Fleet Street, 1786). [Tr.]

which is good I find not. For the good that I would I do not: but the evil which I would not, that I practise. But if what I would not, that I do, it is no more I that do it, but sin which dwelleth in me.

I know that in me, that is, in my flesh, dwelleth no good thing. To know that *in me dwelleth no good thing* is the second requirement of the religious man. This knowledge follows at once from the first requirement. Here again we run up against the "peculiarity" of all to whom the revelation of God is entrusted (iii. 1–20), namely that they, as such, can and ought to know this. Into this sinister secret men are initiated also through the revelation which is in Christ Jesus, precisely because it is the revelation of Revelation. "Paul, good man that he was, longed to be without sin, but to it he was chained. I too, in common with many others, long to stand outside it, but this cannot be. We belch forth the vapours of sin; we fall into it, rise up again, buffet and torment ourselves night and day; but, since we are confined in this flesh, since we have to bear about with us everywhere this stinking sack, we cannot rid ourselves completely of it, or even knock it senseless. We make vigorous attempts to do so, but the old Adam retains his power until he is deposited in the grave. The Kingdom of God is a foreign country, so foreign that even the saints must pray: 'Almighty God, I acknowledge my sin unto thee. Reckon not unto me my guiltiness, O Lord.' There is no sinless Christian. If thou chancest upon such a man, he is no Christian, but an anti-Christ. Sin stands in the midst of the Kingdom of Christ, and wherever the Kingdom is, there is sin; for Christ has set sin in the House of David" (Luther). *For I know* (vii. 14) is, then, not peculiar to some few men. Every religious man has this knowledge concerning himself. *I am flesh* (iii. 20), this is what he knows. We must, of course, bear in mind the meaning of the word *flesh:* unqualified, and finally unqualifiable, worldliness; a worldliness perceived by men, and especially by religious men; relativity, nothingness, non-sense. That is what I am! The man of property or of fashion may not be required to have this opinion of himself. How, indeed, could he, or ought he, to speak thus of himself? for his knowledge of himself may be a ray from the pity of God, which is more powerful than His wrath. No! it is rather the man dedicated to God who must speak of himself thus; the man of genuine and serious religious experience, the prophet, apostle, reformer; the man to whom the oneness of God's holiness and mercy has become the personal problem of his own existence. *Why callest thou me good? none is good save one, even God* (Mark x. 18). So Jesus spake; and because He spake thus, we cannot dismiss the recognition that God and man, that is, the man that I am, do not cohere together, as though it proceeded from a purely pessimistic view of life. Indeed, we have already attained this perception from our knowledge of the Spirit (vii. 14). It is clear, then, that what we have established from the consideration of human experience corresponds with the real and logical situation, and that THIS knowledge about men is the proper rider to the knowledge of God.

For to will is present with me, but to perform that which is good I find not. For the good that I would I do not: but the evil which I would not, that I practise. My will merely reminds me of the good which is not in me, and agrees with my knowledge that the law is divine (vii. 14); for I cannot know what is divine without willing it. *To will is present with me.* But what is meant by *to will*? It means, presumably, to strive after, desire, demand, question, seek, pray, knock; in other words, it constitutes the theme and purpose of all preaching and of all pastoral work. Appealing to the cloud of witnesses in all ages, preachers and pastors breathlessly repeat this theme with every conceivable variation and with all manner of emphasis. How desperately simple the theme is! and, because of its simplicity, it is the final word of religion. If it does not entice men, what can? And they are assuredly attracted by it. The exhortation to "seek God" does not fall on deaf ears; for it is the final exhortation which the human ear is able to receive. It is certain that the number of those who genuinely *will* and who genuinely *seek after God* is far greater than the casual observer would suppose. Who can be deprived of this earnest *will?* Do I not also perhaps *seek after God? To will is present with me.* Maybe it is so! but the comfortable nook into which I am tempted to creep, when I have said this, is no more comfortable than that other place over which is inscribed the words: *What I would not, that I do* (vii. 16). As there, so here, everything depends upon action, upon the performance of *that which is good.* I require that the good should exist in me. But it is quite certain that the most sincere, most upright, most deep-seated vigour of *will* remains uncrowned by the performance of *that which is good.* Consider once again that vast cemetery where lies the history of the Church and of Christian piety. Surely there was there no lack of upright *will!* What is it, then, which distinguishes the *doing* of Jeremiah from the *doing* of the false prophets, with whom he is so sharply contrasted? What distinguishes the "success" of Primitive Christianity which reached its zenith with Constantine—untheologically-minded historians please understand!—from the contemporary "success" of the worship of Mithras and of Cybele? What distinguishes the "success" of the Reformers of Wittenberg, Zürich, and Geneva, from the "success" of the Roman Pontiffs and of the architects of the loftiest towers of Babel? What distinguishes the "achievement" in delineating the inner piety which shines out of the eyes of the Sistine Madonna from the "achievement" in delineating the bigotry which peers out of the eyes of the Madonnas of El Greco? May we not conclude that we should be right in setting every human achievement upon one single ladder, although perhaps upon different rungs of that ladder? Are they not, at best, parables of an achievement which lies on a wholly different plane? Yes, no doubt; but nevertheless, must we not also say that the Lord permits to some human achievements a maturity which is lacking in others, even though the distinction which we note and with which we are satisfied cannot be identified with a human will-to-achieve? Are we not bound to own that the path which leads from our will-to-achieve to the "success" bestowed by the Lord lies wholly beyond our comprehension? We know nothing beyond the frontier which bounds our work and renders it fragmentary and incomplete: *the good that I would I do not: but the evil I would not, that I practise.* The religious man must answer questions concerning human "success," by saying that, so far as he succeeds, his success lies beyond the competence of his will. I cannot identify my will to do good with the good itself. The characteristic mark of the good is that it persistently demands realization, for action is the end of knowledge and of will. But this end is foreign to me. I do not practise what is good; I perform all manner of evil that I would not. And so the question arises once again: Who then am I? I am he that wills and he that does not perform: I am intolerably both at once. When my will is most steadfast, it does but remind me that the good is—not in me.

But if what I would not, that I do, it is no more I that do it, but sin which dwelleth in me. Seen from the standpoint of my will, there is, then, no performance of *that which is good* (vii. 18b, 19). We return therefore to the decisive question: What is performed? Answer: *I do what I would not.* I am therefore no more justified by the nobility of my desire to do good than I am by my desire not to do evil (vii. 16, 17). For the second time the judgement pronounced by myself upon myself is wholly justified: *it is no more I that do it.* Excluded from responsibility for what is happening in my house, I am thrust up against the wall merely as an observer. An appeal to my goodwill only proves that *sin dwelleth in me.* It is sin that acts, sin that performs, and to sin that the "success" belongs. And yet, this does not mean that I am, in fact, released from all responsibility: it means, rather, that I stand self-condemned. I have no reason to suppose that the EGO which performs and the EGO which disapproves can escape identification. Reality, even the reality of religion, knows but one man, and I, and not some other, am that man. It is one man that wills and does not perform; one man that does not will, and yet performs: within the four walls of the house of sin dwells but one man. Religious experience, then, simply bears witness to the fact that sin is all-embracing.

Conclusion from the evidence: vv. 21–23. *I find then the reality of the law exposed in that, to me who would do good, evil is present. For I delight in the law of God after the inward man: but I see a different law in my members, warring against the law of my mind, and bringing me into captivity under the law of sin which is in my members.*

Religion spells disruption, discord, and the absence of peace. A man at one with himself is a man still unacquainted with the great problem of his union with God. Our whole behaviour proves us to be in no way at one with ourselves; and for this reason, our relation to God is a disturbed relation. Happy the man who is able to deny this evident truth! May he long remain innocent of his own questionableness! The reality of religion, however, lies precisely in the utter questionableness of my EGO, confronted, as it is, by my inability to do what I would and by my ability to do what I would not. The subject of these contrasted predicates —my EGO—becomes an *x*, capable neither of life nor of death. By the law, through which I know God, I am enabled *to will to do good:* by the same law, through which I am known by God, my success in *doing evil* is clearly exposed. Thus my noblest capacity becomes my deepest perplexity; my noblest opportunity, my uttermost distress; my noblest gift, my darkest menace. It is almost incredible that, on the day when Schleiermacher finished writing his "Lectures about Religion," his joy in creation, apparently suddenly, was crossed by the fear of death. "What a shame it would be," he said, "were I to die to-night!" One would have supposed that, whilst writing so many beautiful and moving words "about religion"(!) he would have been faced continually by the fact of death. Is it possible to recommend religion to men who long sincerely and simply for peace? Can religion be presented, not merely as a tolerable thing, but as a thing of such absorbing interest that it may be welcomed as an enrichment of life, a valuable addition to civilization, or even as a substitute for it? When men are already sufficiently burdened by the inner uncertainty which attaches both to civilization and to barbarism, is it credible that religion should be brought triumphantly into connexion with science, art, ethics, socialism, the State, Youth Movements and Race, as though we had not had abundant experience of the waste land of "Religion and . . ."? Is it possible to justify these strange prophets, when we see hosts of men and women flocking to enlist willingly under their banners, eager to lay hold of religion, in order that their complacent capacities may be sanctioned, developed, and consecrated; when we behold them zealous to add to their passions one further emotion, the emotion of eternity, and to their other capacities yet one more good thing, the capacity for piety? We may be surprised that all this should go on before our eyes; but surprise cannot alter the fact that all of them, teachers and taught alike, are busily engaged in sawing off the branch upon which they are sitting, in setting fire to the house in which they dwell, and in scuttling the ship in which they are sailing into the "maelstrom." Those who are genuinely concerned to preserve their own peace of mind, to retain humanism on an even keel, and to assist the steady progress of culture—or of barbarism!—will, with Lessing, Lichtenberg, and Kant, so long as they are able, do their best to prevent the intrusion of religion into this world. They will lift up their voices to warn those careless ones, who, for aesthetic or historical or political or romantic reasons, dig through the dam and open up a channel through which the flood of religion may burst into the cottages and palaces of men, after first overwhelming those thoughtless pioneers! Such warning guardians of humanity will, at any rate, have displayed more sense for reality than the futile amateurs in piety—How cruel, in fact, these dilettantes are!—who, without knowing what they are doing, with romantic enthusiasm conjure up the spirits of religion but are powerless to exorcize them. But such warning wisdom is unavailing, since the capacity for religion is deep-seated and cannot be disregarded. Even our western civilization is powerless to protect men from it. The watchman at the gate of humanity has only to take care lest, at the eleventh hour, he too may be compelled to conclude a short armistice with the adversary of whom he is so terrified. Religion, though it come disguised as the most intimate friend of men, be they Greeks or barbarians, is nevertheless the adversary. Religion is the KRISIS of culture and of barbarism. Apart from God, it is the most dangerous enemy a man has on this side of the grave. For religion is the human possibility of remembering that we must die: it is the place where, in the world of time and of things and of men, the intolerable question is clearly formulated—Who, then, art thou? "The Law of God brings men under condemnation; for, in so far as they are under law, they are slaves of sin, and consequently guilty of death" (Calvin).

For I delight in the law of God after the inward man: but I see a different law in my members, warring against the law of my mind, and bringing me into captivity under the law of sin which is in my members. In religion, dualism makes its appearance. The man who conceals this with the fine-sounding phrases of monism is the "supreme betrayer of religion" (Overbeck), and does the greatest possible disservice to those who are satisfied with them. But the secret he endeavours to conceal cannot be hidden. The bomb, which he has so carefully decked out with flowers, will sooner or later explode. Religion breaks men into two halves. One half is the *spirit* of the inward man, which delights in the law of God.—Am I to identify myself with this *spirit?* Am I merely *inward?* But no one dares to make this claim. The other half is the *natural* world of my members; a world swayed by a wholly different law, by a quite different vitality and possibility. This latter wars against the *law of my mind,* and denies what it affirms. This corporeality, this essential second factor, this emergent opposition to my soul, is manifestly the supreme law and the supreme human possibility; and here undoubtedly is the sin by which I am imprisoned. Am I to be identified with this sin-laden *nature?*—Who dares to claim this? The contrast may be defined as inwardness and outwardness, idealism and materialism, that side and this side. But to which dost thou belong? Who art thou? Art thou "Spirit" or "Nature"? Thou canst not deny "Spirit," and hold thee only to "Nature"; for, as a religious man, thou hast knowledge of God, and thy most particular perception is that "Nature" desires to be altogether "Spirit." Neither canst thou deny "Nature," and hold thee only to "Spirit"; for, as a religious man, thou hast knowledge of God, and thou knowest only too well that "Spirit" desires to be altogether "Nature." Am I then both together?! Well, try: Art thou "Spirit–Nature" or "Nature–Spirit" . . .?! Once attempt any such arrogant anticipation, and thou wilt soon perceive that the desired union cannot be manœuvred merely by ranging the two alongside one another, or by amalgamating them, or by conglomerating them. The more thou dost madly endeavour to synthesize things which are directly opposed to one another, the more surely do they break apart and become manifestly antithetic. And thou thyself art harried hither and thither, from one to the other, but never wholly attaining the one or the other. At one moment one has excluded the other—and yet not finally or mortally; for, when the banished one seems weakest, there always remains a way for it to return in the fullness of its power.

vv. 24, 25a. *O wretched man that I am! who shall deliver me out of this body of death? I thank God through Jesus Christ our Lord.*

And so we retrace our steps to the place from which we set out at the beginning of the chapter. We know only the religious man, the man of human possibilities, the man of this world, the man *as long as he liveth* (vii. I). Such a one can never be what he is, and he is not what he ought to be. Indissolubly and undistinguishably one with his mortal body, he bears about with him always the reminder that he—yes, precisely he—must die. Yet, once the reality of religion is established, there arises an ultimate ambiguity concerning the future of the man of the earth. He can neither live nor die! In his piety he is suspended between heaven and earth. But what does this ambiguity profit me? In spite of all the contortions of my soul, of all the gymnastics of my dialectic, the brutal fact remains that *I am*—a man. And it is precisely my religion which compels me to recognize this so clearly. No other possibility is open to me except the possibility of being a man of the earth—*O wretched man that I am!* We have seen at last the reality of religion; we have recognized what men are. How vast a gulf separates the nineteenth-century conquering-hero attitude to religion from that disgust of men at themselves, which is the characteristic mark of true religion! —But Jesus Christ is the new man, standing beyond all piety, beyond all human possibility. He is the dissolution of the man of this world in his totality. He is the man who has passed from death to life. He is—what I am not—my existential I—I—the I which in God, in the freedom of God—I am! Thanks be to God: through Jesus Christ our Lord I am not the wretched man that I am.

v. 25b. *So then I myself,* as a man, *with the mind serve the law of God; but with the flesh the law of sin.*

Wretched man that I am! We must not deprive this *am* of its heavy significance. Paul is not describing the situation before his conversion! If conversion means the dissolution of the man of the earth, what relevance has this preposition "before"? What Paul is here asserting was well understood by the Reformers; but it is misunderstood by those modern theologians who read him through the spectacles of their own piety. Paul describes his past, present, and future existence. He portrays a situation as real after the episode on the road to Damascus as before it. He is writing about a man, broken in two by the law, but who, according to the law, cannot be thus broken. Paul is thrust into a dualism which contradicts itself. He is shattered on God, without the possibility of forgetting Him. Do we now understand the meaning of the Grace of God and of His Freedom?

The Diagnosis of Religious Man

Friedrich Nietzsche

Friedrich Nietzsche (1844–1900) was professor of philology at Basel. Nietzsche wrote many books, including *The Will to Power, Beyond Good and Evil, The Antichrist, Thus Spake Zarathustra,* and *The Geneology of Morals.* A severe critic of existing morality and culture, Nietzsche advocated a "transvaluation of all values," a rejection of Christian morality, and the development of what he calls a "master morality."

Mankind does *not* represent a development toward something better or stronger or higher in the sense accepted today. "Progress" is merely a modern idea, that is, a false idea. The European of today is vastly inferior in value to the European of the Renaissance: further development is altogether *not* according to any necessity in the direction of elevation, enhancement, or strength.

In another sense, success in individual cases is constantly encountered in the most widely different places and cultures: here we really do find a *higher type,* which is, in relation to mankind as a whole, a kind of overman. Such fortunate accidents of great success have always been possible and *will* perhaps always be possible. And even whole families, tribes, or peoples may occasionally represent such a *bull's-eye.*

Christianity should not be beautified and embellished: it has waged deadly war against this higher type of man; it has placed all the basic instincts of this type under the ban; and out of these instincts it has distilled evil and the Evil One: the strong man as the typically reprehensible man, the "reprobate."

From *The Portable Nietzsche,* trans. and ed. by Walter Kaufman (New York, 1954), pp. 571–586, 606–612. Copyright © 1954 by The Viking Press, Inc. All rights reserved. Reprinted by permission of the Viking Press, Inc.

Christianity has sided with all that is weak and base, with all failures; it has made an ideal of whatever *contradicts* the instinct of the strong life to preserve itself; it has corrupted the reason even of those strongest in spirit by teaching men to consider the supreme values of the spirit as something sinful, as something that leads into error—as temptations. The most pitiful example: the corruption of Pascal, who believed in the corruption of his reason through original sin when it had in fact been corrupted only by his Christianity.

It is a painful, horrible spectacle that has dawned on me: I have drawn back the curtain from the *corruption* of man. In my mouth, this word is at least free from one suspicion: that it might involve a moral accusation of man. It is meant —let me emphasize this once more—*moraline-free*. So much so that I experience this corruption most strongly precisely where men have so far aspired most deliberately to "virtue" and "godliness." I understand corruption, as you will guess, in the sense of decadence: it is my contention that all the values in which mankind now sums up its supreme desiderata are *decadence-values*.

I call an animal, a species, or an individual corrupt when it loses its instincts, when it chooses, when it prefers, what is disadvantageous for it. A history of "lofty sentiments," of the "ideals of mankind"—and it is possible that I shall have to write it—would almost explain too *why* man is so corrupt. Life itself is to my mind the instinct for growth, for durability, for an accumulation of forces, for *power:* where the will to power is lacking there is decline. It is my contention that all the supreme values of mankind *lack* this will—that the values which are symptomatic of decline, *nihilistic* values, are lording it under the holiest names.

Christianity is called the religion of *pity*. Pity stands opposed to the tonic emotions which heighten our vitality: it has a depressing effect. We are deprived of strength when we feel pity. That loss of strength which suffering as such inflicts on life is still further increased and multiplied by pity. Pity makes suffering contagious. Under certain circumstances, it may engender a total loss of life and vitality out of all proportion to the magnitude of the cause (as in the case of the death of the Nazarene). That is the first consideration, but there is a more important one.

Suppose we measure pity by the value of the reactions it usually produces; then its perilous nature appears in an even brighter light. Quite in general, pity crosses the law of development, which is the law of *selection*. It preserves what is ripe for destruction; it defends those who have been disinherited and condemned by life; and by the abundance of the failures of all kinds which it keeps alive, it gives life itself a gloomy and questionable aspect.

Some have dared to call pity a virtue (in every *noble* ethic it is considered a weakness); and as if this were not enough, it has been made *the* virtue, the basis and source of all virtues. To be sure—and one should always keep this in mind —this was done by a philosophy that was nihilistic and had inscribed the *negation of life* upon its shield. Schopenhauer was consistent enough: pity negates life and renders it *more deserving of negation*.

Pity is the *practice* of nihilism. To repeat: this depressive and contagious instinct crosses those instincts which aim at the preservation of life and at the enhancement of its value. It multiplies misery and conserves all that is miserable, and is thus a prime instrument of the advancement of decadence: pity persuades men to *nothingness!* Of course, one does not say "nothingness" but "beyond" or "God" or "*true* life," or Nirvana, salvation, blessedness.

This innocent rhetoric from the realm of the religious-moral idiosyncrasy appears much less innocent as soon as we realize which tendency it is that here shrouds itself in sublime words: *hostility against life.* Schopenhauer was hostile to life; therefore pity became a virtue for him.

Aristotle, as is well known, considered pity a pathological and dangerous condition, which one would be well advised to attack now and then with a purge: he understood tragedy as a purge. From the standpoint of the instinct of life, a remedy certainly seems necessary for such a pathological and dangerous accumulation of pity as is represented by the case of Schopenhauer (and unfortunately by our entire literary and artistic decadence from St. Petersburg to Paris, from Tolstoi to Wagner)—to puncture it and make it *burst.*

In our whole unhealthy modernity there is nothing more unhealthy than Christian pity. To be physicians *here,* to be inexorable *here,* to wield the scalpel *here*—that is *our* part, that is *our* love of man, that is how *we* are philosophers, we *Hyperboreans.*

It is necessary to say whom we consider our antithesis: it is the theologians and whatever has theologians' blood in its veins—and that includes our whole philosophy.

Whoever has seen this catastrophe at close range or, better yet, been subjected to it and almost perished of it, will no longer consider it a joking matter (the free-thinking of our honorable natural scientists and physiologists is, to my mind, a joke: they lack passion in these matters, they do not suffer them as their passion and martyrdom). This poisoning is much more extensive than is generally supposed: I have found the theologians' instinctive arrogance wherever anyone today considers himself an "idealist"—wherever a right is assumed, on the basis of some higher origin, to look at reality from a superior and foreign vantage point.

The idealist, exactly like the priest, holds all the great concepts in his hand (and not only in his hand!); he plays them out with a benevolent contempt for the "understanding," the "senses," "honors," "good living," and "science"; he considers all that *beneath* him, as so many harmful and seductive forces over which "the spirit" hovers in a state of pure for-itselfness—as if humility, chastity, poverty, or, in one word, *holiness,* had not harmed life immeasurably more than any horrors or vices. The pure spirit is the pure lie.

As long as the priest is considered a *higher* type of man—this *professional* negator, slanderer, and poisoner of life—there is no answer to the question: what *is* truth? For truth has been stood on its head when the conscious advocate of nothingness and negation is accepted as the representative of "truth."

Against this theologians' instinct I wage war: I have found its traces everywhere. Whoever has theologians' blood in his veins, sees all things in a distorted and dishonest perspective to begin with. The pathos which develops out of this condition calls itself *faith:* closing one's eyes to oneself once and for all, lest one suffer the sight of incurable falsehood. This faulty perspective on all things is elevated into a morality, a virtue, a holiness; the good conscience is tied to faulty vision; and no *other* perspective is conceded any further value once one's own has been made sacrosanct with the names of "God," "redemption," and "eternity." I have dug up the theologians' instinct everywhere: it is the most widespread, really *subterranean*, form of falsehood found on earth.

Whatever a theologian feels to be true *must* be false: this is almost a criterion of truth. His most basic instinct of self-preservation forbids him to respect reality at any point or even to let it get a word in. Wherever the theologians' instinct extends, *value judgments* have been stood on their heads and the concepts of "true" and "false" are of necessity reversed: whatever is most harmful to life is called "true"; whatever elevates it, enhances, affirms, justifies it, and makes it triumphant, is called "false." When theologians reach out for *power* through the "conscience" of princes (*or* of peoples), we need never doubt what really happens at bottom: the will to the end, the *nihilistic* will, wants power.

.   .   .

Let us not underestimate this: *we ourselves,* we free spirits, are nothing less than a "revaluation of all values," an *incarnate* declaration of war and triumph over all the ancient conceptions of "true" and "untrue." The most valuable insights are discovered last; but the most valuable insights are the *methods*. *All* the methods, *all* the presuppositions of our current scientific outlook, were opposed for thousands of years with the most profound contempt. For their sake, men were excluded from the company of "decent" people and considered "enemies of God," despisers of the truth, and "possessed." Anyone with a scientific bent was a Chandala.

We have had the whole pathos of mankind against us—their conception of what truth *ought* to be, of what the service of the truth *ought* to be: every "thou shalt" has hitherto been aimed against us. Our objectives, our practice, our quiet, cautious, mistrustful manner—all these were considered utterly unworthy and contemptible.

In the end one might well ask whether it was not really an *aesthetic* taste that kept mankind in blindness for so long: a picturesque effect was demanded of the truth, and the lover of knowledge was expected to make a strong impression on the senses. Our *modesty* offended men's taste longest of all. How well they divined that, these turkeycocks of God!

We have learned differently. We have become more modest in every way. We no longer derive man from "the spirit" or "the deity"; we have placed him back among the animals. We consider him the strongest animal because he is the most cunning: his spirituality is a consequence of this. On the other hand, we oppose the vanity that would raise its head again here too—as if man had been the great hidden purpose of the evolution of the animals. Man is by no means the crown of creation: every living being stands beside him on the same level of perfection. And even this is saying too much: relatively speaking, man is the most bungled of all the animals, the sickliest, and not one has strayed more dangerously from its instincts. But for all that, he is of course the most *interesting*.

As regards the animals, Descartes was the first to have dared, with admirable boldness, to understand the animal as *machina*: the whole of our physiology endeavors to prove this claim. And we are consistent enough not to except man, as Descartes still did: our knowledge of man today goes just as far as we understand him mechanistically. Formerly man was given a "free will" as his dowry from a higher order: today we have taken his will away altogether, in the sense that we no longer admit the will as a faculty. The old word "will" now serves only to denote a resultant, a kind of individual reaction, which follows necessarily upon a number of partly contradictory, partly harmonious stimuli: the will no longer "acts" or "moves."

Formerly, the proof of man's higher origin, of his divinity, was found in his consciousness, in his "spirit." To become *perfect,* he was advised to draw in his sense, turtle fashion, to cease all intercourse with earthly things, to shed his mortal shroud: then his essence would remain, the "pure spirit." Here too we have considered: the development of consciousness, the "spirit," is for us nothing less than the symptom of a relative imperfection of the organism; it means trying, groping, blundering—an exertion which uses up an unnecessary amount of nervous energy. We deny that anything can be done perfectly as long as it is still done consciously. The "pure spirit" is a pure stupidity: if we subtract the nervous system and the senses—the "mortal shroud"—*then we miscalculate*—that is all!

In Christianity neither morality nor religion has even a single point of contact with reality. Nothing but imaginary *causes* ("God," "soul," "ego," "spirit," "free will"—for that matter, "unfree will"), nothing but imaginary *effects* ("sin," "redemption," "grace," "punishment," "forgiveness of sins"). Intercourse between imaginary *beings* ("God," "spirits," "souls"); an imaginary *natural* science (anthropocentric; no trace of any concept of natural causes); an imaginary *psychology* (nothing but self-misunderstandings, interpretations of agreeable or disagreeable general feelings—for example, of the states of the *nervus sympathicus*—with the aid of the sign language of the religio-moral idiosyncrasy: "repentance," "pangs of conscience," "temptation by the devil," "the presence of God"); an imaginary *teleology* ("the kingdom of God," "the Last Judgment," "eternal life").

This *world of pure fiction* is vastly inferior to the world of dreams insofar as the latter *mirrors* reality, whereas the former falsifies, devalues, and negates reality. Once the concept of "nature" had been invented as the opposite of "God," "natural" had to become a synonym of "reprehensible": this whole world of fiction is rooted in *hatred* of the natural (of reality!); it is the expression of a profound vexation at the sight of reality.

But this explains everything. Who alone has good reason to lie his way out of reality? He who suffers from it. But to suffer from reality is to be a piece of reality that has come to grief. The preponderance of feelings of displeasure over feelings of pleasure is the cause of this fictitious morality and religion; but such a preponderance provides the very formula for decadence.

A critique of the *Christian conception of God* forces us to the same conclusion. A people that still believes in itself retains its own god. In him it reveres the conditions which let it prevail, its virtues: it projects its pleasure in itself, its feeling of power, into a being to whom one may offer thanks. Whoever is rich wants to give of his riches; a proud people needs a god: it wants to *sacrifice.* Under such conditions, religion is a form of thankfulness. Being thankful for himself, man needs a god. Such a god must be able to help and to harm, to be friend and enemy—he is admired whether good or destructive. The *anti-natural* castration of a god, to make him a god of the good alone, would here be contrary to everything desirable. The evil god is needed no less than the good god: after all, we do not owe our own existence to tolerance and humanitarianism.

What would be the point of a god who knew nothing of wrath, revenge, envy, scorn, cunning, and violence? who had perhaps never experienced the delightful *ardeurs* of victory and annihilation? No one would understand such a god: why have him then?

To be sure, when a people is perishing, when it feels how its faith in the future and its hope of freedom are waning irrevocably, when submission begins to appear to it as the prime necessity and it becomes aware of the virtues of the subjugated as the conditions of self-preservation, then its god *has to* change too. Now he becomes a sneak, timid and modest; he counsels "peace of soul," hate-no-more, forbearance, even "love" of friend and enemy. He moralizes constantly, he crawls into the cave of every private virtue, he becomes god for everyman, he becomes a private person,[1] a cosmopolitan.

Formerly, he represented a people, the strength of a people, everything aggressive and power-thirsty in the soul of a people; now he is merely the good god.

Indeed, there is no other alternative for gods: *either* they are the will to power, and they remain a people's gods, *or* the incapacity for power, and then they necessarily become *good*.

Wherever the will to power declines in any form, there is invariably also a physiological retrogression, decadence. The deity of decadence, gelded in his most virile virtues and instincts, becomes of necessity the god of the physiologically retrograde, of the weak. Of course, they do not *call* themselves the weak; they call themselves "the good."

No further hint is required to indicate the moments in history at which the dualistic fiction of a good and an evil god first became possible. The same instinct which prompts the subjugated to reduce their god to the "good-in-itself" also prompts them to eliminate all the good qualities from the god of their conquerors; they take revenge on their masters by turning their god into the *devil*. The *good* god and the devil—both abortions of decadence.

How can anyone today still submit to the simplicity of Christian theologians to the point of insisting with them that the development of the conception of God from the "God of Israel," the god of a people, to the Christian God, the quintessence of everything good, represents *progress*? Yet even Renan does this. As if Renan had the right to be simple-minded! After all, the opposite stares you in the face. When the presuppositions of *ascending* life, when everything strong, brave, masterful, and proud is eliminated from the conception of God; when he degenerates step by step into a mere symbol, a staff for the weary, a sheet-anchor for the drowning; when he becomes the god of the poor, the sinners, and the sick par excellence, and the attribute "Savior" or "Redeemer" remains in the end as the one essential attribute of divinity— just *what* does such a transformation signify? what, such a *reduction* of the divine?

To be sure, "the kingdom of God" has thus been enlarged. Formerly he had only his people, his "chosen" people. Then he, like his people, became a

---

[1] Literal translation of the Greek *idiotes*....

wanderer and went into foreign lands; and ever since, he has not settled down anywhere—until he finally came to feel at home anywhere, this great cosmopolitan—until "the great numbers" and half the earth were on his side. Nevertheless, the god of "the great numbers," the democrat among the gods, did not become a proud pagan god: he remained a Jew, he remained a god of nooks, the god of all the dark corners and places, of all the unhealthy quarters the world over!

His world-wide kingdom is, as ever, an underworld kingdom, a hospital, a *souterrain*[2] kingdom, a ghetto kingdom. And he himself: so pale, so weak, so decadent. Even the palest of the pale were able to master him: our honorable metaphysicians, those concept-albinos. They spun their webs around him until, hypnotized by their motions, he himself became a spider, another metaphysician. Now he, in turn, spun the world out of himself—*sub specie Spinozae*. Now he transfigured himself into something ever thinner and paler; he became an "ideal," he became "pure spirit," the "Absolute," the "thing-in-itself." The deterioration of a god: God became the "thing-in-itself."

The Christian conception of God—God as god of the sick, God as a spider, God as spirit—is one of the most corrupt conceptions of the divine ever attained on earth. It may even represent the low-water mark in the descending development of divine types. God degenerated into the *contradiction* of life, instead of being its transfiguration and eternal Yes! God as the declaration of war against life, against nature, against the will to live! God—the formula for every slander against "this world," for every lie about the "beyond"! God—the deification of nothingness, the will to nothingness pronounced holy!

That the strong races of northern Europe did not reject the Christian God certainly does no credit to their religious genius—not to speak of their taste. There is no excuse whatever for their failure to dispose of such a sickly and senile product of decadence. But a curse lies upon them for this failure: they have absorbed sickness, old age, and contradiction into all their instincts—and since then they have not *created* another god. Almost two thousand years—and not a single new god! But still, as if his existence were justified, as if he represented the ultimate and the maximum of the god-creating power, of the *creator spiritus* in man, this pitiful god of Christian monotono-theism! This hybrid product of decay, this mixture of zero, concept, and contradiction, in which all the instincts of decadence, all cowardices and wearinesses of the soul, find their sanction!

. . .

In the whole psychology of the "evangel" the concept of guilt and punishment is lacking; also the concept of reward. "Sin"—any distance separating God and man—is abolished: *precisely this is the "glad tidings."* Blessedness is not promised, it is not tied to conditions: it is the only reality—the rest is a sign with which to speak of it.

The consequence of such a state projects itself into a new practice, the genuine evangelical practice. It is not a "faith" that distinguishes the Christian: the

---

[2] *L'esprit souterrain* was the title of the first volume by Dostoevski that Nietzsche picked up in 1887, in French translation.

Christian *acts,* he is distinguished by acting *differently:* by not resisting, either in words or in his heart, those who treat him ill; by making no distinction between foreigner and native, between Jew and not-Jew ("the neighbor"— really the coreligionist, the Jew); by not growing angry with anybody, by not despising anybody; by not permitting himself to be seen or involved at courts of law ("not swearing"); by not divorcing his wife under any circumstances, not even if his wife has been proved unfaithful. All of this, at bottom one principle; all of this, consequences of one instinct.

The life of the Redeemer was nothing other than *this* practice—nor was his death anything else. He no longer required any formulas, any rites for his intercourse with God—not even prayer. He broke with the whole Jewish doctrine of repentance and reconciliation; he knows that it is only in the *practice* of life that one feels "divine," "blessed," "evangelical," at all times a "child of God." Not "repentance," not "prayer for forgiveness," are the ways to God: *only the evangelical practice* leads to God, indeed, it *is* "God"! What was disposed of with the evangel was the Judaism of the concepts of "sin," "forgiveness of sin," "faith," "redemption through faith"—the whole Jewish *ecclesiastical* doctrine was negated in the "glad tidings."

The deep instinct for how one must *live,* in order to feel oneself "in heaven," to feel "eternal," while in all other behavior one decidedly does *not* feel oneself "in heaven"—this alone is the psychological reality of "redemption." A new way of life, *not* a new faith.

If I understand anything about this great symbolist, it is that he accepted only *inner* realities as realities, as "truths"—that he understood the rest, everything natural, temporal, spatial, historical, only as signs, as occasions for parables. The concept of "the son of man" is not a concrete person who belongs in history, something individual and unique, but an "eternal" factuality, a psychological symbol redeemed from the concept of time. The same applies once again, and in the highest sense, to the *God* of this typical symbolist, to the "kingdom of God," to the "kingdom of heaven," to the "filiation of God." Nothing is more unchristian than the *ecclesiastical crudities* of a god as person, of a "kingdom of God" which is to come, of a "kingdom of heaven" beyond, of a "son of God" as the second person in the Trinity. All this is—forgive the expression—like a fist in the eye—oh, in what an eye!—of the evangel—a *world-historical cynicism* in the derision of symbols. But what the signs "father" and "son" refer to is obvious—not to everyone, I admit: the word "son" expresses the *entry* into the over-all feeling of the transfiguration of all things (blessedness); the word "father" expresses *this feeling itself,* the feeling of eternity, the feeling of perfection. I am ashamed to recall what the church has made of this symbolism: Has it not placed an Amphitryon story at the threshold of the Christian "faith"? And a dogma of "immaculate conception" on top of that? *But with that it has maculated conception.*

The "kingdom of heaven" is a state of the heart—not something that is to come "above the earth" or "after death." The whole concept of natural death is lacking in the evangel: death is no bridge, no transition; it is lacking because it belongs to a wholly different, merely apparent world, useful only insofar as it furnishes signs. The "hour of death" is *no* Christian concept—an "hour," time, physical life and its crises do not even exist for the teacher of the "glad tidings." The "kingdom of God" is nothing that one expects; it has no yesterday and no day after tomorrow, it will not come in "a thousand years"—it is an experience of the heart; it is everywhere, it is nowhere.

This "bringer of glad tidings" died as he had lived, as he had taught—*not* to "redeem men" but to show how one must live. This practice is his legacy to mankind: his behavior before the judges, before the catchpoles, before the accusers and all kinds of slander and scorn—his behavior on the *cross*. He does not resist, he does not defend his rights, he takes no step which might ward off the worst; on the contrary, he *provokes* it. And he begs, he suffers, he loves *with* those, *in* those, who do him evil. *Not* to resist, *not* to be angry, *not* to hold responsible—but to resist not even the evil one—to *love* him.

Only we, we spirits who have *become free,* have the presuppositions for understanding something that nineteen centuries have misunderstood: that integrity which, having become instinct and passion, wages war against the "holy lie" even more than against any other lie. Previous readers were immeasurably far removed from our loving and cautious neutrality, from that discipline of the spirit which alone makes possible the unriddling of such foreign, such tender things: with impudent selfishness they always wanted only their own advantage; out of the opposite of the evangel the church was constructed.

If one were to look for signs that an ironical divinity has its fingers in the great play of the world, one would find no small support in the *tremendous question mark* called Christianity. Mankind lies on its knees before the opposite of that which was the origin, the meaning, the *right* of the evangel; in the concept of "church" it has pronounced holy precisely what the "bringer of the glad tidings" felt to be *beneath* and *behind* himself—one would look in vain for a greater example of *world-historical irony.*

Our age is proud of its historical sense: How could it ever make itself believe the nonsense that at the beginning of Christianity there stands the *crude fable of the miracle worker and Redeemer*—and that everything spiritual and symbolical represents only a later development? On the contrary: the history of Christianity, beginning with the death on the cross, is the history of the misunderstanding, growing cruder with every step, of an *original* symbolism. With every diffusion of Christianity to still broader, still cruder masses of people, more and more lacking in the presuppositions to which it owed its birth, it became more necessary to *vulgarize,* to *barbarize* Christianity: it has swallowed doctrines and rites of all the *subterranean* cults of the *imperium Romanum* as well as the nonsense of all kinds of diseased reason. The destiny of Christianity lies in the necessity that its faith had to become as diseased, as base and vulgar, as the needs it was meant to satisfy were diseased, base, and vulgar. In the church, finally, *diseased barbarism* itself gains power—the church, this embodiment of mortal hostility against all integrity, against all *elevation* of the soul, against all discipline of the spirit, against all frank and gracious humanity. *Christian* values—*noble* values: only we, we spirits who have *become free,* have restored this contrast of values, the greatest that there is!

At this point I do not suppress a sigh. There are days when I am afflicted with a feeling blacker than the blackest melancholy—*contempt of man*. And to leave no doubt concerning what I despise, whom I despise: it is the man of today, the man with whom I am fatefully contemporaneous. The man of today—I suffocate from his unclean breath. My attitude to the past, like that of all lovers of knowledge, is one of great tolerance, that is, *magnanimous* self-mastery: with gloomy caution I go through the madhouse world of whole millennia, whether it be called "Christianity," "Christian faith," or "Christian church"—I am careful not to hold mankind responsible for its mental disorders. But my feeling changes, breaks out, as soon as I enter modern times, *our* time. Our time *knows better*.

What was formerly just sick is today indecent—it is indecent to be a Christian today. *And here begins my nausea*. I look around: not one word has remained of what was formerly called "truth"; we can no longer stand it if a priest as much as uses the word "truth." If we have even the smallest claim to integrity, we must know today that a theologian, a priest, a pope, not merely is wrong in every sentence he speaks, but *lies*—that he is no longer at liberty to lie from "innocence" or "ignorance." The priest too knows as well as anybody else that there is no longer any "God," any "sinner," any "Redeemer"—that "free will" and "moral world order" are *lies:* seriousness, the profound self-overcoming of the spirit, no longer permits anybody *not* to know about this.

All the concepts of the church have been recognized for what they are, the most malignant counterfeits that exist, the aim of which is to devalue nature and natural values; the priest himself has been recognized for what he is, the most dangerous kind of parasite, the real poison-spider of life. We know, today our *conscience* knows, what these uncanny inventions of the priests and the church are really worth, *what ends they served* in reducing mankind to such a state of self-violation that its sight can arouse nausea: the concepts "beyond," "Last Judgment," "immortality of the soul," and "soul" itself are instruments of torture, systems of cruelties by virtue of which the priest became master, remained master.

Everybody knows this, *and yet everything continues as before*. Where has the last feeling of decency and self-respect gone when even our statesmen, an otherwise quite unembarrassed type of man, anti-Christians through and through in their deeds, still call themselves Christians today and attend communion? A young prince at the head of his regiments, magnificent as an expression of the selfishness and conceit of his people—but, *without* any shame, confessing himself a Christian! *Whom* then does Christianity negate? *What* does it call "world"? That one is a soldier, that one is a judge, that one is a patriot; that one resists; that one sees to one's honor; that one seeks one's advantage; that one is proud. Every practice of every moment, every instinct, every valuation that is translated into *action* is today anti-Christian: what a *miscarriage of falseness* must modern man be, that he is *not ashamed* to be called a Christian in spite of all this!

Spiritual Discipline: Methods of Religious Search

INTRODUCTION

Do the great religious traditions of the world offer more than an uncompromising diagnosis of the human condition and a set of profound ideals? If not, then even where they are psychologically most penetrating and spiritually most inspiring they would be powerless to help man.

Between the perception of what is wrong with man and the vision of what he can become, there must exist a bridge. This bridge is religious "method," the "technique" of the religious search, the practical discipline by which religion effects psychological and spiritual change in individual human lives.

An important aspect of the new sense of the religious in America is the rediscovery of the idea of religious method. The neglect of this idea in recent times is perhaps one reason why our established religious institutions felt challenged by the birth of psychology and by the techniques of modern psychotherapy. Perhaps the change that psychotherapy effected in men was far less than that of which religion spoke. But at least the therapists had a method and a practical program. In this chapter, we shall be exploring the possibility that religion offers not only a transcendent vision of human growth but also precise methods for actualizing that vision.

Once the religions of man are looked at from this point of view, it becomes apparent that the variety of methods or "skillful means," as the Hindus and Buddhists call them, is enormous. We introduce our chapter with two powerfully contemporary formulations of one of the most fundamental of these methods, meditation. This word commonly denotes the process of quietly thinking through some vital question. Lately, however, Westerners have begun to return to the strong, perennial meaning of "meditation" as a method for direct self-knowledge.

Both **Chögyam Trungpa** and **Thomas Merton**, in the first and second selections of this chapter, characterize meditation as the art of inner self-acceptance in the midst of the relationships of life. Students of comparative religion will be interested to note the subtle ways in which even here the differences appear between the Buddhist tradition, with its emphasis on dispelling illusion, and the Christian tradition, with its emphasis on resisting the impulses of pride. Yet the similarities are even more striking, providing some small evidence in support of the idea that the differences among religions narrow as one comes closer to their practical side (this, incidentally, is one of the main ideas discussed in the concluding selection of this chapter).

To show something of the way a spiritual master works with a pupil, we might have gone to any one of a number of familiar sources, East or West. Instead, we have chosen for the third selection of this chapter the opening episode from the celebrated book by **Carlos Castaneda**, *The Teachings of Don Juan.* What is valuable about this selection is that the language is entirely fresh, and thus the pedagogical power of the *event* that the teacher calls into being is perhaps clearer to see, stripped, as it is, of familiar theological or philosophical associations. One cannot presume to say what, exactly, a spiritual master teaches, but it is clear from this example that religious knowledge transmitted in this way is bought at an existential price. Can an example such as this, remote as it is in language, time, and setting from, say, the teaching of Jesus or the Buddha, give us a glimpse of what it may have meant to be a disciple of the Master?

The fourth selection, from **Immanuel Kant**, may contain a surprise for students of Western philosophy. We are accustomed to the Kant of the *Critiques* with their awesome theoretical architecture. But here the great German philosopher evidences a delicate psychological understanding of the practical needs of a pupil struggling to find his way in the path of Christianity. In this short selection, a fresh sort of connection is made between Christian instruction and philosophical dialogue.

The fifth selection is **Leo Baeck's** essay on the way of Judaism, in which we are asked to see that religious method involves more than mere technique, which may be abandoned after a time. To Baeck, all real spiritual method is an indication of how to live and thus may be understood as the basis for a spiritually effective ethical life. Baeck argues that the genius of Judaism is that it never allows men to separate religious experience from the commitment to action, the mystery of the divine presence from the commandment to act under divine law. It would be interesting to compare this strong statement by Baeck to the Eastern idea of method as a "boat" to bring men to the "other shore" and then to be left behind. What really *is* the relationship between a way of living one's whole life and the forms of spiritual discipline? What is the relationship between ethics and method?

Was philosophy once such a method in the West? Our concluding selection, by **Jacob Needleman**, explores this idea by asking why Plato and Maimonides, for example, insisted that philosophy must not be studied early in a man's life. Perhaps wisdom, the goal of philosophy, must be understood as a state of being not entirely different from *nirvana* or union with God. If so, this essay suggests, modern philosophy may have radically misunderstood not only its own original purposes but the purposes of the way of religion itself.

J. N.

Suggested Readings

Black Elk and Brown, Joseph Epes. *The Sacred Pipe.* New York: Penguin Books, 1971.

Bloom, Archbishop Anthony. *Beginning to Pray.* New York: Paulist Press, 1970.

Castaneda, Carlos. *A Separate Reality.* New York: Simon & Schuster, 1971.

———. *The Teachings of Don Juan.* New York: Ballantine, 1969.

Eliade, Mircea. *Yoga: Immortality and Freedom.* Bollingen Series LVI. Princeton, N.J.: Princeton University Press, 1969.

Huber, Jack. *Through an Eastern Window.* Boston: Houghton Mifflin, 1967.

Merton, Thomas. *Contemplative Prayer.* New York: Herder & Herder, 1969.

Reymond, Lizelle. *To Live Within.* New York: Doubleday, 1971.

Suzuki, Shunryu. *Zen Mind, Beginner's Mind.* New York: Walker/Weatherhill, 1970.

Trungpa, Chögyam. *Meditation in Action.* Berkeley, Calif.: Shambala, 1969.

Meditation
Chögyam Trungpa

Chögyam Trungpa (1939–   ) was born in Tibet, as an incarnate lama of high rank. During the takeover of Tibet by the Chinese in 1959, he escaped to India in a dramatic flight described in his first book, *Born in Tibet.* He emigrated to Great Britain, attended Oxford University, and went on to establish a Buddhist center in Scotland. He now lives and teaches in America, principally at his centers in Boulder, Colorado, and Barnet, Vermont.

Meditation is a vast subject and there have been many developments throughout the ages and many variations among the different religious traditions. But broadly speaking the basic character of meditation takes on one of two forms. The first stems from the teachings which are concerned with the discovery of

From Chögyam Trungpa, *Meditation in Action* (Berkeley, Calif., 1969), pp. 51–64. Used by permission from the publisher, Shambala Publications, 1409-5th St., Berkeley, Calif. 94710.

the nature of existence; the second concerns communication with the external or universal concept of God. In either case meditation is the only way to put the teachings into practice.

Where there is the concept of an external, "higher" Being, there is also internal personality—which is known as "I" or the Ego. In this case meditation practice becomes a way of developing communication with an external Being. This means that one feels oneself to be inferior and one is trying to contact something higher, greater. Such meditation is based on devotion. This is basically an inward, or introvert practice of meditation, which is well known in the Hindu teachings, where the emphasis is on going into the inward state of samadhi, into the depths of the heart. One finds a similar technique practised in the Orthodox teachings of Christianity, where the prayer of the heart is used and concentration on the heart is emphasised. This is a means of identifying oneself with an external Being and necessitates purifying oneself. The basic belief is that one is separate from God, but there is still a link, one is still part of God. This confusion sometimes arises, and in order to clarify it one has to work inwards and try to raise the standard of individuality to the level of a higher consciousness. This approach makes use of emotions and devotional practices which are aimed at making contact with God or gods or some particular saint. These devotional practices may also include the recitation of mantra.

The other principal form of meditation is almost entirely opposite in its approach, though finally it might lead to the same results. Here there is no belief in higher and lower; the idea of different levels, or of being in an under-developed state, does not arise. One does not feel inferior, and what one is trying to achieve is not something higher than oneself. Therefore the practice of meditation does not require an inward concentration on the heart. There is no centralising concept at all. Even such practices as concentrating on the chakras, or psychic centres of the body, are approached in a different way. Although in certain teachings of Buddhism the concept of chakras is mentioned, the practices connected with them are not based on the development of an inward centre. So this basic form of meditation is concerned with trying to see what *is*. There are many variations on this form of meditation, but they are generally based on various techniques for opening oneself. The achievement of this kind of meditation is not, therefore, the result of some long-term, arduous practise through which we build ourselves up into a "higher" state, nor does it necessitate going into any kind of inner trance state. It is rather what one might call "working meditation" or extrovert meditation, where skilful means and wisdom must be combined like the two wings of a bird. This is not a question of trying to retreat from the world. In fact without the external world, the world of apparent phenomena, meditation would be almost impossible to practise, for the individual and the external world are not separate, but merely co-exist together. Therefore the concept of trying to communicate and trying to become one with some higher Being does not arise.

In this kind of meditation practise the concept of *nowness* plays a very important part. In fact, it is the essence of meditation. Whatever one does, whatever one tries to practise, is not aimed at achieving a higher state or at following some theory or ideal, but simply, without any object or ambition, trying to see what is here and now. One has to become aware of the present moment through such means as concentrating on the breathing, a practise which has been developed in the Buddhist tradition. This is based on developing the knowledge of nowness, for each respiration is unique, it is an expression of *now*. Each breath is separate from the next and is fully seen and fully felt, not in a visualised form, nor simply as an aid to concentration, but it should be fully and properly dealt with. Just as a very hungry man, when he is eating, is not even conscious that he is eating food. He is so engrossed in the food that he completely identifies himself with what he is doing and almost becomes one with the taste and enjoyment of it. Similarly with the breathing, the whole idea is to try and see through that very moment in time. So in this case the concept of trying to become something higher does not arise at all, and opinions do not have much importance. In a sense opinions provide a way to escape; they create a kind of slothfulness and obscure one's clarity of vision. The clarity of our consciousness is veiled by prefabricated concepts and whatever we see we try to fit into some pigeon-hole or in some way make it fit in with our preconceived ideas. So concepts and theories—and, for that matter, theology—can become obstacles. One might ask, therefore, what is the point of studying Buddhist philosophy? Since there are Scriptures and texts and there is surely some philosophy to believe in, wouldn't that also be a concept? Well, that depends on the individual, but basically it is not so. From the start one tries to transcend concepts, and one tries, perhaps in a very critical way, to find out what *is*. One has to develop a critical mind which will stimulate intelligence. This may at first cause one to reject what is said by teachers or what is written in books, but then gradually one begins to feel something and to find something for oneself. That is what is known as the meeting of imagination and reality, where the feeling of certain words and concepts meets with intuitive knowledge, perhaps in a rather vague and imprecise way. One may be uncertain whether what one is learning is right or not, but there is a general feeling that one is about to discover something. One cannot really start by being perfect, but one must start with something. And if one cultivates this intelligent, intuitive insight, then gradually, stage by stage, the real intuitive feeling develops and the imaginary or hallucinatory element is gradually clarified and eventually dies out. Finally that vague feeling of discovery becomes very clear, so that almost no doubt remains. Even at this stage it is possible that one may be unable to explain one's discovery verbally or write it down exactly on paper, and in fact if one tried to do so it would be limiting one's scope and would be rather dangerous. Nevertheless, as this feeling grows and develops one finally attains direct knowledge, rather than achieving something which is separate from oneself. As in the analogy of the hungry man, you become one with the subject. This can only be achieved through the practice of meditation. Therefore meditation is very much a matter of exercise—it is a working practice. It is not a question of going into some inward depth, but of widening and expanding outwards.

These are the basic differences between the two types of meditation practice. The first may be more suitable for some people and the second may be more suitable for others. It is not a question of one being superior or more accurate than the other. But for any form of meditation one must first overcome that great feeling of demand and ambition which acts as a major obstacle. Making demands on a person, such as a Guru, or having the ambition to achieve something out of what one is doing, arises out of a built-up desire or wantingness;

and that wantingness is a centralised notion. This centralized notion is basically blind. It is like having only one eye, and that one eye being situated in the chest. When you try to walk you cannot turn your head round and you can only see a limited area. Because you can see in only one direction the intelligence of turning the head is lacking. Therefore there is a great danger of falling. This wantingness acts as a veil and becomes an obstacle to the discovery of the moment of nowness, because the wanting is based either on the future or on trying to continue something which existed in the past, so the nowness is completely forgotten. There may be a certain effort to focus on the nowness, but perhaps only twenty per cent of the consciousness is based on the present and the rest is scattered into the past or the future. Therefore there is not enough force to see directly what is there.

Here, too, the teaching of selflessness plays a very important part. This is not merely a question of denying the existence of Ego, for Ego is something relative. Where there is an external person, a higher Being, or the concept of something which is separate from oneself, then we tend to think that because there is something outside there must be something here as well. The external phenomenon sometimes becomes such an overwhelming thing and seems to have all sorts of seductive or aggressive qualities, so we erect a kind of defence mechanism against it, failing to see that that is itself a continuity of the external thing. We try to segregate ourselves from the external, and this creates a kind of gigantic bubble in us which consists of nothing but air and water or, in this case, fear and the reflection of the external thing. So this huge bubble prevents any fresh air from coming in, and that is "I"—the Ego. So in that sense there is the existence of Ego, but it is in fact illusory. Having established that, one generally wants to create some external idol or refuge. Subconsciously one knows that this "I" is only a bubble and it could burst at any moment, so one tries to protect it as much as one can—either consciously or subconsciously. In fact we have achieved such skill at protecting this Ego that we have managed to preserve it for hundreds of years. It is as though a person has a very precious pair of spectacles which he puts in a box or various containers in order to keep it safe, so that even if other things are broken this would be preserved. He may feel that other things could bear hardship, but he knows that this could not, so this would last longer. In the same way, Ego lasts longer just because one feels it could burst at any time. There is fear of it being destroyed because that would be too much, one would feel too exposed. And there is such character, such a fascinating pattern established outside us, although it is in fact our own reflection. That is why the concept of Egolessness is not really a question of whether there is a Self or not, or, for that matter, whether there is the existence of God or not; it is rather the taking away of that concept of the bubble. Having done so, one doesn't have to deliberately destroy the Ego or deliberately condemn God. And when that barrier is removed one can expand and swim through straight away. But this can only be achieved through the practice of meditation which must be approached in a very practical and simple way. Then the mystical experience of joy or Grace, or whatever it might be, can be found in every object. That is what one tries to achieve through Vipassana, or "Insight" meditation practice. Once we have established a basic pattern of discipline and we have developed a regular way of dealing with the situation—whether it is breathing or walking or what-have-you—then at some stage the technique gradually dies out. Reality gradually expands so that we do not have to use the technique at all. And in this case one does not have to concentrate inwards, but one can expand outwards more and more. And the more one expands, the closer one gets to the realisation of centreless existence.

That is the basic pattern of this kind of meditation, which is based on three fundamental factors: firstly, not centralising inwards; secondly, not having any longing to become higher; and thirdly, becoming completely identified with here and now. These three elements run right through the practice of meditation, from the beginning up to the moment of realisation.

Q. You mentioned nowness in your talk, and I was wondering how it is possible to become aware of the absolute through awareness of a relative moment in time?

A. Well, we have to start by working through the relative aspect, until finally this nowness takes on such a living quality that it is no longer dependent on a relative way of expressing nowness. One might say that *now* exists all the time, beyond the concept of relativity. But since all concepts are based on the idea of realitivity, it is impossible to find any words which go beyond that. So nowness is the only way to see directly. First it is between the past and the future—now. Then gradually one discovers that nowness is not dependent on relativity at all. One discovers that the past does not exist, the future does not exist, and everything happens now. Similarly, in order to express space one might have first to create a vase, and then one has to break it, and then one sees that the emptiness in the vase is the same as the emptiness outside. That is the whole meaning of technique. At first that nowness is, in a sense, not perfect. Or one might even say that the meditation is not perfect, it is a purely man-made practice. One sits and tries to be still and concentrates on the breathing, and so on. But then, having started in that way, one gradually discovers something more than that. So the effort one has put into it—into the discovery of nowness, for example—would not be wasted, though at the same time one might see that it was rather foolish. But that is the only way to start.

Q. For meditation, would a student have to rid himself of Ego before he started, or would this come naturally as he is studying?

A. This comes naturally, because you can't start without Ego. And basically Ego isn't bad. Good and bad doesn't really exist anywhere, it is only a secondary thing. Ego is, in a sense, a false thing, but it isn't necessarily bad. You have to start with Ego, and use Ego, and from there it gradually wears out, like a pair of shoes. But you have to use it and wear it out thoroughly, so it is not preserved. Otherwise, if you try to push Ego aside and start perfect, you may become more and more perfect in a rather one-sided way, but the same amount of imperfection is building up on the other side, just as creating intense light creates intense darkness as well.

Q. You mentioned that there are two basic forms of meditation—devotional practice, or trying to communicate with something higher, and the other one, which is simply awareness of what is—but this devotional practice still plays a part in Buddhism as well, and you have devotional chants and so on, but I am not quite sure how this comes in. I mean, the two appear to be different, so can they in fact be combined?

A. Yes, but the kind of devotional practice which is found in Buddhism is merely a process of opening, of surrendering the Ego. It is a process of creating a

346 / Spiritual Discipline: Methods of Religious Search

container. I don't mean to condemn the other kind of devotion, but if one looks at it from the point of view of a person who has an unskilful way of using that technique, then devotion becomes a longing to free oneself. One sees oneself as being very separate, and as being imprisoned and imperfect. One regards oneself as basically bad, and one is trying to break out. In other words the imperfection part of oneself is identified with "I" and anything perfect is identified with some external being, so all that is left is trying to get through the imprisonment. This kind of devotion is an overemphasised awareness of Ego, the negative aspect of Ego. Although there are hundreds of variations of devotional practice in Buddhism, and there are many accounts of devotion to Gurus, or being able to communicate with the Guru, and of achieving the Awakened State of mind through devotion. But in these cases devotion is always begun without centralising on the Ego. In any chants or ceremonies, for example, which make use of symbolism, or the visualisation of Buddhas, before any visualisation is created there is first a formless meditation, which creates an entirely open space. And at the end one always recites what is known as the Threefold Wheel: "I do not exist; the external visualisation does not exist: and the act of visualising does not exist"—the idea being that any feeling of achievement is thrown back to the openness, so one doesn't feel that one is collecting anything. I think that is the basic point. One may feel a great deal of devotion, but that devotion is a kind of abstract form of devotion, which does not centralise inwardly. One simply identifies with that feeling of devotion, and that's all. This is perhaps a different concept of devotion, where no centre exists, but only devotion exists. Whereas, in the other case devotion contains a demand. There is an expectation of getting something out of it in return.

Q. Is there not a great fear generated when we get to this point of opening up and surrendering?

A. Fear is one of the weapons of Ego. It protects the Ego. If one reaches the stage where one begins to see the folly of Ego, then there is fear of losing the Ego, and fear is one of its last weapons. Beyond that point fear no longer exists, because the object of fear is to frighten somebody, and when that somebody is not there, then fear loses its function. You see, fear is continually given life by your response, and when there is no one to respond to the fear—which is Ego loss—then fear ceases to exist.

Q. You are talking about the Ego as an object?

A. In what sense?

Q. In the sense that it is part of the external environment.

A. Ego is, as I have already said, like a bubble. It is an object up to a point, because although it does not really exist—it is an impermanent thing—it in fact shows itself as an object more than actually being one. That is another way of protecting oneself, of trying to maintain Ego.

Q. This is an aspect of the Ego?

A. Yes.

Q. Then you can't destroy the Ego, or you would lose the power to recognise, the power to cognate.

A. No, not necessarily. Because Ego does not contain understanding, it does not contain any insight at all. Ego exists in a false way all the time and can only create confusion, whereas insight is something more than that.

Q. Would you say that Ego is a secondary phenomenon rather than a primary phenomenon?

A. Yes, very much so. In a sense Ego is wisdom, but Ego happens to be ignorant as well. You see, when you realise that you are ignorant, that is the beginning of the discovery of wisdom—it is wisdom itself.

Q. How does one decide in oneself whether Ego is ignorance or wisdom?

A. It is not really a question of deciding. It is simply that one sees in that way. You see, basically there is no solid substance, although we talk about Ego existing as a solid thing having various aspects. But in fact it merely lives through time as a continual process of creation. It is continually dying and being reborn all the time. Therefore Ego doesn't really exist. But Ego also acts as a kind of wisdom: when Ego dies, that is wisdom itself, and when Ego is first formulated that is the beginning of ignorance itself. So wisdom and Ego are not really separate at all. It seems rather difficult to define, and in a way one would be happier if there was clear-cut black and white, but somehow that is not the natural pattern of existence. There is no clear-cut black and white at all, and all things are interdependent. Darkness is an aspect of light, and light is an aspect of darkness, so one can't really condemn one side and build up everything on the other. It is left entirely to the individual to find his own way, and it is possible to do so. It is the same for a dog who has never swum—if he was suddenly thrown in the water he could swim. Similarly, we have a kind of spiritual instinct in us and if we are willing to open ourselves then somehow we find our way directly. It is only a question of opening up and one doesn't have to have a clear-cut definition at all.

Q. Would you care to sum up the purpose of meditation?

A. Well, meditation is dealing with purpose itself. It is not that meditation is for something, but it is dealing with the aim. Generally we have a purpose for whatever we do: something is going to happen in the future, therefore what I am doing now is important—everything is related to that. But the whole idea of meditation is to develop an entirely different way of dealing with things, where you have no purpose at all. In fact meditation is dealing with the question of whether nor not there is such a thing as purpose. And when one learns a different way of dealing with the situation, one no longer has to have a purpose. One is not on the way to somewhere. Or rather, one is on the way and one is also at the destination at the same time. That is really what meditation is for.

Q. Would you say, then, that it would be a merging with reality?

A. Yes, because reality is there all the time. Reality is not a separate entity, so it is a question of becoming one with reality, or of being in reality—not *achieving* oneness, but becoming identified with it. One is already a part of that reality, so all that remains is to take away the doubt. Then one discovers that one has been there all the time.

Q. Would it be correct to describe it as the realisation that the visible is not reality?

A. The visible? Can you define a bit more?

Q. I am thinking of William Blake's theory of the merging of the observer with the observed, and the visible not being the reality at all.

A. Visible things in this sense are reality. There is nothing beyond nowness, therefore what we see is reality. But because of our usual way of seeing things, we do not see them exactly as they are.

Q. Would you say, then, that each person is an individual and must find an individual way towards that?

A. Well, I think that brings us back to the question of Ego, which we have been talking about. You see, there is such a thing as personality, in a way, but we are not really individuals as separate from the environment, or as separate from external phenomena. That is why a different approach is necessary. Whereas, if we were individuals and had no connection with the rest of things, then there would be no need for a different technique which would lead to oneness. The point is that there is appearance of individuality, but this individuality is based on relativity. If there is individuality, there must also be oneness as well.

Q. Yes, but it is the individuality that makes for oneness. If we weren't individuals we couldn't be one. Is that so?

A. Well, the word "individual" is rather ambiguous. At the beginning individuality may be overemphasised, because there are various individual aspects. Even when we reach the stage of realisation there is perhaps an element of compassion, an element of wisdom, an element of energy and all sorts of different variations. But what we describe as an individual is something more than that. We tend to see it as one character with many things built onto it, which is a way of trying to find some sort of security. When there is wisdom, we try to load everything onto it, and it then becomes an entirely separate entity, a separate person—which is not so. But still there are individual aspects, there is individual character. So in Hinduism one finds different aspects of God, different deities and different symbols. When one attains oneness with reality, that reality is not just one single thing, but one can see from a very wide angle.

Q. If a student has a receptive mind and wishes to make himself at one with Nature, can he be taught how to mediate, or does he have to develop his own form?

A. Nature? How do you mean?

Q. If he wishes to study, can he accept other people's teaching, or can he develop them himself?

A. In fact it is necessary to receive oral instruction, oral teaching. Though he must learn to give before he can accept anything, he must learn to surrender. Secondly, he finds that the whole idea of learning stimulates his understanding. Also this avoids building up a great feeling of achievement, as though everything is "my own work"—the concept of the self-made man.

Q. Surely that is not sufficient reason for going to receive instruction from a teacher, just to avoid the feeling that otherwise everything is self-made. I mean, in the case of someone like Ramana Maharshi, who attained realisation without an external teacher, surely he shouldn't go and find a Guru just in case he might become big-headed?

A. No. But he is exceptional, that is the whole point. There is a way, it is possible. And basically no one can transmit or impart anything to anybody. One has to discover within oneself. So perhaps in certain cases people could do that. But building up on oneself is somehow similar to Ego's character, isn't it? One is on rather dangerous ground. It could easily become Ego's activity, because there is already the concept of "I" and then one wants to build up more on that side. I think—and this may sound simple, but it is really the whole thing—that one learns to surrender gradually, and that surrendering of the Ego is a very big subject. Also, the teacher acts as a kind of mirror, the teacher gives back one's own reflection. Then for the first time you are able to see how beautiful you are, or how ugly you are.

Perhaps I should mention here one or two small points about meditation, although we have already discussed the general background of the subject.

Generally, meditation instruction cannot be given in a class. There has to be a personal relationship between teacher and pupil. Also there are certain variations within each basic technique, such as awareness of breathing. But perhaps I should briefly mention the basic way of meditating, and then, if you want to go further, I am sure you could do so and receive further instruction from a meditation teacher.

As we have mentioned already, this meditation is not concerned with trying to develop concentration. Although many books on Buddhism speak of such practices as *Samatha* as being the development of concentration, I think this term is misleading in a way. One might get the idea that the practice of meditation could be put to commercial use, and that one would be able to concentrate on counting money or something like that. But meditation is not just for commercial uses, it is a different concept of concentration. You see, generally one cannot really concentrate. If one tries very hard to concentrate, then one needs the thought that is concentrating on the subject and also something which makes that accelerate further. Thus there are two processes involved and the second process is a kind of watchman, which makes sure that you are doing it properly. That part of it must be taken away, otherwise one ends up being more self-conscious and merely aware that one is concentrating, rather than actually being in a state of concentration. This becomes a vicious circle. Therefore one cannot develop concentration alone, without taking away the centralised watchfulness, the trying to be careful—which is Ego. So the *Samatha* practice, the awareness of breathing, is not concerned with concentrating on the breathing.

The cross-legged posture is the one generally adopted in the East, and if one can sit in that position, it is preferable to do so. Then one can train oneself to sit down and meditate anywhere, even in the middle of a field, and one need not feel conscious of having a seat or of trying to find something to sit on. Also, the physical posture does have a certain importance. For instance, if one lies down this might inspire one to sleep; if one stands one might be inclined to walk. But for those who find it difficult to sit cross-legged, sitting on a chair is quite good, and, in fact, in Buddhist iconography the posture of sitting on a chair is known as the *Maitreya asana*, so it is quite acceptable. The important thing is to keep the back straight so that there is no strain on the breathing. And for the breathing itself it is not a matter of concentrating, as we have already said, but of trying to become one with the feeling of breath. At the beginning some effort is needed, but after practising for a while the awareness is simply kept on the verge of the movement of breath; it just follows it quite naturally and one is not trying particularly to bind the mind to breathing. One tries to feel the breath—outbreathing, inbreathing, outbreathing, inbreathing—and it usually happens that the outbreathing is longer than the inbreathing, which helps one to become aware of space and the expansion of breathing outwards.

It is also very important to avoid becoming solemn and to avoid the feeling that one is taking part in some special ritual. One should feel quite natural and spontaneous, and simply try to identify oneself with the breath. That is all there is to it, and there are no ideas or analysing involved. Whenever thoughts arise, just observe them *as thoughts*, rather than as being a subject. What usually happens when we have thoughts is that we are not aware that they are thoughts at all. Supposing one is planning one's next holiday trip: one is so engrossed in the thoughts that it is almost as though one were already on the trip and one is not even aware that these are thoughts. Whereas, if one sees that this is merely thought creating such a picture, one begins to discover that it has a less real quality. One should not try to suppress thoughts in meditation, but one should just try to see the transitory nature, the translucent nature of thoughts. One should not become involved in them, nor reject them, but simply observe them and then come back to the awareness of breathing. The whole point is to cultivate the acceptance of everything, so one should not discriminate or become involved in any kind of struggle. That is the basic meditation technique, and it is quite simple and direct. There should be no deliberate effort, no attempt to control and no attempt to be peaceful. This is why breathing is used. It is easy to feel the breathing, and one has no need to be self-conscious or to try and do anything. The breathing is simply available and one should just feel that. That is the reason why technique is important to start with. This is the primary way of starting, but it generally continues and develops in its own way. One sometimes finds oneself doing it slightly differently from when one first started, quite spontaneously. This is not classified as an advanced technique or a beginner's technique. It simply grows and develops gradually.

Contemplative Prayer

Thomas Merton

Thomas Merton (1915–1968) was born in Prades, in Southern France. In 1941, he entered the Trappist Monastery at Gethsemani, Kentucky. Among his numerous and influential books are *The Seven Storey Mountain, Seeds of Contemplation,* and *Mystics and Zen Masters.* He died while visiting Bangkok in December 1968.

. . . We see that in meditation we should not look for a "method" or "system," but cultivate an "attitude," an "outlook": faith, openness, attention, reverence, expectation, supplication, trust, joy. All these finally permeate our being with love in so far as our living faith tells us we are in the presence of God, that we live in Christ, that in the Spirit of God we "see" God our Father without "seeing." We know him in "unknowing." Faith is the bond that unites us to him in the Spirit who gives us light and love.

Some people may doubtless have a spontaneous gift for meditative prayer. This is unusual today. Most men have to learn how to meditate. There are *ways* of meditation. But we should not expect to find magical methods, systems which make all difficulties and obstacles dissolve into thin air. Meditation is sometimes quite difficult. If we bear with hardship in prayer and wait patiently for the time of grace, we may well discover that meditation and prayer are very joyful experiences. We should not, however, judge the value of our meditation by "how we feel." A hard and apparently fruitless meditation may in fact be

From Thomas Merton, *Contemplative Prayer* (New York, 1969), pp. 39–49, 98–110. Reprinted by permission of Herder and Herder, the publisher.

much more valuable than one that is easy, happy, enlightened and apparently a big success.

There is a "movement" of meditation, expressing the basic "paschal" rhythm of the Christian life, the passage from death to life in Christ. Sometimes prayer, meditation and contemplation are "death"—a kind of descent into our own nothingness, a recognition of helplessness, frustration, infidelity, confusion, ignorance. Note how common this theme is in the Psalms.[1] If we need help in meditation we can turn to scriptural texts that express this profound distress of man in his nothingness and his total need of God. Then as we determine to face the hard realities of our inner life, as we recognize once again that we need to pray hard and humbly for faith, he draws us out of darkness into light—he hears us, answers our prayer, recognizes our need, and grants us the help we require—if only by giving us more faith to believe that he can and will help us in his own time. This is already a sufficient answer.

This alternation of darkness and light can constitute a kind of dialogue between the Christian and God, a dialectic that brings us deeper and deeper into the conviction that God is our all. By such alternations we grow in detachment and in hope. We should realize the great good that is to be gained only by this fidelity to meditation. A new realm opens up, that cannot be discovered otherwise: call it the "Kingdom of God." Any effort and sacrifice should be made in order to enter this Kingdom. Such sacrifices are amply compensated for by the results, even when the results are not clear and evident to us. But effort is necessary, *enlightened, well-directed* and *sustained*.

Right away we confront one of the problems of the life of prayer: that of learning when one's efforts are enlightened and well-directed, and when they spring simply from our confused velleities and our immature desires. It would be a mistake to suppose that mere good will is, by itself, a sufficient guarantee that all our efforts will finally attain to a good result. Serious mistakes can be made, even with the greatest good will. Certain temptations and delusions are to be regarded as a normal part of the life of prayer, and when a person thinks he has attained to a certain facility in contemplation, he may find himself getting all kinds of strange ideas and he may, what is more, cling to them with a fierce dedication, convinced that they are supernatural graces and signs of God's blessing upon his efforts when, in fact, they simply show that he has gone off the right track and is perhaps in rather serious danger.

For this reason, humility and docile acceptance of sound advice are very necessary in the life of prayer. Though spiritual direction may not be necessary in the ordinary Christian life, and though a religious may be able to get along to some extent without it (many have to!), it becomes a moral necessity for anyone who is trying to deepen his life of prayer. Hence the traditional importance, in monastic life, of the "spiritual father," who may be the abbot or another experienced monk capable of guiding the beginner in the ways of prayer, and of immediately detecting any sign of misguided zeal and wrong-headed effort. Such a one should be listened to and obeyed, especially when he cautions against the use of certain methods and practices, which he sees to be out of place and harmful in a particular case, or when he declines to accept certain "experiences" as evidence of progress.

[1] See, for instance, Psalms 56, 39, etc.

The right use of effort is determined by the indications of God's will and of his grace. When one is simply obeying God, a little effort goes a long way. When one is in fact resisting him (though claiming to have no other intention than that of fulfilling his will) no amount of effort can produce a good result. On the contrary, the stubborn ability to go on resisting God in spite of ever clearer indications of his will, is a sign that one is in great spiritual danger. Often the one who is concerned will not be able to see this himself. This is another reason why a spiritual father may be really necessary.

The work of the spiritual father consists not so much in teaching us a secret and infallible method for attaining to esoteric experiences, but in showing us how to recognize God's grace and his will, how to be humble and patient, how to develop insight into our own difficulties, and how to remove the main obstacles keeping us from becoming men of prayer.

Those obstacles may have very deep roots in our character, and in fact we may eventually learn that a whole lifetime will barely be sufficient for their removal. For example, many people who have a few natural gifts and a little ingenuity tend to imagine that they can quite easily learn, by their own cleverness, to master the methods—one might say the "tricks"—of the spiritual life. The only trouble is that in the spiritual life there are no tricks and no short cuts. Those who imagine that they can discover special gimmicks and put them to work for themselves usually ignore God's will and his grace. They are self-confident and even self-complacent. They make up their minds that they are going to attain to this or that, and try to write their own ticket in the life of contemplation. They may even appear to succeed to some extent. But certain systems of spirituality—notably Zen Buddhism—place great stress on a severe, no-nonsense style of direction that makes short work of this kind of confidence. One cannot begin to face the real difficulties of the life of prayer and meditation unless one is first perfectly content to be a beginner and really experience himself as one knows little or nothing, and has a desperate need to learn the bare rudiments. Those who think they "know" from the beginning will never, in fact, come to know anything.

People who try to pray and meditate above their proper level, who are too eager to reach what they believe to be "a high degree of prayer," get away from the truth and from reality. In observing themselves and trying to convince themselves of their advance, they become imprisoned in themselves. Then when they realize that grace has left them they are caught in their own emptiness and futility and remain helpless. *Acedia* follows the enthusiasm of pride and spiritual vanity. A long course in humility and compunction is the remedy!

We do not want to be beginners. But let us be convinced of the fact that we will never be anything else but beginners, all our life!

Another obstacle—and perhaps this one is more common—is spiritual inertia, inner confusion, coldness, lack of confidence. This may be the case of those who, after having made a satisfactory beginning, experience the inevitable let-down which comes when the life of meditation gets to be serious. What at first seemed easy and rewarding suddenly comes to be utterly impossible. The mind will not work. One cannot concentrate on anything. The imagination and the emotions wander away. Sometimes they run wild. At this point, perhaps, in the midst of a prayer that is dry, desolate and repugnant, unconscious fantasies may take over. These may be unpleasant and even frightening. More often, one's inner life simply becomes a desert which lacks all interest whatever.

This may no doubt be explained as a passing trial (the "night of the senses") but we must face the fact that it is often more serious than that. It may be the result of a wrong start, in which (due to the familiar jargon of books on prayer and the ascetic life) a cleavage has appeared, dividing the "inner life" from the rest of one's existence. In this case, the supposed "inner life" may actually be nothing but a brave and absurd attempt to evade reality altogether. Under the pretext that what is "within" is in fact real, spiritual, supernatural, etc., one cultivates neglect and contempt for the "external" as wordly, sensual, material and opposed to grace. This is bad theology and bad asceticism. In fact it is bad in every respect, because instead of accepting reality as it is, we reject it in order to explore some perfect realm of abstract ideals which in fact has no reality at all. Very often, the inertia and repugnance which characterize the so-called "spiritual life" of many Christians could perhaps be cured by a simple respect of the concrete realities of every-day life, for nature, for the body, for one's work, one's friends, one's surroundings, etc. A false supernaturalism which imagines that "the supernatural" is a kind of Platonic realm of abstract essences totally apart from and opposed to the concrete world of nature, offers no real support to a genuine life of meditation and prayer. Meditation has no point and no reality unless it is firmly rooted in *life*. Without such roots, it can produce nothing but the ashen fruits of disgust, *acedia*, and even morbid and degenerate introversion, masochism, dolorism, negation. Nietzsche pitilessly exposed the hopeless mess which results from this caricature of Christianity![2]

Beginners may get off to another kind of false start, which ends up in a mixture of presumption and inertia. Having learned to enjoy some of the fruits of the spiritual life and having tasted some little success, when this is all lost to them they start looking around for reasons. They are convinced that someone is "to blame" and since they see no reason to blame themselves (for after all, perhaps it is not a matter of anyone being "to blame") they look for an explanation in the monastic society in which they live. Now we must admit that with monasticism in a full crisis of renewal, with all observances and even ideals called into question every day, there is no difficulty in finding things to criticize. The fact that the criticisms may have some basis does not, however, make them in every case entirely reasonable; especially when the criticism is purely negative and is resorted to principally as an outlet for frustration and resentment.

Many of the obstacles to the life of thought and love which is meditation come from the fact that people insist on walling themselves up inside themselves in order to cherish their own thoughts and their own experiences as a kind of private treasure. They misinterpret the gospel parable of the talents, and as a result they bury their talent in a napkin instead of putting it to work and increasing it. Even when we come to live a contemplative life, the love of others and openness to others remain, as in the active life, the condition for a living and fruitful inner life of thought and love. The love of others is a stimulus to interior life, not a danger to it, as some mistakenly believe.

Abbé Monchanin, a great contemplative of our time, a French priest who went to found a Christian ashram in southern India, said:

---

[2] See Emmanuel Mounier, *The Spoils of the Violent*.

Let us keep alive the flame of thought and love: they are one and the same flame. Let us communicate to those around us the desire to understand and to give (and also to receive). There are too many walled-up consciences.[3]

Many serious and good monks, idealists, desire to make of their lives a work of art according to an approved pattern. This brings with it an instinct to study themselves, to shape their lives, to remodel themselves, to tune and re-tune all their inner dispositions—and this results in full-time meditation and contemplation of *themselves*. They may unfortunately find this so delightful and absorbing that they lose all interest in the invisible and unpredictable action of grace. In a word, they seek to build their own security, to avoid the *risk* and *dread* implied by submission to the unknown mystery of God's will.

Other obstacles:

Discouragement—we lose all confidence, become secretly convinced that we cannot get anywhere in prayer. In reality this too can be due to fatal subjectivism, which may have led us in the past to seek the wrong results—the cultivation of feelings and "fulfillment" on an immature level. There is danger of psychological regression here. If we are prepared to go forward, to *lose ourselves*, there is no need for discouragement. The remedy—*hope*.

Confusion, helplessness—a sense of incapacity again due to abuse of subjectivism—imprisoned in ourselves we become paralyzed. The way out is *faith*. What can we do about all these obstacles? The New Testament does not offer us techniques and expedients: it tells us to turn to God, to depend on his grace, to realize that the Spirit is given to us, wholly, in Christ. That he prays in us when we do not know how to pray:

If the Spirit of him who raised Jesus from the dead dwells in you, he who raised Christ Jesus from the dead will give life to your mortal bodies also through his Spirit which dwells in you. . . . For all who are led by the Spirit of God are sons of God. For you did not receive the spirit of slavery to fall back into fear, but you have received the spirit of sonship. When we cry "Abba! Father!" it is the Spirit himself bearing witness with our spirit that we are children of God. . . . Likewise the Spirit helps us in our weakness; for we do not know how to pray as we ought, but the Spirit himself intercedes for us with sighs too deep for words. And he who searches the hearts of men knows what is the mind of the Spirit, because the Spirit intercedes for the saints according to the will of God.[4]

The activity of the Spirit within us becomes more and more important as we progress in the life of interior prayer. It is true that our own efforts remain necessary, at least as long as they are not entirely superseded by the action of God "in us and without us" (according to a traditional expression). But more and more our efforts attain a new orientation: instead of being directed toward ends we have chosen ourselves, instead of being measured by the profit and pleasure we judge they will produce, they are more and more directed to an obedient and cooperative submission to grace, which implies first of all an increasingly attentive and receptive attitude toward the hidden action of the Holy Spirit. It is precisely the function of meditation, in the sense in which we speak of it here, to bring us to this attitude of awareness and receptivity. It also gives

[3] *Ecrits Spirituels*, p. 125.
[4] Romans 8 : 11, 14–16, 26–27.

us strength and hope, along with a deep awareness of the value of interior silence
in which the mystery of God's love is made clear to us.

.   .   .

Meditation is not merely the intellectual effort to master certain *ideas about
God* or even to impress upon our minds the mysteries of our Catholic faith.
Conceptual knowledge of religious truth has a definite place in our life, and that
place is an important one. Study plays an essential part in the life of prayer.
The spiritual life needs strong intellectual foundations. The study of theology
is a necessary accompaniment to a life of meditation. But meditation itself is not
"study" and is not a purely intellectual activity. The purpose of meditation is
not merely to acquire or to deepen objective and speculative knowledge of God
and of the truth revealed by him.

In meditation we do not seek to know *about* God as though he were an
object like other objects which submit to our scrutiny and can be expressed in
clear scientific ideas. We seek to know God himself, beyond the level of all the
objects which he has made and which confront us as "things" isolated from one
another, "defined," "delimited," with clear boundaries. The infinite God has
no boundaries and our minds cannot set limits to him or to his love. His presence
is then "grasped" in the general awareness of loving faith, it is "realized"
without being scientifically and precisely known, as we know a specimen under
a microscope. His presence cannot be verified as we would verify a laboratory
experiment. Yet it can be spiritually realized as long as we do not insist on
verifying it. As soon as we try to verify the spiritual presence as an object of
exact knowledge, God eludes us.

Returning to the classical passages of St. John of the Cross on the "dark
night" of contemplation, we see that his doctrine about faith is often mis-
represented. To some readers, he seems to be saying no more than that if you
turn away from sensible and visible objects, you will come to see invisible objects.
This is Neoplatonism, not the doctrine of St. John of the Cross. On the contrary,
he teaches that the soul

> . . . must not only be in darkness with respect to that part that concerns the creatures and temporal
> things . . . but likewise it must be blinded and darkened according to the part which has respect
> to God and spiritual things, which is the rational and higher part. . . . It must be like to a blind man
> leaning upon dark faith, taking it for guide and light, and leaning upon none of the things that he
> understands, experiences, feels and imagines. For all these are darkness and will cause him to
> stray; and faith is above all that he understands, experiences, feels and imagines. And if he be not
> blinded as to this, and remain not in total darkness, he attains not to that which is greater—namely,
> that which is taught by faith.[5]

Once again, however, this darkness is not merely negative. It brings with it
an enlightenment which escapes the investigation and control of the understanding. "For who shall prevent God from doing that which he wills in the
soul that is resigned, annihilated and detached?"[6]

This teaching of St. John of the Cross is not to be set aside merely as a peculiar
form of "Carmelite spirituality." It is in the direct line of ancient monastic and
patristic tradition, from Evagrius Ponticus, Cassian and Gregory of Nyssa on

[5] *Ascent of Mount Carmel*, II, iv, 2.
[6] *Ibid.*

down through Gregory the Great and the followers of Pseudo-Dionysius in the West.

St. John Chrysostom writes of the "incomprehensibility of God":

Let us invoke him as the inexpressible God, incomprehensible, invisible and unknowable; let us avow that he surpasses all power of human speech, that he eludes the grasp of every mortal intelligence, that the angels cannot penetrate him nor the seraphim see him in full clarity, nor the cherubim fully understand him, for he is invisible to the principalities and powers, the virtues and all creatures without exception; only the Son and the Holy Spirit know him.[7]

St. Gregory of Nyssa describes the "mystical night":

Night designates the contemplation (theoria) *of invisible things after the manner of Moses who entered into the darkness where God was, this God who makes of darkness his hiding place.*[8] *Surrounded by the divine night the soul seeks him who is hidden in darkness.* She possesses indeed the love of him *whom she seeks, but the Beloved escapes the grasp of her thoughts. . . .* Therefore abandoning the search *she recognizes him whom she desires by the very fact that his knowledge is beyond understanding. Thus she says, "Having left behind all created things and abandoned the aid of the understanding, by faith alone I have found my Beloved. And I will not let him go, holding him with the grip of faith, until he enters into my bedchamber." The Chamber is the* heart, which is capable *of the indwelling when it is restored to its primitive state.*[9]

And Evagrius says (in the *Treatise on Prayer*, long attributed to St. Nilus): "Just as the light that shows us all has no need of another light in order to be seen, so God, who shows us all things, has no need of a light in which we may see him, for he is himself light by essence,"[10] and "See no diversity in yourself when you pray, and let your intelligence take on the impression of no form; but go immaterially to the immaterial and you will understand. . . . Aspiring to see the face of the Father who is in heaven, seek for nothing in the world to see a form or figure at the time of prayer."[11]

Returning to the mystics of the Rhineland we find John Tauler saying typically: "All that a man rests in with joy, all that he retains as a good belonging to himself is all worm-eaten except for absolute and simple vanishing in the pure, unknowable, ineffable and mysterious good which is God, by renunciation of ourselves and of all that can appear in him."

And Ruysbroeck:

The interior man enters into himself in a simple manner, above all activity and all values, to apply himself to a simple gaze in fruitive love. There he encounters God without intermediary. And from the unity of God there shines into him a simple light. This simple light shows itself to be darkness nakedness and nothingness. In this darkness, the man is enveloped and he plunges in a state without modes, in which he is lost. In nakedness, all consideration and distraction of things escape him, and he is informed and penetrated by a simple light. In nothingness he sees all his works come to nothing, for he is overwhelmed by the activity of God's immense love, and by the fruitive inclination of his Spirit he . . . becomes one spirit with God.[12]

---

[7] *Incomprehensibility of God*, III, p. 166.
[8] Psalm 17 : 12.
[9] P.G. 44 : 892–893.
[10] See Hausherr, *Les Leçons d'un Contemplatif* (Paris, 1960), p. 145.
[11] *Ibid.*
[12] *The Adornment of the Spiritual Marriage*, II.

The doctrine of purity of heart and "imageless" contemplation is summed up in the *Philokalia*: "That heart is pure which, always presenting to God a formless and imageless memory, is ready to receive nothing but impressions which come from him and by which he is wont to desire to become manifest to it."[13]

In a word, God is invisibly present to the ground of our being: our belief and love attain to him, but he remains hidden from the arrogant gaze of our investigating mind which seeks to capture him and secure permanent possession of him in an act of knowledge that gives *power over him*. It is in fact absurd and impossible to try to grasp God as an object which can be seized and comprehended by our minds.

The knowledge of which we are capable is simply knowledge *about* him. It points to him in analogies which we must transcend in order to reach him. But we must transcend ourselves as well as our analogies, and in seeking to know him we must forget the familiar subject-object relationship which characterizes our ordinary acts of knowing. Instead we know him in so far as we become aware of ourselves as known through and through by him. We "possess" him in proportion as we realize ourselves to be possessed by him in the inmost depths of our being. Meditation or "prayer of the heart" is the active effort we make to keep our hearts open so that we may be enlightened by him and filled with this realization of our true relation to him. Therefore the classic form of "meditation" is repetitive invocation of the names of Jesus in the heart emptied of images and cares.

Hence the aim of meditation, in the context of Christian faith, is not to arrive at an objective and apparently "scientific" knowledge about God, but to come to know him through the realization that our very being is penetrated with his knowledge and love for us. Our knowledge of God is paradoxically a knowledge not of him as the object of our scrutiny, but of ourselves as utterly dependent on his saving and merciful knowledge of us. It is in proportion as we are known to him that we find our real being and identity in Christ. We know him in and through ourselves in so far as his truth is the source of our being and his merciful love is the very heart of our life and existence. We have no other reason for being, except to be loved by him as our Creator and Redeemer, and to love him in return. There is no true knowledge of God that does not imply a profound grasp and an intimate personal acceptance of this profound relationship.

The whole purpose of meditation is to deepen the consciousness of this basic relationship of the creature to the Creator, and of the sinner to his Redeemer.

It has been said above that the doctrine of mystical "unknowing," by which we ascend to the knowledge of God "as unseen" without "form or figure" beyond all images and indeed all concepts, must not be misunderstood as a mere turning away from the ideas of material things to ideas of the immaterial. The mystical knowledge of God, which already begins in a certain inchoative manner in living faith, is not a knowledge of immaterial and invisible essences as distinct from the visible and material. If in a certain sense *nothing* that we can see or understand can give us a fully adequate idea of God (except by remote analogy), then we can say that images and symbols and even the material which enters into sacramental signs and works of art regain a certain dignity in their own right,

---

[13] Kadloubovsky and Palmer, *Writings from the Philikalia* (London, 1957), p. 23.

since they are no longer rejected in favor of other "immaterial" objects which are considered to be superior, as if they were capable of making us "see" God more perfectly. On the contrary, since we are well aware that images, symbols and works of art are only material, we tend to use them with greater freedom and less risk of error precisely because we realize the limitations of their nature. We know that they can only be means to an end, and we do not make "idols" out of them. On the contrary, today the more dangerous temptation is to raise ideas and ideologies to the status of "idols," worshipping them for their own sakes.

So we can say here, if only in passing, that image, symbol, art, rite and of course the sacraments above all, rightly and properly bring material things into the life of prayer and meditation, using them as means to enter more deeply into prayer. Denis de Rougement has called art "a calculated trap for meditation." The aesthetic aspect of the life of worship must not be neglected, especially today when we are barely recovering from an era of abomination and desolation in sacred art, due in part to a kind of manichaean attitude toward natural beauty on the one hand, and a rationalistic neglect of sensible things on the other. So, all that has been said above in quotations from St. John of the Cross and other doctors of Christian mysticism about "dark contemplation" and "the night of sense" must not be misinterpreted to mean that the normal culture of the senses, of artistic taste, of imagination, and of intelligence should be formally renounced by anyone interested in a life of meditation and prayer. On the contrary, such culture is *presupposed*. One cannot go beyond what one has not yet attained, and normally the realization that God is "beyond images, symbols and ideas" dawns only on one who has previously made a good use of all these things, who has a thorough and mature "monastic culture,"[14] and having reached the limit of symbol and idea goes on to a further stage in which he does without them, at least temporarily. For even if these human and symbolic helps to prayer lose their usefulness in the higher forms of contemplative union with God, they still have their place in the ordinary everyday life even of the contemplative. They form part of the environment and cultural atmosphere in which he usually lives.

The function of image, symbol, poetry, music, chant, and of ritual (remotely related to sacred dance) is to open up the inner self of the contemplative, to incorporate the senses and the body in the totality of the self-orientation to God that is necessary for worship and for meditation. Simply to neglect the senses and body altogether, and merely to let the imagination go its own way, while attempting to plunge into a deeply abstracted interior prayer, will end in no result even for one who is proficient in meditation.

All religious traditions have ways of integrating the senses, on their own level, into higher forms of prayer. The greatest mystical literature speaks not only of "darkness" and "unknowing" but also, and almost in the same breath, of an extraordinary flowering of "spiritual senses" and aesthetic awareness

[14] The term "monastic culture" is beginning to be seriously discussed today. It implies the development of a set of tastes and skills, of openness to certain specifically monastic values in all the arts and disciplines that have relation to the monastic life in all its fullness. One could say for example that for a twentieth-century Christian monk, "monastic culture" would imply not only an education in all that is living and relevant in monastic theology, tradition, and literature, as well as art, architecture, poetry, etc., but also in other religious cultures. Hence a certain knowledge of Zen, of Sufism, of Hinduism can rightly claim a place in the monastic culture of the modern monk of the West.

underlying and interpreting the higher and more direct union with God "beyond experience." In fact, what is beyond experience has to be mediated, in some way, and interpreted in the ordinary language of human thought before it can be deeply reflected upon by the subject himself, and before it can be communicated to others. Of course, there is no denying that one may enter into deep contemplative prayer without being able to reflect on it, still less communicate anything whatever of the experience to others. But in mystical literature, which obviously implies communication through images, symbols and ideas, we find that contemplation in "unknowing" is generally accompanied by unusual poetic and theological gifts, whenever the fruit of contemplation is to be shared with others.

We find St. John of the Cross, for instance, describing the "Living Flame of Love" in very concrete and beautiful language which obviously reflects an even more concrete and beautiful experience which is here translated into symbolic terms. But he says without any ambiguity that what he is describing is "the savor of eternal life" and "an experience of the life of God" and the activity of the Holy Spirit. He says:

How can we say that this flame wounds the soul, when there is nothing in the soul to be wounded, since it is wholly consumed by the fire of love? It is a marvelous thing: for, as love is never idle, but is continually in motion, it is continually throwing out sparks, like a flame, in every direction; and, as the office of love is to wound, that it may enkindle with love and cause delight, so, when it is as it were a living flame, within the soul, it is ever sending forth its arrow-wounds, like most tender sparks of delicate love, joyfully and happily exercising the arts and wiles of love. Even so, in his palace, at his marriage, did Ahasuerus show forth his graces to Esther his bride, revealing to her there his riches and the glory of his greatness. Thus that which the Wise Man said in Proverbs is now fulfilled in this soul, namely: I was delighted every day as I played before him always, playing over the whole earth, and my delight is to be with the sons of men, namely, by giving myself to them. Wherefore these wounds, which are the playing of God, are the sparks of these tender touches of flame which touch the soul intermittently and proceed from the fire of love, which is not idle, but whose flames, says the stanza, strike and wound

My soul in its deepest center.

For this feast of the Holy Spirit takes place in the substance of the soul, where neither the devil nor the world nor sense can enter; and therefore the more interior it is, the more it is secure, substantial and delectable; for the more interior it is the purer is it, and the more of purity there is in it, the more abundantly and frequently and widely does God communicate himself. And thus the delight and rejoicing of the soul and the spirit is the greater herein because it is God that works all this and the soul of its own power does naught therein; for the soul can do naught of itself, save through the bodily senses and by their help, from which in this case the soul is very free and very far removed; its only work is to receive God in the depths of the soul, who alone, without the aid of the senses, can move the soul in that which it does.[15]

When St. John of the Cross himself says that we must not attempt to attain to union with God by trying to conjure up images of such experiences in our hearts, he is obviously not invalidating what he has said in an attempt to communicate an experience of God *after* the fact. He is on the contrary trying to protect his reader against an egocentric and spiritually blind manipulation of images and concepts in order to attain to a supposed knowledge of God as an object which the mind of man can understand and enjoy on intellectual and

[15] *Living Flame of Love*, I, 8–9.

aesthetic terms. There is indeed a certain kind of knowledge of God attained by images and reasoning but this is not at all the kind of experiential knowledge that St. John of the Cross describes. Indeed, the use of image and concept can become very dangerous in a climate of egocentricity and false mysticism.

The dangerous abuse of image and symbol is seen, for example, in the case of someone who tries to conjure up the "living flame" by an exercise of will, imagination and desire, and then persuades himself that he has "experienced God." In such a case, this obvious fabrication would be paid for dearly, because there is all the difference in the world between the *fruits* of genuine religious experience, a pure gift of God, and the results of mere imagination. As Jakob Boehme bluntly said: "Where does it stand in Scripture that a harlot can become a virgin by issuing a decree?"

The living experience of divine love and the Holy Spirit in the "flame" of which St. John of the Cross is speaking is a true awareness that one has died and risen in Christ. It is an experience of mystical renewal, an inner transformation brought about entirely by the power of God's merciful love, implying the "death" of the self-centered and self-sufficient ego and the appearance of a new and liberated self who lives and acts "in the Spirit." But if the old self, the calculating and autonomous ego, merely seeks to imitate the effects of such regeneration, for its own satisfaction and advantage, the effect is exactly the opposite—the ego seeks to confirm itself in its own selfish existence. The grain of wheat has not fallen into the ground and died. It remains hard, isolated and dry and there is no fruit at all, only a lying and blasphemous boast—a ridiculous pretense! If lying and fabrication are psychologically harmful even in ordinary relations with other men (a sphere where a certain amount of falsification is not uncommon) all falsity is disastrous in any relation with the ground of our own being and with God himself, who communicates with us through our own inner truth. To falsify our inner truth under pretext of entering into union with God would be a most tragic infidelity to ourselves first of all, to life, to reality itself, and of course to God. Such fabrications end in the dislocation of one's entire moral and intellectual existence.

Instruction in Self-discovery: An Example

Carlos Castaneda

Carlos Castaneda (1931–   ) teaches in the department of anthropology at UCLA. While doing graduate work in anthropology, he spent five years in Mexico as a student of a Yaqui Indian teacher and has written two celebrated books about his experiences with don Juan: *The Teachings of Don Juan* and *A Separate Reality.*

Sunday, June 25, 1961

I stayed with don Juan all afternoon on Friday. I was going to leave about 7 P.M. We were sitting on the porch in front of his house and I decided to ask him once more about the teaching. It was almost a routine question and I expected him to refuse again. I asked him if there was a way in which he could accept just my desire to learn, as if I were an Indian. He took a long time to answer. I was compelled to stay because he seemed to be trying to decide something.

Finally he told me that there was a way, and proceeded to delineate a problem. He pointed out that I was very tired sitting on the floor, and that the proper thing to do was to find a "spot" (*sitio*) on the floor where I could sit without fatigue. I had been sitting with my knees up against my chest and my arms locked around my calves. When he said I was tired, I realized that my back ached and that I was quite exhausted.

I waited for him to explain what he meant by a "spot," but he made no overt attempt to elucidate the point. I thought that perhaps he meant that I should change positions, so I got up and sat closer to him. He protested my movement and clearly emphasized that a spot meant a place where a man could feel naturally happy and strong. He patted the place where he sat and said it was his own spot, adding that he had posed a riddle I had to solve by myself without any further deliberation.

What he had posed as a problem to be solved was certainly a riddle. I had no idea how to begin or even what he had in mind. Several times I asked for a clue, or at least a hint, as to how to proceed in locating a point where I felt happy and strong. I insisted and argued that I had no idea what he really meant because I couldn't conceive the problem. He suggested I walk around the porch until I found the spot.

I got up and began to pace the floor. I felt silly and sat down in front of him.

He became very annoyed with me and accused me of not listening, saying that perhaps I did not want to learn. After a while he calmed down and explained

From Carlos Castaneda, *The Teachings of Don Juan: A Yaqui Way of Knowledge* (Berkeley, Calif., 1968), pp. 14–34. Originally published by the University of California Press; reprinted by permission of The Regents of the University of California.

to me that not every place was good to sit or be on, and that within the confines of the porch there was one spot that was unique, a spot where I could be at my very best. It was my task to distinguish it from all the other places. The general pattern was that I had to "feel" all the possible spots that were accessible until I could determine without a doubt which was the right one.

I argued that although the porch was not too large (12 × 8 feet), the number of possible spots was overwhelming, and it would take me a very long time to check all of them, and that since he had not specified the size of the spot, the possibilities might be infinite. My arguments were futile. He got up and very sternly warned me that it might take me days to figure it out, but that if I did not solve the problem, I might as well leave because he would have nothing to say to me. He emphasized that he knew where my spot was, and that therefore I could not lie to him; he said this was the only way he could accept my desire to learn about Mescalito as a valid reason. He added that nothing in his world was a gift, that whatever there was to learn had to be learned the hard way.

He went around the house to the chaparral to urinate. He returned directly into his house through the back.

I thought the assignment to find the alleged spot of happiness was his own way of dismissing me, but I got up and started to pace back and forth. The sky was clear. I could see everything on and near the porch. I must have paced for an hour or more, but nothing happened to reveal the location of the spot. I got tired of walking and sat down; after a few minutes I sat somewhere else, and then at another place, until I had covered the whole floor in a semisystematic fashion. I deliberately tried to "feel" differences between places, but I lacked the criteria for differentiation. I felt I was wasting my time, but I stayed. My rationalization was that I had come a long way just to see don Juan, and I really had nothing else to do.

I lay down on my back and put my hands under my head like a pillow. Then I rolled over and lay on my stomach for a while. I repeated this rolling process over the entire floor. For the first time I thought I had stumbled upon a vague criterion. I felt warmer when I lay on my back.

I rolled again, this time in the opposite direction, and again covered the length of the floor, lying face down on all the places where I had lain face up during my first rolling tour. I experienced the same warm and cold sensations, depending on my position, but there was no difference between spots.

Then an idea occurred to me which I thought to be brilliant: don Juan's spot! I sat there, and then lay, face down at first, and later on my back, but the place was just like all the others. I stood up. I had had enough. I wanted to say good-bye to don Juan, but I was embarrassed to wake him up. I looked at my watch. It was two o'clock in the morning! I had been rolling for six hours.

At that moment don Juan came out and went around the house to the chaparral. He came back and stood at the door. I felt utterly dejected, and I wanted to say something nasty to him and leave. But I realized that it was not his fault; that it was my own choice to go through all that nonsense. I told him I had failed; I had been rolling on his floor like an idiot all night and still couldn't make any sense of his riddle.

He laughed and said that it did not surprise him because I had not proceeded correctly. I had not been using my eyes. That was true, yet I was very sure he had said to feel the difference. I brought that point up, but he argued that one can feel with the eyes, when the eyes are not looking right into things. As far as I was concerned, he said, I had no other means to solve this problem but to use all I had—my eyes.

He went inside. I was certain that he had been watching me. I thought there was no other way for him to know that I had not been using my eyes.

I began to roll again, because that was the most comfortable procedure. This time, however, I rested my chin on my hands and looked at every detail.

After an interval the darkness around me changed. When I focused on the point directly in front of me, the whole peripheral area of my field of vision became brilliantly colored with a homogeneous greenish yellow. The effect was startling. I kept my eyes fixed on the point in front of me and began to crawl sideways on my stomach, one foot at a time.

Suddenly, at a point near the middle of the floor, I became aware of another change in hue. At a place to my right, still in the periphery of my field of vision, the greenish yellow became intensely purple. I concentrated my attention on it. The purple faded into a pale, but still brilliant, color which remained steady for the time I kept my attention on it.

I marked the place with my jacket, and called don Juan. He came out to the porch. I was truly excited; I had actually seen the change in hues. He seemed unimpressed, but told me to sit on the spot and report to him what kind of feeling I had.

I sat down and then lay on my back. He stood by me and asked me repeatedly how I felt; but I did not feel anything different. For about fifteen minutes I tried to feel or to see a difference, while don Juan stood by me patiently. I felt disgusted. I had a metallic taste in my mouth. Suddenly I had developed a head-ache. I was about to get sick. The thought of my nonsensical endeavours irritated me to a point of fury. I got up.

Don Juan must have noticed my profound frustration. He did not laugh, but very seriously stated that I had to be inflexible with myself if I wanted to learn. Only two choices were open to me, he said: either to quit and go home, in which case I would never learn, or to solve the riddle.

He went inside again. I wanted to leave immediately, but I was too tired to drive; besides, perceiving the hues had been so startling that I was sure it was a criterion of some sort, and perhaps there were other changes to be detected. Anyway, it was too late to leave. So I sat down, stretched my legs back, and began all over again.

During this round I moved rapidly through each place, passing don Juan's spot, to the end of the floor, and then turned around to cover the outer edge. When I reached the center, I realized that another change in coloration was taking place, again on the edge of my field of vision. The uniform chartreuse I was seeing all over the area turned, at one spot to my right, into a sharp verdigris. It remained for a moment and then abruptly metamorphosed into another steady hue, different from the other one I had detected earlier. I took off one of my shoes and marked the point, and kept on rolling until I had covered the floor in all possible directions. No other change of coloration took place.

I came back to the point marked with my shoe, and examined it. It was located five to six feet away from the spot marked by my jacket, in a south-easterly direction. There was a large rock next to it. I lay down there for quite some time trying to find clues, looking at every detail, but I did not feel anything different.

I decided to try the other spot. I quickly pivoted on my knees and was about to lie down on my jacket when I felt an unusual apprehension. It was more like a physical sensation of something actually pushing on my stomach. I jumped up and retreated in one movement. The hair on my neck pricked up. My legs had arched slightly, my trunk was bent forward, and my arms stuck out in front of me rigidly with my fingers contracted like a claw. I took notice of my strange posture and my fright increased.

I walked back involuntarily and sat down on the rock next to my shoe. From the rock, I slumped to the floor. I tried to figure out what had happened to cause me such a fright. I thought it must have been the fatigue I was experiencing. It was nearly daytime. I felt silly and embarrassed. Yet I had no way to explain what had frightened me, nor had I figured out what don Juan wanted.

I decided to give it one last try. I got up and slowly approached the place marked by my jacket, and again I felt the same apprehension. This time I made a strong effort to control myself. I sat down, and then knelt in order to lie face down, but I could not lie in spite of my will. I put my hands on the floor in front of me. My breathing accelerated; my stomach was upset. I had a clear sensation of panic, and fought not to run away. I thought don Juan was perhaps watching me. Slowly I crawled back to the other spot and propped my back against the rock. I wanted to rest for a while to organize my thoughts, but I fell asleep.

I heard don Juan talking and laughing above my head. I woke up.

"You have found the spot," he said.

I did not understand him at first, but he assured me again that the place where I had fallen asleep was the spot in question. He again asked me how I felt lying there. I told him I really did not notice any difference.

He asked me to compare my feelings at that moment with what I had felt while lying on the other spot. For the first time it occurred to me that I could not possibly explain my apprehension of the preceding night. He urged me in a kind of challenging way to sit on the other spot. For some inexplicable reason I was actually afraid of the other place, and did not sit on it. He asserted that only a fool could fail to see the difference.

I asked him if each of the two spots had a special name. He said that the good one was called the *sitio* and the bad one the enemy; he said these two places were the key to a man's well-being, especially for a man who was pursuing knowledge. The sheer act of sitting on one's spot created superior strength; on the other hand, the enemy weakened a man and could even cause his death. He said I had replenished my energy, which I had spent lavishly the night before, by taking a nap on my spot.

He also said that the colors I had seen in association with each specific spot had the same overall effect either of giving strength or of curtailing it.

I asked him if there were other spots for me like the two I had found, and how I should go about finding them. He said that many places in the world would be comparable to those two, and that the best way to find them was by detecting their respective colors.

It was not clear to me whether or not I had solved the problem, and in fact I was not even convinced that there had been a problem; I could not avoid feeling that the whole experience was forced and arbitrary. I was certain that don Juan had watched me all night and then proceeded to humor me by saying that wherever I had fallen asleep *was* the place I was looking for. Yet I failed to see a logical reason for such an act, and when he challenged me to sit on the other spot I could not do it. There was a strange cleavage between my pragmatic experience of fearing the "other spot" and my rational deliberations about the total event.

Don Juan, on the other hand, was very sure I had succeeded, and, acting in accordance with my success, let me know he was going to teach me about peyote.

"You asked me to teach you about Mescalito," he said, "I wanted to find out if you had enough backbone to meet him face to face. Mescalito is not something to make fun of. You must have command over your resources. Now I know I can take your desire alone as a good reason to learn."

"You really are going to teach me about peyote?"

"I prefer to call him Mescalito. Do the same."

"When are you going to start?"

"It is not so simple as that. You must be ready first."

"I think I am ready."

"This is not a joke. You must wait until there is no doubt, and then you will meet him."

"Do I have to prepare myself?"

"No. You simply have to wait. You may give up the whole idea after a while. You get tired easily. Last night you were ready to quit as soon as it got difficult. Mescalito requires a very serious intent."

Monday, August 7, 1961

I arrived at don Juan's house in Arizona about seven o'clock on Friday night. Five other Indians were sitting with him on the porch of his house. I greeted him and sat waiting for them to say something. After a formal silence one of the men got up, walked over to me, and said, "Buenas noches." I stood up and answered, "Buenas noches." Then all the other men got up and came to me and we all mumbled "buenas noches" and shook hands either by barely touching one another's fingertips or by holding the hand for an instant and then dropping it quite abruptly.

We all sat down again. They seemed to be rather shy—at a loss for words, although they all spoke Spanish.

It must have been about half past seven when suddenly they all got up and walked toward the back of the house. Nobody had said a word for a long time. Don Juan signaled me to follow and we all got inside an old pickup truck parked there. I sat in the back with don Juan and two younger men. There were no cushions or benches and the metal floor was painfully hard, especially when we left the highway and got onto a dirt road. Don Juan whispered that we were going to the house of one of his friends who had seven Mescalitos for me.

I asked him, "Don't you have any of them yourself, don Juan?"

"I do, but I couldn't offer them to you. You see, someone else has to do this."

"Can you tell me why?"

"Perhaps you are not agreeable to 'him' and 'he' won't like you, and then you will never be able to know 'him' with affection, as one should; and our friendship will be broken."

"Why wouldn't he like me? I have never done anything to him."

"You don't have to *do* anything to be liked or disliked. He either takes you, or throws you away."

"But, if he doesn't take me, isn't there anything I can do to make him like me?"

The other two men seemed to have overheard my question and laughed.

"No! I can't think of anything one can do," don Juan said.

He turned half away from me and I could not talk to him anymore.

We must have driven for at least an hour before we stopped in front of a small house. It was quite dark, and after the driver had turned off the headlights I could make out only the vague contour of the building.

A young woman, a Mexican, judging by her speech inflection, was yelling at a dog to make him stop barking. We got out of the truck and walked into the house. The men mumbled "Buenas noches" as they went by her. She answered back and went on yelling at the dog.

The room was large and was stacked up with a multitude of objects. A dim light from a very small electric bulb rendered the scene quite gloomy. There were quite a few chairs with broken legs and sagging seats leaning against the walls. Three of the men sat down on a couch, which was the largest single piece of furniture in the room. It was very old and had sagged down all the way to the floor; in the dim light it seemed to be red and dirty. The rest of us sat in chairs. We sat in silence for a long time.

One of the men suddenly got up and went into another room. He was perhaps in his fifties, dark, tall, and husky. He came back a moment later with a coffee jar. He opened the lid and handed the jar to me; inside there were seven odd-looking items. They varied in size and consistency. Some of them were almost round, others were elongated. They felt to the touch like the pulp of walnuts, or the surface of cork. Their brownish color made them look like hard, dry nutshells. I handled them, rubbing their surfaces for quite some time.

"This to be chewed [*esto se masca*]" don Juan said in a whisper.

I had not realized that he had sat next to me until he spoke. I looked at the other men, but no one was looking at me; they were talking among themselves in very low voices. This was a moment of acute indecision and fear. I felt almost unable to control myself.

"I have to go the bathroom," I said to him. "I'll go outside and take a walk."

He handed me the coffee jar and I put the peyote buttons in it. I was leaving the room when the man who had given me the jar stood up, came to me, and said he had a toilet bowl in the other room.

The toilet was almost against the door. Next to it, nearly touching the toilet, was a large bed which occupied more than half of the room. The woman was sleeping there. I stood motionless at the door for a while, then I came back to the room where the other men were.

The man who owned the house spoke to me in English: "Don Juan says you're from South America. Is there any mescal there?" I told him that I had never even heard of it.

They seemed to be interested in South America and we talked about the Indians for a while. Then one of the men asked me why I wanted to eat peyote. I told him that I wanted to know what it was like. They all laughed shyly.

Don Juan urged me softly, "Chew it, chew it [*Masca, masca*]."

My hands were wet and my stomach contracted. The jar with the peyote buttons was on the floor by the chair. I bent over, took one at random, and put it in my mouth. It had a stale taste. I bit it in two and started to chew one of the pieces. I felt a strong, pungent bitterness; in a moment my whole mouth was numb. The bitterness increased as I kept on chewing, forcing an incredible flow of saliva. My gums and the inside of my mouth felt as if I had eaten salty, dry meat or fish, which seems to force one to chew more. After a while I chewed the other piece and my mouth was so numb I couldn't feel the bitterness any-more. The peyote button was a bunch of shreds, like the fibrous part of an orange or like sugarcane, and I didn't know whether to swallow it or spit it out. At that moment the owner of the house got up and invited everybody to go out to the porch.

We went out and sat in the darkness. It was quite comfortable outside, and the host brought out a bottle of tequila.

The men were seated in a row with their backs to the wall. I was at the extreme right of the line. Don Juan, who was next to me, placed the jar with the peyote buttons between my legs. Then he handed me the bottle, which was passed down the line, and told me to take some of the tequila to wash away the bitterness.

I spat out the shreds of the first button and took a sip. He told me not to swallow it, but to just rinse out my mouth with it to stop the saliva. It did not help much with the saliva, but it certainly helped to wash away some of the bitterness.

Don Juan gave me a piece of dried apricot, or perhaps it was a dried fig—I couldn't see it in the dark, nor could I taste it—and told me to chew it thoroughly and slowly, without rushing. I had difficulty swallowing it; it felt as if it would not go down.

After a short pause the bottle went around again. Don Juan handed me a piece of crispy dried meat. I told him I did not feel like eating.

"This is not eating," he said firmly.

The pattern was repeated six times. I remember having chewed six peyote buttons when the conversation became very lively; although I could not distinguish what language was spoken, the topic of the conversation, in which everybody participated, was very interesting, and I attempted to listen carefully so that I could take part. But when I tried to speak I realized I couldn't; the words shifted aimlessly about in my mind.

I sat with my back propped against the wall and listened to what the men were saying. They were talking in Italian, and repeated over and over one phrase about the stupidity of sharks. I thought it was a logical, coherent topic. I had told don Juan earlier that the Colorado River in Arizona was called by the early Spaniards "el rio de los tizones [the river of charred wood]"; and someone misspelled or misread "tizones," and the river was called "el rio de los tiburones [the river of the sharks]." I was sure they were discussing that story, yet it never occurred to me to think that none of them could speak Italian.

I had a very strong desire to throw up, but I don't recall the actual act. I asked if somebody would get me some water. I was experiencing an unbearable thirst.

Don Juan brought me a large saucepan. He placed it on the ground next to the wall. He also brought a little cup or can. He dipped it into the pan and handed it to me, and said I could not drink but should just freshen my mouth with it.

The water looked strangely shiny, glossy, like a thick varnish. I wanted to ask don Juan about it and laboriously I tried to voice my thoughts in English, but then I realized he did not speak English. I experienced a very confusing moment, and became aware of the fact that although there was a clear thought in my mind, I could not speak. I wanted to comment on the strange quality of the water, but what followed next was not speech; it was the feeling of my unvoiced thoughts coming out of my mouth in a sort of liquid form. It was an effortless sensation of vomiting without the contractions of the diaphragm. It was a pleasant flow of liquid words.

I drank. And the feeling that I was vomiting disappeared. By that time all noises had vanished and I found I had difficulty focusing my eyes. I looked for don Juan and as I turned my head I noticed that my field of vision had diminished to a circular area in front of my eyes. This feeling was neither frightening nor discomforting, but, quite to the contrary, it was a novelty; I could literally sweep the ground by focusing on one spot and then moving my head slowly in any direction. When I had first come out to the porch I had noticed it was all dark except for the distant glare of the city lights. Yet within the circular area of my vision everything was clear. I forgot about my concern with don Juan and the other men, and gave myself entirely to exploring the ground with my pinpoint vision.

I saw the juncture of the porch floor and the wall. I turned my head slowly to the right, following the wall, and saw don Juan sitting against it. I shifted my head to the left in order to focus on the water. I found the bottom of the pan; I raised my head slightly and saw a medium-size black dog approaching. I saw him coming toward the water. The dog began to drink. I raised my hand to push him away from my water; I focused my pinpoint vision on the dog to carry on the movement, and suddenly I saw him become transparent. The water was a shiny, viscous liquid. I saw it going down the dog's throat into his body. I saw it flowing evenly through his entire length and then shooting out through each one of the hairs. I saw the iridescent fluid traveling along the length of each individual hair and then projecting out of the hairs to form a long, white, silky mane.

At that moment I had the sensation of intense convulsions, and in a matter of instants a tunnel formed around me, very low and narrow, hard and strangely cold. It felt to the touch like a wall of solid tinfoil. I found I was sitting on the tunnel floor. I tried to stand up, but hit my head on the metal roof, and the tunnel compressed itself until it was suffocating me. I remember having to crawl toward a sort of round point where the tunnel ended; when I finally arrived, if I did, I had forgotten all about the dog, don Juan, and myself. I was exhausted. My clothes were soaked in a cold, sticky liquid. I rolled back and forth trying to find a position in which to rest, a position where my heart would not pound so hard. In one of those shifts I saw the dog again.

Every memory came back to me at once, and suddenly all was clear in my mind. I turned around to look for don Juan, but I could not distinguish anything or anyone. All I was capable of seeing was the dog becoming iridescent; an intense light radiated from his body. I saw again the water flowing through him, kindling him like a bonfire. I got to the water, sank my face in the pan, and drank with him. My hands were in front of me on the ground and, as I drank, I saw the fluid running through my veins setting up hues of red and yellow and green. I drank more and more. I drank until I was all afire; I was all aglow. I drank until the fluid went out of my body through each pore, and projected out like fibers of silk, and I too acquired a long, lustrous, iridescent mane. I looked at the dog and his mane was like mine. A supreme happiness filled my whole body, and we ran together toward a sort of yellow warmth that came from some indefinite place. And there we played. We played and wrestled until I knew his wishes and he knew mine. We took turns manipulating each other in the fashion of a puppet show. I could make him move his legs by twisting my toes, and every time he nodded his head I felt an irresistible impulse to jump. But his most impish act was to make me scratch my head with my foot while I sat; he did it by flapping his ears from side to side. This action was to me utterly, unbearably funny. Such a touch of grace and irony; such mastery, I thought. The euphoria that possessed me was indescribable. I laughed until it was almost impossible to breathe.

I had the clear sensation of not being able to open my eyes; I was looking through a tank of water. It was a long and very painful state filled with the anxiety of not being able to wake up and yet being awake. Then slowly the world became clear and in focus. My field of vision became again very round and ample, and with it came an ordinary conscious act, which was to turn around and look for that marvelous being. At this point I encountered the most difficult transition. The passage from my normal state had taken place almost without my realizing it: I was aware; my thoughts and feelings were a corollary of that awareness; and the passing was smooth and clear. But this second change, the awakening to serious, sober consciousness, was genuinely shocking. I had forgotten I was a man! The sadness of such an irreconcilable situation was so intense that I wept.

Saturday, August 5, 1961
Later that morning, after breakfast, the owner of the house, don Juan, and I drove back to don Juan's place. I was very tired, but I couldn't go to sleep in the truck. Only after the man had left did I fall asleep on the porch of don Juan's house.

When I woke up it was dark; don Juan had covered me up with a blanket. I looked for him, but he was not in the house. He came later with a pot of fried beans and a stack of tortillas. I was extremely hungry.

After we had finished eating and were resting he asked me to tell him all that had happened to me the night before. I related my experience in great detail and as accurately as possible.

When I finished he nodded his head and said, "I think you are fine. It is difficult for me to explain how and why. But I think it went all right for you. You see, sometimes he is playful, like a child; at other times he is terrible, fearsome. He either frolics, or he is dead serious. It is impossible to know beforehand what he will be like with another person. Yet, when one knows him well—sometimes. You played with him tonight. You are the only person I know who has had such an encounter."

"In what way does my experience differ from that of others?"

"You're not an Indian; therefore it is hard for me to figure out what is what. Yet he either takes people or rejects them, regardless of whether they are Indians or not. That I know. I have seen numbers of them. I also know that he frolics, he makes some people laugh, but never have I seen him play with anyone."

"Can you tell me now, don Juan, how does peyote protect . . ."

He did not let me finish. Vigorously he touched me on the shoulder.

"Don't you ever name him that way. You haven't seen enough of him yet to know him."

"How does Mescalito protect people?"

"He advises. He answers whatever questions you ask."

"Then Mescalito is real? I mean he is something you can see?"

He seemed to be baffled by my question. He looked at me with a sort of blank expression.

"What I meant to say, is that Mescalito . . .'

"I heard what you said. Didn't you see him last night?"

I wanted to say that I saw only a dog, but I noticed his bewildered look.

"Then you think what I saw last night was him?"

He looked at me with contempt. He chuckled, shook his head as though he couldn't believe it, and in a very belligerent tone he added, "A poco crees que era tu—mamá [Don't tell me you believe it was your—mama]?" He paused before saying "mamá" because what he meant to say was "tu chingada madre," an idiom used as a disrespectful allusion to the other party's mother. The word "mamá" was so incongruous that we both laughed for a long time.

Then I realized he had fallen asleep and had not answered my question.

Sunday, August 6, 1961

I drove don Juan to the house where I had taken peyote. On the way he told me that the name of the man who had "offered me to Mescalito" was John. When we got to the house we found John sitting on his porch with two young men. All of them were extremely jovial. They laughed and talked with great ease. The three of them spoke English perfectly. I told John that I had come to thank him for having helped me.

I wanted to get their views on my behavior during the hallucinogenic experience, and told them I had been trying to think of what I had done that night and that I couldn't remember. They laughed and were reluctant to talk about it. They seemed to be holding back on account of don Juan. They all glanced at him as though waiting for an affirmative cue to go on. Don Juan must have cued them, although I did not notice anything, because suddenly John began to tell me what I had done that night.

He said he knew I had been "taken" when he heard me puking. He estimated that I must have puked thirty times. Don Juan corrected him and said it was only ten times.

John continued: "Then we all moved next to you. You were stiff, and were having convulsions. For a very long time, while lying on your back, you moved your mouth as though talking. Then you began to bump your head on the floor, and don Juan put an old hat on your head and you stopped it. You shivered and whined for hours, lying on the floor. I think everybody fell asleep then; but I heard you puffing and groaning in my sleep. Then I heard you scream and I woke up. I saw you leaping up in the air, screaming. You made a dash for the water, knocked the pan over, and began to swim in the puddle.

"Don Juan brought you more water. You sat quietly in front of the pan.

Then you jumped up and took off all your clothes. You were kneeling in front of the water, drinking in big gulps. Then you just sat there and stared into space. We thought you were going to be there forever. Nearly everybody was asleep, including don Juan, when suddenly you jumped up again, howling, and took after the dog. The dog got scared and howled too, and ran to the back of the house. Then everybody woke up.

"We all got up. You came back from the other side still chasing the dog. The dog was running ahead of you barking and howling. I think you must have gone twenty times around the house, running in circles, barking like a dog. I was afraid people were going to be curious. There are no neighbors close, but your howling was so loud it could have been heard for miles."

One of the young men added, "You caught up with the dog and brought it to the porch in your arms."

John continued: "Then you began to play with the dog. You wrestled with him, and the dog and you bit each other and played. That, I thought, was funny. My dog does not play usually. But this time you and the dog were rolling on each other."

"Then you ran to the water and the dog drank with you," the young man said. "You ran five or six times to the water with the dog."

"How long did this go on?" I asked.

"Hours," John said. "At one time we lost sight of you two. I think you must have run to the back. We just heard you barking and groaning. You sounded so much like a dog that we couldn't tell you two apart."

"Maybe it was just the dog alone," I said.

They laughed, and John said, "You were barking there, boy!"

"What happened next?"

The three men looked at one another and seemed to have a hard time deciding what happened next. Finally the young man who had not yet said anything spoke up.

"He choked," he said, looking at John.

"Yes, you certainly choked. You began to cry very strangely, and then you fell to the floor. We thought you were biting your tongue; don Juan opened your jaws and poured water on your face. Then you started shivering and having convulsions all over again. Then you stayed motionless for a long time. Don Juan said it was all over. By then it was morning, so we covered you with a blanket and left you to sleep on the porch."

He stopped there and looked at the other men who were obviously trying not to laugh. He turned to don Juan and asked him something. Don Juan smiled and answered the question. John turned to me and said, "We left you here on the porch because we were afraid you were going to piss all over the rooms."

They all laughed very loudly.

"What was the matter with me?" I asked. "Did I . . ."

"Did you?" John sort of mimicked me. "We were not going to mention it, but don Juan says it is all right. You pissed all over my dog!"

"What did I do?"

"You don't think the dog was running because he was afraid of you, do you? The dog was running because you were pissing on him."

There was general laughter at this point. I tried to question one of the young men, but they were all laughing and he didn't hear me.

John went on: "My dog got even though: he pissed on you too!"

This statement was apparently utterly funny because they all roared with laughter, including don Juan. When they had quieted down, I asked in all earnestness, "Is it really true? This really happened?"

Still laughing, John replied: "I swear my dog really pissed on you."

Driving back to don Juan's place I asked him: "Did all that really happen, don Juan?"

"Yes," he said, "but they don't know what you saw. They don't realize you were playing with 'him.' That is why I did not disturb you."

"But is this business of the dog and me pissing on each other true?"

"It was not a dog! How many times do I have to tell you that? This is the only way to understand it. It's the only way! It was 'he' who played with you."

"Did you know all this was happening before I told you about it?"

He vacillated for an instant before answering.

"No, I remembered, after you told me about it, the strange way you looked. I just suspected you were doing fine because you didn't seem scared."

"Did the dog really play with me as they say?"

"Goddammit! It was not a dog!"

Thursday, August 17, 1961

I told don Juan how I felt about my experience. From the point of view of my intended work it had been a disastrous event. I said I did not care for another similar "encounter" with Mescalito. I agreed that everything that had happened to me had been more than interesting, but added that nothing in it could really move me toward seeking it again. I seriously believed that I was not constructed for that type of endeavor. Peyote had produced in me, as a postreaction, a strange kind of physical discomfort. It was an indefinite fear or unhappiness; a melancholy of some sort, which I could not define exactly. And I did not find that state noble in any way.

Don Juan laughed and said, "You were beginning to learn."

"This type of learning is not for me. I am not made for it, don Juan."

"You always exaggerate."

"This is not exaggeration."

"It is. The only trouble is that you exaggerate the bad points only."

"There are no good points so far as I am concerned. All I know is that it makes me afraid."

"There is nothing wrong with being afraid. When you fear, you see things in a different way."

"But I don't care about seeing things in a different way, don Juan. I think I am going to leave the learning about Mescalito alone. I can't handle it, don Juan. This is really a bad situation for me."

"Of course it is bad—even for me. You are not the only one who is baffled."

"Why should you be baffled, don Juan?"

"I have been thinking about what I saw the other night. Mescalito actually played with you. That baffled me, because it was an indication [omen]."

"What kind of an indication, don Juan?"

"Mescalito was pointing you out to me."

"What for?"

"It wasn't clear to me then, but now it is. He meant you were the 'chosen man' [*escogido*]. Mescalito pointed you out to me and by doing that he told me you were the chosen man."

"Do you mean I was chosen among others for some task, or something of the sort?"

"No. What I mean is, Mescalito told me you could be the man I am looking for."

"When did he tell you that, don Juan?"

"By playing with you, he told me that. This makes you the chosen man for me."

"What does it mean to be the chosen man?"

"There are some secrets I know [*Tengo secretos*]. I have secrets I won't be able to reveal to anyone unless I find my chosen man. The other night when I saw you playing with Mescalito it was clear to me you were that man. But you are not an Indian. How baffling!"

"But what does it mean to me, don Juan? What do I have to do?"

"I've made up my mind and I am going to teach you the secrets that make up the lot of a man of knowledge."

"Do you mean the secrets about Mescalito?"

"Yes, but those are not all the secrets I know. There are others, of a different kind, which I would like to give to someone. I had a teacher myself, my benefactor, and I also became his chosen man upon performing a certain feat. He taught me all I know."

I asked him again what this new role would require of me; he said learning was the only thing involved, learning in the sense of what I had experienced in the two sessions with him.

The way in which the situation had evolved was quite strange. I had made up my mind to tell him I was going to give up the idea of learning about peyote, and then before I could really make my point, he offered to teach me his "knowledge." I did not know what he meant by that, but I felt that this sudden turn was very serious. I argued I had no qualifications for such a task, as it required a rare kind of courage which I did not have. I told him that my bent of character was to talk about acts others performed. I wanted to hear his views and opinions about everything. I told him I could be happy if I could sit there and listen to him talk for days. To me, *that* would be learning.

He listened without interrupting me. I talked for a long time. Then he said:

"All this is very easy to understand. Fear is the first natural enemy a man must overcome on his path to knowledge. Besides, you are curious. That evens up the score. And you will learn in spite of yourself; that's the rule."

I protested for a while longer, trying to dissuade him. But he seemed to be convinced there was nothing else I could do but learn.

"You are not thinking in the proper order," he said. "Mescalito actually played with you. That's the point to think about. Why don't you dwell on that instead of on your fear?"

"Was it so unusual?"

"You are the only person I have ever seen playing with him. You are not used to this kind of life; therefore the indications [omens] bypass you. Yet you are a serious person, but your seriousness is attached to what you do, not to what goes on outside you. You dwell upon yourself too much. That's the trouble. And that produces a terrible fatigue."

"But what else can anyone do, don Juan?"

"Seek and see the marvels all around you. You will get tired of looking at yourself alone, and that fatigue will make you deaf and blind to everything else."

"You have a point, don Juan, but how can I change?"

"Think about the wonder of Mescalito playing with you. Think about nothing else: The rest will come to you of itself."

Sunday, August 20, 1961

Last night don Juan proceeded to usher me into the realm of his knowledge. We sat in front of his house in the dark. Suddenly, after a long silence, he began to talk. He said he was going to advise me with the same words his own benefactor had used the first day he took him as his apprentice. Don Juan had apparently memorized the words, for he repeated them several times, to make sure I did not miss any:

"A man goes to knowledge as he goes to war, wide-awake, with fear, with respect, and with absolute assurance. Going to knowledge or going to war in any other manner is a mistake, and whoever makes it will live to regret his steps."

I asked him why was it so and he said that when a man has fulfilled those four requisites there are no mistakes for which he will have to account; under such conditions his acts lose the blundering quality of a fool's acts. If such a man fails, or suffers a defeat, he will have lost only a battle, and there will be no pitiful regrets over that.

Then he said he intended to teach me about an "ally" in the very same way his own benefactor had taught him. He put strong emphasis on the words "very same way," repeating the phrase several times.

An "ally," he said, is a power a man can bring into his life to help him, advise him, and give him the strength necessary to perform acts, whether big or small, right or wrong. This ally is necessary to enhance a man's life, guide his acts, and further his knowledge. In fact, an ally is the indispensable aid to knowing. Don Juan said this with great conviction and force. He seemed to choose his words carefully. He repeated the following sentence four times:

"An ally will make you see and understand things about which no human being could possibly enlighten you."

"Is an ally something like a guardian spirit?"

"It is neither a guardian nor a spirit. It is an aid."

"Is Mescalito your ally?"

"No! Mescalito is another kind of power. A unique power! A protector, a teacher."

"What makes Mescalito different from an ally?"

"He can't be tamed and used as an ally is tamed and used. Mescalito is outside oneself. He chooses to show himself in many forms to whoever stands in front of him, regardless of whether that person is a brujo or a farm boy."

Don Juan spoke with deep fervor about Mescalito's being the teacher of the proper way to live. I asked him how Mescalito taught the "proper way of life," and don Juan replied that Mescalito *showed* how to live.

"How does he show it?" I asked.

"He has many ways of showing it. Sometimes he shows it on his hand, or on the rocks, or the trees, or just in front of you."

"Is it like a picture in front of you?"

"No. It is a teaching in front of you."

"Does Mescalito talk to the person?"

"Yes. But not in words."

"How does he talk, then?"

"He talks differently to every man."

I felt my questions were annoying him. I did not ask any more. He went on explaining that there were no exact steps to knowing Mescalito; therefore no one could teach about him except Mescalito himself. This quality made him a unique power; he was not the same for every man.

On the other hand, the acquiring of an ally required, don Juan said, the most precise teaching and the following of stages or steps without a single deviation. There are many such ally powers in the world, he said, but he was familiar with only two of them. And he was going to lead me to them and their secrets, but it was up to me to choose *one* of them, for I could have only one. His benefactor's ally was in *la yerba del diablo* (devil's weed), he said, but he personally did not like it, even though his benefactor had taught him its secrets. His own ally was in the *humito* (the little smoke), he said, but he did not elaborate on the nature of the smoke.

I asked him about it. He remained quiet. After a long pause I asked him:

"What kind of a power is an ally?"

"It is an aid. I have already told you."

"How does it aid?"

"An ally is a power capable of carrying a man beyond the boundaries of himself. This is how an ally can reveal matters no human being could."

"But Mescalito also takes you out of the boundaries of yourself. Doesn't that make him an ally?"

"No. Mescalito takes you out of yourself to teach you. An ally takes you out to give you power."

I asked him to explain this point to me in more detail, or to describe the difference in effect between the two. He looked at me for a long time and laughed. He said that learning through conversation was not only a waste, but stupidity, because learning was the most difficult task a man could undertake. He asked me to remember the time I had tried to find my spot, and how I wanted to find it without doing any work because I had expected him to hand out all the information. If he had done so, he said, I would never have learned. But, knowing how difficult it was to find my spot, and, above all, knowing that it existed, would give me a unique sense of confidence. He said that while I remained rooted to my "good spot" nothing could cause me bodily harm, because I had the assurance that at that particular spot I was at my very best. I had the power to shove off anything that might be harmful to me. If, however, he had *told* me where it was, I would never have had the confidence needed to claim it as true knowledge. Thus, knowledge was indeed power.

Don Juan said then that every time a man sets himself to learn he has to labor as hard as I did to find that spot, and the limits of his learning are determined by his own nature. Thus he saw no point in talking about knowledge.

He said that certain kinds of knowledge were too powerful for the strength I had, and to talk about them would only bring harm to me. He apparently felt there was nothing else he wanted to say. He got up and walked toward his house. I told him the situation overwhelmed me. It was not what I had conceived or wanted it to be.

He said that fears are natural; that all of us experience them and there is nothing we can do about it. But on the other hand, no matter how frightening learning is, it is more terrible to think of a man without an ally, or without knowledge.

Ethical Combat
Immanuel Kant

Immanuel Kant (1724–1804) exerted an enormous influence on all modern thought with his unique synthesis of rationalist and empiricist philosophy. His most famous work is *The Critique of Pure Reason.*

ETHICAL DIDACTIC

Although virtue cannot be based on anthropological knowledge drawn from experience, the very concept of virtue implies that virtue must be acquired (that it is not innate). For man's capacity for moral action would not be virtue were it not produced by the *strength* of his resolution struggling with such powerful inclinations to the contrary. Virtue is the product of pure practical reason, in so far as reason, aware of its supremacy (on grounds of freedom), wins ascendancy over the inclinations.

That virtue can and must be *learned* follows directly from the fact that it is not innate. The theory of virtue is, therefore, a *doctrine*. But one does not, merely by the theory of how one should behave in keeping with the concept of virtue, acquire the strength to put the rule into practice. Hence the Stoics [in denying that virtue can be learned] meant only that virtue cannot be *learned* through the mere presentation of duty or through admonitions, but must rather be cultivated (by discipline) and *practiced* by being put to the proof of combat with the inner enemy in man; for one *cannot* straightaway do all that one *wills* to do, without having first tried and practiced one's strength. But the *resolution* to practice virtue must be made all at once and in its entirety, since the intention (*animus*) of surrendering at times to vice, in order gradually to break away from it, would in itself be impure and even immoral. Consequently this attitude could also produce no virtue (in so far as virtue is based on a single principle).

From Immanuel Kant, *Doctrine of Virtue*, trans. Mary J. Gregor (New York, 1964), pp. 149–158.

Now as for the doctrinal method (and *methodic* treatment is essential to any scientific doctrine—otherwise the exposition of it would be chaotic), this too must be systematic and not fragmentary if the doctrine of virtue is to present itself as a science. —But the doctrine can be delivered either in a *lecture,* as when all those to whom it is directed are a mere audience, or by the method of *questioning,* in which the teacher asks his pupil what he wants to teach him. And this method of questioning is, in turn, divided into the method of *dialogue* and that of *catechism,* depending on whether the teacher addresses his questions to the pupil's *reason* or merely to his *memory.* For if the teacher wants to question his pupil's reason he must do this in a dialogue in which teacher and pupil reciprocally question and answer each other. The teacher, by his questions, guides the pupil's thinking merely by presenting him with situations in which his disposition for certain concepts will develop (the teacher is the midwife of the pupil's thoughts). The pupil, who thus sees that he is able to think for himself, provides, by his questions about obscurities or doubts in the propositions admitted, occasion for the *teacher* to *learn* how to question skilfully, according to the saying *docendo discimus.* —(For logic has not yet taken sufficiently to heart its task of furnishing us with rules as to the appropriate way of searching for things: that is to say, logic should not limit itself to giving rules for *determinant* judgments but should also provide rules for *preparatory* judgments (*iudicia praevia*), by which one is led to conceptions. Such a doctrine can be a guide even to the mathematician in his inventions, and moreover he often makes use of it.)

For the still untrained pupil the first and most essential *doctrinal* instrument of the theory of virtue is a moral *catechism.* This must precede the religious catechism. It cannot be interwoven, as a mere interpolation, in the teachings of religion but must rather be presented separately, as a self-subsistent whole. For it is only by pure moral principles that the transition from the doctrine of virtue to religion can be made, since otherwise the avowals of religion would be impure. —For their own part, even the worthiest and most eminent theologians have hesitated to draw up a catechism for statutory religion which they would personally answer for, although one would have thought this the least that could be expected from the vast treasury of their learning.

But a *moral* catechism, the basic teaching of the doctrine of virtue, involves no such scruple or difficulty since, so far as its content is concerned, it can be developed from ordinary human reason and, so far as its form is concerned, it needs only to be adapted to the didactic rules appropriate to the earliest instruction. The formal principle of such instruction does not, however, permit Socratic *dialogue* as the method of teaching, since the pupil has no idea what questions to ask; and so the teacher alone does the questioning. But the answer which he methodically draws from the pupil's reason must be written down and preserved in precise terms which cannot easily be altered, and so be committed to the pupil's *memory.* In this way the *catechetical method* differs from both the *dogmatic method* (in which only the teacher speaks) and the *method of dialogue* (in which both teacher and pupil question and answer each other).

The *experimental* (technical) means to the formation of virtue is *good example* of the part of the teacher (his exemplary conduct) and *cautionary* example in others. For, to the as yet unformed human being, imitation is what first determines him to embrace the maxims that he afterwards makes his own. —To become conditioned to something is to establish a permanent inclination apart from any maxim, by the often repeated satisfaction of that inclination; it is a mechanism of sense rather than a principle of thought (and one that is easier to *make* than to *break* after it has been acquired). —As for the power of *examples*[1] (good or bad) which can be held up to the propensity for imitation or presented as warnings, what is given to us by others can establish no maxim of virtue. For a maxim of virtue consists precisely in the subjective autonomy of each man's practical reason, and so implies that the law itself, not the conduct of other men, serves as one's motive. Thus the teacher will not tell his pupil "Take an example from that good (orderly, diligent) boy!" For this would only cause the pupil to hate that boy, who puts him in an unfavorable light. Good example (exemplary conduct) should not serve as a model but only as a proof that it is really possible to act in accordance with duty. Thus it is not comparison with any other man whatsoever (with men as they are), but comparison with the Idea of humanity (with what man ought to be) and so with the law, that must serve as the constant standard of the teacher's instruction.

Note: Fragments of a Moral Catechism. The teacher questions the pupil's reason about what he wants to teach him; and should the pupil sometimes not know how to answer the question, the teacher, guiding his reason, suggests the answer.

1. Teacher: What is your greatest, in fact your whole, desire in life?
   Pupil: (is silent)
   Teacher: That everything should always go the way you want it to.
2. Teacher: What do we call such a state?
   Pupil: (is silent)
   Teacher: We call it *happiness* (continuous well-being, enjoyment of life, complete contentment with one's state).
3. Teacher: Now if it were up to you to dispose of all the happiness possible in the world, would you keep it all for yourself or would you share it with your fellow-men?
   Pupil: I would share it with others and make them happy and contented too.
4. Teacher: Now that shows that you have a good enough *heart*; but let us see whether you show good *understanding* along with it. —Would you really give the lazy fellow a soft cushion so that he could pass away his life in sweet idleness? Or would you see to it that the drunkard is never short of wine and whatever else he needs to get drunk? Would you give the swindler a charming air and manner to dupe other people? And would you give the brutal man audacity and strong fists so that he

---

[1] The German words "instance [*Beispiel*]" and "example [*Exempel*]", though commonly used as synonyms, do not really have exactly the same meaning. To take an *example* of something and to bring forward an *instance* to clarify a term are altogether different concepts. An example is a particular case of a *practical* rule, in so far as this demonstrates the feasibility or impracticability of an action, whereas an *instance* is only the particular (*concretum*), presented as contained under the general by means of concepts (*abstractum*), and is merely a theoretical illustration of a concept.

could crush other people? Each of these things is a means that somebody wants in order to be happy in his own way.

Pupil: No, I would not.

5. Teacher: You see, then, that if you had all happiness in your hands and,
along with it, the best will, you still would not straightaway give it to
anyone who put out his hand for it; instead you would first try to find
out to what extent each is *worthy* of happiness. —But as for yourself,
would you at least have no scruples about first giving yourself everything that you count in your happiness?

Pupil: I would have none.

Teacher: But doesn't it occur to you to ask, again, whether you yourself are
worthy of happiness?

Pupil: Of course.

Teacher: Now the force in you that strives only toward happiness is *inclination*; but the power that limits your inclination to the condition of
your first being worthy of happiness is your *reason*; and your power
to restrain and overcome your inclination by your reason is the freedom
of your will.

6. Teacher: As to how you should set about participating in happiness and also
becoming at least not unworthy of it, the rule and instruction in this
lies in your *reason* alone. This means that you need not learn this rule
for your conduct from experience or be taught it by other men. Your own
reason teaches you what you have to do and directly commands it.
For example, suppose a situation in which you could get a great benefit
for yourself or your friends by making up a little lie that would harm no
one: what does your reason say about it?

Pupil: That I ought not to lie, no matter how great the benefits to myself
and my friend might be. Lying is *base* and makes a man *unworthy* of
happiness. —Here we find an unconditional necessitation through a
command (or prohibition) of reason, which I must obey; and in the
face of it all my inclinations must be silent.

Teacher: What do we call this necessity, which reason lays directly upon a
man, of acting in conformity with a law of reason?

Pupil: It is called *duty*.

Teacher: So a man's fulfillment of his duty is the universal and sole condition of his worthiness to be happy, and his fulfillment of duty is one
with his worthiness to be happy.

7. Teacher: But even if we are conscious of a good and active will in us, by
virtue of which we consider ourselves worthy (or at least not unworthy)
of happiness, can we base on this the sure hope of participating in
happiness?

Pupil: No, not merely on this. For it is not always within our power to
make ourselves happy, and the course of nature does not of itself conform
with merit. Our happiness in life (our welfare in general) depends,
rather, on circumstances that, by and large, are not under man's control.
So our happiness always remains a mere wish which cannot become
a hope unless some other power is added.

8. Teacher: Has reason, in fact, grounds for admitting the reality of such a
power, which apportions happiness according to man's merit or guilt

—a power ordering the whole of nature and ruling the world with supreme wisdom?

Pupil: Yes. For we see in the works of nature, which we can judge, a wisdom so widespread and profound that we can explain it to ourselves only by the ineffably great art of a creator of the world. And from this we have cause, when we turn to the moral order, which is the highest adornment of the world, to expect there a rule no less wise. In other words, we have cause to hold that if we do not make ourselves *unworthy of happiness* by violating our duty, we can also hope to *share* in happiness.

In this catechism, which must be carried through all the articles of virtue and vice, the greatest care must be taken *not* to base the command of duty on the fact that it is actually observed by the men it is supposed to obligate nor even on the advantage or detriment to others flowing from it. It must be based quite purely on the moral principle, and only casual mention should be made of advantage and detriment, as of an adjunct which could really be dispensed with but which is serviceable, as a mere instrument, for the taste of those who are weak by nature. It is the *shamefulness* of vice, not its *harmfulness* (to the agent himself), that must be emphasized above all. For unless the dignity of virtue is exalted above everything else in actions, then the concept of duty itself vanishes and dissolves into mere pragmatic precepts, since man's consciousness of his own nobility then disappears and he is for sale and can be bought for a price that the seductive inclinations offer him.

Now when this is wisely and carefully developed out of man's own reason, with regard for the differences in age, sex, and position which he gradually encounters, then at the end there must be something more—something that moves the soul inwardly and puts man in a position such that he can look upon himself only with the greatest wonder at the original disposition dwelling in him, the impression of which is never erased. When at the end of his instruction he once more, by way of summary, recounts his duties in their order (recapitulates them); and when, in the case of each of them, his attention is drawn to the fact that none of the pains, hardships, and sufferings of life—not even the threat of death—which may befall him because he attends faithfully to his duty can make him lose his consciousness of being their master and superior to them all; then it is time for the question: what is it in you that can be trusted to enter into combat with all the powers of nature in you and around you and, if they come into conflict with your moral principles, to conquer them? Although the answer to this question completely surpasses the power of speculative reason, the question arises of itself. And if he takes it to heart, the very incomprehensibility of this self-knowledge must produce an exaltation in his soul which only inspires it the more to keep its duty holy, the more it is assailed.

In this catechetical instruction in morality it would be most helpful to the pupil's moral development to raise some casuistical questions in the analysis of every duty and to let the assembled children put their reason to the test of how each would go about resolving the tricky problem put before him. The advantage of this is not only that, as a method of *cultivating reason*, casuistry is most suitable to the capacity of the undeveloped (since questions about duty can be decided far more easily than speculative questions), and so is the most appropriate way to sharpen the reason of young people in general. Its advantage lies especially in the fact that it is natural for man to *love* a subject which he has, by his own handling, brought to a science (in which he is now proficient); and so, by this sort of practice, the pupil is drawn unwittingly to an *interest* in morality.

But it is of foremost importance in this instruction not to present the moral catechism mixed with the religious one (to combine them into one) or, what is worse yet, to let it follow upon the religious catechism. On the contrary, the pupil must always be brought to a clear insight into the moral catechism, which should be presented with the greatest diligence and completeness, For otherwise the religion that the pupil afterwards professes will be nothing but hypocrisy: he will embrace duties out of fear and feign an interest in them which is not in his heart.

ETHICAL ASCETIC

The rules for practicing virtue (*exercitiorum virtutis*) aim at a frame of mind that is *brave* and *cheerful* in the observance of duty (*animus strenuus et hilaris*). For in order to overcome the obstacles with which it has to contend, virtue must collect all its strength and at the same time sacrifice many of the pleasures of life, the loss of which can well make the mind morose and surly at times. But what we do cheerlessly and merely as compulsory service has no intrinsic value for us, and so also if we attend to our duty in this way; we do not love it but rather shirk as much as we can the occasion for practicing it.

The cultivation of virtue, *i.e.* moral *asceticism*, takes as its motto for the vigorous, spirited, and courageous practice of virtue the *Stoic* saying: accustom yourself *to bear* the contingent ills of life and *to do without* the equally super-fluous pleasures (*assuesce incommodis et desuesce commoditatibus vitae*). It is a kind of *hygiene* that man should practice to keep himself morally *healthy*. But health is only the *negative* side of well-being: it cannot itself be felt. Something must be added to it—something which, though it is purely moral, offers a pleasant enjoyment of life—and this is the habitually cheerful heart, as the virtuous *Epicurus* conceived it. For who should have more cause for a cheerful spirit, without finding it his duty to acquire such a frame of mind and make it habitual, than the man who is aware of no intentional transgression in himself and is secured against falling into such a transgression? (*hic murus aheneus esto etc., Horat.*) On the other hand monastic asceticism, which, out of superstitious fear or hypocritical self-loathing, goes to work with self-torture and crucifixion of the flesh, does not aim at virtue but rather at fantastic atonement; it inflicts self-punishment and, instead of requiring moral *repentance* for a fault (that is, repentance with a view to self-improvement) insists on *penance* for it. But a self-chosen and self-inflicted punishment is a contradiction (because punishment must always be inflicted by another person); moreover it cannot produce the cheerfulness that accompanies virtue, but much rather brings with it secret hatred for virtue's command. —Ethical gymnastic, therefore, consists only in combatting the impulses of nature to the extent that we are able to master them when a situation comes up in which they threaten morality; hence it is a combat which gives us courage and makes us cheerful in the consciousness of our restored freedom. To *repent* of something and to impose a *penance* on oneself (for example, a fast) not from hygienic but from pious considerations are, morally considered, two very different precautionary measures. To repent of a past transgression when we recall it is inevitable and, in fact, we even have a duty not to let this recollection atrophy; but self-punishment, which is cheerless, morose, and surly, makes virtue itself hated and drives away its followers. Hence the training (discipline) which man exercises on himself can become meritorious and exemplary only by the cheerfulness that accompanies it.

Judaism as the Way of Action
Leo Baeck

Leo Baeck (1873–1956) was born in Prussia and died in London. During the Hitler years, Baeck was, in effect, the leader of Germany's Jews, helping many to emigrate and alleviating the lot of those who remained. In 1943, Baeck was deported to Theresienstadt concentration camp but escaped liquidation through a fortunate mistake. After the war, he divided his time between London and Hebrew Union College in Cincinnati, where he taught. He is also the author of *The Essence of Judaism.*

There are two experiences of the human soul in which the meaning of his life takes on for a man a vital significance: the experience of mystery and the experience of commandment; or, as we may also put it, the knowledge of what is real and the knowledge of what is to be realized.

When man wants to be certain of his existence, when he therefore listens intently for the meaning of his life and life in general, and when he thus feels the presence of something lasting, of some reality beneath the surface, then he experiences the mystery: he becomes conscious that he was created, brought into being—conscious of an undetectable and, at the same time, protective power. He experiences that which embraces him and all else. He experiences, in the words of the ancient metaphor in the Blessing of Moses, "the arms of eternity."

And when man looks beyond the present day, when he wishes to give his life direction and lead it toward a goal, when he thus grasps that which defines his life and is clear about it, then he is always confronted with the commandment, the task, that which he is to realize. The foundation of life is the mystery; the way of life is the revealed. The one is from God; the other to be achieved by man. To cite another thought from the Bible: "That which is concealed belongs unto the Lord our God, but that which is revealed belongs unto us and unto our children forever, that we may do all the words of this Torah." And both, mystery as well as commandment, represent certainty—the certainty of life, the certainty of the self.

From Leo Baeck, *Judaism and Christianity* (Philadelphia, 1970), pp. 171–185. Reprinted by permission of The Jewish Publication Society of America.

This twofold experience could also be called humility and reverence. The humility of man is his recognition that his life is framed by infinity and eternity, by that which transcends all human knowledge and apprehension, and surpasses all that is natural and existent; that his life is absolutely dependent; that the unknowable and unnamable, the unfathomable and unthinkable enters into his life. Humility is the feeling for that deep and mysterious sphere in which man is rooted; the feeling, in other words, for that which remains in being and is real—the great quiet, the great devotion in all philosophy and all wisdom. And reverence is man's feeling that something higher confronts him; and whatever is higher is ethically superior and therefore makes demands and directs, speaks to man and requires his reply, his decision. It can reveal itself in the small and weak no less than in the sublime; it can manifest itself in the other as well as in oneself. Reverence is thus the recognition of the holy, that which is infinitely and eternally commanding, that which man is to accept into his life and realize through his life—the great impelling force, the active aspect of wisdom.

This twofold experience can also be intimated in this way: the consciousness that we have been created versus the consciousness that we are expected to create. The former is our certainty of that through which all that lives has life; our certainty that, at heart and in truth, we are related to the oneness of all life; our certainty of that which is omnipresent and enduring. It is the capacity of the soul for grasping the invisible in the visible, the lasting in the momentary, the eternal in the transitory, and the infinite in the earthly and limited. It is this faith which ever and again grasps that which has reality and which is the principle and source of life. The latter, on the other hand, is the capacity to be aware of the demand and determination of the hour; it is the certainty of the task, of that which admonishes, points ahead, and directs our life; the certainty that every man's life can do its share and accomplish its function; that man has some quality that lifts him out of the universe which has been created even as he himself has been created—a quality which gives man a quite personal aspect, a quite individual place and a unique direction and freedom, a capacity for decision by virtue of which man comprehends again and again what he is supposed to fulfill.

These are the two experiences of the meaning of life. And what is peculiar to Judaism is that these two experiences have here become one, and are experienced as one, in a perfect unity. And it is thus that the soul becomes conscious of its own unity and totality; it is thus that piety springs up in the soul. From the one God come both mystery and commandment, as one from the One, and the soul experiences both as one. Every mystery means and suggests also a commandment; and every commandment means and suggests also a mystery. All humility also means and suggests reverence, and all reverence, humility; all faith, the law, and all law, faith. All consciousness that we have been created means and suggests the demand to create, and every demand to create means and suggests the consciousness that we have been created. What is evident is here rooted in that which is concealed, and what is concealed always has its evident aspect for man. The profundity of life cannot be grasped without its also speaking to us of duty in life; and not a single duty of life is perceived truly without at the same time proclaiming the profundity of life. We cannot have knowledge of the foundation of our life without at the same time beholding our way, and we cannot understand this way without penetrating to the foundation of our life.

We cannot fully take to heart that we are the creatures of God without apprehending also that we ought to be the creators of our own lives; and we cannot be in full possession of this commandment to create unless we remain aware that we ourselves have been created—created by God that we ourselves may create, and creating because we have been created by God. This unity of both experiences in the human soul constitutes Jewish piety and Jewish wisdom; the meaning of life reveals itself here in this form.

Therefore Judaism is not marred by the split which is introduced by other conceptions of God. Judaism lacks any foundation for the conflict between transcendence and immanence. Jewish piety lives in the paradox, in the polarity with all its tension and compactness. That which is a contradiction in the abstract world of mere theory is made a unity and a whole in the religious consciousness. For this consciousness there is no such thing as this world without any beyond, nor a beyond without this world; no world to come without the present world, and no human world without that which transcends it. Whatever is on this side is rooted in the beyond, and whatever is beyond demands completion on this side by man. The infinite appears in the finite, and whatever is finite bears witness to the infinite. The life of man leads from God to man and from man to God. God is He in whom is all being, and God is also He that is positively different. God gives man life, and God demands man's life from him. Our soul is what is divine in us, it is our mystery and shares the mystery of all souls; and yet it shows also our individual stamp, that which is unique within us, our very self, that which belongs to it alone. The human dwells in the divine, and the divine demands of every man his humanity. This unity of both, the meaning which emerges from this opposition, alone is truth and pregnant with thoroughgoing certainty.

Hence any opposition between mysticism and ethics has no place here either. The religious consciousness here is never without its immediacy, its experience —nor without that which has been commanded and still is to be realized in life. No experience without tasks and no tasks without experience; life dwells only where both are present. In Judaism, all ethics has its mysticism and all mysticism its ethics. This applies to the whole far-flung history of its ideas. For Jewish mysticism the energies welling up out of God are energies of the will. Floods of mystery full of commandments and floods of commandment full of mystery issue from God. And the deed which fulfills God's commandment opens up a gate through which these floods surge into man's day. All absorption in the profundity of God is always also an absorption in the will of God and His commandment. And all Jewish ethics is distinguished by being an ethic of revelation or, one might almost say, an ethic of experience of the divine: it is the tidings of the divine. Every "thou shalt" is confronted with another word which introduces it and simultaneously replies to it—another word which is at the same time the word of mystery: "Thus saith the Lord." And it is followed by this same word both as a conclusion and a new beginning: "I am the Lord thy God." Ethics is here rooted in the profundity of living experience, and it is significant that in the Hebrew language of the Middle Ages the same word is used to designate an ethical disposition and a mystical absorption. The history of Judaism from ancient times to the present could be written as a history of mysticism; and the history of Judaism from its origins until now could also be written as a history of "the Law"—and it would be the same history. And for the most part it would be the history of the very same men. Many of the most influential and decisive teachers of the law have been mystics; for example, the author of the oft-cited *Shulhan Arukh*.

Of course, mystery and commandment were not always emphasized equally in Judaism. Now the one was stressed more, now the other; and this distinguishes different spheres and epochs. Only where one or the other was supposed to constitute the whole of religion, only where the whole of piety was exclusively identified with one or the other, did the religion cease to be Judaism. Judaism ceases where the mood of devotion, that which is at rest and restful, would mean everything; where faith is content with itself, content with mystery; where this mere faith finally extends its darkling glimmer to the point where it drowns the world and dreams become the stuff of life. The religion of mere passivity, devoid of commandments, is no longer Judaism. Nor is Judaism to be found where the commandment is content with itself and is nothing but commandment; where the whole sphere of life is supposed to be embraced by commandments and only that which lies under the rays of their cold light is presumed to be the meaning of life; where man thinks that he has seen everything when he sees the way on which he is to proceed. The religion of mere activity without devotion—this religion which becomes an ethic of the surface, or no more than the custom of the day—is not Judaism. The world of Judaism is to be found only where faith has its commandment, and the commandment its faith.

This is why Paul left Judaism when he preached *sola fide* (by faith alone) and thereby wound up with sacrament and dogma. Mystery became everything for him, not only that which is concealed but also that which is manifest. Hence mystery finally had to become for him something tangible, namely, sacraments, and something that can be molded, namely, dogma. For it is always thus: sacraments are a mystery into which man enters, a mystery of which man can take hold; and dogma, like myth, is a mystery which man can build up and shape. The gospel—that old gospel which had not yet been adapted for the use of the Church and made to oppose Judaism—was still wholly a part of Judaism and conformed to the Old Testament. It is relatively less important that it was written in the language of the Jewish land and thus was a piece of Jewish literature. A full understanding of Jesus and his gospel is possible only in the perspective of Jewish thought and feeling and therefore perhaps only for a Jew. And his words can be heard with their full content and import only when they are led back into the language he spoke. The boundary of Judaism was crossed only by Paul at the point where mystery wanted to prevail without commandment, and faith without the law.

Judaism, however, can be abandoned no less on the other side. The very ground on which it rests is abandoned when these other developments take place: when it is assumed to be merely an ethic or the support for an ethic; when it becomes a mere edifice of ideas, a doctrine; or when that which the mystery intimates is no longer supposed to be the foundation of man's life but merely some postulate of his thought—when Judaism is taken to be a Judaism without paradox. There is no such thing as a Judaism which is nothing but Kantian philosophy or ethical culture, nor a Judaism in which the idea of God is merely a decorative embellishment or a crowning pinnacle. And the distinctive essence of Judaism is lost, too, where the abundance of its laws may still prevail, but merely as something that is performed, severed from its roots in mystery, void of devotion.

Jewish piety and Jewish wisdom are found only where the soul is in possession of the unity of that which is concealed and that which is evident, of the profound and the task—the unity of devotion and deed. What matters is the unity experienced in the soul, a unity which is born of a reality and points toward a truth—not a mere synthesis, and least of all syncretism. A synthesis merely puts two things alongside each other or at best into each other; but however closely it connects them, it merely connects one thing with another. A unity, on the other hand, involves no mere connection but a revelation: one thing is grasped and experienced through the other and each receives its meaning only from the other. Mystery and commandment are not merely connected and interwoven but proclaim each other and give each other their distinctive essences. The commandment is a true commandment only because it is rooted in mystery, and the mystery is a true mystery because the commandment always speaks out of it. Because it is rooted in mystery, the commandment is unconditional and absolute, independent of the ephemeral and useful, urgent and triumphant. It has the force of unconditional unity, of the unity of morality, or—and this is merely another way of putting it—it has the capacity for taking itself absolutely seriously, to think itself through; and this gives it its entire meaning. And because mystery here cannot be without commandment, it has its own blessing and creative power, and remains fertile; it has the power to demand real life and to give real life; it can let the wall of profundity rise into the light of day and introduce the eternal into the present hour; it has the gift of being in everything and giving unity to everything or—and this is just another way of putting it—the gift of being real instead of merely existent. And it is this alone that gives mystery its full meaning. This totality and unity—this peculiar way in which each is grasped by way of the other—this is Judaism.

Not only the individual's life but history, too, receives its meaning from this. There is history because there is a unity of creation and future. Creation is unthinkable apart from a future, and the idea of the future is inseparable from the certainty of the divine creation. Every commandment that issues from God, every commandment through which God speaks to man whom He has created, has its own infinity, its everlasting future. It creates and begets, it commands on and on, it transcends itself; every duty begets another duty. This endlessness of the law impressed Paul particularly; and it was his opposition to this, his rebellion against that which could not be fulfilled once and for all, that troubled his soul and eventually gave birth to his faith in a redemption that was fulfilled, in a salvation that had been accomplished. For Judaism, however, this endlessness is something positive, it gives man something. A commandment that can be fulfilled completely is merely a human law. The commandment of God is a commandment which leads into the future and involves a mission which, in the words of the Bible, continues "from generation unto generation." It contains a promise, it has a life that continually comes to life, it has a messianic aspect. All creation has its future; in the words of an ancient Jewish parable: "The creation of the world contained the idea of the Messiah." Thus the future is not merely something historical or a mere result, not merely a synthesis of theses and antitheses of the past, but it signifies the certainty that God has created. All future issues from creation; it is the reply to the question of man's nature; it is that which man must expect—not miracle, nor myth, nor fate, but the future of the way, life begotten by Life. Creation and future, mission and confidence depend on each other and reveal each other. And all ages, too, have their unity. God has made a lasting covenant with man.

Therefore religion is not, in our case, a faith in redemption from the world and its demands, but rather—and this has often been called the realism of Judaism—trust in the world or, to be more precise, the assurance of reconciliation. All reconciliation is the reconciliation of the day with eternity, of the limited with infinity, of that which is near with that which is distant, of existence with being, with that which is real and therefore shall be realized. Reconciliation is the liberating assurance that even now, during our life on earth, while we are coping with what is given and assigned, we are related to God. When we speak of the meaning of life, we have in mind such reconciliation. Wherever we find both mystery and commandment, we also encounter the possibility of such reconciliation; for there it is possible for man to become certain of his origin as well as of his way, and so turn back to devotion and to the task of his life—he can always return to himself. Reconciliation and redemption are correlative here. Redemption here is not redemption from the world, but in the world, consecration of the world, realization of the kingdom of God. Mere redemption means that the spheres of mystery and commandment, of this world and the beyond, are separated as two realms which are in a sense opposed to each other. Reconciliation, however, means that they belong together and that everything is unified in the one God. Whatever is beyond enters into this world, and this world bears witness to the beyond. A sentence in the Talmud exhibits the paradox which characterizes Judaism: "One hour of returning to God and good deeds in this world is more than all the life of the world to come; one hour of peace in the world to come is more than all the life of this world." The kingdom of God comprehends everything: mystery and commandment, the beyond and this world; it is the kingdom of reconciliation. "The whole world is full of His glory."

Thus religion is everything here. It permeates the whole of life, carries the meaning of all days, and comprehends the meaning of all ways. There is nothing left that could be called mere "world," and nothing set aside as basically merely "everyday"; there is no mere prose of existence. That which is seemingly commonplace speaks, too, with a voice that comes from the depths; and all prose is also a parable and speaks of that which is concealed. Religion here is nothing isolated, nothing that is shut off; it does not exist only alongside our life or only under or above our life. There is no mystery outside of life and no life outside the commandment. Even all solitude is the solitude of life and has its place in the social sphere. Again there is a unity even in opposition. The depth of life always leads to solitude because it leads us away from the merely human to God; and the task of life leads us into the social realm because it is to be fulfilled by man among men. Yet every commandment should issue from the depths of the self, from that solitude in which the human is surrounded by the divine and in which man perceives the voice of God; and all depth, all solitude is here meant to be the beginning of that way on which the commandment guides us and where we hear the voice of our fellow men. And all thinking of God and searching for God, too, places us in the midst of life. Knowledge of God is not the conclusion of some speculation or the end of some ecstacy, but the ethical, the commandment, something demanded and demanding, a challenge to man's personality. The prophetic dictum places it alongside faithfulness and love. It is owned by piety, by humble reverence for the Lord, by the fear of God. "Behold, the fear of God is wisdom."

As soon as we understand these traits and trends of Jewish religion, we can also comprehend that which many would consider its only aspect: the profusion of rules and customs with which the community surrounds itself, its so-called Law. In Judaism the attempt has been made to give life its style by causing religion to invade every day and penetrate the whole of every day. Everything is in a sense divine service and has its mood and its dignity. In the view of the earthly, the spirit is to be safeguarded; and in the view of the desire, the freedom is to be kept. Judaism cannot do without this ascetic trait unless it wants to forego all that is inward and religious. It does not lead man out of his everyday world, but relates him to God within it. Every partition of life into the profane and the sacred is to be avoided, and the sanctuary dare not possess merely one day beside all the other days. The word "remember" is inscribed above this law: "That you may remember and do all my commandments and be holy unto your God." Thoughtlessness is the true Godlessness; it is the homelessness of the soul. And the Law would guard man against this state in which he is without mystery and commandment; it would give every surface its symbolic function and every bit of prose its parable. Every man is to be made the priest of his own life. Therefore are we confronted with such an abundance of customs, arrangements, and orders which surround everything, "when thou sittest in thy house, and when thou walkest by the way, and when thou liest down, and when thou risest up"—all the way to the ample prose of eating and drinking. All this has helped to consecrate the day and especially also the evening; and it is in his evenings perhaps even more than in his days that man really lives, and it is in his evenings that he dies. A form of life has been fashioned here, though it is, of course, not entirely free from the danger which confronts every style of life: it may cease to be something personal and alive and degenerate into something purely external, into mere tradition. The "Law," too, has sometimes been degraded in this way: that which was meant to be consecration has at times become a mere routine, the fulfillment of something handed down. But even then it was preferable to pure lack of style. And it contains the power of always coming to life again and retrieving its soul.

The whole love of the "Law" has been lavished on and has cherished the Sabbath. As the day of rest, it gives life its balance and rhythm; it sustains the week. Rest is something entirely different from a mere recess, from a mere interruption of work, from not working. A recess is something essentially physical, part of the earthly everyday sphere. Rest, on the other hand, is essentially religious, part of the atmosphere of the divine; it leads us to the mystery, to the depth from which all commandments come, too. It is that which recreates and reconciles, the recreation in which the soul, as it were, creates itself again and catches its breath of life—that in life which is sabbatical. The Sabbath is the image of the messianic; it proclaims the creation and the future; it is the great symbol. In the words of the Bible, it is "a sign between God and Israel"; or, in the words of the Talmud, it is "the parable of eternity." In the Sabbath, life possesses the great contradiction of any end, a perpetual renaissance. A life without Sabbath would lack the spring of renewal, that which opens the well of the depth again and again. An essential and fruitful aspect of Judaism would dry up in such a life; it could still be an ethical life, but it would lack that which defines the Jewish life. Therefore the Jewish community clings to the Sabbath as its possession in spite of all civic difficulties and troubles. The care for the Sabbath is one of the fundamental cares of Judaism.

The Law, and quite especially the sabbatical element in it, has educated that capacity in man which is born only of the depth of life—the capacity to be different. Without this, life cannot be unique. Whoever experiences mystery and commandment becomes unique among men, different, an individual within the world. Whoever knows only mystery becomes merely unique and knows only the day of silence. Whoever knows only the tasks is only among men and knows only the days of work and times of recess. But whoever experiences both, both in unity, lives in the world and yet is different, is different and yet is in the world, lives for other men and with other men and yet within himself, within himself and yet also for other men and hence also with them. This is the gift and possession of Judaism. And it may well be its historic task to offer this image of the dissenter, who dissents for humanity's sake.

It is one of the capacities of religion to sustain, to conserve; and the old spirit of China created a religion in this sense—but only in this sense. Elsewhere we find that it is also one of the capacities of religion to assuage and to still, to teach denying and diverting; and the soul of India was able to do this—and this alone. The distinctive feature of Judaism—and its history also lives on in those religions which issued from it either immediately or mediately—is the power to liberate and renew, this messianic energy. Wherever Jewish piety is found, we encounter this strong drive to create, to fashion for the sake of God, to build the kingdom of God. We encounter this urge to exhibit the strength which is derived from the source of all things, from that which is beyond all strength; we encounter this decision which grows only in the man who knows mystery, not to bow and not to yield, to speak out and contradict. This demanding faith, this demand prompted by faith, is encountered where the soul experiences its depth and its task, that which is concealed and that which is evident, each in the other and each through the other. It is found in the religion of paradox and reconciliation, that religion which lives on the strength of the unity of mystery and commandment in the soul of man.

Philosophy as a Religious Quest

Jacob Needleman

Jacob Needleman (1934–   ) teaches philosophy and comparative religion at San Francisco State College. His recent book, *The New Religions,* is a report and analysis of the "spiritual revolution" among the new generation. He is also author of *Being-in-the-World,* a critical study of existential psycho-analysis, and general editor of the Penguin Metaphysical Library.

WHY PHILOSOPHY IS EASY

In *The Guide for the Perplexed* (Part I, Chapter XXXIV) Maimonides explains why the pursuit of metaphysical knowledge is reserved for the very few and why, even for them, it must not begin until they have reached fullest maturity. The subject, he says, is difficult, profound, and dangerous. He who seeks this knowledge, which is equated with wisdom, must first submit to a long and difficult preparation—mental, moral, and physical. Only then can he risk the incomparably more difficult and lengthy ascent to wisdom.

This naturally calls to mind Plato's plan of education in which the highest pursuit, philosophy, is also to be the last in line. With Plato, as with Maimonides, we read that the direct search for wisdom is to be preceded by a certain training of all the natural faculties of man: the body, the emotions, and the intellect.

Note that it is not only wisdom that is so high and so difficult of attainment, and which requires such remarkable preparation. It is also the search for wisdom, the love of wisdom—*philosophy,* properly so-called—which requires this preparation. And so the question arises: how is it that in the modern era philosophy is no longer difficult in this rather special sense? Has something been gained or lost? Are our sights lower or is our aim better?

To this last question, many—perhaps very many—modern thinkers would reply that philosophy has simply freed itself from a certain grandiose illusion, and that in "lowering" its sights it has indeed raised them toward what is possible and realistic. Detached from the goals of religion, practical ethics, and therapy, it seeks primarily to *think well* about problems that are most fundamental in human experience and cognition. The modern philosopher, in his philosophizing, no longer loves, i.e., searches for a condition of the self, a new state of being.

It is the abandonment of this objective, more than any single conceptualized point of view, that distinguishes modern philosophy from so much of ancient and medieval philosophy. When Plato speaks of the realignment of the elemental functions of the soul as the goal of the philosopher, when the ancient Sceptics speak of *ataraxia*, the Stoics of an inner collectedness and "indifference," and, of course, when so many of the medieval philosophers intertwine the aim of their

From Jacob Needleman, "Why Philosophy Is Easy," *The Review of Metaphysics,* XXII, No. 1 (September 1968), 3–14. Reprinted by permission.

thinking with the aims of the religious process, they are all speaking and thinking in a language that modern philosophy finds unacceptable. To be sure, there
are still very many philosophers who approve these goals as such. It is just that
we cannot understand or accept that they are to be attained or sought after in
our philosophical activity.

In liberating itself from the influence of theology, modern philosophy sought,
of course, to rest itself on the touchstone of experience. By and large, every
modern philosophical effort ultimately bases itself on the evidence of experience
—be it the experience of existentially crucial situations, the experience of perception, the experience of linguistic usage, the experience of moral decisions, the
experience of emotions, or the experience of thinking and judging.

It would be belaboring the obvious to spell out this point in great detail.
Certainly it is no exaggeration to say that, in this sense, common human experience is the touchstone of almost all modern philosophical thought. Experience is something we all have, and we have only to apply our thought in one
way or another to the test of experience to determine the rightness or wrongness
of our philosophy. Naturally, there are great problems, great difficulties in
definition, communication, the assessment of evidence, the selection of experience, etc. But *in principle* we all have the wherewithal with which to test
our philosophy. To say of any system or philosophical position that it does not
accord with experience is to condemn it beyond redemption.

How could it be otherwise? Yet, in an enormously important sense, it has
been otherwise with philosophy. Indeed, it is this emphasis on and trust in our
experience which makes modern philosophy "easy." The Platonic philosophy
is exemplary of philosophy as *difficult* precisely because the appeal to given
experience is never the basis of a line of thought. At most, general human
experience is used to exemplify a line of thought whose ultimate purpose is to
undermine man's reliance on experience.

In fact, it could be said that for Plato—and for the others in the tradition
that takes philosophy to be difficult—man has no experience; or, to put it
another way, his experience is not anything like what he imagines it to be.
Therefore, the education toward philosophy must involve the acquisition by
man of the ability to have genuine experience. The love of wisdom can fully
emerge in a man only after he has acquired at least a small degree of this ability.
It is, in any case, not something men are born with or which they acquire in the
ordinary, general process of "maturation" and "education." Now, what does
this mean?

To try to explicate this it will be most helpful here to make use of the Platonic
psychology—though one could as well use several other ancient or medieval
philosophies. Staying with Plato will enable us to put off until later the highly
charged issue of the relationship between philosophy and religion. For the moment, what will be explored is the idea that the quality of the true philosopher's
experience stands to common human experience much in the way that what
we take to be our common human experience stands to the experience of those
we call psychotic.

Consider for a moment what this would mean if it were true. Why, in the
plainest possible sense, do we profoundly distrust the experience of the mentally
ill? Though this is neither the time or place to go into the various theories of
psychopathology, may we not say that, for whatever reason and in the light

of whatever psychological theory we adopt, the perceptions and judgments of the mentally ill are to an extraordinary degree ruled by certain powerful fears or desires, of which they are not aware? This is surely the primary element we have in mind when we say of the psychotic that he cannot see reality, that he lives in a dream or nightmare, that he is the slave of his subjectivity, etc.

The mentally ill may, and very often do, think about philosophical problems. In fact, speaking quantitatively of course, there is more philosophical activity on many mental wards than is to be found even in our academic departments of philosophy. Thought, and even systems of thought about the nature of reality, the existence of God, the mind-body problem, the problem of other minds, the concept of goodness, the reality of evil, can be found there in great abundance. And no one who has ever had extensive first-hand acquaintance with the mentally ill will tell you their thought lacks logical consistency and systematic coherence. Of course, their philosophy is bad because their experience is bad. The experience which their philosophy explains is bad experience. And, again, the reason it is bad experience is that their desires and fears govern their power to perceive and judge. For such people philosophy is even easier than it is for us.

For Plato our common human experience is of a similar quality, and his diagnosis of the human condition is, in essential aspects, such as to relegate all men to the insane asylum. As we know, the inner human condition, life in the cave, is described as a state of affairs in which the lower element in man, the multiform desires and fears, rules the higher elements, *thumos* and *nous*. Unregenerate man spends his life as a pawn of these desires and fears (the appetitive element) which themselves do not seek knowledge, but only a sort of gratification much like the scratching of an itch.

This idea of the passive submission to the appetitive is what lies at the basis of Plato's derogation of sensory experience. That is, it is this particular sort of passivity—the very opposite of self-mastery—that characterizes unregenerate man's sensory life. Man's immediate contact with the world is not just through the senses, but also and equally through the appetitive reaction to the data of the senses. Thus it is not that the senses deceive; it is that the appetitive reaction is not in the interest of truth, but only in the interest of its immediate and—with respect to the whole of man—partial gratification.

Even so, man's situation would not be so bad were it not that this passive submission to the appetites extends also to the realm of thought and judgment. For here, too, the thoughts that fly through the mind like birds in an aviary are accepted or rejected according to the likes and dislikes that are sourced in the appetitive element. That is to say, the very same part of man which automatically seeks pleasure and avoids pain with regard to the data of the senses also seeks pleasure and avoids pain with regard to the concepts of the mind. This general state of affairs, or condition of the psyche, is termed *doxa*, opinion. With regard to the senses only, it is called *eikasia*, imagination.

But this is not all. Plato tells us that there is in man a certain power or function—perhaps, in modern terms, a certain emotional force—called *thumos,* "the spirited element" which, serving the desires and fears, locks man even more deeply in his psychic cave. For without the aid of *thumos* the "multitude in the soul" could never have the strength—simply because it is such a "rabble"—to cause man constantly and passionately to trust in and fight for the goals of this multitude. And this, ironically, in the name of victory, conquest, achievement, "hard struggle," devotion, self-realization, or—most ironically—love.

So that, with *thumos* thus serving the appetites, the force that could help turn the psyche toward genuine freedom and self-mastery plunges man into the darkness of the "double lie" or "veritable lie," a state of inner deception in which falsehood is passionately and proudly held fast. As Cushman has observed,[1] here lies the source of *hubris,* false pride: the misdirected *dunamis* of the "spirited element" in its attachment to the multiform and inconstant appetitive element. In modern terms it might be possible to speak of this as the origin of the "ego."

If experience is understood to be that which happens to us, it is clear that from the above perspective all that happens to us—or, rather, in us—is the satisfaction or dissatisfaction of our appetites. In a way, *nothing* happens to us, to *me,* but only to "the multitude in the soul." In such a case, truth becomes that which satisfies one or another of this multitude, and the desire for truth becomes the desire to "master" reality, rather than to experience it: the desire to obtain pleasure and avoid pain. And thus the ability to have experience becomes the first goal, rather than the unquestioned assumption, of the seeker of truth.

Clearly, the first step toward this ability is the knowledge of one's own condition of delusion. Presumably, this is the first real experience possible for a man whose inner life is in such chaos. That is, the first real experience is the experience that one has no veridical experience. But where in a man can this experience come from? Certainly not the appetitive element, and certainly not the spirited element. Nor from or in the thought that serves these elements.

In the Platonic psychology real experience can be obtained only through the functioning of the highest element in the psyche, *nous.* Now, the state in which this element can function, uninfluenced by the other elements is called *wisdom.* Thus, to realize one's own inability to experience already requires the active functioning of that which *can* experience. And thus, on strictly psychodynamic and structural terms, the Delphic Oracle is vindicated: Socrates *is* wise in knowing his ignorance. That is, wisdom is a state of being, a condition of psychic organization, and has little, if anything, to do with the lodgment in thought of "correct" propositions about the universe, man, or even oneself.

Obviously, until this reorganization of the psyche has begun to take place, until the experience of certainty—which is sourced only in the active functioning of *nous*—has been touched, philosophical speculation may be anything but a help toward the attainment of wisdom. For, the very idea of what knowledge is and the purposes it may serve is, in unregenerate man, a direct or distant product of his desires and fears. And what he therefore "achieves" when he achieves satisfying explanations or criticism is to become that much more fixed in the condition of the psyche termed *opinion.*

Thus, the search for wisdom—*philo-sophia*—requires a uniquely extensive preparation and is the proximal goal of education. Philosophy is thus, in this sense, not a part of education, but its first end-purpose. If philosophical speculation is presented or given to the appetites, which have their own utilitarian manner of thinking, it may lead to the illusion that wisdom or the ability to know is already present in a man when in fact he may have never had the real experience

[1] *Therpeia* (Chapel Hill, 1958), p. 75.

of certainty about anything, himself or the universe; and if by chance he has experienced it, this experience will have been used and distorted by the appetites. The whole body of Plato's pedagogical prescriptions may, I think, be understood as part of a method that would lead a sufficiently interested man toward this sense of philosophy.

For the philosopher, to know is to experience *via* the activity of the *nous*. And so the age-old philosophical questions become for him directives for possible experiencing. But unregenerate man approaches philosophical knowledge as propositional and deductive—and based, of course, on his now questionable experience. To put it another way, the philosopher seeks in the act of thinking to embody with the whole of his psyche the structure of reality. This is, perhaps, the primal sense of the activity of reflection and speculation: a psychodynamic mirroring of the structure of reality. Such a task requires consciousness and, ultimately, control of the appetites which, for their part and in their moment, throw up standards of satisfaction not necessarily congruent with the laws of the universe. By struggling against a passive submission to the appetitive element, the philosopher in the act of reflecting seeks to incarnate the functional and structural order of the universe.

Obviously, such a goal if accepted prematurely could easily lead to the most preposterous sort of self-inflation, and it is for this reason, among others, that the study of metaphysics is so dangerous. Only a man who has experienced the nullity of his ordinary experience—such as a Socrates—and who can therefore be more or less persistently watchful of himself, could seriously undertake the study of metaphysics, i.e., the perfection of wisdom that leads to a man's inner life mirroring the *entire* scale of cosmic order.

Logical-deductive thought in itself, *dianoia,* may be a useful aid in giving the pupil a taste, so to say, of an activity uninfluenced by the appetites. But precisely because it is removed from the lower elements, it is blind to them. As an activity of the psyche, it requires a severing of parts, not a mastery of the lower by the higher. It requires concentration, a psychological withdrawal, and cannot therefore, as an activity, mirror an organic cosmic order. It can serve *any* cognitive purpose and in the hands of an ordinary man it can maintain him in his ignorance —at any point blithely withstanding the test of "experience" and allowing him to move on, unchecked, to consistency and systematic error.

I believe there is a widespread misconception about the roots of Western philosophy. It is often said that Eastern thought differs radically from the mainstream of Western thought in that it does not separate philosophy and religion. That is, there are many who believe that only in the East is the effort to think about the nature of reality inextricably bound up with the project of transforming the nature of man. Certainly this is true of the way Eastern thought differs from modern Western philosophy, by which I mean philosophy since the scientific revolution. And perhaps this is why there has recently been a growing interest in various Eastern philosophies: Buddhism in its several forms, Vedanta, Taoism, etc. But by identifying the whole of Western philosophy with the temper of modern philosophy, one may well read this temper into much of ancient and medieval philosophy. One may fail to sense that its form and method may have been an attempt at a practical embodiment of its discursive content, and that its deepest purpose was, perhaps, to awaken in the listener or reader the beginnings of a hunger for wisdom in the sense we have described. One may fail to sense this even while spending one's life espousing its content. Just as modern philosophy is "easy," so it has, perhaps become "easy" to read the ancients.

The separation of the goals of philosophy from the goals of religion may therefore be a typically modern, rather than a typically Western, phenomenon. If so, if there is a way of understanding philosophy and religion as tending toward a common goal, then some interesting questions also arise about the modern Western understanding of religion. Is the attainment of wisdom the goal of the religious process? Did Western religion itself change in such a way as to encourage the philosopher to be quite sure he could think more reliably, and ultimately guide his life, without its help? Did it, too, fall away from its primary goals? Finally, was Western philosophy once a religious way, or an essential part of a religious way?

This last question may be, if not answered, at least approached by attempting to place religion as it is known to us in the perspective of our discussion of Platonic wisdom. To do this it will be helpful to expand upon a certain well-known simile concerning the ultimate unity of the various religions of the world:

One often comes across the idea that the various religions are to each other like the spokes of a wheel in that they emanate from a common center; therefore, as one comes to understand any one religion one comes to understand all religion. Let us assume that this center is the state of being or realignment of psychic functions which Plato and others have called wisdom. And let us assume that, with respect to individual men, it is the ultimate task of religion to bring man from his ordinary psychological condition to this state of wisdom.

It may already seem that we are begging the question by assuming this to be the ultimate goal of religion. But, among the things this simile is designed to illustrate is both the particular difficulty of deciding such an issue, and the fact that this extraordinary difficulty is no argument against there actually being a goal that is common to all genuine religion.

Our simile shall be geographical; we locate the center at some point on the surface of the earth, say the top of a particular mountain. Instead of spokes, we shall speak of paths or routes proceeding from a number of locations quite distant both from each other and from the mountain, and which therefore exhibit great differences with respect to climate, terrain, social and biological conditions, and so forth. One path proceeds from the tropics, another from the polar regions, another from the desert, another from a large city. We shall further assume that, compared to conditions on the mountain, the state of wisdom, these other places are bad places; the desert is dry and barren; the jungle dangerous, the arctic cold and isolated, the cities crowded and artificial, and so forth. It is therefore the ultimate task of religion to enable the inhabitants of these places to find their way to the mountain. To this end, certain sets of directions, handbooks, maps, practical advice, and—most important—guides are made available to the various inhabitants.

Thus, the farther away from the mountain, the greater will be the difference in the travel advice. Those starting from the desert, for example, might be told "Thou shalt carry great quantities of water," something that might be unnecessary and even a hindrance to those proceeding from the jungle. And the prescription to wear warm clothing would be disastrous to both these groups, whereas it would be a vital necessity to those starting in the polar regions.

A crucial element in this interpretation of religion is already apparent—namely, that the primal significance of religious forms (and imperatives) is their *instrumentality*, that their root function is to serve as a means toward psychological transformation. Now, obviously, an effective set of instructions for travelling through a particular region must be based on solid knowledge about the terrain, its dangers, its problems, etc. So that, *for someone who does not wish to leave the region*, these instructions could be taken as ways to improve his life *in* the region. Obviously, much of what would help us travel *out* of the desert could also serve to make life *in* the desert easier or more efficient, *thus reinforcing our satisfaction with where we are.*

There are many ways in which this state of affairs can be translated into the problems of this essay. One that immediately springs to mind is the taking of instrumental formulations as *dogma*, in the modern, pejorative sense of the term. Another possible translation would be the taking of a set of ideas designed to help us change our orientation toward the quality of our experience of the universe as themselves finalistic explanations of that experience. In short, *theology*.

What is being suggested here as a possibility is that dogmatic theology, as we generally understand it, is an instance of transforming the instrumental into the finalistic. An identical situation exists as a possibility with regard to what are termed the moral imperatives of religion. "Thou shalt carry water" is an imperative only as long as we are in dry places. But if we wish to stay in the desert it becomes an absolute imperative and thereby ceases to work as a help toward bringing us out of the desert.

Let us say that it is this form or stage of religion that modern philosophy rejected. By identifying this level of religion with religion as such it unwittingly lost the possibility of moving beyond that level. For, philosophy's rejection is based, in part, on the idea that it can improve upon the explanations of dogmatic theology. And, in a certain limited sense, perhaps it can. But by seeking only to do better what dogmatic theology seemed to do, it fixes itself at what is only an early way-station on the path to wisdom—even, perhaps, while using the word "wisdom" to express its goal. Thus, there may be even more efficient ways of living well in the desert.

Consequently, philosophy, while detaching itself in this way from a relatively elementary form of religion, remains itself—with regard to the actual attainment of wisdom—forever bogged down on that same elementary level. No matter how intricate, subtle, or comprehensive its thought becomes, it will never move from that level. And thus, when an even more efficient way of "living in the desert" comes along—Western natural science—it is quick to recognize this as its master, or at least as that to which it must direct most of its energies. From the point of view of the actual attainment of wisdom, the development of philosophy from Descartes through Locke, Hume, Kant, and the contemporary schools thus represents little more than the rationalization of the chains that hold man in the cave. Philosophy becomes easy.

Our simile can be used to express several other things about the religions of the world. For example, to many people one of the most repugnant aspects of some religions is their claim to exclusiveness and the concomitant condemnation of other religions. But if we take this as instrumental, it can become more understandable. If we are living in the desert, then only a certain limited set of directions can help us get out of the desert. To follow an arctic handbook would kill us. Or, seen from another angle, if one considers the psychological and environmental conditions of a certain period and place, the most *useful* imperative might well involve the necessity of submission to some form of authority.

In other conditions, or at a certain point along the way—say, when we are safely out of the desert—it may be more *useful* to us (as judged by the guide) to try to understand that there are other paths as well. In any event, as the paths get closer to the center, the terrain naturally becomes more and more similar for everyone no matter where they started from; therefore, the various sets of directions become more alike until, finally, they are all mountain-climbing directions, differing only with respect to the face of the mountain that is being scaled. It is only as one climbs the mountain, however, that one can actually *see* some of the other paths and the people travelling them; only then can one actually verify that the various religions lead to a common center.

Thus, the question as to whether the state of wisdom is the end-purpose of the religions cannot really be decided until one is rather far along towards wisdom. Otherwise, it would mean placing our trust in that quality of experience which it is the first lesson of wisdom to distrust. Consequently, there is no neutral ground upon which to stand in judging either the goals of the religious ways or in comparing the ways themselves. "Neutral ground" in this case would mean: to be on no path at all, i.e., the darkest part of the cave (and, incidentally, the place where philosophy is "easiest").

This now brings us to what is perhaps the most important aspect of our whole problem. For one may very well ask: does all this mean we are to surrender our critical faculties, our philosophical methods, our trust in science and in our own moral sense, abandoning all our present intellectual goods, feeble as they may well be when compared to the ideal of wisdom and self-perfection?

One may well ask this, having heard of such notions as "the crucifixion of reason," "belief by virtue of the absurd," having read of the methods of the Zen Buddhists, and having studied the writings of the great mystics, many of whom seem to exhort us to cast away our rationality, such as it is.

We know, most of us, that we cannot do this. We cannot even wish to do this, not even if we felt able to. And not even though we might, somewhere in ourselves, agree that this rationality by itself may never lead us to a certain quality of thought which we might have hoped for in answer to the fundamental life-questions that first brought many of us to the study of philosophy. Even so, we are not able to give it up.

But perhaps to see this fact about ourselves is already to have glimpsed a most crucial aspect of *our* condition here and now, one feature, so to say, of our "geographical" situation. It would be from here, then, that our movement towards wisdom would have to begin; from *here*, and not from some other starting-place where the sacrifice of the mind is required. Just as, on another path, Kierkegaard sought to make Christianity the most difficult thing in the world, so we philosophers may wish to find a way to help us make philosophy more difficult.

Toward a Sacred Universe: Religion and the Cosmic

INTRODUCTION

Ancient man regarded the universe as a living organism, a vast moving structure of energies and purposes animated throughout by the absolute intelligence of God. Moreover, the laws governing this universe were as rigorous and inexorable as any that modern science has discovered. But, as time went by, this vision of a sacred universe, replete with value and mind, was interpreted in a sentimental way and was justly criticized as a fable. Against this sort of interpretation, modern science struck like lightning, reminding men of their tendency to project on reality meanings that pleased them or magnified their importance.

But now, in the despair of our time, men are putting old questions to the universe in a way that is no longer sentimental or academic. Is life a basic property of reality or a fragile and recent outcropping of the planet Earth, unsupported by the fundamental forces of the universe? Is man a metaphysical cul-de-sac or an arm of divinity, reflecting in his potentialities the furthest purposes of his creator? In short, is the universe like a sacred book that we have forgotten how to read or is it only an ocean of force less conscious than the mind that seeks to understand it?

Our opening selection in this chapter is a classic statement by the scientific mind regarding a universe devoid of meaning. In it, the young **Bertrand Russell** finds the cue for courage in the need to forge ideals without dependence on a blind universe in which man's only end is death. No essay of modern times more eloquently forces us to ask for a more realistic sense of the religious. Is the religion that Russell denies the only sort of religion that can exist?

According to **Hans Jonas,** in the second selection of this chapter, ancient man's "animistic" view of the universe has been sadly underestimated by the modern mind. So habituated have we become to seeing reality as unalive, says Jonas, that we fail to realize we are operating on a metaphysical premise that is only one philosophical option among many. For ancient man, death—not life—was the phenomenon that needed to be explained, because for him life was a fundamental property of reality.

Another answer to Russell is given by the eminent physicist and historian of science **Pierre Duhem**, in the third selection of this chapter. The problem, Duhem tells us, is not that science has too rigorously denied a metaphysical sense of the cosmos but that its interpreters have not seen the genuine rigor of natural science. Science has nothing to say one way or the other about meaning in the universe. To claim otherwise is surreptitiously to endow science with a metaphysical bias that would undermine its usefulness as a pragmatic tool for the ordering of data. Here speaks the pure positivist, who, contrary to many popular opinions about positivism, can without contradiction be a believing Christian and an exact scientist at the same time.

In the fourth selection, **Teilhard de Chardin** chooses quite another direction. Taking biology, rather than physics, as the science that offers the most important message for modern man, he extrapolates from the laws of evolution to a factor that reconciles religious belief and scientific fact. The present community of man with all its apparent difficulties wrought by technology is, for Teilhard, like a new creature struggling to be born, a "creature" of spiritualized matter that has not yet existed in the universe.

From the intensely Western mind of Teilhard de Chardin, we turn, in the fifth selection, to the most ancient of Eastern cosmological and psychological systems—the Samkhya, neatly exposited by **John M. Koller.** The Samkhya lies at the heart of almost every spiritual teaching that India has brought forth. Nature is understood as a great organic mechanism whose unending rhythms may be studied impartially within the consciousness of ordinary man. Here, then, is a system of the world that is both impersonal and highly spiritual, where rigorous laws of cause and effect are also the laws by which men can transform their inner lives and attain to a divine intelligence. This selection shows that it is not necessary to sacrifice the idea of conscious universe for the sake of scientific precision.

In our final selection, **S. H. Nasr** details the steps by which modern science let go of the sacred dimension in the universe. After the Renaissance, he says, the cosmos was secularized. Instead of being man's teacher, nature became an object for intellectual and physical exploitation. In calling for a return to pure metaphysics, Nasr is at the same time calling on modern men to search for a contact within themselves with that "active intellect" or intuition that enables a human being, according to traditional teachings, to grasp divine purposes in a sacred universe.

J. N.

Suggested Readings

Burckhardt, Titus. "Cosmology and Modern Science." *The Sword of Gnosis.* New York: Penguin Books, 1973.

Eliade, Mircea. *Cosmos and History.* New York: Harper Torchbooks, 1959.

Nasr, S. H. *The Encounter of Man and Nature.* London: Allen & Unwin, 1968.

Needham, Joseph. *Science and Civilization in China.* Vol. II. Cambridge: Cambridge University Press, 1962.

Nicholson, Marjorie Hope. *The Breaking of the Circle.* New York: Columbia University Press, 1960.

Nicoll, Maurice. *Living Time.* London: Vincent Stuart, 1964.

de Santillana, Giorgio, and von Dechend, Hertha. *Hamlet's Mill.* Boston: Gambit, 1969.

Teilhard de Chardin, Pierre. *The Phenomenon of Man.* Translated by Bernard Wall. New York: Harper, 1959.

White, Andrew Dickson. *A History of the Warfare of Science with Theology in Christendom.* New York: Free Press, 1965.

A Free Man's Worship

Bertrand Russell

Bertrand Russell (1872–1970), the grandson of Lord John Russell, a prime minister under Queen Victoria, was born in Wales. He studied mathematics and philosophy at Trinity College, Cambridge from 1890 to 1894. He was a fellow at Trinity from 1895 to 1901 and a lecturer in philosophy there from 1910 to 1916. In 1916, Russell was dismissed from his position because of his pacifist activities. Then, in 1918, he was sentenced to six months in prison because of an allegedly libelous article in which he expressed his opposition to World War I and his desire for peace. Russell was a fellow of the Royal Society, an honorary fellow of the British Academy, and a recipient of the Order of Merit. He was awarded the Noble Prize for literature in 1950. In the area of logic, Russell wrote *Principles of Mathematics, Principia Mathematica* (with A. N. Whitehead, three volumes, 1910–1913), and *Introduction to Mathematical Philosophy.* His works in epistemology and metaphysics include *Our Knowledge of the External World, The Analysis of Matter,* and *Human Knowledge, Its Scope and Limits.* Among his books on social issues are *Marriage and Morals* and *Education and the Social Order.*

From Bertrand Russell, *Why I Am Not a Christian* (New York, 1957), pp. 105–116. Copyright © 1957 by Allen and Unwin. Reprinted by permission of Simon and Schuster, Inc.

To Dr. Faustus in his study Mephistopheles told the history of the Creation, saying,

The endless praises of the choirs of angels had begun to grow wearisome; for, after all, did he not deserve their praise? Had he not given them endless joy? Would it not be more amusing to obtain undeserved praise, to be worshiped by beings whom he tortured? He smiled inwardly, and resolved that the great drama should be performed.

For countless ages the hot nebula whirled aimlessly through space. At length it began to take shape, the central mass threw off planets, the planets cooled, boiling seas and burning mountains heaved and tossed, from black masses of cloud hot sheets of rain deluged the barely solid crust. And now the first germ of life grew in the depths of the ocean and developed rapidly in the fructifying warmth into vast forest trees, huge ferns springing from the damp mold, sea monsters breeding, fighting, devouring, and passing away. And from the monsters, as the play unfolded itself, Man was born with the power of thought, the knowledge of good and evil, and the cruel thirst for worship. And Man saw that all is passing in this mad, monstrous world, that all is struggling to snatch, at any cost, a few brief moments of life before Death's inexorable decree. And Man said, "There is a hidden purpose, could we but fathom it, and the purpose is good; for we must reverence something, and in the visible world there is nothing worthy of reverence." And Man stood aside from the struggle, resolving that God intended harmony to come out of chaos by human efforts. And when he followed the instincts which God had transmitted to him from his ancestry of beasts of prey, he called it Sin, and asked God to forgive him. But he doubted whether he could be justly forgiven, until he invented a divine Plan by which God's wrath was to have been appeased. And seeing the present was bad, he made it yet worse, that thereby the future might be better. And he gave God thanks for the strength that enabled him to forgo even the joys that were possible. And God smiled; and when he saw that Man had become perfect in renunciation and worship, he sent another sun through the sky, which crashed into Man's sun; and all returned again to nebula.

"Yes," he murmured, "it was a good play; I will have it performed again."

Such, in outline, but even more purposeless, more void of meaning, is the world which science presents for our belief. Amid such a world, if anywhere, our ideals henceforward must find a home. That man is the product of causes which had no prevision of the end they were achieving; that his origin, his growth, his hopes and fears, his loves and his beliefs, are but the outcome of accidental collocations of atoms; that no fire, no heroism, no intensity of thought and feeling, can preserve an individual life beyond the grave; that all the labors of the ages, all the devotion, all the inspiration, all the noonday brightness of human genius, are destined to extinction in the vast death of the solar system, and that the whole temple of man's achievement must inevitably be buried beneath the debris of a universe in ruins—all these things, if not quite beyond dispute, are yet so nearly certain that no philosophy which rejects them can hope to stand. Only within the scaffolding of these truths, only on the firm foundation of unyielding despair, can the soul's habitation henceforth be safely built.

How, in such an alien and inhuman world, can so powerless a creature as man preserve his aspirations untarnished? A strange mystery it is that nature, omnipotent but blind, in the revolutions of her secular hurryings through the abysses of space, has brought forth at last a child, subject still to her power, but gifted with sight, with knowledge of good and evil, with the capacity of judging all the works of his unthinking mother. In spite of death, the mark and seal of the parental control, man is yet free, during his brief years, to examine, to criticize, to know, and in imagination to create. To him alone, in the world with which he is acquainted, his freedom belongs; and in this lies his superiority to the resistless forces that control his outward life.

The savage, like ourselves, feels the oppression of his impotence before the powers of nature; but having in himself nothing that he respects more than power, he is willing to prostrate himself before his gods, without inquiring whether they are worthy of his worship. Pathetic and very terrible is the long history of cruelty and torture, of degradation and human sacrifice, endured in the hope of placating the jealous gods: surely, the trembling believer thinks, when what is most precious has been freely given, their lust for blood must be appeased, and more will not be required. The religion of Moloch—as such creeds may be generically called—is in essence the cringing submission of the slave, who dares not, even in his heart, allow the thought that his master deserves no adulation. Since the independence of ideals is not yet acknowledged, power may be freely worshipped and receive an unlimited respect, despite its wanton infliction of pain.

But gradually, as morality grows bolder, the claim of the ideal world begins to be felt; and worship, if it is not to cease, must be given to gods of another kind than those created by the savage. Some, though they feel the demands of the ideal, will still consciously reject them, still urging that naked power is worthy of worship. Such is the attitude inculcated in God's answer to Job out of the whirlwind: the divine power and knowledge are paraded, but of the divine goodness there is no hint. Such also is the attitude of those who, in our own day, base their morality upon the struggle for survival, maintaining that the survivors are necessarily the fittest. But others, not content with an answer so repugnant to the moral sense, will adopt the position which we have become accustomed to regard as specially religious, maintaining that, in some hidden manner, the world of fact is really harmonious with the world of ideals. Thus man created God, all-powerful and all-good, the mystic unity of what is and what should be.

But the world of fact, after all, is not good; and, in submitting our judgment to it, there is an element of slavishness from which our thoughts must be purged. For in all things it is well to exalt the dignity of man, by freeing him as far as possible from the tyranny of nonhuman power. When we have realized that power is largely bad, that man, with his knowledge of good and evil, is but a helpless atom in a world which has no such knowledge, the choice is again presented to us: Shall we worship force, or shall we worship goodness? Shall our God exist and be evil, or shall he be recognized as the creation of our own conscience?

The answer to this question is very momentous and affects profoundly our whole morality. The worship of force, to which Carlyle and Nietzsche and the creed of militarism have accustomed us, is the result of failure to maintain our own ideals against a hostile universe: it is itself a prostrate submission to evil, a sacrifice of our best to Moloch. If strength indeed is to be respected, let us respect rather the strength of those who refuse that false "recognition of facts" which fails to recognize that facts are often bad. Let us admit that, in the world we know, there are many things that would be better otherwise, and that the ideals to which we do and must adhere are not realized in the realm of matter. Let us preserve our respect for truth, for beauty, for the ideal of perfection which life does not permit us to attain, though none of these things meet with the approval of the unconscious universe. If power is bad, as it seems to be, let us reject it from our hearts. In this lies man's true freedom: in determination to worship only the God created by our own love of the good, to respect only the heaven which inspires the insight of our best moments. In action, in desire, we must submit perpetually to the tyranny of outside forces; but in thought, in aspiration, we are free, free from our fellow men, free from the petty planet on which our bodies impotently crawl, free even, while we live, from the tyranny of death. Let us learn, then, that energy of faith which enables us to live constantly in the vision of the good; and let us descend, in action, into the world of fact, with that vision always before us.

When first the opposition of fact and ideal grows fully visible, a spirit of fiery revolt, of fierce hatred of the gods, seems necessary to the assertion of freedom. To defy with Promethean constancy a hostile universe, to keep its evil always in view, always actively hated, to refuse no pain that the malice of power can invent, appears to be the duty of all who will not bow before the inevitable. But indignation is still a bondage, for it compels our thoughts to be occupied with an evil world; and in the fierceness of desire from which rebellion springs there is a kind of self-assertion which it is necessary for the wise to overcome. Indignation is a submission of our thoughts but not of our desires; the Stoic freedom in which wisdom consists is found in the submission of our desires but not of our thoughts. From the submission of our desires springs the virtue of resignation; from the freedom of our thoughts springs the whole world of art and philosophy, and the vision of beauty by which, at last, we half reconquer the reluctant world. But the vision of beauty is possible only to unfettered contemplation, to thoughts not weighted by the load of eager wishes; and thus freedom comes only to those who no longer ask of life that it shall yield them any of those personal goods that are subject to the mutations of time.

Although the necessity of renunciation is evidence of the existence of evil, yet Christianity, in preaching it, has shown a wisdom exceeding that of the Promethean philosophy of rebellion. It must be admitted that, of the things we desire, some, though they prove impossible, are yet real goods; others, however, as ardently longed for, do not form part of a fully purified ideal. The belief that what must be renounced is bad, though sometimes false, is far less often false than untamed passion supposes; and the creed of religion, by providing a reason for proving that it is never false, has been the means of purifying our hopes by the discovery of many austere truths.

But there is in resignation a further good element: even real goods, when they are unattainable, ought not to be fretfully desired. To every man comes, sooner or later, the great renunciation. For the young, there is nothing unattainable; a good thing desired with the whole force of a passionate will, and yet impossible, is to them not credible. Yet, by death, by illness, by poverty, or by the voice of duty, we must learn, each one of us, that the world was not made for us, and that, however beautiful may be the things we crave, Fate may nevertheless forbid them. It is the part of courage, when misfortune comes, to bear without repining the ruin of our hopes, to turn away our thoughts from vain regrets. This degree of submission to power is not only just and right: it is the very gate of wisdom.

But passive renunciation is not the whole of wisdom; for not by renunciation alone can we build a temple for the worship of our own ideals. Haunting foreshadowings of the temple appear in the realm of imagination, in music, in architecture, in the untroubled kingdom of reason, and in the golden sunset magic of lyrics, where beauty shines and glows, remote from the touch of sorrow, remote from the fear of change, remote from the failures and disenchantments of the world of fact. In the contemplation of these things the vision of heaven will shape itself in our hearts, giving at once a touchstone to judge the world about us and an inspiration by which to fashion to our needs whatever is not incapable of serving as a stone in the sacred temple.

Except for those rare spirits that are born without sin, there is a cavern of darkness to be traversed before that temple can be entered. The gate of the cavern is despair, and its floor is paved with the gravestones of abandoned hopes. There self must die; there the eagerness, the greed of untamed desire, must be slain, for only so can the soul be freed from the empire of Fate. But out of the cavern, the Gate of Renunciation leads again to the daylight of wisdom, by whose radiance a new insight, a new joy, a new tenderness, shine forth to gladden the pilgrim's heart.

When, without the bitterness of impotent rebellion, we have learned both to resign ourselves to the outward rule of Fate and to recognize that the nonhuman world is unworthy of our worship, it becomes possible at last so to transform and refashion the unconscious universe, so to transmute it in the crucible of imagination, that a new image of shining gold replaces the old idol of clay. In all the multiform facts of the world—in the visual shapes of trees and mountains and clouds, in the events of the life of man, even in the very omnipotence of death—the insight of creative idealism can find the reflection of a beauty which its own thoughts first made. In this way mind asserts its subtle mastery over the thoughtless forces of nature. The more evil the material with which it deals, the more thwarting to untrained desire, the greater is its achievement in inducing the reluctant rock to yield up its hidden treasures, the prouder its victory in compelling the opposing forces to swell the pageant of its triumph. Of all the arts, tragedy is the proudest, the most triumphant; for it builds its shining citadel in the very center of the enemy's country, on the very summit of his highest mountain; from its impregnable watchtowers, his camps and arsenals, his columns and forts, are all revealed; within its walls the free life continues, while the legions of death and pain and despair, and all the servile captains of tyrant Fate, afford the burghers of that dauntless city new spectacles of beauty. Happy those sacred ramparts, thrice happy the dwellers on that all-seeing eminence. Honor to those brave warriors who, through countless ages of warfare, have preserved for us the priceless heritage of liberty and have kept undefiled by sacrilegious invaders the home of the unsubdued.

But the beauty of tragedy does but make visible a quality which, in more or less obvious shapes, is present always and everywhere in life. In the spectacle of death, in the endurance of intolerable pain, and in the irrevocableness of a vanished past, there is a sacredness, an overpowering awe, a feeling of the vastness, the depth, the inexhaustible mystery of existence, in which, as by some strange marriage of pain, the sufferer is bound to the world by bonds of sorrow. In these moments of insight, we lose all eagerness of temporary desire, all struggling and striving for petty ends, all care for the little trivial things that, to a superficial view, make up the common life of day by day; we see, surrounding the narrow raft illumined by the flickering light of human comradeship, the dark ocean on whose rolling waves we toss for a brief hour; from the great night without, a chill blast breaks in upon our refuge; all the loneliness of humanity amid hostile forces is concentrated upon the individual soul, which must struggle alone, with what of courage it can command, against the whole weight of a universe that cares nothing for its hopes and fears. Victory, in this struggle with the powers of darkness, is the true baptism into the glorious company of heroes, the true initiation into the overmastering beauty of human existence. From that awful encounter of the soul with the outer world, renunciation, wisdom, and charity are born; and with their birth a new life begins. To take into the inmost shrine of the soul the irresistible forces whose puppets we seem to be—death and change, the irrevocableness of the past, and the powerlessness of man before the blind hurry of the universe from vanity to vanity—to feel these things and know them is to conquer them.

This is the reason why the past has such magical power. The beauty of its motionless and silent pictures is like the enchanted purity of late autumn, when the leaves, though one breath would make them fall, still glow against the sky in golden glory. The past does not change or strive; like Duncan, after life's fitful fever it sleeps well; what was eager and grasping, what was petty and transitory, has faded away; the things that were beautiful and eternal shine out of it like stars in the night. Its beauty, to a soul not worthy of it, is unendurable; but to a soul which has conquered Fate it is the key of religion.

The life of man, viewed outwardly, is but a small thing in comparison with the forces of nature. The slave is doomed to worship Time and Fate and Death, because they are greater than anything he finds in himself, and because all his thoughts are of things which they devour. But, great as they are, to think of them greatly, to feel their passionless splendor, is greater still. And such thought makes us free men; we no longer bow before the inevitable in Oriental subjection, but we absorb it and make it a part of ourselves. To abandon the struggle for private happiness, to expel all eagerness of temporary desire, to burn with passion for eternal things—this is emancipation, and this is the free man's worship. And this liberation is effected by contemplation of Fate; for Fate itself is subdued by the mind which leaves nothing to be purged by the purifying fire of time.

United with his fellow men by the strongest of all ties, the tie of a common doom, the free man finds that a new vision is with him always, shedding over every daily task the light of love. The life of man is a long march through the night, surrounded by invisible foes, tortured by weariness and pain, toward a goal that few can hope to reach, and where none may tarry long. One by one, as they march, our comrades vanish from our sight, seized by the silent orders of omnipotent death. Very brief is the time in which we can help them, in which their happiness or misery is decided. Be it ours to shed sunshine on their path, to lighten their sorrows by the balm of sympathy, to give them the pure joy of a never-tiring affection, to strengthen failing courage, to instill faith in hours of despair. Let us not weigh in grudging scales their merits and demerits, but let us think only of their need—of the sorrows, the difficulties, perhaps the blindnesses, that make the misery of their lives; let us remember that they are fellow sufferers in the same darkness, actors in the same tragedy with ourselves. And so, when their day is over, when their good and their evil have become eternal by the immortality of the past, be it ours to feel that, where they suffered, where they failed, no deed of ours was the cause; but wherever a spark of the divine fire kindled in their hearts, we were ready with encouragement, with sympathy, with brave words in which high courage glowed.

Brief and powerless is man's life; on him and all his race the slow, sure doom falls pitiless and dark. Blind to good and evil, reckless of destruction, omnipotent matter rolls on its relentless way; for man, condemned today to lose his dearest, tomorrow himself to pass through the gate of darkness, it remains only to cherish, ere yet the blow fall, the lofty thoughts that ennoble his little day; disdaining the coward terrors of the slave of Fate, to worship at the shrine that his own hands have built; undismayed by the empire of chance, to preserve a mind free from the wanton tyranny that rules his outward life; proudly defiant of the irresistible forces that tolerate, for a moment, his knowledge and his condemnation, to sustain alone, a weary but unyielding Atlas, the world that his own ideals have fashioned despite the trampling march of unconscious power.

A Universe of Life and a Universe of Death

Hans Jonas

Hans Jonas (1903–   ) is professor of philosophy in the graduate faculty of the New School for Social Research in New York. The author of numerous articles in the areas of history of religion, phenomenology, existentialism, and philosophy of science, his most influential book is *Gnosis und spätantiker Geist,* which appeared in English under the title *The Gnostic Religion.*

When man first began to interpret the nature of things—and this he did when he began to be man—life was to him everywhere, and being the same as being alive. Animism was the widespread expression of this stage, "hylozoism" one of its later, conceptual forms. Soul flooded the whole of existence and encountered itself in all things. Bare matter, that is, truly inanimate, "dead" matter, was yet to be discovered—as indeed its concept, so familiar to us, is anything but obvious. That the world is alive is really the most natural view, and largely supported by prima-facie evidence. On the terrestrial scene, in which experience is reared and contained, life abounds and occupies the whole foreground exposed to man's immediate view. The proportion of manifestly lifeless matter encountered in this primordial field is small, since most of what we now know to be inanimate is so intimately intertwined with the dynamics of life that it seems to share its nature. Earth, wind, and water—begetting, teeming, nurturing, destroying—are anything but models of "mere matter." Thus primitive panpsychism, in addition to answering powerful needs of the soul, was justified by rules of inference and verification within the available range of

From Hans Jonas, "Life, Death, and the Body in the Theory of Being," in *The Phenomenon of Life* (New York, 1966), pp. 7–26. Copyright © by Hans Jonas. Reprinted by permission of Harper & Row, Publishers, Inc.

experience, continually confirmed as it was by the actual preponderance of life in the horizon of its earthly home. Indeed not before the Copernican revolution widened this horizon into the vastness of cosmic space was the proportional place of life in the scheme of things sufficiently dwarfed so that it became possible to disregard it for most of what henceforth was to be the content of the term "nature." But to early man, standing on his earth arched by the dome of its sky, it could never occur that life might be a side issue in the universe, and not its pervading rule. His panvitalism was a perspective truth which only a change of perspective could eventually displace. Unquestioned and convincing at the beginning stands the experience of the omnipresence of life.

In such a world-view, the riddle confronting man is *death:* it is the contradiction to the one intelligible, self-explaining, "natural" condition which is the general life. To the extent that life is accepted as the primary state of things, death looms as the disturbing mystery. Hence the *problem* of death is probably the first to deserve this name in the history of thought. Its emergence as an express problem signifies the awakening of the questioning mind long before a conceptual level of theory is attained. The natural recoil from death takes courage from the "logical" outrage which the fact of mortality inflicts on panvitalistic conviction. Primeval reflection thus grapples with the riddle of death, and in myth, cult, and religious belief endeavors to find a solution to it.

That death, not life, calls for an explanation in the first place, reflects a theoretical situation which lasted long in the history of the race. Before there was wonder at the miracle of life, there was wonder about death and what it might mean. If life is the natural and comprehensible thing, death—its apparent negation—is a thing unnatural and cannot be truly real. The explanation it called for had to be in terms of life as the only understandable thing: death had somehow to be assimilated to life. The question it inspired faces backward and forward: how and why did death come into the world whose essence it contradicts? And whereto is it the transition, since whatever it may lead to must still belong to the total context of life? Early metaphysics attempts to answer these questions; or, despairing of an answer, remonstrates with the incomprehensible law. It is the question of Gilgamesh—the answer of the funeral cult. As early man's practice is embodied in his tools, so his thought is embodied in his tombs which acknowledge and negate death at the same time. Out of the tombs arose pristine metaphysics in the shape of myth and religion. That all is life and that all life is mortal is the basic contradiction it strives to resolve. It meets the profound challenge; and to save the sum of things, death had somehow to be denied.

Any problem is essentially the collision between a comprehensive view (be it hypothesis or belief) and a particular fact which will not fit into it. Primitive panvitalism was the comprehensive view; ever-recurring death, the particular fact: since it seemed to deny the basic truth, it had to be denied itself. To seek for its meaning was to acknowledge its strangeness in the world; to understand it was—in this climate of a universal ontology of life—to negate it by making it a transmutation of life itself. Such a negation is the belief in a survival after death which primeval burial customs express. The cult of the dead and the belief in immortality of whatever shape, and the speculations into which they evolve, are the running argument of the life-creed with death—an argument which could also recoil on the embattled position and eventually lead to its breaking-up. At first, any settling of the contradiction, any solution of the riddle, could only be in favor of life; or the riddle remained, an outcry without answer; or the original position was abandoned and a new stage of thought ushered in. Both the first two alternatives attest the original ontological dominance of life. This is the paradox: precisely the importance of the tombs in the beginnings of mankind, the power of the death motif in the beginnings of human thought, testify to the greater power of the universal life motif as their sustaining ground: being was intelligible only as living; and the divined constancy of being could be understood only as the constancy of life, even beyond death and in defiance of its apparent verdict.

Modern thought which began with the Renaissance is placed in exactly the opposite theoretic situation. Death is the natural thing, life the problem. From the physical sciences there spread over the conception of all existence an ontology whose model entity is pure matter, stripped of all features of life. What at the animistic stage was not even discovered has in the meantime conquered the vision of reality, entirely ousting its counterpart. The tremendously enlarged universe of modern cosmology is conceived as a field of inanimate masses and forces which operate according to the laws of inertia and of quantitative distribution in space. This denuded substratum of all reality could only be arrived at through a progressive expurgation of vital features from the physical record and through strict abstention from projecting into its image our felt aliveness. In the process the ban on anthropomorphism was extended to zoomorphism in general. What remained is the residue of the reduction toward the properties of mere extension which submit to measurement and hence to mathematics. These properties alone satisfy the requirements of what is now called exact knowledge: and representing the only knowable aspect of nature they, by a tempting substitution, came to be regarded as its essential aspect too: and if this, then as the only real in reality. This means that the lifeless has become the knowable par excellence and is for that reason also considered the true and only foundation of reality. It is the "natural" as well as the original state of things. Not only in terms of relative quantity but also in terms of ontological genuineness, nonlife is the rule, life the puzzling exception in physical existence.

Accordingly, it is the existence of life within a mechanical universe which now calls for an explanation, and explanation has to be in terms of the lifeless. Left over as a borderline case in the homogeneous physical world-view, life has to be accounted for by the terms of that view. Quantitatively infinitesimal in the immensity of cosmic matter, qualitatively an exception from the rule of its properties, cognitively the unexplained in the general plainness of physical things, it has become the stumbling block of theory. That there is life at all, and how such a thing is possible in a world of mere matter, is now the problem posed to thought. The very fact that we have nowadays to deal with the theoretical problem of life, instead of the problem of death, testifies to the status of death as the natural and intelligible condition.

Here again, the problem consists in the collision between a comprehensive view and a particular fact: as formerly panvitalism, so now panmechanism is the comprehensive hypothesis; and the rare case of life, realized under the exceptional, perhaps unique conditions of our planet, is the improbable particular that seems to elude the basic law and therefore must be denied its autonomy—that is, must be integrated into the general law. To take life as a problem is here to acknowledge its strangeness in the mechanical world which is *the* world; to explain it is—in this climate of a universal ontology of death— to negate it by making it one of the possible variants of the lifeless. Such a negation is the mechanistic theory of the organism, as the funeral rites of prehistory were a negation of death. *L'homme machine* signifies in the modern scheme what conversely hylozoism signified in the ancient scheme: the usurpation of one, dissembled realm by the other which enjoys an ontological monopoly. Vitalistic monism is replaced by mechanistic monism, in whose rules of evidence the standard of life is exchanged for that of death.

In the new monism, too, one face of the question is turned backward: no longer, how did death, but how did life come into the world, the lifeless one? Life's place in this world has shrunk to that of the organism, a problematical speciality in the configurations of extended substance. In it alone do "extended" and "thinking" being meet, after they had first been sundered into two onto- logical spheres of which only the first is "world," and the second not even belongs to the world. Their meeting in the organism then becomes an insoluble riddle. But since the organism, as a corporeal thing, is a case of the extended, thus a piece of "world," however particular a configuration of its parts, it cannot be essentially different from the rest of the world, i.e., from the general being of the world.

In itself this argument, of course, cuts both ways: If there is to be homo- geneity, then either the general can be seen in the image of the particular (which is first and nearest in experience), or the particular in the image of the general— i.e., either world-nature in the image of the organism, or the organism in the image of world-nature. But what the general nature of the world is, has been decided in advance: mere matter in space. Therefore, since organism represents "life" in the world, the question regarding life now poses itself thus: How does the organism stand in the total context already defined, how is this special order or function of it reducible to its general laws—how, in short, is life reducible to nonlife? To reduce life to the lifeless is nothing else than to resolve the particular into the general, the complex into the simple, and the apparent exception into the accepted rule. Precisely this is the task set to modern biological science by the goal of "science" as such. The degree of approximation to this goal is the measure of its success; and the unresolved remainder left at any time denotes its provisional limit, to be advanced in the next move.

The earlier goal, we have seen, was to interpret the apparently lifeless in the image of life and to extend life into apparent death. Then, it was the corpse, this primal exhibition of "dead" matter, which was the limit of all understanding and therefore the first thing not to be accepted at its face-value. Today the living, feeling, striving organism has taken over this role and is being unmasked as a *ludibrium materiae,* a subtle hoax of matter. Only when a corpse is the body plainly intelligible: then it returns from its puzzling and unorthodox behavior of aliveness to the unambiguous, "familiar" state of a body within the world of bodies, whose general laws provide the canon of all comprehensibility. To approximate the laws of the organic body to this canon, i.e., to efface in *this* sense the boundaries between life and death, is the direction of modern thought on life as a physical fact. Our thinking today is under the ontological dominance of death.

One may object here that we speak of "death" when we mean the mere indifference of matter, which is a neutral character whereas "dead" has an antithetical meaning applying only to what is (or could be, or once was) alive. But in fact, though this is forgotten, the cosmos once *was* alive as perceived by man, and its more recent lifeless image was built up, or left over, in a continuous process of critical subtraction from its fuller original content: at least in this historical sense the mechanistic conception of the universe does contain an antithetic element and is not simply neutral. Moreover, that "subtraction" was set in motion and for long sustained, not by the critical understanding, but by dualistic metaphysics which has demonstrable roots in the experience of mortality. *Dualism* is the link that historically mediated between the two extremes which so far we have opposed to each other unhistorically: it was indeed the vehicle of the movement which carried the mind of man from the vitalistic monism of early times to the materialistic monism of our own as to its unpremeditated, even paradoxical result; and it is difficult to imagine how the one could have been reached from the other without this gigantic "detour."

In more ways than one, the rise and long ascendancy of dualism are among the most decisive events in the mental history of the race. What matters for our context is that, while it held sway, and in an otherwise varied career, dualism continued to drain the spiritual elements off the physical realm—until, when its tide at last receded, it left in its wake a world strangely denuded of such arresting attributes. One clearly recognizable component (there are others) in its origin and motivational history is the death theme. The "unto dust shalt thou return" which every corpse calls out to the living, the finality of the state which its decay opposes to the transience of life, must have first and ever again forced "matter" as bare and lifeless into the reluctant human view, and it never ceased to renew the challenge which panvitalistic creed, in the funeral cult, could appease but not silence. Whether and when this contradiction came to a crisis depended on historical circumstances with which the "death" motif had to ally itself so that at some time it could overwhelm the "life motif." But when this happened, the naïve monism broke up into a dualism, with whose growth the traits of the bewildering sight from which it had started—the sight of the corpse—could progressively spread over the face of the physical All. Death in fact conquered external reality.

Soma–sema, the body–a tomb: this Orphic formula expressed the first dualistic answer to the problem of death—now conceived (as that of life, which only now became a problem too) in terms of the interrelation of two different entities, body and soul. The body as such is the grave of the soul, and bodily death is the latter's resurrection. Life dwells like a stranger in the flesh which by its own nature—the nature of the corporeal—is nothing but corpse, seemingly alive by favor of the soul's passing presence in it. Only in death, relinquished by its alien visitor, does the body return to its original truth, and soul to hers.

The discovery of the "self," made first in earnest (for the West) in the Orphic religion and culminating in the Christian and gnostic conception of an entirely nonmundane inwardness in man, had a curiously polarizing effect on the general picture of reality: the very possibility of the notion of an "inanimate universe" emerged as the counterpart to the increasingly exclusive stress laid on the *human* soul, on its inner life and its incommensurability with anything in nature.[1] The fateful divorce, stretched to the point of a complete foreignness which left nothing in common between the parted members, henceforth qualified them both by this mutual exclusion. As the retreating soul drew about itself all spiritual significance and metaphysical dignity, contracting them and itself alike within its innermost being, it left the world divested of all such claims and, though at first decidedly demonic, in the end indifferent to the very question of value either way.

At the peak of the dualistic development, in Gnosticism, the *soma–sema* simile, in its origin purely human, had come to extend to the physical universe. The whole world is tomb (prison house, place of exile, etc.) to the soul or spirit, that alien injection in what is otherwise unrelated to life. There, one might be tempted to say, the matter rests to this day—with the difference that the tomb has meanwhile become empty. With the critical evaporation of the hypostasized spiritual entity, of the "something" which could be thought of as enclosed in that grave or prison, only the walls remained, but these exceedingly solid. This is, metaphorically speaking, the position of modern materialism, which inherited the estate of a defunct dualism, or what was left of it. Thus the splitting of reality into self and world, inner and outer existence, mind and nature, long sanctioned by religious doctrine, prepared the ground for the postdualistic successors.

If dualism was the first great correction of the animistic-monistic one-sideness, materialist monism which remained as its residue is then the no less one-sided, total triumph of the death experience over the life experience. In this sense, the theoretical shock that once issued from the corpse has turned into a constitutive principle, and in a universe formed after the image of the corpse the single, actual corpse has lost its mystery. All the more does the one unresolved remainder clash with the universal norm: the living organism, which seems to resist the dualistic alternative as much as the alternative dualism–monism itself. The quest for its analysis on the terms of general physical law is the running argument with the refractory from the position of the ontology of death—an argument, this too, which may yet turn back on the position itself and cause its exclusive claim to be reappraised. In its heyday, when the new ontology ruled unchallenged, any settling of the contradiction, any solution of the riddle, could only be in favor of death; or the riddle remained, an annoying dualistic rest: either case testifies to the ontological dominance of death. This dominance is the inverted monism with which mankind emerged at the far shore from the waters of dualism which long ago it had entered with the archaic monism of the soul.

[1] Illuminating in this connection are some of the charges which in the sixth century A.D. Simplicius, one of the last of the Platonists, leveled against his Christian contemporary Johannes Philoponus. He accuses him of blasphemy for likening the light of the heavens to ordinary fire and to glowworms, its color to that of fishscales (in *Arist. de caelo*, p. 88, 28 ff. Heiberg; he also takes him to task for denying, against Aristotle, the eternity of the world, *ibid.*, p. 66, 10). It was a gallant protest of the doomed cosmos-piety against the indignity done to nature under the dispensation of transcendental religion: the submersion of its hierarchy in the common status of mere created things. Almost one thousand years earlier Anaxagoras had been charged by the Athenians with blasphemy for declaring the sun to be a mass of heated metal or stone. Between the two events lie the rise and fall of cosmological religion. The dualistic challenge was more radical than the naturalistic one of the Ionians who were potentially "pantheists." A naturalism, coming after dualism had done its work, was accordingly bound to be more thoroughgoing.

But precisely the nakedness of the new monism from which the general life had been banished and which no transcendent pole complemented anymore, exposed to view the particular, finite life in its metaphysically expatriated identity —and left it to be appraised in its "own" terms after it had so long been measured by other ones. Its solely remaining here-and-now, suspended between beginning and end, acquires a prominence which both preceding views had denied to it. The attention to its peculiar nature, belonging to nothing else, has increased in proportion as, in retreat from both the diffusion of animism and the width of dualistic tension, it has become narrower—in proportion, that is, as the locus of life within being has shrunk to the special case of the organism in its conditioning earthly environment. The conditioning, life-enabling character of that environment is in turn an improbable accident of a universe alien to life and indifferent in its material laws. All modern theories of life are to be understood against this backdrop of an ontology of death, from which each single life must coax or bully its lease, only to be swallowed up by it in the end.

The road through dualism here briefly indicated marks the irreversible time-order of the two positions, and dualism itself represents so far the most momentous phase in the history of thought, whose achievement, however overtaken, can never be undone. The discovery of the separate spheres of spirit and matter, which split primeval monism asunder, created forever a new theoretical situation. From the hard-won observation that there can be matter without spirit, dualism inferred the unobserved reverse that spirit can also be without matter. Irrespective of the tenability of the ontological thesis, the essential difference of the two had now come into view, and their dualistic separation inspired the resolute spelling-out of both their natures in their stark otherness, which was never to be confounded again. Every conception of being that can come thereafter is in essence, not merely in time, postdualistic, as the preceding one was essentially predualistic. As in the latter the specificness and difference of the two fundamental dimensions was not yet discovered (so that its monism was naïvely unproblematic, disturbed only by the experience of death and gradually eroded by technology—until intellectually self-conscious dualism spelled the end of this and all naïveté), so has any postdualistic theory of being inescapably to deal with the two pieces which dualism left behind and concerning which it can be monistic only at the price of choosing between them, i.e., of opting for one of them: at least so long as the dualistic heritage still enforces the recognition of its alternative. With this alternative at its point of departure, any postdualistic monism includes a decision which it has made for one or the other side; that is to say, it is itself of an alternative and thus partial nature, having its opposite as the excluded possibility with it.

It follows that in the postdualistic situation there are, on principle, not one but two possibilities of monism, represented by modern materialism and modern idealism respectively: they both presuppose the ontological polarization which dualism had generated, and either takes its stand in one of the two poles, to comprehend from this vantage point the whole of reality. They are thus in their origin, though certainly not in their intention, partial monisms, unlike the integral monism of prehistory in which the two sides were still fused undifferentiated. There is no returning to this: dualism had not been an arbitrary invention, for the two-ness which it asserts is grounded in reality itself. A new, integral, i.e., philosophical monism cannot undo the polarity: it must absorb it into a higher unity of existence from which the opposites issue as faces of its being or phases of its becoming. It must take up the problem which originally gave rise to dualism.

The problem is still the same: the existence of feeling life in an unfeeling world of matter which in death triumphs over it. If its dualistic solution is theoretically unsatisfactory, the two partial monisms—materialism and idealism—at bottom evade it, each in its own manner of one-sidedness. Their means of unification, i.e., of reduction to the chosen denominator, is the distinction of primary and secondary reality: of substance and function (or "epiphenomenon") in the case of materialism, of consciousness and appearance in the case of idealism. As an ontological position, i.e., as serious monism, either standpoint claims totality for itself and thus excludes the other. But since the point of departure in either case is partial with respect to integral reality, they severally embody the internal contradiction of a partial monism—a contradiction which betrays itself in the failure of their reduction of one element to the other. In the case of materialism, this failure happens in relation to consciousness, in that of idealism —in relation to the thing-in-itself.

Both standpoints, it is true, can dissemble their monistic, i.e., ontological character and, rather than for total views of being, try to pass for a division of labor in the cultivation of two separate fields of reality—their own separateness thus resting first on the difference of their subjects, which naturally also demands different methods. We then would have a phenomenology of consciousness and a physics of extension, and the method of one discipline would be as necessarily idealistic as that of the other materialistic. Their separation would then be not ontological, according to alternative concepts of being, but "ontic," according to subject matter. Here the mutual relation of the two seems to be that, not of alternative, but of complementation: "sciences of nature–sciences of mind." But this peaceful coexistence presupposes that the two "fields" are in fact separate, and can be isolated from each other. Precisely this is not the case. The fact of life, as the psychophysical unity which the organism exhibits, renders the separation illusory. The actual coincidence of inwardness and outwardness in the *body* compels the two ways of knowledge to define their relation otherwise than by separate subjects. Otherwise also than as complementary descriptions of the same subject from different "sides" which can eschew the question of how those abstract aspects concretely cohere in being. For such a descriptive abstention, which is to insure metaphysical neutrality, could be maintained only on condition that the two fields of phenomena are closed in themselves at least *qua* phenomena and do not transcend themselves by their own contents: that either one, thus, can be described entire without drawing in the other. Yet precisely our living body constitutes that very self-transcendence in either direction and thereby makes the methodological *epochē* founder on its rock. It must be described as extended and inert, but equally as feeling and willing—and neither of the two descriptions can be carried to its end without trespass into the sphere of the other and without prejudging it. The physical-outward description cannot be carried to its end without compromising the freedom and thus the genuine reality of the mind; the vitalistic-inward description not without compromising the total determination and autarky of the "extended" realm.

Dualism, when its work was done, had left behind the "extended" as the lifeless and unfeeling, and the body undeniably is a part of this extended: either, then, it is essentially the same as the extended in general—then its being alive is not understood; or it is *sui generis*—then the exception claimed for it is not to be understood and calls into question the whole rule, i.e., the materialist interpretation of substance as such along the pure properties of indifferent extension. The same goes, *mutatis mutandis,* for the other side, that of idealist consciousness. Dualism had left it behind as the uncorporeal absolutely, the unextended and purely inward *per se,* and the "body" as the sensible field of feeling and volition belongs to this inwardness itself: either, then, as part of the total phenomenal extension it is but one among the "external ideas" ("cogitations") of consciousness—then its being the body *of* this consciousness, its being *my* body, my extended I and my share in the world of extension, is not understood; or life and inwardness are really extended through it ("to the tips of my fingers"), it really is " I "—then it is, even though phenomenally extended, not an *idea* of consciousness but the actual outward extent of its own inner spatiality which itself occupies space in the world: and therewith it calls into question the whole idealist interpretation of consciousness as opposed to the entire world of extension.

Thus the organic body signifies the latent crisis of every known ontology and the criterion of "any future one which will be able to come forward as a science." As it was first the body on which, in the fact of *death,* that antithesis of life and nonlife became manifest whose relentless pressure on thought destroyed primitive panvitalism and caused the image of being to split, so it is conversely the concrete unity manifest in its *life* on which in turn the dualism of the two substances founders, and again this bi-unity which also brings to grief both alternatives branching off from dualism, whenever they—as they cannot help doing—enlarge themselves into total ontologies. Indeed, it is this very bi-unity which compels them thus to enlarge themselves, i.e., to transgress their boundaries, and prevents them from sheltering in the seeming neutrality of mere part areas or part aspects. The living body that can die, that has world and itself belongs to the world, that feels and itself can be felt, whose outward form is organism and causality, and whose inward form is selfhood and finality: this body is the memento of the still unsolved question of ontology, "What is being?" and must be the canon of coming attempts to solve it. These attempts must move beyond the partial abstractions ("body and soul," "extension and thought," and the like) toward the hidden ground of their unity and thus strive for an integral monism on a plane above the solidified alternatives.

The problem of life, centered in the problem of the body, is thus a cardinal theme for ontology and the constant disturbance of its latter-day antithetical positions in materialism and idealism alike. It is characteristic of the post-dualistic situation that the problem poses itself today as that of life and not of death: this inversion is the end result of that contraction of life from the whole of nature into its distinct singularity which began with the first dawn of dualistic lightening of the indistinctness. Against the enormous boundary transgression of primordial monism which made life coextensive with being, discrimination could only mean, first, discovery of lifeless matter as such, and then, ever increasing expansion of the extent of the lifeless—until this in turn became coextensive with being. Now obviously, as expression of this postdualistic theoretical situation, materialism is the more interesting and more serious variant of modern ontology than idealism. For among the totality of its objects—bodies in general—materialism lets itself in earnest also encounter the living body; and since it is bound to subject it, too, to its principles it exposes itself to the real ontological test and with it to the risk of failure: it gives itself the opportunity of knocking against its limit—and there against the ontological problem. Idealism is able to evade it: it can always from the secure standpoint of pure consciousness, artificial as it is, interpret "the body," like all other bodies, as external "idea" or "phenomenon" in its international horizon and can thus disown the corporeality of the self: by this means it saves itself the problem of life as well as of death. This was the reason why at the outset we have chosen materialism as the representative of postdualistic ontology (the "ontology of death") and as the true counterpart to the predualistic ontology of panvitalism. Materialism is the real ontology of our world since the Renaissance, the real heir to dualism, i.e., to its residual estate, and with it must be our discourse. Only with a "realist" standpoint can there be fruitful discourse anyway, whereas an idealistic one can slip through its fingers.

Moreover, it can be shown that the idealism of the philosophy of consciousness is itself but a complementarity, an epiphenomenon as it were, of materialism and thus in the strict sense also one face of the ontology of death. This shall here be indicated in just one respect. Only a world objectified to pure extensive outwardness, as materialism conceived it, leaves opposite itself a pure consciousness which has no share in it, in its dimension and its function—which no longer acts but merely beholds. And vice versa, it is this bodyless, merely beholding consciousness for which reality must turn into series of points juxtaposed in space and succeeding in time: points of extensity necessarily as external to one another as they all together are to consciousness, and therefore offering no other rules of order than those of extraneous collocation and sequence. Indeed, without the body by which we are ourselves an actual part of the world and experience the nature of force and action in self-performance, our knowledge—a merely "perceptive," beholding knowledge—of the world (in that case truly "external world" with no real transition from myself to it) would really be reduced to Hume's model, viz., to sequences of contents external and indifferent to one another, regarding which there could not even arise the suspicion of an inner connection, of any relation other than the spatio-temporal ones, nor the least justification for postulating it. Causality here becomes a fiction—on a psychological basis left groundless itself.

At this agnostic resignation modern physics has arrived from its own end, i.e., from its materialist premises which by the road of absolute externalization must lead to the same skeptical framing of the concept of causality as the theory of consciousness must by its road of absolute internalization. Neither can do otherwise, and both from the same cause: pure consciousness is as little alive as the pure matter confronting it. Accordingly, the one can as little generate the aliveness of active connection in its understanding as the other can present it to perception. Both are fission products of the ontology of death to which the dualistic anatomy of being had led. Note that this renders them helpless, not just in dealing with life, but already on the subject of general causality. In the latter field, that of mechanical law, transcendental and materialist theory alike had claimed their principal triumph, for which to forgo the knowledge of organic teleology seemed not too high a price to pay. However, it seems that in the long run no part of a whole can profit from what that whole loses in another part, and in the end even general causality loses in intelligibility what the elimination of life was meant to secure for it in terms of scientific knowledge. The fate of the causality problem in idealist epistemology on the one hand and in materialist physics on the other bespeaks the fact that both positions, considered ontologically, are fragmentary, residual products of dualism, and both are merely consistent when they, each by its own kind of skepsis, acknowledge the inevitable outcome of their isolation, to wit: the inexplicability of that which through the sundering has become inexplicable. The artificial sundering of *res cogitans* and *res extensa* in the heritage of dualism, with the extrusion between them of "life": this double-faced ontology of death creates problems, which it has rendered unsolvable from the start.

But is there not here a contradiction? Has not the discrimination of the lifeless and the living first made possible the distinct articulation of what is peculiar to life? And has this not benefited the "spirit," which as it were drew to itself what there was of life in the universe and concentrated it within itself as "consciousness"? If matter was left dead on one side, then surely consciousness, brought into relief against it on the other side and becoming heir to all animistic vitality, should be the repository, even the distillate of life? But life does not bear distillation; it is somewhere between the purified aspects—in their concretion. The abstractions themselves do not live. In truth, we repeat, the pure consciousness is as little alive as the pure matter standing over against it—and, by the same token, as little mortal. It lives as departed spirits live and cannot understand the world anymore. To it the world is dead as it is dead to the world. The dualistic antithesis leads not to a heightening of the features of life through their concentration on one side, but to a deadening of both sides through their separation from the living middle. This deadening exacts its revenge in the fact that—not to speak of the riddle of life—even for the interpretation of the external regularity in the movements of matter, the image of a causality by active force no longer finds legitimation in any admitted firsthand givenness.

Here we recall Kant's answer to Hume's skeptical challenge which claimed to supply just that legitimation, not indeed in a "given," but in an a priori structure of the mind. However, the transcendental solution of the problem which heroically undertakes to ground causality and its objective meaning in the pure consciousness alone, does not escape the truth that you cannot derive the concreteness from one of its abstractions. The success of Kant's attempted solution depends, *inter alia,* essentially on the proof that "causation" is indeed a concept of the pure understanding (after that, on showing why it should be valid objectively). But an unprejudiced examination will find that not the pure understanding but only the concrete bodily life, in the actual interplay of its self-feeling powers with the world, can be the source of "idea" of force and thus of cause. The understanding as such knows merely of reason and consequence, not of cause and effect: the latter denote a connection of reality, by means of force, not of ideality, by means of form. The experience of living force, one's own namely, in the acting of the body, is the experiental basis for the abstractions of the general concepts of action and causation; and the "schematism" of directed bodily *movement,* not of neutrally receptive intuition, mediates between the formality of the understanding and the dynamics of the real.

Causality is thus not an a priori basis of experience, but itself a basic experience. That experience has its seat in the *effort* I must make to overcome the resistance of worldly matter in my acting and to resist the impact of worldly matter upon myself. This happens through and with my body, with its extensive outwardness and its intensive inwardness at once, which both are genuine aspects of myself. And advancing from my body, nay, myself advancing bodily, I build up in the image of its basic experience the dynamic image of the world—a world of force and resistance, action and inertia, cause and effect. Thus causality is not the a priori of experience in the understanding but the universal extrapolation from propriobodily prime experience into the whole of reality. It is rooted in just the point of actual, live "transcendence" of the self, the point where inwardness actively transcends itself into the outward and continues itself into it with its actions. This point is the intensive–extensive body in which the self exists, at once, for itself (intensive) and in the midst of the world (extensive).

Causality is primarily a finding of the practical, not of the theoretical, self, of its activity, not of its perception—an experience of the one, not a law of the other. . . .

Admittedly, whether the universal extrapolation which in fact, and irresistibly, we do make from propriobodily experience is also rationally justified, is a question of philosophical critique which we must here leave open. It is, however, in the first place an ontological and not an epistemological question. Into ontology also belongs the problem of anthropomorphism in the widest sense which at this point raises its head. The anathema on any kind of anthropomorphism, even of zoomorphism, in connection with nature—this in its absoluteness specifically dualistic and postdualistic prohibition, may well turn out to be, in this extreme form, a prejudice. . . . Perhaps, rightly understood, man *is* after all the measure of all things—not indeed through the legislation of his reason but through the exemplar of his psychophysical totality which represents the maximum of concrete ontological completeness known to us: a completeness *from which*, reductively, the species of being may have to be determined by way of progressive ontological subtraction down to the minimum of bare elementary matter (instead of the complete being constructed from this basis by cumulative addition). The question is still open whether life is a quantitative complexification in the arrangement of matter, and its freedom and purposiveness nothing but an apparent blurring of its simple, unambiguous determinacy through the massed complexity as such (a fact of our bafflement rather than of its own nature)—or whether, contrariwise, "dead" matter, as one extreme of a spectrum, represents a limiting mode of the properties revealed by feeling life, their privative reduction to the near-dwindling point of inchoateness: in which case its bare, inertial determination would be dormant, as yet unawakened freedom. The ontological justification for this question lies in the fact that the living body is the archetype of the concrete, and being *my* body it is, in its immediacy of inwardness and outwardness in one, the *only* fully given concrete of experience in general. Its actual, concrete fullness teaches us that matter in space, otherwise experienced only from without, may have an inner horizon too and that, therefore, its extended being need not be its whole being. Seen from the only true concreteness furnished to us, both pure "extension" and pure "thought" may well appear to be mere abstractions.

Independently, however, of this metaphysical question of a unity of being and the propositions derivable from it if granted, independently also, therefore, of the question concerning the *right* of the de facto extrapolation from our corporeality, there is the plain fact that *without* the body and its elementary self-experience, without this "whence" of our most general, all-encompassing extrapolation into the whole of reality, there could be no idea whatever of force and action in the world and thus of a dynamic connection of all things: no idea in short, of any "nature" at all. Idealism—in that respect the faithful mirror image of materialism—by ranging the body entirely among the external objects, thus understanding it as an object of experience and not its source, as datum for the subject and not as active–passive reality of the subject, has deprived itself of the possibility to go beyond a rule of external orders of sequences and grasp a real connection of things rooted in their own nature—be it in the form of efficient, be it of final causation (on this, the transcendental standpoint has no say anyway, whatever its historical preference). But whichever causality it be, on this point Hume's critique was right that it is not met with any perception, and that the nexus between the data is not a datum itself—not a perceived content. Force indeed is not a datum, but an "actum" humanly present in effort. And effort is surely not a percept, even less a form of the synthesis of percepts. But objectifying thought is wedded to perception ("intuition" = "presentational immediacy") and thus cannot encounter what is not contained therein.

Thus it appears that waiving the intelligibility of life—the price which modern knowledge was willing to pay for its title to the greater part of reality—renders the world unintelligible as well. And the reduction of teleological to mechanical causality, great as its advantages are for analytical description, has gained nothing in the matter of comprehending the nexus itself: the one is no less mysterious than the other.

Our reflections were intended to show in what sense the problem of life, and with it that of the body, ought to stand in the center of ontology and, to some extent, also of epistemology. Life means material life, i.e., living body, i.e., organic being. In the body, the knot of being is tied which dualism does not unravel but cut. Materialism and idealism, each from its end, try to smooth it out but get caught in it. The central position of the problem of life means not only that it must be accorded a decisive voice in judging any given ontology but also that any treatment of itself must summon the whole of ontology. To this whole belong the hitherto, in its history, realized possibilities of ontology, even if they happen to teach more on posing than on solving the problem. Our considerations have shown that not even "animism," i.e., the panvitalism of the dawn, is to be excluded from the ontological evidence that has to be weighed: the principle of the interpretation of being which it, however preconceptually, represents is not really done with even from the perspective of modern knowl edge.[2] Yet the decisive phase in the unfolding of the problem, so we found, was

[2] We may refer to the panpsychism of a Teilhard de Chardin, or (on a considerably higher philosophical plane) of Whitehead's theory of all actuality as "feeling."

dualism, which also in other respects represents the most pregnant chapter in the history of man's interpretation of being and himself. At its hands, the paradox of life received its most pointed antithetical articulatión and, on its expiration, was left behind in its most irreconcilable form. Lastly, we found that of the postdualistic positions which divided the dualistic legacy between them, materialism has an advantage over idealism as a meeting ground with the problem of life, since it can be less easily evaded there. One sign of this is that materialism, herein more faithful to the dualistic bequest, knows of death whereas idealism has forgotten it. Also, the thinker himself is here less easily bribed. In materialism, he looks his own negation in the eye; but since he at the same time, in what he does by thinking, exemplifies the very case to which his thought denies a place, he is here less in danger to forget one side of the question than is the following of idealism, which with the primacy of thought, so flattering to the thinker, has in advance taken his side.

Physics of a Believer
Pierre Duhem

Pierre Maurice Marie Duhem (1861–1916), French physicist and mathematician and a pioneer in the field of thermodynamics, was also a profound student of the history of cosmological systems. His massive study of this subject, *Le Système du Monde,* maintains an orthodox Roman Catholic viewpoint.

It has been fashionable for some time to oppose the great theories of physics to the fundamental doctrines on which spiritualistic philosophy and the Catholic faith rest; these doctrines are really expected to be seen crumbling under the ramming blows of scientific systems. Of course, these struggles of science against faith impassion those who are very poorly acquainted with the teachings of science and who are not at all acquainted with the dogmas of faith; but at times they preoccupy and disturb men whose intelligence and conscience are far above those of village scholars and café physicists.

Now, the system we have expounded gets rid of the alleged objections that physical theory would raise to spiritualistic metaphysics and Catholic dogma; it makes them disappear as easily as the wind sweeps away bits of straw, for according to this system these objections are, and can never be anything but, misunderstandings.

What is a metaphysical proposition, a religious dogma? It is a judgment bearing on an objective reality, affirming or denying that a certain real being

From Pierre Duhem, *The Aim and Structure of Physical Theory* (Princeton, N.J., 1954), pp. 283–291.

does or does not possess a certain attribute. Judgments like "Man is free," "The soul is immortal," "The Pope is infallible in matters of faith" are metaphysical propositions or religious dogmas; they all affirm that certain objective realities possess certain attributes.

What will be required for the possibility that a certain judgment, on one side, is in agreement or disagreement with a proposition of metaphysics or theology, on the other side? Of necessity it will be required that this judgment have certain objective realities as its subject, and that it affirm or deny certain attributes concerning them. In effect, between two judgments not having the same terms but bearing on the same subjects, there can be neither agreement nor disagreement.

The facts of experience—in the current meaning of the words, and not in the complicated meaning these words take on in physics—and empirical laws—meaning the laws of ordinary experience which common sense formulates without recourse to scientific theories—are so many affirmations bearing on objective realities; we may, therefore, without being unreasonable, speak of the agreement or disagreement between a fact or law of experience, on the one hand, and a proposition of metaphysics or theology, on the other. If, for example, we noticed a case in which a Pope, placed in the conditions provided by the dogma of infallibility, issued an instruction contrary to the faith, we should have before us a fact which would contradict a religious dogma. If experience led to the formulation of the law, "Human acts are always determined," we should be dealing with an empirical law denying a proposition of metaphysics.

That being settled, can a principle of theoretical physics be in agreement or disagreement with a proposition of metaphysics or of theology? Is a principle of theoretical physics a judgment involving objective reality?

Yes, for the Cartesian and the atomist, and for anyone who makes of theoretical physics a dependency or a corollary of metaphysics; a principle of theoretical physics is a judgment which bears on a reality. When the Cartesian affirms that the essence of matter is extension in length, breadth, and thickness or when the atomist declares that an atom moves with uniform rectilinear motion so long as it does not hit another atom, the Cartesian and the atomist really mean to assert that matter is objectively just what they say it is, that it really possesses the properties they attribute to it, and that it is deprived of the properties they refuse to give it. Consequently, it is not meaningless to ask whether a certain principle of Cartesian or atomistic physics is or is not in disagreement with a certain proposition of metaphysics or of dogma; it may reasonably be doubted that the law imposed by atomism on the motion of atoms is compatible with the action of the soul on the body; it may be maintained that the essence of Cartesian matter is irreconcilable with the dogma of the real presence of the body of Jesus Christ in the Eucharist.

Yes, also, for the Newtonian; a principle of theoretical physics is a judgment involving objective reality for one who, like the Newtonian, sees in such a principle an experimental law generalized by induction. Such a person will see, for instance, in the fundamental equations of dynamics a universal rule whose truth experiment has disclosed and to which all the motions of objectively existing bodies are subject. He will be able to speak without illogicality of the conflict between the equations of dynamics and the possibility of free will, and investigate whether this conflict is resolvable or not.

Thus, the defenders of the schools of physics that we have put in combat may legitimately speak of agreement or disagreement between the principles of physical theory and metaphysical or religious doctrines. This will not be the case with those whose reason has accepted the interpretation of physical theory we proposed, for they will never speak of a conflict between the principles of physical theory and metaphysical or religious doctrines; they understand, in fact, that metaphysical and religious doctrines are judgments touching on objective reality, whereas the principles of physical theory are propositions relative to certain mathematical signs stripped of all objective existence. Since they do not have any common term, these two sorts of judgments can neither contradict nor agree with each other.

What indeed is a principle of theoretical physics? It is a mathematical form suited to summarize and classify laws established by experiment. By itself this principle is neither true nor false; it merely gives a more or less satisfactory picture of the laws it intends to represent. It is these laws which make affirmations concerning objective reality, and which may, therefore, be in agreement or disagreement with some proposition of metaphysics or theology. However, the systematic classification that theory gives them does not add or take away anything concerning their truth, their certainty, or their objective scope. The intervention of the theoretical principle summarizing and ordering them can neither destroy the agreement between these laws and metaphysical or religious doctrines when such agreement existed before the intervention of this principle, nor reinstate such agreement if it did not exist previously. *In itself and by its essence, any principle of theoretical physics has no part to play in metaphysical or theological discussions.*

Let us apply these considerations to an example:

Is the principle of the conservation of energy compatible with free will? That is a question often debated and resolved in different ways. Now, does it even have a meaning such that a man conscious of the exact import of the terms it employs can reasonably think about answering it with either yes or no?

Of course, this question has a meaning for those who make of the principle of the conservation of energy an axiom applicable in all strictness to the real universe, either when they draw this axiom from a philosophy of nature or when they arrive at it by starting from experimental data with the help of a broad and powerful induction. But we do not accept either side. For us the principle of the conservation of energy is by no means a certain and general affirmation involving really existent objects. It is a mathematical formula set up by a free decree of our understanding in order that this formula, combined with other formulas postulated analogously, may permit us to deduce a series of consequences furnishing us a satisfactory representation of the laws noted in our laboratories. Neither this formula of the conservation of energy nor the formulas that we associate with it can be said, properly speaking, to be true or false, since they are not judgments bearing on realities; all that we can say is that the theory composing a group of laws is a good one if its corollaries represent these laws we intend to classify with a sufficient degree of exactness, and that the theory is a bad one in the contrary case. It is already clear that the question, Is the law of the conservation of energy compatible with free will or not? cannot have any meaning for us. If it had any, in effect it would be the following: Is the objective impossibility of free acts a consequence of the principle of the conservation of energy, or not? Now the principle of the conservation of energy has no objective consequence.

And furthermore, let us insist on this.

How would one go about deriving from the principle of the conservation of energy and from other analogous principles the corollary, "Free will is impossible"? We should observe that these various principles are equivalent to a system of differential equations ruling the changes of state of the bodies subject to them; that if the state and motion of these bodies are given at a certain instant, their state and motion would then be determined unambiguously for the whole course of time; and we should conclude from this that no free movement can be produced among these bodies, since a free movement would be essentially a movement not determined by previous states and motions.

Now, what is such an argument worth?

We selected out differential equations or, what comes to the same thing, the principles they translate, because we wished to construct a mathematical representation of a group of phenomena; in seeking to represent these phenomena with the aid of a system of differential equations, we were presupposing from the very start that they were subject to a strict determinism; we were well aware, in fact, that a phenomenon whose peculiarities did not in the least result from the initial data would rebel at any representation by such a system of equations. We were therefore certain in advance that no place was reserved for free actions in the classification we had arranged. When we note afterwards that a free action cannot be included in our classification, we should be very naïve to be astonished by it and very foolish to conclude that free will is impossible.

Imagine a collector who wishes to arrange sea shells. He takes seven drawers that he marks with seven colors of the spectrum, and you see him putting the red shells in the red drawer, the yellow shells in the yellow drawer, etc. But if a white shell appears, he will not know what to do with it, for he has no white drawer. You would, of course, feel very sorry for his reason if you heard him conclude in his embarrassment that no white shells exist in the world.

The physicist who thinks he can deduce from his theoretical principles the impossibility of free will deserves the same feeling. In manufacturing a classification for all phenomena produced in this world, he forgets the drawer for free actions!

OUR SYSTEM DENIES PHYSICAL THEORY ANY METAPHYSICAL OR APOLOGETIC IMPORT

That our physics is the physics of a believer is said to follow from the fact that it so radically denies any validity to the objections obtained from physical theory to spiritualistic metaphysics and the Catholic faith! But it might just as well be called the physics of a nonbeliever, for it does not render better or stricter justice to the arguments in favor of metaphysics or dogma that some have tried to deduce from physical theory. It is just as absurd to claim that a principle of theoretical physics contradicts a proposition formulated by spiritualistic philosophy or by the Catholic doctrine as it is to claim that it confirms such a proposition. There cannot be disagreement or agreement between a proposition touching on an objective reality and another proposition which has no objective import. Every time people cite a principle of theoretical physics in support of a metaphysical doctrine or a religious dogma, they commit a mistake, for they attribute to this principle a meaning not its own, an import not belonging to it.

Let us again explain what we are saying by an illustration.

In the middle of the last century, Clausius, after profoundly transforming Carnot's principle, drew from it the following famous corollary: The entropy of the universe tends toward a maximum. From this theorem many a philosopher maintained the conclusion of the impossibility of a world in which physical and chemical changes would go on being produced forever; it pleased them to think that these changes had had a beginning and would have an end; creation in time, if not of matter, at least of its aptitude for change, and the establishment in a more or less remote future of a state of absolute rest and universal death were for these thinkers inevitable consequences of the principles of thermodynamics.

The deduction here in wishing to pass from the premises to these conclusions is marred in more than one place by fallacies. First of all, it implicitly assumes the assimilation of the universe to a finite collection of bodies isolated in a space absolutely void of matter; and this assimilation exposes one to many doubts. Once this assimilation is admitted, it is true that the entropy of the universe has to increase endlessly, but it does not impose any lower or upper limit on this entropy; nothing then would stop this magnitude from varying from $-\infty$ to $+\infty$ while the time itself varied from $-\infty$ to $+\infty$; then the allegedly demonstrated impossibilities regarding an eternal life for the universe would vanish. But let us confess these criticisms wrong; they prove that the demonstration taken as an example is not conclusive, but do not prove the radical impossibility of constructing a conclusive example which would tend toward an analogous end. The objection we shall make against it is quite different in nature and import: basing our argument on the very essence of physical theory, we shall show that it is absurd to question this theory for information concerning events which might have happened in an extremely remote past, and absurd to demand of it predictions of events a very long way off.

What is a physical theory? A group of mathematical propositions whose consequences are to represent the data of experiment; the validity of a theory is measured by the number of experimental laws it represents and by the degree of precision with which it represents them; if two different theories represent the same facts with the same degree of approximation, physical method considers them as having absolutely the same validity; it does not have the right to dictate our choice between these two equivalent theories and is bound to leave us free. No doubt the physicist will choose between these logically equivalent theories, but the motives which will dictate his choice will be considerations of elegance, simplicity, and convenience, and grounds of suitability which are essentially subjective, contingent, and variable with time, with schools, and with persons; as serious as these motives may be in certain cases, they will never be of a nature that necessitates adhering to one of the two theories and rejecting the other, for only the discovery of a fact that would be represented by one of the theories, and not by the other, would result in a forced option.

Thus the law of attraction in the inverse ratio of the square of the distance, proposed by Newton, represents with admirable precision all the heavenly motions we can observe. However, for the inverse square of the distance we could substitute some other function of the distance in an infinity of ways such that some new celestial mechanics represented all our astronomical observations with the same precision as the old one. The principles of experimental method would compel us to attribute exactly the same logical validity to both these different celestial mechanics. This does not mean that astronomers would not keep the Newtonian law of attraction in preference to the new law, but they would keep it on account of the exceptional mathematical properties offered by the inverse square of the distance in favor of the simplicity and elegance that these properties introduced into their calculations. Of course, these motives would be good to follow; yet they would constitute nothing decisive or definitive, and would be of no weight the day when a phenomenon would be discovered which the Newtonian law of attraction would be inept to represent and of which another celestial mechanics would give a satisfactory representation; on that day astronomers would be bound to prefer the new theory to the old one.[1]

That being understood, let us suppose we have two systems of celestial mechanics, different from the mathematical point of view, but representing with an equal degree of approximation all the astronomical observations made until now. Let us go further: let us use these two celestial mechanics to calculate the motions of heavenly bodies in the future; let us assume that the results of one of the calculations are so close to those of the other that the deviation between the two positions they assign to the same heavenly body is less than the experimental errors even at the end of a thousand or even ten thousand years. Then we have here two systems of celestial mechanics which we are bound to regard as logically equivalent; no reason exists compelling us to prefer one to the other, and what is more, at the end of a thousand or ten thousand years, men will still have to weight them equally and hold their choice in suspense.

It is clear that the predictions from both these theories will merit equal degrees of confidence; it is clear that logic does not give us any right to assert that the predictions of the first theory, but not those of the second theory, will be in conformity with reality.

In truth these predictions agree perfectly for a lapse of a thousand or ten thousand years, but the mathematicians warn us that we should be rash to conclude from this that this agreement will last forever, and by concrete examples they show us to what errors this illegitimate extrapolation could lead us. The predictions of our two systems of celestial mechanics would be peculiarly discordant if we asked these two theories to describe for us the state of the heavens at the end of ten million years; one of them might tell us that the planets at that time would still describe orbits scarcely different from those they describe at present; the other, however, might very well claim that all the bodies of the solar system will then be united into a single mass, or else that they will be dispersed in space at enormous distances from one another.[2] Of these two forecasts, one proclaiming the stability of the solar system and the other its instability, which shall we believe? The one, no doubt, which will best fit our extra-scientific preoccupations and predilections; but certainly the logic of the physical sciences will

---

[1] This is what they did, in fact, the day when, by introducing the idea of molecular attraction, they complicated the formula of Newtonian attraction in order to be able to represent the laws of capillarity.

[2] Thus the trajectories of the planets under the simultaneous action of Newtonian attraction and capillary attraction might very well not differ over a period of ten thousand years to any appreciable extent from the trajectories of the same bodies subject only to Newtonian attraction; and yet, we could suppose without absurdity that the effects of capillary attraction accumulating over a period of 100 million years might appreciably disturb a planet from the path which Newtonian attraction alone would have made it follow.

not provide us with any fully convincing argument to defend our choice against an attacking party and impose it on him.

So it goes with any long-term prediction. We possess a thermodynamics which represents very well a multitude of experimental laws, and it tells us that the entropy of an isolated system increases eternally. We could without difficulty construct a new thermodynamics which would represent as well as the old thermodynamics the experimental laws known until now, and whose predictions would go along in agreement with those of the old thermodynamics for ten thousand years; and yet, this new thermodynamics might tell us that the entropy of the universe after increasing for a period of 100 million years will decrease over a new period of 100 million years in order to increase again in an eternal cycle.

By its very essence experimental science is incapable of predicting the end of the world as well as of asserting its perpetual activity. Only a gross misconception of its scope could have claimed for it the proof of a dogma affirmed by our faith.

There you have, then, a theoretical physics which is neither the theory of a believer nor that of a nonbeliever, but merely and simply a theory of a physicist; admirably suited to classify the laws studied by the experimenter, it is incapable of opposing any assertion whatever of metaphysics or of religious dogma, and is equally incapable of lending effective support to any such assertion. When the theorist invades the territory of metaphysics or of religious dogma, whether he intends to attack them or wishes to defend them, the weapon he has used so triumphantly in his own domain remains useless and without force in his hands; the logic of positive science which forged this weapon has marked out with precision the frontiers beyond which the temper given it by that logic would be dulled and its cutting power lost.

The Ultimate Earth

Pierre Teilhard de Chardin

Pierre Teilhard de Chardin (1881–1955), Jesuit priest and anthropologist, was the author of numerous influential works that attempted to bring together Christian doctrine and the theory of evolution. In addition to his major work, *The Phenomenon of Man,* he also wrote *The Divine Mileu* and *The Hymn of the Universe.*

PROGNOSTICS TO BE SET ASIDE

When the end of the world is mentioned, the idea that leaps into our minds is always one of catastrophe.

Generally we think of a sidereal cataclysm. There are so many stars hurtling around and brushing past; there are those exploding worlds on the horizon; so, surely, by the implacable laws of chance, our turn will come sooner or later and we shall be stricken and killed; or, at the least, we shall have to face a slow death in our prison.

Since physics has discovered that all energy runs down, we seem to feel the world getting a shade chillier every day. That cooling-off to which we were condemned has been partially compensated for by another discovery, that of radioactivity, which has happily intervened to compensate and delay the imminent cooling. The astronomers are now in a positon to guarantee that, if all goes as it should, we have at any rate several hundred million years ahead of us. So we can breathe again. Yet, though the settlement is postponed, the shadow grows longer.

And will mankind still be there to watch the evening fall? In the interim, apart from the cosmic mishaps that lie in wait for us, what will happen in the living layer of the earth? With age and increasing complication, we are ever more threatened by internal dangers at the core of both the biosphere and the noosphere.* Onslaughts of microbes, organic counter-evolutions, sterility, war, revolution—there are so many ways of coming to an end. Yet perhaps anything would be better than a long-drawn-out senility.

We are well aware of these different eventualities. We have turned them over in our minds. We have read descriptions of them in the novels of the Goncourts, Benson and Wells, or in scientific works signed by famous names. Each one of them is perfectly feasible. We could very well, and at any moment, be crushed by a gigantic comet. And, equally true, tomorrow the earth might quake and collapse under our feet. Taken individually, each human will can repudiate the

From Pierre Teilhard de Chardin, *The Phenomenon of Man,* trans. by Bernard Wall (New York, 1959), pp. 274–290, 296–299. Copyright Ⓒ 1955 by Editions du Seuil. Copyright Ⓒ 1959 in the English translation by Wm. Collins Sons & Co. Ltd., London, and Harper & Row, Publishers, New York. Reprinted by permission of Harper & Row, Publishers, Inc., and Wm. Collins Sons & Co. Ltd.

* [" *Noosphere* ": Word coined by the author likening the appearance of human consciousness on earth to a new sort of "atmosphere."—Eds.]

task of ascending higher towards union. And yet, on the strength of all we learn from past evolution, I feel entitled to say that we have nothing whatever to fear from these manifold disasters *in so far as* they imply the idea of premature accident or failure. However possible they may be in theory, we have higher reasons for being sure *that they will not happen.*

All pessimistic representations of the earth's last days—whether in terms of cosmic catastrophe, biological disruptions or simply arrested growth or senility—have this in common: that they take the characteristics and conditions of our individual and elemental ends and extend them *without correction* to life as a whole. Accident, disease and decrepitude spell the death of men; and therefore the same applies to mankind.

But have we any right to generalise in this simple way? When an individual disappears, even prematurely, another is always there to replace him. His loss is not irreparable from the point of view of the continuation of life. But what about mankind? In one of his books the great palaeontologist Matthew has suggested that if the human branch disappeared, another thinking branch would soon take its place. But he does not tell us where this mysterious shoot could be expected to appear on the tree of life as we know it, and doubtless he would be hard put to it to do so.

If we take the whole of history into consideration, the biological situation seems to me to be quite otherwise.

Once and once only in the course of its planetary existence has the earth been able to envelop itself with life. Similarly once and once only has life succeeded in crossing the threshold of reflection. For thought as for life there has been just one season. And we must not forget that since the birth of thought man has been the leading shoot of the tree of life. That being so, the hopes for the future of the noosphere (that is to say, of biogenesis, which in the end is the same as cosmogenesis) are concentrated exclusively upon him as such. How then could he come to an end before his time, or stop, or deteriorate, unless the universe committed abortion upon itself, which we have already decided to be absurd?

In its present state, the world would be unintelligible and the presence in it of reflection would be incomprehensible, unless we supposed there to be a secret complicity between the infinite and the infinitesimal to warm, nourish and sustain to the very end—by dint of chance, contingencies and the exercise of free choice—the consciousness that has emerged between the two. It is upon this complicity that we must depend. *Man is irreplaceable.* Therefore, however improbable it might seem, *he must reach the goal,* not necessarily, doubtless, but infallibly.

What we should expect is not a halt in any shape or form, but an ultimate progress coming at its biologically appointed hour; a maturation and a paroxysm leading ever higher into the Improbable from which we have sprung. It is in this direction that we must extrapolate man and hominisation if we want to get a forward glimpse of the end of the world.

THE APPROACHES

Without going beyond the limits of scientific probability, we can say that life still has before it long periods of geological time in which to develop. Moreover, in its thinking form, it still shows every sign of an energy in full expansion. On the one hand, compared with the zoological layers which preceded it whose average duration is at least in the order of eighty million years, mankind is so young that it could almost be called newborn. On the other hand, to judge from the rapid developments of thought in the short period of a few dozen centuries, this youth bears within it the indications and the promises of an entirely new biological cycle. Thus in all probability, between our modern earth and the ultimate earth, there stretches an immense period, characterised not by a slowing-down but a speeding up and by the definitive florescence of the forces of evolution along the line of the human shoot.

Assuming success—which is the only acceptable assumption—under what form and along what lines can we imagine progress developing during this period?

In the first place, *in a collective and spiritual form*. We have noticed that, since man's advent, there has been a certain slowing down of the passive and somatic transformations of the organism in favour of the conscious and active metamorphoses of the individual absorbed in society. We find the artificial carrying on the work of the natural; and the transmission of an oral or written culture being superimposed on genetic forms of heredity (chromosomes). Without denying the possibility or even probability of a certain prolongation in our limbs, and still more in our nervous system, of the orthogenetic process of the past,[1] I am inclined to think that their influence, hardly appreciable since the emergence of *Homo sapiens*, is destined to dwindle still further. As thought regulated by a sort of quantum law, the energies of life seem unable to spread in one region or take on a new form except at the expense of a lowering elsewhere. Since man's arrival, the evolutionary pressure seems to have dropped in all the non-human branches of the tree of life. And now that man has become an adult and has opened up for himself the field of mental and social transformations, bodies no longer change appreciably; they no longer need to in the human branch; or if they still change, it will only be under our industrious control. It may well be that in its individual capacities and penetration our brain has reached its organic limits. But the movement does not stop there. From west to east, evolution is henceforth occupied elsewhere, in a richer and more complex domain, constructing, with all minds joined together, *mind*. Beyond all nations and races, the inevitable taking-as-a-whole of mankind has already begun.

With that said, we have now to ask: *along what lines* of advance, among others—judging from the present condition of the noosphere—are we destined to proceed from the planetary level of psychic totalisation and evolutionary upsurge we are now approaching?

I can distinguish three principal ones in which we see again the predictions to which we were already led by our analysis of the ideas of science and humanity. They are: the organisation of research, the concentration of research upon the subject of man, and the conjunction of science and religion. These are three natural terms of one and the same progression.

The Organisation of Research. We are given to boasting of our age being an age of science. And if we are thinking merely of the dawn compared to the darkness that went before, up to a point we are justified. Something enormous

---

[1] Taken up again and prolonged reflectively, artificially—who knows?—by biology (assault on the laws and springs of heredity, use of hormones, etc....)

has been born in the universe with our discoveries and our methods of research. Something has been started which, I am convinced, will now never stop. Yet though we may exalt research and derive enormous benefit from it, with what pettiness of spirit, poverty of means and general haphazardness do we pursue truth in the world today! Have we ever given serious thought to the predicament we are in?

Like art—indeed we might almost say like thought itself—science was born with every sign of superfluity and fantasy. It was born of the exuberance of an internal activity that had outstripped the material needs of life; it was born of the curiosity of dreamers and idlers. Gradually it became important; its effectiveness gave it the freedom of the city. Living in a world which it can justly be said to have revolutionized, it has acquired a social status; sometimes it is even worshipped. Yet we still leave it to grow as best it can, hardly tending it, like those wild plants whose fruits are plucked by primitive peoples in their forests. Everything is subordinated to the increase in industrial production, and to armaments. The scientist and the laboratories which multiply our powers still receive nothing, or next to nothing. We behave as though we expected discoveries to fall ready-made from the sky, like rain or sunshine, while men concentrate on the serious business of killing each other and eating. Let us stop to think for a moment of the proportion of human energy devoted, here and now, to the pursuit of truth. Or, in still more concrete terms, let us glance at the percentage of a nation's revenue allotted in its budget for the investigation of clearly-defined problems whose solution would be of vital consequences for the world. If we did we should be staggered. Less is provided annually for all the pure research all over the world than for one capital ship. Surely our great-grandsons will not be wrong if they think of us as barbarians?

The truth is that, as children of a transition period, we are neither fully conscious of, nor in full control of, the new powers that have been unleashed. Clinging to outworn habit, we still see in science only a new means of providing more easily the same old things. We put Pegasus between the traces. And Pegasus languishes—unless he bolts with the waggon! But the moment will come—it is bound to—when man will be forced by disparity of the equipage to admit that science is not an accessory occupation for him but an essential activity, a natural derivative of the overspill of energy constantly liberated by mechanisation.

We can envisage a world whose constantly increasing "leisure" and heightened interest would find their vital issue in fathoming everything, trying everything, extending everything; a world in which giant telescopes and atom smashers would absorb more money and excite more spontaneous admiration than all the bombs and cannons put together; a world in which, not only for the restricted band of paid research-workers, but also for the man in the street, the day's ideal would be the wresting of another secret or another force from corpuscles, stars, or organised matter; a world in which, as happens already, one gives one's life to be and to know, rather than to possess. That, on an estimate of the forces engaged,[2] is what is being relentlessly prepared around us.

[2] External forces of planetary compression obliging humanity to totalise itself organically in itself; and internal forces (ascendent and propulsive) of spiritualisation, unleashed or exalted by technico-social totalisation.

In some of the lower organisms the retina is, as it were, spread over the whole surface of the body. In somewhat the same way human vision is still diffuse in its operation, mixed up with industrial activity and war. Biologically it needs to individualise itself independently, with its own distinct organs. It will not be long now before the noosphere finds its eyes.

The Discovery of the Human Object. When mankind has once realised that its first function is to penetrate, intellectually unify, and harness the energies which surround it, in order still further to understand and master them, there will no longer be any danger of running into an upper limit of its florescence. A commercial market can reach saturation point. One day, though substitutes may be found, we shall have exhausted our mines and oil-wells. But to all appearances nothing on earth will ever saturate our desire for knowledge or exhaust our power for invention. For of each may be said: *crescit eundo*.

That does not mean that science should propagate itself indifferently in any and every direction at the same time like a ripple in an isotropic medium. The more one looks, the more one sees. And the more one sees, the better one knows where to look. If life has been able to advance, it is because, by ceaseless groping, it has successively found the points of least resistance at which reality yielded to its thrust. Similarly, if research is to progress tomorrow, it will be largely by localising the central zones, the sensitive zones which are "alive," whose conquest will afford us an easy mastery of all the rest.

From this point of view, if we are going towards a human era of science, it will be eminently an era of human science. Man, the knowing subject, will perceive at last that man, "the object of knowledge," is the key to the whole science of nature.

Carrel referred to man as "the unknown." But man, we should add, is the solution of everything that we can know.

Up to the present, whether from prejudice or fear, science has been reluctant to look man in the face but has constantly circled round the human object without daring to tackle it. Materially our bodies seem insignificant, accidental, transitory and fragile; why bother about them? Psychologically, our souls are incredibly subtle and complex: how can one fit them into a world of laws and formulas?

Yet the more persistently we try to avoid man in our theories, the more tightly drawn become the circles we describe around him, as though we were caught up in his vortex. As I said in my Preface, at the end of its analyses, physics is no longer sure whether what is left in its hands is pure energy or, on the contrary, thought. At the end of its constructions, biology, if it takes its discoveries to their logical conclusion, finds itself forced to acknowledge the assemblage of thinking beings as the present terminal form of evolution. We find man at the bottom, man at the top, and, above all, man at the centre—man who lives and struggles desperately in us and around us. We shall have to come to grips with him sooner or later.

Man is, if I have not gone astray in these pages, an object of study of unique value to science for two reasons. (i) He represents, individually and socially, the most synthesised state under which the stuff of the universe is available to us. (ii) Correlatively, he is at present the most mobile point of the stuff in course of transformation.

For these two reasons, to decipher man is essentially to try to find out how the world was made and how it ought to go on making itself. The science of man is the practical and theoretical science of hominisation. It means profound study of the past and of origins. But still more, it means constructive experiment pursued on a continually renewed object. The programme is immense and its only end or aim is that of the future.

What is involved, firstly, is the care and improvement of the human body, the health and strength of the organism. So long as its phase of immersion in the "tangential" lasts, thought can only be built up on this material basis. And now, in the tumult of ideas that accompany the awakening of the mind, are we not undergoing physical degeneration? It has been said that we might well blush comparing our own mankind, so full of misshapen subjects, with those animal societies in which, in a hundred thousand individuals, not one will be found lacking in a single antenna. In itself that geometrical perfection is not in the line of our evolution whose bent is towards suppleness and freedom. All the same, suitably subordinated to other values, it may well appear as an indication and a lesson. So far we have certainly allowed our race to develop at random, and we have given too little thought to the question of what medical and moral factors *must replace the crude forces of natural selection* should we suppress them. In the course of the coming centuries it is indispensable that a nobly human form of eugenics, on a standard worthy of our personalities, should be discovered and developed.

Eugenics applied to individuals leads to eugenics applied to society. It would be more convenient, and we would incline to think it safe, to leave the contours of that great body made of all our bodies to take shape on their own, influenced only by the automatic play of individual urges and whims. "Better not interfere with the forces of the world!" Once more we are up against the mirage of instinct, the so-called infallibility of nature. But is it not precisely the world itself which, culminating in thought, expects us to think out again the instinctive impulses of nature so as to perfect them? Reflective substance requires reflective treatment. If there is a future for mankind, it can only be imagined in terms of a harmonious conciliation of what is free with what is planned and totalised. Points involved are: the distribution of the resources of the globe; the control of the trek towards unpopulated areas; the optimum use of the powers set free by mechanisation; the physiology of nations and races; geo-economy, geo-politics, geo-demography; the organisation of research developing into a reasoned organisation of the earth. Whether we like it or not, all the signs and all our needs converge in the same direction. We need and are irresistibly being led to create, by means of and beyond all physics, all biology and all psychology, *a science of human energetics*.

It is in the course of that creation, already obscurely begun, that science, by being led to concentrate on man, will find itself increasingly face to face with religion.

The Conjunction of Science and Religion. To outward appearance, the modern world was born of an anti-religious movement: man becoming self-sufficient and reason supplanting belief. Our generation and the two that preceded it have heard little but talk of the conflict between science and faith; indeed it seemed at one moment a foregone conclusion that the former was destined to take the place of the latter.

But, as the tension is prolonged, the conflict visibly seems to need to be resolved in terms of an entirely different form of equilibrium—not in elimination, nor duality, but in synthesis. After close on two centuries of passionate struggles, neither science nor faith has succeeded in discrediting its adversary. On the contrary, it becomes obvious that neither can develop normally without the other. And the reason is simple: the same life animates both. Neither in its impetus nor its achievements can science go to its limits without becoming tinged with mysticism and charged with faith.

Firstly *in its impetus*. We touched on this point when dealing with the problem of action. Man will only continue to work and to research so long as he is prompted by a passionate interest. Now this interest is entirely dependent on the conviction, strictly undemonstrable to science, that the universe has a direction and that it could—indeed, if we are faithful, it *should*—result in some sort of irreversible perfection. Hence comes belief in progress.

Secondly *in its construction*. Scientifically we can envisage an almost indefinite improvement in the human organism and human society. But as soon as we try to put our dreams into practice, we realise that the problem remains indeterminate or even insoluble unless, with some partially super-rational intuition, we admit the convergent properties of the world we belong to. Hence belief in unity.

Furthermore, if we decide, under the pressure of facts, in favour of an optimism of unification, we run into the technical necessity of discovering— in addition to the impetus required to push us forward and in addition to the particular objective which should determine our route—the special binder or cement which will associate our lives together, vitally, without diminishing or distorting them. Hence, belief in a supremely attractive centre which has personality.

In short, as soon as science outgrows the analytic investigations which constitute its lower and preliminary stages, and passes on to synthesis—synthesis which naturally culminates in the realisation of some superior state of humanity —it is at once led to foresee and place its stakes on the *future* and on the *all*. And with that it out-distances itself and emerges in terms of *option* and *adoration*.

Thus Renan and the nineteenth century were not wrong to speak of a Religion of Science. Their mistake was not to see that their cult of humanity implied the re-integration, in a renewed form, of those very spiritual forces they claimed to be getting rid of.

When, in the universe in movement to which we have just awakened, we look at the temporal and spatial series diverging and amplifying themselves around and behind us like the laminae of a cone, we are perhaps engaging in pure science. But when we turn towards the summit, towards the *totality* and the *future,* we cannot help engaging in religion.

Religion and science are the two conjugated faces or phases of one and the same complete act of knowledge—the only one which can embrace the past and future of evolution so as to contemplate, measure and fulfil them.

In the mutual reinforcement of these two still opposed powers, in the conjunction of reason and mysticism, the human spirit is destined, by the very nature of its development, to find the uttermost degree of its penetration with the maximum of its vital force.

THE ULTIMATE

Always pushing forward in the three directions we have just indicated, and taking advantage of the immense duration it has still to live, mankind has enormous possibilities before it.

Until the coming of man, life was quickly arrested and hemmed in by the specialisations into which it was forced to mould itself so as to act, and became fixed, then dispersed, at each forward bound. Since the threshold of reflection, we have entered into an entirely new field of evolution—thanks to the astonishing properties of "artifice" which separate the instrument from the organ and enable one and the same creature to intensify and vary the modalities of its action indefinitely without losing anything of its freedom; and thanks to the prodigious power of thought to bring together and combine in a single conscious effort all the human particles. In fact, though the study of the past may give us some idea of the resources of organised matter in its dispersed state, *we have as yet no idea of the possible magnitude* of "noospheric" effects. We are confronted with human vibrations resounding by the million—a whole layer of consciousness exerting simultaneous pressure upon the future and the collected and hoarded produce of a million years of thought. Have we ever tried to form an idea of what such magnitudes represent?[3]

In this direction, the most unexpected is perhaps what we should most expect. Under the increasing tension of the mind on the surface of the globe, we may begin by asking seriously whether life will not perhaps one day succeed in ingeniously forcing the bars of its earthly prison, either by finding the means to invade other inhabited planets or (a still more giddy perspective) by getting into physical touch with other focal points of consciousness across the abysses of space. The meeting and mutual fecundation of two noospheres is a supposition which may seem at first sight crazy, but which after all is merely extending to psychical phenomena a scope no-one would think of denying to material phenomena. Consciousness would thus finally construct itself by a synthesis of planetary units. Why not, in a universe whose astral unit is the galaxy?

Without in any way wishing to discourage such hypotheses—whose realisation, though enormously enlarging the dimensions, would leave unchanged both the convergent form and hence the final duration of noogenesis—I consider their probability too remote for them to be worth dwelling on.

The human organism is so extraordinarily complicated and sensitive, and so closely adapted to terrestrial conditions, that it is difficult to see how man could acclimatise himself to another planet, even if he were capable of navigating through interplanetary space. The sidereal durations are so immense that it is difficult to see how in two different regions of the heavens, two thought systems could co-exist and coincide at comparable stages of their development. For

[3] Over and above the intellectual value of isolated human units, there are thus grounds for recognising a collective exaltation (by mutual support or reverberation) when those units are suitably arranged. It would be difficult to say whether there are any Aristotles, Platos or St. Augustines now on earth (how could it be proved: on the other hand why not?) But what is clear is that, each supporting the other (making a single arch or a single mirror), our modern souls see and feel today a world such as (in size, inter-connections and potentialities) escaped all the great men of antiquity. To this progress in consciousness, could anyone dare to object that there has been no corresponding advance in the profound structure of being?

these two reasons among others I adopt the supposition that our noosphere is destined to close in upon itself in isolation, and that it is in a psychical rather than a spatial direction that it will find an outlet, without need to leave or overflow the earth. Hence, quite naturally, the notion of change of state recurs.

Noogenesis rises upwards in us and through us unceasingly. We have pointed to the principal characteristics of that movement: the closer association of the grains of thought; the synthesis of individuals and of nations or races; the need of an autonomous and supreme personal focus to bind elementary personalities together, without deforming them, in an atmosphere of active sympathy. And, once again: all this results from the combined action of two curvatures—the roundness of the earth and the cosmic convergence of mind—in conformity with the law of complexity and consciousness.

Now when sufficient elements have sufficiently agglomerated, this essentially convergent movement will attain such intensity and such quality that mankind, *taken as a whole,* will be obliged—as happened to the individual forces of instinct —to reflect upon itself at a single point;[4] that is to say, in this case, to abandon its organo-planetary foothold so as to shift its centre on to the transcendent centre of its increasing concentration. This will be the end and the fulfilment of the spirit of the earth.

The end of the world: the wholesale internal introversion upon itself of the noosphere, which has simultaneously reached the uttermost limit of its complexity and its centrality.

The end of the world: the overthrow of equilibrium, detaching the mind, fulfilled at last, from its material matrix, so that it will henceforth rest with all its weight on God-Omega.

The end of the world: critical point simultaneously of emergence and emersion, of maturation and escape.

We can entertain two almost contradictory suppositions about the physical and psychical state our planet will be in as it approaches maturation. According to the first hypothesis which expresses the hopes towards which we ought in any case to turn our efforts as to an ideal, evil on the earth at its final stage will be reduced to a minimum. Disease and hunger will be conquered by science and we will no longer need to fear them in any acute form. And, conquered by the sense of the earth and human sense, hatred and internecine struggles will have disappeared in the ever-warmer radiance of Omega. Some sort of unanimity will reign over the entire mass of the noosphere. The final convergence will take place *in peace.*[5] Such an outcome would of course conform most harmoniously with our theory.

But there is another possibility. Obeying a law from which nothing in the past has ever been exempt, evil may go on growing alongside good, and it too may attain its paroxysm at the end in some specifically new form.

There are no summits without abysses.

Enormous powers will be liberated in mankind by the inner play of its cohesion: though it may be that this energy will still be employed discordantly

[4] Which amounts to saying that human history develops between two points of reflection, the one inferior and individual, the other superior and collective.

[5] Though at the same time—since a critical point is being approached—in *extreme tension.* There is nothing in common between this perspective and the old millenary dreams of a terrestrial paradise at the end of time.

tomorrow, as today and in the past. Are we to foresee a mechanising synergy under brute force, or a synergy of sympathy? Are we to foresee man seeking to fulfil himself collectively upon himself, or personally on a greater than himself? Refusal or acceptance of Omega? A conflict may supervene. In that case the noosphere, in the course of and by virtue of the process which draws it together, will, when it has reached its point of unification, split into two zones each attracted to an opposite pole of adoration. Thought has never completely united itself here below. Universal love would only vivify and detach finally a fraction of the noosphere so as to consummate it—the part which decided to "cross the threshold," to get outside itself into the other. *Ramification once again, for the last time.*

In this second hypothesis, which is more in conformity with traditional apocalyptic thinking, we may perhaps discern three curves around us rising up at one and the same time into the future: an inevitable education in the organic possibilities of the earth, an internal schism of consciousness ever increasingly divided on two opposite ideals of evolution, and positive attraction of the centre of centres at the heart of those who turn towards it. And the earth would finish at the triple point at which, by a coincidence altogether in keeping with the ways of life, these three curves would meet and attain their maximum at the very same moment.

The death of the materially exhausted planet; the split of the noosphere, divided on the form to be given to its unity; and simultaneously (endowing the event with all its significance and with all its value) the liberation of that percentage of the universe which, across time, space and evil, will have succeeded in laboriously synthesising itself to the very end.

Not an indefinite progress, which is an hypothesis contradicted by the convergent nature of noogenesis, but an ecstasy transcending the dimensions and the framework of the visible universe.

Ecstasy in concord; or discord; but in either case by excess of interior tension: the only biological outcome proper to or conceivable for the phenomenon of man.

Among those who have attempted to read this book to the end, many will close it, dissatisfied and thoughtful, wondering whether I have been leading them through facts, through metaphysics, or through dreams.

But have those who still hesitate in this way really understood the rigorous and salutary conditions imposed on our reason by the coherence of the universe, now admitted by all? A mark appearing on a film; an electroscope discharging abnormally; that is enough to force physics to accept fantastic powers in the atom. Similarly, if we try to bring man, body and soul, within the framework of what is experimental, man obliges us to readjust completely to his measure the layers of time and space.

To make room for thought in the world, I have needed to "interiorise" matter: to imagine an energetics of the mind; to conceive a noogenesis rising upstream against the flow of entropy; to provide evolution with a direction, a line of advance and critical points: and finally to make all things double back upon *someone*.

In this arrangement of values I may have gone astray at many points. It is up to others to try to do better. My one hope is that I have made the reader feel both the reality, difficulty, and urgency of the problem and, at the same time, the scale and the form which the solution cannot escape.

The only universe capable of containing the human person is an irreversibly "personalising" universe.

. . .

[CHRISTIANITY: THE RELIGION OF THE FUTURE]

For almost all the ancient religions, the renewal of cosmic outlook characterising "the modern mind" has occasioned a crisis of such severity that, if they have not yet been killed by it, it is plain they will never recover. Narrowly bound to untenable myths, or steeped in a pessimistic and passive mysticism, they can adjust themselves neither to the precise immensities, nor to the constructive requirements, of space-time. They are out of step both with our science and with our activity.

But under the shock which is rapidly causing its rivals to disappear, Christianity, which might at first have been thought to be shaken too, is showing, on the contrary, every sign of forging ahead. For, by the very fact of the new dimensions assumed by the universe as we see it today, it reveals itself both as inherently more vigorous in itself and as more necessary to the world than it has ever been before.

More vigorous. To live and develop the Christian outlook needs an atmosphere of greatness and of coherence. The bigger the world becomes and the more organic become its internal connections, the more will the perspectives of the Incarnation triumph. That is what believers are beginning, much to their surprise, to find out. Though frightened for a moment by evolution, the Christian now perceives that what it offers him is nothing but a magnificent means of feeling more at one with God and of giving himself more to him. In a pluralistic and static Nature, the universal domination of Christ could, strictly speaking, still be regarded as an extrinsic and super-imposed power. In a spiritually converging world this "Christic" energy acquires an urgency and intensity of another order altogether. If the world is convergent and if Christ occupies its centre, then the Christogenesis of St. Paul and St. John is nothing else and nothing less than the extension, both awaited and unhoped for, of that noogenesis in which cosmogenesis—as regards our experience—culminates. Christ invests himself organically with the very majesty of his creation. And it is in no way metaphorical to say that man finds himself capable of experiencing and discovering his God in the whole length, breadth and depth of the world in movement. To be able to say literally to God that one loves him, not only with all one's body, all one's heart and all one's soul, but with every fibre of the unifying universe—that is a prayer that can only be made in space-time.

More necessary. To say of Christianity that, despite appearances to the contrary, it is acclimatising itself and expanding in a world enormously enlarged by science, is to point to no more than one half the picture. Evolution has come to infuse new blood, so to speak, into the perspectives and aspirations of Christianity. In return, is not the Christian faith destined, is it not preparing, to save and even to take the place of evolution?

I have tried to show that we can hope for no progress on earth without the primacy and triumph of the *personal* at the summit of *mind*. And at the present moment Christianity is the *unique* current of thought, on the entire surface of the noosphere, which is sufficiently audacious and sufficiently progressive to lay hold of the world, at the level of effectual practice, in an embrace, at once already complete, yet capable of indefinite perfection, where faith and hope reach their fulfilment in love. *Alone,* unconditionally alone, in the world today, Christianity shows itself able to reconcile, in a single living act, the All and the Person. Alone, it can bend our hearts not only to the service of that tremendous movement of the world which bears us along, but beyond, to embrace that movement in love.

In other words can we not say that Christianity fulfils all the conditions we are entitled to expect from a religion of the future; and that hence, through it, the principal axis of evolution truly passes, as it maintains?

Now let us sum up the situation:

i.   Considered objectively as a phenomenon, the Christian movement, through its rootedness in the past and ceaseless developments, exhibits the characteristics of a *phylum*.

ii.   Reset in an evolution interpreted as an ascent of consciousness, this phylum, in its trend towards a synthesis based on love, progresses precisely in the direction presumed for the leading-shoot of biogenesis.

iii.   In the impetus which guides and sustains its advance, this rising shoot implies essentially *the consciousness of being in actual relationship* with a spiritual and transcendent pole of universal convergence.

To confirm the presence at the summit of the world of what we have called the Omega point,[6] do we not find here the very cross-check we were waiting for? Here surely is the ray of sunshine striking through the clouds, the reflection onto what is ascending of that which is already on high, the rupture of our solitude. The palpable influence on our world of *an other* and supreme Someone . . . Is not the Christian phenomenon, which rises upwards at the heart of the social phenomenon, precisely that?

In the presence of such perfection in coincidence, even if I were not a Christian but only a man of science, I think I would ask myself this question.

[6] To be more exact, "to confirm the presence at the summit of the world of something in line with, but still more elevated than, the Omega point." This is in deference to the theological concept of the "supernatural" according to which the binding contact between God and the world, *hic et nunc* inchoate, attains to a super-intimacy (hence also a super-gratuitousness) of which man can have no inkling and to which he can lay no claim by virtue of his "nature" alone.

Self and World in Samkhya Yoga
John M. Koller

John M. Koller (1938–   ) is professor of philosophy at Rensselaer Poly-
technic Institute. In addition to *Oriental Philosophies,* he has written several
articles for scholarly journals and is now completing a study of the
philosophy of Mao Tse-tung.

The ethical, social, political, and religious philosophies of the epics, *Dharma
shastras,* and the *Gita* presuppose certain relationships between the empirical
self that is the social organism and the ultimate Self that is pure subject. This
presupposition is obvious from the emphasis placed on the various prescriptions
for life in society in order to realize *Atman.* Unless there were a connection
between the empirical self and the *Atman,* the activities of the empirical self
would be irrelevant to *Atman*-realization. The Upanishads appear to be so full
of excitement over the discovery of the *Atman* that they are not, for the most
part, concerned to analyze the nature of the non-*Atman* nor to analyze the relations between what is *Atman* and what is not *Atman.* It is not surprising then,
that at a later time philosophical and critical minds should inquire into these
matters and attempt to show what, if any, relations existed between Self and not-
Self, between the ultimate and the empirical. The underlying question is, How
can one be the self of flesh and bones and desires and habits and also be the
Atman, unchanging and identical with the ultimate reality of the universe?

SUBJECT AND OBJECT

The oldest philosophical school to take up this question of the relation between
the Self and the not-Self was the school of Samkhya. The teachings of this school
suggest that it grew directly out of those portions of the Upanishads emphasizing
the reality of the non-*Atman,* or the non-*Brahman.* In the Upanishads, *Brahman*
is said to have created the universe and then entered into it.[1] The world of objects
cannot be unreal, for it consists of *Atman,* which is object as well as subject. In
the *Brihadaranyaka Upanishad* it is said that *Atman* entered into the universe
"up to the fingertips, as a knife is hidden in its sheath, or the all-sustaining fire in
the fire-preserving wood."[2] Such passages indicate two basic realities; that of
Brahman and that of the objective world of empirical selves and things.

There is no doubt that for the most part the tendency in the Upanishads is to
regard *Brahman* as "more real" than the empirical or objective world. Nevertheless, as seen earlier, knowledge of *Brahman* is not an ordinary kind of knowledge,

[1] *Taittiriya,* II.6; *Chandogya,* VI.3.2.
[2] *Brihadaranyaka,* I.4.7.

and exclusive of *Brahman* knowledge, one has no choice but to take seriously the reality of the empirical self and the objective world, for there is no other reality in evidence. Furthermore, the empirical and the objective must always be the starting point for any investigation of reality, which means that at this level at least, the reality of the empirical must be acknowledged.

It appears that Samkhya, disposed to accept the reality of the empirical, perhaps partially on the basis of certain realistic remarks in the Upanishads, felt keenly the need to analyze carefully the relationship between the empirical and the ultimate realities.

The felt need to establish the relationship between the empirical and the ultimate arose from two considerations. On the one hand, the Upanishads had taught that realization of *Atman* would bring an end to suffering. Therefore, to find ways to realize this *Atman* and put an end to pain and suffering, it was necessary to discover the relationship between the empirical and the *Atman,* and to determine the sorts of things that would lead to the experience of *Atman.* Ishvara Krishna begins his discourse on Samkhya with the statement: "From torment by three-fold misery arises the inquiry into the means of terminating it. . . ."[3]

The other consideration is a matter of the basic human urge to know and render intelligible all human experiences by the exhibition of certain relationships inhering in them.

Focusing attention on ordinary human knowledge and the ordinary world known by such knowledge, the Samkhya philosophers argue that the entire world that can be experienced is fundamentally of the same nature. That is to say, desires, feelings, intelligence, etc., are not basically different from colors, sounds, odors, etc., all of which are fundamentally like sticks and stones. But all of this —the world that can, in principle, be experienced—is of the nature of object (or potential object), or not-self, as opposed to the Self that is always experiencer, that is ultimately and finally Subject. It would seem that the ultimate Subject is of a different nature and order than the world, since what is ultimate Subject can never become object, and what is object cannot be ultimate Subject. The difference between Self and the world is fundamentally the difference between subject and object.

The starting point for any analysis of the world and the self must be the experience of the self and the world one has available for analysis. This experience reveals the existence of a knowing self in a changing world. Nothing is more obvious than that we and the world around us are changing. It is with this obvious fact that the Samkhya philosophers begin, and from which they derive the conclusion that all experience and all that is experienced is fundamentally of the same nature, though basically different from the ultimate experiencing subject.

CAUSALITY

The orderliness and regularity of the experienced world cannot be dismissed as the result of chance. Changes are caused. Whatever is or will be, is or will be due

[3] *Samkhya-Karika*, I, ed. and trans. by S. S. Suryanaranyana Sastri (Madras: University of Madras, 1935), and reprinted in *A Source Book in Indian Philosophy* (Princeton: Princeton University Press, 1957), p. 425 ff.

to various causes. The first important consequence of this is that human knowledge that comes to be must be caused. It is the effect of some prior cause. But since causality is unintelligible unless the dominant features of the effect be derived from the cause, it follows that the effect must be essentially like the cause. Therefore, our knowledge must be essentially like the world that is known. Since knowledge is the result of ordering experiences, the nature of experience must be basically the same as the world. Hence the claim that experience and the experiencable are fundamentally the same.

The analysis of causality provides the main reasons for the claims made about the world and the self by Samkhya. The theory of causality adopted is called *satkaryavada*, which means that the effect preexists in the cause. Now if it is admitted that nothing can occur without a cause and also that every effect has prior existence in the cause, it follows that in an important sense the effect does not provide any new reality, for it is simply a matter of making explicit what already existed implicitly.

The Samkhya theory of the nature of causation is summed up by Ishvara Krishna when he says: "The effect is existent (pre-existent): (1) because what is non-existent cannot be produced; (2) because there is a definite relation of the cause with the effect; (3) because all is not possible; (4) because the efficient can do only that for which it is efficient; (5) because the effect is of the same essence as the cause."[4]

The reason for claiming that effects exist is that the reality of the effect can be denied only upon denial of the cause, as a cause is a cause only to the extent it produces its effects. Therefore if there are no real effects then there are no real causes. Furthermore, the effect is as real as the cause, for the effect is simply a transformation of the cause. If one were to deny the existence of both cause and effect one would be forced to deny the whole starting point of one's analysis, which would make all the conclusions contradictory. Consequently, the existence of effects cannot be denied.

The claim that the effect is of the same essence as the cause is crucially important to Samkhya, for it is the main support of the claim that all objective reality is ultimately of the same nature, the connection being that all of objective reality is simply the result of various transformations of some one ultimate stuff.

To see the force of the Samkhya argument here it is helpful to consider some of the objections that might be raised against this theory of causation. It might be objected that the effect is a new whole different from the constituent parts, and not simply a transformation of them. Evidence is provided for this objection by the fact that no effect can be known before it is produced. But if it were essentially the same as its cause it could be known by knowing the cause prior to the production of the effect. According to Samkhya this objection is not valid, for it makes no sense to say that a whole is different from its material cause. Take the case of a table. The pieces of wood, which are the material cause of the table when arranged in a certain way, are not different from the table. If it were different, one could perceive the table independently of its parts. But this is clearly impossible. And to argue that the effect and the cause are independent and separate because they are perceived as separate and independent is to beg the question. The Samkhya claim is that perceiving an effect is simply perceiving the

---

[4] *Samkhya-Karika*, IX.

cause in transformation. To go on from this to say, "and therefore seeing the effect is seeing a new entity," is not to present an objection at all, but to beg the question.

Another objection that might be raised is that if Samkhya is right in maintaining that causality is simply a matter of transformation and not the production of something new, then the activity of the agent, or efficient cause, would be unnecessary, for the effect was already in existence. But if the effect preexisted, then no efficient cause is required to bring the effect into existence. This objection is addressed by considering the assumption that the effect does not preexist in the cause. If the effect did not preexist in the cause, then causality would be the bringing into existence of something out of nothing. (Hence the claim, "What is non-existent cannot be produced.") If we look at some non-existent things, such as square circles, it will be discovered that no amount of exertion can bring them into existence. To claim that what is can be caused by what is not is not to provide an alternative view of causation but to deny causality completely. Furthermore, if you do not admit that the effect preexists, then you have to say that it does not exist until it is caused. This is tantamount to saying that the non-existent effect belongs to the cause. But since the effect does not exist there is really nothing to belong to the cause, for a relation of belonging is possible only between existing things. Thus, if the effect can be said to belong to the cause it must be admitted that it preexists in the cause. But then what of the objection that in this case no cause is needed? The answer is that the agent or efficient cause simply manifests or makes explicit what was implicit and unmanifest, and does not create something new.

Another reply to the objection that cause and effect are distinct entities is that the preexistence of the effect can be seen from the fact that nothing can be gotten out of a cause which was not in the cause. For example, curd is gotten from milk because it preexisted in the milk. It cannot be gotten from water or oil because it did not preexist in them. If it were not the case that the effect preexisted in the cause it would be possible for any effect to proceed from any cause. But this is obviously not the case; for example, you cannot produce iron from water.

Now if it is the case that only certain causes can produce certain effects, then obviously some causes are potent with respect to some effects, but not with respect to others. But this shows that the effect preexists in the cause; otherwise it would make no sense to say that a cause is potent with respect to a given effect. The reason is that the potent cause of an effect has some power related to the effect, and without the preexistence of the effect there is nothing for the power to be related to, and then it makes no sense to talk about potent causes or potentiality.

Another objection that might be raised is that to talk about manifestation and transformation is to smuggle the notion of causality, in the sense of production of new events and objects, back into the picture in disguised form. This is answered by showing that the nature of transformation has nothing to do with the cessation of preexisting attributes nor with the coming-to-be of a pre-non-existent attribute. Rather, transformation means the manifestation of an attribute or characteristic implicitly present in the substance, and alternatively, the relapse of the manifested attribute into the unmanifest condition.

To clinch the case, the Samkhya philosopher argues that the very concept of causal possibility requires the preexistence of the effect in the cause. Non-being, the non-existent, requires no cause. So if the effect were non-existent, at any time there would be no question of locating its cause. But it does make sense to talk about the possibility of effects which do not yet exist and to try to determine what will cause these effects to come into existence. This, however, makes sense only upon the assumption that the effect preexists in some sense, for that which is absolutely non-existent has no possibility of coming into existence.

The foregoing are all arguments essentially designed to support the claim that causes and effects are essentially the same. Cause is here being considered in the sense of material cause—the stuff out of which something comes to be. No effect can exist in a place different from its material cause. Hence cause and effect are numerically the same. An example given of the essential sameness of cause and effect is the tortoise going in and out of his shell. The spread-out tortoise is the effect, the contracted tortoise, the cause (and vice versa). But this does not involve the production of something new. Another example is a piece of gold which can be pressed into many shapes and pieces. But changing its shape does not make the effect something totally new. The flower made of gold is basically gold, as is the tree that is made of gold; the difference involves only name and form, and not the stuff out of which they are made.

EVOLUTION OF THE WORLD

Having established that the causality that must be assumed to exist in order to make sense out of human experience is of the nature of *satkaryavada* (meaning that the effect necessarily preexists in the cause), the Samkhya philosophers proceed to argue that this implies some one ultimate principle, which as the result of its transformations is experienced in its effects as the objective world. This claim follows once one admits that the present world exists as the result of previous changes and that change is not the production of something radically new. If this is admitted, then in order to avoid ultimate infinite regress it must be admitted that there is some one ultimate material cause, which in its various transformations or manifestations constitutes the world of experience. From this it follows that the entire world of experience is of the same fundamental nature as this ultimate material cause, for everything is basically only a transformation of this first cause. In this way Samkhya comes to the conclusion that the entire experiencable world is of the nature of *prakriti*, which is the name given to the ultimate causal principle.

This conclusion brings to the fore another question, however. How does the pluralistic world of experience derive, through a series of transformations, from this basic reality called *prakriti*? Obviously, if there are no effects except those that preexisted in the cause, then all of the effects that constitute the experienced world must have preexisted in *prakriti*. Consequently, *prakriti* itself must be composed of different tendencies, or characteristics. Accordingly, *Samkhya* posits various tendencies: *sattva*, which is the tendency responsible for the self-manifestation and self-maintenance of *prakriti; rajas*, the tendency of motion and action; and *rajas*, and *tamas* are the principles responsible for pleasure, pain, and indifference, respectively. By various combinations of these differing principles it is possible to account for the evolution of the whole world. The varying proportions of these embodied principles account for all the diversity found in the world.

But what caused the evolution of *prakriti*? If the world is looked at as evolving it is implied that there was a logical time when the principles constituting *prakriti* were in a quiet state of equilibrium. If this is the case, it is necessary to suppose another principle of reality in the world, a principle responsible for disturbing the equilibrium of the tendencies, and thereby setting in motion the evolution of *prakriti*. This second reality is called *purusha,* and it is considered to be of the nature of pure consciousness, being ultimate Subject. It is, in fact, the Samkhya version of the Upanishadic *Atman* or *Brahman*.

It is the existence of *purusha* that accounts for the evolution of *prakriti*. It is not that *purusha* actually has anything to do with *prakriti,* but simply because of the existence and presence of *purusha,* the equilibrium of *prakriti* is upset and the evolutionary process begins.

A summation of the arguments given for the existence of *purusha* is given by Ishvara Krishna as follows: "(a) Because all composite objects are for another's use, (b) because there must be absence of the three attributes and other properties, (c) because there must be control, (d) because there must be someone to experience, and (e) because there is a tendency toward "isolation" or final beatitude, therefore, the *purusha* must be there."[5]

Arguments (a) and (b) rest on the premises that (1) all experienced objects consist of parts, these parts being ordered in such a way as to serve the purposes of other objects or beings so that the whole of nature hangs together as an ordered whole, and (2) unless there is that which is not composed of parts for the sake of which those things composed of parts exist we are caught in an infinite regress. The conclusion is that the world of *prakriti,* which is the world of objects, exists for the sake of another, proving the existence of a principle other than *prakriti*. This principle is *purusha*.

Argument (c) assumes that material objects, the objects constituting the world of *prakriti,* could not work together, each being directed to its proper end, unless there be some principle of intelligence guiding this world. The conclusion is that *purusha* must exist in order that the world be ordered as it is.

Argument (d) claims that from the psychological point of view all the objects of the world are of the nature of pleasure, pain, or indifference. But pleasure and pain cannot exist without an experiencer. The conclusion is that the world of *prakriti* must exist for some experiencer, and therefore *purusha* as the principle of experiencer must exist.

Argument (e) claims that *purusha* must exist because of the desire of the individual to transcend himself. In an ordered universe it couldn't happen that the universal tendency toward the infinite—toward self-realization—would be self-frustrating. Consequently, the *purusha* must be there to be realized, since it is being sought.

But aside from arguments, the existence of *purusha* is put beyond question or doubt by the experience of those who have transcended the world of *prakriti*.

That *purusha* is regarded as being independent of *prakriti* is clear from the claim that "from the repeated study of the truth, there results that wisdom, 'I do not exist [as *prakriti*], naught is mine, I am not [*prakriti*],' which leaves no residue to be known, is pure, being free from ignorance, and is absolute."[6]

---

[5] *Samkhya-Karika,* XVII.
[6] *Samkhya-Karika,* LXIV.

But if *purusha* is independent of *prakriti*, are not the questions of how they are related, and how the empirical self can realize the *purusha* within, even more enigmatic than ever? The clue to the reply is contained in the above quotation according to which it is wisdom that releases the *purusha* from *prakriti*. If the *purusha* were *really* caught up in the *prakriti* and constrained by it, then to say that the *purusha* is completely different from and independent of *prakriti* would be nonsensical. But the Samkhya view is that the relation between *prakriti* and *purusha* has its basis in ignorance. In this ignorance a tragic mistake is made, and *purusha* is confused with *prakriti*.

In order to explain how an illusory connection between *purusha* and *prakriti* can cause the real evolution of *prakriti* it is necessary to see how the mere existence and presence of *purusha* affects *prakriti*. Imagine that *purusha* were a shining light and *prakriti* a pool of water reflecting the light. Without *purusha* doing anything more than shining by its own light, the reflection in *prakriti* reflects on itself. But this is not the true light of *purusha*; it is a reflection in *prakriti* and therefore essentially of the nature of *prakriti*. Now in this reflection, which is the reflection of *purusha* in *prakriti*, *purusha* is lost sight of, and *prakriti* is taken to be the ultimate reality. Due to this mistake, the illumination of the empirical self which enables a person to see, hear, feel, think, desire, etc., is not recognized to proceed from the great light that is *purusha*. Consequently, as *prakriti* continues to evolve, *purusha* is not discriminated from *prakriti* but is identified with the evolutes of *prakriti*.

The order of evolution of *prakriti* sketched in the Samkhya philosophy regards the first illumination of *prakriti* by *purusha* as *Buddhi*, or *Mahat*—the "great one." This reflection becoming aware of itself is the "I-Maker" (*ahamkara*) responsible for individuation in nature. From these evolutes proceed the mind and the organs of sensation as well as the organs of actions and the essences of the things that are sensed and acted upon. Finally the gross objects of the world evolved. In this way the origin of all of experienced reality is accounted for by Samkhya.

SELF-DISCIPLINE

The preceding account of the nature of the empirical self and world, and their relation to the *purusha,* or ultimate Self, provides a rational basis for the techniques of discipline known as *yoga*. The practice of *yoga* is required to achieve the wisdom whereby the ignorance wherein the *purusha* is confused with *prakriti* is alleviated and the essential nature of the Self as *purusha* is realized.

The basic question of *yoga* is, How can that wisdom be achieved wherein the *purusha,* pure subject, recognizes itself for what it is; simply the spectator of *prakriti,* not actually a part of it or connected to it? When this wisdom is achieved there is no longer suffering, for the *purusha* is no longer mistakenly attached to the changing and suffering *prakriti*. Consequently, the afflictions of *prakriti* have nothing to do with *purusha,* and cannot cause suffering.

How the relationship between *purusha* and *prakriti* results in suffering, as explained by Samkhya, can be pictured by imagining a person in a room surrounded by audio-visual devices. These devices lead the person to identify himself with a person being picked up out of the sea, wafted to the peak of a jagged cliff high over the water, and plummeted down to be dashed against the rocks below. Time after time the process is repeated; each time the broken pieces are fused together again and the process commenced anew. For the person who has mistaken this image for himself there is the pain and suffering of a thousand horrible deaths. Nothing could be more wonderful than to escape this horrible fate. But when the person realizes that he has identified himself with a self created out of film and sound he recognizes that nothing that happens to that self has anything to do with him and he is free of the suffering with which he had identified himself. The point is that the person was really free from suffering all of the time, but ignorance prevented this realization. It was neither the audio-visual material in itself nor the person himself that caused the suffering. It was the mistaken identification of the one with the other that led to suffering. In an analogous way, neither *purusha* nor *prakriti* themselves are capable of suffering, but a wrong identification of *purusha* with *prakriti* leads to suffering. To overcome the suffering of the self something must be done to remove the ignorance leading to the mistaken identification of the pure Self with the not-Self.

To this end the *Yoga* aphorisms of Patanjali prescribes *yoga*, or self-discipline. The first four aphorisms indicate the nature and purpose of *yoga*: "Now the exposition of *yoga*. *Yoga* is the restriction of the fluctuations of the mind-stuff (*citta*). Then the Seer [that is, the Self] abides in himself. At other times it [the Self] takes the same forms as the fluctuations [of mind stuff]."[7]

What is here called "mind-stuff" corresponds to what in Samkhya is called the *Buddhi,* or *Mahat*, the "great one." The fluctuations or movements in *Buddhi,* or mind-stuff, lead to the identification with these fluctuations which are due to the not-Self, or *prakriti*. When the changes or fluctuations of the mind-stuff cease there is no foundation for the mistaken identification of *purusha* with *prakriti* and the independence of *purusha* is realized. But when the fluctuations occur they are mistaken for the real Self, the *purusha*. It is as though the light of *purusha* is caught by the rippling dirtied waters of the pool and is therefore regarded as changing and dirty. When the pool is calmed and the dirt allowed to settle, the light is no longer obscured. Accordingly, the important feature of *yoga* is the disciplining and controlling of the mind-stuff.

The eight aids to *yoga* indicate that since the mind-stuff has already identified with the ego, the mind, the senses, and bases of action, one restricts the fluctuations through self-discipline, by bringing under control the other aspects of *prakriti* that have evolved as empirical self—the habits, desires, physical self, etc.

The eight aids to the achievement of the goal of *yoga* are listed as: (1) abstinence from injury, falsehood, theft, incontinence, and the acceptance of gifts; (2) cleanliness, contentment, self-castigation, study, and devotion to the Ishvara; (3) stable and easy posture, accompanied by the relaxation of effort, or by a state of balance; (4) restraint of breath; (5) withdrawal of the senses; (6) not allowing the mind-stuff to wander; (7) focusing the mind-stuff, or contemplation; (8) concentration, wherein the object of contemplation is transcended and duality destroyed.[8]

[7] *Yoga Sutras of Patanjali*, I, 1–4, trans. by James Haughton Woods, *Harvard Oriental Series*, XVII (Cambridge: Harvard University Press, 1914).
[8] *Yoga Sutras*, II, III.

The first five aids are indirect or preliminary steps in that they prepare the empirical self for the discipline of the mind-stuff that is taken up in the last three steps. Essentially, the discipline of *yoga* is a matter of bringing under control the various evolutes of *prakriti* as shaped by mind-stuff, the reflected *purusha*. It is thus really the reverse process of the evolution of *prakriti*; the involution of *prakriti* back to the stage where the original mistake took place. When this occurs the *purusha* will no longer be regarded as constrained by matter and the Self will be realized in its pure subjectivity.

The explanation of the relation between the empirical and the ultimate by Samkhya, and the nature of the mistake causing bondage and suffering which is to be remedied by the discipline of *yoga*, is nicely summed up in an old and favorite Indian story. The story deals with a little tiger raised by wild goats who mistook himself for a goat and had to be instructed by a master and provided with the right kinds of experience in order to realize his true nature—that of a tiger.

The tiger's mother had died giving birth, and the infant was left all alone in the world. Fortunately, the goats were compassionate and adopted the little fellow, teaching him how to eat grass with his pointed teeth and how to bleat like they did. Time passed and the tiger assumed that he was just like the rest of the band of goats. But one day an old male tiger came upon this little band of goats. They all fled in terror, except for the tiger-goat, now about half-grown, who for some unknown reason felt no fear. As the savage jungle beast approached, the cub began to feel self-conscious and uncomfortable. To cover his self-consciousness he began to bleat a bit and nibble some grass. The old tiger roared at the little one in amazement and anger, asking him what he thought he was doing eating grass and bleating like a goat. But the little one was too embarrassed by all this to answer, and continued to nibble grass. Thoroughly outraged by this behavior, the jungle tiger grabbed him by the scruff of his neck and carried him to a nearby pool. Holding him over the water he told him to look at himself. "Is that the pot face of a tiger or the long face of a goat?" he roared.

The cub was still too frightened to answer, so the old tiger carried him to his cave, and thrust a huge chunk of juicy, red, raw meat between his jaws. As the juices trickled into his stomach the cub began to feel a new strength and a new power. No longer mistaking himself for a goat the little tiger lashed his tail from side to side and roared like the tiger he was. He had achieved Tiger-realization! He no longer took himself to be what he appeared to be in his ignorance, but realized his true nature, which had nothing to do with the world of goats.

Why Science Lost the Cosmic

S. H. Nasr

Seyyed Hossein Nasr (1933–   ) is dean of the faculty of arts and letters at Tehran University and professor of the history of science and philosophy. He received his early education in Tehran, after which he studied physics at MIT and took his doctorate at Harvard. Among his many books are *Three Muslim Sages, Ideals and Realities of Islam,* and *Sufi Essays.*

THE INTELLECTUAL AND HISTORICAL CAUSES

A great deal of the blame for the neglect of other conceptions of science and failure to grasp the true significance of ancient and medieval cosmologies and other sciences of nature rests upon the manner in which these sciences are studied today. The investigation of the history of science, which during this century has become an important academic discipline, has concentrated more on glorifying modern science or searching for its historic roots than in making a study in depth of conceptions of nature in different civilizations and epochs of history or penetrating into the metaphysical significance of the ancient and medieval sciences. Most scholars in this field have turned their sole attention to those elements and factors in ancient and medieval or, for that matter, Renaissance science that resemble, anticipate or have influenced modern science.[1] In fact, modern science has been taken by most science historians as the only legitimate and possible form of science of nature, and all other cosmological sciences have been considered either as early anticipations of this form of science or as deviations which have hindered modern science. The use of the word "science" in English is particularly significant and indicative of the point of view in question.[2]

We do not, however, belittle the significance of the studies made in the domain of the history of science in which, through the historical approach, the roots of a particular science and its past information are clarified. The pioneering work of such men as Berthelot, Mach, Duhem, Sarton, Tannery, Thorndike and others has contributed immensely to our understanding of the scientific activity of other ages. But few of these works can help in solving the problem of the modern crisis of the encounter of man and nature. This is because rather than become independent judges of ancient and medieval sciences and objective observers or even critics of modern science they have completely adopted the point of view

From S. H. Nasr, *The Encounter of Man and Nature* (London, 1968), pp. 51–80, 105–106. Reprinted by permission of George Allen & Unwin Ltd.

[1] "Historians of science have, until recently, committed the same error as historians of the early Church in the fourth and fifth centuries; they have written as if the only events of importance in the previous period were those which directly anticipated and promoted the current orthodoxy of their own day." Raven, *Natural Religion and Christian Theology,* I, p. 7.

[2] Whereas science in English should logically mean the *scientia* of Latin or *Wissenschaft* of German it has come to acquire a very restricted meaning in most quarters leaving the English language without a general term corresponding to *Wissenschaft,* or *scientia.* Recently in certain circles the full meaning of "science" has been re-instated but this more universal meaning is far from being widely accepted or employed.

that the only possible and legitimate form of science is the modern one.

There has been in the professional ranks of science historians, particularly before the nineteen-fifties, a singular neglect of the symbolic meaning of the ancient and medieval sciences and a tendency to read into older texts meanings and concepts proper to modern science. Many have written about the concepts of matter or motion in the ancient world as if in those days people held the same views about the physical world as the contemporary ones. Pre-Socratic philosophers have been hailed as forerunners of modern physicists as if the water of Thales were the water of modern chemistry; or the Babylonians are held as the first astronomers in the modern sense, while the religious significance of their astronomical observations is forgotten completely. No doubt Babylonian mathematics is a brilliant chapter in the history of mathematics but we wonder if it is "scientifically" correct to speak of Babylonian science as if its only meaning were that which modern mathematicians understand by it. The symbolic significance of the seven planets, their motion and relation to the earthly domain is, for those who understand it, as exact as that part of Babylonian science which is treated as "exact science" through standards placed upon it by modern scholars who hold a view totally alien to that of the Babylonians.

Alternatively, we could question whether Islamic science is only that element which contributed to the rise of modern science; or when we speak of medieval science whether we should concentrate only on those thirteenth- and fourteenth-century theologians and philosophers like Ockham, Oresme, Buridan, Grosseteste and others who anticipated the mathematical and physical works of Benedetti, Galileo and other founders of modern science. The existence of interest in dynamics and mechanics amongst late medieval nominalists is surely of importance, but with the same certainty we can also assert that this is not the whole of medieval science but is merely the view of modern historians of science as to what, in fact, medieval science was. If we wish to use the history of science beneficially to solve the acute problems modern science and its applications have brought about, we cannot be satisfied merely with the current method of studying the history of science. We must also study the sciences of nature of other civilizations and periods, independently of their contribution, or lack of it, to modern science. We must consider these sciences as being independent views about nature some of which may be of considerable aid in the solution of contemporary problems[3] and as providing a background for the criticism of certain aspects of modern science. It is in this light that we turn, therefore, to the history of science in the hope of discovering the intellectual and historical causes of the present situation.

The historical background of both science itself and Greek and Christian philosophy and theology is important for any present-day discussion, because the individual as well as the culture in which he lives inevitably carries within him the deep roots of his past. The present day encounter of man and nature, and all the philosophical, theological and scientific problems connected with it, carry within themselves elements connected with Christian civilization[4] as well as with

---

[3] Fortunately, in the past few years, some historians of science have turned their attention to the study of ancient and medieval science as related to the total world view of the cultures of these ages rather than as simply historical preludes to modern science. Due to the lack of metaphysical knowledge and disregard for the science of symbolism, this approach has not been widespread.

the civilization of Antiquity which Christianity came to replace. In order then to discover the deep causes of contemporary problems we are forced to return to the beginning and to consider those causes, both intellectual and historical, which still exist today.

The ancient Greeks possessed a cosmology similiar to that of other Aryan peoples of Antiquity. The elements, and nature itself, were still inhabited by the Gods. Matter was alive with spirit and the spiritual and corporeal substances had not as yet become distinct. The rise of philosophy and science in the sixth century BC was not so much the discovery of a new realm as an attempt to fill a vacuum created by the fact that the Olympian Gods had deserted their earthly abode. The basic ideas of *phusis, dike, nomos* and the like which are fundamental to Greek science and philosophy are all terms of religious significance which have been gradually emptied of their spiritual substance.[5] The pre-Socratic philosophers, far from being early examples of modern naturalists and scientists, were still searching for the universal substance which is both spiritual and corporeal and they can be quite legitimately compared to the Hindu cosmologists of the school of Sāmkhya. The water of Thales is not what flows in rivers and streams but is the psycho-spiritual substratum and principle of the physical world.

With the gradual increase in decadence of the Greek Olympian religion, more and more the substance of nature itself became divorced from its spiritual significance, and cosmology and physics tended toward naturalism and empiricism. In the same way that from the Orphic-Dionysian dimension of Greek religion there developed the Pythagorean-Platonic school of philosophy and mathematics, so from the body of Olympian religious concepts, emptied of their meaning, arose a physics and a natural philosophy which sought to fill the vacuum and to provide a coherent explanation for a world no longer inhabited by the gods.[6] The general movement was from symbolic interpretation of nature to naturalism, from contemplative metaphysics to rationalistic philosophy.

With the birth of Aristotle, philosophy as understood in the West began and as understood in the East terminated.[7] After Aristotle, rationalism as expressed in the Stoic, Epicurean and other late schools became prevalent in the Roman empire, a rationalism which, however, contributed little to the natural sciences[8]

---

[4] One hardly need re-assert how many modern scholars insist on the close nexus between science and Christian thought. Some take into consideration positive relations and others the reactions between the two. See for example, Smethurst, *Modern Science and Christian Belief,* J. MacMurray, *Reason and Emotion,* London, 1935; J. Baillie, *Natural Science and the Spiritual Life,* London, 1951; and S. F. Mason, *Main Currents of Scientific Thought,* New York, 1956.

[5] See F. Cornford, *Principium sapientiae,* Cambridge, 1952; and W. Jaeger, *Theology of the Early Greek Philosophers,* Oxford, 1947.

[6] See Cornford, *From Religion to Philosophy,* New York, 1958. Also G. DiSantillana, *Foundations of Scientific Thought,* Chicago, 1961.

[7] See F. Schuon, *Light on the Ancient Worlds,* p. 64.

[8] Of course Stoicism has had much importance during the Renaissance and the seventeenth century as a weapon against Aristotelianism and has contributed much to the rise of seventeenth-century physics as shown by S. Sambursky in *Physics of the Stoics,* New York, 1959. But nevertheless it cannot be denied that the scientific achievements of the Stoics, Epicureans and similar late schools that were disseminated in the Roman Empire hardly compare with that of Aristotle or the school of Alexandria in general.

It is also of interest to note that after Aristotle himself his school turned mostly from a study of the organic aspect of nature, as witnessed in the biological works of Aristotle and the botany directly and which showed little concern for the metaphysical and theological significance of the sciences. In Alexandria, however, mystical and religious schools of philosophy developed during a period of intense activity in the mathematical and physical sciences. It was here that Neoplatonic metaphysics, Neopythagorean mathematics and Hermeticism were developed and where the study of mathematical and natural sciences was often carried out in the matrix of a metaphysics that was aware of the symbolic and transparent nature of things. It is of significance that the immediate background of Western civilization, in its external and formal aspect, is Roman while that which Islam received from the Graeco-Hellenistic heritage comes mostly from Alexandria. Christianity, when it was called upon to save a civilization rather than a few souls, was faced with a world in which naturalism, empiricism and rationalism were rampant, where knowledge of a human order had become divinized and where an excessive attraction to nature seemed to the Christian eye a blasphemy that blinded men to the vision of God.

Christianity, therefore, reacted against this naturalism by emphasizing the boundary between the supernatural and the natural and by making the distinction between the natural and supernatural so strict as to come near to depriving nature of the inner spirit that breathes through all things. To save the souls of men in the particular atmosphere in which it found itself, Christianity had to forget and neglect, or at least belittle, the theological and spiritual significance of nature. Henceforth, the study of nature from a theological point of view did not occupy a central place in Western Christianity.[9]

To preserve a correct theology Christianity became opposed to the "cosmic religion" of the Greeks, and some theologians called nature *massa perditionis*. In the dialogue between the Christian and the Greek, in which both sides were expressing an aspect of the truth but each a half truth, the Christian emphasized the nature of God, the human soul and salvation while the Greek emphasized the "divine" quality of the cosmos and the "supernatural" status of intelligence itself which enables man to know the universe.[10] Against this cosmology Christianity opposed its theology and against this emphasis upon knowledge, accented the path of love. To overcome the danger of rationalism divorced from gnosis it made knowledge the handmaid of faith and ignored the supernatural essence of natural intelligence within men. Only in this way was it able to save a civilization and to instill into a decadent world a new spiritual life; but in the process an alienation took place towards nature which has left its mark upon the subsequent history of Christianity. This is one of the deep-lying roots of the present crisis of modern man in his encounter with nature.

---

of Theophrastus, to an interest in mechanics and simple machines as seen in the pseudo-Aristotelian *Mechanics*.

[9] See B. Bavink, "The Natural Sciences" in *Introduction to the Scientific Philosophy of Today*, New York, 1932, where the author writes that except for a few Teutons, St. Francis of Assisi, the German mystics and Luther, Christianity has neglected the study of nature outside of the human being. See particularly p. 576.

[10] Referring to the debate and dialogue between the Christian and the Hellenist Schuon writes, "...a half truth which tends to safeguard the transcendence of God at the expense of the metaphysical intelligibility of the world is less erroneous than a half-truth which tends to safeguard the divine nature of the world at the expense of the intelligibility of God." *Light on the Ancient Worlds*, p. 60.

On the struggle between early Christian theology and the "cosmic religion" of the Greeks see J. Pépin, *Théologie cosmique et théologie chrétienne*, Paris, 1964.

The character of Christianity as a way of love rather than as knowledge needs particular emphasis. In envisaging man as a will rather than an intelligence, Christianity has emphasized the pull of faith and love over knowledge and certitude. Illuminative knowledge or gnosis[11] has existed in Christianity but mostly on the periphery, especially as far as Western Christianity is concerned. Knowledge derived from intelligence without the aid of faith came to be considered as "knowledge according to the flesh," in conformity with the Christian conception of man as an essentially warped will whose wound must be healed through the rite of Baptism. There was not that accent upon the supernatural essence of the intelligence and on that gnosis or illuminative knowledge which is at once the source and meeting ground of both faith and reason. The Greek gnostic saw in man's natural aptitude to know a means of reaching the Absolute Truth itself. It may also be added that Islam in the cadre of Abrahamic monotheism likewise made gnosis central and placed the accent not so much on the will of man, whose wound had to be healed, but on the intelligence which had only to be reminded through revelation of its supernatural essence.

In any case, because of its character as a way of love and the excessively naturalistic background in which it was called upon to fill the spiritual vacuum caused by the decadence of Graeco-Roman religions, Christianity drew a sharp line between the supernatural and the natural, or grace and nature. The official theology left the problem of nature as a positive domain in the religious life out of its central concern, especially after the formulation of the Creeds and the exteriorization of the esoteric way that is Christianity; this followed inevitably, since after its early days Christianity was called upon not only to save a selected few but a whole civilization that was falling apart. The gnostic element continued to exist, but only as a sideline development which periodically, through the history of Christianity, has manifested itself in different forms. It has been the one element which enabled Christianity to develop in the Middle Ages a cosmology of its own and to adapt to its needs those forms of cosmology and sciences of nature that were conformable to its perspective.

The relation between metaphysical and theological principles of a religious tradition such as Christianity and the cosmological sciences must be made clear. Either the cosmological sciences are based on, or drawn from the metaphysical sources of the religion itself, or they are adopted from an alien tradition but integrated into the perspective of the tradition in question. The traditional cosmological sciences—that whole series of sciences dealing with figures, numbers, forms, colours and correspondence between various orders of reality —can only be understood, and their symbolic significance discovered, in the light of a living spirituality. Without the light of a living tradition with its own metaphysics and theology the cosmological sciences become opaque and unintelligible. Seen in this light these sciences become shining crystals that illuminate the multiple phenomena of the Universe and make them intelligible and transparent.[12] It was in this way that both Islam and Christianity integrated Hermetic cosmology into their esoteric dimensions and gave it new life and significance.

[11] By gnosis of course we mean that unitive knowledge which saves and illumines and is inseparable from love and not gnosticism which was banned as a heresy by the Christian councils.

[12] On this question see T. Burckhardt, "Nature de la perspective cosmologique," *Etudes Traditionnelles,* vol. 49, 1948, pp. 216–19; and in the context of Islam, S.H. Nasr, *An Introduction to Islamic Cosmological Doctrines,* Cambridge (U.S.A.), 1964, especially the introduction.

The ambivalent source of Christian cosmology is seen in the fact that there, both Biblical or Hebrew cosmological concepts and Greek ones stand side by side. There is the Biblical cosmogony based on creation *ex-nihilo* and on a drama that occurs in time. Then there are the Greek cosmologies which occur in "space" without regard for temporal and secular change, one in which time is cyclic and the world appears to lack a temporal beginning. Christianity adopted elements of both these cosmological views, and the long disputes among theologians and philosophers as to the creation or eternity of the world and the nature of time and space, reflect this dual origin of cosmology within the Christian perspective. It is this absorption of Graeco-Hellenistic elements into Western Christian civilization, both directly at the beginning of the Christian era and then again in the modified form given to them by Islam during the Middle Ages, that made possible the arts and sciences in the medieval period, and also served as the background for the scientific revolution. One should therefore always remember both the character of the sciences of the Greek world as they came to be known by later ages and the attitude and reaction of Christianity itself *vis-à-vis* this heritage. Both are of basic importance in the attitude of Western man toward nature in all subsequent periods of Western history including the contemporary.

As Christianity grew from the religion of a few to the spiritual life force of a humanity, and began to mould a civilization which was distinctly Christian, it had to develop both its own art, cosmology and sciences of the natural world.[13] If theologically Christianity emphasized a rejection of the "life of this world" and a search for a kingdom which was not of this world, in its total view of things it also had to possess the means of equating the techniques of the artisans with Christian activity and the world in which the Christian man lived with a Christian Universe. It succeeded on both accounts, in creating both an artisanal tradition that could construct the medieval cathedrals which are a microcosmic model of the Christian cosmos, and a total science of the visible Universe which depicted this Universe as a Christian one. When man stands in a medieval cathedral he feels himself at the centre of the world.[14] This could only be brought about through the relation between sacred art and cosmology that existed in medieval Christianity as it has in other traditions. The cathedral recapitulates the cosmos and is its replica on the human plane in the same way that the medieval city with its walls and gates is a model of the bound medieval Universe.[15]

The science of natural objects and the techniques of making things, or art in its most universal sense, were developed together in the new Christian civilization, and both were integrated as a hidden and secret knowledge into the esoteric dimensions of Christianity. The popular knowledge of nature was based on survivals of such works as the *Historia naturalis* of Pliny and other late popular

[13] Traditional cosmology is very much like sacred art which, out of the many forms of the world of multiplicity, chooses a certain number which it moulds and transmutes so as to make of them an intelligible and transparent symbol of the genius of the religious tradition in question. See Burckhardt, "Nature de la perspective cosmologique."

[14] See "Aesthetics and Symbolism in Art and Nature" in F. Schuon, *Spiritual Perspectives and Human Facts,* pp. 24 ff.

[15] It is not accidental that the walls of European cities began to be broken about the same time that heliocentric astronomy destroyed the idea of the world as cosmos or "order" and removed the finite boundary of the Universe.

encyclopaedias, on the writings of Isadore of Seville, Gregory, Bede and similar medieval authors, and on elements of Platonic cosmology as derived from the *Timaeus* and often cited in the writings of some of the Fathers as well as by more popular writers. Yet the most profound elements of the Christian knowledge of nature and things natural were to be found in secret societies, guilds and associations connected with the esoteric aspect of Christianity. Whether unformulated, as among the guild of masons, or articulated as in the case of the secret association of the *Fedeli d'amore* to which Dante belonged, the sciences of nature and cosmology connected with this aspect of medieval Christian civilization represent the most profound aspects of the process of Christianization.

In order to achieve this end, Christianity integrated into its more inward dimensions elements of the Hermetic-Pythagorean cosmological sciences. The Pythagorean science of harmony, of numbers, geometric forms and colours, pervaded the science and art of the Middle Ages. So many of the medieval cathedrals, of which Chartres is an outstanding example, are a synthesis of medieval art and science in which the element of harmony is the guiding principle. The proportions of so many of these sacred structures are notes of music in stone.[16]

As for Hermeticism, it provided Christianity with a sacred science of material objects. The elemental materials of the natural world became so many building blocks which led the soul from the darkness of the *materia prima* to the luminosity of the intelligible world. The Hermetical and alchemical perspective, which in an articulate form entered into the Christian world through Islamic sources, extended the sacramental conception present in the Christian mass to the whole of nature. Through it, the artisan was able to transform the substance of the corporeal world about him so that it could possess and convey spiritual efficacy and significance.[17]

As we glance at the Middle Ages we see on the one hand a popular natural history imbued more and more with Christian values of an ethical order, as reflected in medieval books of animals, and on the other a science of nature associated closely with the craftsman's guilds. In the latter an operative knowledge of nature was primarily emphasized, while the theoretical knowledge remained for the most part unwritten or unformulated. Occasionally an intellectual expression would be given of this religious science of things and of the cosmos as a whole. This we find in the works of Dante and somewhat before him in the school of Chartres.

The type of science of nature which is profoundly Christian, both in its aims and its presuppositions, is however associated more with the contemplative

[16] See the Appendix of E. Levy in O. von Simpson, *The Gothic Cathedral,* New York, 1956; also T. Burckhardt, *Chartres und die Geburt der Kathedrale,* Lausanne and Freiburg, 1962. H. Keyser in many studies such as *Akroasis, die Lehre von Harmonike der Welt,* Stuttgart, 1947, has re-discovered for the modern world this forgotten traditional science of harmony which is so important as an integrating principle of the arts and the sciences. The *trivium* and *quadrivium,* the medieval arts and sciences themselves, come from the Pythagorean seven-fold division of musical scale.

[17] See M. Aniane, "Notes sur l'alchimie, 'yoga' cosmologique de la chrétienté médiévale," in *Yoga, science de l'homme intégral,* Paris, 1953, pp. 243–73; also T. Burckhardt, *Die Alchemie, Sinn und Weltbild,* Osten, 1960; and S. H. Nasr, "The Alchemical Tradition" in *Science and Civilization in Islam,* Cambridge (U.S.A.), 1968.

and metaphysical dimension of Christianity than with the theological. In fact, the cosmological perspective can be integrated only into the metaphysical dimension of a tradition and not into the theological aspect as this term is usually understood. Theology is too rationalistic and man-oriented to be concerned with the spiritual essence and symbolism of cosmic phenomena, unless we understand by theology the apophatic and contemplative theology which is more metaphysical than rationalistic and philosophical. And so, with certain exceptions as in the case of Erigena or the school of Chartres, in theological circles little interest was taken in the symbolic and contemplative view of nature. It was left to St Francis of Assisi to express, within the bosom of Christian spirituality, the profoundest insights into the sacred quality of nature. A few northern European scientists and philosophers like Roger Bacon were to combine observation of nature with a mystical philosophy based on illumination, but this was more of an exception than a rule. Even later Franciscans like the great theologian St Bonaventure, who expressed the necessity of a *sapientia* as a background for *scientia,* were not particularly interested in the study of nature.

Into the world of early medieval Christianity, dominated by Augustinian theology, Dionysian angelology and a Christian cosmology drawn from Platonic, Pythagorean and Hermetic elements, there entered in the eleventh century a new form of learning from the Islamic world. Besides the spread of certain occult sciences like alchemy, and even esoteric contact between Islam and Christianity through the Order of the Temple and other secret organizations,[18] the main result of this contact was acquaintance with Peripatetic philosophy and science as it had been developed by the Muslims for several centuries.

Here, we are not concerned with how this transmission took place nor with the different sciences that became known through this process to the Latin world. Rather, we wish to turn to the effect of this new development in the general view of nature. The Muslims had for several centuries developed Peripatetic science and philosophy as well as mathematics, but at the same time the gnostic, illuminationist dimension associated with Sufism had been alive from the start and continued as the inner life force of this tradition.[19] In fact, Islam turned more and more to this direction during its later history.

In the Occident, however, the translation of Arabic works into Latin, which caused a major intellectual change from the eleventh to the thirteenth centuries, resulted gradually in the Aristotelianization of Christian theology. Rationalism came to replace the earlier Augustinian theology based on illumination and the contemplative view of nature was increasingly pushed aside as the gnostic and metaphysical dimension of Christianity became ever more stifled in an increasingly rationalistic environment.

A case in point is the career of the philosophy of Ibn Sînâ—the Latin Avicenna —the greatest of the Muslim Peripatetics in the West. To the present day Avicenna has continued to exert influence upon Islamic intellectual life. The later reviver of Peripatetic philosophy, Ibn Rushd or Averroes, however, exercised much less influence upon his co-religionists. In the West a somewhat misunderstood

---

[18] See H. Probst-Biraben, *Les Mystères des templiers,* Nice, 1947; also P. Ponsoye, *Islam et le Graal,* Paris, 1957.

[19] As far as the relation between the sciences, philosophy and the gnostic and Sufi dimension within Islam is concerned see S. H. Nasr, *Three Muslim Sages,* Cambridge (U.S.A.), 1964; *An Introduction to Islamic Cosmological Doctrines* and *Science and Civilization in Islam.*

Averroes became, during the thirteenth century, the master of the Latin Averroists who were associated with pre-Christian learning. Yet Avicenna never gained enough disciples in the West to have even the honour of a school of "Latin Avicennism" named after him.[20]

The Aristotelianism of Averroes was much more pure and radical than that of other Muslim philosophers, while Avicenna had combined this philosophy with the tenets of Islam and even developed later in life an "Oriental philosophy" based on illumination.[21] The interpretation of Averroes in the West as an even more rationalistic philosopher than he actually was, and the lack of a systematic acceptance of Avicenna, are the best indication of the movement toward rationalism in the Christian world. This inclination is brought to light particularly when the situation in the Occident is compared with the intellectual life of its sister Islamic civilization during the same period. Through this process, theology came to replace metaphysics or rather rationalistic theology replaced the contemplative theology of earlier centuries. The result of this change was to become evident after an interim period of relative equilibrium.

The career of Avicennian cosmology is of particular pertinence in this development. For Avicenna, cosmology was closely connected to angelology.[22] The Universe was peopled by angelic forces, a view which accorded perfectly well with the religious conception of the world. The spiritual agent in the form of the angel was an integral and real aspect of cosmic reality. As it spread in the West, however, Avicennian cosmology, although accepted in outline, was criticized by men like William of Auvergne who wanted to banish the angels from the Universe. By neglecting the Avicennian souls of the spheres, these scholars had to a certain extent already secularized the Universe and prepared it for the Copernican revolution.[23] This revolution could, in fact, only have occurred in a cosmos from which the symbolic and spiritual meaning had been removed; a cosmos which had become sheer fact drawn away from the bosom of metaphysics and made the subject of a purely physical science.

While the thirteenth century was the golden age of scholasticism and produced the synthesis of St Thomas and a few men like Albertus Magnus, Roger Bacon and Robert Grosseteste who within the matrix of a Christian philosophy were intensely interested in the sciences of nature, the very domination of rationalism during this period soon destroyed the equilibrium established during the century. The balance tilted in the other direction, and in the fourteenth century led to an attack against reason and a scepticism that marked the end of the Middle Ages. Two different but complementary movements can be seen at this time. The first is the destruction of the esoteric organizations within Christendom such as the Order of the Temple. The result was that the gnostic and metaphysical element which had until that time been continuously present began to disperse and gradually disappear, at least as an active living force in the intellectual framework of the Christian West.[24] The second was the foundering of rationalism by its own weight and the introduction of a denial of the power of reason to

[20] See *Three Muslim Sages*, Chapter 1.
[21] See *An Introduction to Islamic Cosmological Doctrines*, pp. 185–91.
[22] See H. Corbin, *Avicenna and the Visionary Recital*, section II; also S. H. Nasr, *Three Muslim Sages*, pp. 28–31.
[23] Corbin, *op cit.*, pp. 101 ff.
[24] See R. Guénon, *Aperçu sur l'ésotérisme chrétien*, Paris, 1954.

reach the truth. If the mystics like Meister Eckhart sought to transcend reason from above, the nominalist theologians rejected rational philosophy, one might say from below, by refusing reason the very possibility of knowing the universal.

The whole debate about universals which goes back to Abelard became at this time the favourite weapon for attacking reason and showing the inconsistencies of its conclusions. Ockham and the Ockhamists created an atmosphere of philosophical doubt which they tried to fill with a nominalist theology that was to play the role of philosophy. Ockham created a theologism which destroyed the certainty of medieval philosophy and led to philosophical scepticism.[25] Meanwhile, in emphasizing particular universal causes and criticizing Peripatetic philosophy and science, Ockham and his followers like Oresme and Nicolas of Autrecourt made important discoveries in mechanics and dynamics, discoveries that form the basis of the seventeenth-century revolution in physics. It is important to note, however, that this interest in the sciences of nature went hand in hand with philosophical doubt and a turning away from metaphysics. For this was substituted a nominalist theology. Once the element of faith became weakened this scientific development was left without any element of philosophical certainty. Rather, it became wedded to doubt and scepticism.

The Middle Ages thus drew to a close in a climate in which the symbolic and contemplative view of nature had been for the most part replaced by a rationalistic view, and this in turn through the criticism of nominalist theologians had led to philosophical scepticism. Meanwhile, with the destruction of the gnostic and metaphysical elements within Christianity the cosmological sciences became opaque and incomprehensible and the cosmos itself was gradually secularized. Furthermore, within Christian circles in general, neither the Dominicans nor Franciscans showed particular interest in the study of nature.[26] The background was thus prepared in every way for that revolution and upheaval which brought to an end the integral Christian civilization of the medieval period and created an atmosphere in which the sciences of nature began to be cultivated outside of the world view of Christianity and where the cosmos gradually ceased to be Christian.

With the Renaissance, European man lost the paradise of the age of faith to gain in compensation the new earth of nature and natural forms to which he now turned his attention. Yet it was a nature which came to be less and less a reflection of a celestial reality. Renaissance man ceased to be the ambivalent man of the Middle Ages, half angel, half man, torn between heaven and earth. Rather, he became wholly man, but now a totally earth-bound creature.[27] He gained his liberty at the expense of losing the freedom to transcend his terrestrial limitations. Freedom for him now became quantitative and horizontal rather than qualitative and vertical, and it was in this spirit that he went on to conquer the earth and with it to open new horizons in geography and natural

[25] E. Gilson, *The Unity of Philosophical Experience*, London, 1938, pp. 62 ff.

[26] "That neither Fransiscans nor Dominicans succeeded in establishing a serious regard for the study of nature within the Church, during the century in which medieval Christendom rose to its splendid zenith, made inevitable the upheavals and revolts of the Renaissance and Reformation." Raven, *Science and Religion*, p. 72.

[27] See F. Schuon, *Light on the Ancient Worlds*, Chapter II, "In the Wake of the Fall."

history. However, there still existed a religious significance in wilderness and nature that had come down through the Christian tradition.[28]

This new conception of an earth-bound man which is closely tied to the humanism and anthropomorphism of this period, coincided with the destruction and gradual disappearance of what was left of the initiatic and esoteric organizations of the Middle Ages. The Renaissance was witness to the destruction of such organizations as the Society of the Rosy Cross, while at the same time all kinds of writings associated with secret organizations and societies such as Hermetical and Kabbalistic works began to appear. The vast number of these works during this period is due, however, first and foremost to the destruction of the depositories of this type of knowledge, thus facilitating their profanation and vulgarization. Secondly it is due to an attempt on the part of certain thinkers to discover a primordial religious tradition ante-dating Christianity so that they turned to all that spoke of the ancient mysteries.[29]

Moreover, when we glance at the sciences of the Renaissance, we see that besides new discoveries in geography and natural history and certain advances in mathematics, the framework is essentially that of the Middle Ages. Renaissance science is continuous with that of the medieval period, despite its accent upon naturalism. This is because what are seen as coming to the fore at this time are the cosmological and occult sciences of the medieval period that are now made to be publicly known and elaborated, albeit sometimes with confusion and distortion. Agrippa, Paracelsus, Basil Valentine, Meier, Bodin and so many other figures belong more to the ancient and medieval tradition of science than to the modern one. Yet the Hermetical and magical schools of the Renaissance have had as significant a role in the creation of modern science as the more frequently studied mathematico-physical school connected with the name of Galileo. Too little attention has been paid to this all important element because of an *a priori* judgement as to what science is.[30]

However, as is to be expected in a period of the eclipse of metaphysical knowledge and even of philosophical doubt, sciences such as alchemy became ever more incomprehensible, opaque and confused until gradually they ceased to be science as such and became the preoccupation of the occultists or the curious. Paracelsus was still at the centre of the scientific stage of his day. By the time Fludd and Kepler were exchanging notes, the Hermetico-alchemical tradition for which Fludd stood had lost the battle, and what was considered as science passed on into the hands of Kepler and his like.

This loss of metaphysical insight and awareness into the symbolic meaning of cosmological sciences is also seen in the rapid transformation of cosmology into cosmography, a movement from content to form. The numerous cosmographies of the Renaissance no longer deal with the content and meaning of the cosmos, but with its form and external description, although they still describe

[28] See G. Williams, *Wilderness and Paradise in Christian Thought,* Chapter III.

[29] For the analysis of this aspect of the question as far as Hermeticism is concerned see M. Eliade, "The Quest for the 'Origin' of Religion," *History of Religions,* vol. IV, no. 1, Summer 1964, pp. 156 ff.

[30] Only a small number of scholars such as W. Pagel and in recent years A. Debus and F. Yates have studied and made known the immense influence of the Paracelsian and alchemical tradition of the Renaissance in seventeenth-century sciences.

the medieval cosmos.[31] All that is left is the body without its inner spirit and meaning. From these cosmographies to the breakdown of the cosmic picture there is but a single step which comes with the Copernican revolution.

The Copernican revolution brought about all the spiritual and religious upheavals that its opponents forecasted would happen precisely because it came at a time when philosophical doubt reigned everywhere, and a humanism, already over a century old, had taken away from man his position as the "divine image" on earth. The proposal that the sun is at the centre of the solar system was not in itself new; for it was known by certain Greek, Islamic and Indian philosophers and astronomers. But its proposal during the Renaissance without an accompanying new spiritual vision of things could only mean a dislocation of man in the cosmos.

Theology and the external formulation of religion begins with man and his needs as an immortal being. Metaphysics and the esoteric aspect of tradition deal with the nature of things as such. The Ptolemaic-Aristotelian astronomy corresponds to the more immediately apparent structure of the cosmos and the profound symbolism that the concentric spheres present to man as the visible aspect of the multiple states of being. In this scheme, man is from one point of view at the centre of the Universe by virtue of his theomorphic nature, and from another point of view he is at the lowest level of existence from which he has to ascend toward the divine. The ascent through the cosmos as we see so plainly in the *Divine Comedy* corresponds also to the ascent of the soul through the degrees of purification and of knowledge. By necessity it corresponds to existence itself. Medieval cosmology had therefore, from the spiritual point of view, the advantage of presenting the visible cosmos to men as a concrete symbol of a metaphysical reality which in any case remains true, independently of the symbols used to convey it. Also, by virtue of remaining faithful to the immediate appearance of things as they present themselves to man, the Ptolemaic-Aristotelian astronomy corresponded more to a theological and exoteric truth while at the same time it remained a most powerful symbol of a metaphysical reality.

The heliocentric system also possesses its spiritual symbolism. By placing the source of light at the centre, an argument to which Copernicus himself referred in the introduction of his book *De revolutionibus orbium coelestium,* this astronomy symbolizes clearly the centrality of the Universal Intellect for which the sun, the supernal Apollo, is the most direct symbol. Moreover, by removing the boundaries of the cosmos and presenting to man the vastness of cosmic space, which symbolizes the illimitable vastness of the Divine Being and man's nothingness before this Reality, this view corresponds more to the esoteric perspective based on the total nature of things than to the exoteric and theological that are concerned with man's needs in order that he should be saved. But this astronomy was not accompanied by a new spiritual vision even if occasionally a man like Nicolas of Cusa pointed to the profound significance of the "infinite universe," "whose centre is everywhere and whose circumference is nowhere."[32] The total effect of the new astronomy was like the profanation

[31] See T. Burckhardt, "Cosmology and Modern Science," pp. 183–4.

[32] Already a century before Copernicus Nicolas of Cusa in his *De docta ignorantia* referred to the earth as a star and believed in an unbounded Universe to whose metaphysical and esoteric significance he pointed more than once. See R. Klibansky, "Copernic et Nicolas de Cuse," in *Léonard de Vinci et l'expérience scientifique du XVIe siècle,* Paris, 1953.

of an esoteric form of knowledge,[33] somewhat like our observations in the case of the alchemical and Kabbalistic sciences. It presented a new vision of the physical Universe without providing also a spiritual interpretation for it. The transformation from the bound to the "infinite universe" also had, therefore, the deepest religious repercussions in the souls of men and was closely intertwined with the whole religious and philosophical development of the Renaissance and the seventeenth century.[34]

It may seem at first as if the Copernican revolution moved counter to the prevalent humanism of the time by removing man from the centre of the Universe. This is only an apparent effect; its deeper effect was to aid the general humanistic and Promethean spirit of the Renaissance. In medieval cosmology man had been placed at the centre of the Universe, not as a purely terrestrial and earth-bound man but as the "image of God." His centrality was due not to anthropomorphic qualities but to theomorphic ones. By removing him from the centre of things, the new astronomy did not bestow upon man the transcendent dimension of his nature; rather it affirmed the loss of the theomorphic nature by virtue of which he had been placed at the centre. Therefore, although on the surface it belittled the position of man in the scheme of things, on a deeper level it assisted the tendency toward anthropomorphism and the Promethean revolt against the voice of heaven.

With the destruction of an immutable set of principles which are the judge of both knowledge and virtue, and the appearance of a purely terrestrial man who became the measure of all things, a trend from objectivism to subjectivism began in Western civilization which continues to this day. No longer was there a metaphysics and a cosmology to judge the truth and falsehood of what men said, but the thoughts of men in each epoch themselves became the criteria of truth and falsehood. The Renaissance, although still following the formal medieval sciences, brought forth a new conception of man which henceforth made all forms of knowledge including science in a certain sense anthropomorphic. It made of "fallen man's" vision of things, to use the Christian terminology, the truth itself and removed to the greatest possible extent any objective criterion of intellectual knowledge. Henceforth, science was only what the mental could grasp and explain. It could not serve the function of transcending the mental itself through the power of symbolism.

The scientific revolution itself came not in the Renaissance but during the seventeenth century when the cosmos had already become secularized, religion weakened through long, inner conflicts, metaphysics and gnosis in the real sense nearly forgotten and the meaning of symbols neglected, which can be seen in the art of this period. It also came after more than two centuries of philosophical scepticism from which the philosophers of the seventeenth century tried to escape and regain access to certainty. Descartes was the heir to the Christian

[33] "The heliocentric system itself admits of an obvious symbolism, since it identifies the source of light with the centre of the world. Its rediscovery by Copernicus, however, produced no new spiritual vision of the world; rather was it comparable to the dangerous popularization of an esoteric truth. The heliocentric system has no common measure with the subjective experiences of the people, in it man had no organic place; instead of helping the human mind to go beyond itself and to consider things in terms of the immensity of the cosmos, it only encouraged a materialistic Prometheanism which, far from being superhuman, ended by becoming inhuman." Burckhardt, "Cosmology and Modern Science," pp. 184-5.

[34] See A Koyré, *From the Closed World to the Infinite Universe,* New York, 1958.

humanists of the late Middle Ages and the Renaissance, of men like Petrarch, Gehrard Groot and Erasmus as well as the whole group of Renaissance philosophers like Telesio, Campanella and Adriano di Corneto. These latter doubted the power of philosophy to reach certainty about ultimate principles and as compensation usually turned toward ethics and morality. Descartes was also most of all heir to the scepticism expressed in the *Essays* of Montaigne to which his *Discours* is an answer in more than one way.[35]

In order to reach certainty in knowledge through his famous method, Descartes had to reduce the rich diversity of external reality to pure quantity and philosophy to mathematics. His was a mathematicism, to use the term of Gilson,[36] and henceforth Cartesian mathematicism became a permanent element of the scientific world view. The physics Descartes constructed through his method was rejected by Newton. His zoology in which he sought to reduce animals to machines was violently attacked and refuted by Henry More and John Ray. But his mathematicism, the attempt to reduce reality to pure quantity with which one could then deal in a purely mathematical way, has become the background of mathematical physics and unconsciously of many other sciences which desperately seek to find quantitative relationships between things by overlooking their qualitative aspect. The distinction made by Galileo in the *Discorsi* between primary and secondary qualities is an affirmation of Descartes' reduction of reality to quantity, although Galileo succeeded in creating a new physics where Descartes failed.

The genius of Newton was able to create a synthesis from the works of Descartes, Galileo and Kepler and to present a picture of the world which Newton, himself a religious man, felt was a confirmation of a spiritual order in the Universe. In fact the background of Newton's thought, connected with such figures as Isaac Burrows and the Cambridge Platonists, was far from being divorced from interest in the metaphysical meaning of time, space and motion. Yet the Newtonian world view led to the well-known mechanistic conception of the Universe and totally away from the holistic and organic interpretation of things. The result was that after the seventeenth century science and religion became totally divorced. Newton was one of the first to realize the adverse theological effects of his discoveries. We must not forget how much effort he spent and how many pages he wrote on the alchemical and Kabbalistic sciences of his day. Perhaps for him the new physics, with its eminent success on the mathematico-physical level, was just a science of material things. For those who followed him it became *the* science, the only legitimate knowledge of the objective world.

Also in the seventeenth century the last step in the secularization of the cosmos took place in the hands of the philosophers and scientists. In the Renaissance elements of traditional philosophy still survived. The anatomy of existence consisted not only of the physical and the purely intelligible worlds but also of the intermediary world between matter and pure spirit, the "imaginal world" (*mundus imaginalis*). This, however, must not be considered in any way unreal or made to correspond to the modern meaning of "imaginary." Such an intermediate world was the immediate principle of nature, and through it the symbolic science of nature was made possible. Among Christian thinkers (albeit

[35] See E. Gilson, *The Unity of Philosophical Experience*, p. 127.
[36] Gilson, *ibid.,* Chapter V.

away from the centre of theological orthodoxy), even after the Renaissance a man like Swedenborg could write a hermeneutic commentary upon the Bible which was also an exposition of a symbolic science of nature and could rely upon this intermediate world as the meeting ground of spiritual and material forms.[37] The Cambridge Platonists, particularly Henry More, were, however, the last of the European philosophers to speak of this domain of reality in the same way that Leibniz was the last major Western philosopher to speak of the angels.

Henceforth the Cartesian surgical operation in which spirit and matter become totally separated dominated scientific and philosophic thought. The domain of science was matter which was a pure "it" divorced completely from any ontological aspect other than pure quantity. Although there were protests here and there especially among English and German thinkers, this view became the very factor that determined the relationship between man and nature, scientifically and philosophically. Thus seventeenth-century rationalism is the unconscious background of all later scientific thought up to the present day. Whatever discoveries are made in the sciences and whatever changes are brought about in conceptions of time, space, matter and motion, the background of seventeenth-century rationalism remains. For this very reason, other interpretations of nature, especially the symbolic, have never been seriously considered and accepted.

In the seventeenth century Hermeticism still continued strongly particularly in England. There was also Jacob Böhme, the remarkable cobbler and theosopher in Germany, whose very appearance at this time is most significant and who influenced deeply the school of *Naturphilosophie* that reacted so severely against the prevalent mechanical philosophy. These developments are of importance as showing the continuity in certain circles, especially of northern Europe, of a spiritual conception of nature. These schools still remained peripheral as far as their influence on modern science was concerned. The centre of the stage continued to be occupied by mechanistic philosophy and science.

During the eighteenth century, while theoretically science continued along lines established in the seventeenth, its philosophic effect was more pronounced. The philosophy of Descartes was drawn to its logical conclusion by the Empiricists, by Hume and by Kant who demonstrated the inability of purely human reason to reach knowledge of the essence of things, thereby opening the door to the irrational philosophies that have followed since his advent. Through the "encyclopedists," Rousseau and Voltaire, a philosophy of man without a transcendent dimension became popularized and truth reduced to utility.[38] If the seventeenth century still considered problems on the level of their theoretical truth or falsehood, the question now became the utility of knowledge

[37] See H. Corbin, *Herméneutique spirituelle comparée* (*I. Swedenborg-II. Gnose ismaélienne*), *Eranos Jahrbuch*, Zürich, 1965.

[38] "With Voltaire, Rousseau and Kant bourgeois unintelligence erects itself into a 'doctrine' and becomes definitely entrenched in European 'thought,' giving birth, through the French Revolution, to positivist science, industry and quantitative 'culture.' Henceforward the mental hypertrophy of the 'cultured' man ekes out the absence of intellectual penetration; all feeling for the absolute and for principles is drowned in a commonplace empiricism, on to which is grafted a pseudo-mysticism with 'positivistic' or 'humanistic' tendencies. Perhaps some people will reproach us with lack of reticence, but we would like to ask where is the reticence of the philosophers who shamelessly slash at the wisdom of countless centuries." F. Schuon, *Language of the Self* (trans. M. Pallis and D. M. Matheson), Madras, 1959, p. 8, nt. 1.

for man, who had now become nothing but a creature of the earth with no other end but to exploit and dominate its riches. This practical and utilitarian bent, crystallized by the French Revolution, accentuated the effect of the new mechanistic science by turning more attention to the empirical sciences and seeking to destroy any vestiges of a contemplative view toward nature that still survived.[39] With the help of the new science the only role left to man was to conquer and dominate nature and to serve his needs as an animal endowed somehow with analytical reason and thought.

The materialistic conception of nature did not go unchallenged during the nineteenth century, particularly in art and literature where the romantic movement sought to re-establish a more intimate bond with nature and the indwelling spirit within nature. The philosophical Romantic poets like Novalis devoted themselves most of all to the theme of nature and its significance for man. One of the foremost among them, Wordsworth, could write in the *Excursion* (Book IX):

> *"To every Form of being is assigned"*
> *Thus calmly spake the venerable Sage,*
> *"An active Principle:—howe'er removed*
> *From sense and observation, it subsists*
> *In all things, in all natures; in the stars*
> *Of azure heaven, the unenduring clouds,*
> *In flower and tree. in every pebbly stone*
> *That paves the brooks, the stationary rocks,*
> *The morning waters, and the invisible air.*
> *Whate'er exists hath properties that spread*
> *Beyond itself, communicating good,*
> *A simple blessing, or with evil mixed;*
> *Spirit that knows no insulated spot,*
> *No chasm, no solitude; from link to link*
> *It circulates, the soul of all the worlds.*
> *This is the freedom of the universe;"*

Likewise a man like John Ruskin saw nature as something divine[40] and spoke of the "spiritual power of air, the rocks, and waters."[41]

The romantic attitude toward nature, however, was more sentimental than intellectual. Wordsworth speaks of "wise passiveness" and Keats of "negative capability." This passive attitude could not make and mould knowledge. Whatever service the romantic movement rendered in re-discovering medieval art or

[39] "At the time of the Revolution of the late eighteenth century, the earth had become definitely and exclusively the goal of man; the 'Supreme Being' was merely a 'consolation' and as such a target for ridicule; the seemingly infinite multitude of things on earth called for an infinity of activities, which furnished a pretext for rejecting contemplation..., man was at last free to busy himself, on the hither side of transcendence, with the discovery of the terrestrial world and the exploitation of its riches; he was at last rid of symbols, rid of metaphysical transparence; there was no longer anything but the agreeable or the disagreeable, the useful or the useless, whence the anarchic and irresponsible development of the experimental sciences." Schuon. *Light on the Ancient Worlds*, p. 30.

[40] "Ruskin looked at the material universe with preternatural vivacity and clarity, and believed that what he saw was divine." J. Rosenberg, *The Darkening Glass, a Portrait of Ruskin's Genius*, New York, 1961, pp. 4–5.

[41] *Ibid.*, p. 7.

the beauty of virgin nature, it could not affect the current of science nor add a new dimension within science itself by which man would be able to understand those aspects of nature that seventeenth century science and its aftermath had failed to consider.

As for the philosophy of the nineteenth century it surrendered the possibility of knowing things in their immutable aspect and so became, with Hegel, bound to process and change. The Absolute itself was made to enter the current of the dialectical process which was equated with a new logic of process and becoming. The vision of a changeless and immutable reality became completely forgotten in a universe where, for some time now, suprasensible reality had lost its objective and ontological status. The intuitions of men like Schelling or Franz von Baader could do little to turn the tide away from a further plunge into the world of sheer becoming and change.

As for science, the major event occurred in biology where the theory of evolution reflects more the "*zeitgeist*" than a scientific theory. In a world where the "multiple states of being" had lost its meaning, where the archetypal reality of species held no significance, where there was no metaphysical and philosophical background to enable men to interpret the appearance of different species on earth as so many successive "dreams of the World Soul," where the hands of the Creator had been cut off from creation through the spread of Deism there could be no other explanation for the multiplicity of the species than temporal evolution. The vertical "chain of being" had to be made temporal and horizontal,[42] whatever absurdities such a view might imply metaphysically and theologically. The result of this theory, besides causing endless bickerings between popularizers of evolution and theologians, brought a further alienation of man from nature by removing from the world of life the immutable form or essence of things which alone can be intellectually contemplated and can become the object of metaphysical knowledge and vision. It also condoned all kinds of excesses in usurping the right of other forms of life in the name of the "survival of the fittest."

The theory of evolution did not provide an organic view for the physical sciences but provided men with a way of reducing the higher to the lower, a magical formula to apply everywhere in order to explain things without the need to have recourse to any higher principles or causes. It also went hand in hand with a prevalent historicism which is a parody of the Christian philosophy of history, but which nevertheless could only take place in the Christian world where the truth itself had become incarnated in time and history. A reaction is always against an existing affirmation and action.

With the breakdown of classical physics at the end of the nineteenth century, there was no spiritual force ready to re-interpret the new science and integrate it into a more universal perspective. Some found in this breakdown a chance to re-assert other points of view which the monolithic mechanistic conception of the Universe had previously prevented. Also, the breakdown meant on the one hand a re-interpretation of science which destroyed even further contact with the macrocosmic world and the immediate symbolism of things. (This can be seen in the case of the change from Euclidian geometry to those of Riemann or

---

[42] On the chain of being and its relation to the theory of evolution see, O. Lovejoy, *The Great Chain of Being*, Cambridge, (U.S.A.), 1933.

Lobachevski.) On the other hand it meant the opening of the gate to all kinds of pseudo-spiritual movements and occult sciences which graft themselves upon the newest theories of physics, but which are usually either degenerate residues of older cosmological sciences, now no longer understood, or simply dangerous and pernicious inventions. From the genuinely religious quarters the breakdown of classical physics did not bring forth a vigorous response that could lead to a meaningful synthesis. For the most part the theological response has been a weak echo that has often adopted discarded ideas of science itself and sometimes, as in the case of Teilhard de Chardin, has sought a synthesis which is metaphysically an absurdity and theologically a heresy.[43]

It is this long history, some of whose features have been pointed out here, that has at last led to the present crisis in the encounter between man and nature. . . . It is only through a re-discovery of true metaphysics, especially the sapiental doctrines of Christianity and the revival of that tradition within Christianity which has done justice to the relation between man and nature, that a hierarchy of knowledge can be again asserted and a symbolic science of nature re-established which will effectively complement the quantitative sciences of today. Only in this way can an equilibrium be created, an equilibrium from which the development of the past few centuries has drawn away with ever greater speed until today the disequilibrium and lack of harmony between man and nature threatens to destroy them both together. . . .

---

[43] "As a symptom of our time, Teilhardism is comparable to one of those cracks that are due to the very solidification of the mental carapace, and which do not open upwards, towards the heaven of true and transcendent unity, but downward towards the realm of the inferior psychism: weary of its own discontinuous vision of the world, the materialist mind lets itself slide toward a pseudo-spiritual intoxication, of which this falsified and materialized faith—or this sublimated materialism—that we have just described marks a phase of particular significance" Burckhardt, "Cosmology and Modern Science," *Tomorrow,* Autumn, 1964, p. 315.

The Sacred Word

INTRODUCTION

Why a chapter on scripture rather than prayer, say, or ritual, or one of the other basic forms of religious expression? Is there something uniquely important about the problem of understanding sacred writing?

We believe that there is, especially for contemporary man. Words are an expression of thought, and if there are sacred words then there exist sacred thought, sacred ideas. Contemporary man is deeply uncertain about the existence of a mind qualitatively higher than his own; this uncertainty is a central aspect of the modern spiritual crisis. And nowhere are this crisis and this uncertainty mirrored more accurately than in our relationship to scripture. Almost every other religious form presupposes to some degree the assent of the mind. Only the great scriptures of the world require nothing of man at the outset except his attention. Here is waged the first battle for the mind's assent not only to the truth of what is written but to the emotions and beliefs that sacred writing evokes.

Our opening selection, by the medieval Jew, **Maimonides**, sounds the problem loudly and clearly. The difficulties and contradictions in the Bible are not accidental, writes Maimonides. They are there to bring the mind to a certain "perplexity" and to serve as pointers to a deeper meaning. To grasp these deeper meanings, a man must be seriously involved in a religious search. Thus, according to Maimonides, the Bible has an inner and an outer meaning, and the worst mistake is to take it only literally. In this view, scripture is the communication of a supreme mind directed to the same quality of mind that is hidden in man beneath the level of his ordinary awarness. As man penetrates deeper into his own spirituality through the religious struggle, layer upon layer of scriptural meaning is there to confirm his understanding and point yet further to new inward horizons. Therefore, according to Maimonides, a sound judgment about scripture can be made only by a mind engaged in spiritual search. The secular scholar or the academic observer can never grasp its real meaning.

Were it otherwise, writes **Søren Kierkegaard**, in the second selection of this chapter, scripture would have no salvational efficacy. All genuine communication—and by this Kierkegaard means spiritual communication—takes place through the awakening of inwardness. Like nature itself, scripture requires of man that he find its religious meaning through his own experience of himself in the creative suffering of passion and decision. Proof, literal obviousness, and external evidence work in an opposite direction and are of use only where what is at issue is something other than a matter of ultimate concern. This is the gist of Kierkegaard's famous concept of "indirect communication."

We then turn, in the third selection, to the thought of **Rudolf Bultmann**, whose call for "demythologization" of the Bible has influenced a whole generation of biblical scholars. The reader is asked to ponder Bultmann's ideas very carefully. Is he saying that the Bible has to be made more palatable to a scientifically minded age, or is he, like Maimonides and Kierkegaard, calling for a search for the inner or existential meaning of scripture? What does he mean by "myth"? Does he stand in the line of Kierkegaard and Maimonides?

The fourth and fifth selections, by **Paul van Buren** and **Daniel Berrigan**, respectively, are very different sorts of efforts to marry scripture to the modern temper. Van Buren seeks to provide a logical account of the Christian faith of the Gospels, an effort that falls in with a dominant trend of contemporary American philosophy of language. Berrigan, on the other hand, seeks to illuminate his own moral and political stance by reference to the New Testament. The question that is as simple and inevitable as it is difficult is: What is gained through such an effort and what is lost? Much hard thinking awaits the reader who tries to answer this question, and yet it is necessary to try if we are to understand our own relationship to the "sacred word."

We conclude, in the sixth selection, by offering **Martin Lings'** little-known but brilliant spiritual interpretation of a "secular" text almost as well known as the Bible. Here we can see more clearly how psychospiritual meanings can be found where one might have easily taken a text in quite another way. If *Hamlet* can justifiably be read in this way, then the question is, is it *scripture?* and, if not, *why?*

J. N.

Suggested Readings

Barth, Karl. *The Epistle to the Romans*. London: Oxford University Press, 1957.

Boman, Thorleif. *Hebrew Thought Compared with Greek*. Philadelphia: Westminster Press, 1960.

Bultmann, Rudolph. *Kerygma and Myth.* New York: Harper Torchbooks, 1961.

Campbell, Joseph. *Oriental Mythology.* New York: Viking Press, 1962.

Maimonides, Moses. *The Guide for the Perplexed.* Translated by M. Friedlander. New York: Dover Publications, 1956.

Nicoll, Maurice. *The New Man.* New York: Penguin Books, 1972.
Scholem, Gershom G. *On the Kabbalah and Its Symbolism.* New York: Schocken, 1965.
Schuon, Frithjof. "Keys to the Bible." *The Sword of Gnosis.* New York: Penguin Books, 1973.

How to Read the Bible
Moses Maimonides

Maimonides (Moses ben Maimon, 1135–1204), rabbi, physician, and philosopher, was the most significant Jewish thinker of the Middle Ages. Among his many famous writings are *The Guide for the Perplexed* and the *Mishnah Torah.*

The object of this treatise* is to enlighten a religious man who has been trained to believe in the truth of our holy Law, who conscientiously fulfils his moral and religious duties, and at the same time has been successful in his philosophical studies. Human reason has attracted him to abide within its sphere; and he finds it difficult to accept as correct the teaching based on the literal interpretation of the Law, and especially that which he himself or others derived from those homonymous, metaphorical, or hybrid expressions. Hence he is lost in perplexity and anxiety. If he be guided solely by reason, and renounce his previous views which are based on those expressions, he would consider that he had rejected the fundamental principles of the Law; and even if he retains the opinions which were derived from those expressions, and if, instead of following his reason, he abandon its guidance altogether, it would still appear that his religious convictions had suffered loss and injury. For he would then be left with those errors which give rise to fear and anxiety, constant grief and great perplexity.

This work has also a second object in view. It seeks to explain certain obscure figures which occur in the Prophets, and are not distinctly characterized as being figures. Ignorant and superficial readers take them in a literal, not in a figurative sense. Even well informed persons are bewildered if they understand these passages in their literal signification, but they are entirely relieved of their perplexity when we explain the figure, or merely suggest that the terms are figurative. For this reason I have called this book *Guide for the Perplexed.*

I do not presume to think that this treatise settles every doubt in the minds of those who understand it, but I maintain that it settles the greater part of their

From Moses Maimonides, *The Guide for the Perplexed*, trans. by M. Friedlander (New York, 1956) pp. 2–8, 9–11. Reprinted through permission of Dover Publications, Inc.

* [This selection is from the Introduction to *The Guide for the Perplexed.*—Eds.]

difficulties. No intelligent man will require and expect that on introducing any subject I shall completely exhaust it; or that on commencing the exposition of a figure I shall fully explain all its parts. Such a course could not be followed by a teacher in a *viva voce* exposition, much less by an author in writing a book, without becoming a target for every foolish conceited person to discharge the arrows of folly at him. Some general principles bearing upon this point have been fully discussed in our works on the Talmud, and we have there called the attention of the reader to many themes of this kind. We also stated (*Mishneh torah*, I. ii. 12, and iv. 10) that the expression *Ma'ase Bereshit* (Account of the Creation) signified "Natural Science," and *Ma'aseh Mercabah* ("Description of the Chariot") Metaphysics, and we explained the force of the Rabbinical dictum, "The *Ma'aseh Mercabah* must not be fully expounded even in the presence of a single student, unless he be wise and able to reason for himself, and even then you should merely acquaint him with the heads of the different sections of the subject" (Babyl. Talm. *Hagigah*, fol. IIb). You must, therefore, not expect from me more than such heads. And even these have not been methodically and systematically arranged in this work, but have been, on the contrary, scattered, and are interspersed with other topics which we shall have occasion to explain. My object in adopting this arrangement is that the truths should be at one time apparent, and at another time concealed. Thus we shall not be in opposition to the Divine Will (from which it is wrong to deviate) which has withheld from the multitude the truths required for the knowledge of God, according to the words, "The secret of the Lord is with them that fear Him" (Ps. xxv. 14).

Know that also in Natural Science there are topics which are not to be fully explained. Our Sages laid down the rule, "The *Ma'aseh Bereshith* must not be expounded in the presence of two." If an author were to explain these principles in writing, it would be equal to expounding them unto thousands of men. For this reason the prophets treat these subjects in figures, and our Sages, imitating the method of Scripture, speak of them in metaphors and allegories; because there is a close affinity between these subjects and metaphysics, and indeed they form part of its mysteries. Do not imagine that these most difficult problems can be thoroughly understood by any one of us. This is not the case. At times the truth shines so brilliantly that we perceive it as clear as day. Our nature and habit then draw a veil over our perception, and we return to a darkness almost as dense as before. We are like those who, though beholding frequent flashes of lightning, still find themselves in the thickest darkness of the night. On some the lightning flashes in rapid succession, and they seem to be in continuous light, and their night is as clear as the day. This was the degree of prophetic excellence attained by (Moses) the greatest of prophets, to whom God said, "But as for thee, stand thou here by Me" (Deut. v. 31), and of whom it is written "the skin of his face shone," etc. (Exod. xxxiv. 29). [Some perceive the prophetic flash at long intervals; this is the degree of most prophets.] By others only once during the whole night is a flash of lightning perceived. This is the case with those of whom we are informed, "They prophesied, and did not prophesy again" (Num. xi. 25). There are some to whom the flashes of lightning appear with varying intervals; others are in the condition of men, whose darkness is illumined not by lightning, but by some kind of crystal or similar stone, or other substances that possess the property of shining during the night; and to them even this small amount of light is not continuous, but now it shines and now it vanishes, as if it were "the flame of the rotating sword."

The degrees in the perfection of men vary according to these distinctions. Concerning those who never beheld the light even for one day, but walk in continual darkness, it is written, "They know not, neither will they understand; they walk on in darkness" (Ps. lxxxii. 5). Truth, in spite of all its powerful manifestations, is completely withheld from them, and the following words of Scripture may be applied to them, "And now men see not the light which is bright in the skies" (Job xxxvii. 21). They are the multitude of ordinary men; there is no need to notice them in this treatise.

You must know that if a person, who has attained a certain degree of perfection, wishes to impart to others, either orally or in writing, any portion of the knowledge which he has acquired of these subjects, he is utterly unable to be as systematic and explicit as he could be in a science of which the method is well known. The same difficulties which he encountered when investigating the subject for himself will attend him when endeavouring to instruct others; viz., at one time the explanation will appear lucid, at another time, obscure; this property of the subject appears to remain the same both to the advanced scholar and to the beginner. For this reason, great theological scholars gave instruction in all such matters only by means of metaphors and allegories. They frequently employed them in forms varying more or less essentially. In most cases they placed the lesson to be illustrated at the beginning, or in the middle, or at the end of the simile. When they could find no simile which from beginning to end corresponded to the idea which was to be illustrated, they divided the subject of the lesson, although in itself one whole, into different parts, and expressed each by a separate figure. Still more obscure are those instances in which one simile is employed to illustrate many subjects, the beginning of the simile representing one thing, the end another. Sometimes the whole metaphor may refer to two cognate subjects in the same branch of knowledge.

If we were to teach in these disciplines, without the use of parables and figures, we should be compelled to resort to expressions both profound and transcendental, and by no means more intelligible than metaphors and similies; as though the wise and learned were drawn into this course by the Divine Will, in the same way as they are compelled to follow the laws of nature in matters relating to the body. You are no doubt aware that the Almighty, desiring to lead us to perfection and to improve our state of society, has revealed to us laws which are to regulate our actions. These laws, however, presuppose an advanced state of intellectual culture. We must first form a conception of the Existence of the Creator according to our capabilities; that is, we must have a knowledge of Metaphysics. But this discipline can only be approached after the study of Physics; for the science of Physics borders on Metaphysics, and must even precede it in the course of our studies, as is clear to all who are familiar with these questions. Therefore the Almighty commenced Holy Writ with the description of the Creation, that is, with Physical Science; the subject being on the one hand most weighty and important, and on the other hand our means of fully comprehending those great problems being limited. He described those profound truths, which His Divine Wisdom found it necessary to communicate to us, in allegorical, figurative, and metaphorical language. Our Sages have said (Yemen Midrash on Gen. i. I), "It is impossible to give a full account of the Creation to man. Therefore Scripture simply tells us, In the beginning God created the heavens and the earth" (Gen. i. I). Thus they have suggested that this subject is a deep mystery, and in the words of Solomon, "Far off and exceedingly deep, who can find it out ?" (Eccles. vii. 24). It has been treated in metaphors in order that the uneducated may comprehend it according to the measure of their faculties and the feebleness of their apprehension, while educated persons may take it in a different sense. In our commentary on the Mishnah we stated our intention to explain difficult problems in the Book on Prophecy and in the Book of Harmony. In the latter we intended to examine all the passages in the Midrash which, if taken literally, appear to be inconsistent with truth and common sense, and must therefore be taken figuratively. Many years have elapsed since I first commenced those works. I had proceeded but a short way when I became dissatisfied with my original plan. For I observed that by expounding these passages by means of allegorical and mystical terms, we do not explain anything, but merely substitute one thing for another of the same nature, whilst in explaining them fully our efforts would displease most people; and my sole object in planning to write those books was to make the contents of Midrashim and the exoteric lessons of the prophecies intelligible to everybody. We have further noticed that when an ill-informed Theologian reads these Midrashim, he will find no difficulty; for possessing no knowledge of the properties of things, he will not reject statements which involve impossibilities. When, however, a person who is both religious and well educated reads them, he cannot escape the following dilemma: either he takes them literally, and questions the abilities of the author and the soundness of his mind—doing thereby nothing which is opposed to the principles of our faith—or he will acquiesce in assuming that the passages in question have some secret meaning, and he will continue to hold the author in high estimation whether he understood the allegory or not. As regards prophecy in its various degrees and the different metaphors used in the prophetic books, we shall give in the present work an explanation, according to a different method. Guided by these considerations I have refrained from writing those two books as I had previously intended. In my larger work, the *Mishnah Torah*, I have contented myself with briefly stating the principles of our faith and its fundamental truths, together with such hints as approach a clear exposition. In this work, however, I address those who have studied philosophy and have acquired sound knowledge, and who while firm in religious matters are perplexed and bewildered on account of the ambiguous and figurative expressions employed in the holy writings. Some chapters may be found in this work which contain no reference whatever to homonyms. Such chapters will serve as an introduction to others; they will contain some reference to the signification of a homonym which I do not wish to mention in that place, or explain some figure; point out that a certain expression is a figure; treat of difficult passages generally misunderstood in consequence of the homonymy they include, or because the simile they contain is taken in place of that which it represents, and *vice versâ*.

Having spoken of similes, I proceed to make the following remark:—The key to the understanding and to the full comprehension of all that the Prophets have said is found in the knowledge of the figures, their general ideas, and the meaning of each word they contain. You know the verse:—"I have also spoken in similes by the Prophets" (Hosea xii, 10); and also the verse, "Put forth a riddle and speak a parable" (Ezek. xvii. 2). And because the Prophets continually employ figures, Ezekiel said, "Does He not speak parables?" (xxi. 5). Again, Solomon begins his book of Proverbs with the words, "To understand a proverb and figurative speech, the words of the wise and their dark sayings"

(Prov. i. 6); and we read in Midrash, *Shir ba-shirim Rabba*, i. I: "To what were the words of the Law to be compared before the time of Solomon? To a well the waters of which are at a great depth, and though cool and fresh, yet no man could drink of them. A clever man joined cord with cord, and rope with rope, and drew up and drank. So Solomon went from figure to figure, and from subject to subject, till he obtained the true sense of the Law." So far go the words of our Sages. I do not believe that any intelligent man thinks that "the words of the Law" mentioned here as requiring the application of figures in order to be understood, can refer to the rules for building tabernacles, for preparing the lulab, or for the four kinds of trustees. What is really meant is the apprehension of profound and difficult subjects, concerning which our Sages said, "If a man loses in his house a sela, or a pearl, he can find it by lighting a taper worth only one issar. Thus the parables in themselves are of no great value, but through them the words of the holy Law are rendered intelligible." These likewise are the words of our Sages; consider well their statement, that the deeper sense of the words of the holy Law are pearls, and the literal acceptation of a figure is of no value in itself. They compare the hidden meaning included in the literal sense of the simile to a pearl lost in a dark room, which is full of furniture. It is certain that the pearl is in the room, but the man can neither see it nor know where it lies. It is just as if the pearl were no longer in his possession, for, as has been stated, it affords him no benefit whatever until he kindles a light. The same is the case with the comprehension of that which the simile represents. The wise king said, "A word fitly spoken is like apples of gold in vessels of silver" (Prov. xxv. 11). Hear the explanation of what he said:—the word *maskiyyoth*, the Hebrew equivalent for "vessels," denotes "filigree network"—i.e., things in which there are very small apertures, such as are frequently wrought by silversmiths. They are called in Hebrew *maskiyyoth* (lit. "transpicuous," from the verb *sakah*, "he saw," a root which occurs also in the Targum of Onkelos, Gen. xxvi. 8), because the eye penetrates through them. Thus Solomon meant to say, "Just as apples of gold in silver filigree with small apertures, so is a word fitly spoken."

See how beautifully the conditions of a good simile are described in this figure! It shows that in every word which has a double sense, a literal one and a figurative one, the plain meaning must be as valuable as silver, and the hidden meaning still more precious; so that the figurative meaning bears the same relation to the literal one as gold to silver. It is further necessary that the plain sense of the phrase shall give to those who consider it some notion of that which the figure represents. Just as a golden apple overlaid with a network of silver, when seen at a distance, or looked at superficially, is mistaken for a silver apple, but when a keen-sighted person looks at the object well, he will find what is within, and see that the apple is gold. The same is the case with the figures employed by prophets. Taken literally, such expressions contain wisdom useful for many purposes, among others, for the amelioration of the condition of society; e.g., the Proverbs (of Solomon), and similar sayings in their literal sense. Their hidden meaning, however, is profound wisdom, conducive to the recognition of real truth.

Know that the figures employed by prophets are of two kinds: first, where every word which occurs in the simile represents a certain idea; and secondly, where the simile, as a whole, represents a general idea, but has a great many points which have no reference whatever to that idea; they are simply required to give to the simile its proper form and order, or better to conceal the idea; the simile is therefore continued as far as necessary, according to its literal sense. Consider this well.

An example of the first class of prophetic figures is to be found in Genesis: —"And, behold, a ladder set up on the earth, and the top of it reached to heaven; and, behold, the angels of God ascending and descending on it" (Gen. xxviii. 12). The word "ladder" refers to one idea; "set up on the earth" to another; "and the top of it reached to heaven" to a third; "angels of God" to a fourth; "ascending" to a fifth; "descending" to a sixth; "the Lord stood above it" (ver. 13) to a seventh. Every word in this figure introduces a fresh element into the idea represented by the figure.

An example of the second class of prophetic figures is found in Proverbs (vii. 6–26):—"For at the window of my house I looked through my casement, and beheld among the simple ones; I discerned among the youths a young man void of understanding, passing through the street near her corner: and he went the way to her house, in the twilight, in the evening, in the black and dark night: and, behold, there met him a woman with the attire of a harlot, and subtil of heart. (She is loud and stubborn; her feet abide not in her house: now she is without, now in the streets, and lieth in wait in every corner.) So she caught him, and kissed him, and with an impudent face said unto him, I have peace offerings with me; this day have I paid my vows. Therefore come I forth to meet thee, diligently to seek thy face, and I have found thee. I have decked my bed with coverings of tapestry, with striped cloths of the yarn of Egypt. I have perfumed my bed with myrrh, aloes, and cinnamon. Come, let us take our fill of love until the morning: let us solace ourselves with loves. For the goodman is not at home, he is gone a long journey: he hath taken a bag of money with him, and will come home at the day appointed. With her much fair speech she caused him to yield, with the flattering of her lips she forced him. He goeth after her straightway, as an ox goeth to the slaughter, or as fetters to the correction of a fool: till a dart strike through his liver; as a bird hasteth to the snare, and knoweth not that it is for his life. Hearken unto me now therefore, O ye children, and attend to the words of my mouth. Let not thine heart decline to her ways, go not astray in her paths. For she hath cast down many wounded: yea, many strong men have been slain by her."

The general principle expounded in all these verses is to abstain from excessive indulgence in bodily pleasures. The author compares the body, which is the source of all sensual pleasures, to a married woman who at the same time is a harlot. And this figure he has taken as the basis of his entire book. We shall hereafter show the wisdom of Solomon in comparing sensual pleasures to an adulterous harlot. We shall explain how aptly he concludes that work with the praises of a faithful wife who devotes herself to the welfare of her husband and of her household. All obstacles which prevent man from attaining his highest aim in life, all the deficiencies in the character of man, all his evil propensities, are to be traced to the body alone. This will be explained later on. The predominant idea running throughout the figure is that man shall not be entirely guided by his animal, or material nature; for the material substance of man is identical with that of the brute creation.

An adequate explanation of the figure having been given, and its meaning having been shown, do not imagine that you will find in its application a corresponding element for each part of the figure; you must not ask what is meant by "I have peace offerings with me" (ver. 14); by "I have decked my bed with coverings of tapestry" (ver. 16); or what is added to the force of the figure by the observation "for the goodman is not at home" (ver. 19), and so on to the end of the chapter. For all this is merely to complete the illustration of the metaphor in its literal meaning. The circumstances described here are such as are common to adulterers. Such conversations take place between all adulterous persons. You must well understand what I have said, for it is a principle of the utmost importance with respect to those things which I intend to expound. If you observe in one of the chapters that I explained the meaning of a certain figure, and pointed out to you its general scope, do not trouble yourself further in order to find an interpretation of each separate portion, for that would lead you to one of the two following erroneous courses; either you will miss the sense included in the metaphor, or you will be induced to explain certain things which require no explanation, and which are not introduced for that purpose. Through this unnecessary trouble you may fall into the great error which besets most modern sects in their foolish writings and discussions; they all endeavour to find some hidden meaning in expressions which were never uttered by the author in that sense. Your object should be to discover in most of the figures the general idea which the author wishes to express. In some instances it will be sufficient if you understand from my remarks that a certain expression contains a figure, although I may offer no further comment. For when you know that it is not to be taken literally, you will understand at once to what subject it refers. My statement that it is a figurative expression will, as it were, remove the screen from between the object and the observer.

.   .   .

There are seven causes of inconsistencies and contradictions to be met with in a literary work. The first cause arises from the fact that the author collects the opinions of various men, each differing from the other, but neglects to mention the name of the author of any particular opinion. In such a work contradictions or inconsistencies must occur, since any two statements may belong to two different authors. Second cause: The author holds at first one opinion which he subsequently rejects; in his work, however, both his original and altered views are retained. Third cause: The passages in question are not all to be taken literally; some only are to be understood in their literal sense, while in others figurative language is employed, which includes another meaning besides the literal one: or, in the apparently inconsistent passages, figurative language is employed which, if taken literally, would seem to be contradictories or contraries. Fourth cause: The premises are not identical in both statements, but for certain reasons they are not fully stated in these passages; or two propositions with different subjects which are expressed by the same term without having the difference in meaning pointed out, occur in two passages. The contradiction is therefore only apparent, but there is no contradiction in reality. The fifth cause is traceable to the use of a certain method adopted in teaching and expounding profound problems. Namely, a difficult and obscure theorem must sometimes be mentioned and assumed as known, for the illustration of some elementary and intelligible subject which must be taught beforehand, the commencement being always made with the easier thing. The teacher must therefore facilitate, in any manner which he can devise, the explanation of those theorems, which have to be assumed as known, and he must content himself with giving a general though somewhat inaccurate notion on the subject. It is, for the present, explained according to the capacity of the students, that they may comprehend it as far as they are required to understand the subject. Later on, the same subject is thoroughly treated and fully developed in its right place. Sixth cause: The contradiction is not apparent, and only becomes evident through a series of premises. The larger the number of premises necessary to prove the contradiction between the two conclusions, the greater is the chance that it will escape detection, and that the author will not perceive his own inconsistency. Only when from each conclusion, by means of suitable premises, an inference is made, and from the enunciation thus inferred, by means of proper arguments, other conclusions are formed, and after that process has been repeated many times, then it becomes clear that the original conclusions are contradictories or contraries. Even able writers are liable to overlook such inconsistencies. If, however, the contradiction between the original statements can at once be discovered, and the author, while writing the second, does not think of the first, he evinces a greater deficiency, and his words deserve no notice whatever. Seventh cause: It is sometimes necessary to introduce such metaphysical matter as may partly be disclosed, but must partly be concealed; while, therefore, on one occasion the object which the author has in view may demand that the metaphysical problem be treated as solved in one way, it may be convenient on another occasion to treat it as solved in the opposite way. The author must endeavour, by concealing the fact as much as possible, to prevent the uneducated reader from perceiving the contradiction.

Inconsistencies occurring in the Mishnah and Boraitot are traceable to the first cause. You meet frequently in the Gemara with passages like the following:
—"Does not the beginning of the passage contradict the end? No; the beginning is the dictum of a certain Rabbi; the end that of another"; or "Rabbi (Jehudah ha-Nasi) approved of the opinion of a certain rabbi in one case and gave it therefore anonymously, and having accepted that of another rabbi in the other case he introduced that view without naming the authority"; or "Who is the author of this anonymous dictum? Rabbi A." "Who is the author of that paragraph in the Mishnah? Rabbi B." Instances of this kind are innumerable.

Apparent contradictions or differences occurring in the Gemara may be traced to the first cause and to the second, as e.g., "In this particular case he agrees with this rabbi"; or "He agrees with him in one point, but differs from him in another"; or "These two dicta are the opinions of two Amoraim, who differ as regards the statement made by a certain rabbi." These are examples of contradictions traceable to the first cause. The following are instances which may be traced to the second cause. "Rabba altered his opinion on that point"; it then becomes necessary to consider which of the two opinions came second. Again, "In the first recension of the Talmud by Rabbi Ashi, he made one assertion, and in the second a different one."

The inconsistencies and contradictions met with in some passages of the prophetic books, if taken literally, are all traceable to the third or fourth cause, and it is exclusively in reference to this subject that I wrote the present Introduction. You know that the following expression frequently occurs, "One verse says this, another that," showing the contradiction, and explaining that either some premise is wanting or the subject is altered. Comp. "Solomon, it is not sufficient that thy words contradict thy father; they are themselves inconsistent, etc." Many similar instances occur in the writings of our Sages. The passages in the prophetical books which our Sages have explained, mostly refer to religious or moral precepts. Our desire, however, is to discuss such passages as contain apparent contradictions in regard to the principles of our faith. I shall explain some of them in various chapters of the present work; for this subject also belongs to the secrets of the Torah.

Contradictions traceable to the seventh cause occurring in the prophetical works require special investigation; and no one should express his opinion on that matter by reasoning and arguing without weighing the matter well in his mind.

Inconsistencies in the writings of true philosophers are traceable to the fifth cause. Contradictions occurring in the writings of most authors and commentators, such as are not included in the above-mentioned works, are due to the sixth cause. Many examples of this class of contradictions are found in the Midrash and the Agada; hence the saying, "We must not raise questions concerning the contradictions met with in the Agada." You may also notice in them contradictions due to the seventh cause. Any inconsistency discovered in the present work will be found to arise in consequence of the fifth cause or the seventh. Notice this, consider its truth, and remember it well, lest you misunderstand some of the chapters of this book.

Having concluded these introductory remarks I proceed to examine those expressions, to the true meaning of which, as apparent from the context, it is necessary to direct your attention. This book will then be a key admitting to places the gates of which would otherwise be closed. When the gates are opened and men enter, their souls will enjoy repose, their eyes will be gratified, and even their bodies, after all toil and labour, will be refreshed.

Scripture as Indirect Communication

Søren Kierkegaard

Søren Kierkegaard (1813–1855), Danish philosopher and theologian, and principal inspiration of the philosophical movement called existentialism, has achieved wide recognition as an important thinker only in the last two generations. His philosophy combines an acceptance of Christian concepts and an extensive rejection of speculative philosophy as represented by Hegelian idealism. His principal philosophical works are *Concluding Unscientific Postscript, Philosophical Fragments,* and *Either-Or.*

THE HISTORICAL POINT OF VIEW

When Christianity is viewed from the standpoint of its historical documentation, it becomes necessary to secure an entirely trustworthy account of what the Christian doctrine really is. If the inquirer were infinitely interested in behalf of his relationship to the doctrine he would at once despair; for nothing is more readily evident than that the greatest attainable certainty with respect to anything historical is merely an *approximation.* And an approximation, when viewed as a basis for an eternal happiness, is wholly inadequate, since the incommensurability makes a result impossible. But the interest of the inquiring subject being merely historical (whether he also has an infinite interest in Christianity in his capacity as believer, in which case the whole enterprise might readily come to involve him in several contradictions; or whether he stands aloof, yet without any passionate negative decision *qua* unbeliever), he begins upon the tremendous task of research, adding new contributions of his own, and continuing thus until his seventieth year. Just two weeks before his death he looks forward to the publication of a new work, which it is hoped will throw light upon one entire side of the inquiry. Such an objective temper is an epigram, unless its antithesis be an epigram over it, over the restless concern of the infinitely interested subject, who surely needs to have such a question answered, related as it is to his eternal happiness. And in any case he will not upon any consideration dare to relinquish his interest until the last moment.

   When one raises the historical question of the truth of Christianity, or of what is and is not Christian truth, the Scriptures at once present themselves as documents of decisive significance. The historical inquiry therefore first concentrates upon the Bible.

The Holy Scriptures.   Here it is necessary for the scholar to secure the maximum of dependability; for men, on the contrary, it is of importance not to make

From Søren Kierkegaard, *Concluding Unscientific Postscript,* trans. by David F. Swenson and Walter Lowrie (Princeton, N.J., 1969), pp. 25–27, 29, 30, 31, 217–221. Copyright 1941, © 1969 by Princeton University Press. Reprinted by permission of Princeton University Press.

a display of learning, or to betray the fact that I have none. In the interest of my problem it is more important to have it understood and remembered that even with the most stupendous learning and persistence in research, and even if all the brains of all the critics were concentrated in one, it would still be impossible to obtain anything more than an approximation; and that an approximation is essentially incommensurable with an infinite personal interest in an eternal happiness.[1]

When the Scriptures are viewed as a court of last resort for determining what is and is not Christian doctrine, it becomes necessary to make sure of the Scriptures historically and critically.[2]

In this connection there are a number of topics that come up for consideration: the canonicity of the individual books, their authenticity, their integrity, the trustworthiness of their authors; and a dogmatic guaranty is posited: Inspiration.[3] When one thinks of the labors which the English have devoted to digging the tunnel under the Thames, the tremendous expenditure of energy involved, and then how a little accident may for a long time obstruct the entire enterprise, one will be able to form a fitting conception of this critical undertaking as a whole. How much time, what great industry, what splendid talents, what distinguished scholarship have been requisitioned from generation to generation in order to bring this miracle to pass. And yet a little dialectical doubt touching the presuppositions may suddenly arise, sufficient for a long time to unsettle the whole, closing the subterranean way to Christianity which one has attempted to construct objectively and scientifically, instead of letting the problem remain subjective, as it is.

. . .

[1] In seizing upon this contradiction, the *Philosophical Fragments* posed or presented the problem in the following manner: Christianity is something historical, in relation to which the best knowledge attainable is merely an approximation, the most masterly historical elucidation is only the most masterly "as good as," an almost; and yet it proposes *qua* historical, and precisely by means of the historical, to have decisive significance for a man's eternal happiness. It goes without saying that the little merit of the piece consisted merely in posing the problem, and in disentangling it from all prating and speculative attempts at explanation, which serve indeed to explain that their authors have no notion of what it is all about.

[2] Even so it is impossible to exclude dialectics. A single generation, or perhaps two, might succeed in maintaining itself undisturbed in the presumption that a barrier had been found which is the end of the world and of dialectics: that is no use. Thus it was for a long time believed that one could keep dialectics away from faith, by saying that its conviction rested upon the basis of authority. If the believer was asked about his faith, i.e. if he was dialectically challenged, he would declare with a certain easy air of confidence that he neither could nor needed to give any account of it, since his trust reposed in others, in the authority of the saints, and so forth. This is an illusion. For the dialectician has merely to shift his point of attack, so as to ask him, i.e. challenge him dialectically to explain, what authority is, and why he regards just these as authorities. He is then not questioned about the faith he has on the basis of his confidence in these authorities, but about the faith he has in these authorities.

[3] The incommensurability between inspiration and critical inquiries is analogous to the incommensurability between an eternal happiness and critical considerations; for inspiration is solely an object of faith. Or is it because the books are inspired that the critical zeal is so great? In that case, the believer who believes that the books are inspired does not know the identity of the books he believes to be inspired. Or does inspiration follow as a consequence of the critical inquiry, so that when criticism has done its work it has also demonstrated that the books are inspired? In that case, one will never be in a position to accept their inspiration, since the critical labors yield in their maximum only an approximation.

I assume, accordingly, that the critics have succeeded in proving about the Bible everything that any learned theologian in his happiest moment has ever wished to prove about the Bible. These books and no others belong to the canon; they are authentic; they are integral; their authors are trustworthy—one may well say, that it is as if every letter were inspired. More than this it is impossible to say, for inspiration is an object of faith and subject to a qualitative dialectic; it is incapable of being reached by a quantitative approximation. Furthermore, there is not a trace of contradiction in the sacred writings. . . .

Well then, everything being assumed in order with respect to the Scriptures— what follows? Has anyone who previously did not have faith been brought a single step nearer to its acquisition? No, not a single step. Faith does not result simply from a scientific inquiry; it does not come directly at all. On the contrary, in this objectivity one tends to lose that infinite personal interestedness in passion which is the condition of faith, the *ubique et nusquam* in which faith can come into being. Has anyone who previously had faith gained anything with respect to its strength and power? No, not in the least. Rather is it the case that in this voluminous knowledge, this certainty that lurks at the door of faith and threatens to devour it, he is in so dangerous a situation that he will need to put forth much effort in great fear and trembling, lest he fall a victim to the temptation to confuse knowledge with faith. . . .

I assume now the opposite, that the opponents have succeeded in proving what they desire about the Scriptures, with a certainty transcending the most ardent wish of the most passionate hostility—what then? Have the opponents thereby abolished Christianity? By no means. Has the believer been harmed? By no means, not in the least. Has the opponent made good a right to be relieved of responsibility for not being a believer? By no means. Because these books are not written by these authors, are not authentic, are not in an integral condition, are not inspired (though this cannot be disproved, since it is an object of faith), it does not follow that these authors have not existed; and above all, it does not follow that Christ has not existed. In so far, the believer is equally free to assume it; equally free, let us note this well, for if he had assumed it by virtue of any proof, he would have been on the verge of giving up his faith. If matters ever came to this pass, the believer will have some share of guilt, in so far as he has himself invited this procedure, and begun to play into the hands of unbelief by proposing to demonstrate.

The communication of results is an unnatural form of intercourse between man and man, in so far as every man is a spiritual being, for whom the truth consists in nothing else than the self-activity of personal appropriation, which the communication of a result tends to prevent. Let a teacher in relation to the essential truth (for otherwise a direct relationship between teacher and pupil is quite in order) have, as we say, much inwardness of feeling, and be willing to publish his doctrines day in and day out; if he assumes the existence of a direct relationship between the learner and himself, his inwardness is not inwardness, but a direct outpouring of feeling; the respect for the learner which recognizes that he is in himself the inwardness of truth, in precisely the teacher's inwardness. Let a learner be enthusiastic, and publish his teacher's praises abroad in the strongest expressions, thus, as we say, giving evidence of his inwardness; this inwardness is not inwardness, but an immediate devotedness; the devout and silent accord, in which the learner by himself assimilates what he has learned, keeping the teacher at a distance because he turns his attention within himself, this is precisely inwardness. Pathos is indeed inwardness, but it is an immediate inwardness, when it is expressed; but pathos in a contrary form is an inwardness which remains with the maker of the communication in spite of being expressed, and cannot be directly appropriated by another except through that other's self-activity: the contrast of the form is the measure of the inwardness. The more complete the contrast of the form, the greater the inwardness, and the less contrast, up to the point of direct communication, the less the inwardness. It may be difficult enough for an enthusiastic genius, who would so gladly make all men happy and bring them to a knowledge of the truth, to learn in this manner to restrain himself, and to give heed to the *nota bene* of reduplication, the truth not being a circular with signatures affixed, but the *valore intrinseco* of inwardness; for an idler and frivolous person this understanding comes more easily. As soon as the truth, the essential truth, may be assumed to be known by everyone, the objective becomes appropriation and inwardness, and here only an indirect form is applicable. The position of an apostle is different, for he has to preach an unknown truth, whence a direct form of communication may in his case have provisional validity.

It is strange that while there is such universal insistence on the positive, and on the direct form of communication, it occurs to no one to register a complaint against God, who as the eternal spirit from whom all spirits are derived, might in communicating the truth, seem to be justified in sustaining a direct relationship to the derivative spirits, in quite a different sense from that in which the relationship is one between derived spirits, who having a common derivation from God, are *essentially* equal. For no anonymous author can more cunningly conceal himself, no practitioner of the maieutic art can more carefully withdraw himself from the direct relationship, than God. He is in the creation, and present everywhere in it, but directly He is not there; and only when the individual turns to his inner self, and hence only in the inwardness of self-activity, does he have his attention aroused, and is enabled to see God.

The immediate relationship to God is paganism, and only after the breach has taken place can there be any question of a true God-relationship. But this breach is precisely the first act of inwardness in the direction of determining the truth as inwardness. Nature is, indeed, the work of God, but only the handiwork is directly present, not God. Is not this to behave, in His relationship to the individual, like an elusive author who nowhere sets down his result in large type, or gives it to the reader beforehand in a preface? And why is God elusive? Precisely because He is the truth, and by being elusive desires to keep men from error. The observer of nature does not have a result immediately set before him, but must by himself be at pains to find it, and thereby the direct relationship is broken. But this breach is precisely the act of self-activity, the irruption of inwardness, the first determination of the truth as inwardness.

Or is not God so unnoticeable, so secretly present in His works, that a man might very well live his entire life, be married, become known and respected as citizen, father, and captain of the hunt, without ever having discovered God in His works, and without ever having received any impression of the infinitude of the ethical, because he helped himself out with what constitutes an analogy to the speculative confusion of the ethical with the historical process, in that he helped himself out by having recourse to the customs and traditions prevailing in the town where he happened to live? As a mother admonishes her child when it sets off for a party: "Now be sure to behave yourself, and do as you see the other well-behaved children do,"—so he might manage to live by conducting himself as he sees others do. He would never do anything first, and he would never have any opinion which he did not first know that others had; for this "others" would be for him the first. Upon extraordinary occasions he would behave as when at a banquet a dish is served, and one does not know how it should be eaten: he would look around until he saw how the others did it, and so forth. Such a man might perhaps know many things, perhaps even know the System by rote; he might be an inhabitant of a Christian country, and bow his head whenever the name of God was mentioned; he would perhaps also see God in nature when in company with others who saw God; he would be a pleasant society man—and yet he would have been deceived by the direct nature of his relationship to the truth, to the ethical, and to God.

If one were to delineate such a man experimentally, he would be a satire upon the human. Essentially it is the God-relationship that makes a man a man, and yet he lacked this. No one would hesitate, however, to regard him as a real man (for the absence of inwardness is not directly apparent); in reality he would constitute a sort of marionette, very deceptively imitating everything human— even to the extent of having children by his wife. At the end of his life, one would have to say that one thing had escaped him: his consciousness had taken no note of God. If God could have permitted a direct relationship, he would doubtless have taken notice. If God, for example, had taken on the figure of a very rare and tremendously large green bird, with a red beak, sitting in a tree on the mound, and perhaps even whistling in an unheard of manner—then the society man would have been able to get his eyes open, and for the first time in his life would be first.

All paganism consists in this, that God is related to man directly, as the obviously extraordinary to the astonished observer. But the spiritual relationship to God in the truth, i.e. in inwardness, is conditioned by a prior irruption of inwardness, which corresponds to the divine elusiveness that God has absolutely nothing obvious about Him, that God is so far from being obvious that He is invisible. It cannot immediately occur to anyone that He exists, although His invisibility is again His omnipresence. An omnipresent person is one that is everywhere to be seen, like a policeman, for example: how deceptive then, that an omnipresent being should be recognizable precisely by being invisible,[4] only and alone recognizable by this trait, since his visibility would annul his omni-

[4] To point out how deceptive the rhetorical can be, I shall here show how one might rhetorically perhaps produce an effect upon a listener, in spite of the fact that what was said was dialectically a regress. Let a pagan religious speaker say that here on earth, God's temples are really empty, but (and now begins the rhetorical) in heaven, where all is more perfect, where water is air and air is ether, there are also temples and sanctuaries for the gods, but the difference is that the gods really dwell in those temples: then we have here a dialectical regress in the proposition that God really dwells in the temple for the fact that He does not so dwell is an expression for the spiritual relationship to the invisible. But rhetorically it produces an effect. I have as a matter of fact, had in view a definite passage by a Greek author, whom I do not, however, wish to cite.

presence. The relationship between omnipresence and invisibility is like the relation between mystery and revelation. The mystery is the expression for the fact that the revelation is a revelation in the stricter sense, so that the mystery is the only trait by which it is known; for otherwise a revelation would be something very like a policeman's omnipresence.

If God were to reveal Himself in human form and grant a direct relationship, by giving Himself, for example, the figure of a man six yards tall, then our hypothetical society man and captain of the hunt would doubtless have his attention aroused. But the spiritual relationship to God in truth, when God refuses to deceive, requires precisely that there be nothing remarkable about the figure, so that the society man would have to say: "There is nothing whatever to see." When God has nothing obviously remarkable about Him, the society man is perhaps deceived by not having his attention at all aroused. But this is not God's fault, and the actuality of such a deception is at the same time the constant possibility of the truth. But if God has anything obviously remarkable, He deceives men because they have their attention called to what is untrue, and this direction of attention is at the same time the impossibility of the truth. In paganism the direct relationship is idolatry; in Christendom, everyone knows that God cannot so reveal Himself. But this knowledge is by no means inwardness, and in Christendom it may well happen to one who knows everything by rote that he is left altogether "without God in the world," in a sense impossible in paganism, which did have the untrue relationship of paganism. Idolatry is indeed a sorry substitute, but that the item *God* should be entirely omitted is still worse.

Not even God, then, enters into a direct relationship with derivative spirits. And this is the miracle of creation, not the creation of something which is nothing over against the Creator, but the creation of something which is something, and which in true worship of God can use this something in order by its true self to become nothing before God. Much less can a human being sustain such a direct relationship to another *in the truth*. Nature, the totality of created things, is the work of God. And yet God is not there; but within the individual man there is a potentiality (man is potentially spirit) which is awakened in inwardness to become a God-relationship, and then it becomes possible to see God everywhere. The sensuous distinctions of the great, the astonishing, the shrieking superlatives of a southern people, constitute a retreat to idolatry in comparison with the spiritual relationship of inwardness. Is this not as if an author wrote one hundred and sixty-six folio volumes, and a reader read and read, just as people look and look at nature, but did not discover that the meaning of this tremendous literature lay in himself; for astonishment over the many volumes, and the number of lines to a page, which is like the astonishment over the vastness of nature and the countless forms of animal life, is not the true understanding.

A direct relationship between one spiritual being and another, with respect to the essential truth, is unthinkable. If such a relationship is assumed, it means that one of the parties has ceased to be spirit. This is something that many a genius omits to consider, both when he helps people into the truth *en masse*, and when he is complaisant enough to think that acclamation, willingness to listen, the affixing of signatures, and so forth, is identical with the acceptance of the truth. Precisely as important as the truth, and if one of the two is to be emphasized, still more important, is the manner in which the truth is accepted. It would help very little if one persuaded millions of men to accept the truth, if precisely by the method of their acceptance they were transferred into error. Hence it is that all complaisance, all persuasiveness, all bargaining, all direct attraction by means of one's own person, reference to one's suffering for the cause, one's weeping over humanity, one's enthusiasm—all this is sheer misunderstanding, a false note in relation to the truth, by which, in proportion to one's ability, one may help a job-lot of human beings to get an illusion of truth.

Demythologization
Rudolf Bultmann

Rudolph Karl Bultmann (1884–   ) is one of the most influential Christian theologians of the twentieth century. He is noted for his "existential" approach to the New Testament. His major works include *Theology of the New Testament* (two volumes, 1948–1953), *History and Eschatology,* and *Jesus Christ and Mythology.*

THE TASK OF DEMYTHOLOGIZING THE NEW TESTAMENT PROCLAMATION

The Problem. The Mythical View of the World and the Mythical Event of Redemption. The cosmology of the New Testament is essentially mythical in character. The world is viewed as a three-storied structure, with the earth in the centre, the heaven above, and the underworld beneath. Heaven is the abode of God and of celestial beings—the angels. The underworld is hell, the place of torment. Even the earth is more than the scene of natural, everyday events, of the trivial round and common task. It is the scene of the supernatural activity of God and his angels on the one hand, and of Satan and his daemons on the other. These supernatural forces intervene in the course of nature and in all that men think and will and do. Miracles are by no means rare. Man is not in control of his own life. Evil spirits may take possession of him. Satan may inspire him with evil thoughts. Alternatively, God may inspire his thought and guide his purposes. He may grant him heavenly visions. He may allow him to hear his word of succour or demand. He may give him the supernatural power of his Spirit. History does not follow a smooth unbroken course; it is set in motion and controlled by these supernatural powers. This aeon is held in bondage by Satan, sin, and death (for "powers" is precisely what they are), and hastens towards its end. That end will come very soon, and will take the form of a cosmic catastrophe. It will be inaugurated by the "woes" of the last time. Then the Judge will come from heaven, the dead will rise, the last judgement will take

From Rudolf Bultmann, *Kerygma and Myth* (New York, 1961), pp. 1–16, 34–38. Reprinted by permission of Harper & Row, Publishers, Inc.

place, and men will enter into eternal salvation or damnation.

This then is the mythical view of the world which the New Testament presupposes when it presents the event of redemption which is the subject of its preaching. It proclaims in the language of mythology that the last time has now come. "In the fulness of time" God sent forth his Son, a pre-existent divine Being, who appears on earth as a man.[1] He dies the death of a sinner[2] on the cross and makes atonement for the sins of men.[3] His resurrection marks the beginning of the cosmic catastrophe. Death, the consequence of Adam's sin, is abolished,[4] and the daemonic forces are deprived of their power.[5] The risen Christ is exalted to the right hand of God in heaven[6] and made "Lord" and "King."[7] He will come again on the clouds of heaven to complete the work of redemption, and the resurrection and judgement of men will follow.[8] Sin, suffering and death will then be finally abolished.[9] All this is to happen very soon; indeed, St. Paul thinks that he himself will live to see it.[10]

All who belong to Christ's Church and are joined to the Lord by Baptism and the Eucharist are certain of resurrection to salvation,[11] unless they forfeit it by unworthy behaviour. Christian believers already enjoy the first instalment of salvation, for the Spirit[12] is at work within them, bearing witness to their adoption as sons of God,[13] and guaranteeing their final resurrection.[14]

The Mythological View of the World Obsolete. All this is the language of mythology, and the origin of the various themes can be easily traced in the contemporary mythology of Jewish Apocalyptic and in the redemption myths of Gnosticism. To this extent *the kerygma is incredible to modern man, for he is convinced that the mythical view of the world is obsolete.* We are therefore bound to ask whether, when we preach the Gospel to-day, we expect our converts to accept not only the Gospel message, but also the mythical view of the world in which it is set. If not, does the New Testament embody a truth which is quite independent of its mythical setting? If it does, theology must undertake the task of stripping the Kerygma from its mythical framework, of "demythologizing" it.

Can Christian preaching expect modern man *to accept the mythical view of the world as true?* To do so would be both senseless and impossible. It would be senseless, because there is nothing specifically Christian in the mythical view of the world as such. It is simply the cosmology of a pre-scientific age. Again, it would be impossible, because no man can adopt a view of the world by his own volition—it is already determined for him by his place in history. Of course such a view is not absolutely unalterable, and the individual may even contribute to its

[1] Gal. 4. 4; Phil. 2. 6ff.; 2 Cor. 8. 9; John 1. 14, etc.
[2] 2 Cor. 5. 21; Rom. 8. 3.
[3] Rom. 3. 23–26; 4. 25; 8. 3; 2 Cor. 5. 14, 19; John 1. 29; 1 John 2. 2, etc.
[4] 1 Cor. 15. 21f.; Rom. 5. 12ff.
[5] 1 Cor. 2. 6; Col. 2. 15; Rev. 12. 7ff., etc.
[6] Acts 1. 6f.; 2. 33; Rom. 8. 34, etc.
[7] Phil. 2. 9–11; 1 Cor. 15. 25.
[8] 1 Cor. 15. 23f., 50ff., etc.
[9] Rev. 21. 4, etc.
[10] 1 Thess. 4. 15ff.; 1 Cor. 15. 51f.; cf. Mark 9. 1.
[11] Rom. 5. 12ff.; 1 Cor. 15. 21ff., 44b, ff.
[12] Απαρχή: Rom. 8. 23, ἀρραβών: 2 Cor. 1. 22; 5. 5.
[13] Rom. 8. 15; Gal. 4. 6.
[14] Rom. 8. 11.

change. But he can do so only when he is faced by a new set of facts so compelling as to make his previous view of the world untenable. He has then no alternative but to modify his view of the world or produce a new one. The discoveries of Copernicus and the atomic theory are instances of this, and so was romanticism, with its discovery that the human subject is richer and more complex than enlightenment or idealism had allowed, and nationalism, with its new realization of the importance of history and the tradition of peoples.

It may equally well happen that truths which a shallow enlightenment had failed to perceive are later rediscovered in ancient myths. Theologians are perfectly justified in asking whether this is not exactly what has happened with the New Testament. At the same time it is impossible to revive an obsolete view of the world by a mere fiat, and certainly not a mythical view. For all our thinking to-day is shaped irrevocably by modern science. A blind acceptance of the New Testament mythology would be arbitrary, and to press for its acceptance as an article of faith would be to reduce faith to works. Wilhelm Herrmann pointed this out, and one would have thought that his demonstration was conclusive. It would involve a sacrifice of the intellect which could have only one result—a curious form of schizophrenia and insincerity. It would mean accepting a view of the world in our faith and religion which we should deny in our everyday life. Modern thought as we have inherited it brings with it criticism of *the New Testament view of the world.*

Man's knowledge and mastery of the world have advanced to such an extent through science and technology that it is no longer possible for anyone seriously to hold the New Testament view of the world—in fact, there is no one who does. What meaning, for instance, can we attach to such phrases in the creed as "descended into hell" or "ascended into heaven"? We no longer believe in the three-storied universe which the creeds take for granted. The only honest way of reciting the creeds is to strip the mythological framework from the truth they enshrine—that is, assuming that they contain any truth at all, which is just the question that theology has to ask. No one who is old enough to think for himself supposes that God lives in a local heaven. There is no longer any heaven in the traditional sense of the word. The same applies to hell in the sense of a mythical underworld beneath our feet. And if this is so, the story of Christ's descent into hell and of his Ascension into heaven is done with. We can no longer look for the return of the Son of Man on the clouds of heaven or hope that the faithful will meet him in the air (1 Thess. 4. 15ff.).

Now that the forces and the laws of nature have been discovered, we can no longer believe in *spirits, whether good or evil.* We know that the stars are physical bodies whose motions are controlled by the laws of the universe, and not daemonic beings which enslave mankind to their service. Any influence they may have over human life must be explicable in terms of the ordinary laws of nature; it cannot in any way be attributed to their malevolence. Sickness and the cure of disease are likewise attributable to natural causation; they are not the result of daemonic activity or of evil spells.[15] The *miracles of the New Testament* have

[15] It may of course be argued that there are people alive to-day whose confidence in the traditional scientific view of the world has been shaken, and others who are primitive enough to qualify for an age of mythical thought. And there also are many varieties of superstition. But when belief in spirits and miracles has degenerated into superstition, it has become something entirely different from what it was when it was genuine faith. The various impressions and

ceased to be miraculous, and to defend their historicity by recourse to nervous disorders or hypnotic effects only serves to underline the fact. And if we are still left with certain physiological and psychological phenomena which we can only assign to mysterious and enigmatic causes, we are still assigning them to causes, and thus far are trying to make them scientifically intelligible. Even occultism pretends to be a science.

It is impossible to use electric light and the wireless and to avail ourselves of modern medical and surgical discoveries, and at the same time to believe in the New Testament world of spirits and miracles.[16] We may think we can manage it in our own lives, but to expect others to do so is to make the Christian faith unintelligible and unacceptable to the modern world.

The mythical eschatology is untenable for the simple reason that the parousia of Christ never took place as the New Testament expected. History did not come to an end, and, as every schoolboy knows, it will continue to run its course. Even if we believe that the world as we know it will come to an end in time, we expect the end to take the form of a natural catastrophe, not of a mythical event such as the New Testament expects. And if we explain the parousia in terms of modern scientific theory, we are applying criticism to the New Testament, albeit unconsciously.

But natural science is not the only challenge which the mythology of the New Testament has to face. There is the still more serious challenge presented by *modern man's understanding of himself.*

Modern man is confronted by a curious dilemma. He may regard himself as pure nature, or as pure spirit. In the latter case he distinguishes the essential part of his being from nature. In either case, however, *man is essentially a unity.* He bears the sole responsibility for his own feeling, thinking, and willing.[17] He is not, as the New Testament regards him, the victim of a strange dichotomy which exposes him to the interference of powers outside himself. If his exterior behavior and his interior condition are in perfect harmony, it is something he has achieved himself, and if other people think their interior unity is torn asunder by daemonic or divine interference, he calls it schizophrenia.

Although biology and psychology recognize that man is a highly dependent being, that does not mean that he has been handed over to powers outside of and distinct from himself. This dependence is inseparable from human nature, and he needs only to understand it in order to recover his self-mastery and organize his life on a rational basis. If he regards himself as spirit, he knows that he is permanently conditioned by the physical, bodily part of his being, but he distinguishes his true self from it, and knows that he is independent and responsible for his mastery over nature.

In either case he finds *what the New Testament has to say about the "Spirit"*

---

speculations which influence credulous people here and there are of little importance, nor does it matter to what extent cheap slogans have spread an atmosphere inimical to science. What matters is the world view which men imbibe from their environment, and it is science which determines that view of the world through the school, the press, the wireless, the cinema, and all the other fruits of technical progress.

[16] Cp. the observations of Paul Schütz on the decay of mythical religion in the East through the introduction of modern hygiene and medicine.

[17] Cp. Gerhardt Krüger, *Einsicht und Leidenschaft, Das Wesen des platonischen Denkens,* Frankfort, 1939, p. 11 f.

(πνεῦμα) *and the sacraments utterly strange and incomprehensible.* Biological man cannot see how a supernatural entity like the πνεῦμα can penetrate within the close texture of his natural powers and set to work within him. Nor can the idealist understand how a πνεῦμα working like a natural power can touch and influence his mind and spirit. Conscious as he is of his own moral responsibility, he cannot conceive how baptism in water can convey a mysterious something which is henceforth the agent of all his decisions and actions. He cannot see how physical food can convey spiritual strength, and how the unworthy receiving of the Eucharist can result in physical sickness and death (1 Cor. 11. 30). The only possible explanation is that it is due to suggestion. He cannot understand how anyone can be baptized for the dead (1 Cor. 15. 29).

We need not examine in detail the various forms of modern *Weltanschauung*, whether idealist or naturalist. For the only criticism of the New Testament which is theologically relevant is that which arises *necessarily* out of the situation of modern man. The biological *Weltanschauung* does not, for instance, arise necessarily out of the contemporary situation. We are still free to adopt it or not as we choose. The only relevant question for the theologian is the basic assumption on which the adoption of a biological as of every other *Weltanschauung* rests, and that assumption is the view of the world which has been moulded by modern science and the modern conception of human nature as a self-subsistent unity immune from the interference of supernatural powers.

Again, the biblical doctrine that *death is the punishment of sin* is equally abhorrent to naturalism and idealism, since they both regard death as a simple and necessary process of nature. To the naturalist death is no problem at all, and to the idealist it is a problem for that very reason, for so far from arising out of man's essential spiritual being it actually destroys it. The idealist is faced with a paradox. On the one hand man is a spiritual being, and therefore essentially different from plants and animals, and on the other hand he is the prisoner of nature, whose birth, life, and death are just the same as those of the animals. Death may present him with a problem, but he cannot see how it can be a punishment for sin. Human beings are subject to death even before they have committed any sin. And to attribute human mortality to the fall of Adam is sheer nonsense, for guilt implies personal responsibility, and the idea of original sin as an inherited infection is sub-ethical, irrational, and absurd.

The same objections apply to *the doctrine of the atonement.* How can the guilt of one man be expiated by the death of another who is sinless—if indeed one may speak of a sinless man at all? What primitive notions of guilt and righteousness does this imply? And what primitive idea of God? The rationale of sacrifice in general may of course throw some light on the theory of the atonement, but even so, what a primitive mythology it is, that a divine Being should become incarnate, and atone for the sins of men through his own blood? Or again, one might adopt an analogy from the law courts, and explain the death of Christ as a transaction between God and man through which God's claims on man were satisfied. But that would make sin a juridical matter; it would be no more than an external transgression of a commandment, and it would make nonsense of all our ethical standards. Moreover, if the Christ who died such a death was the pre-existent Son of God, what could death mean for him? Obviously very little, if he knew that he would rise again in three days!

The *resurrection of Jesus* is just as difficult for modern man, if it means an event whereby a living supernatural power is released which can henceforth be appropriated through the sacraments. To the biologist such language is meaningless, for he does not regard death as a problem at all. The idealist would not object to the idea of a life immune from death, but he could not believe that such a life is made available by the resuscitation of a dead person. If that is the way God makes life available for man, his action is inextricably involved in a a nature miracle. Such a notion he finds incomprehensible, for he can see God at work only in the reality of his personal life and in his transformation. But, quite apart from the incredibility of such a miracle, he cannot see how an event like this could be the act of God, or how it could affect his own life.

Gnostic influence suggests that this Christ, who died and rose again, was not a mere human being but a God-man. His death and resurrection were not isolated facts which concerned him alone, but a cosmic event in which we are all involved.[18] It is only with effort that modern man can think himself back into such an intellectual atmosphere, and even then he could never accept it himself, because it regards man's essential being as nature and redemption as a process of nature. And as for the pre-existence of Christ, with its corollary of man's translation into a celestial realm of light, and the clothing of the human personality in heavenly robes and a spiritual body—all this is not only irrational but utterly meaningless. Why should salvation take this particular form? Why should this be the fulfilment of human life and the realization of man's true being?

The Task Before Us. Not Selection or Subtraction. Does this drastic criticism of the New Testament mythology mean the complete elimination of the kerygma?

Whatever else may be true, we cannot save the kerygma by selecting some of its features and subtracting others, and thus reduce the amount of mythology in it. For instance, it is impossible to dismiss St. Paul's teaching about the unworthy reception of Holy Communion or about baptism for the dead, and yet cling to the belief that physical eating and drinking can have a spiritual effect. If we accept *one* idea, we must accept everything which the New Testament has to say about Baptism and Holy Communion, and it is just this one idea which we cannot accept.

It may of course be argued that some features of the New Testament mythology are given greater prominence than others: not all of them appear with the same regularity in the various books. There is for example only one occurrence of the legends of the Virgin birth and the Ascension; St. Paul and St. John appear to be totally unaware of them. But, even if we take them to be later accretions, it does not affect the mythical character of the event of redemption as a whole. And if we once start subtracting from the kerygma, where are we to draw the line? The mythical view of the world must be accepted or rejected in its entirety.

At this point absolute clarity and ruthless honesty are essential both for the academic theologian and for the parish priest. It is a duty they owe to themselves, to the Church they serve, and to those whom they seek to win for the Church. They must make it quite clear what their hearers are expected to accept and what they are not. At all costs the preacher must not leave his people in the dark about what he secretly eliminates, nor must he be in the dark about it himself. In Karl Barth's book *The Resurrection of the Dead* the cosmic eschatology in the

---

[18] Rom. 5. 12ff.; 1 Cor. 15. 21ff., 44b.

sense of "chronologically final history" is eliminated in favour of what he intends to be a non-mythological "ultimate history." He is able to delude himself into thinking that this is exegesis of St. Paul and of the New Testament generally only because he gets rid of everything mythological in 1 Corinthians by subjecting it to an interpretation which does violence to its meaning. But that is an impossible procedure.

If the truth of the New Testament proclamation is to be preserved, the only way is to demythologize it. But our motive in so doing must not be to make the New Testament relevant to the modern world at all costs. The question is simply whether the New Testament message consists exclusively of mythology, or whether it actually demands the elimination of myth if it is to be understood as it is meant to be. This question is forced upon us from two sides. First there is the nature of myth in general, and then there is the New Testament itself.

The Nature of Myth. The real purpose of myth is not to present an objective picture of the world as it is, but to express man's understanding of himself in the world in which he lives. Myth should be interpreted not cosmologically, but anthropologically, or better still, existentially.[19] Myth speaks of the power or the powers which man supposes he experiences as the ground and limit of his world and of his own activity and suffering. He describes these powers in terms derived from the visible world, with its tangible objects and forces, and from human life, with its feelings, motives, and potentialities. He may, for instance, explain the origin of the world by speaking of a world egg or a world tree. Similarly he may account for the present state and order of the world by speaking of a primeval war between the gods. He speaks of the other world in terms of this world, and of the gods in terms derived from human life.[20]

Myth is an expression of man's conviction that the origin and purpose of the world in which he lives are to be sought not within it but beyond it—that is, beyond the realm of known and tangible reality—and that this realm is perpetually dominated and menaced by those mysterious powers which are its source and limit. Myth is also an expression of man's awareness that he is not lord of his own being. It expresses his sense of dependence not only within the visible world, but more especially on those forces which hold sway beyond the confines of the known. Finally, myth expresses man's belief that in this state of dependence he can be delivered from the forces within the visible world.

Thus myth contains elements which demand its own criticism—namely, its imagery with its apparent claim to objective validity. The real purpose of myth is to speak of a transcendent power which controls the world and man, but that purpose is impeded and obscured by the terms in which it is expressed.

Hence the importance of the New Testament mythology lies not in its imagery but in the understanding of existence which it enshrines. The real question is whether this understanding of existence is true. Faith claims that it is, and faith ought not to be tied down to the imagery of New Testament mythology.

[19] Cp. Gerhardt Krüger, *Einsicht und Leidenschaft*, esp. p. 17f., 56f.

[20] Myth is here used in the sense popularized by the "History of Religions" school. Mythology is the use of imagery to express the other worldly in terms of this world and the divine in terms of human life, the other side in terms of this side. For instance, divine transcendence is expressed as spatial distance. It is a mode of expression which makes it easy to understand the cultus as an action in which material means are used to convey immaterial power. Myth is not used in that modern sense, according to which it is practically equivalent to ideology.

The New Testament Itself. The New Testament itself invites this kind of criticism. Not only are there rough edges in its mythology, but some of its features are actually contradictory. For example, the death of Christ is sometimes a sacrifice and sometimes a cosmic event. Sometimes his person is interpreted as the Messiah and sometimes as the Second Adam. The kenosis of the pre-existent Son (Phil. 2. 6ff.) is incompatible with the miracle narratives as proofs of his messianic claims. The Virgin birth is inconsistent with the assertion of his pre-existence. The doctrine of the Creation is incompatible with the conception of the "rulers of this world" (1 Cor. 2. 6ff.), the "god of this world" (2 Cor. 4. 4) and the "elements of this world" (στοιχεῖα τοῦ κόσμου, Gal. 4. 3). It is impossible to square the belief that the law was given by God with the theory that it comes from the angels (Gal. 3. 19f.).

But the principal demand for the criticism of mythology comes from a curious contradiction which runs right through the New Testament. Sometimes we are told that human life is determined by cosmic forces, at others we are challenged to a decision. Side by side with the Pauline indicative stands the Pauline imperative. In short, man is sometimes regarded as a cosmic being, sometimes as an independent "I" for whom decision is a matter of life or death. Incidentally, this explains why so many sayings in the New Testament speak directly to modern man's condition while others remain enigmatic and obscure. Finally, attempts at demythologization are sometimes made even within the New Testament itself. But more will be said on this point later.

Previous Attempts at Demythologizing. How then is the mythology of the New Testament to be re-interpreted? This is not the first time that theologians have approached this task. Indeed, all we have said so far might have been said in much the same way thirty or forty years ago, and it is a sign of the bankruptcy of contemporary theology that it has been necessary to go all over the same ground again. The reason for this is not far to seek. The liberal theologians of the last century were working on the wrong lines. They threw away not only the mythology but also the kerygma itself. Were they right? Is that the treatment the New Testament itself required? That is the question we must face to-day. The last twenty years have witnessed a movement away from criticism and a return to a naïve acceptance of the kerygma. The danger both for theological scholarship and for the Church is that this uncritical resuscitation of the New Testament mythology may make the Gospel message unintelligible to the modern world. We cannot dismiss the critical labours of earlier generations without further ado. We must take them up and put them to constructive use. Failure to do so will mean that the old battles between orthodoxy and liberalism will have to be fought out all over again, that is assuming that there will be any Church or any theologians to fight them at all! Perhaps we may put it schematically like this: whereas the older liberals used criticism to *eliminate* the mythology of the New Testament, our task to-day is to use criticism to *interpret* it. Of course it may still be necessary to eliminate mythology here and there. But the criterion adopted must be taken not from modern thought, but from the understanding of human existence which the New Testament itself enshrines.[21]

To begin with, let us review some of these earlier attempts at demythologizing. We need only mention briefly the allegorical interpretation of the New Testament

[21] As an illustration of this critical re-interpretation of myth cf. Hans Jonas, *Augustin und das paulinische Freiheitsproblem*, 1930 pp. 66–76.

which has dogged the Church throughout its history. This method spiritualizes the mythical events so that they become symbols of processes going on in the soul. This is certainly the most comfortable way of avoiding the critical question. The literal meaning is allowed to stand and is dispensed with only for the individual believer, who can escape into the realm of the soul.

It was characteristic of the older liberal theologians that they regarded mythology as relative and temporary. Hence they thought they could safely eliminate it altogether, and retain only the broad, basic principles of religion and ethics. They distinguished between what they took to be the essence of religion and the temporary garb which it assumed. Listen to what Harnack has to say about the essence of Jesus' preaching of the Kingdom of God and its coming: "The kingdom has a triple meaning. Firstly, it is something supernatural, a gift from above, not a product of ordinary life. Secondly, it is a purely religious blessing, the inner link with the living God; thirdly, it is the most important experience that a man can have, that on which everything else depends; it permeates and dominates his whole existence, because sin is forgiven and misery banished." Note how completely the mythology is eliminated: "The kingdom of God comes by coming to the individual, by entering into his *soul* and laying hold of it."[22]

It will be noticed how Harnack reduces the kerygma to a few basic principles of religion and ethics. Unfortunately this means that *the kerygma has ceased to be kerygma:* it is no longer the proclamation of the decisive act of God in Christ. For the liberals the great truths of religion and ethics are timeless and eternal, though it is only within human history that they are realized, and only in concrete historical processes that they are given clear expression. But the apprehension and acceptance of these principles does not depend on the knowledge and acceptance of the age in which they first took shape, or of the historical persons who first discovered them. We are all capable of verifying them in our own experience at whatever period we happen to live. History may be of academic interest, but never of paramount importance for religion.

But the New Testament speaks of an *event* through which God has wrought man's redemption. For it, Jesus is not primarily the teacher, who certainly had extremely important things to say and will always be honoured for saying them, but whose person in the last analysis is immaterial for those who have assimilated his teaching. On the contrary, his person is just what the New Testament proclaims as the decisive event of redemption. It speaks of this person in mythological terms, but does this mean that we can reject the kerygma altogether on the ground that it is nothing more than mythology? That is the question.

Next came the History of Religions school. Its representatives were the first to discover the extent to which the New Testament is permeated by mythology. The importance of the New Testament, they saw, lay not in its teaching about religion and ethics but in its actual religion and piety; in comparison with that all the dogma it contains, and therefore all the mythological imagery with its apparent objectivity, was of secondary importance or completely negligible. The essence of the New Testament lay in the religious life it portrayed; its high-watermark was the experience of mystical union with Christ, in whom God took symbolic form.

[22] *What is Christianity?* Williams and Norgate, 1904, pp. 63–4 and 57.

These critics grasped one important truth. Christian faith is not the same as religious idealism; the Christian life does not consist in developing the individual personality, in the improvement of society, or in making the world a better place. The Christian life means a turning away from the world, a detachment from it. But the critics of the History of Religions school failed to see that in the New Testament this detachment is essentially eschatological and not mystical. Religion for them was an expression of the human yearning to rise above the world and transcend it: it was the discovery of a supramundane sphere where the soul could detach itself from all earthly care and find its rest. Hence the supreme manifestation of religion was to be found not in personal ethics or in social idealism but in the cultus regarded as an end in itself. This was just the kind of religious life portrayed in the New Testament, not only as a model and pattern, but as a challenge and inspiration. The New Testament was thus the abiding source of power which enabled man to realize the true life of religion, and Christ was the eternal symbol for the cultus of the Christian Church.[23] It will be noticed how the Church is here defined exclusively as a worshipping community, and this represents a great advance on the older liberalism. This school rediscovered the Church as a *religious* institution. For the idealist there was really no place for the Church at all. But did they succeed in recovering the meaning of the Ecclesia in the full, New Testament sense of the word? For in the New Testament the Ecclesia is invariably a phenomenon of salvation history and eschatology.

Moreover, if the History of Religions school is right, the kerygma has once more ceased to be kerygma. Like the liberals, they are silent about a decisive act of God in Christ proclaimed as the event of redemption. So we are still left with the question whether this event and the person of Jesus, both of which are described in the New Testament in mythological terms, are nothing more than mythology. Can the kerygma be interpreted apart from mythology? Can we recover the truth of the kerygma for men who do not think in mythological terms without forfeiting its character as kerygma?

An Existentialist Interpretation the Only Solution. The theological work which such an interpretation involves can be sketched only in the broadest outline and with only a few examples. We must avoid the impression that this is a light and easy task, as if all we have to do is to discover the right formula and finish the job on the spot. It is much more formidable than that. It cannot be done single-handed. It will tax the time and strength of a whole theological generation.

The mythology of the New Testament is in essence that of Jewish apocalyptic and the Gnostic redemption myths. A common feature of them both is their basic dualism, according to which the present world and its human inhabitants are under the control of daemonic, satanic powers, and stand in need of redemption. Man cannot achieve this redemption by his own efforts; it must come as a gift through a divine intervention. Both types of mythology speak of such an intervention: Jewish apocalyptic of an imminent world crisis in which this present aeon will be brought to an end and the new aeon ushered in by the coming of the Messiah, and Gnosticism of a Son of God sent down from the realm of light,

[23] Cp. e.g. Troeltsch, *Die Bedeutung der Geschichtlichkeit Jesu für den Glauben*, Tübingen, 1911.

entering into this world in the guise of a man, and by his fate and teaching delivering the elect and opening up the way for their return to their heavenly home.

The meaning of these two types of mythology lies once more not in their imagery with its apparent objectivity but in the understanding of human existence which both are trying to express. In other words, they need to be interpreted existentially. A good example of such treatment is to be found in Hans Jonas's book on Gnosticism.[24]

Our task is to produce an existentialist interpretation of the dualistic mythology of the New Testament along similar lines. When, for instance, we read of daemonic powers ruling the world and holding mankind in bondage, does the understanding of human existence which underlies such language offer a solution to the riddle of human life which will be acceptable even to the non-mythological mind of to-day? Of course we must not take this to imply that the New Testament presents us with an anthropology like that which modern science can give us. It cannot be proved by logic or demonstrated by an appeal to factual evidence. Scientific anthropologies always take for granted a definite understanding of existence, which is invariably the consequence of a deliberate decision of the scientist, whether he makes it consciously or not. And that is why we have to discover whether the New Testament offers man an understanding of himself which will challenge him to a genuine existential decision.

DEMYTHOLOGIZING IN OUTLINE

The Christian Interpretation of Being

.   .   .

The Cross. Is the cross, understood as the event of redemption, exclusively mythical in character, or can it retain its value for salvation without forfeiting its character as history?

It certainly has a mythical character as far as its objective setting is concerned. The Jesus who was crucified was the pre-existent, incarnate Son of God, and as such he was without sin. He is the victim whose blood atones for our sins. He bears vicariously the sin of the world, and by enduring the punishment for sin on our behalf he delivers us from death. This mythological interpretation is a mixture of sacrificial and juridical analogies, which have ceased to be tenable for us to-day. And in any case they fail to do justice to what the New Testament is trying to say. For the most they can convey is that the cross effects the forgiveness of all the past and future sins of man, in the sense that the punishment they deserved has been remitted. But the New Testament means more than this. The cross releases men not only from the guilt, but also from the power of sin. That is why, when the author of Colossians says " He [God] . . . having forgiven us all our trespasses, having blotted out the bond written in ordinances that was against us, which was contrary to us; and he hath taken it out of the way, nailing it to the cross" he hastens to add: "having put off from himself the principalities and powers, he made a show of them openly, triumphing over them in it" (Col. 2. 13–15).

[24] *Gnosis und spätantiker Geist. I. Die mythologische Gnosis,* 1934.

The historical event of the cross acquires cosmic dimensions. And by speaking of the Cross as a cosmic happening its significance as a historical happening is made clear in accordance with the remarkable way of thinking in which historical events and connections are presented in cosmic terms, and so its full significance is brought into sharper relief. For if we see in the cross the judgement of the world and the defeat of the rulers of this world (1 Cor. 2. 6ff.), the cross becomes the judgement of ourselves as fallen creatures enslaved to the powers of the "world."

By giving up Jesus to be crucified, God has set up the cross for us. To believe in the cross of Christ does not mean to concern ourselves with a mythical process wrought outside of us and our world, with an objective event turned by God to our advantage, but rather to make the cross of Christ our own, to undergo crucifixion with him. The cross in its redemptive aspect is not an isolated incident which befell a mythical personage, but an event whose meaning has "cosmic" importance. Its decisive, revolutionary significance is brought out by the eschatological framework in which it is set. In other words, the cross is not just an event of the past which can be contemplated, but is the eschatological event in and beyond time, in so far as it (understood in its significance, that is, for faith) is an ever-present reality.

The cross becomes a present reality first of all in the sacraments. In baptism men and women are baptized into Christ's death (Rom. 6. 3) and crucified with him (Rom. 6. 6). At every celebration of the Lord's Supper the death of Christ is proclaimed (1 Cor. 11. 26). The communicants thereby partake of his crucified body and his blood outpoured (1 Cor. 10. 16). Again, the cross of Christ is an ever-present reality in the everyday life of the Christians. "They that are of Christ Jesus have crucified the flesh with the passions and the lusts thereof" (Gal. 5. 24). That is why St. Paul can speak of "the cross of our Lord Jesus Christ, through which the world hath been crucified unto me, and I unto the world" (Gal. 6. 14). That is why he seeks to know "the fellowship of his sufferings," as one who is "conformed to his death" (Phil. 3. 10).

The crucifying of the affections and lusts includes the overcoming of our natural dread of suffering and the perfection of our detachment from the world. Hence the willing acceptance of sufferings in which death is already at work in man means: "always bearing about in our body the dying of Jesus" and "always being delivered unto death for Jesus' sake" (2 Cor. 4. 10f.).

Thus the cross and passion are ever-present realities. How little they are confined to the events of the first Good Friday is amply illustrated by the words which a disciple of St. Paul puts into his master's mouth: "Now I rejoice in my sufferings for your sake, and fill up on my part that which is lacking of the afflictions of Christ in my flesh for his body's sake, which is the Church" (Col. 1. 24).

In its redemptive aspect the cross of Christ is no mere mythical event, but a historic (*geschichtlich*) fact originating in the historical (*historisch*) event which is the crucifixion of Jesus. The abiding significance of the cross is that it is the judgement of the world, the judgement and the deliverance of man. So far as this is so, Christ is crucified "for us," not in the sense of any theory of sacrifice or satisfaction. This interpretation of the cross as a permanent fact rather than a mythological event does far more justice to the redemptive significance of the event of the past than any of the traditional interpretations. In the last resort mythological language is only a medium for conveying the significance of the historical (*historisch*) event. The historical (*historisch*) event of the cross has, in the significance peculiar to it, created a new historic (*geschichtlich*) situation. The preaching of the cross as the event of redemption challenges all who hear it to appropriate this significance for themselves, to be willing to be crucified with Christ.

But, it will be asked, is this significance to be discerned in the actual event of past history? Can it, so to speak, be read off from that event? Or does the cross bear this significance because it is the cross of *Christ?* In other words, must we first be convinced of the significance of Christ and believe in him in order to discern the real meaning of the cross? If we are to perceive the real meaning of the cross, must we understand it as the cross of Jesus as a figure of past history? Must we go back to the Jesus of history?

As far as the first preachers of the gospel are concerned this will certainly be the case. For them the cross was the cross of him with whom they had lived in personal intercourse. The cross was an experience of their own lives. It presented them with a question and it disclosed to them its meaning. But for us this personal connection cannot be reproduced. For us the cross cannot disclose its own meaning: it is an event of the past. We can never recover it as an event in our own lives. All we know of it is derived from historical report. But the New Testament does not proclaim Jesus Christ in this way. The meaning of the cross is not disclosed from the life of Jesus as a figure of past history, a life which needs to be reproduced by historical research. On the contrary, Jesus is not proclaimed merely as the crucified; he is also risen from the dead. The cross and the resurrection form an inseparable unity.

The Meaning of the Gospel

Paul van Buren

Paul van Buren (1924–   ) is an Episcopal minister who teaches in the Department of Religion at Temple University in Philadelphia. His works include *Christ in Our Place,* and *Theological Explorations.*

THE GOSPEL AS THE EXPRESSION OF A HISTORICAL PERSPECTIVE

. . .

A man who has been converted to Christian faith does not ordinarily go about saying, "I have seen the Lord." He may say, "I have seen the light," however, and this suggests how his experience at once resembles and differs from that of the apostles on Easter. Theology has traditionally accounted for his

From Paul van Buren, *The Secular Meaning of the Gospel* (New York, 1963), pp. 135–156. Copyright © 1963 by Paul van Buren. Reprinted with permission of The Macmillan Company.

conversion not by referring to an appearance of Jesus, as in the case of the apostles, but by referring to the work of the Holy Spirit. It should not be necessary at this stage of our argument to explain why saying that a man was brought to faith and freedom "by the operation of the Holy Spirit" is not an empirical assertion, in any unsophisticated sense of the word *empirical*. If a man says this, he may indeed intend to call our attention to certain aspects of how things are in the world, and if we see things as he does, we may also attend to these aspects, which would provide some empirical grounding for his statement. The divine reference ("Holy Spirit") does indicate, for instance, that the new freedom and perspective are received as gifts by the believer and that they are of fundamental importance to him. The divine reference is also at least an indirect reference to Jesus.[1] Christian theology, especially in the classical Protestant tradition, has underscored this reference to Jesus by saying that such an "operation of the Holy Spirit" does not take place apart from the "proclamation of the Word."[2] The story of the man who was free for others even to the point of death, and whose freedom has been contagious, is held up to the listener, who is invited to share in this event.[3] In the context of hearing the Gospel proclaimed, the listener may have an experience of discernment. He may "see" Jesus in a new way and acquire a new perspective upon himself and the whole of life. A long tradition of Christian devotional literature has emphasized the act of historical imagination in which the reader is invited to be "present" at the events of which the Gospel speaks, and this imaginative act has also played its part in much of Christian worship. Although the language of conversion differs from the language of those involved in the Easter event, they function in a remarkably similar manner. The difference between the two lies in the fact that the believers' expression of faith depends logically and historically upon that of the apostles.

The language of faith, whether that of the first apostles or of a modern believer, contains an exclusive element: it claims the universal significance of a particular, historical individual, Jesus of Nazareth. . . . It is evident, however, that there have been other free men in history. We have already suggested some of the dynamics of interpersonal relations which may result from an encounter with a free man. If our reaction is positive, we may feel attracted to him and we may be encouraged to be more free ourselves, or at least challenged to be more free. Our fears may be calmed simply by the presence of one who is unafraid and free from the fears and anxieties which bind us. On the other hand, our reaction may be negative: we may be threatened by a free person; we may feel judged in our insecurity and bondage. This is an odd experience and if we speak of it at all, we will do so with odd words. We might say that there is a certain mystery about it, a mystery of the depths of human personality and relationships.

Jesus of Nazareth may be distinguished, however, from other men who might have a liberating effect upon men. We must grant a "family resemblance" between the language with which we speak of Jesus and the language used to speak of other free men, of course, in order to be able to describe him at all. Nevertheless, we may use a number of the same words in describing two men without denying that the men are actually quite different. When we compared Socrates as portrayed in Plato's *Dialogues,* for example, and Jesus as portrayed

[1] John 15: 26; 16: 14.
[2] Typically, John Calvin, *Institutes,* I, ix, pp. 1–3.
[3] Gal. 3: 1; Heb. 2: 8-9.

in the Gospels, we may say that both men were "free," but we can also see subtle differences. Two different words for "love," *philia* (the attraction of like to like) and *agape* (a love which makes no distinctions and seeks no return on its investment), may serve to indicate something of the difference which we detect between the two descriptions.

The Gospel, however, is not merely about a free man; it is the good news of a free man who has set other men free, first proclaimed by those to whom this had happened. And it has happened again and again during nineteen centuries that, in the context of hearing this apostolic proclamation, men have been liberated. Their response, which the New Testament calls "faith," consists in acknowledging that this has happened by accepting the liberator, Jesus of Nazareth, as the man who defines for them what it means to be a man as the point of orientation for their lives. They are "in Christ," which is to say that their understanding of themselves and their lives and all things is determined by their understanding of Jesus. They are a "new creation" in that this orientation to the whole world is new for them.

There is no empirical ground, however, for the Christian's saying that something of this sort could not happen to a disciple of Socrates. Reading the history of Socrates might conceivably have a liberating effect on a person, who might say that he shared in the freedom of the philosopher. If this were to happen, the Socratic's freedom, presumably, would be defined by the peculiar character of Socrates' freedom. He would acknowledge Socrates as his norm. He would be "in Socrates," let us say, not "in Christ." Perhaps the Socratic, like the Christian, would claim that his was the only valid norm. The exclusiveness of such a claim . . . would express the firmness of his conviction. Understanding the claim of exclusiveness in this way, we take this to be its meaning.

The language of the Gospel contains not only exclusive claims; it has a universal aspect also. It claims that in the history of Jesus of Nazareth something universal, eternal, absolute, something it calls "God," was manifested. . . . Whether formulated in terms of eternity in time, the divine in human form, or the transcendent in the historical, the Gospel is expressed traditionally in language which has its roots in that of the New Testament and which reflects the patristic doctrine of incarnation. Its earliest and most basic form is the confession "Jesus is Lord."[4] This confession is held to be valid regardless of circumstances,[5] but a believer might say that if he never saw any love among men, he would find it almost impossible to make this confession. In that case, part of the meaning of the confession would be to call our attention to the experience of human love. If we grant that human love or its absence is a part of how things are in the world, we can say that the confession has, in this sense, an "empirical" grounding. Our impression from the New Testament, however, is that this confession implies that the believer is saying, "Even if I never saw any love in others, I have nevertheless seen it in the man Jesus and I recognize the claim of love on me." In this case, the empirical anchorage of the confession is in the history of Jesus and in the actions of the believer. The logic of this confession is at least implied by the traditional assertion that there are practical consequences for the man who confesses the Lordship of Jesus, that Christian faith involves a way of life.

[4] Cor. 12:3; Phil. 2:11; O. Cullmann, *Die ersten christlichen Glaubensbekenntnisse* (Zollikon-Zürich: Evang. Verlag, 1943).
[5] Rom. 8:35–39.

Those who first said, "Jesus is Lord," expressed a particular perspective upon life and history.[6] This confession, ascribing universality to a particular man, indicated that faith constituted a certain understanding of self, man, history, and the whole world, and that this universal perspective had its norm in the history of Jesus of Nazareth and Easter. This perspective upon life and the world was understood not as a point of view selected by the believer, but as a "blik"* by which the believer was "grasped" and "held." The perspective of faith was spoken of as a response "drawn from" the believer. The language of the Gospel implies consistently that faith is "given," that the believer cannot and does not want to take any credit for it. By its very nature, faith excludes all boasting.[7]

The issue between those whose perspective on life and history is defined by the history of Jesus and those whose perspective is defined by another reference is notoriously one that cannot be settled by argument. This shows that the function of the Gospel is to indicate not only the norm of the Christian's perspective but also the character of the perspective itself. This perspective cannot be held as one point of view among many. It is not a logical conclusion to a chain of reasoning. Of either of these, a man might say, "This is the position which I chose." The language of faith says, "I did not choose; I was chosen. I did not take this piece of history as the clue to my life and understanding of all history; it took me." The language of faith, by referring to a transcendent element, indicates that something has happened to the believer, rather than that he has done something.

On the other hand, if in response to the proclamation of the free man who has set men free the hearer finds himself to some extent set free, if Jesus of Nazareth has in fact become the historical point of orientation for his own perspective upon history, then this response is certainly his own act also. It is a historical perspective which *he* holds. This paradox finds classic expression in the words of Paul: "I worked harder than any of them, though it was not I, but the grace of God which is with me."[8] This paradox is related linguistically to the peculiarities we have noted in speaking of the effect of a liberated man upon men who are not free. It points to the fact that the new discernment and its accompanying commitment to a way of life is experienced as a response. This perspective arises in connection with hearing the Gospel concerning Jesus of Nazareth and it looks back to him continually as its historical point of orientation. To affirm the Gospel is to express this historical perspective.

The man who says, "Jesus is Lord," is saying that the history of Jesus and of what happened on Easter has exercised a liberating effect upon him, and that he has been so grasped by it that it has become the historical norm of his perspective upon life. His confession is a notification of this perspective and a recommendation to his listener to see Jesus, the world, and himself in this same way and to act accordingly. It is an important perspective and it can be distinguished from other points of view. We may illustrate the difference by comparing the perspective of Christian faith and the point of view of the man whose perspective upon life is founded on the life of his nation. The nationalist understands himself

---

[6] Acts 2:36–42; cf. Phil. 2:1–11.
* [See five paragraphs later for explanation of this term.–Eds.]
[7] Rom. 3:27; I Cor. 1:27–29; Gal. 6:14.
[8] I Cor. 15:10.

first of all as a patriot and he defines his freedom in the context of loyalty to his country. He can understand the Gospel only as making a relative claim at most. He may allow that there is some freedom to be found in Jesus and in loyalty to him, but it is secondary to his freedom as a citizen. For the Christian, however, the situation will be reversed. His assertion, "Jesus is Lord," expresses the fact that Jesus has become his point of orientation, with the consequence that he is freed from acknowledging final loyalty to his nation, family, church, or any other person and is liberated for service to these other centers of relative loyalty. Because he sees not only his own history but the history of all men in the light of the one history of Jesus of Nazareth and Easter, he will not rest content when his nation, family, or church seek to live only for themselves; he will try to set them in the service of others.

He who says, "Jesus is Lord," says that Jesus' freedom has been contagious and has become the criterion for his life, public and private. As Jesus was led, because of his freedom, into the midst of social and political conflict, so it is with one who shares his freedom. The Gospel asserts that Jesus is Lord of the whole world.[9] This means that the freedom for which the Christian has been set free allows him to see the whole world in its light. When the Christian says that Jesus' Lordship is not limited to the church, he is saying that he understands all free men, regardless of where they may say they have found their freedom, as having "caught" their freedom from the same source as he. He will regard them as the ten cleansed lepers of Luke 17:11ff., who were all set free from their burden, although only one acknowledged Jesus as his liberator. If someone were to object that Jesus is the Lord and Saviour only of believers, he would be saying that he does not see the freedom of unbelievers with the perspective arising from his discernment and commitment as a Christian. The difference is more than a case of theological hairsplitting. It is empirically significant and it has led to serious human consequences in history.

This interpretation of Christian faith is related to Hare's concept of *blik*. The language of faith expressed in the Gospel may be understood if it is seen to express, define, or commend a basic presupposition by which a man lives and acts in the world of men. That is why we call it a historical perspective. As Hare has pointed out, a "blik" is not an explanation of the world or of anything else, but without a "blik" there can be no explanations.[10] He appeals to Hume in support of his conclusion that "the difference between *bliks* about the world cannot be settled by observation of what happens in the world." Although the assertions of the Gospel are meaningless if they are taken empirically, they do have a use. As Hare suggests, "The earth is weak and all the inhabitants thereof: I bear up the pillars of it," has a meaning, if it is taken as the formulation of a "blik." As an explanation it would "obviously be ludicrous. We no longer believe in God as an Atlas—*nous n'avons pas besoin de cette hypothèse.*"[11] The "blik" of the Christian finds its adequate expression in the Gospel, however, and it is related always, if sometimes indirectly, to the history of Jesus of Nazareth. This is why we call this perspective *historical*.

---

[9] Matt. 28:18; Eph. 1:20–22; Phil. 2:9–11.
[10] R. M. Hare, essay in *New Essays in Philosophical Theology*, ed. A. Flew and A. MacIntyre (London: SCM [Student Christian Movement] Press, 1955), p. 101.
[11] *Ibid.*

Ramsey has suggested how a "blik" arises. It comes out of what he calls a situation of discernment or disclosure, a situation which is seen suddenly in a new way demanding a commitment of the viewer. The languages of revelation, Easter, the "illumination of the Holy Spirit," and conversion reflect just such a situation. The decisive discernment situation for Christianity is Easter and the Easter proclamation concerning Jesus of Nazareth. Men may come to Christian faith in all sorts of ways, of course. A man may have begun to be a Christian from reading the book of Genesis, or he may have come through a more distant point of entry. When he has "arrived," however, when he has heard and accepted the whole of what the Gospel has to say, the norm of his perspective will always be the history of Jesus and Easter. Because the sources for this history present Jesus as fulfilling the destiny of his people in his own life, his history receives illumination from that of the people from which he came, but in the last analysis, the Christian will read Genesis, Exodus, and all the rest of biblical history in the light of the history of the Gospels.

Our interpretation has underscored an element in Christian faith not immediately evident when it is considered as a "blik" or the consequence of a disclosure situation. We pointed out that on Easter the disciples came to see Jesus in a *new* way. That implies that they *had* seen Jesus in an *old* way. Their new perspective depended upon prior acquaintance with Jesus as a free man. Even Paul had some prior knowledge concerning Jesus. Conversion to the Christian historical perspective depends in part upon some acquaintance with the history of Jesus. To speak of a sheer discernment, whatever that would be, resting on no prior acquaintance with at least some elements of the situation in which it arose, would be like speaking of a sheer experience concerning which we could not say what was experienced. The various illustrations which we have used along the way make the same point. Lincoln's Gettysburg Address presupposed some awareness of the Civil War and the American Revolution. Hamlet's recognition of his father's ghost rested on prior acquaintance with his father. So Easter faith depended on the disciples' memory of Jesus, and Christian faith requires minimal acquaintance with the Gospel narratives.

Miles has spoken of faith as the way of silence qualified by parables. Certainly the Christian possesses no special sources for the scientific description of the universe. Before such questions as whether there is some absolute being, even "Being itself," which is "behind" or "beyond" all we know and are, some final "ground and end of all created things," he will be wise to remain silent. He may qualify his silence, however, by telling something besides a parable. What he has to tell is the history of Jesus and the strange story of how his freedom became contagious on Easter.

Finally, Braithwaite has taken religious statements to be assertions of an intention to act in a certain way, together with the entertainment of certain stories. As far as it goes, this analysis agrees with our interpretation. We would clarify the "intention" with such words as *discernment* and *commitment,* and we would define the "certain way" as a response to and a reflection of the way of Jesus of Nazareth. It is a way characterized by a freedom "caught" from him. We would go further than this, however. In order to live in the "freedom for which Christ has set us free," we need indeed to "entertain" again and again that piece of history, for it does not just provide an encouragement to walk in the way of freedom; it is the context in which the light dawns anew and in which that freedom proves again to be contagious for us. Braithwaite's presentation of the relationship between "entertaining" the story and the "intention to behave" is not adequate to the language of the Gospel of Easter, helpful as it has been in indicating of what sort that language is, because he has not done justice to the historical aspect of the Gospel and has completely neglected the peculiar "story" of Easter.

THE LANGUAGE OF NEW TESTAMENT CHRISTOLOGY

We have seen that Jesus' freedom was freedom for his neighbor, that he was free from self-concern and therefore open to the concerns of others. We might speak of his solidarity with men: he "put himself in their shoes"; he carried their burdens. In addition, by daring to regard men classed as "sinners" as forgiven and by proclaiming their forgiveness, he convinced them that they were released from the burden of guilt and the consequences of their acts.[12] But what can it mean to say, "He *died* for our sins"? The emphasis is on his death, but we need to remember that theology, as well as the New Testament, speaks of the "cross" or the death of Jesus as the consequence of his life. "The cross" and other references to Jesus' death became summary ways of speaking of his whole history, as indeed his end seemed to his disciples, after the fact, to have been foreshadowed in all of his life. Since his life was one of solidarity with men, compassion for them, mercy toward their weakness and wrong, it is not surprising that his death, which was the consequence of his freedom to be related to men in this way, was spoken of as a death "for us." His death (which could so easily have been avoided if he had taken the way of caution, calculation, and self-interest) was regarded as the measure of the freedom for which he set other men free. The man for whom the history of Jesus and of his liberation of his disciples on Easter is a discernment situation of prime importance will say, "He died for me, for my forgiveness and freedom." When the New Testament says that he died not only for "our" sins, "but also for the sins of the whole world,"[13] it reflects the fact that Jesus was free for every man, those who did not acknowledge him as well as those that did, and it articulates a perspective by which all men, not just believers, are seen.

On the basis of these considerations, we can clarify the dilemma posed by Bultmann: "Does he [Jesus] help me because he is God's Son, or is he the Son of God because he helps me?"[14] The question as it stands only invites confusion. We may say that Jesus helps me because of "what" he is ("Son of God"), and we may also say that such titles as "Son of God" were given to him because of the help he provided. When we say both of these, however, we are using the words "Son of God" in two different ways and are also playing tricks with the slippery word "is." The problem is more clearly expressed if we ask: Does the Gospel speak of a "saving" event which has happened already and which is reported to the listener, who is invited to acknowledge and give thanks for it (a so-called "objective" atonement), or does it announce the possibility of a

---

[12] E.g., the story of the woman taken in adultery, usually found in John 8:3–11.
[13] I John 2:2.
[14] Rudolf Bultmann, *Glauben und Verstehen* (Tübingen: J. C. B. Mohr, 1952), Vol. II, p. 252; *Essays Philosophical and Theological*, p. 280.

"saving" event which takes place in the act of acknowledging it (a so-called "subjective" atonement)? Does the Gospel announce a reality accomplished, or a possibility to be actualized by the hearer? This way of phrasing the question makes it clear that we are speaking about *words* (the Gospel) spoken presumably by a believer.

Now of what precisely does the believer speak? He speaks in part of a piece of history, which is certainly in the past. It is the history of a free man and the peculiar character of his freedom. But the Gospel goes on to speak of the moment in which this freedom became contagious in the Easter event, and the speaker, by his very speaking and by the way in which he does it, indicates that this contagious freedom has also touched him. All this constitutes an invitation to the listener to share this discernment and commitment. Perhaps (but also perhaps not) the listener will "see" for the first time, or he will see again, or he will see more clearly than he has in the past. The light will dawn; he will be possessed of a new way of seeing himself, the world, and all things, and he will "catch" something of the contagious freedom of Jesus.

Now, when was he liberated? Or rather, when will he say he was liberated? He will surely say that he became free at the time he acquired his new perspective. But he will be even readier to point to his liberator. It belongs to the language of a discernment situation that we speak of that situation as containing already ("objectively"), prior to its becoming the occasion of a discernment, what was only "seen" at a later time. As the lover might say to his beloved, "I must have passed you a thousand times and spoken to you a hundred, and there you were, the most beautiful girl in the world, and I did not see you. And then, that night, all of a sudden I realized." She did not become the most beautiful girl in the world for him only "that night." He will insist that she always was that, and that he, poor fool, woke up only later to the fact.[15] Such is the language of the "objective" liberation of mankind in the death and resurrection of Jesus. To insist that this is incorrect and that the actual liberation takes place in the moment of believing, which is perfectly true in a psychological sense, is to misunderstand the language appropriate to a situation of discernment which leads one to a commitment embracing all of life.

An analysis of the language of the Christology of "call and response" presented in Chapter 2 [of *The Secular Meaning of the Gospel*] confirms our conclusions about the function of biblical-Christological statements. The statements that Jesus was "called by God" to be the one man who was free to be for all the others, that he "bore the divine election" of Israel to be a light for the Gentiles, that his history "was the enactment of God's eternal plan and purpose," if taken to be cosmological assertions, are meaningless in the terms of the empirical attitudes in which this study is grounded. These statements, however, belong after the words "I believe," and the word *I* is important. The statements, in the form of a confession of faith, reflect or suggest a situation in which the history of Jesus has been or might be seen in a new way. They also express the commitment of the speaker to what he has now "seen." To speak of Jesus' "call" or "election" is to speak of Jesus as one with a history which

---

[15] The case of "love at first sight" is a compressed variation. The "prior acquaintance," which we have already discussed, would in this case be prior acquaintance with other people and prior knowledge of the fact of "falling in love," together with at least the first impression of the beloved as a person distinct from these other people.

is different from that of any other man, and of Jesus as one who is "set apart" from all the others and for all the others. As the language of one who, in seeing Jesus as the free man who has set others free, has also been set free himself, the statement is appropriate and logically meaningful. This clarifies also the statements concerning Jesus' "response," for his response was only the other side of the coin. To speak of Jesus' "response" is another way of speaking of his history as a free man. Since according to the New Testament his response of obedience was authenticated as perfect obedience by the event of Easter, we may say that it is the contagious aspect of his freedom which authenticates the language which the believer uses of Jesus. To say that Jesus embodies the plan of God and that he was perfectly faithful to this election is to make the sort of final statement which Ramsey says takes the form "I'm I." In this case, however, the "I" is what "I" have become as a result of the liberation arising from hearing the story of Jesus, his life, his death, and Easter.

Finally, the "eschatological" hope, in this interpretation of the language of the Gospel, is the conviction that the freedom which the believer has seen in Jesus and which has become contagious for him, and the reconciliation which he sees to be associated with this freedom, will prevail on this earth among all men. That is his conviction, not a prediction. To say that this hope is "eschatological" is to say that one would die rather than abandon it. It indicates the unqualified, undebatable aspect of the Christian's historical perspective.

As Hare points out, there is no arguing about "bliks." Another man may find some other piece of history to be his key to the understanding of life and history: that of the Buddha or Mary Baker Eddy. Or his perspective might be informed by some idea or ideology. It might be a dialectic of history and the Communist Manifesto, an eighteenth-century Declaration of Independence, or the economic theory of Adam Smith. He who has his freedom from Jesus will not agree, however, with those who would say that all sources of freedom are the same. The fact remains that the history of Jesus is not the same as the history of the Buddha, the Communist Revolution, or Henry Ford. It is one thing to say that Christians have always taken the history of Jesus to be indispensable and definitive for their faith, but it is quite another to think that this "uniqueness" can somehow be proved. Christians have never been able, however (and when they were at their best have not tried), to *prove* the "superiority" of their historical perspective over other perspectives. Claims of "finality" are simply the language appropriate to articulating a historical perspective. The logic of these claims can be illuminated by setting them alongside the statement "I'm I."

The meaning of the Gospel is its use on the lips of those who proclaim it. The Christian has seen a man of remarkable and particular freedom, and this freedom has become contagious for him, as it was for the apostles on Easter. The history of this man and of Easter has become a situation of discernment, reorienting his perspective upon the world. If he should have occasion to tell that story, therefore, he can only do so to express, define, or commend this historical perspective, for this is the secular meaning of that Gospel.

That assertion is itself, of course, a recommendation to the reader to see the language of faith in the way expressed, on the assumption that there is a possibility of his holding empirical attitudes similar to those in the light of which this interpretation has been made. This commendation may also be made in the form of two principles which sum up what we have done:

(1) *Statements of faith are to be interpreted, by means of the modified verification principle, as statements which express, describe, or commend a particular way of seeing the world, other men, and oneself, and the way of life appropriate to such a perspective.* A restatement of the Gospel should allow the logical structure of its language to become clear. With this first principle we indicate that we share certain of the empirical attitudes reflected in the "revolution" in modern philosophy. This principle more than meets the concern of the theological "left" to accept the modern criticism of ancient ways of thinking.

(2) *The norm of the Christian perspective is the series of events to which the New Testament documents testify, centering in the life, death, and resurrection of Jesus of Nazareth.* We have approached the problem of Christology by way of an investigation of the peculiar way in which Christians talked from the first about the man Jesus of Nazareth. Following our first principle, we explored the logic of the language of the New Testament authors concerning Jesus. Our aim has been to discover the *meaning* of their words and to find appropriate and clear words with which to express that meaning today, asking after a functional equivalence between a contemporary Christology and the language of the New Testament. With our second principle, we acknowledge the concern of the theological right wing that Christology be central, and that the norm of Christology be Jesus of Nazareth as the subject of the apostolic witness. These two principles have guided us in the constructive task of interpreting the Gospel in a way which may be understood by a Christian whose empirical attitudes are such as to lead us to call him a secular man.

The Word as Liberation
Daniel Berrigan

Daniel Berrigan (1921–   ) is an American Jesuit priest, who recently served a jail sentence for burning draft records in a protest against the war in Southeast Asia. He is the author of many books, including *False Gods, Real Men, They Call Us Dead Men,* and *Consequences: Truth And . . . .*

Christians do not search the scriptures for the sake of justifying their life or law of conduct, for even the devil, we are told, finds words of comfort in God's word. The saying is a salutary one. The motive that drives us back to our sources is a far different one from that of pride; we go to this word in fear and trembling, knowing that the word itself is a judgment, a two-edged sword, as Paul declares. The logos is still a crisis; that is, the word is not meant to offer comfort to the slovenly, to blur the edge of life, to set up a no man's land in which we are free to wander at will, pursuing our pagan adventures unhindered.

From Daniel Berrigan, "The Word as Liberation," in *No Bars to Manhood* (New York, 1970), pp. 44–50. Copyright © 1970 by Daniel Berrigan. Reprinted by permission of Doubleday and Company, Inc.

The word of God is one of crisis. It confronts men, putting their acts under the scrutiny of the God of history, there to be judged. We are familiar with this. We know, too, that out of submission to God's word issue the deepest streams of joy, that this word liberates us from pharisaism, fear, dread of life, the multiple power of death in this world.

But even this is not the deepest meaning of His word to us. That meaning, I take it, is bound up with history and this world, to the degree that His word becomes our own—that we recognize in the Bible our own people, speaking our own tongue, prophets and saints, men and women who lived to the depths the common life of man, with all that implies for our own darkest hours. And finally: The word that comes to us is the mysterious voice of a brother and friend, God's Son, living our life, beckoning to us from the common condition—marketplace, family, courtroom, garden, agony, and death itself.

God's word thus urges forward and extends the range of our human experience. In its light, moreover, all suppositions about what it is to be religious, all self-justification and self-reliance, all obscene olympianism based on technology, race, and religion itself, are confronted and defeated.

One of these invitations of His word—into exodus, into freedom, into death—one scarcely knows how to characterize it—comes to us toward the end of John's gospel. The Lord is summoned into a courtroom, as He declares, to give testimony of the truth. The truth itself is on trial. It must not be presumed, before the fact, that God is speaking the truth; so men say, so the human powers decree. God must submit to the probing of man. It is for God to render account of Himself. So He answers the summons; the docket of Jesus Christ is opened before His fellows.

And this is no mock trial. Its outcome may possibly grant him new prestige, a new and cleansed people, grateful for the truth He has vindicated in the breach. Or the trial may hand Him over to death.

We know that in fact the second outcome occurred. The Lord was convicted and died the death of a malefactor. But more to our point, I would think, is the extraordinary self-conscious and deliberate manner in which the Lord entered upon the courtroom scene, and made it His own scene. He steeled himself for the crisis, He added a cubit to His stature. So that out of Pilate's court come some of the most profound and disturbing of His self-revelations. Consider, for instance: *For this have I been born, for this have I come into the world, to bear witness to the truth.* I suggest to you that the life of Jesus would have lacked something of its majesty and strength had He not stood in the court of Pilate and endured the proceedings there. I suggest, moreover, that we are offered during the trial of Jesus an example that reappears constantly and mysteriously throughout history, at the edge of life and death where the martyrs walk and let their blood. That is to say, the truth is never fully itself apart from the conditions of witness; to be itself, the truth must be summoned to accounting by the powers and dominations. It must endure crisis, it must be purified in the furnace of this world. It is not enough to declare, "I embody the truth," or "I speak the truth." Indeed, such claims are historically very nearly useless. They fall together with innumerable other such claims into the common wastebin of time. Every malcontent and charlatan and quack has claimed the truth. But the range of risk is narrowed, the issue is met, when one testifies under pressure, amid danger, to the sovereignty of a truth that he does not claim or pre-empt but that literally possesses him.

It is necessary above all to be concrete when we speak of these things. Men, even good men, are commonly disposed to submit to the slavery of the actual; they literally cannot imagine themselves in any life situation other than the one in which they live. They inherit a style, a culture, a religion—and they prolong such forms—because they are there; useful, comfortable, logical, venerable. Their minds wear the costumes of their ancestors, a clothing that was once befitting, literally, but is now simply a folklore or a fakeout. So they call a folklore a religion and a fakeout an adult life. And, alas, who shall disenchant them? But let it at least be said, as the Lord implies from His Roman courtroom, such lives as these must not make large claims to the truth.

We can think, for example, of the differing styles of truth offered by Pope Pius XI and Gandhi. They were contemporaries; both were deeply troubled by the course of events; both urged peace on the world. But one man knew at firsthand prison and fasts and marches, the immediate anguish of the masses. When he spoke, he spoke from the villages, the impoverished homes, the prisons —which are conditions of the common life of men in struggle. The other spoke from a baroque palace in the Eternal City. Today, though his words remain unimpeachable, and his tomb is honored, he is all but forgotten. Gandhi's ashes are scattered to the sea, but his words and examples are among the few spiritual legacies that survive the horrors of the past thirty years.

You may recall (we are speaking of witness and the truth) that in 1934 Gandhi was voyaging to England to plead the cause of the freedom of the Indian masses. Pius XI refused to receive him in audience, and Winston Churchill referred to Gandhi contemptuously in Commons as "that half-naked savage." But Gandhi went on to Britain to live among the very people whom his boycott in India was threatening—the mill workers of Liverpool and Birmingham. He moved through their streets, explaining to the people in the simplest possible terms that the cause of the Indian weavers and of the British factory workers was the same cause. And they understood, and gave him a tumultuous welcome, though their own livelihood had been placed in jeopardy by Gandhi's boycott.

Now, when a man consents to live and die for the truth, he sets in motion spiritual rhythms whose outward influences are, in the nature of things, simply immeasurable. I take the courts as one symbol of Gandhi's method. What indeed did he hope for, from that vantage point? He hoped to say to others something that had come to have the deepest meaning for himself. Out of a virile disregard for personal danger and stress, he wished to make it possible for others to live— to be conscious, to be freed of demons, to welcome their brothers. The point, I would think, for Gandhi and Jesus, is not that men would agree with them, or do the same things they did. The point is that others would come to a deepened consciousness; that their sense of existence and human issues would be sharpened to the point where they would "do their thing"—a good thing, a human thing, as they were doing theirs.

The eminent scholar, C. H. Dodd, writing of Christ before Pilate, says:

It is significant that the words we are considering, on witnessing to the truth, are placed in the context of a trial scene. Where the truth is, there men are judged, and it is only the "man who does the truth" who can stand the scrutiny of the light. So here, John treats the question of judgment with typical irony. The Pharisees had sat in judgment on the claims of Jesus and in the end found the tables turned on them; so here Pilate believes himself to be sitting in judgment on Jesus; yet it is himself who is revealed as judged.

Americans who can bear equally with the sight of burning children are enraged and baffled by the sight of burning draft files. Moreover, Americans in the seventies are unable to create new forms of civilized political power to express our tardy sense that a bad war is being waged with our money, in our name, by our sons. We have declared a moratorium on radical or disobedient protest, and have placed our hopes, with a certain despair, in the promise of three successive Presidents to control, mitigate, and end the war. Meantime peace talks opened in Paris; but Americans and Vietnamese in enormous numbers continued to lose their lives. Our political future is clouded, to say the least; it may well be that the next years will rest in the hands of those who believe that Vietnam has established a virtuous norm of international conduct, that despite its cost, it justifies further military adventuring.

After more than four years of struggle, perplexity, and doubt, my own course is at last clear. In a sense, I claim a certain sorry advantage over most of those who have yet to choose the place and time of their response to American violence, a response that will embody their existence and carry their lives captive, in bonds to a choice, in a direction they cannot yet know. Such an hour as Catonsville may still come to them—we have every reason to believe that the price of peace will escalate grievously in the months ahead. And nothing in our history makes such a prospect easily bearable.

We have assumed the name of peacemakers, but we have been, by and large, unwilling to pay any significant price. And because we want the peace with half a heart and half a life and will, the war, of course, continues, because the waging of war, by its nature, is total—but the waging of peace, by our own cowardice, is partial. So a whole will and a whole heart and a whole national life bent toward war prevail over the velleities of peace. In every national war since the founding of the republic we have taken for granted that war shall exact the most rigorous cost, and that the cost shall be paid with cheerful heart. We take it for granted that in wartime families will be separated for long periods, that men will be imprisoned, wounded, driven insane, killed on foreign shores. In favor of such wars, we declare a moratorium on every normal human hope—for marriage, for community, for friendship, for moral conduct toward strangers and the innocent. We are instructed that deprivation and discipline, private grief and public obedience are to be our lot. And we obey. And we bear with it—because bear we must—because war is war, and good war or bad, we are stuck with it and its cost.

But what of the price of peace? I think of the good, decent, peace-loving people I have known by the thousands, and I wonder. How many of them are so afflicted with the wasting disease of normalcy that, even as they declare for the peace, their hands reach out with an instinctive spasm in the direction of their loved ones, in the direction of their comforts, their home, their security, their income, their future, their plans—that five-year plan of studies, that ten-year plan of professional status, that twenty-year plan of family growth and unity, that fifty-year plan of decent life and honorable natural demise. "Of course, let us have the peace," we cry, "but at the same time let us have normalcy, let us lose nothing, let our lives stand intact, let us know neither prison nor ill repute nor disruption of ties." And because we must encompass this and protect that, and because at all costs—at all costs—our hopes must march on schedule, and because it is unheard of that in the name of peace a sword should fall, disjoining that fine and cunning web that our lives have woven, because it is unheard of that good men should suffer injustice or families be sundered or good repute be lost—because of this we cry peace and cry peace, and there is no peace. There is no peace because there are no peacemakers. There are no makers of peace because the making of peace is at least as costly as the making of war—at least as exigent, at least as disruptive, at least as liable to bring disgrace and prison and death in its wake.

Consider, then, the words of our Savior—Who speaks to us gravely, with the burden of His destiny heavy upon Him, perplexed as we are, solicitous of heart, anxious with a kind of merciless compassion—that we comprehend lucidly, joyously, the cost of discipleship:

You have heard it said to men of old, you shall not kill, whoever kills be liable to judgement. But I say to you that every one who is angry with his brother shall be liable to judgement.
You have heard it said, an eye for an eye and a tooth for a tooth. But I say to you, do not resist one who is evil. But if any one strike you on the right cheek, turn to him the other also.
Blessed are you when men revile you and persecute you and utter all kinds of evil against you falsely on my account. Rejoice and be glad, for your reward is great in heaven, for so men persecuted the prophets who were before you.

And finally,

Pilate said to him, You are a king, then? Jesus answered, You say that I am a king. For this was I born, and for this have I come into the world, to bear witness to the truth. Everyone who is of the truth hears my voice.

The Spiritual Meaning of Hamlet
Martin Lings

Martin Lings (1909–   ) was born in England and now holds the post of keeper of oriental manuscripts and printed books at the British Museum. He was educated at Oxford and London Universities and has taught at the University of Kaunas, Lithuania, and Cairo University. He is the author of *Ancient Beliefs and Modern Superstitions, Shakespeare in the Light of Sacred Art,* and *The Elements and Other Poems.*

THE INTELLECTUALITY OF SACRED ART

In the last few decades there has been a considerable increase of interest in the Middle Ages, which is no doubt partly due to a reaction, but it is also, much more, a case of ignorance giving way to knowledge. In another sense, it is simply a rising to the surface of something that has always been there and is always

From Martin Lings, *Shakespeare in the Light of Sacred Art* (London, 1966), pp. 11–14, 27–41. Reprinted by permission of George Allen & Unwin Ltd.

being rediscovered. Could it not be said that wherever the Middle Ages have not ceased to be accessible, wherever despite the barrier of the Renaissance they have always remained with us, as in the poetry of Dante, for instance, or—to take a more immediately accessible and inescapable example—as in their architecture, their superiority has always been felt at heart? This feeling implies also, if only subconsciously, the acknowledgment of a more general superiority, for it is quite impossible that the great Norman and Gothic cathedrals should have sprung from an age that had no inward excellence to correspond to these superlative outward manifestations.

One of the particular reasons for the present increase of interest in the Middle Ages is in itself highly significant: during the last fifty years Europeans have taken much more interest in the art of other civilizations than ever before, and this has no doubt uprooted many prejudices and opened the door to a certain freshness and objectivity of judgment. Having come to know some of the best examples of Hindu, Chinese and Japanese art and then as it were returning to their own civilization, many people find that their outlook has irrevocably changed. After looking at a great Chinese landscape, for example, where this world appears like a veil of illusion beyond which, almost visibly, lies the Infinite and Eternal Reality, or after having been given a glimpse of that same Reality through a statue of the Buddha, they find it difficult to take seriously a painting such as Raphael's famous Madonna, or Michelangelo's fresco of the Creation, not to speak of his sculpture, and Leonardo also fails to satisfy them. But they find that they *can* take very seriously, more seriously than before, some of the early Sienese paintings such as Lippo Memmi's Annunciation, for example, or the statuary and stained glass of Chartres Cathedral, or the XIIth and XIIIth century mosaics in St. Mark's at Venice, or the ikons of the Orthodox Church.

The reason why mediaeval art can bear comparison with Oriental art as no other Western art can is undoubtedly that the mediaeval outlook, like that of the Oriental civilizations, was intellectual. It considered this world above all as the shadow or symbol of the next, man as the shadow or symbol of God; and such an attitude, to be operative, presupposes the presence of intellectuals, for earthly things can only be referred back to their spiritual archetypes through the faculty of intellectual perception, the insight which pierces through the symbol to the universal reality that lies beyond. In the theocratic civilizations, if an artist himself was not an intellectual, he none the less obeyed the canons of art[1] which had been established on an intellectual basis.

A mediaeval portrait is above all a portrait of the Spirit shining from behind a human veil. In other words, it is as a window opening from the particular on to the universal, and while being enshrined in its own age and civilization as eminently typical of a particular period and place, it has at the same time, in virtue of this opening, something that is neither of the East nor of the West, nor of any one age more than another.

[1] Sacred art in the full sense of the term is art which conforms to canons laid down not by individuals but by the spiritual authority of the civilization in question, as was the case with mediaeval Christian architecture, Gregorain chant, ancient Greek drama, Japanese No plays, Hindu temple dancing and music—to name only a few examples—and such art is always something of a criterion and also a potential source of inspiration for other less central works of art.

If Renaissance art lacks an opening on to the universal and is altogether imprisoned in its own epoch, this is because its outlook is humanistic; and humanism, which is a revolt of the reason against the intellect, considers man and other earthly objects entirely for their own sakes as if nothing lay behind them. In painting the Creation, for example, Michelangelo treats Adam not as a symbol but as an independent reality; and since he does not paint man in the image of God, the inevitable result is that he paints God in the image of man. There is more divinity underlying Simone Martini's painting of Saint Francis than there is in Michelangelo's representation of the Creator Himself.

Shakespeare was born less than three months after Michelangelo's death, and the two are often spoken of in the same breath as being among "the greatest geniuses of the Renaissance." Yet how does Shakespeare stand in the light of an intellectual approach which enhances, if possible, our respect for Dante, but which greatly diminishes our estimate of several others whose pre-eminence had long gone unquestioned? The following chapters are an attempt to answer this question in some detail; but a general answer can be given immediately. Let us quote, as touchstone, a masterly summing up of the difference between Renaissance art and mediaeval art: "When standing in front of a Romanesque or Gothic cathedral, we feel that we are at the centre of the world; when standing in front of a Renaissance, Baroque or Rococo church we are merely conscious of being in Europe."[2] Now without trying to give Shakespeare so essential a place in the art of Christendom as the place which is held by the mediaeval cathedrals or by *The Divine Comedy,* could it not be said that to be present at an adequate performance of *King Lear* is not merely to watch a play but to witness, mysteriously, the whole history of mankind?

But this remark could not possibly be made about the majority of Shakespeare's writings, and if we wish to form any estimate of the mature dramatist whose outlook bestowed on him a universality that is a prolongation of the universality of the Middle Ages, the first thing to be done is to set most of the plays on one side for the moment so as not to confuse the issue. Few writers can have developed so much during their period of authorship as Shakespeare did. By the end of the XVIth century he had written some twenty-two plays; but none of these can be said to represent his maturity, though some of them,[3] in various ways, give an unmistakable foretaste of what was to come. Just after 1600 there was a sharp and lasting change, not in orientation—that change had come before—but in intensity. It was as if he had suddenly come to grips with the universe after having contemplated it for some time with a half-detached serenity. From being in earnest, he had come to be in very deadly earnest. This change is forced on our attention first of all by *Hamlet;* and except for one or two backward glances, mostly in the direction of *Romeo and Juliet* and *Henry IV,* the scope of this book lies inclusively between *Hamlet* and Shakespeare's last complete play, *The Tempest.*

. . .

[2] Frithjof Schuon, *The Transcendent Unity of Religions* (Faber, 1953) p. 84, *note.*
[3] *Romeo and Juliet,* for example, *A Midsummer Night's Dream, Henry IV, As You Like It,* and *Twelfth Night.*

HAMLET

The basic theme of *Hamlet* is summed up in the Prince's own words:

> *Virtue cannot so inoculate our old stock*
> *but we shall relish of it.*   (III, I).

This means : "It is no use plastering one or two superficial virtues over our old stock, that is, the original sin which permeates our nature, since in spite of all such virtues, we shall still continue to reek of the old stock." But in order to express fully what is in Hamlet's mind here we must add : "There is only one thing which can effectively wipe out the stench of our old stock and that is *revenge,* or in other words a complete reversal of the state of affairs which caused the Fall."

In its immediate impact upon us sacred art[4] is like a stone thrown into water. The ever widening ripples illustrate the limitless repercussions that are made, or can be made, upon the soul by this impact, fraught as it is with several meanings at different levels. One meaning can, as we have seen, open out on to another deeper meaning[5] that lies beyond it. In this way sacred art often conveys far more than it appears to convey, far more sometimes even than the mind in question is conscious of or could take in by way of ordinary didactic teaching.

Needless to say, the initial impact itself must captivate the mind and the emotions. According to the literal meaning of *Hamlet*, our sense of Queen Gertrude's culpability goes far beyond the sin of marriage to a dead husband's brother, just as we are given many strong and obvious reasons why Hamlet should kill Claudius, enough at any rate even to make us forget for the moment that revenge is unchristian. None the less, it would be true to say that there is no common measure between the literal meaning of this play and the deep sense of urgency that Shakespeare instils into us. There is something mysteriously unfathomable about the Queen's guilt. Moreover, so long as we are in the theatre we are not far from feeling that revenge is the most important thing in the world; and we are right, for there *is* nothing more important, and indeed nothing more Christian, than what revenge stands for here.

The Ghost's revelation to Hamlet is, as regards its symbolic meaning, like a puzzle with a few missing pieces which it is not difficult for us to supply in the light of those pieces which we are given—the garden with its fruit trees, the serpent, the guilty woman. The *Genesis* narrative is undoubtedly here. There is also, explicitly, the first-fruit of the Fall, the sin of fratricide. But the Fall itself, was in fact a murder also, the slaying or making mortal of Adam by the serpent, and the forbidden fruit was the "poison" through which that murder was effected.

The Queen is not merely Hamlet's mother; she is his whole ancestral line going back to Eve herself; and inasmuch as she is Eve, she represents, in general, the fallen human soul, especially in its passive aspect. In other words, she represents that passivity which in man's primordial state was turned towards Heaven

[4] Shakespeare's plays cannot be considered as sacred art in the full and central sense of the term, but they can be considered as an extension of it, and as partaking both of its qualities and its function.

[5] Needless to say, not every detail in this text has a deeper meaning. Conversely, there are some details which only make good sense on the deepest plane of all.

and which after it lost contact with the Spirit has come more or less under the sway of the devil or, in the words of the play, having *sated itself in a celestial bed* has come to *prey on garbage*. Like the father and son in *Henry IV*, mother and son here can each be taken separately as representing "Everyman," but above all they are to be taken together as constituting fallen human soul, Hamlet himself being the personification of its active aspect—its conscience and its intelligence. The attitude of the son towards his mother, which many people consider to be something of an enigma and which has prompted more than one grotesque explanation, is amply explained if we consider that allegorically mother and son are one person, different faculties of one and the same soul.

Unlike the writer of epic, the dramatist has very limited space at his disposal. Consequently he often chooses to build a house of more than one storey. In *Hamlet* the soul is not only represented by the Prince and his mother; its state is also reflected in the condition of the country. Not that there is actually a subplot of civil war as in *Henry IV,* but none the less

> Something is rotten in the state of Denmark

and *The time is out of joint* and needs to be *set right*. Moreover, as a parallel to the whole action of the play, the soul of King Hamlet is being purified in Purgatory.

But the dead King has also another aspect. Just as Adam was not only the man who fell but also the most perfect of all creatures, made in the image of God, so also King Hamlet, who in a sense corresponds to Adam, is not only a purgatorial pilgrim but also a symbol of man's lost Edenic state. It is in virtue of this that he refers to his own marriage with Gertrude as a *celestial bed,* and is spoken of by Hamlet in terms of human perfection:

> A combination and a form indeed
> Where every god did seem to set his seal
> To give the world assurance of a man.   (III, 4).

It is also in virtue of this aspect that he acts as spiritual guide to his son.

The difference between simple piety and mysticism might almost be summed up by saying that the averagely pious man looks at the story of the Garden of Eden for the most part objectively, whether he takes it literally or allegorically. The mystic, on the other hand, looks at it subjectively as something which intensely, directly and presently concerns himself. Again, the averagely pious man is aware of the existence of the devil, but in fact, if not in theory, he imagines him to be more or less harmless and has little idea of the extent of his own subservience to him. In general he is extremely subject to the illusion of neutrality. But the mystic knows that most of what seems neutral is harmful, and that *one may smile and smile and be a villain.* The Ghost initiates Hamlet into the Mysteries by conveying to him the truth of the Fall not as a remote historical fact but as an immediate life-permeating reality, an acute pain which will not allow his soul a moment's rest; and every man in fact is in exactly the same situation as the Prince of Denmark, did he but know it, that is, if he were not

> Duller . . . than the fat weed
> That roots itself at ease on Lethe wharf.   (I, 4).

What the Ghost says to Hamlet could almost be paraphrased: "Latterly you have been feeling that *all is not well.* I come to confirm your worst suspicions and to show you the remedy. Since man has been robbed by the devil of his birthright, there is only one way for him to regain what is lost and that is by taking revenge upon the robber."

With all the ardour of the novice, in answer to his father's last injunction *Remember me!* the Prince replies:

> *Remember thee?*
> *Yea, from the table of my memory*
> *I'll wipe away all trivial fond records,*
> *All saws of books, all forms, all pressures past,*
> *That youth and observation copied there;*
> *And thy commandment all alone shall live*
> *Within the book and volume of my brain,*
> *Unmix'd with baser matter.*   (I, 4).

Spiritual wisdom, from a wordly point of view, is a kind of madness; and so madness can be made to serve, in certain contexts, as a symbol of spiritual wisdom. Shakespeare avails himself of this possibility more than once in his plays; and in *Hamlet,* in addition to its more outward meaning as a stratagem and a blind, the *antic disposition* which the Prince puts on serves above all to underline the drastic change that has taken place in his life. In his soliloquies he shows no trace of madness; but as soon as he has to face the world, that is, when Horatio and Marcellus enter, shortly after the exit of the Ghost, the new found spiritual outlook which fills his soul almost to bursting point has to find an outlet in what Horatio describes as *wild and whirling words.* It is under cover of this "wildness" that Shakespeare momentarily allows the deeper meaning of the play to come to the surface, for what Hamlet says is:

> *And so without more circumstance at all,*
> *I hold it fit that we shake hands and part;*
> *You, as your business and desire shall point you;*
> *For everyman hath business and desire,*
> *Such as it is; and, for mine own poor part,*
> *Look you, I'll go pray.*

And prayer, which in the widest sense of the word may be said to comprise all forms of worship, is in fact man's chief weapon of "revenge."[6]

It is not however Horatio and Marcellus who represent the world in *Hamlet.* They do so in this scene only incidentally, because they are the first living creatures that the newly initiated Prince is called upon to face. But he soon takes them both half into his confidence, and later he confides everything to Horatio. The world, not only in its incomprehension, but also in its allurements, everything in "ordinary life" which it is difficult to give up but which the man who has taken

---

[6] The already quoted line:
> *Let me wipe it* (my hand) *first; it smells of mortality*
which brings the deeper meaning of *King Lear* to the surface, is spoken by Lear when he is mad. The fact that Hamlet's madness is feigned whereas Lear's is not makes no difference to its symbolism. Another kind of "madness" which has the same significance is the "folly" of the professional fool.

his vows must break with altogether and leave behind him is summed up in the person of Ophelia. Hamlet's subsequent visit to her, which she describes to her father, would seem to be prompted by the vain hope that it may not be necessary to turn his back on the world altogether, or that it may be possible as it were to take the world with him. But when he looks into her face he sees that he must go his way alone; she would be quite incapable of sharing his secret; and so he leaves her without saying a word.

In the "nunnery scene," where we first see them together, Shakespeare once more allows the deeper meaning of the play to rise to the surface under cover of Hamlet's "madness." The first part of the spiritual path is "the descent into Hell." The deeper meaning of Dante's *Inferno*[7] is the descent of Dante into the hidden depths of his own soul. The novice has first to learn the meaning of "original sin"; he must come to know the evil possibilities which lie, almost unsuspected, beneath the surface illusion of being *indifferent honest*. The gist of all that Hamlet says to Ophelia in this scene is in the following speech:

Get thee to a nunnery; why wouldst thou be a breeder of sinners? I am myself indifferent honest; but yet I could accuse me of such things that it were better my mother had not borne me. I am very proud, revengeful, ambitious; with more offences at my beck than I have thoughts to put them in, imagination to give them shape, or time to act them in. What should such fellows as I do, crawling between heaven and earth? We are arrant knaves all; believe none of us. Go thy ways to a nunnery.

(III, 1).

Elsewhere "the descent into Hell," that is, the discovery of sinful propensities in the soul which were hitherto unknown, takes the form of actually committing the sins in question, as happens, for example, with Angelo in *Measure for Measure* and with Leontes in *The Winter's Tale*. The same may be said also of Macbeth. . . .

Despite Hamlet's *antic disposition,* all that he says to Ophelia in the "nunnery scene" makes profound sense. But "the world" is quite uncomprehending; for Ophelia it is all nothing more than

Sweet bells jangled, out of tune and harsh.

In *The Divine Comedy* the discovery of the soul's worst possibilities and purification from them are treated separately. The *Inferno* and the *Purgatorio* correspond to an altogether exhaustive Confession followed by a full Absolution. The "architecture" of Dante's poem demands this separate treatment, as also the fact that it has an eschatological as well as a mystical meaning. Occasionally, as we shall see, Shakespeare also treats the two phases separately, but more often, as in *Hamlet,* he represents them as taking place simultaneously. The killing of Claudius will mean reaching not only to the bottom of Hell but also the top of the Mountain of Purgatory, for revenge means purification.

When Hamlet, on his way to speak with his mother, suddenly comes upon Claudius praying and is about to kill him, he refrains from doing so on the grounds that to kill him while at prayer would amount to sending him to heaven

---

[7] The references here and elsewhere to Dante do not mean to suggest that Shakespeare owes anything to him directly. Of this we know nothing. *The Divine Comedy* can none the less help to throw light on certain aspects of these plays because it is based on principles with which no intellectual of Shakespeare's time could fail to be familiar.

which would be *hire and salary, not revenge.* According to the more outward meaning, that is, according to *Hamlet* as a morality play, the Prince's failure to kill Claudius at this juncture springs from the inability to take decisive action, the readiness to snatch at any pretext for procrastination. At this level a more or less blind eye has to be turned to the actual pretext given. None the less, it is difficult to pass it over altogether as an unpremeditated excuse which flashes across Hamlet's mind and is seized on without being weighed, because later in the play Hamlet deliberately sends Rosencrantz and Guildenstern to a sudden death, *no shriving time allowed,* without even knowing whether they are in the plot against his life or not—and in all probability they are not. We can accept the normal idea of revenge without too much difficulty, even in a morality play, for revenge is or can be a name for justice. But what sin can compare with the implacable determination to send a soul to Hell?[8] And how is such appalling malevolence to be reconciled with the fact that Hamlet is unquestionably a man of great nobility and magnanimity of character, with a profound love of good and hatred of evil and with even much of the priest in his nature—witness the wise, benign and moving sermon he preaches to his mother in the next scene? It must be admitted, with regard to these questions, that the play's deeper meaning strains here the outward sense almost to breaking point. But once the deeper meaning is understood, the difficulties vanish. Revenge on the devil must be absolute. It requires no apologies. There must be no scruples and no compromise. But the time is not yet ripe. There would be no revenge, and therefore no self-purification, in killing Claudius at that moment because Claudius is not himself. Sometimes the soul's worst possibilities may manifest themselves only partially, in such a way that it would be quite easy to overcome them. But nothing final could be hoped for from resisting them on such an occasion; it is only when those possibilities really show themselves for what they are, when they are rampant in all their iniquity, only then is it possible, by stifling them, to give them the death-blow or mortally wound them. As Hamlet says:

> When he is drunk asleep, or in his rage,
> Or in the incestuous pleasure of his bed,
> At gaming, swearing, or about some act
> That has no relish of salvation in't;
> Then trip him, that his heels may kick at heaven
> And that his soul may be as damn'd and black
> As hell, whereto it goes.   (III, 3).

In this scene the devil is far from manifesting himself fully in Claudius. The dragon has not yet come out into the open. Or in other words, Hamlet has not nearly reached the bottom of Hell. He has not even had yet *any direct* experience of the full villainy of Claudius. All that he has learnt so far is relatively indirect compared for example with what he finds when he opens the letter to the King

---

[8] As answer to this question we may quote from *Measure for Measure* (written about the same time as *Hamlet*) what the Duke says about sending a soul to Hell. He has been trying to prepare Barnardine for death, a criminal justly sentenced to be executed for murder. When asked if Barnardine is ready to die, the Duke replies:

> *A creature unprepared, unmeet for death;*
> *And to transport him in the mind he is*
> *Were damnable.*   (IV, 3).

of England and reads Claudius' instructions to have him beheaded immediately on arrival; but the very bottom of Hell is only reached when the Queen lies dead and Hamlet's own body has tasted the poison. Meantime, before he can kill the great devil he has first of all to account for the lesser devils—Polonius, Rosencrantz and Guildenstern; and like Dante's "cruelty" towards some of the sufferers he sees in Hell, who are really elements in his own soul, Hamlet's attitude becomes immediately understandable and acceptable and reconcilable with his nobility of nature if we realize that all the victims of his revenge are in a sense part of himself.

What has so far most impeded Hamlet upon his path is a certain apathy, sluggishness and lack of fervour. *Lapsed in time and passion* is the way he describes himself. The basic cause of this half-heartedness, the chief reason why it is out of the question that Claudius should be killed at this moment of the play is that the soul is divided against itself, being still, in so far as it is represented by the Queen, largely under the Devil's domination. It is only in the next scene that a certain unity of soul is achieved when Hamlet wins his mother over to his side.

This scene is as it were the centre of the play. Personifying the soul that is afraid of its conscience the Queen is afraid of her son and has been holding him at bay. Even now, when the two are to be alone together at last, she has contrived, or rather let us say willingly consented, to have a third party present, one of the devil's spies, hiding behind the arras. Polonius is the embodiment of hypocrisy. His presence at the beginning of this scene means the presence, in the soul, of the determination to brazen things out. The Queen's first words to Hamlet, referring to Claudius as his "father," are shameless in their effrontery:

> *Hamlet, thou hast thy father much offended.* (III, 4).

But when Hamlet's sword pierces the body of Polonius, conscience pierces through the soul's mask of self-justification and with all possibility of intervention at an end the soul is forced to listen to its better self:

> *Leave wringing of your hands. Peace, sit you down*
> *And let me wring your heart; for so I shall*
> *If it be made of penetrable stuff,*
> *If damned custom have not braz'd it so*
> *That it is proof and bulwark against sense.*

The Queen is eventually driven to say:

> *O Hamlet, speak no more!*
> *Thou turn'st mine eyes into my very soul;*
> *And then I see such black and grained spots*
> *As will not leave their tinct.*[9]

No sooner is the soul's repentance assured than its good angle appears. Gertrude, representing the lower part of the soul, cannot sense directly the spiritual power which the ghost of her dead husband represents; but Hamlet sees and hears it, and under its inspiration he tells his mother what she must do.

---

[9] Nothing I can say to myself will make them leave their black tint to take on a lighter colour.

In this scene, which is really an epitome of the whole play, even the literal sense rises to heights that are almost mystical. It is as if the drama's outer meaning, in virtue of which it is a morality play, had been drawn up to the level of its inner meaning. For whether we consider the Prince to be addressing another person or to be addressing his own soul, he is in any case speaking with an exalted penetration worthy of a spiritual master who has years of practical experience of the mystic path behind him.

According to the First Quarto[10] version of this scene Hamlet succeeds in destroying once and for all Claudius' hold over Gertrude. Moreover she promises to help Hamlet to accomplish his revenge. This is left out of the masterly revised text of the Second Quarto,[11] which leaves the audience with the impression, not that Gertrude has completely conquered her weakness for Claudius but that she is well on her way to doing so and that she is sincerely repentant and determined to giver her son all the passive support she can. They feel that like Hamlet himself she still has some obstacles to overcome; and indeed if she had not, and if Hamlet had not, Claudius would have to die then and there.

To judge from the cuts in the first Folio edition of *Hamlet,* published only seven years after Shakespeare's death, we may assume that the full text of this play was considered then, as now, too long for the requirements of theatrical performance. Unfortunately one of the passages nearly always sacrificed is Act IV, scene 4, without which the balance of the play as a whole is seriously upset. In this scene Hamlet, on his way to the Danish coast to set sail for England, has a glimpse of Fortinbras, the young Prince of Norway, who is leading his army through Denmark to fight against the Poles; and this glimpse reveals to Hamlet a hero endowed with all those virtues which he himself most needs to develop.

Fallen man stands between two perfections, one past and one future, that which was lost and that which is to be gained. In this play it is the dead King Hamlet who stands for the past perfection and its loss, whereas Fortinbras represents the perfection in which the redeemed soul, after its purification, will be reborn. It is he whom the dying Hamlet is to name as his heir. The analogy between the symbolism of this play and that of *Henry IV* is by no means exact in every detail; but the dead King Hamlet largely corresponds to the dead King Richard II, whereas Queen Gertrude and her son, taken together, correspond to the synthesis of King Henry IV and his son,[12] while Fortinbras in a sense corresponds to that son regenerated as King Henry V. But this scene, where Fortinbras first appears, is needed above all in that it marks a stage in the development of Hamlet, who drinks a new strength into his soul from his vision of Fortinbras. In the soliloquy which is prompted by this foretaste of his own true self there is a ring of confidence and resolution which we have not heard before. It must be remembered in this connection that the symbolism of honour throughout this play is inextricably connected with the symbolism of revenge. In other words, as the incentive to revenge, honour means spiritual aspiration.

---

[10] 1603.

[11] 1604.

[12] Needless to say there is no exact correspondence here between parent and parent and between son and son. It is true that Gertrude is burdened with guilt towards King Hamlet just as Henry IV is burdened with guilt towards King Richard; but Prince Hamlet, the censurer of self and others, also has much in common with Henry IV, whereas Gertrude in some respects comes closer, symbolically, to the repentant prodigal Prince Hal.

In *Hamlet,* as also in *King Lear,* the play begins with worldly wisdom in a state of triumph. It is as if Shakespeare had set up a pair of scales, and to begin with he allows the weight of worldly wisdom in one scale to lift the opposite scale of spiritual wisdom right up into the air, so that it appears as "light" as folly. But as the play goes on, more and more weight is thrown into the spiritual scale until, even before the last act, it has sunk down to rest on a solid, sober foundation. By the time *King Lear* is drawing to its close the Fool has disappeared, Edgar has ceased to feign madness, and Lear has recovered his sanity. Similarly in *Hamlet* we see no more of the Prince's "madness" after he has left for England; and when he returns he astonishes Horatio with his new-found strength and determination. Meantime it is the scale of worldly wisdom which, found sadly wanting, hangs poised aloft in insecure suspense; and the "lightness" of this world, unstable and transitory as it is, racing towards decay, ruin and death, is pictured in the madness of Ophelia. For her there are only two categories—the dead and the dying.

> And will he not come again?
> And will he not come again?
> No, no, he is dead.
> Go to thy death bed.
> He never will come again.   (IV, 5).

Ophelia's madness is like a mirror for the failure of all wordly aspirations, the shattering of all worldly hopes; and it is significant, considering what she stands for in the play as a whole, that the corpse which is being buried in the churchyard scene is none other than hers.

In this scene, Hamlet, who is himself to die the next day, has the inevitable certainty of death brought home to him with a concrete realism which makes his bones ache, and those of the audience too. He is made to hear death in the knocking together of dead men's bones as the grave-digger throws down one against another; he sees, touches and smells death as he takes the jester's skull in his hands; he even almost tastes death as he remembers how often as a child he had put his lips against what is now no more than two rows of teeth set in two jaw-bones:

> Here hung those lips that I have kissed I
> know not how oft.   (V, 1).

Moreover the scene is to end with the actual burial of everything that had represented, for Hamlet, the possibility of earthly happiness.[13] His own days are numbered too, for it comes out that the grave-digger had taken up his profession on the day that Hamlet was born, thirty years previously; and for him the Prince is already almost a thing of the past, one who has not only come but gone. There is a strange and sudden chill about the words, spoken with the objectivity of a chronicle:

> It was the very day that young Hamlet was born;
> he that is mad, and sent into England.

[13] There is a strong suggestion of death agony in the convulsive violence of Hamlet's outburst over Ophelia's grave—his *towering passion* as he regretfully describes it the next day.

We are reminded by this scene that more than one mystic has sought before now to familiarize himself with death by laying himself out in a coffin; and this is precisely what Hamlet is made to do here. It leads up to his speech in the final scene where he expresses his readiness to die at any time. What does it matter if a man die young, since no man really ever possesses any of the things he leaves behind him at death?

> *Since no man has aught of what*
> *he leaves, what is't to leave betimes?*

We have come a long way from the fears expressed about death in the most famous of his soliloquies.

That soliloquy, *To be or not to be . . .*, marks Hamlet's lowest ebb. As has already been pointed out in an earlier chapter, he goes somewhat back after the first encounter with his father before he begins to go forward. We cannot start to trace the development of the soul he represents until the play-scene, in which doubts are altogether removed and faith confirmed. Onwards from there, the soul gains singleness and sincerity from the reconciliation between Hamlet and his mother; confidence, resolution, a sense of true greatness and even a foretaste of perfection from the glimpse of Fortinbras; resignation to death and a foretaste of death from the churchyard scene; and complete trust in Providence from the discovery of Claudius' letter to the King of England. Hamlet's discovery of his plot to have him killed in England takes place shortly after he sees Fortinbras, but we only hear of it in the last scene of the play. He ascribes, with considerable insistence, every detail of his escape to Divine intervention, and his account of what happened enables trust in Providence to take its place as cornerstone in the remarkable image of royalty which Shakespeare gives us in Hamlet at the beginning of this scene. Without the least arrogance, but with an altogether objective sense of values, he dismisses Rosencrantz and Guildenstern as *baser natures* who have perished for daring to step between two *mighty opposites,* that is, between himself and Claudius—*mighty* because, as we may interpret, since all Heaven is on his side, as he now knows beyond doubt, the clash is ultimately between Michael and Lucifer.

> *Why, what a king is this!*

exclaims Horatio in wonderment. It is significant also that only here, for the very first time, does Hamlet mention among Claudius' other iniquities, that he has robbed him of his rightful crown; and when Horatio implies that there is no time to be lost because news of what has happened will shortly come from England and when Hamlet replies:

> *It will be short; the interim is mine;*
> *And a man's life's no more than to say "One"*

we know that Claudius has not long to live.

The keynote of this opening passage to the final scene is maturity—readiness in every sense of the word, and it is summed up in the words *the readiness is all.* "Everyman" knows that he has almost come to the end of his journey and that the end will be victory but also, necessarily, death. The confidence in the one and the foreboding of the other are expressed in Hamlet's words to Horatio:

> *I shall win at the odds. But thou*
> *wouldst not think how ill all's*
> *here about my heart.*

These words, with their combination of victory and death, are equivalent to Henry IV's:

> *And wherefore should these good news make me sick?*
> (IV, 4).

as he hears of his victory over the rebels. Symbolically the two situations are identical; Henry IV here corresponds exactly to Hamlet before the fencing match. All that remains to be achieved, in either case, is the complete redemption of the other aspect of the soul, represented in *Henry IV* by the Prince and in *Hamlet* by the Queen. As regards the Queen, "the return of the prodigal" has in a sense already taken place; but art demands that it should be clinched beyond all doubt. In this respect, what is generally accepted today as the final text is almost certainly more elliptical than Shakespeare originally intended it to be when he conceived the play. After the King and Laertes withdraw together at the end of Act IV, scene 5, the First Quarto has a scene in which Horatio tells the Queen of Claudius' unsuccessful attempt to have Hamlet killed in England and of Hamlet's return. When the Queen learns that her son is back in Denmark, she tells Horatio:

> *Bid him awhile*
> *Be wary of his presence, lest he fail*
> *In that he goes about*

which means, freely paraphrased: "Tell him to make quite sure that Claudius does not kill him before he kills Claudius." But although this scene is left out in all the later editions of the play, according to the final text a letter is brought from Hamlet to his mother, presumably telling her everything. Moreover, on the basis of Claudius' remark at the end of the churchyard scene:

> *Good Gertrude, set some watch upon your son,*

we may imagine that mother and son have ample time to discuss the whole situation. However that may be, the Queen would be certain that Hamlet's life was in the greatest danger, and she would be watching Claudius' every move. It is very likely, to say the least, that she is suspicious of the drink that Claudius has prepared for her son, and that she drinks from it herself to test it. Though not clear from the text, this can be made clear by the actress. But even if we do not accept this interpretation, Shakespeare has completed his symbolism beyond all doubt by making this last action on the part of the Queen an act of direct disobedience to Claudius who had forbidden her to drink, and by making her final words whole-heartedly on the side of her son:

> *No, no, the drink, the drink,—O my dear Hamlet,—*
> *The drink, the drink!—I am posion'd.*

As to Hamlet's last words, it is perhaps significant that they are a message to Fortinbras. This, together with the entry of Fortinbras immediately after Hamlet's death makes a certain continuity between the dead prince and the living one. There is a suggestion—nothing more—that Hamlet is mysteriously reborn in Fortinbras, though Shakespeare does not indicate this "alchemy" explicitly here as he does in *Henry IV*. At the end of *Hamlet* the stress lies rather on the fruit of rebirth. "Except a man be born again . . ." If the play as a whole corresponds to an interpenetration of Dante's *Inferno* and *Purgatorio,* the *Paradiso* is none the less not merely implicit. It is expressly anticipated in Horatio's farewell prayer for Hamlet:

Flights of angels sing thee to thy rest!

The Struggle
with Death

INTRODUCTION

By now, the readings in this book have surely made it clear that the religious understanding of reality is far more tough-minded than has often been supposed by modern critics. Yet now we shall read several selections that, in one way or another, deny that death is man's absolute enemy. Does this mean that on this subject religion finally turns sentimental or unrealistic?

Quite the contrary. We will find here no naive representation of a life beyond the grave—understood as a continuation of this life in a heaven freed from all unpleasantness or in a hell stripped of all happiness. What we do find is a placing of the question of death in relationship to the weaknesses and terrors that afflict unintegrated man.

We begin with what is perhaps the most powerful presentation in modern literature of the horror of death. Freud once wrote that a man is unable to imagine his own death, but, in the first selection of this chapter, **Fyodor Dostoyevsky** comes close to putting us inside the mind of a man about to die. In reading this selection, we learn a little of what it is men avoid with their comfortable day-to-day sense that, in Heidegger's words, "one dies, but not right now." We see that this condemned man (this selection, by the way, is based on Dostoyevsky's own experience) tastes what little life he has left with extraordinary intensity, and it might be argued that such an awareness of death is precisely what could bring all men to a deeper experience of their own life.

Our second selection, by **Johannes von Saaz**, is a late Medieval poetic dialogue that bares the unwillingness of man to accept the death of a loved one, no matter what reasons are given in justification. By the end of this remarkable dialogue, we see a man chastened in his thinking, struggling anew to connect his personal pain to the sense of a higher order in the universe. Where does life come from? Of what whole is it a part? What is man's proper relationship to this life, to which he clutches without considering the entire scheme of creation?

In our third selection, **Nicholai Berdyaev** pours forth a flood of insights based on the intuition that it is death that gives life meaning. For Berdyaev, the mystery and horror of death and its all-pervasiveness are signs that there is an invisible dimension to the world that we cannot grasp without a spiritual struggle. Death is the invasion of eternity into the world we see and cling to. The fact of death compels all men to choose between the unseen order of God's Reality and the visible order that by itself is meaningless and hopeless.

The fourth selection, from **Evelyn Underhill's** monumental study of mysticism, suggests that man's tormented response to death cannot be separated from his tormented relationship to his own body with its pains and pleasures. The great ascetics, she tells us, struggled not simply with the desires of the flesh but mainly with the human tendency to form a picture of oneself on the basis of bodily sensations. The ascetic's struggle is to not sell himself short, to not identify his real nature with the transitory energies of the body. For us, the implication is that we can never approach death with real inner freedom until we can approach the body with freedom. According to Underhill, man's enemy is not death but the false ego.

In the last selection, the great modern theologian **Paul Tillich** argues that the enemy of a valid human life is not death but anxiety in the face of the unknown. This anxiety clouds man's understanding of his own possibilities, the greatest of which is to affirm oneself in spite of the threat against the individual self. For Tillich, man comes into real relationship to God only if he has the courage to be in the face of the possible loss of everything that men ordinarily take as a support for their sense of self. Death is precisely this loss and therefore precisely the fact that man must face with help from nowhere. Only then does help from God appear.

J. N.

Suggested Readings

St. Augustine. *Confessions.* Book IV. Translated by R. S. Pine-Coffin. Baltimore: Penguin Books, 1966.

Camus, Albert. *Resistance, Rebellion and Death.* Translated by Justrn O'Brien. New York: Knopf, 1961.

Epectetus, *The Manual.*

Evans-Wentz, Walter. *The Tibetan Book of the Dead.* London/New York: Oxford University Press, 1957.

Flew, A. G. N. "Death." *New Essays in Philosophical Theology.* Edited by A. Flew and A. Macintyre. London: SCM Press, 1955.

Krishnamurti, J. "On Death." *The First and Last Freedom.* Wheaton, Ill.: Theosophical Publishing House, 1968. Chapter 23.

MacKinnon, D. M. "Death." *New Essays in Pilosophical Theology.* Edited by A. Flew and A. Macintyre. London: SCM Press, 1955.

Needleman, Jacob. "The Moment of Grief." *Death and Bereavement.* Edited by Austin H. Kutscher. Springfield, Ill.: C. C. Thomas, 1969.

———. "The Perception of Mortality." *Review of Existential Psychology and Psychiatry,* VI, No. 2 (Spring 1966), 168–170.

Plato, *Phaedo.*

———. *Symposium.*

Suzuki, D. T. *Zen and Japanese Culture.* Bollingen Series LXIV. Princeton, N.J.: Princeton University Press, 1970. Chapters IV, V, and VI on Zen, the Samurai, and Swordsmanship.

Tolstoy, Leo. "The Death of Ivan Illich." *The Works of Leo Tolstoy.* Vol. XV. London: Oxford University Press, 1934.

Whitman, Cedric H. "Achilles: Evolution of a Hero." *Homer and the Heroic Tradition.* New York: Norton, 1958. Chapter IX.

The Last Experience

Fyodor Dostoyevsky

Fyodor Dostoyevsky (1822–1881) was one of the two or three greatest Russian novelists. Some of his famous novels are *Crime and Punishment* (1866), *The Idiot* (1868), and *The Brothers Karamazov* (1880).

"There may be two opinions about life in prison," said Myshkin. "A man who spent twelve years in prison told me something. He was one of the invalids in the care of my professor. He had fits; he was sometimes restless, wept, and even tried to kill himself. His life in prison had been a very sad one, I assure you, but not at all petty. Yet he had no friends but a spider and a tree that grew under his window. . . . But I'd better tell you how I met another man last year. There was one very strange circumstance about it,—strange because such things rarely happen. This man had once been led out with others to the scaffold and a sentence of death was read over him. He was to be shot for a political offence. Twenty minutes later a reprieve was read to them, and they were condemned to another punishment instead. Yet the interval between those two sentences, twenty minutes or at least a quarter of an hour, he passed in the fullest conviction that he would die in a few minutes. I was always eager to listen when he recalled his sensations at that time, and I often questioned him about it. He remembered it all with extraordinary distinctness and used to say that he never would forget those minutes. Twenty paces from the scaffold, round which soldiers and other people were standing, there were three posts stuck in the ground, as there were

From Fyodor Dostoyevsky, *The Idiot,* trans. by Constance Garnett.

several criminals. The three first were led up, bound to the posts, the death-dress (a long white gown) was put on, and white caps were pulled over their eyes so that they should not see the guns; then a company of several soldiers was drawn up against each post. My friend was the eighth on the list, so he had to be one of the third set. The priest went to each in turn with a cross. He had only five minutes more to live. He told me that those five minutes seemed to him an infinite time, a vast wealth; he felt that he had so many lives left in those five minutes that there was no need yet to think of the last moment, so much so that he divided his time up. He set aside time to take leave of his comrades, two minutes for that; then he kept another two minutes to think for the last time; and then a minute to look about him for the last time. He remembered very well having divided his time like that. He was dying at twenty-seven, strong and healthy. As he took leave of his comrades, he remembered asking one of them a somewhat irrelevant question and being particularly interested in the answer. Then when he had said good-bye, the two minutes came that he had set apart for *thinking* to himself. He knew beforehand what he would think about. He wanted to realise as quickly and clearly as possible how it could be that now he existed and was living and in three minutes he would be *something*—some one or something. But what? Where? He meant to decide all that in those two minutes! Not far off there was a church, and the gilt roof was glittering in the bright sunshine. He remembered that he stared very persistently at that roof and the light flashing from it; he could not tear himself away from the light. It seemed to him that those rays were his new nature and that in three minutes he would somehow melt into them. . . . The uncertainty and feeling of aversion for that new thing which would be and was just coming was awful. But he said that nothing was so dreadful at that time as the continual thought, 'What if I were not to die! What if I could go back to life—what eternity! And it would all be mine! I would turn every minute into an age; I would lose nothing, I would count every minute as it passed, I would not waste one!' He said that this idea turned to such a fury at last that he longed to be shot quickly."

Myshkin suddenly ceased speaking; every one expected him to go on and draw some conclusion.

"Have you finished?" asked Aglaia.

"What? Yes," said Myshkin, rousing himself from a momentary dreaminess.

"But what did you tell that story for?"

"Oh . . . something in our talk reminded me of it. . . ."

"You are very disconnected," observed Alexandra. "You probably meant to show, prince, that not one instant of life can be considered petty, and that sometimes five minutes is a precious treasure. That's all very laudable, but let me ask, how did that friend who told you such horrors . . . he was reprieved, so he was presented with that 'eternity of life.' What did he do with that wealth afterwards? Did he live counting each moment?"

"Oh no, he told me himself. I asked him about that too. He didn't live like that at all; he wasted many, many minutes."

"Well, there you have it tried. So it seems it's impossible really to live 'counting each moment.' For some reason it's impossible."

"Yes, for some reason it is impossible," repeated Myshkin. "I thought so myself . . . and yet I somehow can't believe it . . ."

.   .   .

"One thought came into my mind just now," Myshkin said to her, growing rather more eager again (he seemed easily roused to confiding eagerness), "when you asked me for a subject for a picture, to suggest that you should paint the face of the condemned man the moment before the blade falls, when he is still standing on the scaffold before he lies down on the plank."

"The face? The face alone?" asked Adelaïda. "That would be a strange subject. And what sort of picture would it make?"

"I don't know. Why not?" Myshkin insisted warmly. "I saw a picture like that at Bâle not long ago. I should like to tell you about it. . . . I'll tell you about it some day. . . . It struck me very much."

"You shall certainly tell us afterwards about the picture at Bâle," said Adelaïda; "and now explain the picture of this execution. Can you tell me how you imagine it to yourself? How is one to draw the face? Is it to be only the face? What sort of a face is it?"

"It's practically the minute before death," Myshkin began with perfect readiness, carried away by his memories and to all appearance instantly forgetting everything else, "that moment when he has just mounted the ladder and has just stepped on to the scaffold. Then he glanced in my direction. I looked at his face and I understood it all. . . . But how can one describe it? I wish, I do wish that you or some one would paint it. It would be best if it were you. I thought at the time that a picture of it would do good. You know one has to imagine everything that has been before—everything, everything. He has been in prison awaiting execution for a week at least; he has been reckoning on the usual formalities, on the sentence being forwarded somewhere for signature and not coming back again for a week. But now by some chance this business was over sooner. At five o'clock in the morning he was asleep. It was at the end of October; at five o'clock it was still cold and dark. The superintendent of the prison came in quietly with the guard and touched him carefully on the shoulder. He sat up, leaning on his elbow, saw the light, asked 'What's the matter?' 'The execution is at ten o'clock.' He was half awake and couldn't take it in, and began objecting that the sentence wouldn't be ready for a week. But when he was fully awake he left off protesting and was silent—so I was told. Then he said, 'But it's hard it should be so sudden. . . .' And again he was silent and wouldn't say anything more. The next three or four hours are spent on the usual things: seeing the priest, breakfast at which he is given wine, coffee and beef (isn't that a mockery? Only think how cruel it is! Yet on the other hand, would you believe it, these innocent people act in good faith and are convinced that it's humane); then the toilet (do you know what a criminal's toilet is?); and at last they take him through the town to the scaffold. . . . I think that he too must have thought he had an endless time left to live, while he was being driven through the town. He must have thought on the way, 'There's a long time left, three streets more. I shall pass through this one, then through the next, then there's that one left where there's a baker's on the right. . . . It'll be a long time before we get to the baker's!'

"There were crowds of people, there was noise and shouting; ten thousand faces, ten thousand eyes—all that he has had to bear, and, worst of all, the thought, 'They are ten thousand, but not one of them is being executed, and I am to be executed.' Well, all that is preparatory. There is a ladder to the scaffold. Suddenly at the foot of the ladder he began to cry, and he was a strong manly fellow; he had been a great criminal, I was told. The priest never left him for a moment; he drove with him in the cart and talked with him all the while. I doubt whether he heard; he might begin listening and would not understand more than two words. So it must have been. At last he began going up the ladder; his ladder; his legs were tied together so that he could only move with tiny steps. The priest, who must have been an intelligent man, left off speaking and only gave him the cross to kiss. At the foot of the ladder he was very pale, and when he was at the top and standing on the scaffold, he became as white as paper, as white as writing paper. His legs must have grown weak and wooden, and I expect he felt sick—as though something were choking him and that made a sort of tickling in his throat. Have you ever felt that when you were frightened, or in awful moments when all your reason is left, but it has no power? I think that if one is faced by inevitable destruction—if a house is falling upon you, for instance —one must feel a great longing to sit down, close one's eyes and wait, come what may. . . . When that weakness was beginning, the priest with a rapid movement hastily put the cross to his lips—a little plain silver cross—he kept putting it to his lips every minute. And every time the cross touched his lips, he opened his eyes and seemed for a few seconds to come to life again, and his legs moved. He kissed the cross greedily; he made haste to kiss, as though in haste not to forget to provide himself with something in case of need; but I doubt whether he had any religious feeling at the time. And so it was till he was laid on the plank. . . . It's strange that people rarely faint at these last moments. On the contrary, the brain is extraordinarily lively and must be working at a tremendous rate—at a tremendous rate, like a machine at full speed. I fancy that there is a continual throbbing of ideas of all sorts, always unfinished and perhaps absurd too, quite irrelevant ideas: 'That man is looking at me. He has a wart on his forehead. One of the executioner's buttons is rusty.' . . . and yet all the while one knows and remembers everything. There is one point which can never be forgotten, and one can't faint, and everything moves and turns about it, about that point. And only think that it must be like that up to the last quarter of a second, when his head lies on the block and he waits and . . . *knows,* and suddenly hears above him the clang of the iron! He must hear that! If I were lying there, I should listen on purpose and hear. It may last only the tenth part of a second, but one would be sure to hear it. And only fancy, it's still disputed whether, when the head is cut off, it knows for a second after that it has been cut off! What an idea! And what if it knows it for five seconds!

"Paint the scaffold so that only the last step can be distinctly seen in the foreground and the criminal having just stepped on it; his head, his face as white as paper; the priest holding up the cross, the man greedily putting forward his blue lips and looking—and aware of everything. The cross and the head— that's the picture. The priest's face and the executioner's, his two attendants and a few heads and eyes below might be painted in the background, in half light, as the setting. . . . That's the picture!"

Myshkin ceased speaking and looked at them all.

. . .

"Hm! . . . Courts of Justice. . . . It's true there are Courts of Justice. And how is it abroad, are their courts better than ours?"

"I don't know [said Myshkin]. I've heard a great deal that's good about ours. We've no capital punishment, you know."

"Why, do they execute people there then?"

"Yes. I saw it in France, at Lyons. Dr. Schneider took me with him."

"Do they hang them?"

"No, in France they always cut off their heads."

"Do they scream?"

"How could they? It's done in an instant. They make the man lie down and then a great knife is brought down by a heavy, powerful machine, called the guillotine. . . . The head falls off before one has time to wink. The preparations are horrible. When they read the sentence, get the man ready, bind him, lead him to the scaffold—that's what's awful! Crowds assemble, even women, though they don't like women to look on. . . ."

"It's not a thing for them!"

"Of course not, of course not! Such a horrible thing! . . . The criminal was an intelligent, middle-aged man, strong and courageous, called Legros. But I assure you, though you may not believe me, when he mounted the scaffold he was weeping and was as white as paper. Isn't it incredible? Isn't it awful? Who cries for fear? I'd no idea that a grown man, not a child, a man who never cried, a man of forty-five, could cry for fear! What must be passing in the soul at such a moment; to what anguish it must be brought! It's an outrage on the soul, that's what it is! It is written 'Thou shalt not kill,' so because he has killed, are we to kill him? No, that's impossible. It's a month since I saw that, but I seem to see it before my eyes still. I've dreamt of it half a dozen times."

Myshkin was quite moved as he spoke, a faint colour came into his pale face, though his voice was still gentle. The footman followed him with sympathetic interest, so that he seemed sorry for him to stop. He, too, was perhaps a man of imagination and strainings after thought.

"It's a good thing at least that there is not much pain," he observed, "when the head falls off."

"Do you know," Myshkin answered warmly, "you've just made that observation and every one says the same, and the guillotine was invented with that object. But the idea occurred to me at the time that perhaps it made it worse. That will seem to you an absurd and wild idea, but if one has some imagination, one may suppose even that. Think! if there were torture, for instance, there would be suffering and wounds, bodily agony, and so all that would distract the mind from spiritual suffering, so that one would only be tortured by wounds till one died. But the chief and worst pain may not be in the bodily suffering but in one's knowing for certain that in an hour, and then in ten minutes, and then in half a minute, and then now, at the very moment, the soul will leave the body and that one will cease to be a man and that that's bound to happen; the worst part of it is that it's *certain*. When you lay your head down under the knife and hear the knife slide over your head, that quarter of a second is the most terrible of all. You know this is not only my fancy, many people have said the same. I believe that so thoroughly that I'll tell you what I think. To kill for murder is a punishment incomparably worse than the crime itself. Murder by legal sentence is immeasurably more terrible than murder by brigands. Anyone murdered by brigands, whose throat is cut at night in a wood, or something of that sort, must surely hope to escape till the very last minute. There have been instances when a man has still hoped for escape, running or begging for mercy after his throat was cut. But in the other case all that last hope, which makes dying ten times as easy, is taken away *for certain*. There is the sentence, and the whole awful torture lies in the fact that there is certainly no escape, and there is no torture in the world more terrible. You may lead a soldier out and set him facing the cannon in battle and fire at him and he'll still hope; but read a sentence of certain death over that same soldier, and he will go out of his mind or burst into tears. Who can tell whether human nature is able to bear this without madness? Why this hideous, useless, unnecessary outrage? Perhaps there is some man who has been sentenced to death, been exposed to this torture and has then been told 'you can go, you are pardoned.' Perhaps such a man could tell us. It was of this torture and of this agony that Christ spoke, too. No, you can't treat a man like that!"

Death and the Plowman
Johannes von Saaz

Johannes von Saaz lived in Bohemia around the turn of the fifteenth century. Although this work was the first and greatest literary expression of German humanism, almost nothing is known about the life of its author.

A DISPUTATION AND A CONSOLATION FROM THE YEAR 1400...ADAPTED[1] INTO ENGLISH BY JACOB NEEDLEMAN

Death and the Plowman, or The Bohemian Plowman, was written in the early 15th century by a certain Johannes von Saaz, about whom we know practically nothing.[2] There may be no other work in Western literature that expresses man's hatred of death with more force and understanding.

The form of the work is that of a legal dispute between plaintiff (the Plowman—his "plow" being the quill pen of a writer) and defendant (Lord Death). The Plowman's complaint concerns the death of his young wife, a complaint which he unremittingly hurls in the face of all the arguments that Death can muster. Much of the work's power comes from the Plowman's constant repetition that he is in pain. No matter what Death says, the agony and the reality of his loss remain the Plowman's heaviest counter arguments.

Lord Death's defense is that he is part of the natural order of God's creation: in this consists his "reasonableness" and "justice." The man, therefore, who violently laments Death's sovereignty is, in fact, refusing to understand reality. Such a man is a fool. Indeed, it is foolishness itself which has

---

[1] Those familiar with the German texts will immediately see why this version is termed an adaptation, rather than a translation. I have tried, however, to take only those liberties with the text which may help to convey some of the force of the original. A fine scholarly English translation, to which I am greatly indebted, is that by Ernest N. Kirrmann: *Death and the Plowman*. Chapel Hill. The University of North Carolina Press, 1958.

[2] See Kirrmann's translation, pages XII-XIV, for a complete summary of the meager biographical information that is available to us.

brought the Plowman's pain in the first place, in the form of his inability to love wisely. Ultimately, Death's counsel to the Plowman is that he must acquire wisdom. He must learn that everything he sees, loves, desires, or hates, including himself, will soon be destroyed by death. Contained in this counsel is Death's devaluation of all the Plowman holds dear: man, woman, marriage, love, "holiness"—all the primary emotions and beliefs and relationships of human life.

The Plowman is neither willing nor able to accept this. Nothing can lessen his pain. No recompense for his loss is possible. He cannot believe that God created a world in which wisdom lies along the lines that Death draws. No argument, however telling, can persuade him that death is not evil. He unyieldingly asserts his own sense of values and finds unacceptable what in the light of these values is surely an injustice: his young wife's death and the pain now weighing upon him. He has, in this sense, eaten of the tree of the knowledge of good and evil; thus death becomes his destroyer.

The final judgment of God reveals the prespective in which both the Plowman and Death are in error: death and life serve higher purposes than either the Plowman or Death is aware of. Yet such is the supremacy of the Divine rule that even this error makes relative sense and serves its function, as we see in the concluding Plowman's Prayer to God. This prayer expresses the Plowman's turning to God, not for the consolation and recompense he had hitherto sought, but for a newly understood *help* from God's created reality (which now *includes* death), a prayer for the tranquillity of heart without which it is impossible truly to mean "amen": so be it.

J. N.

1. THE PLOWMAN

Grim undoer of the world, baleful outlaw unto all mankind, fearful murderer of the good, Death, be you accursed! God, your maker, hate you; endless affliction dwell upon you, fierce disaster rule within your house, be forever scourged to the inners of your being! Dread, want and grievance never leave your side; sorrow, misery and anguish plague your ways; lacerations, presentiments of deep disgrace and crippling punishments all, in all their power, everywhere oppress you! Heaven, earth, sun, moon, stars, ocean, river, mountain, field, valley, meadow, the deepest pits of Hell, and everything that has a life or being, hold you as its bitter, loathsome enemy maledicted unto all eternity! Be consumed by evil, disappear into the sorest grief, and dwell beyond recall for now and all the time to come within the heaviest contempt of God, man, and God's creation! Shameless miscreant, may the evil that you are turn and endlessly prevail upon you; may terror and fear never let you free; may there be ever wringing of the hands and cries of murder shrieked at you by all men and by myself!

2. DEATH

Listen! Listen! Listen! What new wonder be this now!!
Terrible and most unprecedented curses do assail Us.

And whence they come we do not know.
Surely, We have long and everywhere withstood
Threats, laments, cries of murder, wringings of the hands,
And abuse of every sort. Therefore, man,
Declare thyself; announce thy name and let Us hear
What sorrow We have let thee know that thou with such
Unseemly words dost now address Us. To such a thing
We are not as yet accustomed,
Though many be the stalks that we have reaped,
Those rich in knowledge, noble, beautiful and powerful,
Whereby widows and orphans, nations and entire races have also
Known their share of pain. Thou dost comport thyself
As though an earnest need gives thee much oppress,
Thy lament has no rhyme,
Whereby We gather that thou wouldst not sacrifice
Thy understanding to the excellence of sound or rhythm.
But if a raging fury hath the better of thy sense, then
Hold thy tongue, and wait; be not rash and quick to level
Heavy maledictions that in better time shall plague thee
With remorse. Suffer not to think that thou canst
To any small degree divide Us from Our mastery and thorough might.
So name thyself and if thy need be speech, tell Us
Of the matter that thou hast from Us so strongly suffered.
We shall soon acquit Ourself; thou shalt mark Our honesty.
But We do not know as yet whyfore thou dost so fervently
Assail Us.

3. THE PLOWMAN

I'm called a plowman, my plow the sharpened feather of a bird, and I live in the country of Bohemia. I will never cease hating you. You have most fearfully ripped away the thirteenth letter of my alphabet and with it my entire store of happiness. As though they were but weeds, you pitilessly tore the gentle summer flowers from the meadow in my heart; and with the cunning of a thief you kidnapped my greatest and my only gladness, my chosen bird of joy; you have plundered from me what is not to be replaced. Judge for yourself if it is for nothing that I bring forth such anger, fury, and lament, now to face a joyless life, because you robbed me of it, a life deprived of its only source of rapture. Until now every hour was for me one full of happiness and cheer; the days and nights were short and never anything but pleasant; every year was for me a year of grace. Now suddenly I'm told: forget it, I'm told to spend my days now crying and ceaselessly lamenting, full of misery and sadness, drinking muddy wine, clinging to a brittle, withered bough! So now you see me blown by every wind, straining in a wild, angry flood, ever at the mercy of the waves, vainly weighing anchor. Therefore will I shriek without end: Death, be you accursed!

4. DEATH

Wonder seizes Us at such unprecedented hate, the likes of which
We have never yet encountered. Now if thou be a plowman

Who maketh home there in Bohemia,
Then we think thou doest Us unjustly. The time is long
Since We have there worked anything essential,
Save for our recent lying in the hilly confines
Of a charming village there, wherein
Four letters of the alphabet, the nineteenth, first, third
And twenty-sixth twined themselves into a wreath. There
We administered Our graces to an honest, cheerful lady
Who bore, indeed, the thirteenth letter. She was
Completely virtuous, immaculate. Let none dispute Our right
To say "immaculate," for We were present at her birth.
And at that time Dame Honor sent to her a cloak and wreath of honor,
Both of which Dame Happiness dispatched to her. Now to her grave
She took that cloak untattered and unblemished, that wreath
Unviolated. May He who knoweth all things bear witness to Our part
And hers. She was above all others in the goodness
Of her conscience, her honesty, fidelity, and most especially
In charity of heart. Truly, it is seldom that we meet so excellent
A woman. If it be not this of whom thou speakest, then who it is
We know not.

5. THE PLOWMAN

My Lord, I was her husband, she was my wife. You took her from me, my
eyes' delight; she is gone, my shield of peace; gone is my oracle, my seer. Dead is
dead! Here I stand, poor plowman, alone; gone is my gently guiding star; the
sun of my well-being has set, never again to rise! Never will the star of all my
mornings rise, its light has paled; gone is the soother of pain, night veils my eyes,
my eyes are veiled by darkest night. Truly, I do not think there is anything that
can ever bring me proper joy again; for the proud banner of my joy is broken.
Murder! To arms! Be this ever the unending cry, shrieked from the heart's own
source into the empty anxious days to come as my own adamantine luster dims,
as my guiding staff is torn unmercifully from my hands, and as the way is barred
that leads me to the fountain of my health. Oh, endless, endless, eternally
unburdened grief, ruin, desolation and eternal downfall be your proper legacy,
oh Death! Die without honor, gnashing your teeth while you rot in Hell and
while the sickening bile of degradation fills your mouth! God revoke your power
and scatter you like powder in the wind! Oh, be yours an unending devilish existence!

6. DEATH

A fox struck a sleeping lion on the cheek;
For that his skin was flayed.
A rabbit bit a wolf;
Today he is still without a tail.
A cat scratched a dog;
From that time on she had the dog's infernal enmity to bear.

Thou seekest now to vex Us in like manner.
Still, We do believe a vassal is a vassal,
But a lord remaineth a lord. We would give thee proof
That we weigh justly, judge justly, and justly do proceed
Within the world; that we do not heed estate of birth,
Nor honor deeds, nor even look upon such things as beauty,
Talent, love, sorrow, age or youth when We approach the scales.
We do as doth the sun who shineth on both good and evil.
We take both good and evil in our fold.
The genius who is able to compel the muses
Must, at Our command, surrender up to Us his muses;
And neither whores nor temptresses withstand Us, nor
Doth it serve them if they ride on crutches or on goats.
Physicians who prolong the lives of other men
Also are compelled to give Us part; neither roots, herbs, salves,
Nor any number of apothecary measures will assist them.
Had We the interest to prolong a life because of sacrifices,
Gifts, love or sorrow, then might We today be king of all the world;
All sovereigns would have gladly set their crowns upon Our head,
Placed in Our hands their scepters;
We would own the papal seat and its triune mitre.
Indeed, were we now to give a reckoning of every butterfly
Or grasshopper—there'd be no end to it!
Leave off thy cursing and enumerate no babbling romances.
Do not beat the air above thee and splinters will not fall
Into thine eyes.

7. THE PLOWMAN

Could I but curse you, could I but castigate you, could I but damn you until a power more evil than evil itself destroyed you, it would be no more than you have earned from me. For great pain brings forth great lament and I would be less than human did I not bewail the passing of my gift from God, this gift which God alone could give. These tears can never leave me, the falcon of pride has escaped. And in this I am right so to lament her death, for she was noble of birth, rich in honor, beautiful, singular among her friends in wisdom and excellence of form, fine and true in words, modest in body, and with others ever of good cheer. I say no more, for I have not the strength to number all those virtues with which God Himself provided her. Lord Death, you know this yourself. With such sorrow in my heart I have no choice but to come to you with lamentation. Truly, if there were any good in you, you too would be moved to pity. I will turn my back on you, I will speak no good of you, I will forever be your enemy. May all God's creation stand by me in opposing you. May you be condemned and hated by all that is in Heaven, Earth and Hell!

8. DEATH

The heavenly throne was willed by God unto the angels;
Unto evil spirits fell the abysmal domains of Hell;

And unto Us, this realm of Earth.
God commanded that the virtuous shall earn the endless peace
Of Heaven,
And that the pains of Hell shall be the punishment for sin;
Just so, the earth, the air, the seas and all that dwell therein
Were set within Our sovereignty
That We might stand between abundance and plethora.
Now, foolish man, just think
And with thy thinking plow the fields of Reason;
Thou wilt see: since that time when God first formed man out of clay
Had We not started rooting out amid the vast increase
Of men upon the earth,
Animals and worms in deserts and in wild fields,
Scaly and slimy fish within the seas and waters,
Then for the very multitude of flying bugs
No one could exist;
For the very fear of wolves no one would venture from his house.
Men would seek to eat each other, as would each animal
And every living thing; for they would all of them
Lack nourishment. The Earth would be too small.
He is a fool who laments a mortal's death.
Let go! The living to the living, the dead to the dead,
As it hath always been.
Foolish man, be wiser in thy purposes or cease lament.

9. THE PLOWMAN

My stores are gone beyond recalling; shall I not despair? Condemned as I am to fill my life with pain, shall I not cry out? Oh merciful God, oh mighty Lord, grant that vengeance be mine against this evil gardener of despair! You have divided me from every rapture of my life, disappropriated me of honor. For I would have had great honor were my noble, august queen still playing with her children in their righteous place of birth. But those little chicks have lost their mother hen. Oh God, mighty Lord, how dear it was to see her ply her gentle corrections so that all who saw her blessed her, saying: "Praise and honor to this fine woman; may God grant her and her children all good." If my power had been equal to the gratitude I owed to God, then gladly would I have thanked Him in full measure. What poor man ever owned such great treasure? Say what you will, he to whom God gives a noble, pure and beautiful wife has a gift beyond all earthly gifts. Oh Almighty, Lord of Heaven, how happy he is, blessed with a faultless wife! Rejoice, honorable husband, over your virtuous wife; rejoice, God gives you both great joy! What does he know of this, that foolish man who has never drunk from this fountain of youth? Although bitter sorrow overwhelms me, I thank you, God, inwardly, that I have known such a wife. As for you, evil Death, enemy of all men, may God hate you unto all eternity!

10. DEATH

We mark, however, from thy words
That thou hast not drunk from wisdom's fountain.

Thou has not seen into nature's workings,
Nor looked into the contexts of worldly things,
Nor at all perceived the necessary changes in the Earth;
Thou art, in truth, a witless dolt.
Mark how the gorgeous roses and the aromatic lilies in the garden,
How the robust weeds and comely flowers of the meadows,
How the sturdy rocks and towering trees in the wild fields,
How the mighty bears and powerful lions
In the woods and fearful jungles,
How the valiant warriors,
How the nimble, the exceptional, the learned,
And masters and all-powerful men,
And how all earthly creatures,
No matter how intelligent, how clever, how strong they are,
And how long they hold themselves erect, and carry out their will:
Mark how every one of them, how each of them,
Doth come to nothing and falls and is destroyed.
And now
If all men
And all kinds of men, who ever were or are or shall be,
Must pass from being into nothingness, how, then, shall it be
That she whom thou dost praise and endlessly lament
Shall not deserve the fate of every other and all others like her?
Though now thou hast it not in mind, thou also wilt not escape Us.
All in their turn: each of you must come to terms.
Thy lament is vain; it shall not help thee;
It falleth on fallow ground.

11. THE PLOWMAN

I trust in God whose power holds us both in sway to shelter me from you and mightily to avenge the heinous wrong you have brought to bear on me. Like a conjurer you come before me, veiling what is true with falsehood and vainly seeking to remove from me the enormous sorrow of my senses, my mind and my heart. You cannot; I remain in agony upon my bitter loss. Day and night she never wearied. She was my restorative against all sorrow and adversity, my holy servant, guardian of my will and caretaker of my body, sentinel of her renown and mine. Whatever was entrusted to her was ever rendered back whole, pure—aye and increased. God was her never-failing counsel. And God, for her sake, was ever gracious and favorful to me; for her sake God gave me health, joy, and success in all my undertakings. This she earned and deserved for the purity of our house. Reward and gracious meed give unto her, oh benevolent Disburser, Almoner of faithfulness, most bountiful God! Be merciful to her beyond my own wishes! Oh! Oh! Oh! Shameless murderer, Lord Death, evil iniquitor! The hangman be your judge to bind you, by your speech, upon the torture-rack!

12. DEATH

Couldst thou but rightly weigh, measure or determine,
Thou wouldst prevent such talk from spilling from thy shallow head.
Thy cursing and thy vengeful summonings want insight and excuse.
Wherefore this braying, ass? Must We recite again?
All things noble, brave, good, or excellent in any fashion—
All things which live must perish by our hand.
And yet thou whinest and dost maintain
That all thy happiness depended on thy chaste and
Noble wife.
If, truly, thou dost believe that happiness depends on woman,
We would offer thee ripe counsel on the matter.
Tell Us: when thou tookst the renowned woman
As thy wife—
Didst find her excellent?
Or hast made her so?
When the one, then cast about with circumspection;
Thou shalt even better, purer women find upon the earth,
One of which would matrimonially suit thee.
But if the other, if thou hast *made* her all-excelling,
Then rejoice! Thou art the living master craftsman
Who full well dost know the means to fashion
And upbring still one more excelling wife.
And now one final confidence:
The more of love thou hast, the greater sorrow will be thy part.
Hadst withheld thyself from love,
Wouldst now be free of pain.
Great love for what one hath, great pain to be bereft of it.
Wife, child, riches and all that is good on earth
Must yield more sorrow at its end than joy at its beginning;
All earthly things and love must turn to pain.
Pain is the end of love;
Sadness is the end of joy;
Revulsion is the end of pleasure;
Ill-will the end of willing.
Such is life's course; learn it better
If thou wouldst put wit in thy braying!

13. THE PLOWMAN

Insult follows injury: a law well known to all who are oppressed. Just so, you heap abuse on me. You have weaned me from love to pain and I must suffer this from you as long as God so wills. But though I may seem stupid, and though I have garnered little wisdom from learned masters, I know one thing: you have robbed me of honor, thieved my joy, stolen the goodness of my days, murdered my ecstasy and are the destroyer of all that assured me joyous life. Now what shall I celebrate? Where seek consolation? Where refuge? Where shall I find asylum and cure? Where find true counsel? Dead is dead. Dead before its time is all my happiness. Dead too soon. All too soon you have torn away the dear and lovely one and have mercilessly made me to a widower and my children to orphans. Helpless, alone, and filled with sorrow, I remain unrequited by you; no amends could ever come from you. How is that, Sir Death, adulterer of all men's marriage bed? No one can expect a good from you; after foul crimes you would give to no one satisfaction, to no one recompense. I mark that in you there is no mercy to be found; your way is but to curse, to inflict. Such kindness as you show men, the mercies men receive from you, the recompense you give, the ends that you prepare for men, let all these in like measure be sent to you by Him who has power over life and death. O, Ruler of the heavenly legions, reimburse me for my loss, my harm, my affliction, my desolation! Avenge me thereof on Death, Oh God, Avenger of all evildoing!

14. DEATH

Better not to say it than to say it stupidly.
For foolish talk must lead to quarrel;
Quarrel to enmity;
Enmity to unrest;
Unrest to outrage
Outrage to pain,
And after pain, remorse must come to every muddled man.
Wouldst quarrel with Us;
Wouldst lament that We have done thee ill
In the person of thy much-beloved wife.
Thou canst not see how gracious her share of Us hath been.
We received her youth, her proud body,
The best of her life, the best of her dignity, the best of her time,
And honor.
That was Our kindness,
Which hath been praised and desired by all philosophers
Who say: Best to die when one seeketh most to live.
He hath not died well who desired death;
To call for Us is the sorrow of a life too long.
Woe and privation to those doubled with age;
Amid all riches, that is still their poverty.
In this six-thousand-five-hundred-and-ninety-ninth year of the world,
One thousand, four hundred years of the Christ,
We let thy blessed mortal die from thee
And from the tinseled miseries of Earth,
To come, in good reward, to the joy,
The life,
And the peace of God.
Though thou dost spite Us, We would wish thee well,
Thy soul with hers in its heavenly mansion,
Thy bodies limb to limb in this grave of earth.
We would be thy bondsman,

And her good works would stand thee in good stead.
And therefore hold thy tongue!
Thou canst as little separate light from the sun,
Coldness from the moon, heat from fire,
Or wetness from water,
As thou canst divide from Us
Our power.

15. THE PLOWMAN

The guilty have always had their rhetoric, and so do you. To those you would defraud you show yourself as sweet and bitter, gentle and hard, kind and severe. That I now know. But no matter how you ornament yourself I know that because of your grim enmity I have lost my good and beautiful wife. And I also know that none but God and you have such power. But this torment comes not from God. For had I gone against God—as, to my shame, I have often done—then He would have taken vengeance on me, or my immaculate wife would have righted it for me. No, you have done this evil. Therefore, I would know: who are you? what are you? whence are you? what is your excellence that you are granted such power to bring me such evil so suddenly? To have withered my joyous green. To have undermined my tower of strength and brought it to its fall. Oh God, Comforter of all troubled hearts, comfort me and recompense me, poor, anguished, miserable, lonely man! Oh Lord, bring torment and lay payment upon grim Death, grasp and destroy him who is enemy to You and all Your beings! Truly, Lord, in all Your creation there is nothing more dreadful, nothing more abominable, nothing more terrible, nothing more bitter, nothing more unjust than Death! His work is to defile and confuse all Your earthly lordship; he'd take away the good before the bad; he'd leave the malignant, old, sick and useless while raking in the worthy and the useful. Judge, O Lord, judge the false judge!

16. DEATH

Men who do not think name evil good and good evil,
As thou dost.
Thou dost accuse Us of judging falsely,
And doest Us injustice, as We shall prove:
Wouldst ask who We be?
We are Lord Death, God's implement,
And honest working reaper.
Our scythe precedeth Us, leveling white, red,
Green, blue, gray, yellow and every color of bloom
And grass, unmindful of its brilliance, its strength,
Or its value. Its beautiful color does not serve the violet,
Nor its rich fragrances, nor its delicious juices.
Behold, that is justice.
Romans and poets have known Us well and understood Our honesty.

Wouldst ask what We be?
We are nothing, and yet are something.
Being neither life, nor essence,
Neither form, nor quality, nor spirit,
We are nothing;
Being the end of life, the end of being, the beginning of non-being,
The region between them;
We are something; We are a fate;
We befall everyone.
Great giants must topple before Us;
Everything that liveth must suffer Our transfiguration.
Our victory is therefore just.
Wouldst ask how We be?
We are not to be described,
Save that a painted wall in a Roman temple
Showeth a blindfolded man astride an ox,
Carrying in his right hand a cleaver,
And in his left a shovel. These weapons
Against a great swarm of people, shooting, throwing,
Fighting him. All sorts of people, each carrying the tool of his trade—
Even a nun with the Psalter—
Attack the man upon the ox, pelt him, strike at him.
We understand this picture:
This embattled legion will be conquered, all,
And buried. It is the picture of a man with basilisk eyes,
Before whom all living creatures must die.
Wouldst ask whence We come?
From everywhere, and yet from nowhere.
We dwell in every corner of the world,
But are composed of what is not.
We are sourced in the earthly paradise;
There God created Us and rightly named Us, saying:
"On the day that thou eatest of the fruit of this tree
Thou shalt die of Death."
Therefore We sign Our name thus:
"We, Death, on Earth, in the air, and on the waters of the sea,
Lord and Ruler."
Wouldst ask what use We be?
Thou hast already heard We bring the world more benefit than harm.
Desist, then, and be content;
Thank us that We have been kind to thee.

17. THE PLOWMAN

Old men tell strange tales, learned men speak of the unknown, and travelers to
distant lands prevaricate. If you be one of these, your fictions are nothing ill.
But if as a reaper you claim your descent from paradise, and if you aim at
right, then your scythe cuts all unevenly. It roots out vigorous flowers and leaves

the thistle standing; weeds remain and good herbs must perish. You say your scythe precedes you. How is it then that more thistles than good flowers, more rodents than tame animals, more evil men than good are left intact? With your mouth tell me, with your fingers show me: where are the capable, upright men of other times? I think you have them. And my love is with them; only dust is left to me. Where are they gone who dwelled on Earth and spoke with God and earned His grace and mercy? Where are they gone who lived on Earth under Heaven and computed the planets and the stars? Where are they gone, those rich in knowledge, the masterly, just, gifted men so spoken of in our chronicles? You have murdered them all, and with them my beloved; but the despicable still exist. Who is guilty? Sir Death, if you dared acknowledge the truth, you would name yourself. You boast of your justice, sparing no one, all in their turn falling before your scythe. But I was present and saw with my own eyes two mighty armies—each numbered over three thousand men—warring in a green field. They waded in blood up to their calves. You were whirling and buzzing among them from one end to the other. You killed many in these armies and many you left standing. Yet I saw more masters lying dead than servants. I saw you claw particular men from the midst of their fellows like rotten fruit plucked from a basket. Is that your honest reaping? Your justice? Is that the straight path of your blade? Well, then, dear children, come! come! come here and let us ride out together to meet him and offer him honor and speak praise to Death who judges so rightly. The justice of God is hardly as fair!

18. DEATH

He who doth not understand a thing cannot speak of it.
Thus it is with Us.
We did not know thou wert so capable a man.
We have known thee long, but we had forgotten it.
For were we not there when Dame Sybil gave thee wisdom?
When King Solomon, dying, gave thee his wisdom?
When God assigned to thee the power given Moses in Egypt
As thou slew'st the lion in the mountain of Timnah?
We saw thee number the stars,
Compute the sands of the sea and its fish,
Count the drops of rain.
With pleasure We watched thee outrace Asahel,
Taste in Babylon the meat and wine of honor.
And when thou didst bear against Darius
The pennant of King Alexander,
We looked on and wished thee well.
Our special joy was thy cleverness in Athens
When thou bested in debate the wisest heads of the academies,
Men who also understood many high matters.
And when thou imparted morals and patience to Nero.
We marvelled when thou didst navigate the wooden ship of Julius Caesar
Over the wild sea, through the stormy blast.

In thy workshop we watched thee fashion a glorious garment
From the rainbow,
Wherein thou didst weave forms of angels,
Beasts, birds, fishes—even the owl and the ape.
But we laughed aloud and boasted of thee at Paris,
Seated on the fortune-wheel, capering upon the cowhide,
Working black magic and banishing the devil into a grotesque glass.
And finally, when God summoned thy counsel over the fall of Eve,
We knew, truly, thy great wisdom.
Had We but recognized thee earlier, We would have bowed before Thee;
We would have left thy wife and all mankind to live forever—
Solely in thy honor.
For thou art verily a most clever jackass!

19. THE PLOWMAN

For the sake of truth, men often must endure mockery and vile abuse. So must I. You praise me for impossible things and fantastic deeds. Your anger seeks to cut me. Yet it is I who have been treated basely, and I who howl with grief. May I then not even speak of it without suffering as well your resentment and scorn? He who does evil and will not bend his pleasure to listen to reproofs, let him beware lest great enmity be his own reward. Pray, follow my example: you have been sharp with me, contemptuous, irate, unjust, but I have tolerated it and take no revenge, no matter how warranted. And even now if I have wronged you or if my manner has been unseemly, pray tell me and I will gladly make amends. But if not, then it is you who must make amends for the harm done me, or teach me how my heart may be made whole. Truly, no man has ever been so hurt! Yet I would have you take note of my forbearance. Either undo the wrong done me, my children, and my wife, or stand with me before Almighty God to be judged. You could easily entreat me, for I would gladly leave the matter with you. I have trusted that you yourself would see the injustice you have done and yourself would give me satisfaction. Act with insight, or otherwise the hammer shall strike the anvil, iron upon iron, come what may!

20. DEATH

Kind words do soothe a man;
Understanding bringeth peace,
And forbearance, honor.
An angry man doth take no heed of justice.
Hadst thou before been gracious with Us,
Then Our part were also gentle
In showing thee the error of thy grief and lamentation.
Hast not heard of Seneca?
A philosopher who wanted to die in his bath.
Hast not read in his books
That none should lament the death of mortals?

If thou dost not know it, then know it now:
As soon as a man is born he hath begun to die.
The end is the twin of all beginning.
He who was sent out is required to return.
Strive not against what is ordained to happen,
Nor quarrel with what each must suffer.
What is borrowed must be given back.
All men live upon the Earth as in a foreign land,
Proceeding from being to nothingness. A man's life
Is a swift runner. Now alive, done
At the flip of a hand.
In short,
Every man oweth Us a dying
And his inheritance is death.
Thy wife's youth?
But the moment a man is born he is old enough to die.
Thou dost perhaps deem age to be a precious good?
Not so; it is a burden, a sickness, ugly, cold,
And bringeth no pleasure to any man. It is useless;
It is good for nothing.
The over-ripe apple falleth in dung;
The rotted pear falleth into the slough.
Her beauty? Thou wouldst be a child to shed tears for that.
For all beauty must be ruined by age or death,
All rosy lips drained of their color;
Red cheeks must turn pale,
Brilliant eyes, dull.
Hast not read the philosopher Hieronymous
Who teacheth men to beware of a woman's beauty,
Saying: Beauty, even with all carefulness
Is difficult to hold because so coveted;
Ugliness, however, is an easy thing to hold,
For it bringeth no pleasure to any one.
Let go, Plowman!
Lament no loss thou canst not undo.

21. THE PLOWMAN

I have heard that a wise man ought graciously to accept good admonition. I will
bear this reprimand of yours. But if he who censures well ought counsel well,
then, pray, help me and teach me how I may expunge from heart, mind and
sense this unspeakable pain, this grief, this immeasurable sorrow. My God, my
heart is broken beyond saying now that the true and constant honor of my house
is torn away. O Lord Death, the whole world cries out against you as I do, that
there could never be one so evil that in him not any good existed. So counsel me,
help me by showing how I can tear such sorrow from my heart, and how my
children are to be repaid for the loss of their unblemished mother. Else I'll be
forever without spirit and they will despair forever. And this you cannot hold

against me for I have seen unreasoning animals, out of instinct, mourn the death
of a mate. Help, counsel and restitution are what you owe me, for you alone
have done me injury. Should this not be given, then even if vengeance were
beyond the reach of Almighty God, vengeance would still be done—even if once
again the shovel and the cleaver must be used.

22. DEATH

Quack, quack, quack! cackles the goose,
Preach to him what one may.
Hast thou not already heard from Us
That one must not lament the death of men who die?
Why dost thou persist in setting thyself against
Things that are. We *are*
The appointed taker of the toll,
Whom all men must pay by yielding Us their life.
Verily, he doth outwit himself who undertaketh to deceive Us.
Let it sink into thy brain:
Life is made for dying;
Were there no life, We too would not be,
Our handiwork would not be,
Nor with it would there be the very order of the world.
Now, either thy pain is great,
Or thy stupidity.
If the latter, then pray thou to God for understanding.
But if it be thy grief, then have done with it,
Let go, and consider that man's life on Earth
Is wind. Wouldst seek counsel how to purge thy heart of sorrow?
But Aristotle long ago hath taught thee that joy,
Sorrow, fear and hope, these four,
Bring all the world to grief,
And those, especially, who know not how to fend them off.
Time is compressed by joy and fear,
Spun out by sorrow and hope.
Who doth not drive these four completely from his heart
Must be evermore enmeshed by care. Unhappiness
Must follow joy, and love must always come to grief, here,
On Earth.
Love and sorrow are linked. The end of one
Is ever the beginning of the other.
They are naught else than when a man doth clench
A thing in his mind he will not release—
Just as the contented man cannot be poor
Nor the discontented rich,
For peace lieth not in the having of things,
But dwelleth in the heart.
Who will not drive an old love from his heart
Must ever endure a present grief.

Drive from thy heart, thy mind, and thy sense
The very memory of love,
And thou shalt in one stroke defeat all sadness.
The moment thou hast lost a thing
And canst not win it back,
Act as though it never were thine own:
Thy sadness will leave thee forthwith.
And if thou wilt not do this thing,
Much grief lies yet before thee;
Each child's death will break thy heart anew,
And thy death theirs, and every parting will lay new sorrows
In all and for all.
Thou wouldst that the mother's loss be rectified.
Canst thou bring back years that have passed,
Words spoken, maidenhood deflowered?
Then canst thou bring back the mother to thy children.
We have counseled thee enough.
Canst comprehend it, thou dull pickaxe?

23. THE PLOWMAN

They say that to study long is to learn a little; in due time one understands the truth of this. Your homely sayings are sweetly agreeable—*Pfui!* Cast love, happiness, rapture and pleasure from the world and leave it a sickly remnant? Now *I* will cite the ancient Romans. They practiced it themselves and taught their children to esteem pleasure and spend their leisure time in gymnastics, jousting, dancing, wagering, games of running and jumping so that they would not fall prey to evil. For the soul of man can never run idle. Either the good or the bad must ever engage it, even in the dreams of sleep. Deprive the mind of its worthy thought, and corruption will rush in to take its place. Out the good, in the bad; out the bad, in the good: this interchange must last as long as the world. Ever since joy, modesty, propriety and other good manners have been driven from the world, it has been full of meanness, treachery, faithlessness and infamy. Were I therefore to drive thoughts of the beloved out of my mind, my soul would be corrupted. All the more, then, will I think of her. When a great love of the heart is suddenly transformed to heartbreak, who can forget it in the blinking of an eye? Only an evil man can do that; good friends are always rooted in each other's thoughts. Great distances, long years are no obstacles to those who love. If, then, she is physically dead to me, she will continue to live in my thoughts. Sir Death, your counsel must ring truer if it is to help me. Otherwise, fluttering bat, you must further endure the enmity of birds.

24. DEATH

Love that is not too dear,
Pain that is not in excess
Shall be the wise man's loss and gain,
But, alas, not thine.

Who seeketh counsel and will not heed it
Cannot well be guided. Our well-meant counsel
Fails to thrive with thee. Well,
Be it pleasing to thee or not, we would bring truth
Into the light of day,
And let him attend to it who may.
Thy dwarfed understanding, thy chopped-off thoughts,
Thy insubstantial heart yearn to make of men
More than they can be. But make of him what thou wilt,
Man, We say—begging leave of all chaste women—
Is this:
He is conceived in sin,
Nourished in the body of his mother
With unclean, unspeakable filth.
He is born into the world naked, and grimy as a beehive;
An abomination is man, a pocket of dung, a meal for worms,
A stinkhouse, a filthy swill tub, a flyblown carcass,
A mildewed cannister, a sack without bottom,
A bag full of holes, a windy bellows,
A voracious gullet, a stinking sewer,
A fraudulent pinchbeck,
A birdlimed twig,
A paper anchor,
And a garishly painted graveyard.
Let him hear it who may: every roundly made man
Hath nine holes in his body, all of which exude
Such abominable filth the likes of which can scarce be found.
Were never so beautiful a man to come before thee,
And hadst thou the eyes of a lynx,
And couldst thou espy what lay within,
Pale Shuddering would seize thee.
Tear away the arts of the tailor from even the fairest woman,
And thou seest a wretched puppet,
A fast-fading flower of momentary luster,
A clod of earth rushing to its decay.
Show Us a handful of beauty
—not painted on a wall—
In all the women who lived but a hundred years ago,
And take the Emperor's crown for thine own!
Therefore, let go of love,
Let go of sorrow,
Let the Rhine flow as do the other waters,
Thou wise blockhead of donkeytown!

25. THE PLOWMAN

I spit on you, vile slanderbag! That you degrade and besmirch the best beloved of God's creatures, and with it cast your filth upon the very Godhead Itself! I know now that you lied and were not, as you maintained, created in paradise. Else you would know that God created man and all things in their perfection, and gave to man dominion over all, and placed all creation at his feet that he should rule over the animals on the land, the birds in the air, the fish in the waters, and the abundance of all the fruits of the earth, as, in truth, he does. Were man as miserable, evil and unclean as you say, then would God have made a useless and a vile thing; He would be a Creator to be scorned instead of praised. And then the given Word would be false that God made the world and saw that it was good. Lord Death, make an end to your senseless braying. You defile God's sublimest works. Angels, devils, hobgoblins, wraiths—these are spirits under God's compulsion; but man is the greatest of God's works, the most perfect, the most free. It was said on the day of creation: In His own image hath He made him. When has ever a workman made so deft and rich a thing as that small and marvelous sphere that is the head of man—wherein such powers operate that reflect the processes of God Himself? There in the apple of the eye resides the most faithful of instruments masterfully formed as to a mirror, reaching to the clear circles of Heaven. There in the ear the sense of hearing, perfectly concealed behind a thin membrane, proves and determines from afar sweet sounds of every kind. There in the nose the sense of smell going in and coming out through two openings artfully adapted for the pleasures of all delicate and voluptuous fragrances. There in the mouth the teeth day after day grind the body's nourishments; there, too, the thin leaf of the tongue makes known the thoughts of men to men; and there, too, are the pleasures of the taste and test of food. Further: in man's head come thoughts from the very depths of the heart, thoughts that reach to the infinite, to the very Godhead Itself and beyond. Man alone possesses Reason, the noblest of treasures. His alone that fair configuration which none but God could have made, in which all meaning and art is quickened with wisdom. Let it be, Sir Death. You are the enemy of man and therefore speak no good of him.

26. DEATH

Scolding, cursing, extravagant dreams,
However much of them there be,
Can fill no sack,
No matter how small. Words are useless
Against a blabberer. However it be, Plowman,
With your claim that man is the epitome
Of Beauty, Truth and Good,
He will still fall into Our net,
Be caught up in Our snare.

Grammar, the basis of all good speech,
Cannot help him with clear and well-set words.
Rhetoric, the florid ground of splendid style,
Cannot help him with the colors and the tones of language.
Logic, the arbiter of truth and falsity,
Cannot help him with her hidden turns and labyrinthine paths to Truth.
Geometry, surveyor and appraiser of the Earth,
Cannot help him with her faultless measures and unerring weights.

Arithmetic, the queen of numbers,
Cannot help him with her calculations and her clever integers.
Astronomy, the mistress of the firmament,
Cannot help him with the influence of planets or the strength of stars.
Music, cordial deliverer of melody and song,
Cannot help him with her sweet sounds and high-wrought voices.
Philosophy, the acre of wisdom plowed crosswise and seeded
With the natural light of Reason and the will to goodness,
Cannot help him; nor can
Physics, with her many helpful droughts;
Geomancy, stipulator of the zodiac;
Pyromancy, reader of the fire;
Hydromancy, seer of the water;
Astrology, keeper of the supernatural lens;
Chiromancy, comely oracle of the hand;
Necromancy, wielder of the spirits of the dead;
Alchemy, strange transfigurer of metals;
Neither availeth the *Augur's*
Understanding of the voice of birds and his vision of the future;
Nor the *Haruspex's*
Consultations of the smoke that issueth from sacrificial altars;
Nor the *Paedomant* who from the innards of calves,
Nor the *Ornomant* who from the innards of partridges,
Ply their conjurations.
Nor the inconstant and ambiguous judgments of
The *Jurist,* that unconscionable Christian
Who doth braid together right and wrong along the crooked lines
Of his stunted articles of law.
Neither these nor any other;
Neither any nor all together with their arts and powers
Have help to offer. Each man must someday be toppled by Us,
Thrashed in Our fulling-mill,
And scoured in Our whirling barrel.
Thou mayst well believe it, thou blustering bumpkin!

27. THE PLOWMAN

One ought not repay evil with evil; a man must be patient. Such is the path of
virtue, which I will follow—and perhaps you, too, will become patient after your
impatience. I take it from your speech that you mean well and would advise me
truly. Then if there is truth in you, give me true counsel as one bound by an
oath. In what manner shall I now pursue my life? Till now I have lived within
the joy of marriage; what shall I do now? Shall I remain a worldly man or enter
the holy order? Both stand open to me now. In my mind I have examined all
kinds of lives, weighed them and judged them carefully, and I have found they are
all imperfect, frail and tainted with sin. I am in despair as to where to turn, for all
human paths seem laden with flaws. Lord Death, give me counsel! I stand in
need of counsel! In my heart I find, and I believe it to be true, that I shall never

again have such a home as the one her existence made for me. By my soul I tell you: If I knew that once again I would find such a wife then I would live a married man for all my days. Happy and blessed no matter where he be is the man who has found a good wife. To such a man it is a joy to strive for the necessities of life and to vie for honor. And to such a man it is as well a joy to repay honor with honor, faith with faith, blessing with blessing. He need not watch over her, for the best watch is that which a virtuous wife keeps upon herself. The man who cannot trust in his wife will be constantly beset with care. Lord of the heavens, Lord of every dwelling place, happy is he whose bed is blessed with so pure a companion! He should look to Heaven every day and raise his hands in thanks. Do your best, Lord Death, most capable lord!

28. DEATH

To praise without end; to revile without purpose;
This is the habit of the mass of men in all their undertakings.
But praise and blame must be fitly measured
That one may have them at one's hand when they are truly needed.
Thou dost now sing extravagant praises
Of the joys of marriage; yet
—begging leave of all virtuous women—
We would tell thee something:
The moment a man taketh a wife,
The two of them are in Our prison.
At once he hath obligation and care,
A drag-sled, a yoke, a horse-collar,
A burden, a heavy load, an incisored devil,
A daily rasp of which he cannot be free
'Til We bestow Our graces on him.
Day upon day a married man hath thunder in his house.
And hailstones, and foxes and serpents.
A wife always straineth to be master; if he draw up,
She draweth down; will he this,
She would that; will he hither,
She would thither. Of this game he'll have his fill,
And end each day without a victory.
She can deceive,
And at the same time flatter,
And at the same time cajole,
And cheat, with it all, while smiling as well,
And also weeping,
While all the while she is most heavily obstructing;
All this is inborn in her.
Too ill to work,
But well enough for lust,
She is tame or wild when it doth fit her purposes.
In the art of rebuttal she hath scant need of lawyers;

Her practise is ever to do what is forbidden,
While resisting what is asked of her.
That is too sweet for her,
That is too sour;
That is too much for her,
That is too little;
And if it be not too late for her,
It is surely too early.
If she should praise a thing,
It must first be warped upon a turner's lathe,
And even then her praise is spotted with derision.
For the married man help cometh never:
Be he too kind or be he too stern,
He receiveth equal portions of abuse—
Equal, indeed, to that which he doth earn by being then
Half-kindly and half-stern; help there is none.
Each day bringeth another imposition
—or a scolding;
Each week bringeth outlandish demands
—or growling;
Each month bringeth novel sorts of obnoxious filth
—or crimson wrath;
Each year bringeth new apparel
—or a daily recipe of rancor and contention;
And there is no help.
Of the vexations of the night, We will say nothing,
For at Our age we are ashamed of them.
And were We not minded now to spare the women who are virtuous,
We could sing thee still other songs of the dishonest ones.
Therefore, Plowman, know what thou dost praise;
Thou canst not tell gold from lead!

29. THE PLOWMAN

Revilers of women must be themselves reviled, say the masters of truth. What then shall be done with you, Lord Death? This unreasoning slander, even if permitted you by women, is most contemptible and a great offense to women. In the books of many a wise man it is said that without the guidance of a woman no man finds his way to happiness, for having wife and child is not the meanest part of earthly happiness. With this truth, Mistress Philosophy brought peace of mind to the Roman Boethius, himself the artist of consolations. Every thoughtful and wise man will bear me witness: no man is schooled save in the schools of women. Say what you will: a well-bred, beautiful and chaste wife surpasses all earthly goods that one may ever behold. Never have I seen a true man and a brave man who did not find his strength in the help of a woman. Wherever the worthiest assemble one may see it every day: in the market place, in the courts, in tournaments, in every summons to arms it is always women who bring about the best. He who is truly committed to a woman will not do evil. In the school of an upright woman one learns propriety and honor. It is women who have power over all earthly pleasures; they bring it about that everything festive and delightful is done in their honor. A brave man is threatened more by the wag of a woman's finger than by all force of arms. In short and clear: good women are the sustenance, the mainstay and the increase of every man. Of course, with gold there will be lead, with wheat weeds, with true coin counterfeit, and there will be vixens among women. But the good ought not suffer for the bad. How to that, Captain of Inverted Hills!

30. DEATH

A lump of dirt for a nugget of gold,
A turd for a topaze,
A pebble for a ruby—so taketh the fool—
A haystack is a castle,
The Danube is the sea,
A buzzard is the peregrine; thus nameth the fool.
And thou, as well, praiseth the raptures of the eye,
But seest not the root of things,
And knoweth not that everything there is
Is desire of the flesh,
The covetousness of eyes,
Or the aspirings of pride.
Flesh seeketh lust; the eye, possession; pride, honors.
Possession bringeth avarice; lust maketh wanton; honors breed vanity.
Couldst thou but know this,
Thou wouldst encounter suffering and joy with greater grace,
And wouldst leave Us in peace.
But sooner will the jackass comprehend the harpist's art
Than thou wilt recognize the truth.
For this reason We are so much troubled for thy sake.
When We tore young Pyramus from the maiden Thisbe,
Who were one heart and soul,
When We took away the world from Alexander,
When We destroyed young Paris of Troy and Helena of Greece,
We were never so sorely plagued as We are by thee.
Nor were We thus vexed by the Emperor Charles,
Or the Margrave William, or Theodoric of Verona,
Or the powerful Boppe, or Siegfried the invulnerable.
There are many mourners still for Aristotle and Avicenna,
Yet they leave Us in peace. When the mighty King David
And King Solomon the wise came to dying,
More thanks than cursing was Our share.
They who once lived are all of them gone;
Thou, and all who now are and are yet unborn,
Will follow behind. Despite all,
We, Death, here remain Lord!

31. THE PLOWMAN

Out of his own mouth a man is often condemned, especially he who speaks now this way, now that way. You have said before that you were something and yet nothing, that you are no spirit and yet are the end of life and that all men on earth were in your keeping. But now you say we must all pass away and you, Sir Death, remain here Lord! Contradictory words cannot together be true. If we must all leave this life, and if all earthly life must have an end, and if you, as you say, are the end of life, then I ask: when there is no more life, there will be no more dying and no more death. Where will you go then, Lord Death? Not to Heaven, for none but good spirits dwell there and you are, as you say, no spirit. If, then, there is nothing more on Earth for you to do, and if Earth exists no more, you must needs go straightaway to Hell, there to groan for all eternity. And then, too, the living and the dead will be avenged on you. No man can be guided by your contradictory words. Are all things on Earth created and fashioned in a manner so evil, pitiful and useless? Of that the Almighty God has never been accused. God has ever loved virtue, hated evil, punished and forgiven sin down to the present day. I think that He will always do so. Since I was a youth, I have read and learned from books how God created all things. You say that all being and life on Earth shall have an end. But opposed to this, Plato and other philosophers say that for all things the destruction of one is the birth of another, and that all things are based on rebirth, and that events of Heaven and Earth are conjoined in a whirl of everlasting change. With your double-edged speech, upon which no one may build, you would affright me from my suit. Therefore, Lord Death, my Destroyer, I convoke us before God, my Redeemer. And may He deliver to you an evil Amen.

32. DEATH

Oft when a man hath begun to speak
He cannot stop till he be interrupted.
From such a die hast thou been stamped.
We have once said it, and will again say it,
And with it make an end to it:
The Earth and all that it contains is built on shifting sand.
And now, indeed, it is more changeable than ever,
For everything is changed about:
The back is made the front, the front is back,
The top is undermost and what is under is on top;
The masses have made perversion into law.
But We have brought them all, all generations,
To the constancy of flames.
To find a good, true and helpful friend
Is, on Earth, almost as possible as to grasp a beam of light.
All men are more disposed to evil than to any good in them.
And should one do the good, he does it out of fear of Us.
All the activity of men is vanity and noise.
Their body, their wife and children, their honor,
Their possessions and all their powers fly away,

Vanish in an instant and are scattered with the wind;
Neither shape nor shadow can remain.
Look about thee and behold what the children of men
Do hasten after here on Earth:
How they plumb mountain and valley,
Wood and wilderness, the depths of ocean and earth
For the sake of worldly goods;
How they dig deep mines and probe in the earth
To bleed her veins of the shining ores they prize
Above all else. How they hew down trees
And, like sparrows, weave together walls and houses.
Plant orchards and set graftings,
Plow their fields, stake their vineyards,
Build their mills, exact their taxes,
Hunt and fish, gather together great herds of animals,
And countless servants and maids,
Ride high upon their horses,
Stock their houses and their coffers full of precious stones,
Gold, silver, and voluptuous apparel,
Surrendering themselves by night and by day
To the lusts and raptures they are ever seeking.
What is all that?
It is all vanity upon vanity, and confusion of the soul,
As fleeting as a day already past.
With war and thievery they make their gains,
For the more they have the more they have robbed.
And what they have they leave as an inheritance
For new quarreling and dissension.
Alas, mortal man liveth always in fear, in misery,
In sorrow, in care, in dread, in terror,
In sickness and pain, in sadness and woe, in wailing and moaning,
And in adversity of sundry kind. The more of earthly goods,
The more compounded his adversity.
But the greatest burden is that he cannot know when, where, or how
We shall pounce on him and drive him hence
Along the way of mortal flesh.
It is a burden to be borne by masters and slaves,
Men and women, rich and poor, good and evil.
O painful certainty, how little thou art heeded by fools!
When it is too late, they would all of them be pious.
Therefore, O man, let go of thy complaint.
Enter what course of life thou wouldst,
Thou wilt find it frail and vain as any other.
But turn thyself from evil and do good,
Seek peace and pursue it ever,
Prize above all earthly things
A conscience that is clear.
And to prove Our counsel hath been true,
We shall stand with thee before God,
The Eternal, The Great, The Almighty.

33. THE JUDGMENT OF GOD

Spring, Summer, Fall and Winter,
The four quickeners and helpers of the year,
Fell once into a great dispute,
Each boasting of his own good will
In wind, rain, thunder, snow
And weather of every grade and hue,
Each claiming that his work was best.
Spring said he vivified all fruit and brought abundance;
Summer that he brought all fruit its form and time of ripeness;
Fall said that for the other two he brought fruit home
Into cellars, barns and houses; while Winter said
He ate the fruit and drove away the venomous worm.
And each, in the eagerness of his claim,
And in the zeal of argument,
Forgot from whence his power came.
Now both of you do likewise:
The plaintiff mourns his loss as though it were his rightful due;
He gives no thought that it was loaned to him by Us.
And Death, as well, boasts of a warranted dominion
For which We alone indentured him.
The one bewails what is not his;
The other vaunts a power he does not himself possess.
Yet the quarrel is not without its sense,
And you have both fought well.
Sorrow drives the former to bring suit,
And, in the face of this, the latter is constrained to tell the truth.
Therefore:
To you, Plowman, honor;
To you, Death, victory.
Each man must give his life to Death, his body to earth,
His soul to Us.

34. THE PLOWMAN'S PRAYER TO GOD

Ever watchful Keeper of the world, God above all gods,
Wonderful Lord above all lords, all-powerful Spirit above all spirits,
Wellspring of all good, Source of all holiness,
Crown and giver of crowns, Reward and giver of rewards,
O hear me!

O Light that needs no light, in whom all other light is darkness,
Light that breaks upon all shadow,
Light that said "Let there be light!"
O Fire forever burning, O beginning and End,
Hear me!

Holy one above all holiness, Path without turning,
Best, Life of all life, Truth of all truth, Issuer of strength,
Perceiver of all evil, Helper of all in need of help,
Comforter and Rock of all celestial harmony,
Sculptor of the face of man, Law of the heavenly order, bright Sun,
Hear me!

Physician of all illness, sole Father of creation,
Almighty Companion from womb to grave, Hater of all corruption,
Judge and Unifier, Firm Knot which no man can unravel,
Hunter to whom no trail is hidden, Measurer, Arbiter, Conciliator,
O hear me!

Perfect Being in whose hand all perfection lies, Creator and Destroyer,
Host, Ministrant and Friend to all good men,
Mingler of the inconstant air, Kindler of fire, Lode-star,
Emperor in whose service none may fail, Cause of all causes,
Hear me!

Good above all goods, most worthy Lord Jesus,
Graciously receive the soul of my dearly beloved wife,
Grant her eternal rest, lave her with the dew of Your grace,
Keep her in the shadow of Your wings. Take her, O Lord, into
Your perfect peace.

I grieve for Margaret, my chosen wife. Grant her, Most Gracious
Lord, eternally to see into the mirror of Your divinity.

May all things that live under God help me to say with tranquil heart:
"Amen!"

Death and Immortality
Nikolai Berdyaev

Nikolai Berdyaev (1874–1948) was a famous Russian religious philosopher
who was exiled after falling into disfavor with the revolutionary regime in
1922. He died in Paris. His major works include *Dream and Reality, The
Destiny of Man,* and *The Beginning and the End.*

Ordinary systems of philosophical ethics do not deal with the problems of
eschatology. If they treat of immortality, they do so without going deep into the
question of death but discuss it chiefly in connection with man's moral responsibility, rewards and punishments, or, at best, with the need of satisfying his
longing for infinity. The conception of immortality has been defended on the

From Nicholas Berdyaev, *The Destiny of Man* (London, 1960), pp. 249–265. Reprinted by permission
of Geoffrey Bles.

ground of naturalistic metaphysics and the idea of the soul as a substance. It left completely untouched the problem of death, so fundamental for the religious and especially for the Christian consciousness. Death is a problem not only for metaphysics but also for ontological ethics. Thinkers like Kierkegaard and Heidegger recognize this. It also acquires a central significance in Freud. It is the problem of death, inseverably connected with that of time, that has a primary significance; the problem of immortality is secondary, and as a rule it has been wrongly formulated. The very word "immortality" is inexact and implies a rejection of the mysterious fact of death. The question of the immortality of the soul forms part of a metaphysic that is utterly out of date. Death is the most profound and significant fact of life, raising the least of mortals above the mean commonplaces of life. The fact of death alone gives true depth to the question as to the meaning of life. Life in this world has meaning just because there is death; if there were no death in our world, life would be meaningless. The meaning is bound up with the end. If there were no end, i.e. if life in our world continued for ever, there would be no meaning in it. Meaning lies beyond the confines of this limited world, and the discovery of meaning presupposes an end here. It is remarkable that although men rightly feel the horror of death and rightly regard it as the supreme evil, they are bound to connect with it the final discovery of meaning. Death—the supreme horror and evil—proves to be the only way out of the "bad time" into eternity; immortal and eternal life prove to be only attainable through death. Man's last hope is connected with death, which manifests so clearly the power of evil in the world. This is the greatest paradox of death. According to the Christian religion death is the result of sin and is the last enemy, the supreme evil which must be conquered. And at the same time in our sinful world death is a blessing and a value. It inspires us with terror not merely because it is an evil, but because the depth and the greatness of it shatter our everyday world and exceed the powers accumulated by us in this life to meet this world's requirements. Spiritual enlightenment and an extraordinary intensity of spiritual life are needed to give us a right attitude towards death. Plato was right in teaching that philosophy was the practice of death. The only trouble is that philosophy as such does not know how one ought to die and how to conquer death. The philosophic doctrine of immortality does not show the way.

It might be said that ethics at its highest is concerned with death rather than with life, for death manifests the depth of life and reveals the end, which alone gives meaning to life. Life is noble only because it contains death, an end which testifies that man is destined to another and a higher life. Life would be low and meaningless if there were no death and no end.

Meaning is never revealed in an endless time; it is to be found in eternity. But there is an abyss between life in time and life in eternity, and it can only be bridged by death and the horror of final severance. When this world is apprehended as self-sufficient, completed and closed in, everything in it appears meaningless because everything is transitory and corruptible—i.e. death and mortality in this world is just what makes it meaningless. This is one-half of the truth seen from a narrow and limited point of view. Heidegger is right in saying that the herd-mentality (*das Man*) is insensitive to the anguish of death.[1] It feels merely a low fear of death as of that which makes life meaningless. But there

[1] See *Sein und Zeit*, chapter *Das mögliche Ganzsein des Daseins und das Sein zum Tode*.

is another half of the truth, concealed from the ordinary point of view. Death not merely makes life senseless and corruptible: it is also a sign, coming from the depths, of there being a higher meaning in life. Not base fear but horror and anguish which death inspires in us prove that we belong not only to the surface but to the depths as well, not only to temporal life but also to eternity. While we are in time, eternity both attracts and horrifies us. We feel horror and anguish not only because all that we hold dear dies and comes to an end, but still more because we are conscious of a yawning abyss between time and eternity. Horror and anguish at having to cross the abyss contain at the same time a hope that the final meaning shall be revealed and realized. Death holds hope as well as horror for man, though he does not always recognize this or call it by an appropriate name. The meaning that comes from the other world is like a scorching flame to us and demands that we should pass through death. Death is not only a biological and psychological fact but a spiritual fact as well. *The meaning of death is that there can be no eternity in time and that an endless temporal series would be meaningless.*

But death is a manifestation of life, it is found on this side of life and is life's reaction to its own demand for an end in time. Death cannot be understood merely as the last moment of life followed either by non-being or by existence in the world beyond. Death is an event embracing the whole of life. Our existence is full of death and dying. Life is perpetual dying, experiencing the end in everything, a continual judgment passed by eternity upon time. Life is a constant struggle against death and a partial dying of the human body and the human soul. Death within life is due to the impossibility of embracing the fullness of being, either in time or in space. Time and space are death-dealing, they give rise to disruptions which are a partial experience of death. When, in time, human feelings die and disappear, this is an experience of death. When, in space, we part with a person, a house, a town, a garden, an animal, and have the feeling that we may never see them again, this is an experience of death. The anguish of every parting, of every severance in time and space, is the experience of death. I remember what anguish I felt as a boy at every parting. It was so all-embracing that I lived through mortal anguish at the thought of never seeing again the face of a stranger I met, the town I happened to pass through, the room in which I spent a few days, a tree or a dog I saw. This was, of course, an experience of death within life.

Space and time cannot enfold the wholeness of being but condemn us to severances and separations, and death always triumphs in life; it testifies that meaning is to be found in eternity and in fullness of being, that in the life in which meaning will triumph there shall be no parting, no dying, no corruption of human thoughts and feelings. We die not only in our own death but in the death of those we love. We have in life the experience of death, though not the final experience of it. And we cannot be reconciled to death—to the death neither of human beings nor of animals, plants, things or houses. The striving for eternity of all that exists is the essence of life. And yet eternity is reached only by passing through death, and death is the destiny of everything that exists in this world. The higher and more complex a being is, the more it is threatened with death. Mountains live longer than men, although their life is less complex and lower in quality; Mont Blanc appears to be more immortal than a saint or a genius. Things are comparatively more stable than living beings.

Death has a positive significance, but at the same time it is the most terrible and the only evil. Every kind of evil in the last resort means death. Murder, hatred, malice, depravity, envy, vengeance are death and seeds of death. Death is at the bottom of every evil passion. Pride, greed, ambition are deadly in their results. There is no other evil in the world except death and killing. Death is the evil result of sin. A sinless life would be immortal and eternal. Death is a denial of eternity and therein lies its ontological evil, its hostility to existence, its striving to reduce creation to non-being. Death resists God's creation of the world and is a return to the original non-being. Death wants to free the creature by bringing it back to primeval freedom that preceded the creation of the world. There is but one way out for the creature which in its sin resists God's conception of it—death. Death is a negative testimony to God's power and to the Divine meaning manifested in the meaningless world. It might be said that the world would carry out its godless plan of an endless (but not eternal) life if there were no God; but since God exists, that plan is not realizable and ends in death. The son of God, the Redeemer and Saviour, absolutely sinless and holy, had to accept death, and thereby He sanctified death. Hence the double attitude of Christianity to death. Christ has destroyed death by His death. His voluntary death, due to the evil of the world, is a blessing and a supreme value. In worshipping the cross we worship death which gives us freedom and victory. In order to rise again we must die. Through the cross death is transfigured and leads us to resurrection and to life. The whole of this world must be made to pass through death and crucifixion, else it cannot attain resurrection and eternity.

If death is accepted as a part of the mystery of life, it is not final and has not the last word. Rebellion against death in our world is rebellion against God. But at the same time we must wage a heroic struggle against death, conquer it as the last evil and pluck out its sting. The work of Christ in the world is in the first instance victory over death and preparation for resurrection and eternity. The good is life, power, fullness and eternity of life. Death proves to be the greatest paradox in the world, which cannot be understood rationally. Death is folly that has become commonplace. The consciousness that death is an ordinary everyday occurrence has dulled our sense of its being irrational and paradoxical. The last achievement of the rationalized herd-mind is to try to forget about death altogether, to conceal it, to bury the dead as unobtrusively as possible. It is the very opposite of the spirit expressed in the Christian prayer "ever to remember death." In this respect modern civilized people are incomparably inferior to the ancient Egyptians.

The paradox of death takes an aesthetic as well as a moral form. Death is hideous, the acme of hideousness, it is dissolution, the loss of all image and form, the triumph of the lower elements of the material world. But at the same time death is beautiful, it ennobles the least of mortals and raises him to the level of the greatest, it overcomes the ugliness of the mean and the commonplace. There is a moment when the face of the dead is more beautiful and harmonious than it had been in life. Ugly, evil feelings pass away and disappear in the presence of death. Death, the greatest of evils, is more noble than life in this world. The beauty and charm of the past depends upon the ennobling influence of death. It is death that purifies the past and puts upon it the seal of eternity. Death brings with it not only dissolution but purification as well. Nothing perishable, spoiled and corruptible can stand the test of death—only the eternal can. Terrible as it is to admit it, the significance of life is bound up with death and is only revealed in the face of death. Man's moral worth is manifested in the test of death, which abounds in life itself.

But at the same time struggle with death in the name of eternal life is man's main task. The fundamental principle of ethics may be formulated as follows: act so as to conquer death and affirm everywhere, in everything and in relation to all, eternal and immortal life. It is base to forget the death of a single living being and to be reconciled to it. The death of the least and most miserable creature is unendurable, and if it is irremediable, the world cannot be accepted and justified. All and everything must be raised to eternal life. This means that the principle of eternal being must be affirmed in relation to human beings, animals, plants and even inanimate things. Man must always and in everything be a giver of life and radiate creative vital energy. Love for all that lives, for every creature, rising above the love for abstract ideas, means struggle against death in the name of eternal life. Christ's love for the world and for man is victory over the powers of death and the gift of abundant life.

Asceticism means struggle with death and with the mortal elements within oneself. Struggle with death in the name of eternal life demands such an attitude to oneself and to other people as though both I and they were on the point of death. Such is the moral significance of death in the world. Conquer the low animal fear of death, but always have a spiritual fear of it, a holy terror before its mystery. It was death that first gave man the idea of the supernatural. Enemies of religion such as Epicurus thought they disproved it by showing that it originated in the fear of death. But they will never succeed in disproving the truth that in the fear of death, in the holy terror of it, man comes into touch with the deepest mystery of being and that death contains a revelation. The moral paradox of life and of death can be expressed by a moral imperative: treat the living as though they were dying and the dead as though they were alive, i.e. always remember death as the mystery of life and always affirm eternal life both in life and in death.

Life, not in its weakness but in its strength, intensity and super-abundance, is closely connected with death. This is felt in the Dionysian cults. This is revealed in love which is always connected with death. Passion, i.e. the expression of the highest intensity of life, always holds the menace of death. He who accepts love in its overwhelming power and tragedy, accepts death. He who attaches too much value to life and avoids death, runs away from love and sacrifices it to other tasks of life. In erotic love the intensity of life reaches its highest pitch and leads to destruction and death. The lover is doomed to death and involves the loved one in his doom. In the second act of *Tristan and Isolde* Wagner gives a musical revelation of this. The herd-mind tries to weaken the connection between love and death, to safeguard love and settle it down in this world. But it is not even capable of noticing love. It organizes the life of the race and knows only one remedy against death—birth. Life seems to conquer death through birth. But the victory of birth over death has nothing to do with personality, with its fate and its hopes; it is concerned with life of the race only. The victory over death through birth is an illusion. Nature does not know the mystery of conquering death; the victory can come only from the supernatural world. Throughout their whole history men have tried to struggle against death, and this gave rise to various beliefs and theories. Sometimes the struggle took the form of forgetting about death and sometimes of idealizing it and revelling in the thought of destruction.

The philosophical idea of the natural immortality of the soul deduced from its substantiality leads nowhere. It ignores the fact of death and denies the tragedy of it. From the point of view of such a doctrine there is no need to struggle against death and corruption for the sake of eternal life. It is rationalistic metaphysic without any tragic element in it. Scholastic spiritualism is not a solution of the problem of death and immortality, but is a purely abstract and academic theory. In the same way idealism does not solve the problem or indeed does not even face it. The idealism of the German metaphysics has no place for personality, regards it merely as a function of the world-spirit or idea, and therefore the tragedy of death does not exist for it. Death is a tragedy only when there is an acute awareness of personality. It is only because personality is experienced as eternal and immortal that death is felt to be a tragedy. The death of that which is eternal and immortal in its meaning and destination is alone tragic; there is nothing tragic about the death of the temporal and the transitory. The death of personality in man is tragic because personality is God's eternal idea of him. It is unendurable that a complete personality containing the unity of all human powers and possibilities should die. Personality is not born of the father and the mother, it is created by God. There is no such thing as immortality of man as a natural being, born in the generic process; there is no natural immortality of his soul and body. In this world man is a mortal being. But he is conscious of the Divine image and likeness in him and feels that he belongs not only to the natural but to the spiritual world as well. Man regards himself, therefore, as belonging to eternity, and yearns for eternity. What is eternal and immortal in man is not the psychical or the physical element as such but the spiritual element which, acting in the other two, constitutes personality and realizes the image and likeness of God. Man is immortal and eternal as a spiritual being belonging to the incorruptible world, but his spirituality is not a naturally given fact; man is a spiritual being in so far as he manifests himself as such, in so far as the spirit in him gains possession of the natural elements. Wholeness and unity may result from the work of the spirit in the psychic and bodily elements and constitute personality. But the natural individual as such is not yet a personality, and immortality is not characteristic of him. Natural immortality belongs to the species or to the race but not to the individual. Immortality has to be won by the person and involves struggle for personality.

Idealism affirms the immortality of the impersonal or the superpersonal spirit, of the idea and value, but not of the person. Fichte and Hegel have nothing to say about personal human immortality. Human personality and its eternal destiny are sacrificed to the idea, the value, the world-spirit, world-reason, etc. There is an element of truth in this. It is true that it is not the natural, empirical man who is immortal and eternal but the spiritual, ideal, valuable element in him. The idealists, however, fail to recognize that this spiritual, ideal and valuable element forms an eternal personality and transmutes all man's powers for eternity; they are wrong in separating it out and abstracting it into an ideal heaven as an impersonal and non-human spirit, abandoning the rest of man to death and corruption. A realized and completed personality is immortal. But in the spiritual world there are no self-contained personalities, they are united with God, with other personalities and with the cosmos.

Materialists, positivists and followers of similar theories accept death, legitimize it, and at the same time try to forget about it, building up life on the graves. Their views show a lack of "memory of death" and are therefore shallow and commonplace. The theory of progress is entirely taken up with the future of the species, of the race, of the coming generations, and has no concern with personality and its destiny. Progress, like evolution, is absolutely impersonal. For the progressing species death is an unpleasant fact, but one that has nothing deep or tragic about it. The species has an immortality of its own. It is only for the person and from the personal point of view that death is tragic and significant.

Theories of a nobler variety take up a sad and resigned attitude towards death. They recognize the tragic nature of it, but as conceived by them the human personality, though conscious of itself, has not the spiritual force to struggle with death and conquer it. The Stoic or the Buddhist attitude to death shows impotence in the face of it, but it is nobler than the naturalistic theories which completely ignore death. The emotional as distinct from the spiritual attitude to death is always melancholy and coloured by the sadness of memory which has no power to raise the dead; only the spiritual attitude to death is victorious. The pre-Christian view of it implies resignation to fate. Christianity alone knows victory over death.

The ancient Hebrews were not familiar with the idea of personal immortality. We do not find it in the Bible. Personal self-consciousness had not yet awakened. The Jewish people were conscious of the immortality of their race but not of persons. Only in the book of Job there is awareness of personal destiny and its tragedy. It was not until the Hellenistic era, just before the coming of Christ, that the spiritual element in the Jewish religion came to be to some extent disentangled from the naturalistic, or, in other words, that personality was liberated and no longer dissolved in the collective, racial life. But the idea of immortality was truly revealed in the Greek and not in the Jewish thought.[2] The development of that idea in Greece is very instructive. At first man was recognized as mortal. Gods were immortal, but not men. Immortality was an attribute of the divine and not of the human nature. It came to be ascribed to man in so far as the divine, superhuman element was manifested in him. Not ordinary men but demigods, heroes and demons were immortal. The Greeks knew well the heart-rending grief caused by death. Greek tragedy and poetry is full of it. Man was resigned to inevitable death; he was denied immortality which the gods appropriated for themselves alone. The mortal human and the immortal divine principles were dissevered and became united only in heroes and supermen. Man descended into the subterranean realm of shadows and nothing could be sadder than his destiny. The melancholy, characteristic of the Greek and alien in this form to the Hebraic feeling for life, was rooted in the fact that the Greeks were able to reveal the human principle but not to connect it with the divine. It was the humanity of the Greeks that gave rise to the melancholy. And it was from the Greeks we heard the words that it was better for man not to be born. This is not the Indian metaphysical pessimism which denies man and regards the world as an illusion. It is an expression of human sadness for which both man and the world are real. Greeks were realists. But the Greek genius could not endure for ever the

---

[2] See Erwin Rohde, *Psyche, Seelenkult und Unsterblichkeitsglaube der Greichen.*

hiatus between the divine and the human world that doomed men to death and reserved immortality for the gods. A struggle for human immortality began.

The religious mythological consciousness of Greece recognized that although the divine principle was immortal and the human mortal, man's thought brought him into communion with the divine and enabled him to rise up to it and acquire it. This was the teaching of the Mysteries, of the Orphics and of Plato's philosophy. The human soul contains a divine element, but it must be freed from the power of matter; only then will man become immortal. Immortality means that the divine element of the soul forsakes the lower, material world and does not transfigure it. Immortality is ideal and spiritual. It belongs only to that which is immortal in its metaphysical nature, but is not won for elements that are mortal and corruptible, i.e. death and corruption are not conquered. According to the Orphic myth the soul descends into the sinful material world, but it must be freed from it and return to its spiritual home. That myth had a great influence upon Plato, as can be seen particularly from *Phaedo,* and is one of the most profound human myths. It is connected with the ancient doctrine of reincarnation—one of the few attempts to understand the destiny of the soul in its past and future. And Orphism does contain a certain eternal truth. Christianity teaches of resurrection, of the victory over death for every life, for all the created world, and in this it is infinitely superior to the Greek conception of immortality which dooms a considerable part of the world to death and corruption. But the Christian view does not make clear the mystery of the genesis of the soul. The presence of the eternal element in the soul means eternity not only in the future but in the past as well. That which has an origin in time cannot inherit eternity. If the human soul bears the image and likeness of God, if it is God's idea, it arises in eternity and not in time, in the spiritual and not in the natural world. But Christian consciousness can interpret this dynamically and not statically as Platonism does. In eternity, in the spiritual world, there goes on a struggle for personality, for the realization of God's idea. Our natural earthly life is but a moment in the process which takes place in the spiritual world. This leads to the recognition of pre-existence in the spiritual world, which does not by any means involve reincarnation on earth.

The fact that man belongs to the eternal spiritual world does not imply a natural immortality of the spirit. Our natural world is the arena of the struggle for eternity and immortality, i.e. of the struggle for personality. In this struggle the spirit must gain possession of the natural elements of the soul and body for their eternal life and resurrection. Christianity teaches not so much of natural immortality which does not presuppose any struggle as of resurrection which presupposes the struggle of spiritual gracious forces with the powers of death. Resurrection means spiritual victory over death, it leaves nothing to death and corruption, as abstract spiritualism does. The doctrine of resurrection recognizes the tragic fact of death and means victory over it—which is not to be found in any doctrines of immortality, whether Orphic or Platonic or theosophical. Christianity alone faces death, recognizes both its tragedy and its meaning, but at the same time refuses to reconcile itself to it and conquers it. Eternal and immortal life is possible for man not because it is natural to the human soul, but because Christ rose from the dead and conquered the deadly powers of the world—because in the cosmic miracle of the Resurrection meaning has triumphed over meaninglessness.

The doctrine of the natural immortality of the human soul severs the destiny of the individual soul from the destiny of the cosmos, of the world-whole. It is metaphysical individualism. But the doctrine of the Resurrection links up the destiny of man with world-destiny. The resurrection of my body is at the same time the resurrection of the body of the world. "Body" in this connection means of course "spiritual body" and not the material frame. A complete personality is connected with the body and the eternal form of it and not merely with the soul. If it had not been for the coming of Christ and for His Resurrection, death would have triumphed in the world and in man. The doctrine of immortality is paradoxical: man is both mortal and immortal, he belongs both to the death-dealing time and to eternity, he is both a spiritual and a natural being. Death is a terrible tragedy, and death is conquered by death through Resurrection. It is conquered not by natural but by supernatural forces.

Two Russian religious thinkers have said remarkable things about life and death, from two entirely opposed points of view—V. Rozanov and N. Feodorov. For Rozanov all religions fall into two categories according as to whether they are based on the fact of birth or of death. Birth and death are the most important and significant events in life, and in the experience of them we catch a glimpse of the divine. Judaism and almost all pagan religions are for Rozanov religions of birth, while Christianity is the religion of death. Religions of birth are religions of life, since life springs from birth, i.e. from sex. But Christianity has not blessed birth, has not blessed sex, but enchanted the world with the beauty of death. Rozanov struggles against death in the name of life. In his view death is conquered by birth. Life is for ever triumphant through birth. But then death is conquered by life only for the newly born and not for the dead. To regard birth as victory over death is only possible if one is utterly insensitive to the human personality and its eternal destiny. For Rozanov the primary reality and the bearer of life is the genus and not the individual. In birth the genus triumphs over the personality: the genus lives for ever, the person dies. But the tragic problem of death is the problem of personality and not of the genus, and it is experienced in all its poignancy when personality is conscious of itself as a true reality and the bearer of life. However flourishing the life of the new generations may be, it does not remedy the unendurable tragedy of the death of a single living being. Rozanov knows nothing about eternal life, he knows only the endless life through child-bearing. It is a kind of sexual pantheism. Rozanov forgets that it was not with Christ that death came into the world and that the last word of Christianity is not death, not Calvary, but Resurrection and eternal life. Rozanov seeks escape from the horror of death in the vital intensity of sex. But sex in its fallen state is the very source of death in the world, and it is not for it to conquer death.

For N. Feodorov the problem is quite different. No one in the whole of human history has felt such pain at the thought of death as did Feodorov, nor such a burning desire to restore to life all who died. While Rozanov thinks of the children that are being born and finds comfort in the thoughts of life in the future, Feodorov thinks of the dead ancestors, and finds a source of sorrow in the thought of death in the past. For Feodorov death is the worst and only evil. We must not passively resign ourselves to it; it is the source of all evils. Final victory over death consists, in his view, not in the birth of a new life but in raising up the old, in bestowing resurrection upon the dead ancestors. This feeling for the dead shows how lofty was Feodorov's moral consciousness. Man ought to be a giver of life and affirm life for all eternity. This is the supreme moral truth, whatever we may think of Feodorov's "plan" of raising the dead.

There was a great deal of truth, but also a great deal of error, in Feodorov's attitude to death. He wrongly understood the mystery of it. Feodorov was a believing Christian, but he apparently failed to grasp the mystery of the Cross and to accept the redeeming meaning of death. Death was not for him an inner moment of life, through which every sinful life must inevitably pass. While Rozanov was blind to the Resurrection, Feodorov failed to see the Cross, and its redeeming significance. Both wanted to struggle with death in the name of life and to conquer death—one through birth and the other through raising the dead to life. There is more truth in Feodorov's view, but it is a one-sided truth. Death cannot be conquered by denying all meaning to it, i.e. by denying its metaphysical depth. Heidegger rightly says that the source of death is "anxiety," but that is a source visible from our everyday world. Death is also a manifestation of eternity, and in our sinful world eternity means terror and anguish. The paradoxical fact that a man may be afraid of dying in an accident or from a contagious disease, but is not afraid of dying on the battlefield or as a martyr for his faith, shows that eternity is less terrifying when we rise above the level of commonplace everyday existence.

Both individual death and the death of the world inspire horror. There is a personal and a cosmic Apocalypse. Apocalyptic mood is one in which the thought of death reaches its highest intensity, but death is experienced as the way to a new life. The Apocalypse is the revelation about the death of the cosmos, though death is not the last word of it. Not only the individual man is mortal, but also races, civilizations, mankind as a whole, all the world and all created things. It is remarkable that the anguish of this thought is even greater than that of the anticipation of personal death. The fate of the individual and of the world are closely interconnected and intertwined by thousands of bonds. Man suffers anguish not only because he is doomed to death but because all the world is doomed to it. During historical epochs which were not marked by apocalyptic moods a man's death was softened by the thought of the race continuing for ever and preserving the results of his life and activity. But Apocalypse is the end of all perspectives of racial or cosmic immortality; in it every creature and all the world is directly faced with the judgment of eternity. There can be no comfort in the thought that we shall be immortal in our children and that our work will last for ever, for the end is coming to all consolations that are in time. Apocalypse is a paradox of time and eternity that cannot be expressed in rational terms. The end of our world will come in time, in time as we know it. But it is also the end of time as we know it and therefore lies beyond its limits. This is an antinomy similar to Kant's antinomies of pure reason.[3] When the end comes there shall be no more time. And therefore we must paradoxically think of the end of the world both as in time and in eternity. The end of the world, like the end of each individual man, is an event both immanent and transcendent. Horror and anguish are caused by this incomprehensible combination of the transcendent and the immanent, the temporal and the eternal. For every one of us and for the world as a whole there

---

[3] Kant's genius is seen at its best in his treatment of the antinomies of pure reason. See *Kritik der reinen Vernunft, Die Antinomie der reinen Vernunft.*

comes a catastrophe, a jump across the abyss, a mysterious escape from time which takes place in time. The death of an individual is also a deliverance from time taking place in time. If our sinful temporal world as we know it were endless, this would be an evil nightmare, just like the endless continuation of an individual life. It would be a triumph of the meaningless. And the presentiment of the coming end calls forth, together with horror and anguish, hope and expectancy of the final revelation and triumph of meaning. Judgment and valuation of all that has happened in the world is the final revelation of meaning. The Last Judgment of individuals and of the world, interpreted in an inner sense, is nothing other than the discovery of meaning and the affirmation of qualities and values.

The paradox of time and eternity exists for the destiny both of the world and of the individual. Eternal and immortal life may be objectified and naturalized, and then it is spoken of as life in the world beyond. It appears as a natural realm of being though different from ours. Man enters it after death. But eternal and immortal life regarded from within and not objectified is essentially different in quality from the natural and even the supernatural existence. It is a spiritual life, in which eternity is attained while still in time. If man's existence were wholly taken up into the spirit and transmuted into spiritual life so that the spiritual principle gained final possession of the natural elements of the body and the soul, death as a natural fact would not take place at all. The transition to eternity would be accomplished, without the event which externally appears to us as death. Eternal life is revealed in time, it may unfold itself in every instant as an eternal present. Eternal life is not a future life but life in the present, life in the depths of an instant of time. In those depths time is torn asunder. It is therefore a mistake to expect eternity in the future, in an existence beyond the grave and to look forward to death in time in order to enter in to the divine eternal life. Strictly speaking, eternity will never come in the future—in the future there can only be a bad infinity. Only hell can be thought of in this way. Eternity and eternal life come not in the future but in a moment, i.e. they are a deliverance from time, and mean ceasing to project life into time. In Heidegger's terminology it means the cessation of "anxiety" which gives temporal form to existence.

Death exists externally as a certain natural fact which takes place in the future, and it signifies that existence assumes a temporal form, and life is projected into the future. Inwardly, from the point of view of eternity unfolded in the depths of the moment and not projected into time, death does not exist; it is only an element in the eternal life. Death exists only "on this side of things," in temporal being, in the order of nature. The unfolding of spirituality, the affirmation of the eternal in life and participation in a different order of being mean transcendence of death and victory over it. To transcend death and conquer it is not to forget it or be insensitive to it, but to accept it within one's spirit, so that it ceases to be a natural, temporal fact and becomes a manifestation of meaning which proceeds from eternity.

The personal and the cosmic Apocalypse bring to light our failure to fulfil eternal righteousness in life and are a triumph of righteousness in the dark world of sin. The death of the world and of individuals, of nations, civilizations, customs, historical forms of state and society, is a catastrophic reminder on the part of truth and righteousness of the fact that they have been distorted and not fulfilled. This is the meaning, too, of all great revolutions which indicate an

Apocalypse within history, and the meaning of catastrophic events in the individual life. The Revelation about the coming of the antichrist and his kingdom shows that the Christian truth has not been fulfilled and that men are incapable and unwilling to realize it. Such is the law of spiritual life. If men do not freely realize the Kingdom of Christ, the kingdom of the antichrist will be brought about with necessity. Death comes to all life which does not fulfil the divine meaning and the divine truth. The triumph of irrationality is the revelation of meaning in the darkness of sin. Hence death, both cosmic and individual, is not merely a triumph of meaningless dark forces and a result of sin but also a triumph of meaning. It reminds man of the divine truth and does not allow unrighteousness to be eternal.

Theoretically, N. Feodorov was right in saying that the world and man could pass into eternal life without the catastrophe of the end and the Last Judgment, if humanity were fraternally united for the sake of the common task of realizing Christian righteousness and raising the dead.[4] But the world and mankind have gone too far in the path of evil, and judgment has come upon them already. Irrational, meonic freedom prevents the realization of Feodorov's "plan." He was too optimistic and under-valued the forces of evil. But the affirmation of eternity, of eternal life for every being and for all creation, is a moral imperative. Act so that eternal life might be revealed to you and that the energy of eternal life should radiate from you to all creation.

Ethics must be eschatological. The question of death and immortality is fundamental to a personalistic ethics and confronts us in every act and every expression of life. Insensitiveness to death and forgetfulness of it, so characteristic of the nineteenth and twentieth century ethics, mean insensitiveness to personality and to its eternal destiny, as well as insensitiveness to the destiny of the world as a whole. Strictly speaking, a system of ethics which does not make death its central problem has no value and is lacking in depth and earnestness. Although it deals with judgments and valuations, it forgets about the final judgment and valuation, i.e. about the Last Judgment. Ethics must be framed not with a prospect to happiness in an unending life here, but in view of an inevitable death and victory over death, of resurrection and eternal life. Creative ethics calls us not to the creation of temporary, transitory and corruptible goods and values which help us to forget death, the end, and the Last Judgment, but to the creation of eternal, permanent, immortal goods and values which further the victory of eternity and prepare man for the end.

Eschatological ethics does not by any means imply a passive renunciation of creative activity. Passive apocalyptic moods are a thing of the past, they are a sign of decadence and an escape from life. On the contrary, eschatological ethics based upon apocalyptic experience demands an unprecedented intensity of human creativeness and activity. We must not passively await in horror and anguish the impending end and the death of human personality and the world. Man is called actively to struggle with the deadly forces of evil and creatively to prepare for the coming of the Kingdom of God. Christ's second coming presupposes intense creative activity on our part, preparing both mankind and the world for the end. The end itself depends upon man's creative activity and is determined by the positive results of the cosmic process. We must not passively

---

[4] See *Filosofia obshtchago dela.*

wait for the Kingdom of Christ, any more than for that of antichrist, but must actively and creatively struggle against the latter and prepare for the Kingdom of God which is taken by force.

To regard apocalyptic prophecies with passive resignation means to interpret them in a naturalistic sense, to rationalize them and deny the mysterious combination of Divine Providence and human freedom. It is equally wrong to take up a passive and fatalistic attitude to one's own death, to the death of personality, and regard it as a predetermined natural fact. We must accept death freely and with an enlightened mind, and not rebel against it; but this free and enlightened acceptance of death is a creative activity of the spirit. There is a false activity which rebels against death and refuses to accept it. It leads to unendurable suffering. But there is also the true activity which is the victory of eternity over death. An active spirit does not really fear death—only a passive spirit does. An active spirit experiences an infinitely greater fear and terror than that of death—the fear of hell and eternal torments. It lives through its own eternity; death exists for it not inwardly but merely as an external fact. It experiences terror at the thought of its eternal destiny and of the judgment which is in eternity.

We come here upon a psychological paradox which to many people is unknown and incomprehensible. An active spirit which has a direct inward experience of being eternal and indestructible may, so far from fearing death, actually desire it and envy those who do not believe in immortality and are convinced that death is the end. It is a mistake to imagine that the so-called faith in immortality is always comforting and that those who have it are in a privileged and enviable position. Faith in immortality is a comfort and makes life less hard, but it is also a source of terror and of an overwhelming responsibility. Those who are convinced that there is no immortality know nothing of this responsibility. It would be more correct to say that the unbelievers rather than the believers make life easy for themselves. Unbelief in immortality is suspicious just because it is so easy and comforting; the unbelievers comfort themselves with the thought that in eternity there will be no judgment of meaning over their meaningless lives. The extreme, unendurable terror is not the terror of death but of judgment and of hell. It does not exist for the unbelievers, only the believers know it. A passive spirit seldom experiences it, but an active one experiences it with particular intensity, because it is apt to connect its destiny, and consequently judgment and the possibility of hell, with its own creative efforts. The problem of death inevitably leads to that of hell. Victory over death is not the last and final victory. Victory over death is too much concerned with time. The last, final and ultimate victory is victory over hell. It is wholly concerned with eternity. Still more fundamental than the task of raising the dead, preached by Feodorov, is the task of conquering hell and freeing from it all who are suffering "eternal" torments. The final task, which ethics is bound to set us in the end, is creative liberation of all beings from the temporal and "eternal" torments of hell. If this task is not realized, the Kingdom of God cannot be realized either.

The Mortification of the Flesh

Evelyn Underhill

Evelyn Underhill (1875–1941), British educator, writer, and philosopher, is best known for her monumental study, *Mysticism.* Other works are *The Mystic Way* and *Practical Mysticism.*

Mortification takes its name from the reiterated statement of all ascetic writers that the senses, or "body of desire," with the cravings which are excited by different aspects of the phenomenal world, must be mortified or killed; which is, of course, a description of psychological necessities from their special point of view. All those self-regarding instincts—so ingrained that they have become automatic—which impel the self to choose the more comfortable part, are seen by the awakened intuition of the embryo mystic as gross infringements of the law of love. "This is the travail that a man behoveth, to draw out his heart and his mind from the fleshly love and the liking of all earthly creatures, from vain thoughts and from fleshly imaginations, and out from the love and the vicious feeling of himself, that his soul should find no rest in no fleshly thought, nor earthly affection."[1] The rule of Poverty must be applied to the temper of normal consciousness as well as to the tastes and posessions of the self. Under this tonic influence, real life will thrive; unreal life will wither and die.

This mortifying process is necessary, not because the legitimate exercise of the senses is opposed to Divine Reality, but because those senses have usurped a place beyond their station; become the focus of energy, steadily drained the vitality of the self. "The dogs have taken the children's meat." The senses have grown stronger than their masters, monopolized the field of perception, dominated an organism which was made for greater activities, and built up those barriers of individuality which must be done away if true personality is to be achieved, and with it some share in the boundless life of the One. It is thanks to this wrong distribution of energy, this sedulous feeding of the cuckoo in the nest, that "in order to approach the Absolute, mystics must withdraw from everything, even themselves."[2] "The soul is plunged in utter ignorance, when she supposes that she can attain to the high estate of union with God before she casts away the desire of all things, natural and supernatural, which she may possess," says St. John of the Cross,[3] "because the distance between them and that which takes place in the state of pure transformation in God is infinite."[3]

From Evelyn Underhill, *Mysticism* (New York, 1961), pp. 220–231. Published in a paperback edition in 1961 by E. P. Dutton & Co., Inc., and used with their permission.

[1] Walter Hilton, "The Scale of Perfection," bk. i. cap. 8, xlii.
[2] Récéjac, "Fondements de la Connaissance Mystique." p. 78. This, however, is to be understood of the initial training of the mystic; not of his final state.
[3] "Subida del Monte Carmelo," l. i. cap. v.

Again, "until the desires be lulled to sleep by the mortification of sensuality, and sensuality itself be mortified in them, so that it shall war against the spirit no more, the soul cannot go forth in perfect liberty to union with the Beloved."[4]

The death of selfhood in its narrow individualistic sense is, then, the primary object of mortification. All the twisted elements of character which foster the existence of this unreal yet complex creature are to be pruned away. Then, as with the trees of the forest, so with the spirit of man, strong new branches will spring into being, grow towards air and light. "I live, yet not I" is to be the declaration of the mystic who has endured this "bodily death." The self-that-is-to-be will live upon a plane where her own prejudices and preferences are so uninteresting as to be imperceptible. She must be weaned from these nursery toys: and weaning is a disagreeable process. The mystic, however, undertakes it as a rule without reluctance: pushed by his vivid consciousness of imperfection, his intuition of a more perfect state, necessary to the fulfilment of his love. Often his entrance upon the torments of the Purgative Way, his taking up of the spiritual or material instruments of mortification, resembles in ardour and abruptness that "heroic plunge into Purgatory" of the newly dead when it perceives itself in the light of Love Divine, which is described in the "Treatise" of St. Catherine of Genoa as its nearest equivalent. "As she, plunged in the divine furnace of purifying love, was united to the Object of her love, and satisfied with all he wrought in her, so she understood it to be with the souls in Purgatory."[5]

This "divine furnace of purifying love" demands from the ardent soul a complete self-surrender, and voluntary turning from all impurity, a humility of the most far-reaching kind: and this means the deliberate embrace of active suffering, a self-discipline in dreadful tasks. As gold in the refiner's fire, so "burning of love into a soul truly taken all vices purgeth." Detachment may be a counsel of prudence, a practical result of seeing the true values of things; but the pain of mortification is seized as a splendid opportunity, a love token, timidly offered by the awakened spirit to that all-demanding Lover from Whom St. Catherine of Siena heard the terrible words "I, Fire, the Acceptor of sacrifices, ravishing away from them their darkness, give the light."[6] "Suffering is the ancient law of love," says the Eternal Wisdom to Suso, "there is no quest without pain, there there is no lover who is not also a martyr. Hence it is inevitable that he who would love so high a thing as Wisdom should sometimes suffer hindrances and griefs."[7]

The mystics have a profound conviction that Creation, Becoming, Transcendence, is a painful process at the best. Those who are Christians point to the Passion of Christ as a proof that the cosmic journey to perfection, the path of the Eternal Wisdom, follows of necessity the Way of the Cross. That law of the inner life, which sounds so fantastic and yet is so bitterly true—"No progress without pain"—asserts itself. It declares that birth pangs must be endured in the spiritual as well as in the material world: that adequate training must always hurt

[4] *Op. cit.,* bk. i. cap. xv.
[5] S. Caterina di Genova, "Trattato di Purgatorio," cap. i.
[6] Dialogo, cap. lxxxv.
[7] Leben, cap. iv.

the athlete. Hence the mystics' quest of the Absolute drives them to an eager and heroic union with the reality of suffering, as well as with the reality of joy.[8]

This divine necessity of pain, this necessary sharing in the travail of a World of Becoming, is beautifully described by Tauler in one of those "internal conversations" between the contemplative soul and its God, which abound in the works of the mystics and are familiar to all readers of "The Imitation of Christ." "A man once thought," says Tauler, "that God drew some men even by pleasant paths, while other were drawn by the path of pain. Our Lord answered him thus, 'What think ye can be pleasanter or nobler than to be made most like unto Me? that is by suffering. Mark, to whom was ever offered such a troubled life as to Me? And in whom can I better work in accordance with My true nobility than in those who are most like Me? They are the men who suffer. . . . Learn that My divine nature never worked so nobly in human nature as by suffering; and because suffering is so efficacious, it is sent out of great love. I understand the weakness of human nature at all times, and out of love and righteousness I lay no heavier load on man than he can bear. The crown must be firmly pressed down that is to bud and blossom in the Eternal Presence of My Heavenly Father. He who desires to be wholly immersed in the fathomless sea of My Godhead must also be deeply immersed in the deep sea of bitter sorrow. I am exalted far above all things, and work supernatural and wonderful works in Myself: the deeper and more supernaturally a man crushes himself beneath all things, the more supernaturally will he be drawn far above all things.'"[9]

Pain, therefore, the mystics always welcome and often court: sometimes in the crudely physical form which Suso describes so vividly and horribly in the sixteenth chapter of his Life, more frequently in those refinements of torture which a sensitive spirit can extract from loneliness, injustice, misunderstanding—above all, from deliberate contact with the repulsive accidents of life. It would seem from a collation of the evidence that the typical mystical temperament is by nature highly fastidious. Its passionate apprehension of spiritual beauty, its intuitive perception of divine harmony, is counterbalanced by an instinctive loathing of ugliness, a shrinking from the disharmonies of squalor and disease. Often its ideal of refinement is far beyond the contemporary standards of decency: a circumstance which is alone enough to provide ample opportunity of wretchedness. This extreme sensitiveness, which forms part of the normal psycho-physical make-up of the mystic, as it often does of the equally highly-strung artistic type, is one of the first things to be seized upon by the awakened self as a disciplinary instrument. Then humility's axiom, "Naught is too low for love" is forced to bear the less lovely gloss, "Naught must be too disgusting."

[8] "This truth, of which she was the living example," says Huysmans of St. Lydwine, "has been and will be true for every period. Since the death of Lydwine, there is not a saint who has not confirmed it. Hear them formulate their desires. Always to suffer, and to die! cries St. Teresa; always to suffer, yet not to die, corrects St. Magdalena dei Pazzi; yet more, oh Lord, yet more! exclaims St. Francis Xavier, dying in anguish on the coast of China; I wish to be broken with suffering in order that I may prove my love to God, declares a seventeenth century Carmelite, the Ven. Mary of the Trinity. The desire for suffering is itself an agony, adds a great servant of God of our own day, Mother Mary Du Bourg; and she confided to her daughters in religion that "if they sold pain in the market she would hurry to buy it there," (J. K. Huysmans, "Sainte Lydwine de Schiedam," 3rd edition, p. 225). Examples can be multiplied indefinitely from the lives and works of the mystics of all periods.

[9] Tauler, Sermon on St. Paul ("The Inner Way," p. 114).

Two reasons at once appear for this. One is the contempt for phenomena, nasty as well as nice—the longing to be free from all the fetters of sense—which often goes with the passion for invisible things. Those mystics to whom the attractions of earth are only illusion are inconsistent if they attribute a greater reality to the revolting and squalid incidents of life. St. Francis did but carry his own principles to their logical conclusion, when he insisted that the vermin were as much his brothers as the birds. Real detachment means the death of preferences of all kinds: even of those which seem to other men the very proofs of virtue and fine taste.

The second reason is nobler. It is bound up with that principle of self-surrender which is the mainspring of the mystic life. To the contemplative mind, which is keenly conscious of unity in multiplicity—of God in the world—all disinterested service is service of the Absolute which he loves: and the harder it is, the more opposed to his self-regarding and aesthetic instincts, the more nearly it approaches his ideal. The point to which he aspires—though he does not always know it—is that in which all disharmony, all appearance of vileness, is resolved in the concrete reality which he calls the Love of God. Then, he feels dimly, everything will be seen under the aspect of a cosmic and charitable beauty; exhibiting through the woof of corruption the web of eternal life.

It is told of St. Francis of Assisi, in whom the love of lovely things was always paramount, how he forced himself to visit the lepers whose sight and smell disgusted him: how he served them and even kissed them.[10] "Then as he departed, in very truth that which had aforetime been bitter unto him, to wit, the sight and touch of lepers, now changed into sweetness. For, as he confessed, the sight of lepers had been so grievous unto him that he had been minded to avoid not only seeing them, but even going nigh their dwelling. And if at any time he chanced to pass their abodes, or to see them, albeit he were moved by compassion to do them an alms through another person, yet always would he turn aside his face, stopping his nostrils with his hand. But through the grace of God he became so intimate a friend of the lepers that, even as he recorded in his will, he did sojourn with them and did humbly serve them."

Also, after his great renunciation of all property, he, once a prosperous young man who had been "dainty in his father's home," accustomed himself to take a bowl and beg scraps of food from door to door: and here too, as in the case of the lepers, that which at first seemed revolting became to him sweet. "And when he would have eaten that medley of various meats," says the legend, "at first he shrank back, for that he had never been used willingly even to see, much less to eat, such scraps. At length, conquering himself, he began to eat; and it seemed to him that in eating no rich syrup had he ever tasted aught so delightsome."[11]

The object, then, of this self-discipline is, like the object of all purgation, freedom: freedom from the fetters of the senses, the "remora of desire," from the results of environment and worldly education, from pride and prejudice, preferences and distaste: from selfhood in every form. Its effect is a sharp reaction to the joy of self-conquest. The very act that had once caused in the enchained self a movement of loathing becomes not merely indifferent, but an

[10] Thomas of Celano, Legenda Prima, cap. vii.; 3 Soc. cap. iv.
[11] 3 Soc. cap. vii.

occasion of happiness. So Margery Kempe "had great mourning and sorrowing if she might not kiss a leper when she met them in the way for the love of our Lord, *which was all contrary to her disposition* in the years of her youth and prosperity, for then she abhorred them most."[12]

I spare the sensitive reader a detailed account of the loathsome ordeals by which St. Catherine of Genoa and Madame Guyon strove to cure themselves of squeamishness and acquire this liberty of spirit.[13] They, like St. Francis, St. Elizabeth of Hungary, and countless other seekers for the Real, sought out and served with humility and love the sick and the unclean; deliberately associated themselves with life in its meanest forms; compelled themselves to contact with the most revolting substances; and mortified the senses by the traditional ascetic expedient of deliberately opposing all—even their most natural and harmless—inclinations. "In the first four years after she received the sweet wound from her Lord," says the Life of St. Catherine of Genoa, she "made great penances: so that all her senses were mortified. And first, so soon as she perceived that her nature desired anything, at once she deprived it thereof, and did so that it should receive all those things that it abhorred. She wore harsh hair, ate no meat nor any other thing that she liked; ate no fruit, neither fresh nor dried . . . and she lived greatly submitted to all persons, and always sought to do all those things which were contrary to her own will; in such a way that she was always inclined to do more promptly the will of others than her own." . . . "And while she worked such and so many mortifications of all her senses it was several times asked of her 'Why do you do this?' And she answered 'I do not know, but I feel myself drawn inwardly to do this . . . and I think it is God's will.'"[14]

St. Ignatius Loyola, in the world a highly bred Spanish gentleman of refined personal habits, found in those habits an excellent opportunity of mortification. "As he was somewhat nice about the arrangement of his hair, as was the fashion of those days and became him not ill, he allowed it to grow naturally, and neither combed it nor trimmed it nor wore any head covering by day or night. For the same reason he did not pare his finger or toe nails; for on these points he had been fastidious to an extreme."[15]

Madame Guyon, a delicate girl of the leisured class, accustomed to the ordinary comforts of her station, characteristically chose the most crude and immoderate forms of mortification in her efforts towards the acquirement of "indifference." But the peculiar psychic constitution which afterwards showed itself in the forms of automatism and clairvoyance, seems to have produced a partial anaesthesia. "Although I had a very delicate body, the instruments of penitence tore my flesh without, as it seemed to me, causing pain. I wore girdles of hair and of sharp iron, I often held wormwood in my mouth." "If I walked, I put stones in my shoes. These things, my God, Thou didst first inspire me to do, in order that I might be deprived even of the most innocent satisfactions."[16]

In the earlier stages of their education, a constant *agere contra,* even in appar-

---

[12] "A Short Treatise of Contemplation taken out of the boke of Margery Kempe ancresse of Lynne," London, 1521. Reprinted and ed. by F. Gardner in "The Cell of Self-knowledge," 1910, p. 49.

[13] The curious are referred to the original authorities. For St. Catherine, chapter viii. of the "Vita e Dottrina": for Madame Guyon, Vie, pt. i. ch. x.

[14] "Vita e Dottrina," cap. v.

[15] Testament, cap. ii. (Rix's translation).

[16] Vie, pt. i. cap. x.

ently indifferent things, seems essential to the mystics; till the point is reached at which the changes and chances of mortal life are accepted with a true indifference and do not trouble the life of the soul. This established ascendancy of the "interior man," the transcendental consciousness, over "sensitive nature"—the self in its reactions to the ups and downs and manifold illusions of daily life—is the very object of Purgation. It is, then, almost impossible that any mystic, whatever his religion, character or race, should escape its battles: for none at the beginning of their growth are in a position to dispense with its good offices. Neoplatonists and Mahommedans, no less than the Christian ascetics, are acquainted with the Purgative Way. All realize the first law of Spiritual Alchemy, that you must tame the Green Lion before you give him wings. Thus in 'Attar's allegory of the Valleys, the valley of self-stripping and renunciation comes first.[17] So too Al Ghazzali, the Persian contemplative, says of the period immediately following his acceptance of the principles of Sūfiism and consequent renunciation of property, "I went to Syria, where I remained more than two years; without any other object than that of living in seclusion and solitude, conquering my desires, struggling with my passions, striving to purify my soul, to perfect my character, and to prepare my heart to meditate upon God." At the end of this period of pure purgation circumstances forced him to return to the world; much to his regret, since he "had not yet attained to the perfect ecstatic state, unless it were in one or two isolated moments."[18]

Such gleams of ecstatic vision, distributed through the later stages of purification, seem to be normal features of mystical development. Increasing control of the lower centres, of the surface intelligence and its scattered desires, permits the emergence of the transcendental perceptions. We have seen that Fox in his early stages displayed just such an alternation between the light and shade of the mystic way.[19] So too did that least ascetic of visionaries, Jacob Boehme. "Finding within myself a powerful contrarium, namely the desires that belong to the flesh and blood," he says, "I began to fight a hard battle against my corrupted nature, and with the aid of God I made up my mind to overcome the inherited evil will, to break it, and to enter wholly into the Love of God. . . . This, however, was not possible for me to accomplish, but I stood firmly by my earnest resolution, and fought a hard battle with myself. Now while I was wrestling and battling, being aided by God, a wonderful light arose within my soul. It was a light entirely foreign to my unruly nature, but in it I recognized the true nature of God and man, and the relation existing between them, a thing which heretofore I had never understood, and for which I would never have sought."[20]

In these words Boehme bridges the gap between Purgation and Illumination: showing these two states or ways as co-existing and complementary one to another, the light and dark sides of a developing mystic consciousness. As a fact, they do often exist side by side in the individual experience:[21] and any treatment which exhibits them as sharply and completely separated may be convenient for purposes of study, but becomes at best diagrammatic if considered as a representation of the mystic life. The mystical consciousness, as we have

---

[17] *Supra*, p. 131.
[18] Schmölders, "Essai sur les Écoles Philosophiques chez les Arabes," p. 59.
[19] *Supra*, p. 177.
[20] Hartmann, "Life and Doctrines of Jacob Boehme," p. 50.
[21] Compare the case of St. Teresa already cited, *supra*, p. 213.

seen, belongs—from the psychological point of view—to that mobile or "unstable" type in which the artistic temperament also finds a place. It sways easily between the extremes of pleasure and pain in its gropings after transcendental reality. It often attains for a moment to heights in which it is not able to rest: is often flung from some rapturous vision of the Perfect to the deeps of contrition and despair.

The mystics have a vivid metaphor by which to describe that alternation between the onset and the absence of the joyous transcendental consciousness which forms as it were the characteristic intermediate stage between the bitter struggles of pure Purgation, and the peace and radiance of the Illuminative Life. They call it *Ludus Amoris,* the "Game of Love" which God plays with the desirous soul. It is the "game of chess," says St. Teresa, "in which game Humility is the Queen without whom none can checkmate the Divine King." [22] "Here," says Martensen, "God plays a blest game with the soul." [23] The "Game of Love" is a reflection in consciousness of that state of struggle, oscillation and unrest which precedes the first unification of the self. It ceases when this has taken place and the new level of reality has been attained. Thus St. Catherine of Siena, that inspired psychologist, was told in ecstasy, "With the souls who have arrived at perfection, I play no more the Game of Love, which consists in leaving and returning again to the soul; though thou must understand that it is not, properly speaking, I, the immovable GOD, Who thus elude them, but rather the sentiment that My charity gives them of Me." [24] In other terms, it is the imperfectly developed spiritual perception which becomes tired and fails, throwing the self back into the darkness and aridity whence it has emerged. So we are told of Rulman Merswin [25] that after the period of harsh physical mortification which succeeded his conversion came a year of "delirious joy alternating with the most bitter physical and moral sufferings." It is, he says, "the Game of Love which the Lord plays with His poor sinful creature." Memories of all his old sins still drove him to exaggerated penances: morbid temptations "made me so ill that I feared I should lose my reason." These psychic storms reacted upon the physical organism. He had a paralytic seizure, lost the use of his lower limbs, and believed himself to be at the point of death. When he was at his worst, however, and all hope seemed at an end, an inward voice told him to rise from his bed. He obeyed, and found himself cured. Ecstasies were frequent during the whole of this period. In these moments of exaltation he felt his mind to be irradiated by a new light, so that he knew, intuitively, the direction which his life was bound to take, and recognized the inevitable and salutary nature of his trials. "God showed Himself by turns harsh and gentle: to each access of misery succeeded the rapture of supernatural grace." In this intermittent style, torn by these constant fluctuations between depression and delight, did Merswin, in whom the psychic instability of the artistic and mystic types is present in excess, pass through the purgative and illuminated states. [26] They appear to have coexisted

[22] "Camino de Perfection," cap. xvii.
[23] Martensen, "Meister Eckhart," p. 75.
[24] Dialogo, cap. lxxviii.
[25] Jundt, "Rulman Merswin," pp. 10 and 20.
[26] We recognize here the chief symptoms of the "cyclic type" of mentality, with its well-marked alternations of depression and exaltation. This psychological type is found frequently, but not invariably, among the mystics; and its peculiarities must be taken into account when studying their experiences. For a technical description, see W. McDougall: "An Introduction to Abnormal Psychology," caps. xxii and xxviii.

in his consciousness, first one and then the other emerging and taking control. Hence he did not attain the peaceful condition which is characteristic of full illumination, and normally closes the "First Mystic Life"; but passed direct from these violent alternations of mystical pleasure and mystical pain to the state which he calls "the school of suffering love." This . . . is strictly analogous to that which other mystics have called the "Dark Night of the Soul," and opens the "Second Mystic Life" or Unitive Way.

Such prolonged coexistence of alternating pain and pleasure states in the developing soul, such delay in the attainment of equilibrium, is not infrequent, and must be taken into account in all analyses of the mystic type. Though it is convenient for purposes of study to practise a certain dissection, and treat as separate states which are, in the living subject, closely intertwined, we should constantly remind ourselves that such a proceeding is artificial. The struggle of the self to disentangle itself from illusion and attain the Absolute is a life-struggle. Hence, it will and must exhibit the freedom and originality of life: will, as a process, obey artistic rather than scientific laws. It will sway now to the light and now to the shade of experience: its oscillations will sometimes be great, sometimes small. Mood and environment, inspiration and information, will all play their part.

There are in this struggle three factors.

(1) The unchanging light of Eternal Reality: that Pure Being "which ever shines and nought shall ever dim."

(2) The web of illusion, here thick, there thin; which hems in, confuses, and allures the sentient self.

(3) That self, always changing, moving, struggling—always, in fact, *becoming*—alive in every fibre, related at once to the unreal and to the real; and, with its growth in true being, ever more conscious of the contrast between them.

In the ever-shifting relations between these three factors, the consequent energy engendered, the work done, we may find a cause of the innumerable forms of stress and travail which are called in their objective form the Purgative Way. One only of the three is constant: the Absolute to which the soul aspires. Though all else may fluctuate, that goal is changeless. That Beauty so old and so new, "with whom is no variableness, neither shadow of turning," which is the One of Plotinus, the All of Eckhart and St. John of the Cross, the Eternal Wisdom of Suso, the Unplumbed Abyss of Ruysbroeck, the Pure Love of St. Catherine of Genoa, awaits yesterday, to-day, and for ever the opening of Its creature's eyes.

In the moment of conversion those eyes were opened for an instant: obtained, as it were, a dazzling and unforgettable glimpse of the Uncreated Light. They must learn to stay open: to look steadfastly into the eyes of Love: so that, in the beautiful imagery of the mystics, the "faithful servant" may become the "secret friend."[27] Then it is, says Boehme, that "the divine glimpse and beam of joy ariseth in the soul, being a new eye, in which the dark, fiery soul conceiveth the Ens and Essence of the divine light."[28] So hard an art is not at once acquired in its perfection. It is in accordance with all that we know of the conditions of development that a partial achievement should come first; bewildering moments of lucidity, splendid glimpses, whose brevity is due to the weakness of the newly

[27] See Ruysbroeck, "De Calculo," cap. vii. The metaphor is an ancient one and occurs in many patristic and mediaeval writers.
[28] "The Epistles of Jacob Boehme," p. 19.

opened and unpractised "eye which looks upon Eternity," the yet undisciplined strength of the "eye which looks upon Time." Such is that play of light and dark, of exaltation and contrition, which often bridges the gap between the Purgative and the Illuminative states. Each by turn takes the field and ousts the other; for "these two eyes of the soul of man cannot both perform their work at once."[29]

To use another and more domestic metaphor, that Divine Child which was, in the hour of the mystic conversion, born in the spark of the soul, must learn like other children to walk. Though it is true that the spiritual self must never lose its sense of utter dependence on the Invisible; yet within that supporting atmosphere, and fed by its gifts, it must "find its feet." Each effort to stand brings first a glorious sense of growth, and then a fall: each fall means another struggle to obtain the difficult balance which comes when infancy is past. There are many eager trials, many hopes, many disappointments. At last, as it seems suddenly, the moment comes: tottering is over, the muscles have learnt their lesson, they adjust themselves automatically, and the new self suddenly finds itself—it knows not how—standing upright and secure. That is the moment which marks the boundary between the purgative and the illuminative states.

The process of this passage of the "new" or spiritual man from his awakening to the illuminated life, has been set out by Jacob Boehme in language which is at once poetic and precise. "When Christ the Corner-Stone [*i.e.,* the divine principle latent in man] stirreth himself in the extinguished Image of Man in his hearty Conversion and Repentance," he says, "then Virgin Sophia appeareth in the stirring of the Spirit of Christ in the extinguished Image, in her Virgin's attire before the Soul; at which the Soul is so amazed and astonished in its Uncleanness that all its Sins immediately awake in it, and it trembleth before her; for then the judgment passeth upon the Sins of the Soul, so that it even goeth back in its unworthiness, being ashamed in the Presence of its fair Love, and entereth into itself, feeling and acknowledging itself utterly unworthy to receive such a Jewel. This is understood by those who are of our tribe and have tasted of this heavenly Gift, and by none else. But the noble Sophia draweth near in the Essence of the Soul, and kisseth it in friendly Manner, and tinctureth its dark Fire with her Rays of Love, and shineth through it with her bright and powerful Influence. Penetrated with the strong Sense and Feeling of which, the Soul skippeth in its Body for great Joy, and in the strength of this Virgin Love exulteth, and praiseth the great God for his blest Gift of Grace. I will set down here a short description how it is when the Bride thus embraceth the Bridegroom, for the consideration of the Reader, who perhaps hath not yet been in this wedding chamber. It may be he will be desirous to follow us, and to enter into the Inner Choir, where the Soul joineth hands and danceth with Sophia, or the Divine Wisdom."[30]

---

[29] "Theologia Germanica," cap. vii.
[30] Jacob Boehme, "The Way to Christ," pt. i. p. 23 (vol. iv. of the complete English translation of Boehme's works).

The Courage to Be

Paul Tillich

Paul Tillich (1886–   ), one of the most influential Christian thinkers of the twentieth century, was born in Germany. In 1933, he immigrated to America, where he taught at Union Theological Seminary, Harvard, and the University of Chicago. His major work is the three-volume *Systematic Theology*, but he is author of many other important books, including *Dynamics of Faith, The Courage to Be,* and *Theology of Culture.*

THE INTERDEPENDENCE OF FEAR AND ANXIETY

Anxiety and fear have the same ontological root but they are not the same in actuality. This is common knowledge, but it has been emphasized and over-emphasized to such a degree that a reaction against it may occur and wipe out not only the exaggerations but also the truth of the distinction. Fear, as opposed to anxiety, has a definite object (as most authors agree), which can be faced, analyzed, attacked, endured. One can act upon it, and in acting upon it participate in it—even if in the form of struggle. In this way one can take it into one's self-affirmation. Courage can meet every object of fear, because it is an object and makes participation possible. Courage can take the fear produced by a definite object into itself, because this object, however frightful it may be, has a side with which it participates in us and we in it. One could say that as long as there is an *object* of fear love in the sense of participation can conquer fear.

But this is not so with anxiety, because anxiety has no object, or rather, in a paradoxical phrase, its object is the negation of every object. Therefore participation, struggle, and love with respect to it are impossible. He who is in anxiety is, insofar as it is mere anxiety, delivered to it without help. Helplessness in the state of anxiety can be observed in animals and humans alike. It expresses itself in loss of direction, inadequate reactions, lack of "intentionality" (the being related to meaningful contents of knowledge or will). The reason for this sometimes striking behavior is the lack of an object on which the subject (in the state of anxiety) can concentrate. The only object is the threat itself, but not the source of the threat, because the source of the threat is "nothingness."

One might ask whether this threatening "nothing" is not the unknown, the indefinite possibility of an actual threat? Does not anxiety cease in the moment in which a known object of fear appears? Anxiety then would be fear of the unknown. But this is an insufficient explanation of anxiety. For there are innumerable realms of the unknown, different for each subject, and faced without any anxiety. It is the unknown of a special type which is met with anxiety. It is the unknown which by its very nature cannot be known, because it is nonbeing.

Fear and anxiety are distinguished but not separated. They are immanent within each other: The sting of fear is anxiety, and anxiety strives toward fear. Fear is being afraid of something, a pain, the rejection by a person or a group, the loss of something or somebody, the moment of dying. But in the anticipation of the threat originating in these things, it is not the negativity itself which they will bring upon the subject that is frightening but the anxiety about the possible implications of this negativity. The outstanding example—and more than an example—is the fear of dying. Insofar as it is *fear* its object is the anticipated event of being killed by sickness or an accident and thereby suffering agony and the loss of everything. Insofar as it is *anxiety* its object is the absolutely unknown "after death," the nonbeing which remains nonbeing even if it is filled with images of our present experience. The dreams in Hamlet's soliloquy, "to be or not to be," which we may have after death and which make cowards of us all are frightful not because of their manifest content but because of their power to symbolize the threat of nothingness, in religious terms of "eternal death." The symbols of hell created by Dante produce anxiety not because of their objective imagery but because they express the "nothingness" whose power is experienced in the anxiety of guilt. Each of the situations described in the *Inferno* could be met by courage on the basis of participation and love. But of course the meaning is that this is impossible; in other words they are not real situations but symbols of the objectless, of nonbeing.

The fear of death determines the element of anxiety in every fear. Anxiety, if not modified by the fear of an object, anxiety in its nakedness, is always the anxiety of ultimate nonbeing. Immediately seen, anxiety is the painful feeling of not being able to deal with the threat of a special situation. But a more exact analysis shows that in the anxiety about any special situation anxiety about the human situation as such is implied. It is the anxiety of not being able to preserve one's own being which underlies every fear and is the frightening element in it. In the moment, therefore, in which "naked anxiety" lays hold of the mind, the previous objects of fear cease to be definite objects. They appear as what they always were in part, symptoms of man's basic anxiety. As such they are beyond the reach of even the most courageous attack upon them.

This situation drives the anxious subject to establish objects of fear. Anxiety strives to become fear, because fear can be met by courage. It is impossible for a finite being to stand naked anxiety for more than a flash of time. People who have experienced these moments, as for instance some mystics in their visions of the "night of the soul," or Luther under the despair of the demonic assaults, or Nietzsche-Zarathustra in the experience of the "great disgust," have told of the unimaginable horror of it. This horror is ordinarily avoided by the transformation of anxiety into fear of something, no matter what. The human mind is not only, as Calvin has said, a permanent factory of idols, it is also a permanent factory of fears—the first in order to escape God, the second in order to escape anxiety; and there is a relation between the two. For facing the God who is really God means facing also the absolute threat of nonbeing. The "naked absolute" (to use a phrase of Luther's) produces "naked anxiety"; for it is the extinction of every finite self-affirmation, and not a possible object of fear and courage. . . . But ultimately the attempts to transform anxiety into fear are vain. The basic anxiety, the anxiety of a finite being about the threat of nonbeing, cannot be eliminated. It belongs to existence itself.

TYPES OF ANXIETY

The Three Types of Anxiety and the Nature of Man. Nonbeing is dependent on the being it negates. "Dependent" means two things. It points first of all to the ontological priority of being over nonbeing. The term nonbeing itself indicates this, and it is logically necessary. There could be no negation if there were no preceding affirmation to be negated. Certainly one can describe being in terms of non-nonbeing; and one can justify such a description by pointing to the astonishing prerational fact that there is something and not nothing. One could say that "being is the negation of the primordial night of nothingness." But in doing so one must realize that such an aboriginal nothing would be neither nothing nor something, that it becomes nothing only in contrast to something; in other words, that the ontological status of nonbeing as nonbeing is dependent on being. Secondly, nonbeing is dependent on the special qualities of being. In itself nonbeing has no quality and no difference of qualities. But it gets them in relation to being. The character of the negation of being is determined by that in being which is negated. This makes it possible to speak of qualities of nonbeing and, consequently, of types of anxiety.

Up to now we have used the term nonbeing without differentiation, while in the discussion of courage several forms of self-affirmation were mentioned. They correspond to different forms of anxiety and are understandable only in correlation with them. I suggest that we distinguish three types of anxiety according to the three directions in which nonbeing threatens being. Nonbeing threatens man's ontic self-affirmation, relatively in terms of fate, absolutely in terms of death. It threatens man's spiritual self-affirmation, relatively in terms of emptiness, absolutely in terms of meaninglessness. It threatens man's moral self-affirmation, relatively in terms of guilt, absolutely in terms of condemnation. The awareness of this threefold threat is anxiety appearing in three forms, that of fate and death (briefly, the anxiety of death), that of emptiness and loss of meaning (briefly, the anxiety of meaninglessness), that of guilt and condemnation (briefly, the anxiety of condemnation). In all three forms anxiety is existential in the sense that it belongs to existence as such and not to an abnormal state of mind as in neurotic (and psychotic) anxiety. . . .

The Anxiety of Fate and Death. Fate and death are the way in which our ontic self-affirmation is threatened by nonbeing. "Ontic," from the Greek *on,* "being," means here the basic self-affirmation of a being in its simple existence. (Onto-logical designates the philosophical analysis of the nature of being.) The anxiety of fate and death is most basic, most universal, and inescapable. All attempts to argue it away are futile. Even if the so-called arguments for the "immortality of the soul" had argumentative power (which they do not have) they would not convince existentially. For existentially everybody is aware of the complete loss of self which biological extinction implies. The unsophisticated mind knows instinctively what sophisticated ontology formulates: that reality has the basic structure of self-world correlation and that with the disappearance of the one side, the world, the other side, the self, also disappears, and what remains is their common ground but not their structural correlation. It has been observed that the anxiety of death increases with the increase of individualization and that people in collectivistic cultures are less open to this type of anxiety. The observation is correct yet the explanation that there is no basic anxiety about death in collectivist cultures is wrong. The reason for the difference from more individualized civilizations is that the special type of courage which characterizes collectivism . . . , as long as it is unshaken, allays the anxiety of death. But the very fact that courage has to be created through many internal and external (psychological and ritual) activities and symbols shows that basic anxiety has to be overcome even in collectivism. Without its at least potential presence neither war nor the criminal law in these societies would be understandable. If there were no fear of death, the threat of the law or of a superior enemy would be without effect—which it obviously is not. Man as man in every civilization is anxiously aware of the threat of nonbeing and needs the courage to affirm himself in spite of it.

The anxiety of death is the permanent horizon within which the anxiety of fate is at work. For the threat against man's ontic self-affirmation is not only the absolute threat of death but also the relative threat of fate. Certainly the anxiety of death overshadows all concrete anxieties and gives them their ultimate seriousness. They have, however, a certain independence and, ordinarily, a more immediate impact than the anxiety of death. The term "fate" for this whole group of anxieties stresses one element which is common to all of them: their contingent character, their unpredictability, the impossibility of showing their meaning and purpose. One can describe this in terms of the categorical structure of our experience. One can show the contingency of our temporal being, the fact that we exist in this and no other period of time, beginning in a contingent moment, ending in a contingent moment, filled with experiences which are contingent themselves with respect to quality and quantity. One can show the contingency of our spatial being (our finding ourselves in this and no other place, and the strangeness of this place in spite of its familiarity); the contingent character of ourselves and the place from which we look at our world; and the contingent character of the reality at which we look, that is, our world. Both could be different: this is their contingency and this produces the anxiety about our spatial existence. One can show the contingency of the causal interdependence of which one is a part, both with respect to the past and to the present, the vicissitudes coming from our world and the hidden forces in the depths of our own self. Contingent does not mean causally undetermined but it means that the determining causes of our existence have no ultimate necessity. They are given, and they cannot be logically derived. Contingently we are put into the whole web of causal relations. Contingently we are determined by them in every moment and thrown out by them in the last moment.

Fate is the rule of contingency, and the anxiety about fate is based on the finite being's awareness of being contingent in every respect, of having no ultimate necessity. Fate is usually identified with necessity in the sense of an inescapable causal determination. Yet it is not causal necessity that makes fate a matter of anxiety but the lack of ultimate necessity, the irrationality, the impenetrable darkness of fate.

The threat of nonbeing to man's ontic self-affirmation is absolute in the threat of death, relative in the threat of fate. But the relative threat is a threat only because in its background stands the absolute threat. Fate would not produce inescapable anxiety without death behind it. And death stands behind fate and its contingencies not only in the last moment when one is thrown out of existence but in every moment within existence. Nonbeing is omnipresent and produces anxiety even where an immediate threat of death is absent. It stands behind the experience that we are driven, together with everything else, from the past toward the future without a moment of time which does not vanish immediately. It stands behind the insecurity and homelessness of our social and individual existence. It stands behind the attacks on our power of being in body and soul by weakness, disease, and accidents. In all these forms fate actualizes itself, and through them the anxiety of nonbeing takes hold of us. We try to transform the anxiety into fear and to meet courageously the objects in which the threat is embodied. We succeed partly, but somehow we are aware of the fact that it is not these objects with which we struggle that produce the anxiety but the human situation as such. Out of this the question arises: Is there a courage to be, a courage to affirm oneself in spite of the threat against man's ontic self-affirmation?

The Anxiety of Emptiness and Meaninglessness. Nonbeing threatens man as a whole, and therefore threatens his spiritual as well as his ontic self-affirmation. Spiritual self-affirmation occurs in every moment in which man lives creatively in the various spheres of meaning. Creative, in this context, has the sense not of original creativity as performed by the genius but of living spontaneously, in action and reaction, with the contents of one's cultural life. In order to be spiritually creative one need not be what is called a creative artist or scientist or statesman, but one must be able to participate meaningfully in their original creations. Such a participation is creative insofar as it changes that in which one participates, even if in very small ways. The creative transformation of a language by the interdependence of the creative poet or writer and the many who are influenced by him directly or indirectly and react spontaneously to him is an outstanding example. Everyone who lives creatively in meanings affirms himself as a participant in these meanings. He affirms himself as receiving and trans- forming reality creatively. He loves himself as participating in the spiritual life and as loving its contents. He loves them because they are his own fulfillment and because they are actualized through him. The scientist loves both the truth he discovers and himself insofar as he discovers it. He is held by the content of his discovery. This is what one can call "spiritual self-affirmation." And if he has not discovered but only participates in the discovery, it is equally spiritual self- affirmation.

Such an experience presupposes that the spiritual life is taken seriously, that it is a matter of ultimate concern. And this again presupposes that in it and through it ultimate reality becomes manifest. A spiritual life in which this is not experienced is threatened by nonbeing in the two forms in which it attacks spiri- tual self-affirmation: emptiness and meaninglessness.

We use the term meaninglessness for the absolute threat of nonbeing to spiritual self-affirmation, and the term emptiness for the relative threat to it. They are no more identical than are the threat of death and fate. But in the background of emptiness lies meaninglessness as death lies in the background of the vicissitudes of fate.

The anxiety of meaninglessness is anxiety about the loss of an ultimate con- cern, of a meaning which gives meaning to all meanings. This anxiety is aroused by the loss of a spiritual center, of an answer, however symbolic and indirect, to the question of the meaning of existence.

The anxiety of emptiness is aroused by the threat of nonbeing to the special contents of the spiritual life. A belief breaks down through external events or inner processes: one is cut off from creative participation in a sphere of culture, one feels frustrated about something which one had passionately affirmed, one is driven from devotion to one object to devotion to another and again on to another, because the meaning of each of them vanishes and the creative eros is transformed into indifference or aversion. Everything is tried and nothing satisfies. The contents of the tradition, however excellent, however praised, however loved once, lose their power to give content *today*. And present culture is even less able to provide the content. Anxiously one turns away from all concrete contents and looks for an ultimate meaning, only to discover that it was precisely the loss of a spiritual center which took away the meaning from the special contents of the spiritual life. But a spiritual center cannot be produced intentionally, and the attempt to produce it only produces deeper anxiety. The anxiety of emptiness drives us to the abyss of meaninglessness.

Emptiness and loss of meaning are expressions of the threat of nonbeing to the spiritual life. This threat is implied in man's finitude and actualized by man's estrangement. It can be described in terms of doubt, its creative and its destructive function in man's spiritual life. Man is able to ask because he is separated *from,* while participating *in,* what he is asking about. In every question an element of doubt, the awareness of not having, is implied. In systematic questioning systematic doubt is effective; e.g. of the Cartesian type. This element of doubt is a condition of all spiritual life. The threat to spiritual life is not doubt as an element but the total doubt. If the awareness of not having has swallowed the awareness of having, doubt has ceased to be methodological asking and has become existential despair. On the way to this situation the spiritual life tries to maintain itself as long as possible by clinging to affirmations which are not yet undercut, be they traditions, autonomous convictions, or emotional preferences. And if it is impossible to remove the doubt, one courageously accepts it without surrendering one's convictions. One takes the risk of going astray and the anxiety of this risk upon oneself. In this way one avoids the extreme situation—till it becomes unavoidable and the despair of truth becomes complete.

Then man tries another way out: Doubt is based on man's separation from the whole of reality, on his lack of universal participation, on the isolation of his individual self. So he tries to break out of this situation, to identify himself with something transindividual, to surrender his separation and self-relatedness. He flees from his freedom of asking and answering for himself to a situation in which no further questions can be asked and the answers to previous questions are imposed on him authoritatively. In order to avoid the risk of asking and doubting he surrenders the right to ask and to doubt. He surrenders himself in order to save his spiritual life. He "escapes from his freedom" (Fromm) in order to escape the anxiety of meaninglessness. Now he is no longer lonely, not in existential doubt, not in despair. He "participates" and affirms by participation the contents of his spiritual life. Meaning is saved, but the self is sacrificed. And since the conquest of doubt was a matter of sacrifice, the sacrifice of the freedom of the self, it leaves a mark on the regained certitude: a fanatical self-assertiveness. Fanaticism is the correlate to spiritual self-surrender: it shows the anxiety which it was supposed to conquer, by attacking with disproportionate violence those who disagree and who demonstrate by their disagreement elements in the spiritual life of the fanatic which he must suppress in himself. Because he must suppress them in himself he must suppress them in others. His anxiety forces him to persecute dissenters. The weakness of the fanatic is that those whom he fights have a secret hold upon him; and to this weakness he and his group finally succumb.

It is not always personal doubt that undermines and empties a system of ideas and values. It can be the fact that they are no longer understood in their original power of expressing the human situation and of answering existential human questions. (This is largely the case with the doctrinal symbols of Christianity.) Or they lose their meaning because the actual conditions of the present period are so different from those in which the spiritual contents were created that new creations are needed. (This was largely the case with artistic expression before the industrial revolution.) In such circumstances a slow process of waste of the spiritual contents occurs, unnoticeable in the beginning, realized with a shock as it progresses, producing the anxiety of meaninglessness at its end.

Ontic and spiritual self-affirmation must be distinguished but they cannot be separated. Man's being includes his relation to meanings. He is human only by understanding and shaping reality, both his world and himself, according to meanings and values. His being is spiritual even in the most primitive expressions of the most primitive human being. In the "first" meaningful sentence all the richness of man's spiritual life is potentially present. Therefore the threat to his spiritual being is a threat to his whole being. The most revealing expression of this fact is the desire to throw away one's ontic existence rather than stand the despair of emptiness and meaninglessness. The death instinct is not an ontic but a spiritual phenomenon. Freud identified this reaction to the meaninglessness of the never-ceasing and never-satisfied libido with man's essential nature. But it is only an expression of his existential self-estrangement and of the disintegration of his spiritual life into meaninglessness. If, on the other hand, the ontic self-affirmation is weakened by nonbeing, spiritual indifference and emptiness can be the consequence, producing a circle of ontic and spiritual negativity. Nonbeing threatens from both sides, the ontic and the spiritual; if it threatens the one side it also threatens the other.

The Anxiety of Guilt and Condemnation. Nonbeing threatens from a third side; it threatens man's moral self-affirmation. Man's being, ontic as well as spiritual, is not only given to him but also demanded of him. He is responsible for it; literally, he is required to answer, if he is asked, what he has made of himself. He who asks him is his judge, namely he himself, who, at the same time, stands against him. This situation produces the anxiety which, in relative terms, is the anxiety of guilt; in absolute terms, the anxiety of self-rejection or condemnation. Man is essentially "finite freedom"; freedom not in the sense of indeterminacy but in the sense of being able to determine himself through decisions in the center of his being. Man, as finite freedom, is free within the contingencies of his finitude. But within these limits he is asked to make of himself what he is supposed to become, to fulfill his destiny. In every act of moral self-affirmation man contributes to the fulfillment of his destiny, to the actualization of what he potentially is. It is the task of ethics to describe the nature of this fulfillment, in philosophical or theological terms. But however the norm is formulated man has the power of acting against it, of contradicting his essential being, of losing his destiny. And under the conditions of man's estrangement from himself this is an actuality. Even in what he considers his best deed nonbeing is present and prevents it from being perfect. A profound ambiguity between good and evil permeates everything he does, because it permeates his personal being as such. Nonbeing is mixed with being in his moral self-affirmation as it is in his spiritual and ontic self-affirmation. The awareness of this ambiguity is the feeling of guilt. The judge who is oneself and who stands against oneself, he who "knows with" (conscience) everything we do and are gives a negative judgment, experienced by us as guilt. The anxiety of guilt shows the same complex characteristics as the anxiety about ontic and spiritual nonbeing. It is present in every moment of moral self-awareness and can drive us toward complete self-rejection, to the feeling of being condemned—not to an external punishment but to the despair of having lost our destiny.

To avoid this extreme situation man tries to transform the anxiety of guilt into moral action regardless of its imperfection and ambiguity. Courageously he takes nonbeing into his moral self-affirmation. This can happen in two ways, according to the duality of the tragic and the personal in man's situation, the first based on the contingencies of fate, the second on the responsibility of freedom. The first way can lead to a defiance of negative judgments and the moral demands on which they are based; the second way can lead to a moral rigor and the self-satisfaction derived from it. In both of them—usually called anomism and legalism—the anxiety of guilt lies in the background and breaks again and again into the open, producing the extreme situation of moral despair.

Nonbeing in a moral respect must be distinguished but cannot be separated from ontic and spiritual nonbeing. The anxiety of the one type is immanent in the anxieties of the other types. The famous words of Paul about "sin as the sting of death" point to the immanence of the anxiety of guilt within the fear of death. And the threat of fate and death has always awakened and increased the consciousness of guilt. The threat of moral nonbeing was experienced in and through the threat of ontic nonbeing. The contingencies of fate received moral interpretation: fate executes the negative moral judgment by attacking and perhaps destroying the ontic foundation of the morally rejected personality. The two forms of anxiety provoke and augment each other. In the same way spiritual and moral nonbeing are interdependent. Obedience to the moral norm, i.e. to one's own essential being, excludes emptiness and meaninglessness in their radical forms. If the spiritual contents have lost their power the self-affirmation of the moral personality is a way in which meaning can be rediscovered. The simple call to duty can save from emptiness, while the disintegration of the moral consciousness is an almost irresistible basis for the attack of spiritual nonbeing. On the other hand, existential doubt can undermine moral self-affirmation by throwing into the abyss of skepticism not only every moral principle but the meaning of moral self-affirmation as such. In this case the doubt is felt as guilt, while at the same time guilt is undermined by doubt.

.   .   .

THEISM TRANSCENDED

The courage to take meaninglessness into itself presupposes a relation to the ground of being which we have called "absolute faith." It is without a *special* content, yet it is not without content. The content of absolute faith is the "God above God." Absolute faith and its consequence, the courage that takes the radical doubt, the doubt about God, into itself, transcends the theistic idea of God.

Theism can mean the unspecified affirmation of God. Theism in this sense does not say what it means if it uses the name of God. Because of the traditional and psychological connotations of the word God such an empty theism can produce a reverent mood if it speaks of God. Politicians, dictators, and other people who wish to use rhetoric to make an impression on their audience like to use the word God in this sense. It produces the feeling in their listeners that the speaker is serious and morally trustworthy. This is especially successful if they can brand their foes as atheistic. On a higher level people without a definite religious commitment like to call themselves theistic, not for special purposes but because they cannot stand a world without God, whatever this God may be. They need some of the connotations of the word God and they are afraid of what they call atheism. On the highest level of this kind of theism the name of God is used as a poetic or practical symbol, expressing a profound emotional state or the highest ethical idea. It is a theism which stands on the boundary line between the second type of theism and what we call "theism transcended." But it is still too indefinite to cross this boundary line. The atheistic negation of this whole type of theism is as vague as the theism itself. It may produce an irreverent mood and angry reaction of those who take their theistic affirmation seriously. It may even be felt as justified against the rhetorical-political abuse of the name God, but it is ultimately as irrelevant as the theism which it negates. It cannot reach the state of despair any more than the theism against which it fights can reach the state of faith.

Theism can have another meaning, quite contrary to the first one: it can be the name of what we have called the divine-human encounter. In this case it points to those elements in the Jewish-Christian tradition which emphasize the person-to-person relationship with God. Theism in this sense emphasizes the personalistic passages in the Bible and the Protestant creeds, the personalistic image of God, the word as the tool of creation and revelation, the ethical and social character of the kingdom of God, the personal nature of human faith and divine forgiveness, the historical vision of the universe, the idea of a divine purpose, the infinite distance between creator and creature, the absolute separation between God and the world, the conflict between holy God and sinful man, the person-to-person character of prayer and practical devotion. Theism in this sense is the nonmystical side of biblical religion and historical Christianity. Atheism from the point of view of this theism is the human attempt to escape the divine-human encounter. It is an existential—not a theoretical—problem.

Theism has a third meaning, a strictly theological one. Theological theism is, like every theology, dependent on the religious substance which it conceptualizes. It is dependent on theism in the first sense insofar as it tries to prove the necessity of affirming God in some way; it usually develops the so-called arguments for the "existence" of God. But it is more dependent on theism in the second sense insofar as it tries to establish a doctrine of God which transforms the person-to-person encounter with God into a doctrine about two persons who may or may not meet but who have a reality independent of each other.

Now theism in the first sense must be transcended because it is irrelevant, and theism in the second sense must be transcended because it is one-sided. But theism in the third sense must be transcended because it is wrong. It is bad theology. This can be shown by a more penetrating analysis. The God of theological theism is a being beside others and as such a part of the whole of reality. He certainly is considered its most important part, but as a part and therefore as subjected to the structure of the whole. He is supposed to be beyond the ontological elements and categories which constitute reality. But every statement subjects him to them. He is seen as a self which has a world, as an ego which is related to a thou, as a cause which is separated from its effect, as having a definite space and an endless time. He is a being, not being-itself. As such he is bound to the subject-object structure of reality, he is an object for us as subjects. At the same time we are objects for him as a subject. And this is decisive for the necessity of transcending theological theism. For God as a subject makes me into an object which is nothing more than an object. He deprives me of my subjectivity because he is all-powerful and all-knowing. I revolt and try to make *him* into an object, but the revolt fails and becomes desperate. God appears as the invincible tyrant, the being in contrast with whom all other beings are without freedom and subjectivity. He is equated with the recent tyrants who with the help of terror try to transform everything into a mere object, a thing among things, a cog in the machine they control. He becomes the model of everything against which Existentialism revolted. This is the God Nietzsche said had to be killed because nobody can tolerate being made into a mere object of absolute knowledge and absolute control. This is the deepest root of atheism. It is an atheism which is justified as the reaction against theological theism and its disturbing implications. It is also the deepest root of the Existentialist despair and the widespread anxiety of meaninglessness in our period.

Theism in all its forms is transcended in the experience we have called absolute faith. It is the accepting of the acceptance without somebody or something that accepts. It is the power of being-itself that accepts and gives the courage to be. This is the highest point to which our analysis has brought us. It cannot be described in the way the God of all forms of theism can be described. It cannot be described in mystical terms either. It transcends both mysticism and personal encounter, as it transcends both the courage to be as a part and the courage to be as oneself.

THE GOD ABOVE GOD AND THE COURAGE TO BE

The ultimate source of the courage to be is the "God above God"; this is the result of our demand to transcend theism. Only if the God of theism is transcended can the anxiety of doubt and meaninglessness be taken into the courage to be. The God above God is the object of all mystical longing, but mysticism also must be transcended in order to reach him. Mysticism does not take seriously the concrete and the doubt concerning the concrete. It plunges directly into the ground of being and meaning, and leaves the concrete, the world of finite values and meanings, behind. Therefore it does not solve the problem of meaninglessness. In terms of the present religious situation this means that Eastern mysticism is not the solution of the problems of Western Existentialism, although many people attempt this solution. The God above the God of theism is not the devaluation of the meanings which doubt has thrown into the abyss of meaning-lessness; he is their potential restitution. Nevertheless absolute faith agrees with the faith implied in mysticism in that both transcend the theistic objectivation of a God who is a being. For mysticism such a God is not more real than any finite being, for the courage to be such a God has disappeared in the abyss of meaning-lessness with every other value and meaning.

The God above the God of theism is present, although hidden, in every divine-human encounter. Biblical religion as well as Protestant theology are aware of the paradoxical character of this encounter. They are aware that if God encounters man God is neither object nor subject and is therefore above the scheme into which theism has forced him. They are aware that personalism with respect to God is balanced by a transpersonal presence of the divine. They are aware that forgiveness can be accepted only if the power of acceptance is effective in man—biblically speaking, if the power of grace is effective in man. They are aware of the paradoxical character of every prayer, of speaking to somebody to whom you cannot speak because he is not "somebody," of asking somebody of whom you cannot ask anything because he gives or gives not before you ask, of saying "thou" to somebody who is nearer to the I than the I is to itself. Each of these paradoxes drives the religious consciousness toward a God above the God of theism.

The courage to be which is rooted in the experience of the God above the God of theism unites and transcends the courage to be as a part and the courage to be as oneself. It avoids both the loss of oneself by participation and the loss of one's world by individualization. The acceptance of the God above the God of theism makes us a part of that which is not also a part but is the ground of the whole. Therefore our self is not lost in a larger whole, which submerges it in the life of a limited group. If the self participates in the power of being-itself it receives itself back. For the power of being acts through the power of the individual selves. It does not swallow them as every limited whole, every collec-tivism, and every conformism does. This is why the Church, which stands for the power of being-itself or for the God who transcends the God of the religions, claims to be the mediator of the courage to be. A church which is based on the authority of the God of theism cannot make such a claim. It inescapably develops into a collectivist or semicollectivist system itself.

But a church which raises itself in its message and its devotion to the God above the God of theism without sacrificing its concrete symbols can mediate a courage which takes doubt and meaninglessness into itself. It is the Church under the Cross which alone can do this, the Church which preaches the Crucified who cried to God who remained his God after the God of confidence had left him in the darkness of doubt and meaninglessness. To be as a part in such a church is to receive a courage to be in which one cannot lose one's self and in which one receives one's world.

Absolute faith, or the state of being grasped by the God beyond God, is not a state which appears beside other states of the mind. It never is something separa-ted and definite, an event which could be isolated and described. It is always a movement in, with, and under other states of the mind. It is the situation on the boundary of man's possibilities. It *is* this boundary. Therefore it is both the courage of despair and the courage in and above every courage. It is not a place where one can live, it is without the safety of words and concepts, it is without a name, a church, a cult, a theology. But it is moving in the depth of all of them. It is the power of being, in which they participate and of which they are fragmentary expressions.

One can become aware of it in the anxiety of fate and death when the traditional symbols, which enable men to stand the vicissitudes of fate and the horror of death, have lost their power. When "providence" has become a superstition and "immortality" something imaginary that which once was the power in these symbols can still be present and create the courage to be in spite of the experience of a chaotic world and a finite existence. The Stoic courage returns but not as the faith in universal reason. It returns as the absolute faith which says Yes to being without seeing anything concrete which could conquer the nonbeing in fate and death.

And one can become aware of the God above the God of theism in the anxiety of guilt and condemnation when the traditional symbols that enable men to withstand the anxiety of guilt and condemnation have lost their power. When "divine judgment" is interpreted as a psychological complex and forgiveness as a remnant of the "father-image," what once was the power in those symbols can still be present and create the courage to be in spite of the experience of an infinite gap between what we are and what we ought to be. The Lutheran courage returns but not supported by the faith in a judging and forgiving God. It returns in terms of the absolute faith which says Yes although there is no special power that conquers guilt. The courage to take the anxiety of meaninglessness upon oneself is the boundary line up to which the courage to be can go. Beyond it is mere nonbeing. Within it all forms of courage are re-established in the power of the God above the God of theism. *The courage to be is rooted in the God who appears when God has disappeared in the anxiety of doubt.*

Additional Suggested Readings for the Book

In the opinion of the editors, almost every book cited in this anthology has the power to lead the student into fresh approaches to the study of religion. We add the following few authors and titles in this spirit.

Burch, George Bosworth. *Early Medieval Philosophy.* New York: King's Crown Press, 1951. A lucid and succinct introduction to an area too often bypassed by students of religion.

Coomaraswamy, Ananda K. *The Selected Writings.* Edited by Roger W. Lipsey. Bollingen Series LXXXIX. Princeton; N.J.: Princeton University Press, 1972. A great scholar and penetrating thinker at home in the traditions of East and West, and particularly acute in his analyses of religious art.

Graham, Dom Aelred. *Zen Catholicism.* New York: Harcourt Brace Jovanovich, 1963. A sincere and intelligent effort to connect Western and Eastern religious thought.

James, William. *Varieties of Religious Experience.* New York: Modern Library, 1902. The great classic expression of religious open-mindedness.

Mbiti, John S. *African Religions and Philosophies.* New York: Anchor Books, 1970. A sophisticated and sympathetic account of the African religious mind.

Nygren, Anders. *Agape and Eros.* New York: Harper & Row, 1969. A profound study of the Christian idea of love.

"Studies in Comparative Religion." A distinguished journal published in England, containing articles of uncompromising scholarship and depth about all the religious traditions of man.

Zimmer, Heinrich. *The Philosophies of India.* Edited by Joseph Campbell. Bollingen Series XXVI. Princeton, N.J.: Princeton University Press, 1969. Reliable, clear, and comprehensive.

Index